Organizing African Unity

by
Jon Woronoff

The Scarecrow Press, Inc.
Metuchen, N. J.   1970

<u>Dedication</u> :

To the African leaders

Who combine realism with courage,

And to them alone.

Contents

Illustrations

Foreword

This book is an introduction to a movement that is
all too little known in the world and even on the African
continent itself. Nevertheless, the Pan-African movement
has been with us for over half a century and is now strongly shaping the course of the youngest emerging continent.
Despite its importance to understanding Africa, there is
little idea of where the movement came from and less of
where it is heading. There is not even a real awareness
of its present impact. This book is therefore an attempt
at filling these gaps. It relates not only the accomplishments and prospects, but also the limits and failures, so
that the movement may be seen as it is.

The most significant instrument of Pan-Africanism
today is the Organization of African Unity, and the author
has focused largely on the OAU. Now that it has entered
its seventh year, the time has come for an analysis and summing up of its work. The activities are numerous: in-
tensification of the struggle for liberation, pacification of
internal disputes, a continent-wide approach to economic
and social development, and efforts to promote solidarity.
If one follows each activity, the OAU can be seen as a
whole rather than a disjointed series of meetings and conferences. But there are many other bodies active on the
continent and they, too, must be considered.

In 1963, tremendous hopes were placed in the
Organization of African Unity. Some of them have been
fulfilled. For it did develop a structure to deal with its
many tasks. It introduced all of the activities and rose to
certain challenges. It did not prove as fragile as its
enemies insinuated. Unfortunately, for some time the
Organization has tended to remain on the sidelines, to avoid
rather than deal with the problems. It has lost prestige
because of timidity over Rhodesia and neglect of the tragedy
in Biafra. And there is less optimism about the future.

Still, pessimism is not justified either. Africa has
already proven itself more united and successful in handling

its own affairs than most other parts of the world. It is necessary to find out why it has relaxed its efforts. To this end some criticism is valid. Several flaws are obvious and arise from an unavoidable respect for the sovereignty of its members. Occasionally the policies were poorly chosen. But there has been less damage from actual weaknesses or mistakes than a certain mood in leading circles. At first there was a tendency not to accept unpleasant facts, or worse, to conceal them demagogically. More recently failure has been due to a hesitation to seize the opportunities that existed. More courage and realism will be needed to overcome future difficulties. And all the activities would be promoted by a greater willingness to compromise. With these qualities, certainly the continent could recover its old dynamism and use it to better purpose.

The author has been fortunate enough to see Pan-Africanism develop over past years, during the most fruitful period of its history. His relation with the various organizations was a very exciting experience. He wishes to thank those he has worked with and who helped him understand the movement and those he consulted with or who read the manuscript. Special mention must be made of Professors François Borella of the University of Nancy and I. William Zartman of New York University.

End of chapter notes are in brief form; complete citations will be found in the Bibliography. Annex V, at the back of the book, listing OAU Assembly and Council meeting dates and venues from 1963-1969 may be helpful to the reader following chronologically other political developments on the continent.

Chapter I

Beginning of Pan-Africanism

A. Pan-Negro Prelude

When Pan-Africanism arose in the United States and
the Caribbean at the beginning of the twentieth century, it
was originally a result of the New World Negroes' interest
in their own lot and not a concern with other peoples of
their race. The solidarity that developed was conditioned
by the society in which they lived, one in which they received only nominal equality with the white population. In
the United States especially, after emancipation and the
guarantee of full rights under the Constitution, Negroes had
been re-subjugated in many ways. The time had come to
seek more complete and lasting improvement. As conceived
of by most Negroes in the United States, the movement was
unusual in that it aimed at greater integration in the white
society. Others, to the contrary, wished a break.

Gradually, however, the Negroes became more aware
of their origin in Africa, where the peoples had been subjected to European colonialism. There was a growing feeling of involvement in this homeland which, although vague
and diffuse intellectually, was often powerful emotionally.
The Negroes in the Americas had been uprooted from the
African continent and any links had to be created anew.
Still, since they no longer knew which specific tribe or
region they came from, they could attach themselves to
Africa as a whole, or almost. For there was a definite
pan-Negro tinge to the sentiment. They were only interested in Black Africa, whence they had been brought into
slavery, and where men of their own race lived. Since the
black peoples had been so poorly treated in Africa and
America, they felt the urgency of joining whatever forces
they had to promote a better future.

Equality for the American Negroes.

The first serious efforts at creating a collective
consciousness on a national level were made by Booker T.
Washington. Teaching his policy of "industrial education"
at Tuskegee University, he convinced many Negroes of his
time that a betterment in their position could come only
from within the given structures--including even segregation--
and that a proper education would enable them to improve
their economic standing. This education, specifically
adapted to let him play some role in the industrial society
he was to enter, could help the Negro find a better job,
earn more money, and thus work himself up towards
economic equality. Since there was no call for political
change and it was felt by many that a gradual assimilation
of the Negroes was necessary, this plan was broadly supported by whites as well.

But it was not accepted by all Negroes. As of the
early 1900's, this policy appeared to some to be not only a
capitulation to the social and political supremacy of the
whites, but also a failure in its own terms. For, it was
argued, how could even economic progress be complete if
only menial tasks were reserved to the blacks and talented
young men could aspire to nothing more than an "industrial
education"? Without political equality even the economic
betterment would be illusory and fragile, for discriminatory
legislation or trade union practices could still keep the
Negroes "in their place." Thus it was necessary to take
the leap, as soon as possible, from the economic to the
political level, so as to obtain full equality.

In 1901, the move to civil rights was initiated by
Dr. William Edward Burghardt DuBois, who rejected the
patient and humble approach of Booker T. Washington. In
1906, he was joined by a number of other Negro intellectuals at Harpers Ferry in West Virginia. The battle cry of
DuBois followed that of John Brown, half a century earlier,
in a call for the second emancipation: "We demand every
right--political and social." After this movement had collapsed, DuBois sought other backing for his aims. In 1909,
he joined with sympathetic whites to found the National
Association for the Advancement of Colored People (NAACP).
This body, based on cooperation between the races,
attempted merely to accelerate the restoration of rights to
the Negroes and to seek their "advancement." With the
aid of white liberals opposed to segregation and of the labor

unions, the Negroes were able to gain certain advantages.
But the struggle was a long drawn-out affair and when it
flared up again, in the mid-twentieth century, it was still the
NAACP that tried to rally the good will of both communities so
that the Negroes might cease being second-class citizens and
integrate themselves even more completely in a society that
rejected them.

Cooperation and moderation did not appeal to all Negroes. Marcus Garvey repudiated DuBois even more fiercely
than DuBois had turned on Booker T. Washington. During the
First World War, this demagogue and Black Messiah launched
a vast popular movement. In 1914, he founded the Universal
Negro Improvement Association in Jamaica, and two years later he transferred its headquarters to New York City. His organization grew phenomenally and by 1919, as conditions deteriorated after the boom years of the war, he was able to
claim some two million members. Rather than work with
white "philanthropists" and integrate the Negroes in white society, Garvey met white racism with black racism. Through
his weekly, the "Negro World," he proclaimed the abilities
and talents of the Negro race, their glorious past and promising future, and urged them to throw off their inferiority complex and create their own distinctive society. His program
was complete: an African Orthodox Church with black angels
and a white devil; a Black government with its President in a
Black House; Negro newspapers, an African Legion, and a
Black Cross nursing corps. To crown this edifice, he planned
to create a Black State in the new world, and then to associate
it with an independent Africa. To this purpose he issued a
"Declaration of the Rights of the Negro Peoples of the World"
in 1920.

Unlike the NAACP, the Universal Negro Improvement
Association of Garvey was ephemeral. After having momentarily aroused the passions of the Negroes of Harlem and other
ghettos, it collapsed with the disappearance of its leader.
Nevertheless, half a century later, the same passions took a
similar form with Black Power and within the Black Muslims.

Later on, as well, both W. E. B. DuBois and Marcus
Garvey served as prototypes for the Africans in their struggle
for independence. The first man was a moderate and accepted
many of the given structures, trying to make the best of them,
and thus integrating the Negro community in the broader, all-
embracing society. The second forcefully rejected the structures imposed by another race and sought to build a different

world.   He was unwilling to cooperate even with whites of
similar views in seeking a modus vivendi for the Negroes in
a world that was not of their making.   However, rather than
work towards a synthesis, Garvey only managed to create an
antithesis, differing from the white world in color alone.
What was to make this world truly distinctive could only come
later, when the external structures borrowed from a hated
civilization were given a new and constructive content.

        Their antagonism taught another lesson.   Booker T.
Washington was hissed by the followers of DuBois; they in turn
were the butt of violent reprisals and terrorism by Garvey's
African Legion.   The tension between the moderates, allied
with white liberals, and the radicals, rejecting both the whites
and the "hybrids" like DuBois, degenerated into street fighting
and divided the vital forces of Pan-Negroism in America.   Politically, although the radicalism of Garvey may have encouraged the whites to accept some of DuBois' moderate platform
as a "lesser evil," it also stiffened the resistance of other
whites to all Negro demands.   Whether or not the plus and mi-
nus cancelled out, the split among Pan-Negroists did not help.

Negro Solidarity.

        Fortunately, the source had not run dry with the Negro
movements for equality in the New World.   The solidarity that
developed was extended to the greater Negro community and,
in particular, to those living in Africa.   Despite the fact that
the American Negroes were the descendants of Africans, the
uprooting and cultural assimilation had been so complete that
any solidarity had to be created rather than continued.   This
formidable task was taken up by the same leaders.   Each in
his own way, DuBois and Garvey were able to cast a more or
less tenuous bridge to the ancestral homeland.   Differing greatly in their approaches and antagonistic as ever, they were
nevertheless able to create the links by which Pan-Negroism
was brought to Africa.   But their efforts were often nullified
by the actions or indifference of the American Negroes, so
wrapped up in their own problems that they had no time or energy for the problems and needs of others.

        After having laid the foundation of the struggle for
equality in the United States, DuBois turned to the racial
brothers in Africa.   To encourage new social and political
links, he held five Congresses from 1919 to 1945.   Through
these and other activities he became, in truth, the "father of

Pan-Africanism." Although his was not a mass movement, limited largely to the black "thinking intelligentsia," it did introduce many Americans and Africans to the cause of solidarity among the black peoples. The early Congresses were largely planned and run by DuBois himself. Their aim was to bring the white majority, this time the colonial powers, to respect certain moral obligations towards their "wards" in the colonies, while preparing the latter for their rights and duties. The meetings were inter-racial, attended by white socialists and Laborites, humanitarians and others. With the aid of these white liberals and through various declarations and petitions to European governments and the League of Nations, an attempt was made at improving the situation of the Africans.

Unlike DuBois, whose Congresses at first provided only polite intercourse and the enlightened assistance of the American Negroes for their African brethren, Marcus Garvey conceived a series of schemes for a complete re-union of the Negro race. Almost at the same time that he was planning a Negro State in America, Garvey began his grand design of a "universal confraternity" spreading from the Americas to Africa, and even further--wherever Negroes lived. Already in 1920, he proclaimed the existence of a Negro Empire, convened a Black parliament, and announced that he was the "Provisional President of a Racial Empire of Africa." The delegates, including some Africans, gave him a vague mandate to free Africa from white domination and the struggle was launched. However, the American Negroes were increasingly aware that a Negro State was utopian and that the minority had to come to terms with the majority. Even as it was being proclaimed, the American pillar of the Negro Empire crumbled.

Garvey then turned away from America. He began preaching Black Zionism and his goal became a return to Africa. That the emotion of solidarity and communion with those in the homeland was strong and compelling was shown by Garvey's tremendous success in galvanizing the masses into contributing to his schemes. His Black Star Line, which was to transport the American Negroes to Africa, was a huge success in terms of financing. But, due to maladministration, the company was soon bankrupt and Garvey was condemned to prison for fraud in 1923. He had not yet lost his hold over the Negro masses and a second attempt was made, only to fail as miserably. Finally, after another term in prison and because of his virulent attacks against the NAACP and DuBois, Garvey lost this support and set out alone for Africa. He got no further than London, where he died in 1940, impoverished and ignored.

In addition to the financial difficulties, Garvey's "Back to Africa" movement also suffered moral bankruptcy. For life in the unknown fatherland appealed to very few American Negroes. And it aroused anxiety among the Africans. Wary of Garvey and his friends, the Liberian government turned down his plan for a state to which all Negroes could return and asked the United States not to give him a visa. Very few ever reached the promised land. But arrival, too, was usually a failure. The American Negroes were foreigners to the Africans and they did not feel at one with them when they arrived. Emotionally and morally, the Negroes were alienated from the white world in which they lived, but culturally and intellectually they were very much a part of it. Thus, with few exceptions, the Africans of the diaspora chose to turn their backs on Africa.

But Garvey did not disappear without leaving spiritual heirs in the rising generation. Due largely to Kwame Nkrumah, his ideas and methods were to appear in the new Africa.

Pride of Race and Négritude.

The difficulties of acclimatizing persons of one culture experience in another with which they have only spiritual links were avoided by the distillation of emotions. The transplantation of ideas from the diaspora to the homeland was much more successful. Books by Negro writers in the United States and Caribbean could be read and assimilated in Africa, or more likely in London and Paris, and transformed into a more readily accessible message for the masses. Both DuBois, through his Souls of Black Folk and Dark Waters, and Garvey, in the Philosophy of Marcus Garvey, edited by his wife, were able to influence their African readers.

Another more genuinely literary trend was initiated by Jean Price-Mars, whose diplomatic career as Haitian representative in Paris brought him into close contact with the French-speaking African intelligentsia. His "Ainsi parla l'oncle ...," an ethnographic essay published in 1928, was a source of ideas that became part of the common heritage of cultural Pan-Negroism. His concern with the rehabilitation of Negro-Africa, its animistic religions, and its races and civilizations, was quite different from that of DuBois and Garvey, for he was guided by African and not Negro-American concepts. A number of poems by Alain Locke unleashed similar hidden stores of inspiration in African minds, and these two men were looked upon by Léopold Sedhar Senghor as the spiritual ancestors of the "Négritude" movement.

The relay was taken up by a group of poets and authors, consisting of Senghor and Alioun Diop (both Senegalese), Aimé Césaire (a Martiniquan) and many others, who began to develop the first African school of literature. It was not surprising that it originated in Paris, the gathering place of the educated élite of the French colonies, where it was strongly supported by intellectuals like Jean-Paul Sartre. The French policy of assimilation had forced the Africans to surrender their Africanness or to define and defend their own cultural values. In 1932, the challenge was taken up by an early journal of the group, "Légitime Défense, " and the struggle against assimilation was propagated for years through another periodical, "Présence Africaine."

Négritude was defined by its most prominent founder, Léopold Senghor, as "the whole complex of civilized values-- cultural, economic, social and political--which characterize the black peoples, or, more precisely the Negro-African world. ... the sense of communion, the gift of myth-making, the gift of rhythm, such are the essential elements of Négritude, which you will find indelibly stamped on all the works and activities of the black man."[1] The main contribution of this movement and the other trends of the time was to give more mature and striking expression to the vocabulary of Pan-Negroism. Terms such as alien and exile, ambivalence towards the West, Black solidarity, feelings of inferiority and rejection of inferiority, pride of color, the sense of a lost past and African personality--these expressed emotions felt by Negroes the world over.[2]

Although the movement was primarily cultural, it could not help partaking in the general ferment of the times. Moreover, how could cultural tutelage be rejected without striking at the other manifestations of colonialism? Gradually the writers, those using French or English, became the most noticeable publicists of all forms of independence for the peoples. In September 1956, the first International Congress of Negro Writers and Artists met in Paris. The delegates, stressing the need to restore Negro values, expressed the wish to be genuinely African and not an extension of Europe. Although

rejecting Western ideas and institutions, they hoped to use
them to their own ends. And the most valid end seemed the
redemption of African man and the strengthening of the African
personality. Before separating, the Congress pledged to "defend, illustrate and publicize throughout the world the national
values of their own peoples." The growth of culture, they
added, required an end to colonialism, oppression and racialism.

Early Pan-African Congresses.

        The term Pan-Africanism was first given currency at a
conference called in 1900 by a Trinidad lawyer, Henry Sylves-
ter-Williams. He was a member of the English bar and specialized in land suits, acting as advisor for the Bantus of
South Africa and the Fantis of the Gold Coast to protect their
customary tribal land from the greed of white settlers. He
brought together a number of similarly minded Caribbean and
American Negroes and Africans at a conference held in West-
minster Hall, London. There they drafted a memorial pro-
testing against the poor treatment of the indigenous population
in the African colonies, and in particular the usurpation of
their tribal lands. The success of the meeting--modest as it
was--was due to the good will of British missionaries and abo-
litionists who supported the African cause. Queen Victoria replied to the memorial that Her Majesty's Government "will not
overlook the interests and welfare of the native races."

        The whole matter might have ended there if Dr. DuBois,
who attended the conference, had not revitalized the idea and
convened his first Pan-African Congress in 1919. It met in
Paris after the armistice, at the same time as the Peace Conference, and it was the Negro-Americans' and the Africans'
first real attempt at influencing world politics in favor of those
in the colonies. Speaking on behalf of the hundred thousand
Negroes who served in the ranks of the American forces in
Europe and of thousands of French "rifles," DuBois and his
fellow delegates tried to get the Allies to act upon one of the
main principles President Wilson had laid down for the peace
settlement--the right of self-determination of peoples. However, this particular appeal was not listened to even by the
President.

        Fortunately, another door was opened by a black par-
liamentarian, Blaise Diagne, who represented Senegal in the
French Assembly for some twenty years. With the permission

of George Clemenceau, about sixty delegates were able to
meet and draft a limited, but explicit series of political demands for the peace settlement.   The resolutions proclaimed
the need for international laws to protect the natives, for land
to be held in trust, for prevention of exploitation by foreign
capital, for the abolition of slavery and capital punishment,
and for the right to education; finally, it insisted that "the natives of Africa must have the right to participate in the Government as fast as their development permits."

This time, along with those from the United States and
West Indies, there were more representatives from both the
British and French colonies.   The program was readily endorsed by delegates from all communities and ideological horizons of the Negro world.   It was so toned down and legitimate
that it could even receive some support from white liberals
and politicians.   Although hardly influenced by the Pan-African
Congress, the mandate system of the League of Nations embodied many of the demands in some form.   Whether fact or
fiction, the idea that the former German colonies in Africa
were not just war booty but a trust for humanity, and the
creation of a Mandates Commission to look after the needs of
these wards of the mandatory powers, meant that a break had
been made with the colonialism of the past.

Part of the second Pan-African Congress was held in
London in August 1921.   There DuBois drafted and had adopted a relatively moderate "Declaration to the World," in which
he called for recognition of civilized men as civilized, whatever their race or color.   But the initiative taken in Brussels,
somewhat later, of handing in a petition to the Mandates Commission stressing the absolute equality of the human races was
an important precedent.   It was the first attempt to use an international lever.

Nevertheless, possibly because the outlook was so bleak
or because DuBois was too far ahead of the times, the following Congresses became acts of faith, and then, almost of desperation.   The period was not propitious for action.   Moreover, the Congresses had no real means of acting.   The only
valid effort--and this effort was made by DuBois--could be to
keep the flame burning.   Thus a third Pan-African Congress
met in London, in 1923, where it issued a manifesto stressing
that equal treatment of Negroes was the only path to peace and
progress.   The second session of this Congress, in Lisbon,
received formal pledges that forced labor in Angola and St.
Thomas and Principe Islands would be relaxed.   But the mani-

festo was ignored and the pledges were never kept.

The fourth Pan-African Congress, held in New York in 1927, was able to obtain a record participation, some two hundred delegates from twelve countries. It also made doctrinal headway, sponsoring more explicit proposals on issues like self-government, education, labor and world peace. But there was no means to obtain implementation and, with the 1929 Depression, the Congresses ceased.

Even at that early date, an interesting transformation was taking place in the Pan-Negro audience. The Congresses had originally been called to increase the active interest of the American Negroes in the fate of their racial brothers in Africa. More and more, however, the American Negroes had been sliding back into an almost exclusive concern with civil rights in the United States. The NAACP did not follow its founder on the path towards an uncertain association with Africa, and DuBois found himself increasingly drawn towards African causes and impatient with American provincialism. The other branch of American Pan-Negroism, the radical wing of Marcus Garvey, never ceased attacking DuBois. With their "Back to Africa" movement, Garvey and his followers thought they had a more drastic and satisfactory solution for uniting the Negro family. Finally, the Communists denounced both DuBois and Garvey for their "petty bourgeois Black Nationalism." But, DuBois had been making converts among the Africans he met in the European capitals and his Congresses. They avidly seized upon his ideas, weaving them into their own needs and aspirations thus giving form and content to a new movement that was to arise.

Progress through Communism.

During the period from the great Depression to the end of the Second World War, when even the frail light of Pan-Negroism cast by DuBois' Congresses went out, a glimmer of hope came from another quarter. If, after all, the Pan-African Congresses could only produce appeals and statements of good will, and if its white supporters were involved in the governments of the countries administering colonies, or were out of power, why not turn to the other revolutionary movement of the time--Communism? Where the socialists and Laborites only offered gradual change, why not work with the one international movement that proclaimed colonialism its enemy and swore to overthrow it?

During the twenties, and particularly the thirties, a
number of Pan-Negroists had joined the Communist Party.
They were attracted by Marxist doctrine, which condemned the
capitalist powers as enemies of the proletariat and also as ex-
ploiters of the minorities and colonial peoples. By joining
hands with the working class, these Americans and Africans
hoped to destroy the capitalist-colonialist forces that oppressed them both. From the beginning, the Russian revolution had solicited the minorities and colonized peoples as allies, for the foes of the new Soviet state were also Great
Britain, France and the United States. The Communist International tried to take advantage of this solidarity by disseminating subversive propaganda and forming branches of the
party. Lenin paved the way and Stalin was also interested in
this cooperation.

Until the mid-thirties, the universalism of Marxist
thought was recognized and Negroes, as members of the Communist Party of the Soviet Union or of national branches, adhered to this movement. George Padmore, prominent in the
Comintern's Black Bureau, played a particularly important
role. Many others in the diaspora, in the United States and
Caribbean, or in London and Paris, joined local parties. And
the Communist party was an early channel for dissatisfaction
in South Africa.

The alliance with the colonial peoples was originally a
sincere attempt at cooperation, but differences arose as to
whether capitalism or colonialism should be undone first.
Moreover, as Nazi and Fascist regimes formed along the Soviet frontiers, Stalin's fears for the "Russian motherland" and
the "home of socialism, " had to be given precedence over all
else. From this point on the Soviet Union sought allies among
the Western colonial powers. There was a growing feeling
that Moscow was no longer aiding the minorities and colonial
peoples or, worse, was only using them for its own ends.

The Negroes and Africans who had flirted with Commu-
nism or honestly hoped for cooperation with the Communist
Party turned back to the specific interests of Pan-Negroism.
Although many of them remained scientific socialists and used
Marxist terminology, most of them left the Communist parties.
With the resignation of men like Padmore, Wright, Yergan,
Fanon, Robeson and Césaire, the break with Communism was
quite spectacular. The reason was pointed out most clearly by
Aimé Césaire, long a member of the French Communist Party
and a representative to the National Assembly, in his resound-

ing letter to Maurice Thorez: "What I want is that Marxism
and Communism be placed at the service of black peoples and
not black peoples at the service of Marxism and Communism."
Padmore and others felt that Pan-Africanism should not be an
adjunct to world communism but rather an ideological alternative. And, in the younger generation of Pan-Africanists, people such as Kwame Nkrumah and Sékou Touré tried to use
Soviet aid and Communist tactics to their own advantage without being drawn into the movement.

The basic lesson was that real cooperation between two
revolutionary forces was difficult. Not only was priority in
the Soviet Union given to the destruction of capitalism and not
colonialism, but more essentially both Capitalism and Communism were expressions of white and Western thought. The only movement that could serve the Negroes or Africans exclusively was one of their own conception and making. All other
movements were only fair weather companions. It was not
possible to hitch the wagon of Pan-Africanism to liberalism or
Communism or anything else. This was the beginning of a
new independence and self-reliance, of "African" socialism and
a non-alignment with the East as well as the West.

The Manchester Congress.

When the Second World War came to an end, what neither the Pan-African Congresses of DuBois nor even the mighty
Communist Party could have accomplished had been self-in-
flicted upon Western civilization. The long Depression of the
thirties had sapped the strength of the capitalist states, and
the destructive war of the forties had left the Western colonial
powers a mere shadow of themselves. Power, to the extent
that it existed, was to be found in the United States and the
Soviet Union, but no longer in the countries that ruled over
Africa.

Decolonization did not begin in Black Africa, but it was
clear that it would not halt until the Negro peoples of the African continent were also free. This confidence led to the convening of the last Pan-African Congress that met outside of
the continent. For the first time Dr. DuBois was only the
elder statesman and honorary head of a Congress. Even the
convening was the work of the Pan-African Federation. This
body was the successor of earlier groups like the International
African Friends of Africa, the International African Service
Bureau, student and trade union circles that merged in 1944

under Pan-Africanists and Africans of the new generation:
Padmore, C. L. R. James, Wallace Johnson and Jomo Kenyatta.

At the Manchester Congress, in October 1945, the lead
was finally taken by Africans. There were some two hundred
delegates including many trade unionists and students. Two of
the most prominent were Kwame Nkrumah, an organizing secretary, and Jomo Kenyatta as chairman. Working at the side
of Nkrumah were George Padmore and T. R. Makonnen, both
West Indians. Other Africans from the British Territories
were Chief H. O. Davies and Chief S. L. Akintola of Nigeria,
and Wallace Johnson of Sierra Leone, as well as Peter Abra-
hams from South Africa. There were also several delegates
from French-speaking Africa.

Partially a continuation of the preceding Congresses,
the Manchester meeting nevertheless struck a new note doc-
trinally. The cautious and meek demands of earlier days were
replaced by an analysis and condemnation of colonialism. This
first awkward attempt at drawing up a "scientific" program
was often ambiguous or contradictory, but there was no mis-
taking its general import.

The resolutions of the Congress included a very thorough list of grievances against the colonial powers and an in-
dictment of their policy. Even the supposed reforms were
condemned as half-hearted or ineffectual. Both the political
and economic situations were labelled "systematic exploitation"
and the conditions regarded as worsening rather than improving. For this reason the colonial powers were summoned to
practice their own principles, those of the Atlantic Charter
and democracy (one man, one vote) and to redress the situation for the benefit of the peoples.

Going well beyond this analysis and appeal, the delegates also adopted a "Declaration to the Colonial Powers," in
which they laid down certain demands. The main goals were
expressed simply and compellingly: "We are determined to be
free. We want education. We want the right to earn a decent
living; the right to express our thoughts and emotions, to
adopt and create forms of beauty. We demand for Black Africa autonomy and independence, so far and no further than it
is possible in this One World for groups and peoples to rule
themselves subject to inevitable world unity and federation. "
Broader economic demands were made as well: "We condemn
the monopoly of capital and the rule of private wealth and in-

dustry for private profit alone. We welcome economic democracy as the only real democracy."

But the means to these ends were rather confused, for
although the above statement was bold, the conclusions were a
strange mixture of patience and despair. "The delegates believe in peace. How could it be otherwise, when for centuries
the African peoples have been the victims of violence and slavery? Yet if the Western world is determined to rule mankind
by force, then Africans, as a last resort, may have to appeal
to force in the effort to achieve freedom, even if force de-
stroys them and the world." The final decision of the Congress was to use "positive action," based on Ghandi's non-
violent teachings, and the declaration concluded: "We shall
complain, appeal and arraign. We will make the world listen
to the facts of our condition." But, as a last resort, "We
will fight in every way we can for freedom, democracy and
social betterment."

The Decline of Pan-Negroism.

Although the Manchester Congress had gone furthest
along the path opened half a century earlier by Sylvester-
Williams and DuBois, the solidarity of the Pan-Negro movement was fundamentally altered by the Africans. Dr. DuBois'
vision of Africa had been clearly Pan-Negro. Although not a
racist, he was keenly race-conscious. And he looked upon the
"color line" as the key problem of the twentieth century. Already in 1900 he spoke of the line between the "darker and
lighter races of men" that was to condition the political life of
the century. His concept of the alignments in the world of his
time was racial, and his primary concern was for a broadening and deepening of the tenuous links between the Negroes in
America and those in Africa. When he spoke of Africa, it was
not a geographical expression, for the dark continent was
shorn of its white fringes. Egypt was considered a passage
between the continents rather than a part of Africa and the
states north of the Sahara were associated more closely with
Europe.

All this was changed in Manchester. By analyzing their
condition and problems solely as a result of colonialism and
by launching a struggle against colonial exploitation, the Africans were as parochial as the NAACP. They forgot the Negroes in the new world and turned to the other colonial peoples. By switching the racial alliance for a political alliance,

they struck the second blow of egoism that hastened the decline of the Pan-Negro movement. In the future the friends
of the African Negroes were to be sought in the other colonial
lands and not America. This was shown by the "Declaration
to the Colonial Peoples," laying down the common objectives
and tactics of all colonized peoples, which ended: "Colonial
and subject peoples of the world, Unite!"

Elsewhere, the "Congress expressed the hope that before long the peoples of Asia and Africa would have broken
their centuries-old chains of colonialism. Then, as free nations, they would stand united to consolidate and safeguard
their liberties and independence from the restoration of Western imperialism, as well as the dangers of Communism."
This first Afro-Asian statement totally ignored the American
Negroes. And a first genuinely Pan-African resolution burst
the frontiers of the movement traced by DuBois by demanding
the independence of Algeria, Tunisia and Morocco.

At this time, George Padmore became the theoretician
of a new kind of Pan-Africanism. His thought was summed
up in the book Pan-Africanism or Communism? published in
1955. On page 379, he described his view of the future:

> In our struggle for national freedom, human dignity,
> and social redemption, Pan-Africanism offers an
> ideological alternative to Communism on the one
> side and Tribalism on the other. It rejects both
> white racialism and black chauvinism. It stands
> for racial co-existence on the basis of absolute
> equality and respect for human personality.
>
> Pan-Africanism looks above the narrow confines of
> class, race, tribe, and religion. In other words,
> it wants equal opportunity for all. Talent to be re-
> warded on the basis of merit. Its vision stretches
> beyond the limited frontiers of the nation-state. Its
> perspective embraces the federation of regional
> self-governing countries and their ultimate amalga-
> mation into a United States of Africa.
>
> In such a Commonwealth, all men, regardless of
> tribe, race, colour or creed, shall be free and
> equal. And all the national units comprising the
> regional federations shall be autonomous in all
> matters regional, yet united in all matters of com-
> mon interest to the African Union. This is our

vision of the Africa of Tomorrow--the goal of Pan-
Africanism.

Although feeble, Pan-Negroism was not dead. Exchanges of all sorts, between students and professors, businessmen and politicians, continued to link the branches of the
Negro family informally. Despite mutual incomprehension and
exclusiveness, Negroes on both sides of the ocean were aware
of each others' needs. This consciousness was heightened by
the bitter struggles for comparable goals, civil rights in the
United States, political independence in Africa. Soon, however, the balance in the Negro community began to shift. The
well-organized and influential American Negroes who promoted
African causes were insignificant compared with the new African Heads of State and the locus of power in independent Africa. The stronger part of the family was definitely in the
homeland.

It was there, to Africa, that the new generation of
American Negro leaders turned for help. As the struggle for
civil rights flared up again, almost a century after the Emancipation Proclamation, a renewed sentiment of oneness with
Africa arose in Black America. The NAACP was still working at its tasks and one of its foremost leaders, Martin Lu-
ther King, went on a tour of the African countries. The more
emotional trend, focused in the Black Muslims, felt an even
stronger pull, and Malcolm X left on a double pilgrimage to
Mecca and independent Africa. Proponents of Black Power
such as Stokely Carmichael and Rap Brown turned towards Africa for examples. Finally, the factions rejecting integration
and seeking a Negro personality looked directly to Africa,
even adopting African dress and customs. And the Negro community as a whole became Afro-American.

The moral debt of gratitude to DuBois, Garvey and
other pioneers was not forgotten in Africa either. At the historic summit conference of 1963, the Emperor of Ethiopia paid
tribute to the forerunners of African Unity, many of whom had
never seen Africa. An unexpected sign of solidarity was the
resolution adopted at this conference, stating that it:

> Expresses the deep concern aroused in all African
> peoples and governments by the measures of racial
> discrimination taken against communities of African
> origin living outside the continent and particularly
> in the United States of America;

> Expresses appreciation for the efforts of the Federal Government of the United States of America to put an end to these intolerable mal-practices which are likely seriously to deteriorate relations between the African peoples and governments on the one hand and the people and Government of the United States of America on the other.

Unfortunately, this resolution was faintly reminiscent of earlier resolutions of the Pan-African Congresses, a well-meaning attempt at improving the treatment of Negro brothers abroad. Whether this benevolent attitude would go any further than pious wishes and fraternal resolutions remained to be seen.

Notes

1. West Africa, 4 Nov. 1961, p. 1211.

2. See catalogue in Colin Legum, Pan-Africanism, p. 14-22.

B. The Struggle for Independence

The winds of change that were to turn Africa into a largely independent continent within two decades were but a faint breeze in 1945. In Asia, however, where India and Pakistan were preparing for independence, they already blew more strongly. And they soon became a storm in Indo-China. To the north, in the Maghreb and Egypt, the end of the Second World War was also a time of unrest. Both the moral claims of superiority of the colonial powers and the material backing of these claims were shaken and increasingly demands were made for a revision of status.

Although Black Africa perceived the winds of change, the population was far less articulate and politicized. The few pressure groups, political, intellectual or business, were at most basically reformist. Often they sought little more than an improvement in their own position within the colonial structure. Through cooperation and loyalty, mixed possibly with a bit of Ghandism, they hoped to obtain what they wanted peacefully--although they might have to wait.

The erosion of colonialism in the Asian and Arab lands, subjected to the same yoke by the same powers, strongly impressed the nationalists meeting in Manchester. Some of the delegates, again in particular Kwame Nkrumah and Jomo Kenyatta, were more attuned than others. And they broke with the meek petitions for minor reforms when the Declaration to the Colonial Powers was adopted. This Declaration proclaimed what earlier resolutions had not dared to admit: "We are determined to be free." This determination was even backed by a veiled threat, for the Africans, "as a last resort, may have to appeal to force in the efforts to achieve freedom."

Independence Movements in Africa.

Little would ever come of the bold statements of a group of students and intellectuals meeting in London or discussing politics in Paris. Those who sought independence had to use the best means available--the political parties and other

28

pressure groups back home. During the following two decades
these nationalist bodies played the primary role in Africa,
either under the control of the older leaders or a new "revolutionary" team. From Manchester to Accra, in 1958, there
were no major Pan-African meetings. Each leader was too
busy with the absorbing task of obtaining his own country's
liberty.

By 1946, the West African National Secretariat, founded in Manchester, proclaimed the goal of total independence.
The two main leaders in British West Africa were Dr. Nnamdi
Azikiwe and Kwame Nkrumah. Already in 1946, Dr. Azikiwe
replaced the moderate Herbert Macaulay at the head of the
National Council of Nigeria and Cameroons. The vast and
heterogeneous colony of Nigeria, however, was not a very fertile field for decolonization. The dynamic Ibo party still had
to arouse and mobilize other sectors and regions before a serious campaign could be launched.

The Gold Coast, the most prosperous and advanced colony, was more promising. There already existed a well organized United Gold Coast Convention (UGCC), largely the
spokesman of the local businessmen, whose economic concerns
had political implications. Shortly after the Manchester Congress, Kwame Nkrumah was called back home to serve as the
secretary of this party. But his militant approach was opposed by the older leaders; in 1948, against their better judgement, a strike was called. When the strike was crushed by
the police, leaving several demonstrators and policemen dead,
Nkrumah was repudiated. A split arose on the question of
methods, for the old guard had been frightened into greater
conservatism, whereas Nkrumah drew the conclusion of the
Manchester Declaration. First he had to create his own political base. When he was unable to take over the UGCC from
within, Kwame Nkrumah carried the youth movement with him
and formed his own party--the Convention People's Party
(CPP). With branches in every village, masses of young activists, and a bold plan for independence, the CPP was able to
win every election and represent the people in dealings with
the Crown. Further measures of "positive action" made the
position of the British colonial administration uncomfortable
enough that independence was granted on 6 March 1957.

With a solid base in the new state of Ghana, named
after an ancient Negro Empire, Nkrumah threw himself into a
vastly more ambitious program: independence for all Africa
and unity of the continent. But, when he cast about for allies,

he found that the struggle for independence was making less
headway in the rest of Black Africa and sometimes had not
even been initiated.

British East and Central Africa were not as advanced
politically. The main brake was the dominant position of
white settler minorities. Jomo Kenyatta had returned home
to Kenya in 1946 and the next year he was made President of
the Kenya African Union, a Kikuyu-based political movement
that launched the first campaign for African rights. However,
no headway could be made against the colonial administration
and settlers and in 1950 the first sparks of violence were ignited by the secret Mau Mau society. But even more powerful outbursts only increased the repression and in 1957 Kenyatta was still in jail. Trailing somewhat behind, but un-
hampered by a large settler population, Tanganyika seemed to
be in a better position. In 1954, Julius Nyerere founded the
Tanganyika African National Union (TANU) and started the long
path towards independence. But at the end of December 1957
he resigned from his country's Legislative Council because of
"lack of progress."

The situation in French West and Equatorial Africa was
even less heartening. For despite a long heritage of political
activity and a well-organized inter-territorial political party,
the Rassemblement Démocratique Africain, independence had
not even been made a primary goal. Most of the leaders
came from the older generation of reformists and progressives
and advocated good relations with the metropolis. Few of
them were ready to break away from France. The first
breach did not come until early 1958 when Sékou Touré chose
independence. In the Belgian colonies of Central Africa the
very notion of independence was a dream. Portugal was imposing ever stricter controls on its colonies. And South Africa was an impregnable fortress.

The situation was strikingly different to the north.
Egypt, nominally independent since 1922, had only recovered
its freedom of action when the Farouk regime was swept away
by the coup d'état of 23 July 1953. A more radical break with
the past came when Gamal Abdel Nasser replaced General Ne-
guib and tried to steer a middle course for his country. In
the Maghreb, after years of agitation, Morocco and Tunisia had
become free by 1956. This was done with relatively little violence, but the same was not true in Algeria. At first the
population was amazingly passive. Occasionally timid demands for improvement were made. There seemed to be

little doubt that Algeria would remain an integral part of
France. Then in 1954, by-passing the earlier reformists, a
small but resolute group of nationalists unleashed an unexpected uprising. The Front de Libération Nationale (FLN) had
finally put teeth in the efforts at creating a new nation and its
primary aim was complete independence. Soon the battle was
engaged. Guerrilla actions were launched and a serious effort
was made at educating the people and winning them over to
the cause. Although the National Liberation Army overran
much of the country, the French army was still largely in control. The obstacles to independence beyond the army were the
colonial administration and a stubborn European minority, anxious to prevent "premature" independence and able to put pressure on the French government. With both sides determined
to hold the line, the struggle flared up and grew more violent.

The Pan-African Alliance.

By 1958, when Ghanaian Prime Minister Nkrumah felt
the new state had been sufficiently consolidated, he was ready
to tackle the broader program of independence and unity. His
first step was to create a Department for African Affairs,
staffed by able advisors like George Padmore and T. R. Makonnen, who developed a strategy he could wield. Nkrumah also threw open the doors of Ghana to nationalists from other
parts of the continent, to whom he offered training, equipment
and financing (drawn from the wealth of his country). Militant
nationalists flocked to Ghana and the capital city of Accra
promptly became a center of propaganda and agitation.

But he seriously needed allies in this struggle. The
first contacts had been made at the celebrations for independence, attended by representatives from Liberia, Ethiopia and
the Maghreb. On this occasion, Nkrumah revealed his intention of convening a conference of all the independent states of
the continent. However, among them, the Black African states
of Liberia and Ethiopia were too conservative or even reactionary to give him the support he wanted. So he had to look
elsewhere. The nearest and most logical place to seek help
was in the northern tier of the same continent.

A similar desire for links with the southern part of the
continent was already manifest in the Maghreb and Egypt. Algeria was engaged in a crucial battle for decolonization that
required all its strength and more. Morocco and Tunisia did
their best to help. Along with moral and material aid, enabl-

ing the FLN to maintain a second army along their frontiers,
they spearheaded the diplomatic moves to bring France to the
negotiating table and to grant freedom. Egypt also provided
considerable financial and material support. As of 1958, they
recognized the newly formed Provisional Government as the
sole spokesman of the Algerian people and campaigned for increased aid. Above all they wished to broaden the circle of
states supporting the struggle.

President Nasser also began to show a lively interest.
Egypt had tried to remain free of influence from East and
West. What remained of its ties with the West were swept
away during the Suez crisis in October 1956. But Nasser's
design was not to trade dependence on the West for new bonds
with the Communist bloc. He sought other allies. They had
to be anti-colonial, progressive politically and economically,
and wary of reliance on both blocs. There was also a natural
tendency to seek them closest to home and he developed a
theory of three circles: the Arab circle, the African continent
circle, and the our-brethren-in-Islam circle.

Being the passage from Africa to Asia, and controlling
the Suez Canal joining Europe to eastern Africa, Egypt had an
exceptionally wide choice of international political roles.
President Nasser took an important part in the Arab League
and the Asian-African movement before turning to Black Africa. Nevertheless, after some hesitation, he took a serious
look at the second-best circle, more modest for the present,
but with huge potential for the future. Already in 1953, he
wrote in his "Philosophy of the Revolution"

> We cannot under any condition, even if we wanted
> to, stand aloof from the terrible and terrifying bat-
> tle now raging in the heart of that continent be-
> tween five million whites and two hundred million
> Africans. We cannot stand aloof for one important
> and obvious reason--we ourselves are in Africa.
> Surely the people of Africa will continue to look to
> us--we who are the guardians of the continent's
> northern gate, we who constitute the connecting link
> between the continent and the outer world. We
> certainly cannot, under any condition, relinquish
> our responsibility to help to our utmost in spread-
> ing the light of knowledge and civilization up to the
> very depth of the virgin jungles of the continent.

Despite any inaccuracies or condescension, the important thing was that Egypt did--as indeed it had to--decide in
favor of an African alliance. From the beginning of his regime, Nasser made Cairo one of the major centers of propaganda and training for nationalists from the Arab countries
and Black Africa. Soon the Egyptian radio was broadcasting
to the rest of the continent and funds and equipment were flow-
ing to the liberation movements.

At this point, the alliance was to be concluded. However, its desirability was not evident to all. Ever since the
Pan-African Congresses there had been more or less tenuous
links between the Negro peoples of the continent. In the struggle for independence, these links had grown as the political
parties and leaders formed broader fronts in West Africa,
East and Central Africa, and the French colonies. But there
were as yet no links with the Arab world.

For centuries, indeed, the relations between Arab north
and Negro south had been no better--occasionally even worse--
than those between the Africans and the colonial masters from
Europe. If the Black-Africans were given a choice, some
would have preferred cooperation with the white colonial rulers to aid from the traditional Arab enemies. This was especially so along the east coast of the continent, from the old
slaving station of Zanzibar to the Arab north, and the racial
or religious borders inland, as in the Sudan. Still, even if
the Arab heartland and Egypt were held in suspicion, this la-
tent enmity was much weaker towards the Maghreb.

Moreover, since the yoke of European colonization had
been imposed on Negroes and Arabs alike, the potential division of the continent was slowly replaced by solidarity. The
struggle for decolonization that developed, and was directed
against the same powers, led to an increased willingness to
work with Arabs for a common goal. But the actual decision
was taken by Kwame Nkrumah when he looked for allies in the
struggle for independence and found the states to the north
most suitable. In so doing, he gave a death blow to the lin-
gering Pan-Negroism of an earlier day, and gave life to a new
and genuinely Pan-African movement.

The Conferences of Independent African States.

In the race to establish these broader links, it was
Ghana that won. This was fitting. For Nkrumah was a direct

heir of the oldest movement of solidarity. Trained in the
Pan-African Congress of DuBois, embracing much of the philosophy of Marcus Garvey, he was able for some time to combine these two trends in the promised land of Africa. And
Black Africa was potentially the larger partner in the new
movement.

The first Conference of Independent African States
(CIAS) met in Accra from 15-22 April 1958. This was a
meeting of governments at the highest level of representation
in order that it might both speak with authority and be able to
implement its decisions. If Heads of State were unable to attend, Foreign Ministers took their place. From the outset
the conference was a "historical" one. It was the first meeting of the men who guided the destiny of very different states,
from moderate Liberia to militant Ghana, from the ancient
Empire of Ethiopia to the reborn states of Libya, Morocco
and Tunisia, from Arab Egypt and mixed Sudan. The vast
panorama of races and religions, of ideologies and outlooks,
of histories and futures might have been enough to over-awe
the delegates--if they had not assembled to chart the destiny
of the whole continent, to proclaim its independence and pre-
dict its future.

One stumbling block remained before the alliance could
be concluded. The Arab states, Egypt in particular, were
locked in a bitter struggle against the intruder state of Israel.
But many in Black Africa looked upon Israel as a friend, one
that could bring the benefits of Western civilization without its
perils. And the host country, Ghana, had called upon Israelis
to create a shipping line and collective farms; even the hotel
in which many delegates were lodged was built by Israel. Although in the minority, the Black Africans were able to keep
Egypt from putting Israel on a list of racist and imperialist
powers. The conference limited itself to urging a "just solution" to the Palestine question.

With this problem out of the way, the conference could
get down to business. Prime Minister Nkrumah himself directed many of the debates. Before all else, it was necessary for the delegates to get to know one another and a general discussion covered all problems of common interest. The
most pressing point was to help the still dependent territories
obtain their freedom. But there was also reference to foreign
policy and economic and other matters. The delegates were
pleased--and surprised--by the breadth of the consensus and
they emphasized the need to channel this agreement and forge

stronger links of friendship and cooperation among the states.

The Accra conference was particularly important as the
first occasion the leaders of all the African states had to define a common program. They had to lay down the objectives
and, where possible, also the means of attaining them. However, this program was not defined once and for ever, and
nothing was more certain than that other conferences would
follow to modify or improve it. In fact, there was a meeting
of Foreign Ministers in Monrovia, Liberia, from 4-8 August
1959. And the second Conference of Independent African States
was held, again at a Heads of State level, in Addis Ababa,
Ethiopia, from 15-24 June 1960. These conferences gave
more precision and substance to the program and showed the
trends that were likely to develop.

During these two years, the number of independent
states increased. The eight states of the Accra conference
were joined in Monrovia by Guinea and the informally accredited delegation of the Provisional Government of Algeria. By
the time of the convocation in Addis Ababa, the African family
had grown to fifteen: the Algerian Provisional Government
(now a full member), Cameroon, Ethiopia, Ghana, Guinea, Liberia, Libya, Morocco, Nigeria, Somalia, Sudan, Tunisia,
United Arab Republic, plus the Congo (Léopoldville), and Togo
(not present). There were also observers from Angola, Kenya, Tanganyika, Uganda, Northern and Southern Rhodesia,
South Africa and South West Africa.

Article One - Independence.

As was quite natural, the primary concern of the African leaders was to obtain the liberation of the rest of the continent. There was no doubt that one day all Africa must be
free. But the first approach to the problem of dependent territories was rather circumspect. This was a big step and the
delegates felt obliged to justify their interest in that the continued existence of colonialism was a threat to African security and world peace. For this reason the future of the dependent territories was "not the exclusive concern of the Colonial
Powers but the responsibility of all members of the United Nations and in particular of the Independent African States."
This done, the conference proceeded to condemn categorically
all colonial systems on the continent and demand that a "definite date" be fixed for the attainment of independence.

By the time of this 1960 conference in Addis Ababa, the Heads of State had grown accustomed to their role as leaders of the continent. They began to feel more certain of their footing. As time passed the calls for self-determination and independence became bolder (and somewhat more dramatic), as well as moving from an unspecified date to "the immediate attainment of independence." Even the title of the resolution showed this new self-confidence: "Eradication of Colonial Rule from Africa."

The evolution of the means to implement such a policy was more painstaking and hesitant. As a direct heir to the Manchester Congress, the CIAS in 1958 was still bound to a policy of peaceful emancipation and positive action. This may have been the better part of valour for some of the states, but the most exposed were also the most militant. Still the problem of means was very real and it was unconsciously expressed by a curious pair of goals in the Accra Declaration: "We further assert ... our solidarity with the dependent peoples of Africa as well as our friendship with all nations."

The desire of the young African states to appear as peace-loving members of the world community and to maintain friendly relations with all powers was genuine. So was their eagerness to free the dependent peoples. Unfortunately the two goals were sometimes incompatible. The only way of having the best of both worlds was to use peaceful methods exclusively. This implied a reliance on distressed appeals to the good will of the colonial and administering powers. And appeals were made for an implementation of the United Nations Charter, the granting of independence, cessation of repression, respect of human rights and an end to all forms of discrimination. But what if the colonial powers did not heed the appeals? Then the African leaders were left with the dilemma of how to reconcile their two goals or, if need be, which one to reject.

The quandary appeared in an even cruder light in specific cases of decolonization. One of the mainsprings of the alliance was the need to aid the Algerian liberation movement. Nevertheless, the Accra conference's support was largely platonic. It consisted basically of condemnations and appeals: appeals to France to recognize the right of self-determination, end the hostilities and negotiate a settlement; appeals to all peace-loving states to make France apply the principles of the United Nations Charter and refuse aid for the Algerian operations; and finally, appeals to the African states to consult, in-

form, solicit support and enlighten world opinion. The only
glimmer of hope for effective backing was the vague "determination to make every possible effort to help the Algerian
people towards the attainment of independence."

Pulled in both directions, the African states almost dis-
played a split personality by adopting two separate resolutions
in Addis Ababa. One was pacific, believing that "the conditions for the implementation of the right to self-determination
of the Algerian people must be negotiated by the two parties
concerned." The other was more energetic, asking the African states for material aid and diplomatic support within the
United Nations, periodic consultations and missions to France,
the NATO powers and others. As a tender of good faith, the
Algerian Provisional Government was accepted as a full member of the conference and thereby given enhanced prestige and
a platform.

However, the strongest steps were taken in connection
with the problem of racialism and segregation. This practice
was condemned as evil and inhuman, a "negation of the basic
principle of human rights and dignity ... of such explosive-
ness ... that it may well engulf our Continent in violence and
bloodshed." Yet, at first, the means used to vanquish it were
merely another series of appeals. The main culprits were
listed as the Union of South Africa, the Central African Federation and Kenya.

By 1960, however, the main danger had been pin-point-
ed in South Africa, whose policy of apartheid was decried as
shameful. In view of its contempt for the resolutions of the
United Nations and the continued implementation of this policy,
it was obvious that serious action was needed. This time, the
Heads of State and Foreign Ministers drew up a more forceful
and specific program: severance or refusal of diplomatic relations, the closing of ports to South African vessels, boycott
of goods, and denial of airports and air-space to South African planes. The Arab states were asked to contribute by preventing their oil from being sold to the Union. South Africa
was to be excluded from the Commonwealth. And the United
Nations would be used to introduce further measures.

However, there was a definite trend. In 1958, the independent states had accepted the need to "give all possible
assistance to the dependent peoples in their struggle to achieve
self-determination and independence." But they only offered
facilities for training and education. The second CIAS drifted

closer to serious aid. In any struggle Africa had to be at the side of the African peoples and the conference condemned any aid to the colonial powers, such as the enlistment of Africans "in foreign armed forces to suppress the liberation movements in Africa." Moreover, it was decided to establish an "African Freedom Fund" to finance the liberation movements and to extend assistance to "genuine African political refugees." In return for their aid, the independent states demanded stronger efforts and especially the creation of a "national front" in each territory. To this end they offered "good offices to assist in settling differences among leaders and political parties."

Nevertheless, the heads of the independent states sidestepped the fundamental question of what to do if peaceful means were not enough. This attitude looked a bit unreal, for violent uprisings had already broken out in three parts of the continent. In Kenya, Algeria and Angola the people had grown tired of waiting for the colonial power to heed appeals and had taken the future into their own hands. In so doing they had no qualms about using violence. And still the independent African states only sponsored peaceful means of decolonization-- although giving aid to all those who ignored this precept.

Expanding the Program.

During the (first) Conference of Independent African States came the first time in its history that the continent defined a program towards itself and towards the world. Still at the beginning of their careers, the leaders assembled in Accra were basically optimistic, although they realized that many difficulties and problems lay ahead. The first article of the alliance was independence for the whole continent. But the already independent states could not forget their own concerns. Nor could they help projecting outwards onto the broader world scene.

Introducing the series of resolutions, somewhat unexpectedly, was a declaration on foreign policy. The first exchange of views had been a success and the delegates were pleased with the "unanimity" they achieved on fundamental aims and principles. The purpose of later meetings would be to preserve this fundamental unity of outlook so as to assert "a distinctive African Personality which will speak with a concerted voice in the cause of Peace." The actual newness and immaturity of the continental movement became terribly apparent here, for the basis of this African Personality was to be "unswerving loyalty" to the Charter of the United Nations, adherence to the Bandung principles, and support for a list of intangibles including sovereignty, equality, non-interference and non-aggression.

Obviously, the primary goal of any African foreign policy was basically defensive, to safeguard the hard-won independence and territorial integrity of the states. And the worst dangers in the world they entered arose from the existence of two antagonistic blocs. Africa was painfully aware that for the continent to have any policy of its own, it had to keep from being drawn into the magnetic field of the powers and super-powers. Thus the participating governments were warned to "avoid being committed to any action which might entangle them to the detriment of their interest and freedom." Among the Bandung principles, there was also the "abstention from the use of arrangements of collective defence to serve the particular interests of any of the big powers."

Nevertheless, on this platform borrowed for the occasion, Africa was able to issue its first statement on the problem of international peace. It viewed as the greatest single threat to peace the continued manufacture and testing of nuclear and thermo-nuclear weapons in general, and in the Sahara in particular. There was little they could do to prevent this but, significantly, the African states demanded the right to participate in all international bodies dealing with the problems affecting world peace and in particular United Nations or other bodies on disarmament. When the plenipotentiaries reached Addis Ababa, the campaign had been narrowed down to the critical case of French tests of atomic devices in the Sahara.

Domestically, the most urgent problem faced by the African governments was to overcome the economic backwardness of their countries and to offer their peoples a better life. The CIAS therefore urged that the common effort extend into the economic and other fields. The Accra Declaration stressed the "need to raise the living standards of our peoples," and the resolutions proposed an impressive list of projects: common means of communication, a common market, action against diseases, exchange of professors and teachers, cultural centers, the revision of syllabi and text books, conferences, journals, an annual inter-African sports meeting, and other joint enterprises. This list was lengthened at the Addis Ababa Conference.

Two paths were open to the African states for the development of their economies: inter-African cooperation or cooperation with the outside world. Cooperation among African states was preferred and the second CIAS, in 1960, threw its weight behind the efforts for cooperation and coordination in Africa. But this source was less plentiful because, even if all African states were not equally poor, none of them could provide as much assistance as the former colonial powers or the two rival super-powers.

The weak economic position of the African states meant that they could not really benefit from the give and take of economic life to the extent they desired, since they needed much more than they could give. If they succumbed to the temptation to pay the difference in political coin, they might gradually lose their freedom of action or independence. Awareness of such dangers dawned on most of the states some time before the Addis Ababa conference, for one of its resolutions laid down the "means to prevent new forms of colonialism in Africa." It called upon the colonial powers "to refrain from any action which might compromise the sovereignty and independence of the emerging states" and laid down the general principle that "assistance to emerging States should be without political conditions." The resolution also warned the independent states against "colonial penetration through economic means." And it underlined the need to resist any attempt at "balkanization." The solution offered was a collective system of distributing financial and technical aid.

The All-African Peoples Conferences.

The first inter-governmental conference in Accra had been an undeniable success. But it did not quite meet the expectations of all its promotors. Some wanted a more militant program and immediate efforts to put it into practice; in particular they wanted unstinting aid to Algeria and the other liberation movements. For men like Nkrumah and Nasser, the program was a lowest common denominator and the measures resulting from it derisive. Since the leaders were not ready for action, they turned towards the masses.

At the end of 1958, Kwame Nkrumah decided to convene a second meeting. Instead of the governments, it was the "people" this time that swarmed to Accra to lay down a program. The first All-African Peoples Conference (AAPC), from 5-13 December 1958, brought together the political par-

ties and trade unions, the students' and youth movements and
the men's and women's organizations of Africa. This time
they came not only from the independent states but also from
the colonies and dependent territories or even from the oppositions to existing governments.

There was a very noticeable change in tone. The
AAPC spoke with the voice of "over 300 delegates representing over 200 million Africans." It dealt mainly with political
questions, especially decolonization. And it fired broadside
after broadside at the colonial powers, as the conference "vehemently condemns colonialism and imperialism in whatever
shape or form these evils are perpetuated." It went much
further into detail when analyzing the situations and proposing
means of advancing the independence of these territories.
Priority was given to Algeria and the Congo and the AAPC repeatedly offered new plans of aid. The peoples were also less
patient. They accelerated the timing for decolonization and
took the initiative demanding immediate independence for all of
Africa.

Rather than sitting on the fence when it came to means
of forcing independence, the peoples began to lean with the
wind. Their compromise on the use of violence was strikingly
different from that of the states. For the peoples' representatives declared their full support "to all fighters for freedom
in Africa, to all those who resort to peaceful means of non-
violence and civil disobedience as well as to all those who are
compelled to retaliate against violence to attain national independence and freedom for the peoples."

With many delegates from the dependent territories in
East, Central and Southern Africa, the AAPC also paid closer
attention to the problem of racialism. The abuses in various
parts of the continent were strongly condemned but the Chairman, Tom Mboya of Kenya, insisted that the Africans were
willing to live together with the white and Asian minorities and
would not practice "racism in reverse." The conference correctly perceived the link between minority rule and racialism
and offered thoroughgoing democracy and universal adult franchise as the solution. At the opening session, Prime Minister
Nkrumah had already pointed out that

> ... we are not racialists or chauvinists. We wel-
> come into our midst peoples of all other races,
> other nations, other communities, who desire to
> live among us in peace and equality. But they

> must respect us and our rights, our rights as the
> majority to rule. That, as our Western friends
> have taught us to understand it, is the essence of
> democracy. [1]

Accra was only a beginning. The All-African Peoples
Conference in Tunis, from 25-30 January 1960, recognized
that the struggle was far from over and that increased efforts
were necessary to bring it to a successful conclusion. The
delegates were

> indignant at the savage and inhuman repression ex-
> erted by foreign imperialism on the Africans strug-
> gling to obtain their liberty ... and at the inhuman
> racial discriminatory measures ... and at the ig-
> noble policy of deportation, torture and genocide
> pursued by France in North Africa ... and by
> other colonial powers in other African countries ...

From this point of departure the AAPC was forced to
make even stronger demands. It could no longer appeal for
negotiations in Algeria, as the Heads of State did some months
later. The peoples offered, as their contribution, "the creation of a corps of African Volunteers for the war of the Independence of Algeria." To help destroy the evils of colonialism, they again came up with an idea that could be developed:
"the speedy setting up of an organization designed to coordinate the aid and solidarity of all the independent countries
with regard to helping african peoples engaged in the struggle."

The Algerian Provisional Government and other liberation movements that used violent methods had always played an
important part in these conferences and by the third meeting
they had their weapons added to the arsenal of decolonization.
More consistent in the urge for decolonization than the states,
and less intimidated by the fear of eventual retaliation, the
peoples of the independent states joined with those of the liberation movements to take the fatal leap. At the third All-
African Peoples Conference in Cairo, from 23-31 March 1961,
they announced that "the time has come for intensifying the
struggle." The AAPC took the initiative of "endorsing the necessity in some respects to resort to force in order to liquidate colonialism." Hence it "urges all African freedom fighters whether fighting with violent or non-violent means to intensify their struggle to the maximum."

From conference to conference and condemnation to condemnation, the "peoples" were driven by their own momentum
to adopt increasingly rabid resolutions. The decisive step was
in endorsing violence before this had been officially approved
by the governments of most states. In so doing, they often
outpaced or collided with those states that could not accept
their methods. This led to growing rivalry and even opposition with the inter-governmental meetings. With two spokesmen, the CIAS and AAPC, Africa seemed to speak with two
voices, either of which disagreed with the other almost as
much as with the common enemy.

The Pan-African Freedom Movement.

Although independence was slower in coming to Eastern,
Central and Southern Africa, this did not prevent the nationalist movements from forming broader groupings even as they
began the struggle for liberation. There it was not that simple, since the colonial administration was wary of any gatherings that could undermine its control. Finally, after a number of tries, the Tanganyika African National Union (TANU)
leader, Julius Nyerere, was able to have representatives of
other parties attend a conference in Mwanza, Tanganyika, from
16-18 September 1958. The delegates came from Kenya, Nyasaland, Tanganyika, Uganda and Zanzibar. And they decided
to form an organization called the Pan-African Freedom Movement of East and Central Africa (PAFMECA).

The conference immediately set about drafting a Freedom Charter which would clearly outline its aims, both present
and future. The primary goal was, of course, decolonization.
However, some of the considerations were peculiar to the region. For the path to independence was often obstructed less
by the colonial powers than by the influence exercised locally
by European settlers. Thus the catalogue of enemies to African freedom included, along with colonialism: trusteeship,
partnership, apartheid, multiracialism and white settlerism.
Pressure had to be brought against the British government to
override the objections of these minorities and grant independence. The methods adopted were non-violent. To be more
effective, it was decided to coordinate action among the various nationalist movements and parties. A "caretaker committee" was appointed to this end. And a freedom fund was set
up to aid the poorer movements.

But concern with the influence of racial minorities did
not mean that the African majorities intended to reverse the
situation.   The Freedom Charter stated that there would be no
discrimination, victimization or segregation based on color,
race or religion once self-government was attained.   The governments would be established on a democratic basis and all
those of foreign origin who upheld the principles of parliamentary democracy, social justice and equality would enjoy the full
rights and protection of a citizen.   After self-government, it
would be possible to improve conditions in the countries.
Poverty, ignorance and ill health could be eradicated, there
would be industrialization and use of cooperative methods, full
trade union rights would be recognized, and the principal
means of production would be controlled by the peoples themselves through democratically instituted governments.

At the second PAFMECA conference in Moshi, Tanganyika, again convened by Nyerere in September 1959, there
was also a member from outside the British colonial realm--
the Belgian Congo.   During the preceding year, the efforts for
liberation had been intensified.   Raising their demands, the
delegates approved the principle that "Africans should be given
the right to govern themselves now."   Only in the Congo, however, were things already coming to a head and a resolution
urged the voters in the approaching elections to select candidates who would pledge themselves to securing full, responsible government by 1960.   The resolution further asked the Belgian government to honor its promise of independence, and
warned the Congolese people of any attempts at "divide et im-
pera."

In the British territories the situation had hardly improved.   The campaigns met with ever greater resistance.
Thus the conference denounced the repression of nationalist
movements by Britain while making specific demands: an end
to a seven years' state of emergency in Kenya and the release
of Jomo Kenyatta, an end to the ban on the Nyasaland African
Congress and the release of Dr. Hastings Banda and other
leaders, the observance of human rights and the rule of law in
Uganda and the release of political detainees.   But the greatest problems arose in the multiracial areas and particularly in
South Africa, where the delegates condemned the "gross abuse
of human rights," called for a world-wide boycott of South African goods and asked the transport unions in their countries
to refuse to handle goods from or to South Africa.   Since
PAFMECA still rejected violence, it was all the more necessary to avoid any divisions in the nationalist ranks.   There-

fore an appeal was made to the heads of the two major parties
in Kenya to form a united organization. It also tried to con-
ciliate rival nationalist leaders in Zanzibar, Uganda and the
Rhodesias.

By the third PAFMECA conference in Addis Ababa, in
February 1962, there had been a definite improvement on some
fronts. Tanganyika, Kenya, Uganda and Zanzibar had attained
or were approaching independence and could already think of
the future. At the same time, the organization was expanded
northwards to include Ethiopia and Somalia. The growing number of independent states in PAFMECA had a definite impact
on its program. New goals were set. There was interest in
economic cooperation and the conference asked for a coordination of education, communications and transport. But this did
not relieve them of their obligations in the struggle for freedom elsewhere. The fortunate ones had to increase their aid
to the others, something they could do more effectively now
that they had the strength of a state apparatus behind them.

On other fronts, unfortunately, almost no headway had
been made. The leaders were very worried about the situation in Central and Southern Africa. Resolutions were adopted
on the Portuguese colonies, on the Federation of Rhodesia and
Nyasaland, and on the High Commission Territories. South
Africa was again the major concern. The conference dealt intensively with the question of apartheid and called on the African states to refuse to let South Africa use their ports and
airports, to curtail the flow of African laborers to South Africa, rejected self-government in the Transkei as an "insult to
African people who are demanding complete and genuine freedom and independence for all of South Africa," and demanded
the immediate withdrawal from South West Africa.

The first act of solidarity with the people in Southern
Africa was to accept their independence movements into membership. In Addis Ababa there were already observers from
Basutoland, Bechuanaland, Swaziland, South Africa and South
West Africa. The organization was renamed the Pan-African
Freedom Movement of East, Central, and South Africa
(PAFMECSA). Henceforth these movements would enjoy the
backing of the new states and the organization's committee and
fund. But the newcomers also reversed earlier policy. Pacific means had clearly not impressed the Portuguese or settler regimes and violence had broken out in Angola and had
been approved by many of the movements. Finally,
PAFMECSA also took the step.

The Brazzaville - Casablanca Split.

     The second Conference of Independent African States in 1960 presented the world with the highest common denominator of agreement on the continent. Its program included the various concerns and aspirations (decolonization, an African foreign policy and economic or social goals) as well as the only methods to attain them (peaceful means of liberation and loose cooperation) that had been approved by all the governments. Presumably, nothing should have kept Africa from using the means to attain its ends. Periodic conferences could provide the necessary instructions and mobilize the states for action. But things worked out quite differently. This was the last meeting of all the independent states for some time. And Africa was left without a common policy or, rather, with several competing or contradictory policies.

     The way in which African policy had been chosen in the early days was not far removed from the traditional "palaver." Decisions were not imposed by a majority upon a minority. Rather, an attempt was made at reaching a consensus. This was easy enough at the first CIAS, for it was dominated by the states that had militated for rapid independence. Ethiopia and Liberia, older states which had long been on the sidelines, were only just integrating themselves in the continent. Two years later, the physiognomy of Africa had already begun to change. Guinea, the only French colony to say "no" to de Gaulle's Community, reinforced the Arab states and Ghana. Nigeria and Cameroon were distinctly more moderate. But the dream of "revolutionary" leadership for the continent was shattered in 1960 when a wave of new states turned the balance--especially the former French colonies that had voted "yes."

     It was then that the activists became painfully aware of the drawbacks to palaver. In trying to please the faint-hearted or hesitant, the common policy would be watered down continually until it no longer satisfied the more demanding. The radicals had already begun to switch their backing to the AAPC, where more congenial policies could be voted, and increasingly ignored the possible advantages of the CIAS. The newer members of the independent community were less outward-looking and showed no real interest in reviving the intergovernmental conferences either. Thus, with amazingly little regret, the states on the continent permitted the one official Pan-African organization to disappear.

Changes in the relative number of these states, the
"reformists" and "revolutionaries" as they were called, would
have been unimportant if it were not for the critical problems
with which Africa was confronted. The Algerian war had been
dragging on for years, with each side apparently more resolute than ever and each hope of peaceful settlement an illusion.
The states committed to the struggle stepped up their backing
and expected the same of the newer brothers. Then, only a
few days after the second meeting of Heads of State, the crisis in the Congo broke out and split that country and the whole
continent into feuding camps. These two crises, reacted to
differently by different states, led fatally to a polarization.
This was followed by a more general "ideological" separation
and conflict.

Independence in the thirteen French territories of Black
Africa came--not as the result of a struggle--but smoothly and
reluctantly even for some. General de Gaulle realized that it
was time to reform the French colonial system after the war.
A conference was thus held in Brazzaville in 1944 to consider
the future of the colonies. Although there was no question of
independence, the need for greater administrative decentralization and some self-government was conceded. This was embodied in the second French constitution of 1946 which established "grands conseils" at the federal level and created an
"Assemblée de l'Union Française" in Paris, with elected representatives from the overseas territories. The African leaders in the Assembly often harmonized their positions through
an inter-territorial political party, the Rassemblement Démocratique Africain (RDA), founded in Bamako in the same year.
This party was generally satisfied with autonomy within the
Union, considerably more than in the rest of Africa then, and
did not press for independence.

This experiment in cooperation lasted ten years until
the next step towards independence began seriously eroding the
links with France. The "loi cadre" of 1956 gave the sub-
Saharan colonies even greater self-government. In 1958, de
Gaulle's constitution replaced the Union with a voluntary French
Community, introducing quasi-federal links between France
and the overseas territories. They received internal self-
government aside from foreign affairs, defence, and overall
economic policy, which were handled by the Community Ministers. Coordination was ensured by a meeting of Prime Ministers under the head of the Community, the French President.
There were also joint inter-governmental committees and a
Senate and Court of Arbitration. This offer was put before the

African territories in the referendum of 28 October 1958.
Only Guinea turned it down and was cast into independence
and isolation from France. But the Community was a short
lived hope. It soon began to crumble and the next year, before most of the African leaders, de Gaulle drew his conclusions. He allowed the territories to negotiate independence
while remaining in the Community. Mali was the first to do
so, and by the end of 1960 all the states had obtained total independence.

Only Guinea and Mali, really drew away from France.
The other states d'expression française retained their traditionally close and friendly relations. They remained in the
franc zone and continued their association with the European
Economic Community. Most of them adhered to defence agreements permitting France to intervene in case of external attack or even internal disturbances, and these accords were
backed by a number of military bases and some 28,000 troops.
In questions of external policy, they usually sided with France
and the relations were close enough to appear to some as subordination. The only point at which there might have been a
conflict was policy on Algeria. Therefore the former Community states were anxious for a rapid conclusion to the war.

Already in October 1960, a first meeting was called by
Ivory Coast President (and former French cabinet member)
Félix Houphouët-Boigny to convene in Abidjan, to look into the
possibility of mediating between Algeria and France. But a
larger and more decisive conference was held in Brazzaville,
from 15-19 December 1960. It was attended by the Heads of
State of Cameroon, Central African Republic, Chad, Congo
(Brazzaville), Dahomey, Gabon, Ivory Coast, Niger, Mauritania, Madagascar, Senegal and Upper Volta.

What was peculiar to the Brazzaville Group was certainly not its aims, for the primary one was still the traditional goal of self-determination. What was new was that the
twelve states had solved the predicament of peaceful versus
violent means, left open by the Conferences of Independent African States, by choosing the former. Although they favored
Algerian independence, there was a definite limit to how far
they would go to impose it. The only policy they offered was
one of mediation and persuasion. The approach they adopted
was expressed in the preface to the Brazzaville Declaration:

> Faced with the grave situation of Africa today, they
> are fully aware of their responsibilities. Thus, the

method they have chosen is not to merely appear
to solve problems but to try to solve them concretely, not to take sides but to reconcile the
sides, not to propose any particular compromise
but to invite both sides to a dialogue from which
alone can emerge a solution that constitutes a positive progress for international peace and cooperation.

Ever since 1958, a second group had been forming.
The solidarity of these states was not as old as that of the ex-
French colonies, but it grew rapidly under the pressure of
events. The hard core of this bloc were the states that had
first attained independence and struck their own course in foreign affairs. In most cases, these states had also entered into opposition with the former colonial power and the West.
Gradually they developed similar African ideologies and a
close but informal alliance was maintained on most continental
and international issues.

The solidarity, however, was only political, for the
group consisted of states separated geographically and with different racial, religious or linguistic makeups. The northern
wing, the Maghreb states and Egypt, with Libya and the Sudan
as marginal members, had very close racial and religious
links. The mainspring of their common action was the Algerian war. The southern wing arose with Ghana's support of
Guinea and they were joined later by Mali. The ties between
the two wings were the result of a common attitude on Algeria
and particularly on the Congolese crisis.

Originally these states had been the soul of the Pan-
African movement and they dominated early conferences. However, by 1961, they were a dwindling minority in official African councils. Their policy was no longer followed by the
African Group at the United Nations either. Thus they increasingly felt a need to meet formally to decide upon a common program. When the Brazzaville Group was created, it
was inevitable that this should be taken as a provocation, and
for the militant and activist states to form a counter-bloc.
This was done only two weeks later, when a meeting was held
in Casablanca from 3-7 January 1961, attended by the leaders
of Algeria (Ferhat Abbas), Ghana (Kwame Nkrumah), Guinea
(Sékou Touré), Libya, Mali (Modibo Keita), Morocco (Mohammed V), and the United Arab Republic (Abdel Nasser).

The basic purpose of the Casablanca conference was to reactivate the struggle for decolonization. Only this time the emphasis on liberation was much broader, since it also condemned the post-independence hangovers of colonialism. By so doing, the Casablanca Group struck out on two fronts, against the colonial powers and against any independent states that did not distance themselves from these powers. The stringency of their policy was clear from the preamble to their statement:

> [We] proclaim our determination to liberate the African territories still under foreign domination, by giving them aid and assistance, to liquidate colonialism and neo-colonialism in all their forms, to discourage the maintenance of foreign troops and the establishment of bases which endanger the liberation of Africa and to strive equally to rid the African Continent of political and economic interventions and pressure.

Preliminary Skirmishes.

There were considerable differences in the program and approach of both groupings and they were only accentuated when applied to specific problems. Surprisingly enough, it was the relatively marginal issue of Mauritania that led to the parting of ways. Mauritania, previously part of French West Africa, obtained its independence early in 1960. As did the other former colonies, it requested admission to the United Nations. Meanwhile, Morocco had put forward claims to this territory as part of its historic empire. The Soviet Union supported this stand and vetoed Mauritania's membership.

When the leaders of the former French Community met in Brazzaville, one of their number was President Moktar Ould Daddah. They took this opportunity to sponsor Mauritania's application again and to strike an ironic blow for the cause of the "heroic and pacific struggle for independence." Since the USSR had presented a resolution to the United Nations demanding immediate independence of all colonial territories "through negotiations," these relatively moderate leaders expressed their astonishment that Russia should veto the membership of a country which attained independence by these very means. They then pledged themselves to remedy the situation and called upon all other African states, in the name of liberty and dignity, and also "to avoid the cold war on our continent, " to support Mauritania as well. In this way the "great injustice" of the Russian veto could be undone.

There was an immediate reaction from the King of Morocco, Mohammed V, who called another conference in Casablanca. He hoped to enroll other African states in his campaign against Mauritania. But this issue was a rather poor rallying point. Originally Algeria, Ghana and Libya had not gone along with the Moroccan view and Ghana even sponsored Mauritania's admission to the United Nations. Nevertheless, the states closed their ranks and adopted a hard line. The resolution made the former French colony a test case for the struggle against balkanization and neo-colonialism. The "said" Mauritania was branded a "puppet State" that had been set up "against the will of the people concerned." As such it was just one more artificial barrier in Africa. The main danger was that France was using Mauritania to encircle African countries and as a base for "economic exploitation and strategic use." For these reasons, the conference "approves any action taken by Morocco on Mauritania for the restitution of her legitimate rights. "

Finally there was also a resolution on the problem of Palestine. For some time the Arabs had tried to enlist Black Africa in their crusade against Israel, but the good relations between Israel and many of these states had prevented this. In Casablanca, however, with an Arab majority and President Nkrumah hard pressed on the Congo issue, a resolution could be passed. It regretted that the Arabs of Palestine had been deprived of their legitimate rights. The conference insisted that these rights be restored and denounced Israel "as an instrument in the service of imperialism and neo-colonialism not only in the Middle East but also in Africa and Asia. "

Parallel to this there was a general attack against the policies followed by the moderate states. The main target was the Brazzaville grouping, but the terms were usually broad enough to include any country that maintained close ties with the West and especially the former metropolis. More particularly, there was a condemnation of formal links with external economic blocs and the acceptance of military bases or treaties. As the campaign to liberate Algeria and rescue the Congo from a new colonialism went into high gear, there was also a tendency to criticize any states that did not go all the way. The Casablanca group naturally denounced the recruitment of Africans in the French army, but it was also suspicious of any offer of good offices or appeal for negotiations.

Most of this campaign was undertaken through the All-African Peoples Organization. The AAPO owed its existence largely to the states that financed it and it was not surprising that it followed their political lead. At first it had been a genuine forum in which to discuss the pros and cons of peaceful and violent methods or of the French Community. But the membership changed and was becoming more militant. The former French colonies had never really participated. At the same time, many of the moderates from the English-speaking states dropped out. Both were soon replaced by dissident and oppositional elements from their own countries. And this was reflected in the tenor of the resolutions.

At the Tunis conference, the delegates had issued a warning against the French Community as "a new form of imperialist domination." However, when the Community members became independent and still maintained excellent relations with France, the accusations became more damning. One of the main themes of the AAPO was soon the threat of neo-colonialism and the betrayal of the peoples by leaders who permitted it. The major resolution of the Cairo conference, in March 1961, entered upon very slippery ground.

Neo-colonialism was defined as "the survival of the colonial system in spite of formal recognition of political independence in emerging countries which become victims of an indirect and subtle form of domination by political, economic, social, military or technical means." The aim was seen to "foster disunity and to thwart the struggle towards the true liberation of Africa." A detailed analysis was made of the phenomenon. The manifestations were listed as, among others: puppet governments represented by stooges and fabricated elections, both the regrouping and balkanization of states, economic entrenchment and integration in colonial economic blocs, economic infiltration by investments and loans or direct monetary dependence, and military bases. The agents of neo-colonialism were the colonial embassies and missions, foreign and United Nations technical assistants and, in particular, "puppet governments in Africa being used by imperialists in the furtherance of neo-colonialism, such as the use of their good offices by neo-colonial powers to undermine the sovereignty and aspirations of other African States." The main "perpetrators" of neo-colonialism were the United States, the Federal Republic of Germany, Israel, Britain, Belgium, Holland, South Africa and France. And the worst victims were the Congo, the Federation of Rhodesia and Nyasaland, and the French Community.

At this point the AAPO noisily entered the fray between the Casablanca states and the moderates. Whether or
not it really spoke for the African peoples, as it claimed, it
was increasingly expressing the policy of a small group of
states and criticizing that of the rest. "Down with neo-colonialism" was a particularly disruptive battle cry since it encouraged certain elements in Africa to judge and even condemn policies approved or accepted by the others. Rather
than uniting the continent it was another wedge driving the
nascent blocs apart.

None of these issues were sufficient to consolidate the
split in Africa. The various states eventually fell out over
two issues of seemingly decisive importance for the continent's
future: Algeria and the Congo. For the first time no attempt
at obtaining a common policy was successful and there was a
clash between different and antagonistic approaches.

The Algerian War of Liberation.

On 1 November 1954, a completely unexpected uprising
initiated one of the most harrowing phases of decolonization.
France acted rapidly and massively to defend the integrity of
its "departments" in Algeria and the war began. By 1956 the
National Liberation Front (FLN) had an army of about 20,000
within the country, highly mobile and able to blend in with the
population, that could attack and retreat before the arrival of
French troops. There was a second army double the size
along the borders with Morocco and Tunisia but held at bay by
the French. Still, by materializing suddenly and vanishing,
the FLN was able to harass the French administration and
eventually tie down an army of almost half a million.

In this struggle the Algerian Liberation Front received
generous support from Morocco, Tunisia and Egypt. Its allies
provided numerous services diplomatically and materially, helping to arm and finance the war. Any backing outside the Arab
world was much more limited. It was only natural to look toward the rest of Africa for aid and the matter was discussed
at the first conference of independent states in April 1958.
The FLN attended as an observer and pleaded its case. The
Moroccans and Tunisians also repeated their offer of good offices. And the conference responded as a whole by recognizing the right of the Algerian people to independence and self-
determination. The delegates urged France to recognize this
right as well, cease the hostilities and enter into peaceful ne-

gotiations with the FLN to reach a settlement. There was
general interest in aiding Algeria, but it was ill-defined and
the only commitment was "to make every possible effort to
help the Algerian people."

Somewhat later in the year the Provisional Government
of the Algerian Republic (GPRA) was constituted and made a
bid for recognition. This was soon accorded by Arab states
like Libya, Morocco, Sudan, Tunisia and the United Arab Republic. But there was much less headway in Black Africa.
It was recognized by Ghana but the other states were worried
by French retaliation. There was a tendency for Africa to
fall into groups of strong and lukewarm supporters on this
basis and, in order to restore the common front, a special
conference of Foreign Ministers was convened in Monrovia
from 4-8 August 1959. It was to work out a joint African policy on Algeria, mobilize aid for the nationalists and try to end
the war.

Fortunately, the positions did not seem far apart.
President Tubman of Liberia urged both France and the GPRA
to modify their extreme demands to permit a peaceful conclusion. The Algerian delegation, attending as a full member,
expressed readiness to meet with the French government to
discuss a political settlement. And the conference urged that
a "just, peaceful and democratic solution" be reached by negotiations. In the meantime the African governments were to
maintain their diplomatic support and render material aid as
well (each government deciding itself the kind and amount). In
addition, it was "hoped" that peoples and governments the
world over would recognize the GPRA, but only Guinea did so
immediately.

As early as 16 September 1959, President de Gaulle
admitted the right of the Algerians to determine their own future, although he did not accept the GPRA as their sole representative. Finally, on 14 June 1960, he made an offer of
discussions with the GPRA, to consider the basis for a settlement. Clutching at this straw, the second conference of independent states that opened the day after welcomed de
Gaulle's offer and GPRA willingness to negotiate. It invited
both parties to reach an agreement on "fair and sincere implementation of the right of self-determination." Until then,
the material and diplomatic support would be continued.

However, even acceptance in principle by the President
of the French Republic was not enough to end the conflict.

For there was tremendous pressure to keep "Algérie française"
in the army and the civilian population, primarily among the
settlers but also in France.   There were also other elements
among the Algerians that did not see eye-to-eye with the FLN.
Thus the war for independence went on unabated.   Neither
modern equipment and large concentrations of troops nor barb-
ed wire fences could wipe out the maquis or keep the terrorist squads from launching their raids in the cities.   The bitterness of the attacks from within and the increasingly ruth-
less repression of the Arab population led to exasperation on
both sides.   The French were not able to bring about a complete "reconquest" of the country, but they could also not be
driven out by the FLN.

      Nevertheless, the President maintained his offer and
France was growing weary of the effort.   When the former
colonies entered the scene they reminded de Gaulle of this offer.   In Brazzaville these states adopted a more conciliatory
attitude than had been customary in Africa, but they did not
question the ultimate goal.   The declaration of 19 December
1960 called upon France to persevere in its tradition of decolonization.   Rather than condemn, they spoke as friends to obtain the "honest and democratic application of the principle of
self-determination solemnly proclaimed by General de Gaulle."
Their stand was also dictated by the "fear of watching the Algerian drama degenerate into a world conflict."   Although they
did not extend even moral support to Algeria--or keep their
nationals from serving in the French army--they did plan a
somewhat different campaign in its favor.   They even set a
deadline for fulfillment and "resolved to ask France firmly to
conclude the war in Algeria in 1961."

      Their initiative was not well received in some quarters.
The war had been poisoning inter-African relations and each
state was increasingly judged by its contribution to the struggle.   Even if they did not all give freely, the other independent states had at least gone on record in favor of diplomatic
and material aid to the GPRA.   The French Community members, to the contrary, passively accepted French policy in Algeria and even collaborated by permitting their territory or
men to be used for the military effort.   When they became independent, the older states were uncertain how to react.   For,
although the Brazzaville twelve claimed to desire Algerian independence, they sought it in another way and for other motives.

The Casablanca Group did not hesitate. The declaration was treated as a challenge. For them there were only two categories of states, those aiding the Algerian people and making a "contribution to the liberation of Africa," and those abetting France and committing an "act of hostility directed against Africa as a whole." Those who were the friends of Africa had to recognize the GPRA, reconsider their relations with France and encourage the enlistment of volunteers in the Army of National Liberation. Africa's enemies included the NATO powers and those whose territory was used by France and whose troops served under the French command in Algeria. The Casablanca states decided to back the Algerians "by all means," political, diplomatic and material. But they had no faith in negotiations or mediation. The resolution of 7 January 1961 implicitly denied France's capacity to find a solution and "denounces and condemns all consultations and referendums unilaterally organized by France in Algeria, and the result thereof can in no way commit the Algerian people."

Ignoring this strong stand of the Casablanca Group, not long thereafter the Algerian Provisional Government again put forward propositions for negotiations. Early in 1961, a referendum was held in Algeria and France. The majority in France and 69 percent of those in Algeria approved General de Gaulle's offer to let Algeria vote on self-determination and have the result confirmed by the French people. This was a breakthrough in the process of withdrawal and the French Government decided to open negotiations with the GPRA.

Things bogged down, however, due to French attempts at detaching the Sahara. Negotiations were held and collapsed. The positions stiffened. And there was a further threat from among the settler population of a million. There had already been two uprisings to prevent independence. But this was nothing compared with the last ditch struggle launched by the extremists as Algerian independence became a certainty. The Organisation de l'Armée Secrète (OAS), through unrestricted terrorist acts, drove the country towards the brink of civil war and carried on a two front campaign against the Algerians and the French Government, both in Algeria and metropolitan France. But it could not prevent the Evian Agreement of 19 March 1962. A cease-fire was then proclaimed and the OAS was gradually mopped up. The struggle for liberation had been won. The referendum confirmed this with a massive "yes" from 91.23 percent of the Algerian voters. The French approved as well. Then, on 5 July, Algeria was declared independent.

At this point, one might ask which approach was more
effective, that of Brazzaville or Casablanca. Working on the
principle of the carrot and the stick, the Brazzaville Group
would be the carrot. Arguing its friendship for France and
its respect of French traditions, it tried to prevail on General
de Gaulle to take the decisive step. The Casablanca Group
was a stick. But it was waved more often than it struck.
For, already having bad relations with France and committed
to the Algerian cause, it could do little more. The real
stick was the Army of National Liberation. By making
France's war long and painful, it gained the right of self-determination. The backing of the Casablanca powers was help-
ful--but far from decisive. Moreover, independence was eventually granted on the very basis desired by France and rejected by the Casablanca states: negotiations and referendum.
By allowing France to save face and protect its interests in
Algeria, an acceptable solution could be found. What was
needed were both the carrot and the stick.

The Congolese Embroglio.

Whereas the other African countries obtained their independence as the result of some sign of determination to plot
their own destiny, the Belgian Congo was just dropped. There
had been no real preparation for self-government during Belgium's paternalistic rule and there were very few "intellectuals" to form the core of a future government and administration. Moreover, until the Brussels World Fair, the Congolese
had had few contacts with one another and less with the rest
of the continent. Nevertheless, the Congolese became aware
of the drift towards independence in Africa and Patrice Lumumba attended the AAPO meeting in Accra, in December 1958.
He met the more radical nationalist leaders and was endorsed
as a valid spokesman for the Congo by Prime Minister Nkrumah and others.

After returning to the Congo, Lumumba addressed an
important gathering in Léopoldville. His call for liberty led
to riots and this was the shock that made King Baudouin concede Belgium's intention of granting the Congo independence.
This set off a hectic rush to organize political parties in
which the only point of agreement was the demand for elections and independence. A Round Table Conference in Brussels, in January 1960, after a year of demonstrations and disturbances, ended with Belgian acceptance of provincial and
national elections, the formation of a fully African government

and complete independence--all in six months.

Obviously, this was not enough time to build up genuinely national or ideological parties and voting was largely
along tribal or provincial lines. In the May 1960 elections,
only Patrice Lumumba, leader of the Mouvement National Con-
golais, had some support throughout the country, although most
of his following was in Orientale province. And this party
was soon split by a branch led by Albert Kalondji, Joseph Ileo
and Cyrille Adoula. Elsewhere, parties like the Conakat of
Moise Tshombe in Katanga, the Parti Solidaire Africain (PSA)
of Antoine Gizenga, in Kwilu, and the Alliance des Ba-Kongo
(ABAKO) of Joseph Kasavubu, in Léopoldville, and others were
able to establish bastions in their own regions. It was only
with great difficulty that a government could be put together
with Patrice Lumumba as Prime Minister and Joseph Kasavubu
as Head of State.

Five days after the Congo became independent, on 30
June 1960, the "Force Publique" mutinied against its European
officers and there was an exodus of settlers and civil servants
from the country. When the Kasavubu/ Lumumba government
failed to quell the riots, Brussels by-passed them and sent in
troops to protect its nationals. The return of the Belgians
looked like a re-colonization of the Congo to many Africans,
and a common front was formed in the United Nations to back
the Congolese Government's appeal for aid. On 14 July, the
Security Council decided to send the United Nations Operation
in the Congo (ONUC) to replace the Belgians. Within two days
troops from African, Asian and smaller European states began
to arrive and, by the beginning of September, there were no
more Belgian troops in the Congo.

The second crisis was more serious. On 11 July, the
day after the Belgians arrived, a secession was declared in
Katanga and rapidly consolidated during the Belgian occupation.
The national authorities had no influence in the region, and
Moise Tshombe, the head of the provincial government, quickly built up a 15,000 man "gendarmerie" led by former Belgian
officers, political advisors and mercenaries, to make the secession a reality. His example was followed shortly thereafter
by Albert Kalondji, who proclaimed a "Mining State of Kasai,"
of which he eventually became "king."

In Léopoldville, there was general agreement that any
secession had to be put down, but little agreement on how.
Although President Kasavubu held back, Prime Minister Lu-

mumba had soon gotten into a quarrel with the United Nations
Secretary-General, Dag Hammarskjöld, over the extent to
which the United Nations Force should be used against the
Katangese secession. On August 9, the Security Council endorsed Hammarskjöld's stand and stated that ONUC "will not
be a party to or in any way intervene in or be used to influence the outcome of any internal conflict, constitutional or
otherwise."[2]

Since the United Nations troops would not do his bid-
ding, Prime Minister Lumumba tried to organize his own force
to attack Katanga. Among other things, he accepted Russian
support and transport planes to fly in his troops. In his quest
for African backing, he also called a meeting of independent
African states in Léopoldville. This "Little Summit," where
neither invitations nor participation was universal, met from
25-31 August 1960. The states present were Algeria, Congo
(Léopoldville), Ethiopia, Ghana, Guinea, Libya, Liberia, Morocco, Sudan, Togo, Tanganyika, Tunisia and the UAR. Since
they had been picked by Lumumba, it was assumed that on the
whole these states would be favorable to his views.

The situation was tense in the capital of the Congo and,
as the Prime Minister welcomed the delegates with the words,
"You are now making contact with the realities of the African
Congo," these realities were echoed by the sound of shooting.[3]
Due possibly to this climate, the African leaders maintained
their support of the United Nations as the only alternative to
anarchy and the cold war. Despite Prime Minister Lumumba's
insistence that the UN policy be disavowed and the personal
representative of the Secretary-General, Ralph Bunche, condemned, the conference praised the United Nations and agreed
to send a message of appreciation to Dr. Bunche. The delegates also stressed the importance of "harmonizing" aid to the
Congo within the UN program. Although the Prime Minister's
struggle against the Tshombe regime in Katanga was approved
and the "secession and colonialist manoeuvres" condemned, the
delegates only pledged support for the integrity of the Congo
without laying down any policy for dealing with the secession.
A further deception was that Kwame Nkrumah, who had always
backed Lumumba in the past, was worried by his impetuous
behaviour.

All the while, President Kasavubu had been distancing
himself from Lumumba's schemes. On 5 September 1960, he
disavowed his policy and dismissed the Prime Minister, requesting Joseph Ileo, the President of the Senate, to take his

place. Lumumba then dismissed President Kasavubu. Soon
the rivalry took worse forms and the confusion was complete.
To avoid trouble, the United Nations troops closed down the
airports and radio stations. Still, Lumumba fought back and
might have come out on top, except that on 13 September all
the politicians were "neutralized" by Colonel Joseph Mobutu,
the head of the Congolese national army. Thus began a constitutional crises of eleven months. This third crisis was the
worst for, in the interval, there was no one "legal" government, but rather a country divided into three or more opposed
and armed camps.

   Mobutu's "College of Commissioners" had little authority in the Congo and was rejected by Lumumba. Increasingly,
however, Kasavubu and Ileo began to associate themselves with
Colonel Mobutu. And, when two delegations were sent to the
General Assembly in November, President Kasavubu managed
to have his representatives seated. This was only at the cost
of a split in the Afro-Asian group, with Ghana, Guinea, Mali,
Morocco and the UAR, joined by India and the Communist
countries, voting against him. It was not surprising that Lumumba was more suspicious of the United Nations than ever
and sought a stronger base for action. While trying to flee
Léopoldville he was captured by Mobutu's troops and arrested
on a warrant signed by Kasavubu. Some of his followers, including Antoine Gizenga and Christophe Gbenye, did escape to
Stanleyville and created a Lumumbist stronghold and rival government there in December.

   By the time the Brazzaville conference was held, at
the end of 1960, its members could choose between the competing regimes in Léopoldville, Stanleyville and Katanga. In
some cases, a clear choice was made. When ONUC closed
the airports across the river, President Abbé Fulbert Youlou,
of Congo (Brazzaville), placed the airport of Brazzaville at
the disposal of both Kasavubu and Tshombe. In other ways as
well, he and a number of the moderate leaders showed preference for the Kasavubu regime and greater tolerance for Tshombe's demands of autonomy. Nevertheless, the group held to
its policy of mediation in the Congolese affair as well. Thus,
parallel to the conference, President Youlou had invited representatives of all the factions in the Congo: Kasavubu, Tshombe, Kalondji, Kasongo (a Lumumbist), Justin Bomboko (head
of the "College of Commissioners") and Colonel Mobutu (who
did not attend).

The Conference adopted a stand very similar to the original united front among the African states. It gave full support to the United Nations and its Secretary-General in its efforts to "save the Congo (Léopoldville) from chaos and anarchy" and to keep the cold war out of the Congo. The split between Kasavubu and Lumumba and their two governments was a constant invitation to antagonistic blocs trying to "recolonize" the Congo. What was worse, these blocs worked through the intermediary of certain African states. Therefore, the solution suggested for maintaining the independence of the Congo was continued UN technical assistance only. The other states would have to refrain from all intervention in domestic affairs. Then the Congolese could seek a practical solution at a "Round Table Conference, which would group together the representatives of every party without exception."

Only Thomas Kanza, the head of Lumumba's delegation to the General Assembly, was invited to the Casablanca meeting in January 1961. The more adamant of the leaders there wished to back the Stanleyville regime to the hilt, diplomatically and materially. They repudiated the tame stand of the United Nations and the other African states and sought open commitment to the Lumumbist regime. If the UN did not come into line, they wanted to withdraw their troops from the Congo and help build-up the forces under Gizenga. This policy was resisted by Ghana's President Nkrumah, who feared a further degeneration of the conflict and asked that the troops be left under the UN command while arguing that the "logistics" of keeping Stanleyville supplied made military support impracticable. For the moment, at least, he was able to restrain the Casablanca group.

Ultimately the conference adopted a plan and a warning. It asked the United Nations to "safeguard" the unity and independence of the Republic of the Congo and preserve its territorial integrity." To this purpose, the UN would immediately disarm the "lawless bands" of Mobutu and release the members of the "legitimate" government (including Lumumba) and Parliament; the airports and radio stations would be restored to the government and Parliament reconvened; then ONUC would eliminate all foreign military and para-military personnel from the Congo, and Belgium would be prevented from using Ruanda-Urundi "as a base to commit aggression." The sting was that any failure of the United Nations to implement this plan would cause the Casablanca states to withdraw their troops and possibly also to take "appropriate action."

But Africa had little control over what happened. The Congo operation was run through the Security Council, where the great powers had a privileged position, and in the field through the Secretariat. Africa was largely on the sidelines, although intensely interested in the outcome. All it could do was express its views or criticism in the General Assembly. And this it did, excepting that its effect was dispersed by serious divisions among the states. The Brazzaville members had never liked ONUC's intervention in internal affairs, both on principle and because by leaving the Congolese alone things might well come out as they desired. The Casablanca states urged a forceful UN role at first, but when it went against their man, they reversed their stand and tried to scuttle the whole operation. Others were relatively undecided but usually went along with the UN. To keep an eye on the Secretariat, Dag Hammarskjöld had been prevailed upon to accept an Afro-Asian consultative committee, a body of uncertain effect given its distance from the scene of events. The only real impact Africa had in the Congo derived from the ideas or actions of strategically placed individuals like Robert Gardiner of Ghana and General Kettani of Morocco.

For some time, the Kasavubu/Mobutu regime in Léopoldville had been worried by the strength of the Lumumbist forces. Gradually, the West (especially the advisors of President-elect Kennedy), the United Nations and some moderate African states began to feel that a coalition was necessary. But, neither Kasavubu nor Mobutu were certain what that meant for them. On 18 January they had Patrice Lumumba transferred to prison in Elisabethville, in the heart of Tshombe's Katanga. There, he and two of his companions were brutally murdered.

When the news leaked out, on 13 February 1961, there was a wave of indignation and fury. It came to a head in the United Nations. The world organization had not been able to take the Prime Minister into custody after his arrest and the UN troops at the airport did not even prevent the departure of a battered and bleeding Lumumba. The UN Force remained true to its orders--not to intervene in internal affairs. This indifference was criticized by many of the African delegates and the Soviet Union unleashed a bitter attack against Secretary-General Hammarskjöld, demanding his dismissal. Although the majority of the delegates supported him, it was generally admitted that the United Nations had to change its policy and a stronger resolution was adopted by the Security Council on 21 February. The UN Command was authorized to use force as a last resort to prevent civil war and the necessary measures were to be taken to remove the foreign military advisers and mercenaries from Katanga.

The death of Lumumba ushered in one of the most tragic periods in the history of Pan-Africanism. The common front was gone, even willingness not to aggravate the situation faded, and one after another the African states took sides. The Casablanca Group promptly announced their unconditional backing of the Gizenga regime and increased their harassing of the UN operation. Many moderate states, both the Brazzaville Group and others, came out in favor of the Kasavubu/ Mobutu regime as the only legitimate one and expressed a wish to maintain a United Nations presence to avoid the worst. They also sought to reintegrate Katanga peacefully rather than crush the Tshombe regime. Soon independent Africa was split into opposing camps.

In an effort to heal the rift in the Congo and in Africa, the Brazzaville Group called a Round Table Conference in Tananarive, in Madagascar, from 5-13 March 1961. Gizenga sent no one, but three of the factions did come: Kasavubu, Tshombe and Kalondji. The first was a federalist at heart and the other two heads of break-away provinces, and they agreed in principle that the unitary form of government in the Congo should be replaced by a federal system, with Kasavubu at its head. The Brazzaville states declared their willingness to give military and other assistance to the Congo if this were approved by the rest of the African states. Neither of these proposals, however, was acceptable to the Gizenga regime and its backers, who had always been advocates of strict unity.

A sharp reply to the Round Table Conference came from the All-African Peoples Organization in Cairo. The "meeting of puppets" in Tananarive was denounced as a tool of the imperialists who attempted to "apply their classical methods of 'Divide and Rule'." The ties between Lumumba and the AAPO had always been very deep and he was a permanent member of the Conference's governing body. The resolution of 23 March condemned his "savage assassination" and proclaimed him "Hero of Africa." Immediate punishment was demanded for those responsible for his death: Kasavubu, Mobutu, Tshombe, Kalondji and Dag Hammarskjöld ("equally responsible"). As was done at the Casablanca conference, the AAPO called upon all the African states to recognize the government of Antoine Gizenga as the "only legitimate government of the indivisible Republic of the Congo." The United

Nations was accused of serving the rival "puppet governments"
and urged to cease its "imperialistic military interventions"
in the Congo and "restore law and order by the normal functioning of ... Parliament." As for the peoples and states of
Africa, they were "to help, by every possible means, the
brother people of the Congo to continue their struggle for the
liberation and unification of their territory."

The outlook for reconciliation in the Congo was bleak.
Nevertheless, the three-cornered struggle left an opening for
alliances. After temporary cooperation with the Tshombe regime, President Kasavubu realized that there was little chance
of ending the secession. Negotiations were then initiated with
Gizenga and it was possible to reassemble Parliament under
United Nations protection in July 1961 with all but Tshombe's
Conakat participating. On 2 August, a new national government was formed with Cyrille Adoula as Prime Minister and
Antoine Gizenga as Vice-Prime Minister. Unfortunately this
was only a brief interlude, for the government soon fell out
over the policy to follow towards the Katangan secession.
Antoine Gizenga retreated again to Stanleyville, where he was
arrested and then imprisoned by the central authorities in
January 1962.

The rump government of national unity, under Cyrille
Adoula, still tried to win over Tshombe. When this did not
work, it issued an order for the expulsion of the mercenaries
in Katanga. The aid of ONUC was requested, and it was obvious that the only effective force in the Congo was that of the
United Nations, grown to some 20,000 men. The Belgian government had already ordered its personnel to withdraw from
Katanga, but over 500 military advisers and mercenaries remained. About 300 were rounded up peacefully; the rest went
underground. When the operation was repeated on 28 August,
the UN troops were fired upon by the Katangan gendarmerie.
Hostilities continued during most of September, as the United
Nations tried to obtain a cease-fire. While flying to meet
Tshombe, on 18 September 1961, Secretary-General Hammarskjöld lost his life.

Not long after the fighting ceased temporarily. But the
cease-fire was not observed by the Katangan authorities and
the situation was threatening. In a new resolution, on 24 November, the Security Council permitted the UN Command to
use force--on its own initiative and without order of the Congolese government--to expel the mercenaries and other foreign personnel from Katanga. On 5 December, fighting broke

out again and went on for two weeks until Tshombe gave in
and signed an eight point declaration accepting the "loi fonda-
mentale," recognizing the central government, and promising
to end the secession.

Even then the crisis was not over. Léopoldville began
negotiations with Tshombe and they went on fitfully from
March to June 1962, before collapsing. Eventually a United
Nations "Plan of National Reconciliation" was approved by
Prime Minister Adoula. It provided for a federal system of
government, a general amnesty and a central government representative of all political and provincial groups. The plan
was finally accepted by Tshombe, a federal constitution was
drafted and, in November, President Kasavubu proclaimed the
amnesty.

Nevertheless, back in Katanga, no steps were taken to
fulfill the plan and the situation deteriorated. After six days
of unprovoked fire from the gendarmerie, the UN forces replied and its operations expanded. By 14 January 1963, the
gendarmerie was beaten and Tshombe agreed to end the secession. Fully two-and-a-half years after it had been proclaimed,
the state of Katanga was reintegrated in the Congo.

Inter-State Rivalry and Intervention.

Bad as the verbal warfare at conferences and clashes
over policy on Algeria and the Congo may have been, the situation would not have been as explosive if the militant states
had not made even more active efforts at influencing the destiny of the continent. After having labelled the moderate
states puppets or tools of neo-colonialism, many of the Casablanca states drew the logical conclusion. It was this attempt
at bringing a "real" liberation to the already independent
states that led to the worst abuses in inter-African affairs.

The situation in West Africa was most threatening. The
earlier cordiality and amity among leaders there rapidly faded.
A case in point was the relations between the most dynamic
country, Ghana, and the huge Federation of Nigeria. Coming
on the scene when President Nkrumah of Ghana already seemed to have cornered the Pan-African movement, the Nigerians
wished to escape his tutelage. When Ghana kept them out of
the Non-Aligned Conference, in 1961, the Nigerians were doubly hurt: first, that they should be barred by their rival; secondly, that anyone should dictate foreign policy to them or call

their policy "aligned. " Taking a contrary tack to Ghana in
domestic matters as well, the Nigerians were proud of their
democracy and diversity and criticized each step taken by the
Ghanaian President to crush the opposition, particularly the
Preventive Detention Act of 1958. This was returned in good
measure by Nkrumah. The climax was reached in September
1962, when a conspiracy was uncovered in Nigeria. It was
traced to Chief Obafemi Awolowo's Action Group, but Ghana
was implicated as well.

Elsewhere in the region tension also ran high. Ghana
and Guinea had long backed the Union des Peuples du Cameroun (UPC), giving asylum and a platform to its leader in exile, Félix Moumié. But this active solidarity went further,
including the training and equipping of guerrilla soldiers and
terrorists. This support enabled the UPC to make numerous
raids and slow down the pacification. The situation became so
bad that, at the second Conference of Independent African
States, the Cameroun Foreign Minister attacked Guinea for
supporting the insurrection and accused it of flooding the
Cameroun Republic[4] with Czech weapons.

Liberia, as well, was subject to considerable harassing
by its larger neighbors. This came to a head in September
1961 when Monrovia expelled a member of the Ghanaian embassy for organizing subversive movements. Less than a
week later, it was announced that preparations for a coup
d'état to install a Communist regime had been uncovered and
that it was organized through the Soviet embassy in Guinea.

The worst rivalry was between Prime Minister Nkrumah and President Sylvanus Olympio of Togo. Ghana made no
secret of its designs on its smaller neighbor and was repeatedly involved in oppositional maneuvres in Togo. But Nkrumah also had trouble with his own political and tribal opposition. Many moderate political leaders and tribal heads, especially the Ashanti, objected to his strong rule and used desperate measures to stop him. This ignited a long series of
plots and attempted assassinations in both countries. In May
1961, the Togolese disrupted plans for a revolt and the assassination of President Olympio, which they announced was backed by a "neighboring country." Another plot was uncovered in
December. The plotters were arrested and confessed that
they had been trained in Ghana. On 8 January 1962, the Togolese government officially accused Nkrumah of supporting
the plot. But the Ghanaian government had already countered
this. In October 1961, President Nkrumah had most of the

opposition arrested, accusing it en masse of conspiracy.
When the White Paper came out, on 10 December, it mentioned the "connivence and active support of the Togolese government," explained by the fact that Togo was one of the
countries in Africa "where neo-colonialism has its strongest
hold." Shortly thereafter, another attempt at assassinating
President Olympio failed. In September 1962, President Nkrumah's turn came again, and two bombs went off in his presence. From this point on, reaching a crescendo at the end
of the year, Togo was repeatedly accused of supporting plots
by Ghanaian refugees.

Sékou Touré of Guinea also stirred up trouble in the
region. After Guinea voted "no" in the 1958 French constitutional referendum, it formed a center of great agitation and
more serious resistance against France and against the policies of the states that cooperated with France. Most of the
sparks were purely verbal, directed largely against Félix
Houphouët-Boigny of the Ivory Coast and--after the collapse
of Mali--President Léopold Sédar Senghor of Senegal. But the
other leaders of the Brazzaville Group also felt his ire.

With the collapse of the Mali Federation, Sékou Touré
was joined by Modibo Keita. Although Mali gave asylum to
the Senegalese opposition and was accused of instigating a plot
against Senegal in February 1962 and providing a training
camp for refugees, the relations with the Brazzaville leaders
were not as strained.

In the Arab North, the unity of action for Algerian independence was not enough to prevent a split among unlike-
minded leaders. President Habib Bourguiba's struggle against
Salah ben Youssef's terrorists in southern Tunisia, who were
controlled from rebel headquarters in Cairo, rapidly deteriorated the relations with Egypt. The breach was hastened
when Egypt was implicated in a plot against President Bourguiba's life in March 1958. In October Tunisia broke its diplomatic relations with Cairo because of interference in its internal affairs. By December this degenerated into a war over
the air waves between Presidents Nasser and Bourguiba.

A further split was caused by the Mauritanian affair,
given top priority by Morocco. Tunisia had recognized Mauritania in November 1960 and, after a sharp note, the Moroccans recalled their ambassador. Morocco was also tied up in
the plot against Senegal, one of the main sponsors of Mauritanian independence, and the Senegalese ambassador to Moroc-

co was recalled from Rabat.   All the while, sporadic raids
were launched by a "national liberation council," quartered
somewhere in Mali.   The incursions did not cease even when
Mauritania entered the United Nations.   As late as May 1962,
President Moktar Ould Daddah accused Morocco and Mali of
organizing "attentats" in his country.

Finally, the Congo had its share of intervention from
both sides.   By November 1960, Ghana's active support of
Lumumba had become intolerable and relations were broken.
At the same time, the tension increased with Egypt.   In December when the Gizenga government was set up in Stanleyville, the gulf with the Casablanca Group became unbridgeable.
There were now two groups of states who supported two different governments, each seen as "legitimate," and each claiming exclusive authority over the whole territory of the Congo.
This situation did not cease until August 1961, when a government of national unity was formed.

Trouble arose in another quarter as well.   President
Youlou of the Congo (Brazzaville) had always supported Moise
Tshombe.   After the Tananarive conference, he insisted that
the plan of federation be applied.   On 3 May 1961, he called
upon the Brazzaville states to help impose its implementation
and demanded the release of Tshombe, who had been arrested
at the reconciliation meeting in Coquilhatville.   Two days
later, the Kasavubu government of the Congo (Léopoldville) replied by closing the frontier between the two Congos.

The Inter-Union Feud.

At different times and in different ways trade unions
had sprung up in all parts of the continent.   They were always at the forefront of the struggle for independence and it
was often the unions that, by unleashing strikes or demonstrations, provided the positive action needed to sway the colonial
power.   Many of the men who worked their way up through the
unions also became important leaders in the new states.   Even
after independence it was hard for the rank-and-file or union
officials to be unconcerned with political issues.   But this was
not all to the good.   For rivalries on the political scene
could be drawn into trade union affairs and repeated efforts
were made to capture the movement.

One of the most militant of the union leaders, Sékou
Touré, brought the first impulse of Pan-Africanism to the

trade union movement.   Back in April 1956, he broke with the
French Communist trade union and the leftist international center, the World Federation of Trade Unions (WFTU), and led
the Guinean and Senegalese trade unions into the first strictly
African confederation.   Not long after, a conference was held
in Cotonou, Dahomey, to found the Union Générale des Trav-
ailleurs d'Afrique Noire (UGTAN) with no metropolitan or international affiliations.   Its aims read like a declaration of
independence of trade unionism: "to unite and organize the
workers of black Africa, to co-ordinate their trade union activities in the struggle against the colonial regime and all
other forms of exploitation ... and to affirm the personality
of African trade unionism."

        Although UGTAN at first gained a broad following in the
French territories of Black Africa, the split between Sékou
Touré and the other African leaders had implications for trade
unionism as well.   When Guinea left the French Community
and began to attack it, UGTAN affiliates in the other territories were politicized and began criticizing the policies of their
national leaders.   But they were gradually squeezed out by
state-sponsored unions or merely suppressed.   By the end of
1959, only Guinea still had a section of UGTAN.

        Ghana, at first, lagged behind.   An African regional
conference of the other main international center, the International Confederation of Free Trade Unions (ICFTU), was held
in Accra in 1957.   However, after the Union was formed between Ghana and Guinea, and then expanded to Mali, the
Guinea section of UGTAN was joined by those of Ghana and
Mali.   For President Nkrumah, this was a natural expansion
of his ideas into another field.

        The role of the trade unions in the All-African Peoples
Organization was highly significant.   This was shown by making Tom Mboya, the Secretary-General of the Kenya Federation of Labour, its chairman in Accra.   This first conference
expressed the will of all trade unionists to unite.   But the harmony was soon disturbed.   A second ICFTU regional meeting
had been scheduled for Lagos, Nigeria, in November 1959.
Nevertheless, Ghana called a rival meeting to coincide with
that date.   With two meetings at the same time, the African
trade unions had to make a choice, and the great majority
went to Lagos.   Only Ghana, Guinea, Morocco, the UAR and
one of the Nigerian centers went to Accra, although others
sent observers.   In Accra, the delegates made strong demands
for an all-African trade union federation.   At the same time,

although they agreed with an African federation in principle,
the moderate unions refused any split with the ICFTU. They
did, however, create their own African Regional Organization
(AFRO) within the ICFTU.

At the second AAPO conference in Tunis, in January
1960, the battle was joined again. A major resolution was
adopted on the unity of the African trade union organizations.
But the problem of affiliation had not yet been thrashed out
among the unions and no mention was made of it in the resolution. When AFRO met in Tunis, in November 1960, the
vast majority of the African trade unions (only those of Ghana,
Guinea and the UAR stayed away) accepted the idea of an "all-
African trade union Federation" in principle, but stressed that
they would not be pressured into joining one. They wished to
share in the creation of such a body and to preserve their
principles, one of which was "international solidarity." The
AAPO meeting in Cairo, in March 1961, also called for the
launching of the All-African Trade Union Federation (AATUF)
as a "means of counteracting neo-colonialism."

The actual birth of AATUF was more painful. Not long
after the political division of the continent was consumated by
the Casablanca conference, a second meeting was held there,
in May 1961. This time the trade unionists assembled. The
intention proclaimed by the organizers was to create AATUF,
and in this they were successful. But only through a variety
of irregularities. Some unions had not been invited, the preparatory committee was run by the radical unions and there
was a biased distribution of votes. The final decision was
taken--by acclamation and not by a vote--at a moment when
many of the unions had already walked out in disgust. In an
ultimatum to the moderate unions, the new body summoned
them to break their affiliations within ten months and join
AATUF.

As soon as they returned home, the leaders of the moderate trade unions, like Tom Mboya, Ahmed Tlili (Tunisia)
and Lawrence Borha (Nigeria), protested the proceedings and
principles of the Casablanca conference. The reply, made by
John Tettegah of Ghana, was that AATUF would wage "total
war" on African unions refusing to disaffiliate from other international organizations. "We shall isolate them," he said,
"and enter their countries and form AATUF unions there. It
is as simple as that--total war."[5] He added that Ghana was
already active in various independent countries.

Nevertheless, at the ILO conference in Geneva, in June 1961, a number of labor leaders decided to convene a further meeting in order to bring about a reconciliation and create a Pan-African body acceptable to all. When the president of AATUF informed them that he would not cooperate in holding a conference and that the only basis for a reconciliation was the unconditional acceptance of AATUF, they went ahead and called a meeting for Dakar, Senegal. The only delegations that deliberately stayed away were those of the Casablanca Group. Thus, in January 1962, the moderate trade unionists created a counter-organization, the African Trade Union Confederation (ATUC). Although it was decided that ATUC should not be affiliated to any of the international centers, the individual unions were free to affiliate.

So, at this point, the trade union movement in the African continent was also split into two. Rivalry and controversy raged, mixed with bribery and raiding, formation of splinter groups, and interference.

The Monrovia Conference.

The split between the Brazzaville and Casablanca powers ushered in the darkest period of post-independence African history. The unity of action of the first conferences was replaced by contradictory and antagonistic policies of two rival groups. It was soon evident to many of the leaders that this rivalry could only harm Africa while, at the same time, making it impossible to implement either of the policies. Repeated attempts were made at bringing about a reconciliation.

One of the countries most concerned by the split between radicals and moderates was Senegal. President Senghor, a respected leader of the Brazzaville Group, depended far more on the good will of the Senegalese hinterland in Mali and neighboring Guinea for peace and fruitful cooperation. At his request, President Olympio of Togo consulted with Prime Minister Alhaji Sir Abubakar Tafawa Balewa of Nigeria and President William V. S. Tubman of Liberia, who agreed to sponsor a meeting of all African states. Although relatively moderate, these three leaders were not committed to either bloc. They eventually persuaded Sékou Touré and Modibo Keita to join them as co-sponsors. Later, under pressure from President Nkrumah, the two withdrew. Then, just before the conference was due to open, a meeting of Casablanca states in Cairo demanded that it be postponed.

Thus, the first major attempt at bringing the Casablanca and Brazzaville states together had the opposite effect. A third, Monrovia Group was formed. The conference, from 8-12 May 1961, was the largest gathering of independent states in the history of Africa. The Brazzaville states joined with the moderate English-speaking countries like Ethiopia, Liberia, Nigeria and Sierra Leone, as well as Somalia, Togo, Libya (having left the Casablanca Group) and Tunisia (with only observer status). The only states not represented were Ghana, Guinea, Mali, Morocco, the United Arab Republic and the Sudan (which at first accepted).

The seriousness of the rift was shown by the emphasis on relations among African states. The first order of business was not decolonization but the means of "promoting better understanding and cooperation" in Africa. The conference adopted a series of principles to govern relations in the future. This included the absolute equality of all states and respect for their sovereignty, the right to existence and development of their personality. To this end, there was to be no interference in the internal affairs of states nor outside subversive action by neighboring states. And cooperation was to be based upon "tolerance, solidarity and good-neighbor relations."

The first conferences had assumed the enemy was always outside of independent Africa. Unfortunately, history had already shown that the greatest threats could come from within. The Monrovia conference of 1961 was therefore the first attempt at regulating the continent's internal relations. As a practical step towards reducing friction within Africa, and to avoid the use of more dangerous means, the principle of peaceful settlement of disputes was to be given machinery in the form of a commission.

Only then did the moderate leaders turn to independence. The African and Malagasy states affirmed their "unanimous determination to give material and moral assistance to all dependent territories of colonial powers with a view to accelerating their accession to independence." That they fully grasped the implications of this offer was clear from the preceding admission that the principle of non-interference "applies only to States already independent and sovereign." The conference severely condemned the policy of repression in Angola and the apartheid of South Africa and pledged support to nationalists in both countries as well as urging the immediate application of political and economic sanctions against South

Africa.

However, on the controversial issues, although the
statements were purposely brief and colorless, the tendency
was toward the Brazzaville stand. This was indicated by the
request that Mauritania be admitted to the United Nations.
Due to the improvement in the situation in Algeria and the an-
nouncement of forthcoming negotiations, this issue was side-
stepped by asking both sides to put an end to the war and
France to accord Algeria its independence and territorial integrity. But, the GPRA was not recognized by the conference,
nor was it asked to attend, and no concrete support was offered.

The most delicate item was the Congo crisis, particularly after the assassination of Lumumba and the creation of
the Gizenga government. The Monrovia Group tried to take a
neutral stand by inviting neither party to the conflict and calling on all African states to avoid "taking sides with rival
groups in any form or manner." But the fact that the Monrovia states recognized the Kasavubu government gave a definite
content to the demand that African states "desist from such
activities as the hasty recognition of breakaway regimes in the
Republic of the Congo." The rest of the resolution was a condemnation of "certain non-African states" that encouraged subversion in African states and of "assassination as a means to
attain political power."

Since the main goal of the Monrovia conference had
been to bring about a general reconciliation, it expressed
"deep regret at the absence of some of our sister states."
Yet it could not help becoming part of the rivalry. It was impossible for the conference to deny the position taken by its
individual members. And by not taking sides on Algeria and
the Congo, the Monrovia Group only laid themselves open to
accusations of timidity. The most striking example was the
statement on assassination, which began as a condemnation of
the assassination of Patrice Lumumba and ended as a general
disapproval of interference and violence in African affairs.

The Lagos Conference.

There were no further initiatives for holding a conference of all independent states until the end of 1961. During
the interval there had been some improvement on the political
scene. Mauritania had been admitted to the United Nations

and the question of its recognition was rapidly becoming academic for all but Morocco. In Algeria, despite various setbacks, it had become evident that an agreement would be reached with France on independence. And, in the Congo, although the government of national unity had disintegrated it had no rival.

This time the attempt at reconciliation was made by Nigerian Prime Minister Balewa, a newcomer to Pan-Africanism. As a moderate leader, he could appeal to the Monrovia Group, and as a Muslim, to the North African states. The main problem was to convince the Casablanca Group to attend the meeting in Lagos. At first he succeeded. Only Morocco refused to be seated with Mauritania, and although President Nkrumah insisted the meeting of Heads of States had not been sufficiently prepared he agreed to send his Foreign Minister.

A more serious hurdle arose in connection with the Algerian Provisional Government. The GPRA had not been invited to Monrovia and originally it was not on the list for Lagos, but Balewa later invited it on his own. Since the GPRA was not recognized by the Brazzaville states, they threatened to stay away if Algeria came, and the refusal to admit Algeria led the Casablanca Group and others to refuse to come if Algeria were not present. Unable to settle the matter himself, Sir Abubakar left the choice to a preliminary meeting of Foreign Ministers, where it was assumed all states would be present.

These hopes were dashed a few days before the conference, when the Casablanca Foreign Ministers meeting in Accra decided not to attend the Lagos conference. The Nigerians were furious about the boycott, decided in the capital of their rival, and were disappointed when the Libyan, Tunisian and Sudanese delegations withdrew because of the absence of the GPRA. Eventually twenty independent states (Congo (Léopoldville) and Tanganyika were new) attended the Lagos conference from 25-30 January 1962. But it was clear from the outset that, once again, the attempt at reconciliation had failed. The meeting could only bring another consolidation of the moderate camp politically and institutionally.

At least there was a conscious effort to avoid making the situation worse. The discussions were circumscribed to economic and social questions more than usual. There had been a meeting of economists from nineteen of the Monrovia states at Dakar in July 1961, and the Lagos conference had to

study the findings. Agreement had been reached on a number
of recommendations including the promotion of trade through
customs unions, harmonization of development policies, improvement of communications and ways of overcoming language
barriers. There were also proposals for economic, financial
and social cooperation. The Lagos conference widened this
circle of subjects to include other fields and laid down priorities. It decided to establish a special fund to finance regional
development, create a customs union and set up a training and
research institute. A special committee of Finance Ministers
was to consider the possibility of founding a development bank
and private investment fund as well as reviewing the effects
of association with the European Economic Community.

The Heads of State and Foreign Ministers were particularly careful not to open a controversy when they debated the
major political questions. They again adopted relatively simple and unexceptionable resolutions on all pertinent issues.
Since the political situation had improved considerably since
Monrovia this was somewhat easier. However, although the
resolutions were not a challenge to the Casablanca policy,
they were not a real compromise either.

Unfortunately, relations between individual states had
not improved to the same extent. This was where the moderate states had a bone to pick with the radicals. Nigerian
Governor-General Nnamdi Azikiwe pointed this out in a pene-
trating statement.

> From a general observation, it would appear that
> there is not much to choose between the respective
> accords reached by the member states of the Casa-
> blanca Conference and those of the Monrovia Con-
> ference ... But there is one basic difference ...
> the conspicuous absence of a specific declaration
> on the part of the Casablanca States of their inflex-
> ible belief of the fundamental principles enunciated
> at Monrovia.

The point stressed most was "safety from interference in their
internal affairs through subversive activities engineered by supposedly friendly states." Until these principles were accepted
the weaker states would continue to fear their stronger and
more ambitious neighbors. And Dr. Azikiwe demanded that
the Casablanca powers publicly adhere to them. Some delegates had more specific complaints to make against the absent
states. But others, including the Emperor of Ethiopia, did

their best to calm the tempers and avoid reviving the quarrels.

Disintegration of the Blocs.

        No third attempt at reconciliation was made until well
over a year later. During that time the main divisive issues
lost their immediacy and sharpness. As this happened, the
cohesion within the blocs began to disappear.

        Mauritania had ceased being an African issue. Presi-
dent Nkrumah returned to his position of friendship and received in Ghana an official visit from Mauritania's President
Ould Daddah. Even Mali stopped backing Morocco and put an
end to the incidents along the border by signing a frontier
treaty with Mauritania in February 1963.

        The Casablanca Group had first been convened by Mor-
occo, but kings were rather odd partners for "revolutionaries." Already after the initial meeting, Libya had come to
that conclusion and had left. Now that the other source of
solidarity, Algerian independence had run dry, Morocco also
drifted away from the group. Moreover, when Ben Bella came
out on top in the hectic days after independence, Hassan II
realized that the settlement of certain matters with Algeria
would not be easy and ideological differences pushed them further apart. When the Algerians asked that the meeting of
Heads of State be postponed until after the meeting of reconciliation, this was accepted by Morocco, and the Casablanca
Group faded out.

        Even the threesome of Ghana, Guinea and Mali had
trouble keeping up cooperation as the motives therefore decreased. Already, in the hey-day of the Congolese crisis,
Kwame Nkrumah and Sékou Touré had given contradictory advice to Lumumba and Nkrumah moderated the general policy
of the whole group. With no rival government to support in
the Congo, any joint policy was now pointless. At the same
time, Guinea and Mali tried to patch up their relations with
the former Community states. Cooperation was a must for
land-locked Mali and relations with Senegal were normalized at
the beginning of 1963. Even Touré began to seek a modus
vivendi. Russian collusion in the "teachers' conspiracy" of
December 1962 led him to turn back towards the West and
even cooperate with his former RDA colleagues.

Reconciliation had always been sought by many members of the Monrovia group. The English-speaking states never intended to form a bloc and were pleased to see the barriers fall. The leading member of PAFMECSA, Tanganyika, had always discouraged bloc-building and Julius Kambarage Nyerere had actually obtained an amazing degree of harmony in the region. The Brazzaville Group also relaxed its links. Senegal's President Senghor went half-way to meet the leaders of Mali and Guinea, while at the same time his relations with President Houphouët-Boigny cooled and the competition between Dakar and Abidjan reappeared.

As the two rival groups lost their "raison d'être" more and more leaders began to speak of reconciliation. Once again there was a flurry of diplomatic activity. Sir Abubakar Balewa called for a common policy. And Haile Selassie I, the conciliator at Lagos, made every effort to guarantee the success of the next conference in Addis Ababa. This time there was to be careful preparation and no slip-ups and he sent his envoys about the continent to clear up disagreements and pave the way for accord.

The matter was clinched when, on 5 July 1962, Algeria became independent and there were no longer any outstanding controversies between the blocs. In addition to this, Algerian President Ben Bella, who had become an African hero during his imprisonment, came out in favor of such a meeting. He also sent a mission to various capitals to stress the importance of a united front against the real enemies of Africa in order to liberate the remaining dependent territories. He breathed new life into the original source of Pan-Africanism and united all Africa behind the one constant point of agreement on the continent.

But the blow that shattered the blocs and finally put an end to the inter-conference period was the poisoned fruit of the years of rivalry and antagonism. Despite the general improvement in relations, the almost unbroken series of plots and attempted assassinations, accusations and counter-accusations between Ghana and Togo had not ceased. It reached a peak in the new year when Ghana repeatedly charged Togo with supporting insurgent acts of Ghanaian refugees. Then, on 13 January 1963, a military coup broke out in Lomé. President Olympio was shot down, his government overthrown, and a provisional government was established. The same day, Ghanaian troops were sent to the border.

Ghana was widely suspected of involvement in the coup,
and Dahomey called upon President Nkrumah not to let his
troops cross the border or intervene in Togolese affairs.
This assurance was given. Throughout Africa, the reaction
was one of horror and indignation, and this was not limited
to the friends of President Olympio. In Guinea, Sékou Touré
proclaimed eight days of national mourning. He also asked
for a joint African policy towards the incident and an international investigation of the assassination before recognition of
the provisional government in Togo. Nigeria's Foreign Minister, Jaja Anucha Wachuku, spearheaded the campaign and
called an urgent meeting in Lagos. He added that any recognition of the Togolese government would be regarded as an
"unfriendly act" and called the assassination "cold blooded
murder engineered, organized, directed and financed by some-
body. "

The suspicions were reinforced when, before any investigation could be made, the Ghanaian government recognized the government of Nicholas Grunitsky. This aroused a
protest from Guinea. Then the Inter-African and Malagasy
Organization of the Monrovia Group met to study the political situation. There was no agreement among the Foreign
Ministers on recognition and a mission of enquiry was sent off
to Togo. The conference also decided, for the future, to
break off relations with any state fomenting subversive activities in other independent states.

With the death of Sylvanus Olympio fresh in their minds,
the African Heads of State were more than ever determined to
put an end to the period of rivalry and hatred.

                                Notes

1.   Vernon McKay, <u>Africa in World Politics</u>, p. 95.

2.   On the difficulties of fulfilling such a mandate, see:
        Stanley Hoffmann, "In Search of a Thread: The U.N.
        in the Congo Labyrinth, " <u>International Organization</u>,
        Spring 1962, Vol. 16, No. 7, p. 331-361.

3.   Philippe Decraene, <u>Le Panafricanisme</u>, p. 65.

4.   Presently the nation's official name is "Federal Republic
        of Cameroon, " formed in 1961 by the merger of the
        Cameroun Republic (French UN trust territory until

1960) and the southern half of the Cameroons (British
UN trust territory).

5. West Africa, 10 June 1961, p. 639.

C. The Movement Towards Unity

One of the most striking phenomena of this period of ferment and rebirth in Africa was the almost mystical attachment to the cause of unity. Despite the traditional separations and consolidation in over forty colonies, almost all the leaders of the time pleaded the case of unity. For some, unity already existed and merely required appropriate forms, for others, it had to be nurtured, but no African denied the principle.

Coming from a continent known for its divisions, this attachment to unity was a surprise to many. Although there were some precedents, even the Pan-Negro movement and the DuBois Congresses only went back half a century. And race-consciousness might be expected to split the continent in two rather than unite it. True, with the struggle for decolonization reaching its peak, this racial aspect was tempered by the more recent Bandung brand of solidarity among all colonial peoples. But this was too vast to reinforce continental unity.

There were also more elemental sources, such as the recognition that the peoples of the African continent had been subjugated and exploited for centuries because of their rivalries. Without a far-reaching unity of action, the continent might never be able to throw off the yoke of colonialism. And once the several nations were independent, should new rivalries arise the continent could again fall victim to a policy of divide and rule.

Whatever the sources or the reasons, there was no doubt that a sentiment of unity and solidarity enveloped the continent and powerfully influenced the course of Africa. However, the very diffuseness of the sentiment meant that only time could give it a firm content and a steady direction. Only when it had been distilled and encompassed in an institutional form would it become a serious tool and means of action.

Independence First!

From the beginning, the new generation of Pan-Africanists had a double goal: independence and unity. It was
assumed that they were inseparable and would reinforce one
another. Independence, however, was given priority since it
had to be wrested from the colonial powers. Unity, to the
contrary, was presupposed inherent in every African. It could
be left to a later day, when the barriers raised by the enemies of Africa would crumble and Africa unite. This choice
may have been unavoidable at the time, but it was bound to
affect what followed. For each movement developed largely
on its own and each potential state matured in isolation.

Since most of the time and energy of the African leaders was devoted to the struggle for independence, the history
of African unity during the hectic years of early decolonization
was limited and sporadic. Even in the career of its main advocate, Kwame Nkrumah, unity was only secondary. Back in
1945, at the Manchester Congress, he had formed a West African National Secretariat to coordinate the activities of the
nationalist movements in the region. Another conference in
London, in August 1946, adopted the goal of a West African
Federation as an "indispensable lever" for the achievement of
a United States of Africa. This goal was endorsed by a representative of French-speaking Africa, Sourou Migan Apithy of
what is now Dahomey, and the next year by Dr. Azikiwe, long
a proponent of broader African links. But when Nkrumah returned to the Gold Coast to lead the struggle for independence
he had little time to keep up contacts with the rest of West
Africa.

No further action was taken until Nkrumah called the
first "Pan-African" congress on African soil in December 1953
at Kumasi, capital of the Ashanti region, in the Gold Coast.
There were few delegations present, although Azikiwe came at
the head of a Nigerian group, and Liberia sent observers.
The result was a National Congress of West Africa, created in
1954, to promote unity in the region and convene conferences.
Once again tenuous contacts could be established with Azikiwe
and with Senghor and Apithy in French West Africa. But the
struggle for independence in the Gold Coast was entering a
critical phase and there was another lull. When, as Ghana, it
became independent in 1957, Prime Minister Nkrumah was
finally able to devote himself more completely to the problem
of unity. At the independence festivities in Accra, he announced that he planned to convene a conference of independent

African states.

In the French sub-Saharan territories, although with
some delay, several of the politicians began to orient their
territories towards Pan-Africanism.   In French West Africa
and Equatorial Africa there was something concrete at stake.
As the territories moved towards independence, the metropolis
began decentralizing powers and dismantling the federations.
The majority of the RDA leaders approved this policy and
Félix Houphouët-Boigny very much doubted the viability of such
massive structures.   However, there was also a "federalist"
wing that hoped to rescue the older and larger units.   Active
in this movement were men from Dakar and Brazzaville, the
former federal capitals, and activists like Sékou Touré and
Modibo Keita.   At the initiative of Léopold Sédar Senghor, this
group even created its own Parti du Regroupement Africain.
And the Cotonou Congress, in July 1958, proclaimed the twin
goals of independence and a United States of Africa.   But the
key slogan of the meeting lay down the real order of priorities: "Recherchez d'abord l'indépendance, le reste vous sera
donné par surcroît."   (First seek independence, the rest shall
be added on to you.)

Only Sékou Touré acted upon this in the 1958 referendum, when he campaigned for a vote of "no."   By opting out
of the French Community, he obtained independence for his
country some two years before his colleagues.   But this independence was not followed by unity, rather he was turned
out of the family of French-speaking Africa and the ties were
cut on both sides.   This was the first sign that unity was not
always a fruit of independence.

In Eastern and Central Africa, PAFMECA, a loose co-
ordinating body of liberation movements, also had a place for
unity in its program.   Only, once again, precedence went to
decolonization.   Prior to independence, it was felt, there was
little sense in talking unity.   Although most of the other leaders were concerned almost exclusively with decolonization,
Julius Nyerere reversed the order and offered to postpone Tanganyikan independence to facilitate broader East African links.
But his offer could not be maintained against opposition in his
own party.   So, in East Africa as in all of Africa, unity had
to await independence.

The First Conference of Independent African States.

When Ghana became the first Black African state to have thrown off the colonial yoke, its leader was able to turn to the rest of his program. With much of Africa still struggling for independence, Nkrumah's primary concern was to create a broad front of already independent states to aid them, and thus unity moved into the foreground. Similarly, unity was the key to the preservation of independence and to the development of the new states.

When the first Conference of Independent African States met in Accra, in April 1958, the underlying unity was shown by the rapid success in defining an action program for Africa. The agreement covered principles of international policy and decolonization as well as cooperation in technical fields. Sometimes it even included the ways and means of obtaining these goals. Fortunately, the independent states had so much in common and were faced with such imposing tasks that the first statements were often unanimous. There were as yet no controversies that could distract them from their duties. At no point was the atmosphere of harmony broken.

Speaker after speaker pointed with pride to this African unity. But the success was too easily won to be lasting. That nothing was done to preserve or nurture unity could be seen in the field of foreign policy. As in the past, all action would be undertaken individually or through the United Nations. No effective machinery was created for channelling the solidarity that existed on matters such as decolonization either. Despite the pledge to wipe out colonialism on the continent, no body was created to work for this purpose. And, although the participating governments agreed to cooperate to safeguard their independence, sovereignty and territorial integrity, there was no defensive organization nor indeed any idea as to how this cooperation should take place.

The success was often also too emotional to be real. Indeed, the conference limited itself to "asserting" the existence and "resolving" the preservation of "unity of purpose and action," but it did nothing to increase or direct it. Rather than becoming a tool, unity was an act of faith of a conference that "believes that as long as the fundamental unity of outlook on foreign policy is preserved, the Independent African States will be able to assert a distinctive African Personality which will speak with a concerted voice ... at the United Nations and other international forums."

In various technical matters, however, the plans for
cooperation made more headway--on paper at least. The various states agreed "to co-operate in their economic, technical
and scientific developments and in raising the standard of living of their respective peoples." In a longish resolution, examining the ways and means of promoting economic cooperation, the conference recommended that each state establish an
economic research committee "to survey the economic conditions and to study the economic and technical problems within
the State." These committees would be brought together in a
Joint Economic Research Commission which would, among
other things, coordinate information and planning of the economy and industry, encourage inter-African trade, and obtain
foreign capital and experts. The individual states, on their
own initiative, were also to promote cooperation in various
ways, such as exchange of information, joint enterprises, common markets and so on. In cultural matters, as well, recommendations were made for the promotion of understanding
and mutual appreciation. The task was left largely to the exchange of "visiting missions," and no joint machinery was
created.

Some follow-up was clearly necessary. Yet all the
conference did was to establish an "informal permanent machinery." This consisted of the permanent representatives of
the member states to the United Nations and would coordinate
matters of common concern and examine and make recommendations on "concrete practical steps which may be taken to
implement the decisions" of the CIAS. This body was not
authorized to implement nor to supervise the implementation
by the independent states of the program they had adopted.
The most it could do was to make recommendations thereon.
Thus it could hardly bridge the gap between the ambitious
goals of the conference and the scant means of attaining them.
Moreover, an African Group at the United Nations was far
from "permanent," meeting only during sessions of the General Assembly and even then only intermittently. And it did not
even have a secretariat to provide continuity.

The only hope for an increase in unity could come from
the decision that other conferences would follow. There were
to be meetings of Foreign Ministers and other ministers or
experts, which would be held "from time to time as and when
necessary to study and deal with particular problems of common concern to the African States." There would also be a
CIAS every two years. These meetings would be prepared by
the "informal permanent machinery."

The reasons for the limited tangible success of the con-
ference--as opposed to its overwhelming emotional triumph--
sprung from the attitude towards unity of preceeding years.
It was assumed that unity already existed and only had to be
given the opportunity to manifest itself. This was done in Accra and the world was amazed by the sight of African leaders
from such varying horizons mixing and agreeing with one another so readily. It was also assumed that this unity would
grow as the externally imposed barriers fell, without any conscious effort to promote it, and thus future meetings were
enough to give it periodic form.

However, behind this there lurked a very real danger.
For, although the feelings and words conveyed ample solidarity
and oneness of views, it was impossible to obtain any real
commitment from the various states. There was no willingness to sacrifice dearly won sovereignty in the cause of unity
nor to create genuine machinery that might disapprove of the
policy of a sovereign state or ask it to fulfill pledges made on
the altar of unity.

The All-African Peoples Organization.

Although the Conference of Independent African States
was an undeniable success, it did not meet the expectations of
some of the African leaders. Those who placed themselves
in the vanguard of unity, such as Kwame Nkrumah and Sékou
Touré, realized that no inter-governmental body taking its decisions by "consensus" would follow them. Even the tame
resolutions adopted could not be implemented without some machinery. And periodic meetings were not enough to follow up
and deal with Africa's many problems. Nkrumah soon cast
about for another tool of unity. The first attempt had foundered on the reefs of sovereignty. Turning from the rulers to
the people, he hoped to form a more active and dynamic instrument. President Nasser had already held an Afro-Asian
People's Solidarity Conference in Cairo and Nkrumah decided
to do the same for Africa alone.

The first All-African Peoples Conference met in Accra,
in December 1958. It was attended by delegates from national
political parties, trade unions and men's and women's organizations. This meant that the grass-roots leaders, previously
on the outside looking in, were also consulted about questions
that affected them as much as the first-string leadership.
Movements from the dependent territories were also invited

and the colonial peoples were integrated more closely than in
the CIAS. Finally, the AAPO also accepted oppositional parties from the more moderate states. With a membership un-
encumbered by the obligations of power becoming increasingly
radical, these conferences seemed indeed to be able to adopt
resolutions going much further than those of the governments.

This time the first order of business was to establish
permanent machinery. A constitution for the All-African Peoples Organization was drafted and adopted in Accra already
and amended slightly in Tunis. The governing body of the
AAPO was the college of heads of delegation of the conference when in session. Interim supervision was provided by a
steering committee, elected by the heads of delegation. This
steering committee was to meet at least twice a year, with
"the authority to act on behalf of the Conference in accordance
with the aims and objects of the Conference." There was a
permanent secretariat in Accra. The secretary-general, responsible to the steering committee, was entrusted with many
important administrative and representative tasks, as well as
the catch-all function permitting him to "do all such necessary
things as shall be calculated to further the aims and objects of
the Conference."

Policy decisions were taken by the conference. However, unlike the inter-governmental meetings, the AAPO bodies
took their decisions "by vote of the simple and not absolute
majority," according to the Accra constitution. This was
toned down in Tunis to read simple majority after having tried
to "secure the widest possible measure of agreement."
Amendments could be made to the constitution by two-thirds
majority (simple majority in the Accra version).

Since the people's organization was permanent, it was
necessary to make provision for financing it. The funds, administered by the secretary-general on the basis of a budget
approved by the steering committee, were drawn from the
member organizations, other African organizations, institutions and individuals, and from the African governments.
Since member organizations could be excused from contributing and governments could make voluntary contributions, the
independence that the AAPO gained by having its own budget
was imperiled by its reliance on the states to provide these
funds.

The AAPO had the very same tasks as the inter-governmental meetings, i.e., promotion of unity, liberation of

the continent and technical cooperation. Nevertheless, it gave much higher priority to the development of African unity and was committed to "work for the emergence of a United States of Africa." It was certainly more active in this cause than any other body.

The Accra AAPC adopted the first major resolution on African unity. It was also the strongest. The underlying premise was that boundaries were artificial and even danger- ous barriers between the African peoples who were animated by a desire for unity. As a step towards this goal, a plan was put forward for creating an African Commonwealth. It was restricted to independent states "governed by Africans." First, these states would join together in regional federations or groupings, such as the projected North African Federation and a West African Grouping. In this complete reshaping of the map of Africa, every state would join one unit or another, on the basis primarily of geographic and economic considera- tions, and secondarily, linguistic and cultural affinity. Any decisions would be taken by the people concerned through a referendum. But this was only a start and it was stressed that these federations and groupings should "not be prejudicial to the ultimate objective of a Pan-African Commonwealth."

During this vast process of unification, it was of course necessary to prepare the peoples for closer relations. This entailed an abolition of passports and travel restrictions for African visitors, tourists and students, teaching of both English and French and the organization of inter-territorial enterprises. Furthermore, the radio, press and other media of mass communication would promote Pan-Africanism, as would the political parties in their constitutions and programs. The most far-reaching proposal was to grant reciprocal rights of citizenship for Africans from other territories.

A more extreme aspect of this resolution, however, was the wholesale rejection of existing borders. It denounced the "artificial frontiers drawn by imperialist Powers to divide the peoples of Africa, particularly those which cut across ethnic groups and divide people of the same stock." Its ob- jective was "the abolition or adjustment of such frontiers at an early date." The solution was again to be based on the "true wishes of the people."

At the same time that it sought to topple the external barriers to unity, the conference was worried about the inter- nal obstacles. It was particularly opposed to the "evil prac-

tices" of tribalism and religious separatism. These sources
of division were being exploited by the colonial powers to sap
the drive for liberation in the dependent territories and the
same traditional structures were hampering the modernization
and political evolution of the independent states. The greatest
danger was that tribalism created largely self-contained units
in the new states and resisted national integration and, in the
second degree, the unification of Africa. To eliminate these
evils, the governments were exhorted to pass laws and by
propaganda and education to discourage tribalism and religious
separatism; political, trade union, cultural, and other organizations were also to educate and warn the masses against disintegration.

By its meeting in Tunis, in January 1960, it was clear
that the AAPO had over-reached itself in the resolution on
unity. Although it "enthusiastically" supported the very different recommendations of both Accra conferences, the second
AAPC limited itself to fourteen practical suggestions of a very
general nature: granting of bursaries to students, exchange of
agricultural experts, musical and folklore programs, exchanges
of teachers and students, an African Youth Festival, regional
conferences, abolishment of visas (but not passports), a solidarity fund for refugees, unity in the trade union movement,
and others.

Nevertheless, by the Cairo conference, in March 1961,
it was possible for the AAPO to put forward a practical plan
for an institutional structure linking all the African states.
The organizational machinery consisted of an African Consultative Assembly and a Council of African States. The Assembly,
with members representing the parliaments of the African
states, would meet periodically to "formulate a common policy
of the African States." The Council, whose membership was
not specified, would study and implement the recommendations
of the Assembly.

A Commission of African Experts was to help establish
an economic community based on the coordination of national
development plans. But economic cooperation was only the
means to an end, for the experts were "to elaborate a common economic policy in order to promote and consolidate African political unity." A Cultural Commission was to provide
a common policy for educational and cultural exchanges. A
more striking innovation was the Commission of African Commanders to study, define and organize an "African joint defence." Along with the "consolidation and protection of Afri-

can countries subjected to foreign pressures, " the commission
was to contribute to "the total liberation" of the African dependent countries.

Because of its militant membership and majority votes,
the AAPO was able to lay down a program that went far
enough for the vanguard of the African leaders. However, by
the same token, these resolutions usually went too far for the
less advanced states. Sometimes they went too far even for
the radicals. A case in point was the original statement on
frontiers, boundaries and federations. The idea of an African
Commonwealth was unobjectionable. But the mere thought of
erasing the boundaries between independent states sent a shiver
down certain spines. Neither the moderates nor most of
the radical states dared open the Pandora's box of border disputes. No matter how bad the frontiers were, they were better than a free-for-all among the tribes and social or political
groups. As a consequence, there was a noticeable retreat
from this position within the AAPO, though there was no such
timidity on questions of decolonization and neo-colonialism.
The attacks reached a crescendo in Cairo.

Nevertheless, despite its more energetic program, the
AAPO was actually less effective than the CIAS, for it could
not commit the states. All of its resolutions were accompanied by pleas that they be studied, adopted or implemented
by the states. Each suggestion was addressed to "all Governments of Independent African States." The parties and trade
unions could propose very impressive plans, but they would
remain a dead letter unless endorsed by the national governments. And, since the AAPO was clearly biased against many
of them, there was little chance its proposals would find favor
in the broader African community. Eventually it turned out
to be little more than an incubator of ideas and a testing bank
for institutional machinery, albeit a prolific one.

The Ghana-Guinea Union and the Sanniquellie Declaration.

Shortly after the first people's conference, Kwame
Nkrumah was given a chance to put his ideas on political union
into practice. When Guinea voted "no" in the 1958 referendum,
France retaliated by withdrawing all its personnel and aid,
leaving the country in a desperate situation. Ghana immediately came to the rescue with a spectacular loan of Ł10 million
(drawn from the reserves of the Cocoa Marketing Board).
And, on 23 November 1958, Nkrumah and Sékou Touré amazed

the world by announcing a future union. It was inspired by
the example of the thirteen colonies that created the United
States of America. The two states would immediately facilitate contacts and harmonize policies. Then a constitution
would be framed.

Finally, on 1 May 1959, the contents of this Union
were made public. The project had a double thrust. It was
both to consecrate the close relations between Ghana and
Guinea and to serve as a "nucleus" for a vast Union of Independent African States. The main objectives of the proposed
Union were to help the other African brothers obtain independence, to avoid obedience to any group or bloc, to build a
"free and prosperous African community" and, of course, to
promote greater unity among African states. Nevertheless,
the Ghana-Guinea Union was not as ambitious as might have
been expected after the famous AAPO resolution. There was
no mention of merging the states. Rather, "each State or
Federation which is a member of the Union shall preserve its
own individuality and structure." Even in the future there
would be no surrender of "any portion of sovereignty" without
the approval of the member states.

As for the practical arrangements, the states of the
Union were to have their own foreign representation, although
they could be represented jointly with other members of the
Union in foreign countries. No institution was projected for
aligning policies and each state only pledged to follow the principles of independence, unity, African personality and the interest of the peoples, as well as to refuse to "act in obedience
to any one group or bloc." Instead of instituting joint citizenship, the nationals of each state would have both their own
citizenship and that of the Union; visas would no longer be required. In matters of defence, the Heads of State would determine a common policy, but each state maintained its own
army. Only in the economic field was there any hint of institutional links or eventual supranationality. An economic council, with members designated by the states, would lay down
the general economic policy and study all pertinent questions.
Moreover, there would be a common Union Bank to "issue and
back the respective currencies of the different States or Federations."

But all this was for the future. The only step actually
taken in Conakry was to select a flag. Even then, the union
flag, anthem and motto (independence and unity) were duplicat-
ed by national ones. Thus, Ghana and Guinea's Declaration of

Union was more of a gesture than an immediate reality. Nevertheless, this gesture was already enough to upset the other independent states, worried about the prospect of a continental "union" they had no part in designing. For, according to article one, "membership in the Union shall be open to all independent African States or Federations adhering to the principles on which the Union is based."

The President of Liberia took a particular dislike to the Ghana-Guinea concept of union and he asked Dr. Nkrumah and Sékou Touré to meet him in the village of Sanniquellie. In February 1959, he had circulated his own plan for an Associated States of Africa to the African Group at the United Nations. It envisaged a grouping of African states, maintaining their national sovereignty and identity, and based on a "convention of friendship" for commerce amongst them. From his remarks it could be seen that President Tubman's main concern was not so much to prevent an eventual United States of Africa as to avoid moving too rapidly and leaving no way out but "war, revolt or secession."[1]

Unexpectedly enough, a compromise could be reached and the Sanniquellie Declaration of 19 July 1959 was endorsed by the foremost proponents of unification and the spokesman of national sovereignty. Agreement on the basic goal was relatively easy. Like the Ghana-Guinea Union the primary objectives were independence of the other African territories, a free and prosperous community and unity. But relations with the outside world were more simply based on equality and reciprocity and a further principle was invoked for relations among African states: acceptance by members not to interfere in the internal affairs of other members.

Like the Union, the proposed body was also open to all independent African states. Unlike the Union, it immediately laid down the limit to unity: each state was to "maintain its own national identity and constitutional structure." The institutional machinery was also more rudimentary. The major organ was to be economic, but there would also be councils for culture, science and research. No provision was made for defence, joint citizenship or a bank of issue. The only step taken on the spot was to pick the motto (once again, independence and unity). The choice of a flag and anthem were put off for later.

The main difference was not so much the actual statement or machinery as the mood that presided over them.

Rather than a union or even an association, the new body was
to be called the "community" of independent African states.
Despite its phrasing, the Ghana-Guinea Union had not required
any loss of sovereignty, but it did not make this a principle.
Now, rather than being envisaged as a first step on the long
road towards complete unification, the community was--if not
an end in itself--not necessarily a step towards a higher level
of unity.   For, "it is not designed to prejudice the present or
future international policies, relations and obligations of the
States involved."

This was only the beginning of the great African debate
on unity.   The three Heads of State decided to have the question placed on the agenda of the second CIAS, where the views
of the whole independent continent could be heard.

The Second Conference of Independent African States.

Despite its sketchy structure, the conference was able
to continue its existence and meet periodically.   The Foreign
Ministers held a meeting in Monrovia in August 1959.   Then,
in June 1960, there was another conference of Heads of States.
This gave the African leaders a chance to take stock of the
progress that had been made and to plan a new strategy for
the future.   Although the basic principles and outline of the
program did not change much, there was a striking difference
in organization.   Whereas the first CIAS had decided to work
largely through the United Nations, the second one placed increasing reliance on the African states, singly or collectively,
outside of the world body.

In the field of decolonization, for example, the recommendations laid down more specific and active duties than mere
consultation.   As backing for Algeria, the African states were
to continue their material and diplomatic support within the
United Nations, but also to make joint representation to France,
the capitals of the world and especially the NATO powers.   A
more unprecedented step was the decision to create an African
Freedom Fund to aid the nationalist movements.   This fund
was to receive contributions from the African states and was
to be administered by an organ "to be established" in accordance with rules and regulations "to be adopted" by the Conference.

As for economic cooperation, the (unestablished) commission was to be replaced by an African council of economic

co-operation and the (non-existent) visiting missions were to
become a council for educational, cultural and scientific cooperation in Africa.   In order to institute these bodies, with
increasingly broad goals and competences, there would be an
"immediate" meeting of experts to formulate the functions and
jurisdictions of the councils and, when their report was approved, the first session of the councils would be convened.
The main purpose of the councils would be to give effect to
the resolutions of the conference.

However, in order to provide an adequate framework
for these prospective bodies and to ensure overall supervision,
it was obvious that the conference itself required more than
informal permanent machinery.   In keeping with the Sanniquellie Declaration, the general question of unity was brought before the highest representatives of the independent states.
Here it was that the underlying disagreement on the meaning
of unity and the ways of attaining it came into the open.

It had been assumed that the compromise reached at
Sanniquellie between partisans of the two extremes would serve
as a common platform for the African states.   But Prime
Minister Nkrumah had increasingly become the prophet of rapid and complete unity and his Foreign Minister, Ako Adjei, interpreted the compromise to his own advantage.   "It is clear
from this declaration of principles," he said, "that the Union
of African states which the three leaders discussed and agreed
upon is intended to be a political Union."   He proposed that a
committee of experts be established to work out the details of
such a Union.   It would also deal with concrete projects like
"a Customs Union, the Removal of Trade Barriers and the
Establishment of an African Development Fund."[2]

The Ghanaian proposals received some backing from
Guinea, but the Liberian viewpoint was much more widely and
strongly supported, in particular by the Nigerian delegation.
Its head, Yussuf M. Sule, did not deny that the ultimate goal
was a United States of Africa or even a Union of African
States, but he felt it was still premature.   He insisted on the
preliminary step of "preparing the minds of the different African countries," so as to "start from the known to the unknown."
All he could admit as feasible for the moment was to tear
down the "artificial barriers" by constructing roads, exchang-
ing information, or "lifting any ban on the movement of free
trade and people."[3]

Although the concrete suggestions were largely compatible, no agreement could be reached on the essentials of unity. Although the moderate states were willing to work towards an ultimate union of states, they refused to start with one. Thus they rejected even the modest proposals coming from Ghana just because they were all labelled unions. Dr. Nkrumah, for his part, was constantly insisting on "strong political unity," which he considered a "practical proposition." Warning that "tomorrow may be too late," he called for "the African race united under one federal government."[4] But in fact the plans he proposed made very few demands on his partners. All that was really required was verbal commitment.

What worried the leaders most anyway were the methods used to impose the union. Rather than seeking or abiding by a compromise, a war of propaganda was unleashed against them. Therefore, the Nigerian delegation objected to any "Messiah who has got a mission to lead Africa." Y. M. Sule felt that if "any one of the African countries is not pursuing the right policy let us by all means try to convince that country in a brotherly way to abandon the policy and take to the right one." But he disapproved of any state that would "go all out to campaign against a fellow African country ... simply because we disagree or believe it is a satellite of a foreign country."[5]

Thus, due to semantics and differences of approach, the Addis Ababa conference was unable to find any common denominator for an improved institutional structure. All that could be done was to request the member states to "initiate consultations through diplomatic channels with a view to promoting African unity." It was hoped that by the next conference, two years hence, a consensus could be attained. For the time being, the informal permanent machinery would have "to continue as a transitional organization."

The Brazzaville Group.

By then, Africa's failure at establishing a solid Pan-African body to represent the continent had become patent. There was not enough agreement to give any institutional structure to the Conferences of Independent African States and the elaborate and daring structure of the All-African Peoples Organization was a facade. During 1960, however, things became even worse. Sixteen territories obtained independence in this "year of Africa." Most of them were moderate and the wave of new states tipped the balance in the inter-governmental organization towards slow and cautious policies. The radicals were clearly in a minority and many of them switched their backing to the people's organization.

As the former French Community members entered the particularly turbulent political arena of the time, they were uncertain where they fit in. They were worried and annoyed by the vehement attacks of the AAPO but the CIAS did not offer a haven. Both defensively and to preserve their common heritage, the newly independent states turned towards one another. In so doing they were only continuing a long tradition. Under French colonial rule there had always been some sort of links with the metropolitan power and among the territories.

For decades, the élites of the various colonies had been first trained then assimilated by French culture, a process crowned by a stay in Paris, where the budding African leaders met those of France and came into contact with one another. The relations were particularly close as many of the African statesmen represented their territories in French Assemblies. Such had been the case for Senegal as early as 1848. In addition, France had established two huge agglomerations of colonies with more or less tight federal links: French West Africa with its capital in Dakar and French Equatorial Africa with its capital in Brazzaville. The eight territories in West Africa and the four territories in Equatorial Africa had their own budgets and governors, but they were in turn responsible to the Governor-General in the federal capital, who was ultimately controlled by the French Minister for Colonies. These federal links and capitals, with their governing bodies and universities, fostered an esprit de corps among African leaders. To this was added the activities through the interterritorial political party, the Rassemblement Démocratique Africain, founded by Houphouët-Boigny in 1946.

Then decolonization began eroding this system. The Brazzaville conference in 1944 started the move towards greater self-government through elected territorial assemblies and increased administrative decentralization. Still, the French constitution of 1946 did provide councils at the federal level and a Union Assembly. The next decisive step towards independence seriously relaxed the ties among the colonies when each territory was granted considerable self-government under the "loi cadre" of 1956. At the same time, the binds of the two federations were loosened and the only links were directly

with Paris. This move, approved by Houphouёt-Boigny and
most of the other RDA leaders, was opposed by radicals like
Sékou Touré and moderates like Senghor and Abbé Youlou
(then mayor of Brazzaville), who defended the former federal
capitals. Léopold Senghor was especially concerned by what
he saw as the seeds of "balkanization."

Indeed, when de Gaulle's constitution replaced the Union
with a Franco-African Community in 1958, each of the territories was given full self-government aside from foreign affairs, defence and over-all economic policy. There were still
quasi-federal relations between France and the overseas territories, and coordination was ensured by meetings of Prime
Ministers, joint inter-governmental committees, a Senate, and
a Court of Arbitration for the Community. But even this
structure soon began to crumble. By the end of 1960, all of
the territories had achieved independence. And the French
sub-Saharan colonial empire dissolved into twelve independent
states.

Nevertheless, the personal relations between the African leaders, largely of the same generation, background, and
outlook, as well as of similar former links with France (and
especially with General de Gaulle personally), were still too
important in fact and potential for them not to seek some institutional form for their preservation. Moreover, they belonged to larger monetary, economic and defence unions. For
this reason as well as any other a first conference was called
in Abidjan, Ivory Coast, in October 1960. There it was decided to hold periodic meetings as well as to offer this body
jointly as a mediator in the Algerian crisis.

What became known as the Brazzaville Group took form
at a conference held in December 1960 in the former capital
of French Equatorial Africa. The states attending were:
Cameroun Republic, Central African Republic, Chad, Congo
(Brazzaville), Dahomey, Gabon, Ivory Coast, Madagascar,
Mauritania, Niger, Senegal and Upper Volta. Although the
conference closed with a political statement on various issues,
the twelve states had no inclination to create a bloc or even a
political institution. There was merely an irregular series of
meetings and consultations on African and foreign policy among
like-minded Heads of State as the need arose. Greater attention was directed towards economic cooperation and it was
decided to convene a commission in Dakar to draft a "plan" in
fields such as money and credit, production and marketing,
harmonizing and financing of national plans, investments and

an African and Malagasy investment bank, and relations with
the European Economic Community. These were not academic questions for the Brazzaville states since their interest
arose from the "economic ties which already unite them" and
the "other international commitments to which they have sub-
scribed."

The Afro-Malagasy Heads of State met again in Yaoundé, Cameroun, from 26-28 March 1961, to study the proposals of the Dakar meeting. It was rapidly decided to insti-
tutionalize economic cooperation by establishing an Organisation Africaine et Malgache de Coopération Economique (OAMCE)
to harmonize economic policies and to coordinate development plans. Another major concern was to define a joint policy towards the EEC, with which all members were associated.
The "organe suprême de décision" was to be a council of government representatives taking its decisions unanimously. Although the council could act on its own initiative, it was by
no means supranational, and the final aim was not integration
but only a more complete customs union.

The Casablanca Bloc.

The meetings of the Brazzaville states were taken as a
challenge by the militant leaders of the continent. They felt
that the political declaration had to be disavowed immediately.
And they did not want to leave to the French-speaking moderates the initiative in questions of unity. Very shortly after
the Brazzaville conference, another meeting was held in Casablanca in January 1961. This time it was attended by the Algerian Provisional Government, Ghana, Guinea, Libya, Mali,
Morocco and the UAR.

The solidarity between these states was much more recent and had been shaped by similar attitudes and policies on
specific issues such as Algeria and the Congo. Although they
had somewhat similar concepts of domestic structures, economic development and African socialism, these states did not
form a contiguous block and had no previous trade or financial
ties. Thus the Casablanca Group devoted themselves largely
to laying down a common platform on the key political issues
of the day. But Dr. Nkrumah would not let the opportunity
pass without obtaining agreement on a plan for unity as well.
He urged the other leaders to join him in a political union.
For, he insisted, "the future of Africa lies in a political
union--a political union in which the economic, military and

cultural activities will be co-ordinated for the security of our continent." Despite the modest definition of union, his plea was not accepted by the other radical leaders, who only endorsed "an effective form of co-operation."[6]

Nevertheless, the outline of a Charter of Casablanca was adopted. On paper it went much further than the Brazzaville Group. The cornerstone of the organization was to be an African consultative assembly. Unfortunately, since the time was not yet ripe, this had to be put off until "as soon as conditions permit." In the meanwhile there would be an African political committee, an African economic committee, an African cultural committee and a joint African high command. Cooperation among these bodies would be ensured by a liaison office.

After lengthy consultations, the protocol of the African Charter was signed at Casablance on 5 May by the Foreign Ministers of six states only, as Libya had dropped out. According to the charter, the "highest body for the coordination and unification of the general policy of the member States" was the Political Committee, meeting at Heads of State level at least once a year. The subordinate bodies were at ministerial level and could merely submit reports to the Political Committee. Only the joint high command, composed of chiefs of staff, could submit recommendations, valid when approved by the Political Committee. Although no mention was made of the Foreign Ministers, the fact that they had drafted and signed the protocol showed their importance and they were bound to act as advisors or "accredited representatives" of the Heads of State.

A liaison office was established to provide for the "smooth functioning" of the committees. But it was just a normal secretariat, it even being specified that the office was "administrative." It consisted of a secretary and assistant secretaries, all appointed by the Political Committee, and given certain privileges and immunities. The actual harmony among the bodies was ensured by the exclusive power of the Political Committee to take decisions.

However, it was questionable whether the Political Committee itself could bring about "unification" as opposed to mere coordination of policy. Even though internal decisions, such as amendments, could be taken by a two-thirds vote, there was no indication that the Committee could make majority decisions on policy binding on the member states. Therefore,

the Casablanca machinery, although more intricate than any
organization before it, was a far cry from the political union
demanded by President Nkrumah.

As with his other attempts, Nkrumah meant the Casablanca Charter to be universal and the protocol was open to
"any African State accepting the provisions of the African
Charter and this protocol." Again, what stood in the way of
eventual joining by other states was not so much the loose organization as the principles. For an article was inserted
whereby "the member States declare that the obligations and
commitments they incur by virtue of their international undertakings shall not contradict their obligations and commitments
under the Casablanca African Charter and this protocol and,
in particular, the policy of non-alignment ..." Although willing to proclaim the general principles of African independence
and unity, few if any states were inclined to have their foreign policy judged or their freedom of commitment restricted
by any organization.

This provision seriously hindered the universality of
the Casablanca Group. Moreover, there was good reason to
doubt that the six countries really wished to become the nucleus of a larger group in which they might be outvoted. For,
only three days later, a conference of all the independent
states was due to meet in Monrovia. The Foreign Ministers
debated the advisability of attending this attempt at reconciliation and decided to stay away.

The Monrovia Conference.

Despite the increasing polarization of the continent and
the division into rival Brazzaville and Casablanca Groups, a
number of leaders tried to reunite all of Africa behind a common program in one Pan-African organization. The men connected with the three major attempts, President Tubman of
Liberia, Azikiwe and Balewa of Nigeria, and the Emperor of
Ethiopia, were all moderates. But as elder statesmen standing outside of either group, they attempted to bring Africa
back to its roots. The conferences they sponsored had no
pre-conceived political bias and the primary condition of its
organization was that all independent states participate.

The first attempt at reconciliation was to be made in
Monrovia and the chances of success were enhanced when Sékou Touré and Modibo Keita agreed to join more moderate

leaders in sponsoring the meeting. Unfortunately, under the
pressure of Kwame Nkrumah, his partners withdrew and it
was impossible to have any reconciliation in the absence of
the six radical states. This partial gathering of Heads of
States and Government inevitably went down in history as one
more step towards the schism. The new grouping was important because it included almost all the moderate African states,
old and new, English and French-speaking, and because of its
size: the twelve Brazzaville states, plus Ethiopia, Liberia,
Libya, Nigeria, Sierra Leone, Somalia, Togo, and Tunisia (as
an observer).

As was expected, the moderate states again preferred
a slower and gradualist approach to unity. President Tubman
insisted that although the possibility of a universal political
order was debatable, the need for better cooperation was obvious. It could be based on common economic, social and
cultural ties. President Senghor also stressed these aspects
over political agreement. He was encouraged by Africa's inherent propensity for unity. However, the delegates felt that
the time had not yet come to take a major step. After surveying the situation, they concluded that "the unity that is
aimed to be achieved at the moment is not the political integration of sovereign African states, but unity of aspiration and
of action."

But the Monrovia conference of May 1961 did not forget the "absence of some of our sister states" nor try to profit from this. Rather, it made considerable efforts to avoid
widening the gulf and thus it eased a later reconciliation.
Since the antagonism was largely political, the resolutions
were drafted as neutrally as possible to avoid provoking the
Casablanca states.

Similarly, the potential grouping was purposely given no
institutional form so as to allow the other states to attend any
future meeting. All that was done in Monrovia was to revive
the conference of Heads of State or ministers of the independent states, holding periodic sessions and taking decisions unanimously. It was decided that the next meeting would be convened in Lagos. Still, little as this was, it showed the re-
siliency of this fundamental body and paved the way for the
next attempt.

Wary of political commitments, these leaders showed
no hesitation about handling the more technical aspects of
unity. Taking up where the second CIAS left off, they de-

cided to convene a commission of experts to work out plans
for cooperation in economics, education, culture, science,
technology, communications and transport. Any institutions
proposed would be placed under the conference of Heads of
State and an Inter-African and Malagasy Advisory Organization
was to be created.

The key to the Monrovia terms of unity were the conditions laid down for inter-African relations. Above all, cooperation had to be voluntary. The very idea of primus inter
pares was, according to Tubman, "destructive of African
Unity and Peace." The firmest platform for unity, the moderates agreed, would be "tolerance, solidarity and good-
neighbour relations, periodical exchange of views and non-
acceptance of any leadership." And a number of principles
were enunciated in advance for any future organization: absolute equality, non-interference in the internal affairs of states,
respect for the sovereignty of each state and its inalienable
right to existence and development of its personality, unqual-
ified condemnation of outside subversive action by neighboring
states and peaceful settlement of disputes.

If the members of the Casablanca bloc were willing to
accept these principles and base their policies upon them, reconciliation was indeed possible. However, even during the
Monrovia meeting, Ghana replied with a violent press campaign against the "bogus" conference and the plan of cooperation described as "unity without unification." This may have
been so, but it applied equally to every other scheme developed in Africa. The West African Pilot of Nigeria deduced that
the problem was one of leadership and Dr. Azikiwe's periodical concluded that "the truth is that Dr. Nkrumah must be at
the head of anything or outside it."[7] Although Ghana put an
end to the campaign, the damage had already been done.

The Union of African States.

In practice, the Ghana-Guinea Union did not quite live
up to its name. Only in the question of citizenship and a
Union Bank was there any real basis for close relations. To
this might be added the decision of the Conakry conference of
June 1960, whereby the determination of a common policy in
external affairs and diplomacy, military and economic matters
was left to meetings of the Heads of State and ministers, as
well as the establishment of a resident minister in the partner
country with the right to attend cabinet meetings.

Nevertheless, neither the plans for common citizenship nor the monetary scheme were ever brought to fruition. Although Guinea left the franc zone, Ghana remained in the sterling area and no common currency was created. The resident minister system did not work and conferences were few and far between. There was never any harmonization of national development plans nor even air, ship or telecommunication lines between the two countries. The Union was only held together by the occasional meetings of Nkrumah and Sékou Touré.

Still, the Union grew. On 24 December 1960, it was announced that Mali was joining. This was accompanied by a grant of five million pounds from Ghana. Although hazy on the contents of the new Union, the Declaration of Conakry had a definite sting. Referring to the Brazzaville meeting,

> ... the three Heads of State deplored the attitude taken by certain African Heads of State whose recent stand is likely to jeopardize the unity of Africa and strengthen neo-colonialism. They condemn all forms of African regroupment based on languages of the colonial Powers. They therefore appeal to these Heads of State to follow a higher and more healthy conception of African Unity.

Kwame Nkrumah made one further incursion into West Africa when he got President Maurice Yaméogo of Upper Volta to sign an agreement for "concrete measures quickly to achieve the total independent and effective unity of Africa." The Paga Agreement of 27 June 1961 stipulated that "freedom of movement for persons and goods shall be the rule and the equitable refund of customs dues collected on re-exports from Ghana shall be paid into the Upper Volta Treasury." In addition, Ghana advanced credits of some three-and-a-half million pounds. The Presidents symbolically destroyed a wall between the two states. But Yaméogo had second thoughts and decided that links with the Francophone moderates were safer and more promising.

Then, on 1 July 1961, Ghana, Guinea and Mali took the long-awaited step toward unity. After several months work, the Charter of the Union of African States had been drafted and adopted by the parliaments. This impressive document, in seven sections and fourteen articles, lay down the rules for the "nucleus of the United States of Africa."

The "supreme executive organ" of the Union was a Conference of Heads of State. Meeting once a quarter alternately in the three capitals, the Conference was enabled to pass resolutions "which shall become effective immediately." (Any indication as to whether these resolutions had to be approved by a majority or by all of the Heads of State, thus permitting each one to veto any measures he did not wish to implement, was carefully omitted.) The Conference was to be aided by a preparatory committee, which submitted recommendations on political and diplomatic matters to it, and by an economic committee which did the same for economic and financial questions. Coordination at lower levels was through consultations. There was no permanent secretariat.

This machinery contained two noteworthy innovations. For the first time, a body was created to work at the grassroots level in order to prepare the climate for unity. Coordinating committees of mass organizations for trade unions, women's and youth movements, were "to impart to the said bodies a common ideological orientation which is absolutely necessary for the development of the Union." But no provision was made for initiatives arising at the grassroots level or any representation of the people as such.

Secondly, the section on joint defence read like an active alliance. The states "shall jointly ensure the defence of their territorial integrity. Any aggression against one of the States shall be considered as an act of aggression against the other States of the Union." But it did not specify how or when the other states of the union were involved in war with the aggressor or should come to the aid of the victim. And the "common system of defence" itself was only to be organized later on.

Although the preservation of the sovereignty and identity of the states was not explicitly guaranteed, the Charter did not countenance abandonment of sovereignty either. Moreover, the old supranational measures of the former Ghana-Guinea Union (joint citizenship and bank of issue) were discarded. Indeed, there was not even a common flag, anthem or motto to seal the Union. Despite the ambiguity of the wording, the expanded and renovated Union of African States marked a considerable decrease in unification, and it became obvious that Messrs. Touré and Keita were pouring water into Dr. Nkrumah's wine.

The Afro-Malagasy Union.

Initially the Brazzaville states had not planned to set up a formal organization to channel cooperation among them. It had simply been decided to hold periodic meetings as the need arose. However, once the OAMCE was established to coordinate economic matters, it was necessary for the political will to be formulated somewhere. And, as the controversy over Algeria and the Congo worsened and blocs were formed, a further impulse was given towards the establishment of an overall supervisory body.

The Brazzaville twelve were ready to take this step at the Tananarive, Malagasy conference, from 6-12 September 1961, where they adopted the Charter of the Union Africaine et Malgache (UAM). This organization was intended to coordinate their common policy in external affairs, collective security and the maintenance of peace in Africa and the world. This policy would be determined by the supreme body, a conference of Heads of State, convened twice a year and at special request. The conference elected its president, who held office until the next conference, and who could be entrusted with specific missions on behalf of the other members. There were no other policy-making bodies although meetings of other ministers, experts or representatives could be held. The UAM had its own secretariat and secretary-general, both strictly "administrative." The text carefully avoided any suspicion of supranationality and the sovereignty of the states was explicitly guaranteed. Although most decisions were taken by a majority vote, they were only recommendations and not binding on the members. The UAM was open to other independent states, but only upon unanimous approval.

A convention on diplomatic representation was also signed, making it possible for two or more states to share joint diplomatic representation. It was also decided to have the heads of mission of the member states at important posts (especially Paris) meet periodically and to create an African and Malagasy Group at the United Nations.

Even in the sensitive field of defence the Brazzaville states went ahead and adopted a defence pact. It invoked the United Nations Charter, the duty of peaceful settlement and the desire to live in peace, but provided that the states, individually or jointly, could act continuously and effectively in case of conventional or nuclear armed attacks. Leaving no doubt about where the threat was likely to come from, the pact

also applied in cases of armed or unarmed subversive actions
directed or supported from abroad. Aggression against one
state would be considered aggression against the others. However, to safeguard sovereignty, the reply was not automatic
and took the form of mutual consultations and immediate assistance. The defence organization (UAMD) was placed under
the conseil supérieur du pacte and a permanent secretariat.
However, all policy decisions were taken by the Heads of
State.

Once again, the major concern was with economic matters. Five protocols were adopted to give substance to the
Organisation Africaine et Malgache de Coopération Economique.
Four committees were established. The committee on economic and social development was to harmonize development
and investment and consider setting up a common price stabilization fund. The committee on foreign trade was to study
customs and fiscal arrangements as well as an expansion of
the existing customs unions or the creation of a free trade
area. The committee on monetary questions dealt with the
balance of payments and transfer of funds. And the committee
on scientific and technical research was to coordinate work in
existing institutes and promote new ones. Finally, a permanent secretariat was established for the OAMCE.

In various functional activities, however, the Brazzaville states went even further. At successive meetings a
whole series of agencies were founded, as well as a common
airline. The first tangible project was the company Air-
Afrique, administered jointly with French airlines, and servicing most of the states to avoid unnecessary and costly duplication. There was also a Postal and Telecommunications Union
(UAMPT), an association of development banks, an office of
industrial property, and a development institute.

Thus, by the end of 1961, the Brazzaville Group had
caught up with their Casablanca rivals. Although their charters were not as impressive, the various bodies covered a
broad range of activities. The fact that the organization was
much looser, with four separate institutions--each with its own
secretary-general and headquarters--did not keep the UAM,
UAMD, OAMCE and UAMPT from rapidly getting down to work.
Actually, in the economic and technical fields, the Brazzaville
twelve were well ahead of the Casablanca Group and a number
of concrete projects were initiated. Where they fell behind
was the question of decolonization. No provision had been
made for active solidarity with the dependent territories. And

the proposals of UAM Secretary-General Albert Tevoedjre that
they offer diplomatic and financial backing or take care of
training freedom fighters and political leaders were turned
down. [8]

The Lagos Conference.

Finally, by the end of 1961, the efforts made to bring
the whole African family together at the Conference of Heads
of State and Government in Lagos seemed to be bearing fruit.
Only two states refused to attend any meeting: Morocco, because of Mauritania's presence, and Ghana, because Dr.
Nkrumah complained of insufficient preparatory work.   Then,
unexpectedly, the conference foundered on disagreement over
the representation of the Algerian Provisional Government.
Although a compromise was to be sought at the preparatory
conference of Foreign Ministers, the Casablanca states did not
come.

When the moderate leaders met on 25 January 1962,
they were in the same position as they were at the previous
Monrovia conference and it seemed likely that the result would
be a further polarization of the continent. On the whole,
every effort was made not to perpetuate the split. The resolutions were toned down. But criticism could not be avoided
on one point, the continued refusal of the Casablanca states to
openly adhere to and respect the basic principles that had been
laid down in Monrovia as the basis for any reunion. Governor-General Azikiwe insisted on the inalienable right of all
African states, as then constituted, to legal equality and self-
determination, and the inviolability of their territories from
without and safety from subversion within. Otherwise the suspicions would continue that other states "secretly nurse expansionist ambitions against their smaller and perhaps weaker
neighbours."

Still, some sort of organization was necessary for this
grouping of states. A rather detailed draft charter was presented by Liberia and approved in principle. However, in the
hope that an understanding could be reached and one Pan-African body established, the draft was sent to the absent states
and the actual adoption was put off to later. The draft was
discussed bilaterally during the year and in December 1962 another meeting was held in Lagos. This time a Charter was
adopted for the Inter-African and Malagasy Organization.

Although the IAMO was to assure political and defence
cooperation, it was strongly oriented towards non-political activities like economic development, trade, education, health,
agriculture, transport and communications. The highest body
was to be an Assembly of Heads of State, meeting annually.
It was aided by a Council of Ministers that met twice a year.
There was a permanent Secretariat, elected for three years
and eligible for re-election, with clearly defined tasks. The
major innovation of IAMO was a commission of conciliation to
enquire into disputes among the member states. The organization, with twenty-one members, was the largest political
grouping thus far in the continent. It consisted of over half
of the independent states of Africa.

One Movement or Many?

The ferment of ideas and the multitude of joint actions
throughout the colonial world made Africa and Asia a breeding
place for movements of solidarity. The Conferences of Independent African States were far from being the only manifestation of the period. Almost every dynamic leader or ambitious country claimed its share in the prestige of founding or
backing a movement that was destined to transform the future.
This rivalry was somewhat less divisive. But it was expensive and eventually pitted Nkrumah against Nasser in a struggle for leadership of the continent.

As was natural, the earliest steps to channel the energy and enthusiasm of the times were taken in the most politically articulate regions, often by the recently decolonized
states. The first in the series was the Arab League, created
as a regional body prior to the founding of the United Nations,
by the Cairo Treaty of 22 March 1945. The Arab League
originally had seven members, but it was expanded to include
the other states of this racial and cultural community as they
obtained independence, with the aid and sponsorship of the
League. Its conferences, often at the Heads of State level and
always inter-governmental, were similar to the meetings of
the independent African states, as were the objectives and concerns. With one exception--the attitude towards the State of
Israel. Whereas the Black African states assumed a neutral
or friendly stance towards the Jewish state, the Arabs actively
participated in the bloody war in Palestine and their defeat
marked the beginning of a long feud. Like the Africans, the
Arabs were engaged in a struggle against colonialism and racialism, but the state that embodied that evil for them more

than Portugal or South Africa was Israel. Nevertheless, cooperation with the rest of the continent entailed a sort of division of labor: the Arab League dealing with the "Arab" problem of Palestine, which did not even receive second-best
treatment to the south, while the African organizations dealt
with "African" problems. Any undue insistence to the contrary lay the Arab leaders open to accusations of "Arab first,
Arab last. "

Egypt was not only the heart and soul of the Arab
League, it was also--as the passage between the continents--
one of the key members of the broader Afro-Asian movement
of solidarity. In April 1955, when this movement was begun
at the Bandung Conference, there were only three delegations
present from Black Africa. But, even with the Arab League
members in Africa included, the meeting was overwhelmingly
what it purported to be--Asian-African. It did not arouse any
great enthusiasm even for a revolutionary African like Kwame
Nkrumah, who felt that the Asians were more concerned with
their own needs and struggle than those of Africa. He was
not reconciled when President Nasser brought a section of the
movement to Africa, the Afro-Asian People's Solidarity Organization. The AAPSO, created at the end of 1957 in Cairo,
was open to all African political parties and freedom movements, but it only attracted the more radical varieties. And
its work was first dominated and then paralyzed by the big
brothership of China and the Soviet Union.

Almost at the same time that Prime Minister Nkrumah
convened the first All-African Peoples Conference in Accra,
President Nasser again tried to take the lead. Realizing the
growing importance of the problem of under-development, one
day likely to eclipse decolonization as a common source of
solidarity as more states became independent, he called a major meeting on the subject. In December 1958, an Afro-Asian
economic conference was held in Cairo to chart a program for
development. Despite the similarity of views in Africa, Asia
(and Latin America), the result was not so much to draw the
continent into this new movement as to incite the other African
organizations to devote more attention to economic concerns
and include them in their own programs.

The last serious rival to a purely Pan-African movement was non-alignment, which took rough shape at the Bel-
grade Conference of September 1961. Believing that the smaller uncommitted states' balancing act between East and West,
Capitalism and Communism, would be much easier if a united

front could be formed, Presidents Tito, Nehru and Nasser
sponsored a meeting to give birth to a third or neutral force.
By disqualifying many of the less adventurous African states
as members, the non-aligned group already made African adhesion to the cause en masse impossible. But the recommendations of the conference helped make membership superfluous.
Rather than stick to the original line of political and economic
independence between the two blocs, many states from Africa
and Asia imposed upon the conference their additional policies
of decolonization and economic development. In return for
this, the Africans placed non-alignment and disarmament in
their own program.

Regional Experiments in Former French Africa.

        During the whole period in which the struggle for broad
Pan-African unity was fought out, there was a second controversy as to whether lesser forms of unity were possible or
permissible. The first regional grouping was the Ghana-
Guinea Union which, although supposedly the nucleus of a vast
continental unit, was condemned to be a group of two and then
three states. The Union was called organic by its authors,
but it never got to be more than a loose alliance. However,
the dynamic nature of this Union and the aggressive policies
of its members soon provoked the formation of other regional
groups, especially among the nearby moderate states.

        The lessons that could be drawn from the sub-Saharan
French territories were particularly interesting. Among countries with roughly the same linguistic and colonial heritage and
even level of development, three different regional groupings,
with three different degrees of integration and success were
established. They were all attempts at salvaging something of
the federal structures of the old French West Africa and
French Equatorial Africa.

        The most ambitious project was the work of two mem-
bers of the "federalist" wing of the RDA, Léopold Sédar Senghor and Modibo Keita. Fearing that separate independence of
the territories would dissolve the remaining links between
them, they planned to unite in a broader grouping even before
independence through a federation of Senegal, Soudan, Dahomey
and Upper Volta. A constitutional assembly in Dakar, in January 1959, laid the foundation for the Federation of Mali, with
Dakar as its capital and French as its official language. It
was to be governed through a federal executive, the head of

state and government, who would choose two ministers from each member state for his cabinet; a federal assembly of twelve deputies from each territorial legislature; and an independent judiciary or federal court.

But this federation was stillborn. It had to be approved by the people, through referendums, and was rejected in Dahomey and Upper Volta. Although both territories sponsored the project in Dakar, within a few months "anti-federalist" groups had gained enough strength to replace the former leaders. External pressure also played a role, as France did not favor the federation and may have offered other compensation, such as a deep-water port for Dahomey.

Shortly thereafter, at another conference in Dakar in March 1959, a second Federation of Mali was created. It included only Senegal and Soudan. However, when limited to two, it was hard to find a compromise between opposing attitudes on the distribution of powers in the federation. Modibo Keita, the head of government, sought a unitary state with a single party, whereas Senghor, the head of the assembly, wished looser links and democracy. For some time, it was impossible to choose between the two theories or the two men, one of whom had to be made president of the federation, and the two territories continued their separate existence. Finally, on 20 August 1960, after differences between the leaders and an abortive coup d'état in Senegal, the federation collapsed. All that remained was the name, since Soudan became the Republic of Mali and kept the federal flag and anthem.

A deliberately less ambitious attempt was made by the anti-federalist leader of the RDA, Houphouët-Boigny, who objected in theory to the immense and far-flung federations as unviable. In practice, Abidjan, Ivory Coast, had always been a counter-pole to Dakar, Senegal. Houphouët-Boigny also sought to draw the nearby states into a more natural and profitable relationship with the Ivory Coast. He did not think highly of the Mali Federation and his plan was more pragmatic and looser. The Sahel-Benin Union was founded at a meeting in Abidjan, in May 1959, between the Ivory Coast, Niger, Upper Volta and Dahomey. It was limited in its structures and objectives. The supreme body of the Union was the Conseil de l'Entente. This "council of understanding" expressed the basic philosophy. It was merely a periodic meeting of the Prime Ministers, other ministers and Presidents of the National Assemblies of the four territories. All decisions were taken unanimously and there was not even a regular secretariat.

The system was based on concrete links such as strengthening the customs union by an equitable distribution of duties and taxes, joint operation of the Abidjan-Niger railway, use of the port of Abidjan in common, a court of appeal to settle differences and eventually common postal services. The real cement was the solidarity fund. It drew upon ten percent of the resources of each member and was used to provide a reserve fund (20 percent), running expenses of the Conseil de l'Entente (10 percent) and economic and financial balance of the members (70 percent). Most of the money came from the wealthiest state, the Ivory Coast, which only received back 1/16 of the fund, while the other three partners obtained 5/16 each. This was a shrewder and more lasting scheme than that of Dr. Nkrumah.

Since the relations were made mutually advantageous and flexible, the members were willing to expand them as needs arose. In the ensuing years, frequent meetings among the Heads of State or ministers reinforced the common structures. A secretariat was set up and made permanent. The customs union was adjusted to satisfy Upper Volta and the solidarity fund was enabled to guarantee loans to member states. When the territories became independent, they adopted similar constitutions and organizations for their national army, administration and diplomacy. A regional defence council was established. Increasingly the members supported common economic policies and concerted diplomatic actions. And a fifth state was attracted to the group. Although Togo did not become a member (to avoid Nkrumah's ire), it entered a customs union with Dahomey in 1960 and was an interested observer.

In French Equatorial Africa the endeavors at forming a larger grouping also began well before independence. The broadest scheme was advanced by Barthélémy Boganda of Oubangui-Chari (Ubangi-Shari), the future Central African Republic. He hoped that at least the close links between the four French colonies of the region could be maintained, but in October 1958 he went much further and called for the creation of a United States of Latin Africa, including the French and Portuguese-speaking territories with Latin and Christian traditions. But his plea was ignored by Muslim Chad, Gabon (jealous of its wealth) and even the Congo. Latin Africa came to nought with the untimely death of Boganda in a plane crash in 1959.

From Brazzaville, the former federal capital, Mayor Abbé Fulbert Youlou put forward his own plans. He first supported a United States of Central Africa, a very loose arrangement permitting each state to preserve its own identity. Early in 1960, the Congo, Chad, the to-be (August 13) Central African Republic, and Gabon worked out a Union of Central African Republics, to allow them to accede to independence together. The Union consisted of a council, president and supreme court, its only permanent bodies. But Gabon had dropped out by the time the plan was formally submitted in May 1960, and the Union never materialized.

Fortunately, back in June 1959, the four states had already signed a convention to maintain their customs union, harmonize fiscal legislation and run three joint bodies: a post and telecommunications authority, an institute of mining research and a transport agency. Building on this limited but concrete foundation, the Equatorial Customs Union began to develop. Although Gabon was at first distant, it increasingly participated in joint activities, and Cameroun also began to attend regional meetings. The fields of activity spread to thoughts of a defence council or concrete projects like the construction of a common oil refinery.

Federation in English-Speaking Africa.

There had been few similar ties between the former British territories and no broad federations as in French Africa. The only exception was the vast Federation of Nigeria. Moreover, the Crown did not even encourage serious integration within each one of its colonies, adopting a policy of indirect rule and relative autonomy. Where there were strivings for larger units they often came from the settler elements that wanted to spread their influence. Usually these efforts were only supported lukewarmly by the British Colonial Office and resisted by the nationalists. In West Africa, since the territories were scattered, very few concrete links aside from some common services and a common currency were created. In Eastern and Central Africa the relations were closer. Nevertheless, all the territories had English as a common language (and Swahili in East Africa) and many of the leaders had studied and met in London. After independence, the states stayed in the sterling area and enjoyed certain trade preferences. The only all-embracing framework, the British Commonwealth, was adhered to with surprising goodwill by the new states.

The lack of closer relations between the territories was, in one way, a hindrance to effective schemes of cooperation and integration. The former British colonies often lagged behind the ex-French colonies when it came to forming broader and rather active associations. However, there was less particularism, and the English-speaking states were more often trail-blazers when it came to genuinely Pan-African groups. Nkrumah's Ghana and Nigeria were active in establishing relations with their French-speaking neighbors. In Eastern Africa, despite the close ties between Kenya, Uganda and Tanganyika, their relations were rarely exclusive and all efforts among them had strong repercussions and overflowed onto the surrounding region. Their own links did not prevent them from participating directly in larger movements throughout East, Central and Southern Africa.

Before independence, relatively little had been done towards associating the various British colonies with one another. East Africa, despite several plans, never reached the stage of federation. Nevertheless, a customs union was introduced by the Agreement of 1927, and the Governors of Kenya, Uganda and Tanganyika set up a joint conference system. In 1948, an East African High Commission was established to coordinate a number of common services: communication, finance, commercial and social. Mainly at the initiative of Julius Nyerere, these services were carried over and adapted to post-independence conditions, in which they would be administered by African authorities. And, in December 1961, the old system was turned into the East African Common Services Organization (EACSO). A less auspicious step was taken in 1953, when Northern Rhodesia and Nyasaland were forced into a Central African Federation against the wishes of the nationalists.

The only broader grouping in the region was the Pan-African Freedom Movement of East and Central Africa, created in 1958, and expanded to include Southern Africa in 1962. This was originally a "people's" organization consisting of representatives from the major political parties and nationalist movements. In 1962, it was made a combined operation with liberation movements from the dependent territories and governments of the independent states. But it was always a more disciplined group than the AAPO. Every effort was made at having only one spokesman per territory and there was no question of accepting oppositional parties. A simple structure was established. There was an annual general meeting which elected a co-ordinating freedom council, with one member from each territory, as its governing body. It had a perma-

nent secretariat, a territorial freedom committee in each member territory, and a freedom fund. This makeshift apparatus
had its headquarters in Dar es Salaam and was kept alive
largely by TANU.

As its name denoted, PAFMECSA was primarily concerned with independence and not unity. Its first conference
considered that before independence the question of federation
was even somewhat irrelevant. What little experience the nationalists had with colonial and settler "unity" was negative.
They wanted East African federation only under African rule.
And the Federation of Rhodesia and Nyasaland was a major
obstacle to independence. Ever since its creation it had been
resented or attacked by nationalists in all three territories.
PAFMECSA echoed these views at successive conferences and
condemned the Federation as a threat to peace.

Still, even though unity was not a prominent aim, the
joint struggle for independence could not help but reinforce the
solidarity and mutual relations in the region. This was further enhanced by the pragmatic and collegial approach of its
members. There was no dominant leader or state in
PAFMECSA. The doors were wide open to all, no matter
what the colonial heritage or regime, from ancient and conservative Ethiopia to the newly independent states and the most
radical of liberation movements.[9] This refreshingly smooth
experiment in cooperation drew eighteen territories of the region into the broader movement towards African unity.

With the approach of independence, however, there was
a sudden flurry of interest in some sort of closer links. The
main advocate of this was Julius Nyerere, who went out on a
limb by proposing that Tanganyikan independence be postponed
so that Kenya and Uganda might become free at the same time
and the three merge. Otherwise he feared that sovereignty
and vested interests would be consolidated too rapidly and then
block later integration. But he was overruled by his own party and hampered by Britain's dilatory withdrawal.

When Kenya obtained self-government, a new effort was
made. The leaders of Kenya, Tanganyika and Uganda met in
Nairobi in June 1963 and endorsed the establishment of an
East African Federation. A declaration of intention to feder-
ate was signed and the three leaders went on record that "we
believe that East African Federation can be a practical step
towards the goal of Pan-African unity." The deadline was the
end of 1963. A constitution was prepared. And a serious

pitfall was avoided when Nyerere offered the presidency of the
federation to Kenyatta, obviating any leadership crisis. But
the declaration of intention was not that easy to realize.

In PAFMECSA as well, when the territories reached
the threshold of independence (and states like Ethiopia and
Somalia joined), there was a keener interest in unity.   The
third conference in February 1962 devoted considerable attention to the problems of cooperation.   It was decided to increase the coordination in transport and communications and
to hold a meeting on education.   On a higher level, the delegates agreed to work towards a federation of Eastern Africa
as soon as Kenya, Uganda and Zanzibar attained independence.
Tanganyika, Ethiopia and Somalia would be included in the
broader federation.   Eventually the countries of Central and
Southern Africa would also become members.   The mechanics
of such a federation were not defined although it would certainly be more loosely regulated than the smaller East African
grouping.   A first step was to extend the common market to
Somalia and Ethiopia and both governments were asked to consult with EACSO to this purpose.

Maghreb Unity.

The racial, religious and cultural links among the countries of the Maghreb were so strong as to seem to give new
life to the old dream of unity.   Such a union, to include Morocco, Algeria and Tunisia, possibly with Libya or Mauritania
later, had been given a strong impulse by the states' open and
continued support of the Algerian cause.   But little concrete
could be done so long as Algeria was not independent.

The first step taken towards closer formal relations
was a Maghreb Charter signed as early as May 1945 by the
major political parties, the Istiqlal of Morocco and Neo-Destour of Tunisia.   Cooperation in the ensuing years was necessarily limited to aid to the war of liberation.   Nevertheless,
in April 1958, a Convention was adopted in Tangiers in which
the Istiqlal, Neo-Destour, and the FLN proclaimed the goal of
Maghreb unity and a future federation.   It was even provided
that the national assemblies should convene a consultative assembly "to consider matters of federal and common interest
during the transition period" and that in the interim the three
governments should "refrain from making basic international
agreements on matters of foreign policy or defence until the
federal institutions could be made effective. " Permanent sec-

retariats were created by each member to implement the project.

During the war the dream was well out of reach and all plans were put off until peacetime. However, any intimate union among the three states presupposed a minimum consensus on domestic and foreign policy and despite repeated appeals for Maghreb unity, this agreement was increasingly remote. After seven years of war, only the hard core remained in the Algerian leadership, and when Ben Bella came out on top in the struggle for power, it was clear that Algeria was going to exercise very different foreign and state policy options from its neighbors. Even underlying ideologies in Algeria were often contrary to those in the Kingdom of Morocco and the relatively moderate Tunisia. There were also more specific points of discord. Morocco had already based much of its foreign policy on an irredentist campaign against Mauritania, which was accepted and later recognized by both Algeria and Tunisia. What was worse, its territorial claims also included some of Algeria. For its part, revolutionary Algeria supported the Yussefist faction in Tunisia or men like Ben Barka in Morocco, and relations with the brother states were stormy. Finally, Algeria's closest ally and the most influential Arab power on the continent, Egypt, was strongly opposed to any grouping from which it would be excluded. With such varied forms of government and policies--as well as incipient territorial disputes--the Maghreb states were further than ever from political unity. Their only hope lay in narrow functional arrangements.

Annexationism and Unity.

There were other, less propitious aspects of the strivings for unity--as for example a nation's attempts to integrate part of a divided social or natural unit within itself. It was true that the colonial frontiers were highly artificial, arbitrarily cutting across tribal and racial boundaries, rarely taking into consideration the basic economic and geographical lay of the land. Many a racial, religious or economic grouping had been split in two, three or more parts by the colonial frontiers, and it was a natural concern of the members of these families to seek to restore the unity shattered by the colonial powers. But it was difficult to decide what should be re-united and how, and most particularly: by whom. The re-unification of one group might be at the expense of another and would be strongly resisted by those called upon to make the sacrifice.

Several successful mergers had taken place at the eve
of decolonization, when the territories concerned were still
colonies or United Nations trusts. After a plebiscite in British Togoland in 1956, the United Nations decided that the territory would be joined to the Gold Coast when it became independent. Thus Kwame Nkrumah obtained not only the independence of his country but also a considerable addition to it,
and he had accomplished the first successful "unification" in
Africa. After another plebiscite in February 1961, the United
Nations decided to divide the British Cameroons and unite the
southern part with French Cameroun while incorporating the
northern part in Nigeria.

In many ways these two precedents were important and
even fateful for Africa. It showed that the will of the people
could lead to unification and the creation of larger units. But
there were always losers. Both Togo and Cameroun contested
the elections, the Cameroun Republic even referring the matter to the International Court of Justice. One of the most
painful situations existed for the Ewe tribe, scattered through
the Gold Coast, Togoland and Togo. The Ewes in British
Togoland hoped they could eventually be re-united with those
in Togo. But the referendum of 9 May 1956 was a grave dis-
appointment to them, for the northern peoples obtained 58 percent of the votes for a union with the Gold Coast, where they
could avoid Ewe domination. The minority of 42 percent voting for maintenance of trusteeship (and later union with Togo)
thus lost the possibility of uniting with other Ewes. Nevertheless, Sylvanus Olympio, later president of Togo and head
of the All-Ewe Congress, continued to advocate a new Ewe
state. To the surprise of all, however, he was soon challenged by another potential unifier. Incorporation of the Togoland Ewes had swollen the Ewe population of Ghana and Prime
Minister Nkrumah intimated that Togo might be annexed as
well and the problem thus solved. Ghana also made broad
hints about re-uniting the tribes on its western border, including Nkrumah's Nzima tribe, and seriously aided the attempt at
"liberating" the Sanwi from the Ivory Coast.

Ghana's partner, Guinea, also made claims to some of
the surrounding territory in its bid for a Greater Guinea.
With his eye on part of Liberia (through which its iron ore
had to be brought to the sea) and the Ivory Coast, Sékou
Touré entered a difficult period with his neighbors during
which any demands for unity seemed to hide ulterior motives.

The main territorial problem of the time was in the Maghreb, where the newly independent (1956) state of Morocco laid claim to all the territory ruled over more or less effectively by the previous Moroccan dynasties. This "Greater Morocco" was vast, covering all of Mauritania, the Spanish territories and parts of Algeria. So powerful was the urge for recognition of these claims that King Mohammed V called the conference creating the Casablanca bloc and became part of the radical group in the hope of re-uniting his realm. Thus, more than ever, the pleas and demands for unity by the radical states seemed to hide designs of annexation. For Mali as well had its eye on part of Mauritania and joined Morocco in harassing this emergent state.

The Egyptian brand of unity did not seem much purer to its southern neighbor. There had been some trouble in disposing of the former Anglo-Egyptian Sudan, but the decision had finally been taken in favor of a separate and independent existence. Nevertheless, a Union of the Nile States was almost imposed forcefully by Egypt in 1955. By interfering in the internal affairs of the Sudan when it obtained independence, considerable antagonism was engendered. When, in 1958, Egypt tried to enforce a territorial claim by military action, the relations worsened and the primary concern of the Sudanese government became the maintenance of the independence and integrity of the country. Despite a conscious attempt by President Nasser to improve relations, the suspicion remained.

The most explosive, potentially, of the territorial disputes was in the Horn of Africa. On 1 July 1960, the former British Somaliland and Italian Somalia united in the Somali Republic. But, this was only to be the start, for the constitution and declarations of the political leaders indicated that three further territories were to be brought into the union. One was French Somaliland, two others were parts of Ethiopia and the future Kenya. Vast stretches of these countries were inhabited by Somalis and the ultimate aim was to integrate all the lands inhabited by members of the Somali tribe. Somalia saw this as a legitimate move towards greater and more genuine unity.[10] But Ethiopia and Kenya had reason to fear this would disrupt their own states.

National Unity and African Unity.

The question of unity and federation was not only on the agenda of the international conferences. There were also fair-

ly intense strivings for autonomy by the disparate tribal, racial, or religious groups within most African countries. These
were met by attempts at imposing centralized governments,
presidential regimes and one-party systems upon the dissidents
and making them bow to national unity. However, in a number of the larger countries or where internal differences were
too great or the preparation for independence too hasty, the
urge for separatism often burst the fragile bonds and federation was proposed as a solution to relax unity.

Although the vast Sudan was established as a unitary
state, it had considerable trouble with separatism. A majority of people with Arab blood or speaking Arabic, and a larger
majority of Muslims were in a constant state of tension with
the substantial minority of Negroes, strongly tribalized and
animist or Christian. In 1955, the Negroes agreed to independence but insisted that "federation" be given full consideration. However, when the British withdrew and were replaced
by Arabized Sudanese, discontent grew in the three southern
provinces. Then, in August 1955, a bloody revolt broke out
in which hundreds of northerners were killed. The elections
of 1958 returned a considerable "federalist" bloc to parliament,
largely from the southern provinces. Nevertheless, the central government's reply was to increase the integration of the
south and impose Arabic and Islam. The revolt continued and
met with bloody reprisals, so much so that the demands
switched to complete separation from the Sudan. The forceful imposition of unity had only negative results.

The most serious crisis Africa had to face derived also
from a failure at national unity. Despite the traditional centralized and direct rule of the Belgians, the Congo was too
vast and varied to develop a national consciousness. In the
brief period of preparation for independence it was impossible
to form truly national political parties and all the leaders
drew their strength from a particular tribe or region. Thus,
once the mutiny broke out and the central government fell
apart, the Congo dissolved into self-contained units, each ruled
by its own leaders, and Katanga, Kasai and Kivu sought autonomy or secession.

Even the two main forces for unity were divided on the
correct solution, for Patrice Lumumba wished to impose a
strongly centralized government, by armed might if need be,
whereas President Kasavubu had always been in favor of leaving the provinces some powers. When the split came, the
Lumumbists retired to Stanleyville. In so doing they in-

creased the fragmentation of the Congo. President Kasavubu,
seeking allies, eventually asked the secessionists to moderate
their demands and accept a loose federation. At the Tananarive conference of March 1961, it was decided to establish a
confederation of Congolese States under the presidency of
Kasavubu. But this agreement was rejected by Stanleyville
and never implemented by the secessionists or central government. No genuine compromise was ever obtained on the question of unity.

The handbook model for federation and democracy was
for a time Nigeria. It had been recognized that the country
was too varied and the tribal and religious differences too
sharp for a unitary state. From the outset, Nigeria was made
a federation, consisting of three regions and a federal capital.
This federalism was reflected in the political life of the country by the creation of tribal political parties: the National
Council of Nigerian Citizens (NCNC) of the Eastern Ibos, the
Action Group of the Western Yorubas, and the Northern People's Congress of the Housas. But not all the tribes were
satisfied and, in 1963, it was necessary to create a further
region for the Edo and Bini.

Democracy was the necessary counterpart of federation
and the governments of Nigeria were usually coalitions between
the parties. At first they joined the North and East. However, the oppositional Action Group became thoroughly dissa-
fected and in September 1962 it was accused of planning a
coup. Later, after the 1963 census, it became evident that
the overwhelming preponderance of the northern tribes could
rule Nigeria without the others. This was expressed politically by dissatisfaction in the Ibo NCNC. From then on even
coalition governments were difficult. When the northern-run
Nigerian National Alliance won the 1964 elections, largely boycotted in the south, its leaders were obliged to form a "broad-
based" government or risk the collapse of the federation.

A Fresh Start.

After this initial phase in the movement for unity in
Africa, despite tremendous efforts and drive, the concrete results were disappointingly meager. What originally looked
rather easy turned out to be a sisyphean labor. The more
energetic the endeavors, the greater the setbacks. Unity had
not been attained--far from it. When blocs formed on the continent, the Africans became acutely aware that they were fur-

ther away from unity than ever.

As it turned out, Africa's leaders had clearly underestimated the difficulties. Many just assumed that there was
a natural harmony of things in the continent and that all divisions resulted from external machinations. It was true that
the colonialists had introduced many unnecessary separations.
But the nationalists tended to forget the old barriers which
existed before. Actually, although rarely admitted, the most
serious threats to unity had always been there and occasionally, when the colonial powers withdrew, the unity they had imposed collapsed under factional strains. And the new ruling
classes only added to them. They were unwilling to sacrifice
the sovereignty they had won even to join together with other
Africans. They would not create the sort of machinery that
could direct the continent. Moreover, they injected the worst
of divisions--their own nascent ideologies. On the reefs of
these new and old barriers to unity, the most ambitious projects were bound to founder.

It was thus unwise to aim too high. Organic unity was
an ideal. But how could it be achieved when even before independence most of the territories had structures, élites and
vested interests? Political unity was the hardest to achieve.
And the so-called "unions" were often a mere facade. Greater success was obtained by more modest projects, starting at
lower levels of unity. By excluding or isolating political concerns, it was possible to avoid sudden disruption and collapse.
At the same time, by strengthening what concrete links existed, economic usually, it was possible to lay a solid foundation
for later structures.

Frustration at moving ever further from the ultimate
goal incited the great debate on unity. And this degenerated
into an unending doctrinal controversy about the best path to
unity. Paradoxically, the issue of how to achieve unity had
become one of the principle divisions between African states.[11]
Each leader had his own panacea. Each had some scheme for
unity. The extremes were far apart and the plans varied widely. They ran from Nkrumah's demand for immediate political
union to the moderates' worship of state sovereignty. There
were the integral and functional approaches, groups could be
all-African or regional, things could be done all at once or
progressively.

Yet, this was not entirely in vain, for over the years
all the methods were tried. Gradually the extremes began to

meet. The states which proclaimed the need for rapid and
far-reaching unity were indeed more dynamic. Ghana, Guinea,
Mali and the UAR had already placed in their constitutions the
right to abandon sovereignty for African unity. They also had
similar views on both domestic and foreign policy. They
claimed to be in the vanguard of the march towards unity but,
in practice, the various charters they signed never went very
far.

In theory, the Brazzaville states were a pole away
from the Casablanca Group. They insisted on not sacrificing
sovereignty and strictly limited the scope of their cooperation.
However, in practice, they did create new and stronger bodies.
They had both political and technical activities. And their organizations had no reason to envy those of Casablanca. Even
the Monrovia states were reaching towards a rather complete
organization by the second Lagos meeting.

Thus, during the years of controversy over the ideal
form of African unity--despite even the creation of blocs--Af-
rica was progressing haltingly towards an acceptable common
denominator. The more radical states had been unable to give
any reality to the most ambitious plans and the series of
unions became increasingly modest in their real contents. At
the same time, by trial and error, the more moderate states
also found that (partly under the pressure and stimulus of radical attempts) they could go further than they had originally
thought. By 1963, there was not much difference between the
structures of the three groupings: the Casablanca, the Brazzaville (UAM), and the Monrovia (IAMO).

Still, it was necessary to liquidate the past legacy of
these Groups. Their fundamental weakness was that they were
primarily political and were thus as transient as the causes
which gave birth to them. When the causes disappeared, the
organizations began to disintegrate. This process was strongest in the radical camp, where political fronts had been created more than real organizations, but it was true of Africa in
general as well. With Algerian independence and the end of
the Congo war, much of the will faded. The Casablanca Group
had hastily decreed a military command (even choosing the
commander), a common market and development bank. But
they never really set up any machinery. They decided to wait.
Only the UAM really functioned or had solid non-political links.
But the Brazzaville states were interested in a reconciliation,
too. The Monrovia Group had been created against the better
judgement of many of its members and it was easy to scrap

the charter of the stillborn organization.

In this new atmosphere, with the disappearance of the main contentious issues and the weakening of the blocs, an increasing number of African leaders began to support the forthcoming conference of Addis Ababa. The advocates of reconciliation were in both camps. There were radicals such as Sékou Touré and Modibo Keita and moderates like Senghor and Balewa. Nyerere had kept East Africa largely out of the split. There was also the untiring Emperor of Ethiopia, who worked for the success of the next meeting. The final boost was given by Ben Bella when he recalled the Africans to their primary duty of decolonization.

Then, another voice was heard. After having rejected the first two attempts at reconciliation, President Nkrumah also came out in favor of the meeting. In a personal communication to the Heads of State, he sent his new plan for a political union "along the lines of the USA or the USSR." He urged a "central political organization" consisting of an upper and lower house to formulate a common foreign policy, continental planning of economic and industrial development, a common currency, monetary zone and bank of issue, and a joint defence system. He also published a new book for the occasion: Africa Must Unite!

But this unity could only be restored at a conference in which the wishes of all states were heard and respected. It had been impossible to impose unity on the more recalcitrant. Now it was necessary to find a new and genuine consensus. After three years of strife, Africa had come back to the starting point. It had learned a lot in the meanwhile. And it was willing both to sacrifice--and compromise--for unity.

Notes

1. Philippe Decraene, Le Panafricanisme, p. 86.

2. Colin Legum, Pan-Africanism, p. 188-189.

3. Ibid., p. 191.

4. Kwame Nkrumah, I Speak of Freedom.

5. Legum, op. cit., p. 192.

6. Ibid., p. 57.

7. Ibid., p. 55.

8. See Albert Tevoedjre, Pan-Africanism in Action: U.A.M.

9. See Richard Cox, Pan-Africanism in Practice:
    PAFMECSA.

10. See I. M. Lewis, "Pan-Africanism and Pan-Somalism,"
    Journal of Modern African Studies, June 1963, p. 147-
    162.

11. Erasmus H. Kloman Jr., African Unification Movements,
    p. 387.

D. The Summit Conference of Addis Ababa

Not since June 1960, when the last Conference of Independent African States met in Addis Ababa, had it been possible to assemble all the African states. Despite considerable efforts, both the Monrovia and Lagos conferences failed to end the schism. It was only when Algeria had become independent and there was a lull in the Congo that a further attempt was made. It remained to be seen whether unity could be restored this time.

Unfortunately, not all the omens were favorable. The King of Morocco refused to attend the summit because of the presence of Mauritania and there were signs the new President of Togo might not attend because his government was still opposed by certain states. Once again, it was feared that the Arab countries would press for concerted denouncement of Israel. Trouble could also be expected if association with the European Common Market and French explosions in the Sahara were placed on the agenda. And Somalia wished to bring the whole complex of border problems with its neighbors before the Heads of State.

Still, even these were relatively minor issues compared with Algeria and the Congo and it was assumed that they would not prevent the long desired reconciliation. The third attempt, coming at an opportune moment, and more carefully prepared than the others, stood a much better chance of success. Even before it opened, the Conference of Addis Ababa was destined to go down in history as the end of the interconference period. The members of both blocs, some thirty states, had finally agreed to meet with one another and make a serious effort to overcome all differences. If it had been nothing more than a solemn and ceremonious gathering, it would have left many of Africa's most ardent wishes unanswered.

The Continent in 1970

The Conference of Foreign Ministers.

Two conferences had been scheduled for Addis Ababa.
The first was a preparatory meeting of Foreign Ministers.
This was in keeping with a tradition that had grown up over
the years. The Foreign Ministers were to discuss the general problems, draw up an agenda for the summit, frame a
Charter if need be, and draft various resolutions and recommendations that could serve as working documents for the
Heads of State. While so doing, they could weed out the
points on which no agreement was possible, while reaching a
preliminary agreement on other items. When the Heads of
State met, they would not have to remain away from their
countries too long and they could engage in a relatively smooth
and dignified process of ratification, more becoming to their
prestige and that of Africa than the crude haggling about agenda
and resolutions.

As the Foreign Ministers began to arrive in Addis Ababa, the attention of world public opinion was focused on their
activities and rumors of success or failure began to circulate.
When they first met, on 15 May, they were indeed faced with
certain painful decisions. They were informed by the Foreign
Minister of Morocco that only a delegation of "functionaries"
would be present as observers. Despite considerable efforts,
Togo's President Nicolas Grunitsky's envoys were not able to
obtain an invitation to the conference. But all the other controversial issues were simply put aside and the agenda did not
include Israel, common market association, atomic tests in
the Sahara, or the Somali claims.

The approved agenda included the establishment of an
Organization of African States, charter and permanent secretariat, cooperation in the areas of economics, social affairs
and technology, education, culture and science, collective defence and high command, decolonization, racial discrimination
and apartheid, the effect of regional economic groupings on
African economic development, disarmament, the establishment
of a permanent conciliation commission, and Africa and the
United Nations. The Foreign Ministers had also been seized
with a draft for a Charter of the Organization of African
States, presented by Ethiopia.

In order to deal with these various matters, the Foreign Ministers set up two committees, one on the charter and
cooperation and the other on political questions. After thorough discussion a number of resolutions were adopted along

much the same lines as at previous African conferences. But
there was a big difference. For this time, they were a genuine compromise between the various tendencies in Africa and
not part of the rivalry between opposing groups. In addition,
they went somewhat further than the decisions of previous Pan-
African meetings, if not always as far as the statements of
the Casablanca Group. The only drawback to these resolutions
was that, as usual, they would remain a dead issue unless
some means were provided to supervise or enforce implementation.

In this essential the Ministers had defaulted. They had
not been able to lay the foundation of any general and permanent machinery for the African states. They were not even
certain that the framing of an organization came within their
attributions. Despite all the talk about a Charter, most of
the Foreign Ministers had not been given specific instructions
on the matter and only Ethiopia had submitted a draft. When
the Casablanca and Lagos Charters and Dr. Nkrumah's ideas
for a Union of African States were also thrown in as a basis
for discussion, the Foreign Ministers admittedly had too vast
a range of plans and concepts to pick from. Moreover, the
decisions were highly political and would have to be referred
to the Heads of State. All the Ministers actually did was to
propose that the Ethiopian draft be accepted "as a basis for
discussion" and that the Ethiopian government provide a provisional secretariat to transmit the draft to the member governments so they might present their comments and amendments to another meeting of Foreign Ministers later. The
time and place of this next meeting were not specified.[1]

Finally, when the Foreign Ministers adjourned after a
week's work, the results of the first conference of Addis Ababa were disappointing. No matter how well founded the hesi-
tations, if the Heads of State did nothing more than confirm
the Minister's decisions and return home the long awaited summit would have been a failure.

The Heads of State and Government Take Over.

From this moment on, under a barrage of unsympathe-
tic radio and newspaper coverage, there was talk of failure in
the air. All that was expected were pious resolutions and another meeting, and still another. It seemed that the hopes of
Africa were being betrayed and that Africans were capable of
nothing but prevarication and palaver. By the time the Heads

of State and Government arrived in Addis Ababa to consummate the work of the Foreign Ministers, they had been challenged by Africa and the world to prove their words by action.

As the Kings and Presidents, Princes and politicians arrived the tension mounted. The sight of nearly all Africa's leaders in one city, the capital of the oldest independent African state, was only more striking in the barren reality of Addis Ababa. On May 22, when the Emperor of Ethiopia, Haile Selassie, went to the podium to deliver the key-note address, the tension reached its peak. Like many others, he had worked too hard for that conference to let it succumb. Realizing that the time had come to start along the path of unity and that delay would be fatal, the Negus made a clean break with the preparatory conference of Ministers.

Haile Selassie demanded that

> ... our meeting henceforth proceed from solid accomplishments. Let us not put off, to later consideration and study, the single act, the one decision, which must emerge from this gathering if it is to have real meaning. This Conference cannot close without adopting a single African Charter. We cannot leave here without having created a single African organization ... If we fail in this, we will have shirked our responsibility to Africa and to the peoples we lead. If we succeed, then, and only then, will we have justified our presence here.[2]

In this key point there was almost a consensus. No one expressed agreement more bluntly than President Nasser:

> Let it be an African League.

> Let there be a Charter for all Africa.

> Let there be periodical meetings of the African Heads of State and the peoples' representatives in the continent.

> Let there be anything.

> One thing the United Arab Republic does not want: namely to leave this place with mere enthusiastic words or with formalistic institutional facades.

A strong incentive for seeking results also came from the fact that much of the press and radio and especially the detractors of Africa on the continent and elsewhere wagered that the conference would fizzle. The atmosphere outside the conference hall was described by the President of the Ivory Coast:

>   Certain newspapers will tomorrow bear the head-
>   line: "African Conferences follow one another and
>   are all alike."
>
>   "A lot of speeches, very fine speeches (indeed, in
>   Africa everything is song, symphony and poetry),
>   resolutions, piles of resolutions, but no decisions
>   at all."
>
>   Agreed as we are on the goal, are we going to con-
>   tinue our discussions endlessly, to tear each other
>   to pieces on the choice of means, thus ruining Af-
>   rica's chance of unity, a chance that is greater
>   than that of all the other continents, and to prove
>   our inveterate critics right by the same token?

Houphouët-Boigny's reply to his own questions was an emphatic "NO." This was also the answer of most of the delegates.

"Unite We Must!"

Nevertheless, President Nkrumah hoped to forestall agreement on a halfway house he feared would make "union" impossible. Before the summit conference, he had circulated a plan for the establishment of a "central political organiza-tion," consisting of an upper house (two members per state) and a lower house (on population), with the power to formulate a common foreign policy, common continental planning for eco-nomic and industrial development, a common currency, mone-tary zone and central bank of issue, and a common defence system.

When the Heads of State came together in Addis Ababa, Nkrumah was once again the leader of a "revolutionary" wing on unity. However, he received amazingly little support. The Brazzaville and Monrovia states had never been enticed by his visions. But even his partners in the Union of African States preferred a more limited approach. They made no gesture to-

wards a "union government" or even a super-organization.
The only backing came from rather unexpected quarters.
Speaking for Uganda, the youngest independent state at the con-
ference, Prime Minister Milton Obote made a dramatic appeal:

> I hold the view that however nice one may feel as
> complete master in one's own house the time has
> come, indeed almost overdue, for African Independ-
> ent States to surrender some of their sovereignty
> in favor of an African Central Legislature and Ex-
> ecutive body with specific powers over those sub-
> jects where divided control and action would be un-
> desirable. I refer to such subjects as the estab-
> lishment of an African Common Market, Economic
> Planning on a continent-wide basis, Collective De-
> fence, a Common Foreign Policy, a Common De-
> velopment Bank and a Common Monetary Zone.
> This list is by no means exhaustive ...

Abbé Fulbert Youlou of the Congo (Brazzaville) also put
forward a plan that would be gradual but nevertheless would
tend towards the same solution.

> The independent States may, however, voluntarily
> relinquish part of their national sovereignty in fa-
> vor of a supra-national agency, which could at first
> be consultative and progressively increase its com-
> petence and authority in the sectors for which it
> was responsible.

The initial structure would consist of an African consultative
assembly of two members per state, an African executive acting through periodic conferences of Heads of State, and a permanent secretariat-general. The prerogatives of these bodies
would be defined in a "Charter of the United African States,"
which would ultimately be ratified by the national assemblies
or parliaments of the African states.

The first drawback to these plans was that it would
take considerable time to work out the details, at least six
months and possibly more, and the Heads of State were determined not to return home empty-handed. In addition, the two
plans were vague on the powers and attributions of the bodies,
left to be "blocked in," as well as the relationship between
the legislature and the executive.

The basic flaw, however, was only then becoming visible. Although President Nkrumah originally called for a bicameral legislature, not even mentioning any executive, the situation in Ghana was rapidly giving the lie to any such structure. For the Osagyefo, who had been given life presidency in September 1962, the year 1963 was one of struggle for a single-party state. He very soon reached the point of no return on a path that included the emasculation of the other two branches of government. Similarly, at the time of the summit conference, Abbé Youlou was locked in a struggle for a one party state, and he ruled by decree. The same course was soon being followed throughout Africa, with more or less success, and the generalization of the one party state and strong presidential control made any plea for parliamentary rule in Africa unconvincing. Moreover, no Pan-African institution could any longer reflect the situation without giving all powers to the Heads of State and Government.

This tendency had already led Dr. Nkrumah to alter his earlier stand and, indeed, the only real "Nkrumists" at the summit were Obote and Youlou. The Osagyefo himself hid more than ever behind a veil of words. He still called for political union as a revolutionary act. He promised that "by creating a true political union of all the independent states of Africa, we can tackle hopefully every emergency, every enemy, and every complexity." But his plan was, nonetheless, greatly watered down:

> Unite we must. Without necessarily sacrificing our sovereignties, big or small, we can here and now forge a political union based on Defence, Foreign Affairs and Diplomacy, and a Common Citizenship, an African Currency, an African Monetary Zone and an African Central Bank. We must unite in order to achieve the full liberation of our continent. We need a Common Defence System with an African High Command to ensure the stability and security of Africa.

This proposal raised more questions than it answered. How could any of the goals be achieved without loss of sovereignty? What would be the governing bodies of any such union? There was no hint as to whether they consisted of Heads of State or parliamentarians, or both, and what their inter-relations might be. No proposal was made as to the liberation of the continent. And the clarifications on the economic and defence aspects, the only that were made, left much to be desired.

Despite all this vagueness, the Osagyefo campaigned for a "formal declaration that all the independent African States here and now agree to the establishment of a Union of African States." For, he warned, delay can "set us drifting further and further apart into the net of neo-colonialism, so that our union will become nothing but a fading hope, and the great design of Africa's full redemption will be lost, perhaps forever." To back his demands, Nkrumah appealed over the heads of his fellow leaders to the masses of Africa, whose spokesman he posed as.

> So many blessings must flow from our unity; so many disasters must follow on our continued disunity, that our failure to unite today will not be attributed by posterity only to faulty reasoning and lack of courage, but to our capitulation before the forces of imperialism.

> The hour of history which has brought us to this assembly is a revolutionary hour ...

> The masses of the people of Africa are crying for unity ...

> Our people call for unity ...

> It is the popular determination that must move us on to a Union of Independent African States.

The Future Organization.

President Nkrumah's appeal had no effect on the other heads of state. Their analysis was quite different, taking into account the barriers to unity and rejecting any supranational formula. This attitude was widely shared by the members of the Brazzaville and Monrovia Groups, but it was valid not only for them. The members of the Casablanca Group did not come out for any abandonment of sovereignty either. And even Dr. Nkrumah hedged on his demands. As Prime Minister Balewa said, "there have been only a very few members who spoke on the desirability of having a political union. Almost all the speeches indicate that a more practical approach is much preferred by the majority of the delegations."

By and large, this practical approach meant that the time had come for the mechanism "we still lack, despite the efforts of past years ... a single African organization through which Africa's single voice may be heard, within which Africa's problems may be studied and resolved." Most of the speakers agreed with the Emperor and together they sought to fill in the blanks. Haile Selassie had already suggested "a well-articulated framework, having a permanent headquarters and an adequate Secretariat providing the necessary continuity between meetings of the permanent organs." He also outlined various fields of activity and the Ethiopian draft charter gave further particulars.

Putting aside all reference to parliaments and assemblies, the delegates could agree with President Ahmadou Ahidjo of Cameroon Republic that:

> ... what has to be immediately institutionalized is the periodical meeting of all the African Heads of State. Its task would be to weigh up experiences, decide upon alternatives, harmonize our policies, standardize decisions made on the main affairs of continental importance or which require a common stand to be taken before international opinion.

President Senghor added that the "Conference of Heads of State and Heads of Government" would be the "supreme" institution of the organization and that "its decisions alone would be binding." President Philibert Tsiranana of Malagasy Republic also felt that the Conference should be the "supreme authority" and that "it would take decisions to be implemented immediately." However, he added that "the ideal procedure to respect the principle of sovereignty of the different States would be for decisions to be taken unanimously."

Many of the proposals also included a Council of Ministers, similar to the one that met before the summit, "to draw up drafts for discussion by or recommendation to the Conference," to quote Senghor.

There was no doubt that a permanent headquarters and Secretariat would be needed, but President Senghor interpreted the general consensus when he added that "this would be an administrative body and not a political one; a body which implemented decisions but did not make them."

There was also agreement on the need for subordinate bodies in certain specialized fields. Primary attention was given to economic goals such as common markets, banks of issue, and so on, as well as to a general African economic body to coordinate the whole program. Mention was also made of activities in cultural, scientific and other fields.

Finally, it was admitted that the African Group at the United Nations was ineffective and had to be revitalized and given a specific role and form.

However, the idea of a high command or board for collective security suffered a different fate. For the most part these suggestions were just ignored. But Prime Minister Balewa of Nigeria insisted that any such body was both contrary to Africa's principles and went beyond Africa's means. "Some people have suggested that we should organize ourselves into a Defence Bloc," said Sir Abubakar.

> Well ... all of us have been talking about the bad nature of the armament race. It has been suggested that we should embark on an arms race in Africa. All of us know very well that we are at present incapable of joining in such a race. Our idea is that we should not be talking about an arms race. All we should talk about, sir, is how to stop it, and I would not suggest that we should join in that race at all.

One last element had increasingly been recognized as essential for the future organization. The principle of peaceful settlement had no meaning unless a commission of conciliation or some similar body were established. The Negus of Ethiopia, among others, gave it highest priority.

> Permanent arrangements must be agreed upon to assist in the peaceful settlement of these disagreements which, however few they may be, cannot be left to languish and fester. Procedures must be established for the peaceful settlement of disputes, in order that the threat or use of force may no longer endanger the peace of our continent.

The consensus on both principles and institutions was exceptionally broad. The African leaders felt that there was already enough agreement to forge ahead and they reactivated the plans for unity. Overruling the appeals for a delay of six

months to create a "union," they decided to act immediately
on an acceptable and feasible organization. The assembly thus
convened the "third" conference of Addis Ababa, a special
committee of ministers to draft a charter that could be adopted by the Heads of State before they left.

The Quest for Unity.

The reason for this low level of consensus at the
conference was that certain facts of life had become painfully
clear. The first Pan-African meetings on the continent had
assumed a unity of outlook and action. Yet, when put to the
test in the Algerian and Congolese affairs, that unity was
grievously lacking. The years of rivalry and conflict had
shaken the earlier faith and given rise to a "realistic" school
of unity. Indeed, the reversal was even more complete. By
1963, rather than being an hypothesis, unity had to be proven
and defined, promoted and channelled for the good of Africa.

The African leaders had always known what bound them
together. And, at the summit conference, they made a conscious effort at seeking these common roots. They were most
forcefully summed up by Guinea's President Sékou Touré:

> In the course of their history, the African coun-
> tries have all experienced foreign domination, which
> hampered the normal development of their civiliza-
> tion, of their personality and of their culture and
> also fostered the intensive exploitation of their
> wealth and of their peoples for the benefit of for-
> eign interests ...

> Each of our peoples resisted colonial penetration
> and later colonial exploitation and oppression.
> Each of our peoples fought and accepted all the
> essential sacrifices for regaining its freedom.

> Today, most of the countries have been liberated
> and have built up states whose concerns are still
> the same. They have to eradicate from their pres-
> ent conditions the consequences of foreign domina-
> tion, the spirit of irresponsibility, the causes of
> social distress, and to return to Africa, and for
> Africa, all the structures and resources inherited
> from the colonial system ...

> Is not the essential basis of the African unity which
> is to be constructed this growing awareness by our
> peoples of the identity of the destinies that they ex-
> perienced in the past, that they have in the present
> and that they will necessarily have in the future?

What was new was that the African leaders also conceded openly that there were still tremendous differences.
President Hamani Diori of Niger was just one of many to
stress the divisions:

> A realistic view of the African conjuncture enables
> us to perceive this first crying fact, the great di-
> versity of situations within our continent. People
> of black, white or brown races, whose ways of
> life, languages, beliefs and ethics are very differ-
> ent, alternately separated, opposed, confronted
> sometimes even regrouped by the accidents of his-
> tory, particularly by the "colonial fact," these
> peoples are today situated at super-imposed levels
> of economic and cultural development; their mem-
> bership of large world groups, such as the mone-
> tary zones, seems to condemn them to divergent
> fates.

The most dangerous item had already been placed in this inventory by the Emperor of Ethiopia, "the pitfalls of tribalism."

These lines of cleavage became most disruptive when
they were used by outsiders to impose their will on Africa.
Thus, President Kasavubu described what had happened in the
Congo as "due essentially to a coalition of foreign interests
which could not bring themselves to give up certain regions of
our country, which geologists often have called the 'treasure
chest' of Africa." And Mwami (king) Mwambutsa IV, of
Burundi, warned against those that

> ... seek to perpetuate this state of subordination
> of Africa, particularly by sabotaging efforts to
> unite Africa, according to the imperialist principle
> "Divide et Impera." Our enemies are happy to
> see Africa balkanized. It is certain that a divided
> Africa will always be a dominated Africa.

It was the exploitation of these divisions by outside
powers that led to the urgent need for unity on the continent.
In Addis Ababa, every effort was made to overcome differ-

ences or at least keep them from troubling the reconciliation.
Some success was achieved with what was potentially the most
serious partition--the one between Black Africa and the Arab
North. Although there had been an embarrassing moment during the conference of Foreign Ministers, when Sierra Leone
asked the UAR delegate to show that his African policy was
not subordinate to Arab interests, no similar occurrence arose
among the Heads of State.

Indeed, the hands of friendship were stretched out by
both sides. President Maurice Yaméogo of Upper Volta confirmed that "the bridge between our two worlds has been
thrown by three of our Black African brothers: President
Kwame Nkrumah, Sékou Touré and Modibo Keita." The second bridge was independent Algeria, whose struggle--albeit in
different ways--had been supported by all the states on the
continent.

For their part, the Arab statesmen stressed the common African heritage and goals, and passed over differences
in silence. In a caucus before the conference, they had
agreed not to seek commitment on the Israeli issue, and President Nasser could say with pride:

> We have come here without selfishness: even the
> problem which we consider to be one of our most
> serious problems, namely that of Israel ... we
> shall not submit ... for discussion at this meeting
> in the conviction that the progress of free African
> endeavour will, through trial, reveal the truth, day
> after day and lay it unmasked before African con-
> science.

Subversion and Border Disputes.

Despite any difficulties, a reconciliation was definitely
possible. However, although the African leaders wished to
forgive, they could not forget. They could not forget the nas-
tiness of the rivalry and friction. More than once blood had
been shed. And this united them even more strongly in their
opposition to the methods used against fellow Africans during
the preceding years. It was the blood of Patrice Lumumba
and Sylvanus Olympio, as well as of many unknown victims,
that animated this aspect of the debates.

President Houphouët-Boigny called for "absolute tolerance, scrupulously and religiously observed by all in their dealings with one another." Only this, he insisted,

> ... will bring about the disappearance of the grave threat which hangs over the future of our young states: the subversive intrigues originating in third African States, which are the accomplices of foreign states hostile to our unity, and therefore to our real independence and happiness. [The summit conference was] the place for us to condemn, energetically and in unison, political assassination as a means of government or of assuming power. [This included] assassination or murder organized from abroad, or with the tacit complicity of foreign countries, in order to overturn a government or regime that does not enjoy the favor of the African States organizing or encouraging such actions.

No one gainsaid him. But there was another side to the question. President Modibo Keita of Mali insisted that the best way of preventing outside interference was to remove its causes through national reconciliation.

> It would be desirable for those African states, of which certain citizens have been obliged to take refuge abroad, to extend to them the hand of friendship and facilitate their return to the hearth and home in their common native land.

One last point had to be settled for tranquillity among the states to be assured. It was necessary to stabilize international frontiers--preferably where they were when the states became independent. Unless these "colonial" boundaries were recognized, Africa would fall prey to countless border conflicts. Mali had already settled its frontier disputes with Mauritania; and its President Keita issued the admonishment:

> ... if all of us here present are truly animated by the ardent wish to achieve African unity, we must take Africa as it is, and we must renounce any territorial claims, if we do not wish to introduce what we might call black imperialism in Africa. ... African unity demands of each one of us complete respect for the legacy that we have received from the colonial system, that is to say: maintenance of the present frontiers of our respective

states.

And President Tsiranana of Malagasy, whose country was quite immune to border disputes, made a comment that was echoed during the conference:

> It is no longer possible, nor desirable, to modify the boundaries of Nations, on the pretext of racial, religious or linguistic criteria ... Indeed, should we take race, religion or language as criteria for setting our boundaries, a few States in Africa would be blotted out from the map. Leaving demagogy aside, it is not conceivable that one of our individual States would readily consent to be among the victims for the sake of unity.

President Nkrumah's solution to the problem was the reverse. Rather than accept colonial frontiers, the artificial barriers should be swept away so that Africa could unite. With unity all boundaries would be superfluous. "The people of Africa," he proclaimed, "call for the breaking down of the boundaries that keep them apart."

In certain quarters, however, the debate was less academic. The King of Morocco stayed away from the conference because his country would not recognize the independent existence of Mauritania. And, the only real break in the serenity of the debates arose over the question of frontiers. The President of Somalia, Aden Abdulla Osman Saar, insisted that silence would not eliminate the problem. Not quite unexpectedly he spoke of self-determination for the Somali nation and pleaded the cause of the Somalis living in French Somaliland, Ethiopia and Kenya's Northern Frontier District. He charged that "Ethiopia has taken possession of a large portion of Somali territory without the consent and against the wishes of the inhabitants." He stressed that although "the Somali Government has no ambitions or claims for territorial aggrandizements ... the people of the Republic cannot be expected to remain indifferent to the appeal of its brethren."

The rebuttal came from the Ethiopian Prime Minister Ato Habte-Wold. Intimating that this was only the start, he warned that

> ... it is in the interest of all Africans now to respect the frontiers drawn on the maps, whether

they are good or bad, by the former colonizers,
and that is in the interest of Somalia, too, because
if we are going to move in this direction, then we,
too, the Ethiopians will have claims to make: on
the same basis as Somalia, and for more on historical and geographical reasons.

With this, the debate was closed--at the conference.
For the Heads of State were unable to reach a consensus on
all the matters that threatened the peace and security of the
continent. No one denied the need to ban intervention, subversion or assassination. But, despite the majority in favor
of maintaining colonial frontiers, no hard and fast rule could
be laid down.

Liberation of the African Continent.

A Pan-African organization was meant only to be a tool.
And much of the conference was defining the objectives for
which that tool would be used. The primary goal on any African program was still independence. The Emperor proclaimed this in his key-note address.

Our liberty is meaningless unless all Africans are
free. Our brothers in the Rhodesias, in Mozambique, in Angola, in South Africa cry out in an-
guish for our support and assistance. ... our political and economic liberty will be devoid of meaning for so long as the degrading spectacle of South
Africa's apartheid continues to haunt our waking
hours and to trouble our sleep.

But agreement on the principle was not enough. This
had always been at the top of Africa's list of priorities. What
was needed was greater agreement on the means to the end if
the new tool was to have any value. On that particular, the
continent had for years been divided between the advocates of
violent decolonization and the supporters of pacific change.
Still, most of the Heads of State tended to agree with President Nasser that justice had to be given precedence over peace.
"There can be no peace without justice; accepting the fait ac-
compli without justice means the acceptance of submission ...
and this is as remote from peace as can be."

Since all its leaders denounced colonialism and racial
discrimination as injustices, Africa was already sliding to-

wards the point where peace might have to be sacrificed to obtain justice. Finally, at Addis Ababa, this point was reached
by the entirety of states. The only way to evict colonial or
settler powers that refused to be convinced by arguments or
frightened by diplomatic pressure and civil disobedience, or
even uprisings, was to use force.

Doubtlessly speaking on behalf of the whole Brazzaville
Group, President Houphouẽt-Boigny committed his country,
Ivory Coast, to a new policy of decolonization.

> ... we solemnly declare that our country, over-
> coming the scruples of its devotion to negotiations,
> have requested us to seek, in concert with your-
> selves, the most practical means of putting an end
> to the criminal obstinacy of Portugal, to foreign
> occupation in Africa, and to the apartheid that is
> held in honour in South Africa--that apartheid which
> is the great shame of our continent.

This decision, the result of a slow evolution, meant
that Africa could now forge ahead with its first really active
and integral campaign of decolonization. Now the arsenal was
full. It included the more traditional weapons: diplomatic
pressure by the states individually or as a group in the United
Nations, severance of diplomatic relations, introduction of
economic sanctions and refusal to let Portuguese and South African aircraft overfly or land in the African countries. And
it no longer excluded force.

The most urgent task of the independent states was to
support and aid the nationalist movements, to equip and finance them. To this purpose, it was again suggested that a
liberation fund be established and Sékou Touré decided to "formally propose that each independent African State contributes
one percent of its national budget to the fund at the beginning
of every financial year."

However, the suggestions for active solidarity with the
struggling peoples often went much further. For example,
President Youlou called for military sanctions, the organization of volunteer camps and the interception of ships trans-
porting arms. And President Obote offered Uganda as "a
training ground for the land forces that are necessary for the
liberation forces which are needed in the struggle against colonialism." President Ben Bella announced that since Angola
Day "ten thousand Algerian volunteers have been waiting for a

chance to go to the assistance of their brothers in arms."

Ben Bella, appearing after a seven years' war, put forward the most aggressive program of assistance. According to his plan, the brunt of the struggle would fall to the liberation movements, but they would be supported by the peripheral countries, and these in turn by the rest of Africa. On the borders between the dependent territories and the independent states would arise crisis points, where "African unity must take the form of effective solidarity with those who are still fighting for their liberty." If a colonial or settler power attacked a neighboring African state at these points, it had to "find the whole of Africa united opposing it." Then, in a stunning appeal that left its mark on the conference, he concluded:

> Thus, African brothers agreed to die a little so that Algeria might become an independent State.
>
> So let us all agree to die a little, or even completely, so that the peoples still under colonial domination may be freed and African unity may not be a vain word.

At the end of the debate, President Nyerere was able to sum up and second many of the proposals for the whole conference, which had been transformed by the cause and occasion into a truly militant body. First, he endorsed the proposal of brother Sékou Touré, "that one percent of our national budget should be set aside for the purpose of liberating non-free Africa." And then he assured the gallant brother from Algeria that "we are prepared to die a little for the final removal of the humiliation of colonialism from the face of Africa."

But none of the Heads of State went as far as the freedom fighters themselves. Their representatives had attended the conference as observers and some twenty-one national liberation movements submitted a joint memorandum. Addressing themselves to "our brothers and fellow freedom-fighters, the Heads of African Independent States," the members of these movements proclaimed:

> All Africa must be liberated now! Empty words and pious resolutions will not suffice. This Summit Conference of African Independent States should issue an ultimatum to all colonial and racist powers

in Africa to start immediately the transference of
power to the African peoples ... or else face the
consequences. It should be absolutely clear that
where the ultimatum is not heeded the African Independent States shall intervene directly.

Economic Development.

During the deliberations in Addis Ababa, aside from the
key issues of unity and decolonization, no problem received
greater attention than that of economic development. This was
the first opportunity the African leaders had had to work out a
strategy for what President Ahidjo of Cameroon called "another great battle" of the second half of the twentieth century,
"the economic liberation of the developing countries."

The anomaly of this struggle, however, was that there
was little agreement as to who was the actual enemy. For
some, the task was one of uniting efforts in each country and
then among the countries so as to overcome the mental barriers to economic development and then launching the necessary projects--educational, infrastructural, agricultural and
industrial--to exploit the resources of the continent. For
others, this was only secondary, the real enemy was a group
of persons or states guilty of neo-colonialism, deliberately
keeping Africa underdeveloped and exploiting its peoples.
There were thus considerable differences in the approach.

The real pioneers in economic cooperation were the
members of the UAM; their leaders provided the summit conference with a number of pointers for a continental plan. They
hoped that the same gradual and functional methods they used
among themselves could be spread to the other states.

Since all the African countries were essentially primary producers, there was considerable concern with the
worsening terms of trade of the commodities from which they
lived. Therefore, President Youlou stressed the need for "international machinery capable of maintaining prices and avoiding overproduction," while suggesting inter-African marketing
boards for products such as coffee, cocoa, bananas, citrus
fruit, pineapples, palm oil and others. Secondly, in order to
diversify their predominantly agricultural economies, the African states would have to industrialize. And he emphasized
that "African development depends on industrialization. Only
by producing itself the essential manufactured goods it needs,

can Africa ensure its development and reach a higher standard
of living. "

Another major goal was an African common market.
But most of the leaders felt that continental integration was
something for the future and had to be prepared by suitable
measures. One might, according to President Youlou, start
with preferential treatment for industrial products manufactured
in Africa. Geographically also, it would be necessary to begin with smaller regional groupings. Although these regional
units were "initially indispensable, " President Tsiranana
stressed that "they will be a means to an end and not an end
in themselves. "

The main drawback to any project, however, was that
none of the African states were in a position to finance their
own development. Assistance had to be sought by all of them.
Still, there was a considerable range of opinion between the
view of, say, Habib Ben Ali Bourguiba and that of President
Nasser. The former, President of Tunisia, stressed that "cooperation with the industrialized countries, rich in capital,
cadres and technical experience, is not only desirable but inevitable. " Refusal of this cooperation "through fear of a re-
vival of colonialism" was a position which could be justified
from the sentimental point of view or that of pure logic, "but
it was unrealistic and only means isolating oneself and condemning oneself to stagnation. " The policy of the UAR was
not to reject foreign aid either, although this was regarded as
"an obligation upon those who preceded in progress, towards
the under-developed peoples ... a tax due to others by the big
powers with a colonial past, in compensation for the looting
to which numerous peoples in Africa and Asia have and are
still being exposed. "

Once again, President Nkrumah took an advanced post.
His whole scheme was focused on the struggle against "crushing and humiliating neo-colonialist controls and interference. "
He suggested that "the first step towards our cohesive economy would be a unified monetary zone, with, initially, an
agreed common parity for our currencies. " Then, when this
worked, "there would seem to be no reason for not instituting
one currency and a single bank of issue. " This would be the
foundation for continental planning and industrialization and,
finally, an African common market. (The only concrete offer
that Ghana made, however, was to "change to a decimal system. ") Unlike the moderates who built on what already existed, trying to strengthen the economic and social links until

they could support an independent economy, the Osagyefo started with an act of negation that would impose unity. By cutting all ties with external monetary areas and trade blocs,
Africa would have no choice but to unite. Then the task of
reinforcing the economic and social foundations could begin.
For him, "African Unity is, above all, a political kingdom
which can only be gained by political means. The social and
economic development of Africa will come only within the political kingdom, not the other way around."

African Non-Alignment and the United Nations.

        Another aim all the Heads of State could support, in
principle at least, was non-alignment. While some only paid
lip-service, others, like President Nkrumah, had made non-
alignment an "article of faith." At minimum, these leaders
rejected the acceptance of military bases and cooperation,
political subordination, and overly close economic ties. Africa was urged to break the old links with the colonial masters
and avoid entering into new ones that could bind the states on
the continent too tightly to external powers.

        The most compromising links were the military ones.
Prime Minister Ibrahim Abboud of the Sudan (formerly com-
mander-in-chief of its army) mentioned "foreign military pacts,
foreign military bases" and also made an "outright condemnation of armament." And President Nasser criticized:

            ... making of the lands of the peoples of the con-
            tinent a field for nuclear tests without the consent
            of those peoples, contrary to their aspirations for
            peace and in direct threat to them even in the air
            they breathe on their native soil.

        President Nkrumah had a more ambitious plan for non-
alignment. He felt that liberation from cold war pressure and
involvement could be achieved "only by counter-balancing a
common defence force with a common defence policy based
upon our common desire for an Africa untrammeled by foreign
dictation or military and nuclear presence." His solution: an
"all-embracing African High Command." Although this was
presented as "an essential and indispensable instrument for ensuring stability and security in Africa," he did not give any
details.

This debate was probably where the "spirit of Addis Ababa" was most pervasive. For the attacks against alignments were carefully kept on the level of generalities. There was no criticism of EEC association. There was no condemnation of the countries harboring foreign bases. Nothing was even said specifically about French tests in the Sahara. No names were mentioned. And there was no need to reply or apologize.

However, there was one point where complaints of non-alignment really struck home and where all shades of opinion could agree. Every leader had in mind the disarray in which the Congo crisis found Africa and the damage done their cause by the introduction of the cold war into an African conflict. For this reason, after admitting that the nations of Africa also "from time to time dispute among themselves," the Emperor of Ethiopia pleaded that "these quarrels must be confined to this continent and quarantined from the contamination of non-African interference."

For some time already, Africa had been instinctively groping towards its own brand of non-alignment. Oddly enough, its inspiration was old and alien. Like others, Abbé Fulbert Youlou felt

> ... it is desirable to establish a Monroe Doctrine for Africa, that is to say to secure Africa against any direct interference by a non-African power, in the same way that North and South America have acted with regard to their own continent.

And Sékou Touré spoke of "Africa for the Africans."

For such a policy to work, African nations had to avoid allowing their disputes to fester and thus open the door to foreign involvement. Above all, they had to guard against forming rival blocs to impose contrary solutions. Two leaders expressed serious concern about intervention from without. Houphouët-Boigny cautioned that Africa had "to eliminate all internal elements of discord, so as to be able to stand aside from the competition in which the two rival ideological blocs are engaged, and to ensure that they do not succeed in transposing their rivalry to this continent." Similarly, Modibo Keita declared:

> ... it is no longer possible to tolerate the opposition cleverly fostered between groups of states.

We should be threatened by the cleavage of our
continent into antagonistic blocs and should be preparing the most fertile ground for the dangerous
transplantation of the cold war to the soil of our
common homeland.

In one respect, however, African non-alignment policies were very different from the Monroe Doctrine. For the
Africans were not willing to balance non-intervention in their
own affairs with isolation from world affairs. Rather, according to President Abboud, "we believe that, with Unity, the
African voice will carry more weight; that our role will be
more constructive; and our contribution more positive at this
critical juncture in the affairs of Mankind."

Since the Congolese crisis, the United Nations had also
become a target of the policy of non-alignment in some states.
For this reason there was very little echo to the Emperor's
tribute to the world body. After praising the United Nations
and collective security, he suggested a sort of partnership.

The African Charter of which We have spoken is
wholly consistent with that of the United Nations.
The African organization which We envisage is not
intended in any way to replace in our national or
international life the position which the United Nations has so diligently earned and so rightfully oc-
cupies. Rather, the measures which We propose
would complement and round out programmes undertaken by the United Nations and its specialized
agencies and, hopefully, render both their activities and ours doubly meaningful and effective.

Only the President of the Congo had a good word to say
for the United Nations. But it was overshadowed by the statements of leaders on the opposite side of the fence. President
Nasser spoke of

... those attempts at forging new colonialist tools
which infiltrate under the banner of the United Nations and which brought to the Congo, during its
violent crisis, that appalling tragedy whose victim
was that African revolutionary martyr Patrice Lumumba.

Even those who did not deny the value of the world body
proposed a rather one-sided relationship: Africa would have

to work through the United Nations to attain its own aims.
Thus, Sékou Touré concluded that "it only remains for Africa
to coordinate its action at the United Nations to stimulate its
effectiveness." And Prime Minister Balewa felt "it is absolutely essential that the African continent must have more appropriate representation in the Security Council and all the
bodies of the United Nations, because we have more to gain
thereby." But no mention was made of the role the United
Nations could play in Africa.[3]

The Ministers and the Ethiopian Draft Charter.

While the Heads of State were making speeches, the
Special Committee of Foreign Ministers busily prepared a charter. Although not drawn up by the Heads of State themselves,
it was fully in keeping with their ideas and proposals. For it
was clear to the Ministers that the surest sign of success was
a rapid and unreserved approval of the text.

The Ministers deliberated intensively on 23-24 May and
accomplished their task in record time. True, they were already familiar with the problem of organization from earlier
meetings. But much credit also went to the Ethiopian draft,
a very complete working document which was a fair synthesis
of the previous African charters and organizations. This made
the discussions much more concrete and specific. Gradually
the text was modified and improved upon by a sub-committee
and then by the special committee itself.

The Ethiopian draft consisted of a preamble, a list of
purposes and principles, and an organization. The organization had as its supreme body an Assembly of Heads of State
and Government, seconded by a Council of Ministers. It was
equipped with a permanent Secretariat and a Court of Mediation, Conciliation and Arbitration. Many of its more specialized activities were entrusted to relatively autonomous agencies. The organization's purpose was to coordinate and unify
general policies and cooperation in all fields--but it was not
supranational.

During the discussions, the Foreign Ministers gave the
charter further depth. New items were added to the preamble, more amply reflecting the motives for the momentous
decision of Addis Ababa. The paragraphs were also reshuf-
fled to indicate the relative order of priority. At the top was
the dedication to the "inalienable right of all people to control

their own destiny." This was followed by the ideals and objectives of freedom, equality, justice and dignity for the African peoples. Only then was there any mention of unity or
economic development. These were the goals around which
the Heads of State could rally their peoples and towards the
accomplishment of which they could lead them. However,
there was no reference to the internal situation in the African
countries and the only lines that could have been invoked by
the peoples against their leaders, which briefly slipped into
the sub-committee draft, were striken: "Believing that the
aim of government is the well-being of the governed."

The objectives were broadened by including that of international cooperation, placing the African organization in the
world context. But more significant additions were made in
the principles. The states accepted the duty of peaceful settlement and pledged to refrain from subversion and assassination. Moreover, the primary purpose of decolonization was
made a principle as well, and it was joined by that of non-
alignment. In order to leave no doubt about the organization's
actual role, the veil of words was withdrawn and rather than
being instituted to "unify" policy it was left what in fact it
was, a body to coordinate and "harmonize" policies.

Certain important changes were also made in the institutional machinery proposed in the original Ethiopian document.
In every case this enhanced the position of the Assembly of
Heads of State and Government and the Council of Ministers,
subordinate but working closely with it. The roles and autonomy of the lesser bodies were increasingly restricted and the
lines of command made stricter.

Although the Court of Mediation, Conciliation and Arbitration was to be relatively autonomous, its statute would be
an integral part of the Charter rather than a special treaty.
And the "Court" was eventually made a mere "Commission."
The Secretary-General was first deprived of his only outlet for
direct influence when the sub-committee decided not to specifically authorize him to "participate in all deliberation of the
Institutions of the Organization." Then he was made "administrative" and was even surrounded by several assistants, also
elected by the Assembly.

The specialized committees ceased being principal institutions. Their "technical autonomy" was withdrawn and they
were made directly responsible to the Assembly and the Council. They too were made commissions, consisting of the re-

sponsible ministers, and even the brief description of their
duties was removed. The defence board underwent a greater
mutation when the "board" of chiefs of staff of the armed
forces became a mere "council" and then a Commission of
Defence Ministers. Its competence was also severely reduced
from the original Ethiopian proposal that it be able to recommend "measures of preparation it believes necessary for the
collective self-defence of the African Continent against aggression, as well as the measures of military collaboration it
deems advisable for the collective security of the continent. "

Since the pivot of the whole organization was the team
Assembly/Council, it was necessary for them to be able to
function. This was impeded by the prohibitive rules for majority and quorum. The four-fifths majority for Assembly
resolutions was reduced to two-thirds, and the Council could
decide with a simple majority. The quorum was lowered as
well and became two-thirds of the membership for both. Extraordinary sessions of either body could be convened by two-
thirds of the members.

The final changes were basically an "Africanization" of
the charter. As a potential regional agency within the United
Nations system, it was only natural that the new organization
should profess its conformity with the Charter of the UN.
This had been done, for courtesy sake at least, by all other
regional agencies and even the bodies for collective security.
Nevertheless, the only references to that world organization
were relegated to the preamble and purposes. The Heads of
State were "persuaded that the Charter of the United Nations,
to the principles of which we reaffirm our adherence, provides
a beneficial basis for peaceful and positive co-operation among
states. " And the members were to promote international cooperation, "having due regard to the Charter of the United Nations and the Universal Declaration of Human Rights. "

What was significant, however, was that the only article that completely disappeared from the Ethiopian draft was
the one on the relationship with the United Nations:

> The Member States agree that nothing herein shall
> be understood or interpreted as impairing the com-
> mitments or other rights and obligations of the
> Member States of the Organization of African States
> under the Charter of the United Nations Organiza-
> tion.

Likewise, the article providing that the interpretation of the
African charter should be submitted to the International Court
of Justice was altered. Both interpretation and amendment
were entrusted to the Assembly.

Thus, by 25 May 1963, the Heads of State and Government were able to approve and formally sign the "Charter of
the Organization of African and Malagasy States." Although
there were almost no amendments, one last touch was given.
The body that was henceforth to preside over the destiny of
the African continent was named the "Organization of African
Unity." This proposal was made by President Nkrumah and
welcomed by the other delegates. It marked the Osagyefo's
acceptance of a more modest form of unity. The compromise
may not have satisfied everyone, but it was a beginning. And
he prophesized that "the decisions we have taken here have
made African Unity a reality and we can see clearly a Union
Government of Africa on the horizon."

Agreement and Compromise.

The conclusion that could be drawn from the summit
conference was clear--African solidarity and unity were strong.
They were strong enough, at any rate, to make the Conference
of Addis Ababa a brilliant success. But, how could it have
been otherwise? For all the countries had roughly the same
background of colonialism and under-development. They had
the same problems and goals. This solidarity had been forged
in the common struggle for liberation and progress. Certainly the agreement on principles could easily outweigh any differences on details.

Still, it was important not to lose sight of the limits to
this unity. In Addis Ababa, every effort was made at sealing
the reconciliation. This was often done at the cost of ignoring
or side-stepping causes of disunity. For this reason, even
before the conference met, the Foreign Ministers decided that
the Heads of State should not discuss boundary disputes, the
Togo affair, French testing in the Sahara, or EEC association.
And the Arab leaders shelved the question of Israel. During
the debates, everything was left sufficiently vague and imper-
sonal so that no one could take offence. The speakers carefully avoided making any specific charges. The only rift in
the atmosphere of good will came with the flare-up over the
Somali claims--and even this was brief.

The first compromise to secure broad agreement was to endorse all the various aims without fixing absolute priorities. Nevertheless, there were very noticeable differences in stress at the conference. Some of the leaders gave precedence to decolonization and seemed to assume that little would be done about other matters until the entire continent had been liberated. Others spoke primarily of the needs and concerns of the already independent countries and assumed that the organization would permit them to tackle these problems. Similarly, some of the leaders were interested in political goals and others in economic tasks, some yearned for an African projection in the world and others were satisfied to improve things at home.

The basic division was on priority to independence or development. And one way of distinguishing between the states was to use the old criteria of guns versus butter. The two extremes were President Ben Bella and Mwambutsa IV, king of Burundi. The Algerian leader devoted his whole speech to the war of liberation and dismissed economic concerns with contempt.

> I very much fear that everything we are proposing to do in this domain may be reduced to straightforward agreements enabling us to feed our peoples better. We have no right to think of filling our bellies when our brothers are still dying in Angola, Mozambique and South Africa.

The Mwami, however, felt that "before long, the purely colonial factor will no longer be a major concern for the Africans. Without being a prophet, one can say that within a short time the colonial system will collapse like a pack of cards."

The second compromise was to accept both a hard and soft line on each goal. Sometimes the policies envisaged were even incompatible. Force to obtain independence had finally been accepted by all the African states, but the earlier peaceful means had not been rejected. This meant that in each specific case it would be necessary to choose between violence and pressure. Although neo-colonialism had been denounced, the need for outside technical and financial assistance was obvious to all. The problem was still to decide which links were beneficial and which were neo-colonialistic snares. And non-alignment did not exclude cooperation with the rest of the world.

In order to have as complete agreement as possible,
the speakers had concentrated on Africa's common enemies.
All the states could be rallied by pointing to the dangers coming from the colonial and settler powers or the cold war. On
this basis, a united front was readily achieved and much of
the program consisted of goals vis-à-vis the outside world:
decolonization, non-alignment, neo-colonialism and economic
independence. Much less light was shed on the sources of internal disturbances. Several general principles for positive
relations had been laid down but no effort was made at solving
the existing problems or preventing new ones. The key principle of colonial frontiers that would have helped Africa settle
its border disputes was not confirmed. And the machinery for
peaceful settlement was left to later deliberations.

The final compromise was on organization. None of
the states were willing to sacrifice the least shred of their
sovereignty and only a relatively simple international institution could be established. This body was to be a forum and
a tool. However, since it could make few demands on its
membership, the tool could not be wielded too energetically.
Nevertheless, all the activities entrusted in the new organization required very powerful action, whether it was decolonization, peaceful settlement or economic development. It was
uncertain how well the young organization would hold up under
these demands and whether it could survive crises.

As long as things ran smoothly in Africa, the four compromises were safe. However, when a serious difference
arose, African unity would be put to the test. Where would
the priorities go, to decolonization or development, to guns or
butter? Would violence win out over negotiations and isolation
over cooperation? Would fear of outside interference overcome internal dissension? And, would the new organization
adapt or crack under the strain? Only time would tell.

Notes

1. Proceedings of the Summit Conference of Independent Afri-
    can States, Vol. 1, Sec. 1, Addis Ababa, May 1963.

2. Ibid., Sec. 2, for quotations from the Conference.

3. For earlier, more positive statements, see "Africa Speaks
    to the United Nations," International Organization,
    Spring 1962, p. 303-330.

Chapter II

The Organization of African Unity

Despite the urging of certain leaders, the new organization founded in Addis Ababa was not a drastic departure from the earlier attempts at channelling the continent's efforts. The appeals of the few partisans of sweeping change in state structure and the creation of a supra-national organization or "union government" went unheeded. This, indeed, was the main reason for the success of the summit conference. For the new organization was very down to earth and practicable and even then the more modest commitments of the Charter had to be accepted as an act of faith by some.

The stumbling block to a new order in Africa was still sovereignty and no solution that ignored it was feasible. Nevertheless, within the bounds laid by state sovereignty, the conference was able to turn out an amazingly good second-best. The organization created in Addis Ababa was highly original. The Africans did not copy the standard structure--a broad assembly of government delegates and a narrower governing body--largely adopted in the United Nations family and elsewhere. They also did not add an unreal and powerless "people's" assembly. Rather, they maintained and improved upon the structure that was developing naturally on the continent.

Ever since the first Conference of Independent African States in Accra, back in 1958, the Heads of State had played the primary role in African affairs. In order to prepare and follow up their work, the practice had also emerged of preceding their meetings with one of Foreign Ministers and even of holding further such meetings in the interval between summit conferences. With the decadence of the AAPO, which never really represented the peoples, and the spread of presidential regimes, the idea of having a popular assembly share the power with the Heads of State was discarded. As the independent states became aware of their needs and concerns in the many facets of national life, they repeatedly sought new bodies to plan and coordinate their efforts in each one of them

155

and the scope of any African organization was vastly expanded.
This trend had been followed by all the rival groupings. In
addition, the Casablanca Group clearly showed the importance
of a strong and permanent secretariat, while the Monrovia
Group stressed the need for a commission to settle disputes
among the states.

Thus a new "African" structure of international organization was fashioned and tested over the years and took its
most advanced form in the OAU. The supreme organ was and
could only be a summit conference, finally institutionalized as
an annual Assembly of Heads of State and Government. The
work of the Heads of State would be prepared by a Council of
Ministers, which also had certain responsibilities in the application of decisions. A number of specialized commissions
were created to promote cooperation in fields as varied as defence, health and communications. To handle the administrative work and help prepare the activities of the various bodies,
a permanent and independent Secretariat was obviously necessary. And a Commission of Mediation, Conciliation and Arbitration could offer its services for the peaceful settlement of
any conflicts that arose on the continent.

The Charter of Addis Ababa was drafted and adopted in
record time. So rapidly that, to some, it seemed a miracle.
In the haste, however, although the principles and purposes
were perfectly clear, the competences and tasks of the institutions established to fulfill them were only partly sketched in
or left blank. It was therefore not surprising that some uncertainty existed as to the powers and functions of the various
organs. But this was a result not only of haste. The original Ethiopian draft was much more detailed and explicit. The
revisions of the Foreign Ministers either removed what terms
of reference there were or deliberately left them vague. It
also reduced the standing of most bodies in the Organization.
The reason for this was simple: with strict lines of control
downwards, any gaps could be used by the governing bodies.
In addition, the Assembly had the right to interpret and amend
the Charter. Thus the Heads of State and the member states
could mold the Organization to suit themselves.

As a guide to or description of the functioning of the
OAU, the Charter was soon insufficient. Within the first years
after Addis Ababa, the structure was complete and the various
bodies had been established. It was necessary to adopt additional instruments and documents to define or regulate the activities of these institutions. Then there was some experimen-

tation and running in to adapt them to their tasks and work out the mutual relations. Finally, several new bodies had to be set up to handle specific problems.

As it met and overcame or succumbed to major challenges, the OAU adapted, evolved. Soon the Charter was an unrecognizable or misleading image of the Organization. Real insight could be gained only from a study of both the theory and the practice of its function.

One of the most important facts of African life was the attachment to sovereignty in the newly independent states. Another was a countervailing desire of the leaders and peoples to accomplish the aims enshrined in the Charter despite this attachment to national sovereignty. Within this field of repulsion and attraction the competences of the Organization were restricted or expanded. To identify the compromises between the contradictory trends, it is now necessary to consult the practices consecrated by repetition and time.

A. Assembly and Council

The Organization of African Unity was established at
the behest of the African Heads of State and Government gathered in Addis Ababa and, to some extent, it was cut to their
measure. Since the OAU had been created to attain certain
vital goals, the leaders left no doubt that there should be
strict lines of command from the top down and their control
over all activities was made complete. The African leaders
as a corporate body intended to govern the Organization as
they governed their states and this was reflected by the preamble of the Charter which began: "We, the Heads of African
States and Governments ... "

Nevertheless, the Heads of State were already so bur-
dened with problems and tasks in their home countries that
they could not also keep a permanent watch over the details of
operation of the OAU. In order to maintain their control and
work the Organization into the broader scheme of African activity, the task of supervision had to be shared with a Council
of Ministers. This Council also had extensive command and
was directly responsible to the Heads of State for the functioning of the OAU. It was this team that was to preside over
the work of the fledgling organization and make the OAU a
real tool for Africa.

Assembly of Heads of State and Government: Theory ...

The Assembly consisted of the Heads of State and Government themselves or of their duly accredited representatives.
It met at least once a year and, at the request of any member and on the approval of two-thirds of the member states,
it could also meet in extraordinary session. Its resolutions
were adopted by a two-thirds majority of the members of the
Organization, although procedural questions required only a
simple majority. A quorum was two-thirds of the total membership. The Assembly determined its own rules of procedure.

The Assembly was made the "supreme" organ of the OAU and this was an accurate reflection of the role of the Heads of State on the African continent. The independent states were born of a struggle for liberation. Then, each newly sovereign state (and older ones as well) were faced with a multitude of smaller and partial struggles for viability in every conceivable domain within the nation. The need to militate against factionalism and the requirements of economic development caused the leaders and party that had gained independence further to strengthen their hold over the state. Gradually this trend became pronounced and Africa became a continent of one-party states and strong rulers. It was in recognition of their position that the heads of the various countries were given--or rather, claimed for themselves--the control of the new all-African organization.

Since they had considerable powers in their own states, it was only natural that the corporate body should be given the very widest scope and power. This was expressed by the basic term of reference of the Assembly, to "discuss matters of common concern to Africa with a view to co-ordinating and harmonizing the general policy of the Organization." This wording, however, was rather misleading. The Assembly could debate any matter, ranging from decolonization and non-alignment to cooperation in every technical field. It could also discuss disputes among states or situations that endangered the peace and security of the continent. It could even take decisions and adopt resolutions on all these issues.

But the policy the Assembly coordinated could only be that of the OAU and not the member states. For at the foundation of the Organization was still unrestricted sovereignty. No abandonment of sovereignty could be read from the attitude of the states either at or after the summit conference. Whereas the Charter mentioned respect for national sovereignty among its principles, it was strangely silent on respect for OAU decisions. And there was no definition of the value of Assembly resolutions. So the strong position of the African leaders turned out to be a mixed blessing. Each Head of State had unusually broad powers in his own government but even all of them together could not take decisions binding on any one.

Although the Assembly could not--as some had hoped--coordinate the action of the member states, it could at least coordinate that of the Organization. This was provided by the second term of reference, to "review the structure, functions

and acts of all the organs and any specialized agencies which
may be created in accordance with the present Charter." This
made the Assembly the hierarchical head of the Organization
with a right to guide and direct the other bodies.   The decisions of the "supreme organ" had to be applied by the subordinate ones.   The recommendations and resolutions of the subordinate bodies, however, had to be approved by the Assembly.
The Assembly could also modify the structure of the Organization by creating new bodies and agencies as necessary under
Articles VIII and XX.   In addition, it appointed and could remove the major officials of the OAU: the Administrative Secretary-General and his Assistants and the members of the
Commission of Mediation, Conciliation and Arbitration.

Fundamental transformations could be wrought by amendment of the Charter requiring a two-thirds majority of the
Heads of State.   For ordinary purposes, an interpretation of
the Charter was enough.   Usually, the silence or ambiguity of
the section on institutions left the Heads of State enough leeway to shape the Organization as they desired without introducing formal changes.

... and Practice.

The fact that the Charter did not make the Assembly's
resolutions binding on the member states left the supreme organ in a rather difficult position.   It was enabled to discuss
and deal with the most burning issues on the continent and
adopt resolutions or suggest plans of settlement.   However,
even those generally accepted could not be enforced and the
Organization was constantly dependent on the good will of its
members.

This gap between responsibility and power was inevitable.   In order to permit the Assembly to function at all, the
rule of unanimity had been replaced by majority decisions.
This meant that the dissenting states could not veto decisions.
However, they could ignore or violate those they would have
been able to block under the older, more stringent rule.   Even
unanimous resolutions could be disregarded by a state that
changed its stand or did not wish to make the effort.   Thus
state sovereignty was avoided in the first instance only to be
encountered later.

Nevertheless, the good will of the member states could
be counted upon in many cases.   To encourage this, the As-

sembly usually dealt only with issues of overriding importance and where there was a high degree of dedication and agreement. On items like decolonization and racial discrimination or the maintenance of peace and security in Africa, hesitation could be expected but not a denial of basic principles. On more marginal issues like non-alignment the actual demands were kept vague and the stage of development still left more room for cooperation than competition. Really controversial questions were often avoided. Thus, with few exceptions, the body of resolutions could be supported and applied voluntarily.

At the same time, there was a gradual return to unanimity in practice. Realizing that action could not be imposed on the member states, efforts were increasingly made to draft resolutions that satisfied all of them or at least were not strongly objected to by any. The Assembly tried to obtain the broadest possible consensus on each item. Although the Charter only required a two-thirds majority, it was advisable to have many more support any decision so that it would be put into effect. The closer the Assembly came to the old rule of unanimity, the more likely it was that its policies would be followed.

Then, even though the resolutions were not compulsory, the fact that they had been decided upon openly and freely by the Heads of State endowed them with considerable authority. It could be expected that when a leader returned home he would not act against a decision he had just taken at an OAU conference. Even the dissenters might be persuaded to implement a resolution if it were supported and applied by the rest of the African community.

Still, the paradox that the Heads of State could "discuss" any matter but "implement" none carried with it a very real danger that the Assembly would become a mere debating society. During the first meetings, this was almost what happened. The statesmen did not deliberate on the general situation or problems so much as to merely declaim and make lengthy speeches on general principles and policy. It was soon realized that no headway could be made thus. Especially, when some of the early resolutions went unapplied, the Heads of State had to turn the Assembly into a real working body. The time of the leaders and their prestige was too precious for speech making. Thus they came around to the basic job of direction and supervision.

In order to keep track of all action undertaken in the interim, the Assembly had to work rapidly during its few days of meeting each year. It heard status reports on the various fields of activity. The Heads of State looked into the most important items themselves. Others, usually the less political ones, were dealt with summarily and resolutions were adopted at the proposal of the Council of Ministers. Then it considered the work of the various subordinate bodies. Their recommendations and resolutions were submitted to the Assembly: if approved, they were given the authority of Assembly decisions; if rejected, they were nullified and the bodies had to seek other solutions. The Heads of State also supervised the implementation of their resolutions by both the Organization and the member states. Of the former, they could make specific demands; the member states could only be urged. Sometimes the more lax could be impressed with the need for renewed efforts or embarrassed by the bare facts of their un-African stand, but the Assembly had no means of imposing its will. Finally, the Heads of State had to deal with a number of questions that were so crucial or delicate that only they could recommend action. This happened in particular with the Nigerian civil war.

Unfortunately, with time a feeling of disenchantment spread among the Heads of State. The Organization had not really lived up to the expectations of the delegates at Addis Ababa. Obviously it would take many years of serious effort even to come close to attaining these goals and some impatience was only natural. But there was deeper frustration at the ineffectualness of the OAU as such. Even on critical issues of decolonization or in handling serious crises, there was too much hesitation and reluctance to implement common policies. Due to this and various circumstances or quarrels, which kept particular leaders away from one meeting or another, the attendance of Heads of State at Assemblies sank. Eventually, the "summit" could only be held because lesser personalities had been accredited to represent them.

Council of Ministers: Theory ...

The Council was composed of Foreign Ministers or other ministers designated by the governments of the member states. It met twice a year in ordinary session and could hold extraordinary sessions. Its resolutions were adopted by a simple majority. However, the Charter did not define the effect of Council resolutions either and there was some uncertainty

as to their real value. The decisions were obviously not binding and less authoritative than those of the Assembly. Since
the Council was "responsible" to the Assembly, they could be
reviewed and eventually rejected. But, were Council decisions
valid from the start?

The terms of reference of the Council of Ministers
were described by Article XIII of the Charter and Rule 3 of
its own Rules of Procedure. The Council was conceived of
very much as an assistant or help-mate to the Assembly.
Two of its primary tasks were directly connected with the
meetings of the Assembly. First, it was "entrusted with the
responsibility of preparing conferences of the Assembly." It
had to inform the Heads of State of the work being accomplished by the various organs and any problems encountered.
It also reported on progress made by the member states towards the fulfillment of resolutions. It informed the Assembly about the various items on the agenda and could even present recommendations or resolutions to the Heads of State as
a basis for their decisions.

Then, after the conference, the Council was "entrusted
with the implementation of the decisions of the Assembly."
As Assembly resolutions were not binding on member states,
the meaning of this provision was uncertain. Either the Council could see to the implementation of the only decisions that
were binding, i.e. internal decisions concerning the other
bodies of the Organization, or it could limit itself to supervising or just noting the implementation of resolutions voluntarily by the member states and then reporting back to the
Assembly. But it was out of the question for the Council to
impose implementation or to implement decisions itself in the
place of the member states.

The Council was also the channel through which the Assembly exercised its control over the rest of the Organization.
In accordance with the instructions of the Assembly, the Council was to "co-ordinate inter-African co-operation" under Article II(2) of the Charter. This article referred to the coordination and harmonization of policies in a vast range of fields
including political and defence but also economic and social or
health and research. However, once again, since the Organization could not impose cooperation on its members, the actual role of the Council was to define a consistent and feasible
policy for the Organization. This meant basically that it had
to work the activities of the many commissions and committees
into an overall program and determine priorities.

The power of the Council to coordinate the activities of the various bodies was enhanced in two ways. First of all, it had to approve the rules of procedure of the specialized commissions and the basic documents of the Secretariat. It could thus determine their terms of reference and scope from the outset. Secondly, the Council was empowered to approve the budget, which now usually means trimming expenditures. There was no end to what could be done in each field and the various administrative bodies or specialized commissions could make excessive demands. Those that did might then be supported by the Secretariat eager to expand its own influence. To cut the demands down to size and see that each field received the sum it deserved or, rather, the sum the member states were willing to devote to it, the Council of Ministers had to adapt plans that fit the budget. With this power of the purse, it was able to make its control and coordination felt in the subordinate bodies.

Finally, the Council of Ministers could represent or replace the Assembly in dealing with certain issues. As a catch-all function, "it shall take cognisance of any matter referred to it by the Assembly."

... and Practice.

The exact relationship between the Assembly and the Council was none too clearly defined. Both had the same vast field of activity. However, the Assembly was "supreme" and would presumably take the lead. In practice that was not always so. For the Council had considerable outlets for ambition. It even grew in size. At the first pre-Assembly meeting in Cairo, it was necessary to set up two committees, a political and an administrative one, to handle the many tasks and draw up resolutions or reports on all facets of the work. At the Addis Ababa Assembly, in 1966, it was decided to add a third committee on economic, social and cultural cooperation.

It was not difficult for the Council to influence the Assembly. Its primary task was to prepare and follow up summit conferences. At the preparatory meetings it checked on the implementation of resolutions and supervised the work of the subordinate bodies. Then it drew together the various strands of the OAU's activities. This was then presented to the Heads of State. They therefore saw the situation through the eyes of their Ministers. The chiefs' actions were moti-

vated by their subordinates' reports. And, most often, the
decisions they adopted were based on draft resolutions presented by the Council. Secondly, since the Council of Ministers had to "implement" Assembly resolutions, it had considerable influence on the way they were put into effect.

It was in the political field that the Foreign Ministers
grew most in stature. This was within their competence nationally and they tended to devote most of their time and care
to the political problems of the continent. The Council was
not directly empowered to do so by the Charter. But it could
deal with all matters referred to it by the Assembly, and it
was eventually entrusted with almost all questions of decolonization, non-alignment and the peaceful settlement of African disputes. Moreover, it could also implement and thus
interpret or work out details and tactics for Assembly resolutions. Many issues were also dealt with by the Council in the
first instance. In this way it became a sort of specialized
commission on political questions.

Soon the Council began to overshadow the Assembly.
Since it met at least twice a year, it was in a better position
to follow up matters and often took important decision in the
interim. These decisions could not be immediately approved
or rejected and they were widely accepted as the expression
of OAU policy until the next Summit. Since the Heads of State
repeatedly refused to meet in extraordinary session, whereas
the Foreign Ministers could be called together rapidly in crises, the most urgent and explosive problems were dealt with
by the Council and not the Assembly. When a crisis broke
out, the Foreign Ministers often took the crucial decisions and
Africa came to look towards them as the political trouble
shooters and peace-keepers of the OAU.

During the formative period of the Organization, the
Ministers took the initiative and met often to deal with critical
issues. During the first year the Council met three times in
ordinary session, but also twice in an emergency to deal with
the Algero-Moroccan border dispute, the dispute between Somalia and its neighbors, and the mutinies in Tanganyika. By
the time the Heads of State met in Cairo, the Council had acquired much more experience and played a more important
role than the Assembly. Later, it was the Council that dealt
with the Congolese crisis and Rhodesia. During this time the
decisions of the Council were always accepted tacitly and often
highly praised by the Assembly. And the Council got into the
habit of acting on its own. The first timid resolutions gave

way to bold attempts at solving key problems.

Nevertheless, this extraordinary growth was not without friction. The Council often met under the pressure and exaltation of a serious crisis, whereas the Heads of State avoided meeting in unsettled times and weighed pros and cons at length before acting. The Foreign Ministers were younger and dynamic. Moreover, they were not directly implicated in any action. The Heads of State, who bore a greater responsibility for the consequences any measures might have on their countries, were more cautious and conservative. In the OAU these differences were magnified since the Council adopted its decisions with a simple majority while the Assembly required a two-thirds majority. For these reasons, decisions taken on the same issue by both organs could vary considerably. The Council would tend to move further and faster and, on occasion, the Assembly might refuse to follow it.

In December 1965, the Council of Ministers obviously went too far. It decided that if the United Kingdom did not crush the rebellion in Southern Rhodesia within ten days the African states would break off diplomatic relations. The excitement and indignation following the unilateral declaration of independence by a minority regime swept the Ministers towards a unanimous decision. But, when only a third of the member states actually severed relations, it was obvious that the Council had made a mistake and that no such decision would have been taken by the Assembly, although the deadline left it no time to disapprove officially.

It had never been clear whether the Council of Ministers could make decisions for the Organization and there was some confusion after the ill-fated Rhodesian resolution. Most of the members explained their reasons for not immediately complying with the decision, although some intimated that it had never been valid. To avoid a repetition, it was urged that the conditions for validity of Council resolutions be defined. But the Assembly never provided such a definition. None really seemed necessary. The Africans and their leaders knew perfectly well what could and could not be done by a Foreign Minister. Common sense also indicated that urgent measures of peace-keeping like a cease-fire had to be implemented immediately without referring back to the Assembly while other measures that committed the states should be considered more calmly.

Nevertheless, after this December 1965 incident, the Council of Ministers no longer enjoyed the same freedom of action and the previous ad hoc development was retracted. Once again it presented recommendations to the Assembly for approval. Its resolutions in March 1966 were even specifically held over to the next Assembly, a half year later. Unfortunately, there was another mishap in February 1967. The Council adopted a particularly strong resolution condemning Israel and demanding an immediate withdrawal of its troops. This position went much further than the preceding Assembly resolution or the stand most members had taken in the United Nations. The resolution was already vitiated by the irregular conditions under which it was adopted by "acclamation." But many Heads of State were quite embarrassed when they had to explain a decision they did not really support. Thus, at the Algiers Assembly in September 1967, it was decided that all Council resolutions had to be officially approved by the Assembly. Even then some flexibility was preserved by not writing this into the Charter.

Finally, after years of experimentation, things seemed to be falling into place. The Council of Ministers had been returned to its subordinate position and the Assembly realized that it must not foresake the command of the Organization. An encouraging sign was that the Heads of State dealt with the Nigerian civil war as of its Kinshasa meeting in September 1967, after the Council of Ministers had failed even to include the issue in its agenda. Both the Assembly and the Council were becoming aware of their actual powers and responsibilities. They began to form a team in which each played its role. And together they could govern the OAU--if not Africa.

B. Specialized Commissions

The breadth of the activities assigned to the new organization was exceptional. Along with its many political tasks, it included a vast range of relatively technical matters. Since one of the main concerns of the African leaders was to make their countries grow and prosper, they were keenly interested in development in all fields. The list of proposed fields of cooperation given by Article II (2) of the Charter, although incomplete, was very impressive: economic, including transport and communications; education and culture; health, sanitation, and nutrition; science and technology; and defence and security. In short, the actual or potential scope of the OAU covered virtually every facet of life dealt with by modern governments and in which they wished to join their efforts at a continental level.

It was hoped that the Organization would enable the member states to coordinate and strengthen their endeavors. By pooling their wealth and know-how they could tackle hitherto unsolvable tasks. Through a division of labor they could avoid duplication. And, since the African countries still relied on foreign assistance, it might be safer to channel necessary aid through the common organization. Cooperation in these fields was demanded for another reason as well. Each step towards developing the continent offered considerable opportunities for promoting unity. These activities could help weld the individual states into a more united Africa.

Specialized Commissions: Theory ...

In order to encourage the coordination and harmonization of policies in the various technical fields, the Charter established five specialized commissions and left the door open for the creation of more. The commissions consisted of the ministers concerned or of plenipotentiaries designated by the governments. Despite the high level of membership, there was no wish for them to be autonomous and they were carefully integrated in the system of the OAU in Addis Ababa. The specialized commissions, according to Article XXII, were to

work under regulations approved by the Council of Ministers.
Despite some resistance all of them, under their rules of procedure, were made "answerable" or "responsible" to the Council and the Assembly. Obviously, the Assembly could not constantly supervise such a wide range of fields, but final decisions would have to be deferred to the Heads of State.   The
Council was instrumental as a guide and intermediary between
the Assembly and the commissions and it could effectively coordinate and shape their activities by its power to approve the
budget.

The five specialized commissions established directly
under Article XX of the Charter were:

> Economic and Social Commission;
> Educational and Cultural Commission;
> Health, Sanitation and Nutrition Commission;
> Defence Commission;
> Scientific, Technical and Research Commission.

Nevertheless, within the first year of operation, the Assembly
felt a need to add commissions for certain essential fields
that had not been covered. By a two-thirds vote, the Heads
of State established two additional bodies in July 1964.   The
new-comers were:

> Transport and Communications Commission;
> Commission of Jurists.

The Charter gave no description whatsoever of the responsibilities or powers of the various commissions.   Nevertheless, some insight into their potential work could be gained
by studying the tasks laid down by the preparatory committees at the summit conference.   These enunciations of tasks
became the eventual terms of reference of the commissions
and indicated the future course they would follow.   It was necessary, of course, for each commission to determine its
priorities and then tackle projects one by one.

The program laid down for possible cooperation in economic matters and transport was perhaps the most ambitious:

a)   the establishment of a free trade area between the
     various African countries;

b)   the establishment of a common external tariff to
     protect the emergent industries and the setting up

of a raw material price stabilization fund;

c)   the restructuring of international trade;

d)   the development of trade by the organization and
     participation in African trade fairs and exhibitions
     and the granting of transport and transit facilities;

e)   the co-ordination of means of transport and the es-
     tablishment of road, air and maritime companies;

f)   the establishment of an African Payment and Clear-
     ing Union;

g)   a progressive freeing of national currencies from
     all non-technical external attachments and the es-
     tablishment of a Pan-African monetary zone; and

h) ˙ the ways and means of effecting the harmonization
     of existing and future national development plans.

In the fields of social and labor affairs, the Heads of
State suggested the following program:

a)   the exchange of social and labor legislation;

b)   the establishment of an African Youth Organization;

c)   the organization of an African Scouts Union and an
     annual continental jamboree;

d)   the organization of an annual African Sport Games;

e)   the organization of vocational training courses in
     which African workers will participate;

f)   the establishment of an African Trade Union.

From this it was clear that the Economic and Social
Commission was intended to be one of the major bodies of the
Organization. It was entrusted with highly important--and ar-
duous--tasks that were crucial for the growth and development
of the continent. The programs laid down for the Educational,
Scientific, Cultural and Health Commissions were less ambitious and more strictly technical. However, although the lists
were less complete, they were by no means restrictive.

In the field of education and culture, it was proposed
to establish an Institute of African Studies as the first department in a future African University. To overcome language
barriers and spread knowledge about other parts of the continent, it was suggested to introduce programs in the major African languages and exchange radio and television programs
among the states. And, as a means of escaping the intellectual tutelage of the outside world, it was decided to establish
an African News Agency.

The projects suggested for health, sanitation and nutrition were kept to the level of exchanges. There was to be an
exchange of information about endemic and epidemic diseases
and means to control them, of health legislations, of doctors,
technicians and nurses. There was also need for a reciprocal
offer of scholarships for medical students and the establishment of training courses on health, sanitation and nutrition.

Only in the fields of science, technology and research
did the OAU start with a full action program, largely because
it inherited the Commission for Technical Cooperation in Africa. The CCTA was a going concern that had been established by the colonial powers to provide technical cooperation
in various fields (agriculture, animal health, housing, labor,
etc.) as well as to channel technical aid and know-how. It already had a program and staff, a headquarters in Lagos and
research centers in various countries. What the OAU had to
do was continue this work while turning the CCTA into an African body.

The Transport and Communications Commission was
established in Cairo with the purpose of "drawing up plans and
co-ordinating action for telecommunications and postal services
as well as for air, land and maritime transport." More specific suggestions were also included in the summit program of
economic activities.

The Commission of Jurists grew out of a series of conferences that met in Lagos to discuss questions of interest to
the judges, lawyers and teachers of law in their professional
capacity and as Africans. The Conference on the Rule of Law
met in January 1961 and adopted various resolutions on the
protection of human and individual rights and the position of
the judiciary in Africa.[1] Other meetings were held in August
1963 and January 1964. At the latter it was decided to establish a Pan-African legal organization to promote cooperation
among African jurists, to develop the concept of justice, to

encourage the study of African law, especially customary law
and its progressive codification, to consider international law
in its relations to the problems of the African states and to
examine and make recommendations on legal problems of common interest and those referred to it by member states or the
OAU. The conference also requested the Organization to adopt
it as one of its specialized commissions. This was done at
the Cairo Assembly and the Commission of Jurists was established to study and carry on research into the "specific legal
problems" of Africa.

The Defence Commission was still in flux. Rather than
retain the idea of a board of chiefs of staff to draw up plans
for the collective defence of the continent, this body had been
turned into a specialized commission like the others. Nevertheless, since neither the Charter nor the summit resolutions
provided any mandate for its work, there was immediately a
renewal of proposals to turn it into a more active body. The
approaches varied greatly: the Commission could become a
body for collective defence in case one of the independent
states were attacked; it could become the nucleus of an African army under a "union" high command; it could perform
peace-keeping operations in the independent countries; or, finally, it could be a force for decolonization either to protect
the border states from retaliation by the colonial and settler
powers or even to aid the liberation movements in their struggle against them.

... and Practice.

Africa had been seeking machinery for technical advancement and cooperation for some time and this was given
form in the specialized commissions. Their activities were
vital to the growth and independence of Africa. However, it
was not expected that the goals would be attained in short order nor even that many of them would be tackled for some
time to come. It was only normal to narrow the aims and
choose a small number of concrete projects for the Organization.

Unfortunately, the ministers forged ahead too rapidly at
the first and second meetings of the commissions. The most
important one, the Economic and Social Commission, was unable to pick just one item and decided to handle several at
once, among them economic integration, coordination of national development plans, and monetary arrangements. The lesser

commissions lengthened their lists of activities to appear as
impressive as the economic ones.   Nowhere was a single project chosen as a start.

Obviously, one brief meeting a year was not enough for
the commissions to make headway.   They needed the backing
of a secretariat and experts to prepare reports and studies,
committees to make plans and some sort of permanent body to
follow up implementation.   The Economic and Social Commission soon asked the Secretary-General to appoint a group of
experts on measures leading to rapid economic integration.
The Transport Commission wanted studies on, among other
things, the economic aspects of laying a coaxial submarine cable.   The Health Commission called for a health division in
the Secretariat and the Education Commission wanted an advisory body to help members solve common problems.   The
Defence Commission planned an African Defence Organization
and convened a committee of defence experts.   And the Scientific, Technical and Research Commission even demanded an
executive committee and secretariat of its own, a Scientific
Council for Africa and an African Academy of Sciences.

All at the same time the various commissions tried to
impose their demands on the Organization.   But the ministers
forgot the relatively low priority for all technical questions
within the OAU.   Development was important.   But the OAU
had been created primarily to attain certain political goals.
As long as it had trouble handling top priority items like decolonization and peaceful settlement, it had little time or funds
left over to coordinate technical activities.   Thus the machinery was never created and the projects remained pipe dreams.
All that was left was the ambitious list of aims.

Despite the enthusiasm and appearances, any illusions
collapsed quite abruptly.   The first meeting of all the commissions looked like a success and the ministers were optimistic about the prospects of continent-wide cooperation.   Then,
in December 1964, the Defence Commission failed to attain a
quorum and could be convened only after several months' delay.
Not all the commissions were even that fortunate and some
simply did not meet.   This unexpected apathy was so strong
that none of the commissions was able to hold a third session.

By the Accra Assembly in 1965, disillusionment had set
in and the Heads of State realized that the Organization had
been over-ambitious.   The Institutional Committee they established felt that it was not only necessary to pare down the pro-

grams of the commissions, they had to be amalgamated since
seven statutory bodies was too costly and time-consuming. It
was thus decided to have the Commission of Jurists revert
back to its earlier status without ever having met, and also to
combine certain other commissions. In the new set-up there
was an Economic and Social Commission that included transport and communications in its terms of reference. The second body was the Educational, Scientific, Cultural and Health
Commission, which combined the activities of three previous
commissions. And, finally, the Defence Commission was
maintained. In addition, the commissions were to meet every
second year.

Even this, though, was not enough. Member states
never firmly undertook to attend the meetings and, rather than
miss the quorum, the commissions were left in suspension.
For several years there were no meetings at all. Only the
CCTA section of the second commission preserved more than
a shadow of existence. Its Scientific Council for Africa still
met although attendance was falling and the work of the CCTA
had to be cut back. Only the "Africanization" of the body progressed well.

Nevertheless, these fields of activity were too important to be entirely forgotten, Arrangements were made at the
Addis Ababa Assembly in 1966 which temporarily short-cir-
cuited the commissions. A third committee was established
by the Council of Ministers to deal with economic, social and
technical cooperation. The necessary reports and background
material were provided by the Secretariat. On this basis the
Council adopted resolutions on economic and technical cooperation. The commissions and the interested ministers did not
intervene in this operation. Still, although resolutions could
be adopted, that was certainly not the purpose of any organization.

It could only be hoped that, as more funds became available and as the OAU matured, it would be possible to expand
the work in the technical fields without swamping the Organization. The commissions could be revived and given a more
complete and solid structure. Slowly but surely, concrete projects could be brought to fruition and the member states would
get used to cooperating in the common interest. This sort of
activity might then provide the cement that was necessary to
consolidate African unity. This would be particularly vital
when the goal of decolonization or other political goals receded
and the African states could concentrate more on development.

No matter how ineffectual they were for the moment, the specialized commissions were bound to assume importance in the future.

1. <u>African Conference on the Rule of Law: A Report on the Proceedings</u>. Geneva, Int. Commission of Jurists, 1961.

C. Commission of Mediation, Conciliation and Arbitration

For some time, the Heads of State had recognized that it was necessary to have some machinery for settling disputes that arose among the independent states of the continent. This could reduce friction and animosity and enable them to concentrate on more important matters. At the request of certain speakers at the summit conference, the Charter stressed the need for peaceful settlement. Under Article XIX, the members stated that they:

> ... pledge to settle all disputes among themselves by peaceful means and, to this end, decide to establish a Commission of Mediation, Conciliation and Arbitration, the composition of which and conditions of service shall be defined by a separate Protocol to be approved by the Assembly of Heads of State and Government.

One of the primary tasks of the new Organization was thus to define the membership and tasks of the Commission. This process began already at the first Council of Ministers, in Dakar, where suggestions were made by various states and a first draft could be studied. It was amended at the second Council in Lagos. The Lagos draft, after being revised and expanded by a committee of experts that met in Cairo, was eventually adopted by the first Assembly. The Protocol of the Commission was signed by the Heads of State and Government in Cairo, on 21 July 1964, and became an integral part of the Charter. It was this document that governed the establishment and activities of the Commission.

The Commission: Theory ...

The Commission consisted of twenty-one members elected by the Assembly for a period of five years and eligible for re-election. Election was on the basis of no more than two candidates from each state and the Commission could not contain more than one national of each state. Once chosen, the members could not be removed from office except by a two-thirds majority of the total membership of the Assembly "on the grounds of inability to perform the functions of their office or of proved misconduct." Like other officials of the OAU, the Commission members were not to seek or receive instructions and were covered by the Convention on Privileges and Immunities when engaged in business of the Commission. They were selected on the basis of "recognized professional qualifications," which did not necessarily imply legal training as only the members of the Arbitral Tribunal required legal qualifications. Nevertheless, most of those elected at the Accra Assembly in October 1965 were jurists, although there were also several ambassadors and parlamentarians.

The Commission was placed under a Bureau, i.e. a President and two Vice-Presidents, elected by the Assembly from among the members of the Commission. They were its only full-time members; the other eighteen would be called upon when necessary. The Commission then appointed a Registrar and was empowered to elect such other officers as it deemed necessary. The Commission had its seat in Addis Ababa. Since the Commission itself was not a permanent body but rather a panel of judges who were activated when disputes were brought to it for settlement, there was a considerable economy of means. Flexibility was obtained by providing twenty-one members and allowing the parties a rather broad choice in the composition of the body judging their case. It was also possible for several groups to be established at the same time to deal with several disputes.

The Commission's jurisdiction was restricted to disputes between member states. Its jurisdiction could well have been made broader but, again, the Heads of State would not accept any infringement of their own prerogatives. The Commission could not be seized with a conflict between a state and the Organization. It did not interpret the Charter of the OAU, this being the role of the Heads of State themselves. Nor did it serve as an advisory body for the OAU or give it opinions on legal matters. In particular, despite all talk of human rights and justice, there was no question of an individual's (or corporate body's) being able to seize the Commission or bring suit against a state.

Disputes could be referred to the Commission by one or more parties, by the Council of Ministers, or by the Assembly of Heads of State. If one of the parties refused to submit to the jurisdiction of the Commission, the Bureau could refer the matter to the Council of Ministers. However, the Council

could not impose any obligation on a recalcitrant state. (The
authors of the Protocol had agreed that the Commission's
jurisdiction should be optional and not compulsory, doubtlessly
convinced that the member states would accept no other rule.)[1]
Thus, in the final analysis, the consent of each party was necessary for it to be involved in proceedings before the Commission. This consent could take the form of a prior written
undertaking to resort to the Commission, reference of the
dispute to the Commission or submission to the jurisdiction of
the Commission in a dispute referred to it by another state,
the Council or Assembly.

Once there was mutual consent to the jurisdiction of
the Commission, it was necessary to determine which mode of
settlement to use. The working methods and rules of procedure for each method were left largely to the parties and
Commission. What the Protocol did provide was that the member states "shall refrain from any act or omission that is likely to aggravate a situation." The members of the Commission
engaged in the case were endowed with diplomatic privileges
and immunities. And they were authorized to conduct investigations or inquiries to elucidate facts or circumstances with
the fullest cooperation of the member states.

Mediation could be introduced by the President of the
Commission, who appointed--with the consent of the parties--
one or more mediators chosen from the Commission. In this
way, the parties were not bound to accept the proposals of the
mediators and in no way sacrificed their sovereignty. The
mediators tried to reconcile the views and claims of the parties and made written proposals which might (or might not) become the basis of a protocol of arrangement between them.
If the proposals were not accepted, the mediators could try
again.

A matter could be referred for conciliation by means of
a written petition giving the grounds of the dispute. In forming the Board of Conciliation of five members, only one was
named by each party and the other three by the President of
the Commission. He also chose the Chairman of the Board.
Although the procedure was still rather flexible, it was more
formal than mediation and the question had to be stated precisely in the petition, the parties were represented by agents,
and they could be assisted by counsel and experts. There was
also provision for fact-finding and holding of hearings.

Nevertheless, the duty of the Board was only "to clarify the issues in dispute and to endeavour to bring about an agreement between the parties upon mutually acceptable terms." These terms, if any could be reached, were included in a final report by the Board along with any recommendations for settlement. If no agreement could be reached the report merely stated that it was impossible to effect a settlement. Thus, once again, the parties had the final say as to what the settlement should be. The Board or a party could not even exert pressure on a state by publishing the report, since this was only possible with the consent of all parties.

The most effective form of settlement was arbitration. The machinery and procedure were much more complete. Each party selected one member of the Tribunal and the two members then chose the third. If they could not agree, the Bureau of the Commission made the choice. If so desired, two further members, this time not necessarily drawn from the Commission, could be appointed by the President of the Commission. However, none of the arbitrators could be nationals of the parties, domiciled there or in their service. And no two arbitrators could be from the same country. Finally, only members of the Commission with "legal qualifications" could be selected.

The particulars of the case were set forth in the basic document calling for arbitration, the compromis, which provided that the parties would accept the Tribunal's decision as legally binding, related the subject matter of the controversy, and named the seat of the Tribunal. The compromis could also specify the law to be applied. Otherwise the Tribunal would base its decision on "treaties concluded between the parties, International Law, the Charter of the Organization of African Unity, the Charter of the United Nations, and, if the parties agree, ex aequo et bono." The hearings were to be held in camera, unless the arbitrators decided otherwise, the formal records signed by the arbitrators and the Registrar were alone to be authoritative, and the award, or final judgment, had to be in writing and the reason for its every point clearly stated.

The more juridical and formal nature of arbitration was essential as a guarantee to the states of a just decision, based on law, since this was the only mode of settlement that was directly binding without their approval. Article XXVIII provided that: "Recourse to arbitration shall be regarded as submission in good faith to the award of the Arbitral Tribunal."

No provision was made, however, for imposing execution of
the award upon a state through action of the Council or Assembly.   Although the aggrieved party could bring the matter
before the political bodies, there was little the OAU could do
to make the other party implement a ruling.   The Charter did
not even permit them to decide its expulsion from the Organization.

... and Practice.

        When the summit conference agreed to establish a Com-
mission of Mediation, Conciliation and Arbitration, this was a
seemingly decisive step.   In Africa, like any other part of the
world, conflicts were bound to arise and before the Commission was constituted a number of serious problems had erupted.   There were in particular great expectations that the Commission could calm boundary disputes, and in addition interpret treaties and conventions.   At any rate, there was no
doubt that the Commission had ample scope for its activities.

        Special significance was also attached to the fact that,
for the first time, Africa had its own legal body.   There was
increasing distrust of international law as the creation of the
Western world, all too often used to explain away or legalize
the abuses of colonialism such as the acquisition of territories
and subjection of their peoples.   There was also dissatisfaction with the more traditional tribunals.   The last straw was
the inability of the International Court of Justice to rule in Africa's favor on the South West Africa case.   There was no
longer much chance that the African states would bring their
differences before a largely alien body.

        What Africa wanted was justice of a kind it felt and
trusted and it was assumed that, among other things, the Commission could provide justice for and among Africans and gradually form a body of African law.   For this reason much attention was paid to less binding methods in which a "palaver"
would lead the parties to agree.   By not demanding legal qualifications for members, it was possible to leave room for a
"village elder" type of judge.   And there was far greater like-
lihood that the parties would invoke either customary African
law or the principles of the OAU.

        However, even with an African Commission whose rul-
ings were usually not binding, it was not certain whether the
independent states would relax their grip on sovereignty suffi-

ciently to permit the Commission to function. Although the
member states had pledged to settle their disputes by peaceful
means, this did not necessarily imply that they would have recourse to the Commission. In many cases they might well
prefer direct negotiations or good offices through another state
or the OAU itself. This was certainly the only way in which
they would handle political disputes and for some time almost
every dispute might seem politically loaded. At most they
would come before the Commission when an agreement had
nearly been reached so as to present it as a victory of African unity.

There were two preliminary barriers to an effective
Commission. There was the prior question of consent. Few
if any states would accept a general clause of compulsory
jurisdiction and in each individual case it would first be necessary to obtain the consent of all parties. Then, there was the
choice of method. Unless the binding mode of arbitration was
chosen, which hardly seemed probable, even after rather
lengthy proceedings the proposed solutions could be rejected
and no final settlement reached. During its early years the
OAU was rarely able to jump these hurdles and, despite the
various disputes that arose, only the Algero-Moroccan border
conflict was ever brought before a legal body. And this ad
hoc Commission was at most enabled merely to mediate between the parties.

Until the member states were more willing to cooperate
with the Commission and employ legal means, it had little future. This unhappy fact was recognized by the Commission
itself. It met for the first time on 11 December 1967. Its
president, M. A. Odesanya of the Nigerian Supreme Court,
had convened the members to adopt rules of procedure and set
up a secretariat. But even his presence in Addis Ababa was
not likely to breathe life into the Commission. It had a structure and members, but it was largely decorative until the independent states entrusted it with their differences.

1. See T. O Elias, "The Commission of Mediation, Concilia-
    tion and Arbitration," British Yearbook of International
    Law, 1965, p. 343.

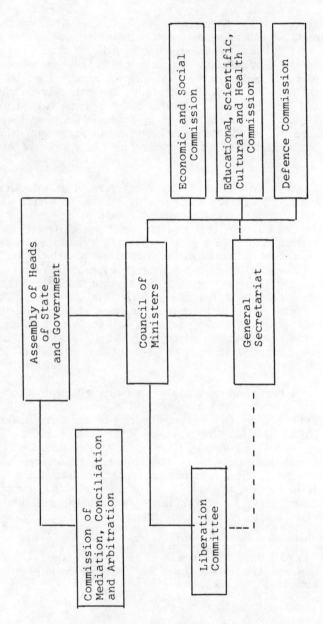

The OAU Administrative Structure

D. Secretariat

The General Secretariat was listed among the principal institutions and there was no doubt it would be an essential pillar of the Organization. It had to prepare the work of the other bodies and carry out any number of day-to-day tasks. But the Secretariat was most significant as the only really permanent machinery. Only the Secretariat could follow up the many activities and see whether the OAU was coming close to its goals. Only the Secretariat could report to the other bodies and inform them of accomplishments or failures and possibly suggest more valid alternatives. Only the Secretariat could keep the member states informed about implementation of the various resolutions or indicate which members were slow to apply approved policies.

It was in the interest of the Organization that the Secretariat should be thoroughly independent of the member states. In this way it could devote itself to the cause of Africa as a whole rather than that of any given tendency. But its importance and autonomy might conceivably lead the Secretariat to try to impose action or restraint on the governing bodies or the states. To forestall any such initiatives and prevent the Secretariat from dictating to them or even advising them as an equal, the Heads of State carefully restricted its competences and placed it on a level definitely below that of the Assembly and the Council.

The General Secretariat: Theory ...

As with the other institutions of the OAU, the outline traced in the Charter left many blanks to be filled in. All it actually specified was that the Assembly was to appoint an Administrative Secretary-General and one or more Assistant Secretaries-General and that the staff's functions and conditions of service were to be contained in regulations approved by the Assembly. In this connection, it stipulated that the officials and the civil servants were to have only one allegiance--to the Organization. Article XVIII included a double undertaking to guarantee this. The personnel of the OAU "shall not seek or

receive instructions from any government or from any other
authority external to the Organization" and "they shall refrain
from any action which might reflect on their position as international officials responsible only to the Organization." And
the member states of the OAU pledged "to respect the exclusive character of the responsibilities of the Administrative
Secretary-General and the staff and not to seek to influence
them in the discharge of their responsibilities."

This was all that remained after the pruning of the
Ethiopian text in Addis Ababa. For the Heads of State had
very firm ideas as to the place of the Secretariat and, in particular, they knew what they did not want: a dynamic Secretary-General who could cast a shadow on their own role. The
new states and their leaders were too jealous of power to tolerate undue pressure from the officials of the common organization. This fear was only heightened by recent events in
other international organizations. Dag Hammarskjöld had
played an increasingly strong role in the United Nations, especially during the Congo crisis. This led to criticism of his
position and the Soviet proposal of a troika. The Afro-Malagasy states also had some experience with an ambitious UAM
Secretary-General.

Thus, the politicians were careful not to put any real
power in the hands of the Secretariat. In Addis Ababa, the
Foreign Ministers revised the Ethiopian draft to further reduce the stature of the Secretary-General. The only opening
for direct influence on decisions, a clause authorizing him to
"participate in all deliberations of the Institutions of the Organization" without a vote, was deleted. Then, the Secretariat
was pointedly made "administrative" and the Secretary-General
was surrounded by a number of assistants independent of his
will.

But it was still necessary to specify the role of the
Secretariat. This meant drafting a number of basic documents
which had to be approved by the Council and Assembly. The
principal document was the Functions and Regulations of the
General Secretariat, which included the terms of reference and
rules under which it would work. Staff rules and regulations
were necessary to determine the exact status of the personnel
recruited to carry out this work. A Convention on Privileges
and Immunities was required to permit both the staff and the
representatives of the states to accomplish their official tasks
in the interest of the Organization. And, finally, an Administrative Tribunal was to deal with disputes between the Organi-

zation and its staff.

As directed by the Functions and Regulations document, an Administrative Secretary-General and four Assistant Administrative Secretaries-General were appointed by the Assembly for a period of four years. The Secretary-General "directs the activities of the General Secretariat and is its legal representative." He was "directly responsible to the Council of Ministers for the adequate discharge of all duties assigned to him." The position of his Assistants was less clear. One of them shall represent the Secretary-General in "all matters assigned to him." Another, or possibly the same one, "shall exercise the functions of the Administrative Secretary-General in his absence." This, however, did not indicate what contribution could be made by four Assistants.

The rest of the personnel consisted of the necessary professional and general categories needed to accomplish the work of the Secretariat. They were to be recruited according to rules that gave precedence to those persons of skill and efficiency. Nevertheless, considerable care was also taken to provide a geographical and especially political distribution of posts. Even questions of language had to be taken into consideration. For example, these factors led the Assembly to choose the Secretary-General from Guinea and his Assistants from Algeria, Dahomey, Kenya and Nigeria, giving a rather large spread. In order to obtain a capable and dynamic staff, the salaries and indemnities had to attract likely candidates to the OAU. The first Council of Ministers, in August 1963, thus decided that "without losing sight of the financial means of our States, a fair remuneration worthy of international civil servants should be granted to the staff of this essential organ of the OAU."[1]

The Functions and Regulations provided the following three departments in the Secretariat: the Political, Legal and Defence Department; the Economic and Social Department; the Administrative, Conference and Information Department. But the structure of the Secretariat was by no means rigid. With the approval of the Council, the Administrative Secretary-General could "create divisions and sub-divisions as he may deem necessary" and establish--or abolish--"such branches and administrative and technical offices as may be deemed necessary." It was on this basis that a key office like the Bureau of Sanctions could be established.

The position and activities of the General Secretariat were defined by a multitude of documents: the Charter, the Functions and Regulations, treaties and agreements among member states and the constant stream of decisions and resolutions of all sorts by the many bodies of the Organization. According to the Functions, the General Secretariat was "a central and permanent organ" of the OAU. In order really to centralize this work, Rule 3 pointed out that the General Secretariat was "the Secretariat of the Assembly of the Council of Ministers, of the Specialized Commissions and other organs of the Organization of African Unity." Although there was no doubt about it being the Secretariat of all the bodies created by the Charter of Addis Ababa, it was more difficult for the Secretariat to impose its control over the secretariats of earlier or largely autonomous bodies such as the Liberation Committee and the African Group at the United Nations.

According to Rule 2, the "General Administrative Secretariat shall supervise the implementation of decisions of the Council of Ministers concerning all economic, social, legal and cultural exchanges of Member States." Here, too, the wording was much stronger than the realities of power. For the Secretariat could not supervise the implementation of decisions. At most, it could keep some watch over their application and report to the governing bodies on progress made. The limited nature of the actual tasks of the Secretariat was highlighted by the adjective "administrative" and the omission of political decisions in the enumeration. It was shown more concretely by the actual duties that were listed in the Functions. Although it was difficult to classify them under a few headings, most of the tasks consisted roughly of servicing the Charter, conference work, preparation of the annual or other reports and program and budget.

The Charter was, in many ways, a living instrument which required the accomplishment of certain operations to grow with the Organization. When a new state asked to adhere or accede to the Charter, the Secretariat had to forward the request to the members and then inform the candidate whether its application had been accepted. It also was to receive notification from states which wished to renounce their membership. For amendment or revision of the Charter, the member states had to make a written request to the Secretariat which then communicated the proposal to the other members and placed it on the agenda of the Assembly. The Secretariat received communications of ratification of instruments or agreements entered into between member states. The Secre-

tariat also prepared the list of candidates nominated as members of the Commission of Mediation, Conciliation and Arbitration in accordance with Article II of the Protocol. Finally,
Article XXX of the Charter authorized the Secretary-General
to accept gifts, bequests and donations on behalf of the Organization.

Most of the activity of the Organization was undertaken
during conferences and meetings. It was therefore essential
for the Secretariat to prepare effectively, help conduct, and
then follow up these conferences. Given the large number of
such meetings, there was even a risk that the Secretariat
would be turned into a conference-processing machine. It had
to prepare the agenda, inserting the items proposed by the
OAU organs and the member states. It drew up the basic
studies and papers. Then, the agenda and documents had to
be sent out to the member states well before the meetings
were held. During the meetings, it provided the material facilities for work, the interpretation and translation, taking of
records, and general policing. And, once the conference was
over, the Secretariat had to pass along the decisions to the
pertinent bodies and start filling the many requests for new
documents and reports. A final service was to store records
and files of the meeting.

The most important documents prepared by the Secretariat were the annual report on the activities of the Organization and the reports on the activities of the specialized commissions or any other reports requested by the Assembly or
Council. In them the Secretariat could analyze and evaluate
the work of the OAU and its bodies. This provided the necessary perspective to see what was being accomplished and where
it was heading. On certain occasions, the Secretariat might
even venture to suggest conclusions.

A particularly delicate task was to prepare the program and budget of the various institutions and the Organization as a whole. The Functions and Regulations therefore included extensive sections on fiscal rules, financial resources
and supervision. It was important for the Secretariat to manage its accounts well and submit a suitable budget. This was
also a chance for the General Secretariat to impose its will on
the more or less autonomous bodies financed by the OAU, such
as the Liberation Committee and the UN African Group, whose
budgets it had to recommend to the Council. But the actual
decisions on the budget were taken by the Council and Assembly and this gave them an opportunity to keep the Secretariat

in its place by rationing out the funds it needed.

... and Practice.

By the time the Conference of Addis Ababa was over,
a new organization had been framed on paper. But it took
much longer for the OAU to assume even a rudimentary form
and the many organs could not be instituted and begin their
tasks without some staff to prepare and hold the first series
of meetings. Fortunately, the Ethiopian government generously agreed to second enough personnel to set up a provisional
secretariat. This was a relatively small but homogeneous
team, under the effective direction of Ato Kifle Wodajo, which
ran the Organization for over a year.

It was not until the Cairo Assembly, in July 1964, that
the Heads of State had the opportunity of appointing the highest
officials of the new, permanent Secretariat. Realizing the import of the decisions, they had some difficulty in choosing the
first Secretary-General. A strong will was needed to shape
the Organization and turn the broader African staff into a team.
But there was concern that the same will might try to bring
the states themselves into line. It was also necessary to balance political and other considerations. The brief hope of a
unanimous decision was dashed when the UAM states presented
their own candidate to run against Guinea's permanent representative to the United Nations, Diallo Telli.[2] The preliminary voting in the Council of Ministers ended in a tie and it
was not possible to recommend one name to the Heads of
State. Nevertheless, with some effort, the Assembly was able
to attain the required two-thirds majority.

Secretary-General Diallo Telli and his four assistants
soon took charge of the Organization. Since his assistants had
not been chosen individually but were appointed and could be
replaced by their governments, he enjoyed somewhat greater
authority and tenure than they. To work them into the structure of the Secretariat, the departments were rearranged so
that each assistant could look after a broad sphere of activity.
One ran the political department which took care of most of
the activities of the Assembly and Council as well as the Defence Commission. Two others served, respectively, the
Economic and Social Commission, and the Educational, Scientific, Cultural and Health Commission and especially the
CCTA. The fourth assistant was directly responsible for the
internal administration and operation of the Secretariat itself.

The four of them were under the overall supervision of the Secretary-General.

With the arrival of the permanent Secretary-General, the Ethiopian staff was partially replaced and supplemented by officials from other states. Gradually a broader African staff was recruited. Due to a shortage of funds and difficulties in finding suitable candidates, it grew slowly to fill the gaps in the manning tables. The Council of Ministers in Nairobi, in February 1965, decided that ultimately the personnel should consist of 250 members, two-thirds of whom would be attached to the central headquarters. At the end of the Secretary-General's first term, there were only about two hundred people working for the OAU. The lower grades, the clerical and administrative posts were rapidly filled. But the professionals and experts were harder to find. And, because of an excessively cautious policy, very few were granted a permanent contract.

But given the OAU's extremely broad and ambitious program, 250 would still be only a skeleton staff. The political division was most generously provided for but even it had trouble handling all the work expected of it. In return, the less popular divisions on economic or technical matters suffered. The few experts or officials they obtained could never have kept up with the shower of demands from the various Commissions. Only the offices of the former CCTA had a considerable number of highly qualified professionals and experts at their disposal. The general services were also faced with a mass of work and often the production of documents and the publication of records fell behind. Thus, completion of the staff and a high level of competence and dedication was a basic prerequesite to the success of the OAU.

After some hesitation, the city of Addis Ababa was chosen as the headquarters of the Organization. The choice was fitting for more reasons than one. It was due largely to the painstaking efforts of Emperor Haile Selassie and the Ethiopian Foreign Office that the Conference of Addis Ababa could be held and a Charter adopted then and there. The Ethiopian government even provided the staff and funds for the first year's operations. This contribution was decisive in getting the Organization established. Until a new headquarters building could be constructed, the OAU was installed in the former police academy, renamed the African Unity House. There it began to grow. Its status was legally fixed by the headquarters agreement signed with Ethiopia on 6 July 1965.

The Secretariat was soon busy at work for the Organization. It endeavored to spread the authority and prestige of the OAU, and to promote the various goals contained in the Charter. However, that same Charter had severely limited the initiatives it could take and it was constantly checked upon by the Council and Assembly. This weighed heavily on the top officials and the early enthusiasm of the staff threatened to give way to apathy. No one was irked more by unwillingness to tackle the many tasks than the Secretary-General. Diallo Telli had never really reconciled himself to the purely administrative nature of his post. Known for his uncompromising stands in the United Nations, he had a very strong personality. And it was not surprising that he was--as would be many of his successors--tempted to play a more active and political role.

Actually, by his mere presence at the meetings and contacts with the delegates, he could get across some of the urgent needs of the Organization. As the person who best knew the functioning of the Secretariat and who followed up the work of the OAU between conferences, he could make many worthwhile suggestions. But he could go even further. In the course of his duties, especially in the reports he submitted to the Council and Assembly, he could do more than describe the situation. By stressing the shortcomings and failures, the prospects and possibilities of future action, the Secretariat could influence decisions. Even the cold recital of facts, as when the Sanctions Bureau or another body revealed which members had, or had not, applied resolutions, could stimulate action.

However, in the political crises and the emergencies the OAU faced, there was no inclination to "let Telli do it." The primary role was usually played by the Council of Ministers or by an ad hoc committee. Nevertheless, the Secretary-General could move faster than any extraordinary session. He could also handle minor difficulties without putting the heavier machinery into operation. Often on his own, the Secretary-General began to act as the representative of the Organization and to make statements on major issues. He gradually tried to introduce an OAU presence in African affairs by accompanying missions of reconciliation, providing good offices and attending other meetings and events.

The chief weapon of the Secretary-General was the press conference. He could report on the progress of the Organization, and appear as its spokesman. In particular, when no major organ was in session or when the outcome of deliberations were kept secret, the Secretary-General was the only link between the OAU and the world. He could also speak as the conscience of a suffering or struggling Africa. By appealing to public opinion, he could even bring pressure to bear against the member states. But he could not afford to pass off the OAU's action or resolutions as more than they actually were or engage in demagogery or bluff. Above all, he could not afford to mistake the policy of his own state for that of the full membership or his own ideological convictions for those of the African people.

Any autonomous development was particularly risky since the Secretary-General could be called to order by the governing bodies at their sessions or tacitly disavowed by events. Since he had no real powers and was not entrusted with implementation, often any interference by the Secretary-General in the Organization met with irritation in the member states and any open or disguised criticism was sharply rejected. Thus, while trying to mobilize the member states and public opinion, the Secretary-General had to tread carefully.

The Council of Ministers, in particular, lost no opportunity to remind the Secretariat that its tasks were purely administrative. Occasionally, individual governments complained of an unnecessarily energetic policy. And, by and large, they managed to restrict the initiatives coming from Addis Ababa. The only serious clash arose when Diallo Telli signed cooperation agreements with the ECA and ILO without previously obtaining the authorization of the Council.[3] After that incident and as election time approached, he was increasingly prudent, although regretting the more active pioneering days.

Politically he came also to lose the backing of many of the member states. Telli's policies worried the moderates and particularly the Francophones, who found them too much aligned with radical stands, most distinctly in the Congo operations but in other matters as well. He had never really been backed by the English-speaking delegations as a whole. Therefore, before the Algiers Assembly, both groups tried to place a candidate. This time the division worked in favor of the incumbent. But the circumstances of the election in September 1968 were most painful. The OCAM states ran a candidate and blocked a two-thirds majority until the sixth ballot. This rather humiliating re-election (his Assistants were re-elected unanimously) further undermined Diallo Telli's authority and served warning that he would have to heed the wishes of all members if he expected their support.

It no longer seemed likely that the Secretary-General would play a dominant part in the work of the OAU. His leadership during the second term would certainly be less vigorous. This might well please the majority of the member states. But it did not obviate the necessity for the Organization to develop a distinct personality and create a noticeable presence on the continent. More than ever it required a trusted and dynamic person to give it a new impulse.

Notes

1. Report of the Sub-Committee on Budget, Dakar 9 Aug. 1963.

2. Secretary-General Telli's name also appears in references as Diallo Telli Boubakar.

3. François Borella, "Le Régionalisme Africain en Crise," Annuaire Français du Droit International, 1966, p. 767.

E.   The Member States

When the independent states decided to establish an organization for the continent, they carefully refrained from giving it any supranational powers.   The OAU was created to put into practice the goals and aspirations of Africa; these were laid down in the Charter.   However, aside from internal matters, none of the bodies of the OAU were actually authorized to implement the resolutions they adopted.   These powers had been reserved by the member states.   Thus, in order for the OAU to have any effect, its decisions and resolutions had to be applied by the member states.   This made them, collectively, the real foundation of the Organization and its major executive arm.   If they were willing to assume the responsibility, they could make the OAU's role on the continent and Africa's role in the world highly effective.   If unwilling to cooperate, the whole Charter would be devoid of meaning.

In order to make the Organization not only a valid spokesman but even the sole official representative of Africa, it was left open to all the independent states of the continent. Nothing seemed more dangerous to the unity and influence of Africa than the existence of splinter or rival organizations, such as existed before the summit conference.   In most cases, the principle of universality prevailed.   Still, there were certain restrictions on membership so as to make the organization truly "African."

Conditions of Membership.

The Organization was established, under Article I, as a regional body in the strict geographic sense since it was to include "the Continental African States, Madagascar and other Islands surrounding Africa."   This, however, was only the ultimate goal.   For the continent was still divided among independent states ruled by the indigenous majority, colonies and countries ruled by settler minorities.   Since the OAU was created by the former primarily as a weapon against the latter, it was obvious that neither the colonial nor settler territories could be accepted as members until they had been decolonized.

Thus it would take some time for the Organization to attain
its goal of full continental membership.

In the meanwhile, membership was open to "each independent sovereign African state." Obviously the Portuguese,
Spanish, French and British colonies were not independent and
could not be represented by the colonial powers nor by people
taking orders from them in an organization keyed for decolonization. South Africa, whose independence had been generally recognized by the world community, was also not acceptable because of an interpretation of sovereignty and independence that differed from traditional international law. Titles
acquired by discovery or colonial conquest were rejected by it
and the OAU denied recognition to South Africa until the indigenous majority ruled. Until then, rather than a state, South
Africa was for them a territory under the alien rule of a
white settler minority. Actually, it was quite simply the term
"African," which needed no definition, that excluded the colonial and settler powers from membership.

The only demand made of the African states eligible for
membership was that they "pledge themselves to observe scrupulously the principles" of the Charter. By and large, there
was no difficulty for any African state to accept this pledge.
The principles, listed under Article III, either provided the
customary guarantees of sovereignty or rules for ensuring
good relations among the members. The final principles of
decolonization and non-alignment were goals approved of by
every African state. In determining the reliability of any such
pledge, the Charter provided no basis on which the internal
policies of the states--as long as they were African-ruled--
could be scrutinized to determine whether the pledge would
actually be honored. There were also no requirements for the
internal system, i.e. that it be either democratic or peace-
loving. Therefore, as a general rule, any sort of regime was
accepted as long as it favored the African ideology.

Recently, however, there have been several delicate
cases. As the membership of the Organization spread southwards, a number of prospective members were located dangerously near the settler and colonial powers. They often had
rather close ties with the enemies of Africa and there was
some doubt they could implement the OAU resolutions calling
for sanctions and aid to the liberation movements. The issue
became more acute when the Prime Minister of Basutoland announced before independence that his government would oppose
sanctions. But he did not feel this should keep his country

from joining the OAU. For the first time there was some
reluctance among the older members to accept states which,
although not rejecting the principles, might not comply with
resolutions adopted to put them into effect. Still, in October
1966, Botswana and Lesotho became members of the organization.

A further, more difficult case was also conceivable.
The Charter of the OAU included the principle of the territorial integrity of the member states. Although no problem arose
from a change of regime, it was uncertain what the OAU and
its members would do in the event of a successful civil war.
If the Republic of Biafra, or any other break-away state, won
its independence and was eventually recognized, it would probably be able to comply with the conditions of membership.
Nevertheless, the refusal of the state it had seceded from to
accept this could create a problem of universality. For it had
rarely been possible to have both parts of a divided state
agree to membership in the same organization, even though
the rest of the members were willing to grant this.

On the basis of the above conditions, the Organization
of African Unity has grown. There was nothing like the original burst with early decolonization, when the number of independent states rose from three to the thirty-two founder members of the OAU. Nevertheless, it gradually reached towards
forty and fifty members and would eventually include every
state located on or near the continent. This expansion was
greatly facilitated by the simplicity of the procedure for admission. No formal debate was required in the bodies of the
OAU and the Charter left the older members no solid ground
on which to refuse membership. Above all, there was no veto
or even high majority vote to serve as a barrier to newcomers.

The procedure for adhesion and accession, outlined by
Article XXVIII of the Charter, was very simple. Any independent sovereign African state could, when it so desired, inform the Secretary-General of its intention to join the Organization. This request was then communicated to the member
states which merely cabled back their acceptance. As soon
as a majority had approved, the Secretary-General informed
the new state thereof and it became a member. This procedure could be followed between sessions so that the independent state was able to attend the next meeting of the OAU as a
full member.

The Charter also provided for cessation of membership.
Under Article XXXII, a state that wished to renounce its membership merely sent written notification to the Secretary-
General. One year later it automatically ceased belonging to
the Organization.

The Charter did not, however, provide for expulsion of
a member. The conditions for membership were so elementary and fundamental that there was little chance a state would
cease fulfilling them. It was hardly conceivable that a state
would stop being sovereign, independent or African. It was
also unlikely that it would openly repudiate its commitment to
the principles of the OAU. Even if it ignored them in practice, it would certainly not proclaim this formally. Nevertheless, the other states could esteem that the principles were
being violated and that the state was a threat to the Organization. The state might also have failed to pay its contributions
and become a deadweight on the others. Despite such valid
reasons, there was no way in which the membership as a
whole could force a state to withdraw. Lack of a clause on
expulsion helped guarantee the continental universality of the
OAU, but it could undermine its effectiveness in other ways.

Although not mentioned in the Charter, full membership
was not the only possibility for participation in the work of the
OAU. From the very beginning, African organizations provided a place for the liberation movements and governments-in-
exile as observers and ad hoc members. The major precedent
was the Algerian GPRA, eventually recognized by many African
states and accepted as a full member or observer at various
African gatherings. By the time of the summit conference in
1963, there were already twenty-one national liberation movements accredited as observers and they submitted a joint memorandum to the Heads of State.

The OAU maintained this tradition. The leaders of
states on the threshold of independence were able to participate
without voting. This possibility was also granted the Angolan
government-in-exile. And most of the other liberation movements were accepted as observers. This system enabled the
OAU to attain a genuine universality by having the African population of the dependent territories represented at its meetings
even before states could be formed. This also enhanced the
position of the governments-in-exile and liberation movements.
It gave them a political forum in which to speak out for their
cause and it facilitated coordination of the struggle for liberation with the independent states. The fact that many (although

not all) of these movements would eventually attain full membership if they were successful in freeing the territory and
assuming power, underscored the second advantage of the system.   This was a sort of apprenticeship for the leaders of the
future independent states.   They could learn how to represent
their countries in African organizations and be worked into the
team.

Role of the Member States: Theory ...

The Organization of African Unity was created by a
community of states extremely jealous of their sovereignty and
attributes.   It was therefore not surprising that the Charter
emphasized the powers of the states while restricting those of
the Organization.   This made the section on "rights and duties
of member states" somewhat lopsided and left considerable
doubt as to the actual extent to which the member states were
bound to support the Organization they created.

The only commitment accepted by the members of the
OAU was "to observe scrupulously the principles" of the Charter.   These principles, however, created a somewhat unbal-
anced situation.   Some of them merely confirmed the sovereignty of the member states and non-interference in their internal affairs.   Others built upon this by prohibiting attacks
against the members' territorial integrity and independence or,
more specifically, the use of subversion and assassination.
Only three principles referred to the aims of the Organization
and implied any duty of the states to fulfill them.   They were
the allusions to peaceful settlement, decolonization and non-
alignment.   However, even these principles were weakened by
calling merely for a "dedication" to the emancipation of the
dependent territories or an "affirmation" of a policy of non-
alignment.   Thus any obligation to work towards goals as opposed to merely observing principles was very weak indeed.

To make an organization a purposeful tool it was, nonetheless, necessary to have some obligation upon the members
to pursue its purposes and aims.   The Charter of the United
Nations provided this in two of its principles: "all Members
... shall fulfil in good faith the obligations assumed by them
in accordance with the present Charter" and "all Members
shall give the United Nations every assistance in any action it
takes in accordance with the present Charter ..."   More specifically, the members of the United Nations undertook "to accept and carry out the decisions of the Security Council in

accordance with the present Charter."[1]   The principal organ,
which had considerable powers in the all-important matter of
maintaining peace and security, could thus adopt measures
that were binding.

Despite this example, the Charter of African Unity imposed no obligations on the member states to act in good faith
or to comply with the decisions of the Organization.   Rather,
there was an odd discontinuity in the Charter.   According to
Article II (2), which clearly outlined the fields of cooperation,
the "Member States shall co-ordinate and harmonize their
general policies" in order to attain the ends of the Organization.   According to Article VIII, which defined the powers of
the Assembly of Heads of State and Government, that supreme
organ of the OAU was to "discuss matters of common concern ... with a view to co-ordinating and harmonizing the general policy of the Organization."   This meant that the member
states co-ordinated their own policies while the Assembly
merely co-ordinated the policy of the Organization--but not the
policies of the member states.   The essential link between the
institutions and the members was missing.

This was not an oversight.   The constant stress on
sovereignty had amply shown the position of the states.   Much
of the summit conference had been an exercise in pruning the
powers of the future organization to maintain those of the state
intact.   Sovereignty was used as an excuse for eliminating any
aspect that could infringe on the state's competences or even
influence its action.   The final outcome was that the member
states had an organization through which they could determine
a common policy although they were not obliged to implement
this policy.   In case of doubt, the principle of non-interference
was a handy means of rejecting any decision of the OAU that
seemed to be directed against a member or merely restricted
its freedom of action.

The African states were also careful to protect their
sovereignty from the influence of the other members of the
OAU.   They wished to prevent coercion, or even just leadership, by the more dynamic or stronger states.   Article V
stressed that all the member states "shall enjoy equal rights
and have equal duties."   This was reaffirmed by the basic
principles.   The principle of "sovereign equality," however,
was not merely a declaration of intention, to some extent it
was actually built into the Organization.   The Assembly and
Council were to include all the members.   The specialized
commissions also had full membership.   Even a limited body

like the Commission of Mediation, Conciliation and Arbitration
was made large enough to include almost half the members
and the Secretariat had five major officials.   Later on other
bodies, committees, or expert groups would certainly also be
broad enough to encompass many shades of opinion.   Since
the subordinate bodies were made directly responsible to the
Council and Assembly, the basic guarantee, stipulated in the
Charter, was that each member had one vote in the governing
bodies.

... and Practice.

In this case, although the Charter was intentionally
vague and imposed no obligations on the member states, the
realities of African affairs were somewhat more encouraging.
The gap between the aims of the Organization and the action
of the members or the non-compulsory nature of the decisions
of the Assembly were, of course, very serious.   An organization was still rudimentary and weak as long as it could not
impose the slightest sacrifice upon its members.   But this did
not mean that the members of their own would not be willing
to make sacrifices.

In the OAU, the Charter was the program of the member states.   All the purposes enshrined in it were deliberately
placed there because the African leaders and their peoples felt
a strong compulsion to attain them.   None of the purposes
was added merely to embellish the document.   The basic goals
of decolonization, non-alignment, peaceful inner-African relations and development in all fields were such as to command
considerable efforts from the member states whether the obligation was written into the Charter or not.   As long as these
goals were preserved there was little danger that the member
states would refuse to implement generally agreed policies.
Moreover, since the goals had almost become "sacred," there
was also some pressure from below for their fulfillment.
Even ill-informed public opinion or a poorly organized opposition could press the governments into adherence to the policies
of the OAU.   And even the members that made no great efforts would at least pay lip-service to the goals.

To avoid forcing any member to reject or violate a decision of the Organization, the various organs tried to make
their resolutions generally acceptable.   In addition, the actual
measures were rarely defined so precisely that a state could
be accused of non-implementation as such.   The resolutions

were left vague enough for each state to pride itself on progress towards their fulfillment no matter how slow this progress might be. In particular, there was a conscious effort
not to direct any resolution against a specific state. The
terms were kept general enough for no member to feel injured or have to reject a resolution as intervention in its internal affairs. Within this framework, it was possible to
count on sufficient good will among the member states to progress gradually towards a definite attainment of goals, no
matter how slow.

Although the decisions and resolutions of the Assembly
were not binding as such, there was a very real link between
the institutions of the OAU and the members. The Organization was so structured that the only ones who could clearly
take valid decisions were the Heads of State and Government
convened in an Assembly. These were the same people who
took the most important decisions in every state. The same
applied to the ministers in other organs. Thus a personal
union provided a very direct connection between the OAU and
its members. What they voted in the OAU bodies, Africa's
leaders would certainly tend to implement in their own countries. To maintain their prestige and authority they were almost compelled to do so. And this link could be far stronger
than the one between a permanent delegate and a more sophis-
ticated institution.

Fortunately, the scope for voluntary cooperation was
particularly great in Africa, since it was one of the few continents in which there was a real equality among the members. Power and influence were spread over the continent so
evenly that there was no serious threat of hegemony. Although some of the African states were outstanding in size or
population, natural resources or human abilities, economic
progress or political experience, none were ahead in all aspects. The tribal, racial and religious patterns were also so
intricate and coincided so little with the national borders that
it was hard for any one state to control the whole of an ethnic
or religious group or use it as a tool for its own policy. At
most, there were regional pace-setters, but no country or
leader could claim predominance on the continent.

In point of fact, the apparently stronger states were not
always the most influential. The advantages of having a larger area or population, or even greater wealth, could be ne-
gated by the difficulty of handling a more heterogeneous entity.
Often the powerful seemed the weakest or were prey to the

worst difficulties. Divided populations in the Congo and Nigeria led to friction and collapse. And even Egypt learned
that the position of a leader was not always enviable. For
some time to come, it seemed as if the smaller and more
compact states might be the more successful and dynamic.

The African situation was quite different from that
found in other continents and regions. Even the most powerful of the forty member states only had a few 40ths more of
the area, population or wealth of the entire continent. One
or a few African nations could never muster the relative power of the United States compared to that of its Latin American
partners in the Organization of American States or even to its
European colleagues in NATO. The Soviet Union's place in
the Warsaw Pact and Comecon or China's in the Asian continent could not be assumed by any state in Africa. Even
Egypt's role in the Arab League was greater than in the OAU.
Africa was, indeed, one of the rare places where sovereign
equality had any meaning.

In practice as well, the potential leaders (Algeria, Congo, Nigeria, UAR or others) usually avoided the limelight in
the OAU. Only President Nkrumah actively tried to mobilize
the Organization and, in so doing, he merely aroused suspicion. The experiences with "leadership" in the past had been
so bad that most of the states tried to avoid too prominent a
role. By not having leaders, the Assembly stood the chance
of being a truly collegial body influencing the course of events
on the continent. This democracy contrasted sharply with the
authoritarianism in almost all the states of the continent. But
it was very healthy for Africa to be able to discuss problems
from various points of view. Only in this way could the OAU
come up with decisions that might, to some extent, please all
the various shades and tendencies. Since there was no leader
in the OAU, every state felt that the Organization could meet
its needs, and inasmuch as all the states worked out a common policy, no state felt it bore an unfair burden.

1.   United Nations Charter, Art. 2, paras. 2 and 5, and Art.
     25.

Chapter III

Decolonization

The strongest impulse for the creation of the various continental alliances over the years had always been the desire to free all Africa from colonialism. This prime mover was also active in the efforts to form the Organization of African Unity. The link between the two was underlined by proclaiming the 15th of May, the day the OAU was founded, "African Liberation Day."

The first wave of decolonization, almost complete by the summit conference, was a glorious and uplifting struggle. With few exceptions it appeared as an inevitable movement that could not be withstood by the colonial powers and merely had to be hastened on to its goal by the African leaders. Already, by the Brazzaville declaration of General de Gaulle and the "wind of change" speech of Macmillan, leading circles in the two main colonial powers accepted the coming of independence and received the nationalists' initiatives with more or less good grace. Although obstacles blocked the path, they were not insurmountable. The only serious difficulties arose where, as in Algeria and Kenya, the settlers had a real say in the matter and the Africans had to prove their will to fight. Even then, the mother countries were able to disengage despite their own citizens.

The second wave, given considerable impetus by the OAU, did not advance with the same speed or confidence. In fact, it soon broke at various points against barriers raised by unyielding colonial and settler regimes. For the first time, Africa as a whole was faced by a resolute enemy that only scoffed at appeals and resolutions, threats and uprisings. Much more would be needed before independent Africa could conquer the last bastions of colonialism on the continent.

The OAU and Decolonization.

One way or another, all the African peoples had suffered from colonialism. For them, as indeed for most of the world, colonialism was an unnatural status that had to be replaced by the natural and just rights of liberty. The Charter of African Unity therefore proclaimed the "inalienable right of all people to control their own destiny." But this was more than a pious wish. For the most ambitious African organization was created in "absolute dedication to the total emancipation of the African territories which are still dependent" and had as its main purpose the "eradicat[ion of] all forces of colonialism from Africa."

Since this "inalienable right" was still denied millions of people on the continent, it was necessary to lay down a concrete policy of decolonization. The Organization of African Unity had made this its primary role. It was endowed with certain competences itself. However, since the methods of attaining the end were so many and varied, its major task was one of coordination. Even if it did not wield all the weapons, it endeavored to keep up a constant barrage against Africa's foes.

The spearhead of the struggle was relatively independent of the Organization. These were the wars of national liberation that had sprung up in all the Portuguese territories and were being ignited in Rhodesia, South Africa and South West Africa. Looked upon as just wars, growing out of the humiliation and indignation of oppressed people, they were a result of exasperation at having no other way of throwing off the colonial yoke. But they were also wars encouraged and supported, to some extent even orchestrated, by the community of independent African states.

The nationalist movements were largely autonomous internally and externally. The rest of Africa had little influence on their choice of leaders, strategy and tactics, military campaigns or ideology. They handled their own external relations and each movement was free to seek allies, ask recognition, establish centers or obtain military and financial backing. Unfortunately, disagreement on various aspects of these policies had created divisions in the nationalist movements and on each front there were two or more bodies with contrasting attitudes and options. Rather than forget all differences during the struggle for freedom, they promoted specific political lines and quarreled with opposing groups.

Since the liberation movements were not strong enough
to win the wars alone, they turned toward free countries in
the rest of Africa for aid. The moral obligations of states so
approached were formally accepted at the summit conference.
Many of the duties of the Organization and its member states
were indicated by the resolution on decolonization, although not
explicitly. Basically, the member states were to give nationalist movements every assistance. The refugees who fled the
colonies had to be fed and housed and the young people, educated. Those who decided to take up arms had to be equipped
and trained and then returned to the territory to continue the
fight. In practice, the heaviest burden fell upon the neighboring countries, where the nationalists were received and set up
their bases. The liberation movements were equipped and
helped by volunteers. And this backing extended even to providing access to the territories and a place to stage attacks.

Africa also pitched in as a whole. The summit conference immediately set up a special fund to give the liberation
movements the materiel and financial aid they needed to pursue the struggle. Funds were used to provide equipment and
stores, lodging, and medicine, and to create training camps.
The member states were obliged to contribute to the Freedom
Fund. But it was also desirable for outside donors to channel
their assistance through a more neutral body like the OAU.
This would help cleanse the aid and limit the direct influence
of both African and non-African sources. The summit therefore established a Co-ordinating Committee for the Liberation
of Africa, "responsible for harmonizing the assistance from
African States and for managing the Special Fund." It was to
propose the amount of the fund and its apportionment among
the member states and then distribute the practical and financial aid to the national liberation movements.

However, in view of its interest and aid, the OAU also
had an obligation to make the struggle as effective as possible.
For this reason, the Heads of State urged the freedom fighters
"to co-ordinate their efforts by establishing common action
fronts wherever necessary so as to strengthen the effectiveness
of their struggle and the rational use of the concerted assistance given them." The Committee's most delicate task was to
eliminate division and discord to make way for a broad strategy in each territory and eventually for all the fronts. Rivalry and even antagonism among the movements were often cited
as the major flaws in the struggle and discouraged active and
wholehearted support by the African community. In July 1964
in Cairo, the Council of Ministers had to regret "the continued

existence of multiple rival liberation movements ... in spite
of the efforts of the Committee of Liberation to reconcile
them." Over the years, repeated appeals had to be made for
unity, committees of good offices or individuals were sent to
reconcile and help movements cooperate or merge.

Thus the Co-ordinating Committee ended up with twin
duties. It was to coordinate aid to the liberation movements
and at the same time, using its authority and power of the
purse, to coordinate the action of the liberation movements.
It was originally a "Committee of Nine" consisting of Algeria,
Congo (Léopoldville), Ethiopia, Guinea, Nigeria, Senegal, Tanzania, Uganda and the UAR. In 1965 Somalia and Zambia
were added. Its headquarters were in Dar Es Salaam, near
the front. It was made a relatively small and compact body,
including some of the major contributors and the all-important
border states, so that it could work more efficiently. But the
Committee was responsible to the Council of Ministers and the
Assembly for its directives and budget. Since the Committee
was Africa's main tool in pursuing decolonization, it was given
considerable leeway, although its actual powers were never
clearly defined.

The Organization's second line of attack was to weaken
its foes politically and economically. Sanctions were introduced to exert further pressure. The Addis Ababa conference
had already resolved "the breaking off of diplomatic and consular relations between all African States and the Governments
of Portugal and South Africa so long as they persist in their
present attitude towards decolonization." But economic measures would be more debilitating and were viewed as a major
weapon in the struggle. The Heads of State called for an "effective boycott of foreign trade of Portugal and South Africa"
by prohibiting imports, closing ports and airports to them and
forbidding their planes to overfly the African states.

The following year, the Cairo Assembly decided to reinforce this side of the efforts by creating machinery to review the implementation of its resolutions both inside and outside Africa. This became the Bureau of Sanctions in the OAU
Secretariat. Its task was to coordinate efforts among the
member states and cooperate with friendly states towards an
effective boycott. Although it was not able to make members
or nations outside Africa apply sanctions, it could keep watch
and inform the OAU, and public opinion, of any progress or
backsliding.

The OAU and the UN.

From the outset it was evident that Africa could not
win the struggle alone. Politically, economically and militarily, it still did not have the force to overcome its enemies.
Thus OAU policy was carefully developed to put certain efforts
into motion on the continent to convince friends and allies elsewhere of Africa's will to fight. Then the OAU had to promote
and coordinate the assistance from those states and to carry
on a world campaign for decolonization.

For example, the colonial and settler powers were not
daunted by the severance of diplomatic relations. Even the
boycott had a limited impact, since independent Africa was
only a marginal trading partner (about five percent of their
trade). For this reason measures initiated by the OAU had
to be spread abroad. The summit resolution served notice on
the world that in this struggle every state had to take sides.
It pointedly "informs the allies of colonial powers that they
must choose between their friendship for the African peoples
and their support of powers that oppress African peoples."
The first test of their goodwill was to call on the governments
with diplomatic, consular and economic relations with South
Africa (and later Portugal) to "break off these relations and
cease any other form of encouragement for the policy of apartheid."

The best way of mobilizing support and obtaining action
on the international level was to work through the United Nations. And the OAU neglected no opportunity to do so. By
using the platforms provided by the various bodies of the world
organization, the delegates could keep up an almost ceaseless
battery of propaganda. Resolutions could be voted continuously
denouncing the policies of the colonial and settler powers and
committees sent off to trouble spots. Any states that did not
participate in this campaign were likely to be branded opponents or lukewarm supporters of Africa.

However, the United Nations offered much more. Under Article 41 of its Charter, measures could be introduced
"not involving the use of armed force." They could take the
form of a severance of diplomatic relations or "complete or
partial interruption of economic relations or of rail, sea, air,
postal, telegraphic, radio and other means of communications."
International isolation or an economic boycott of Rhodesia,
South Africa or Portugal would be vastly more telling than any
steps taken by the OAU. The UN could go even further. For,

if these measures proved inadequate or the boycott were ignored, Article 42 permitted a blockade of their ports.   Finally, enforcement action could be taken including "operations by
air, sea or land forces of Members of the United Nations."
The ultimate goal was thus the application of Chapter VII,
which was not only powerful but compulsory.

However, two hurdles had to be overcome before any
such action could be taken.   First it was necessary for the
Security Council to "determine the existence of any threat to
the peace, breach of the peace or act of aggression."   Although not always conceded, there was undoubtedly some threat
to the peace arising out of the situation in the dependent and
settler territories, as shown by insurrection and repression.
But the second hurdle was tougher, for all decisions on such
matters had to be taken by the Security Council where action
could be blocked by any permanent member.

Over the years, OAU policy was laid down by its political bodies: the Liberation Committee, the Council of Ministers, and the Assembly of Heads of State and Government.
The tactics for imposing this policy in the United Nations were
worked out by the African Group.   To prove they were very
much in earnest about decolonization, the OAU arranged to
have certain member states send their Foreign Ministers to
represent Africa before the world organization on each specific
issue.   This meant a smaller, more authoritative and increasingly specialized group to plead Africa's case.

The main task of the UN's African Group was to obtain
the necessary majorities in favor of African policies.   In the
United Nations, the delegates cleverly used all the levers
available to bring about a gradual escalation of resolutions.
First of all, Africa worked through a body devoted to its
cause.   This was originally the Committee on Information and,
as of 1961, the Special Committee on Decolonization and the
Committee on Apartheid.   In these overwhelmingly anti-colonial
bodies a strong stand could be taken.   When such committees
submitted their recommendations to the General Assembly, they
were usually unpalatable for some.   Still, after a bit of lobby-
ing, a compromise could be found.   Then, the next year, an
even more advanced resolution would be presented and the
former extreme proposals, now more respectable, would be
accepted.

The main difficulty was to have the resolutions of the
General Assembly adopted by the Security Council.   Here the

resistance was greater. Decisions taken by the Council were
more serious, for they had to be followed by action. And the
great powers had a built-in veto. Nevertheless, the same
process was repeated and a relatively acceptable compromise
could be adopted under pressure, only to give way to a stronger compromise the year after. Nevertheless, there were limits to how fast and how far the Security Council could be
moved. There was always a time lag. In addition, once the
Council finally introduced sanctions, certain members tended
to drag their feet until the measures were proven (or disprov-
en). Enforcement action still seemed well out of reach.

The Enemy.

        The opponents of African decolonization, as character-
ized by the OAU, included those who had not read the signs of
the time or denied their validity. They also included amenable states which, for various reasons, were merely slow to
withdraw from the continent. In this grey zone were Great
Britain, France and Spain. The territories concerned were
the High Commission Territories, Djibouti, the Spanish colonies and enclaves, and a number of islands. None of them
were specifically attacked at the summit conference. And the
first meeting of the Liberation Committee, in July 1963,
placed Britain, France and Spain in a special category: states
recognizing the right of self-determination but against which
diplomatic pressures were required to accelerate the pace of
decolonization.[1]

        A month later Madrid announced its intention of giving
the two provinces of Spanish Guinea greater economic and administrative autonomy and an opportunity to "prepare themselves to be administered and governed by their own sons."
It was also willing to return Ifni to Morocco. Although Spain's
pledges were not universally accepted by the liberation movements, which urged the OAU to introduce the full range of
sanctions or condemn the referendum in Río Muni and Fernando Póo, the Organization refused to depart from its policy of
quiet and behind-the-scenes diplomacy. It even seemed to join
in a "deal" to help Spain recover the British "colony" of Gibraltar. At any rate, by October 1968, Equatorial Guinea was
free and united.

        Britain also delivered Basutoland (now Lesotho), Bech-
uanaland (now Botswana), and Swaziland to a rather uncertain
fate as independent states in South Africa's backyard. It

liberated the island of Mauritius, later to be joined by the
French island of Réunion. But the smaller colonies, like
Djibouti, the Spanish Sahara and various islands, were in an
uncomfortable position: they were unviable alone. This
strengthened the hand of the colonial power while firing the
ambition of nearby states. Their progress toward independence was further retarded by the danger that they would be
fought over by rival "unifiers." Moreover, the high investment in liberation, especially for the islands, would have a
low yield. Thus there was a tendency to leave them until
later.

Africa preferred concentrating its efforts against the
major obstacles to decolonization, the colonial and settler powers that refused to recognize the right of self-determination.
They would be harassed by "all means" at the disposal of the
Committee including, according to Tanganyikan (Tanzanian)
Foreign Minister Oscar Kambona, armed intervention.[2] The
vast region covering most of southern Africa was the real
bastion of colonialism. Portugal, the only unrepentant colonial power, was making a last stand in its colonies. It was
joined in this battle by the settler governments in South Africa
and Southern Rhodesia. Although the rear-guard colonialists
were nowhere near as strong materially as Great Britain and
France, they were far more determined to hold their positions
and effectively slowed down or contained the drive for independence.

The first and the last of the colonizers in Africa, Portugal clung to an antiquated view of colonization and refused to
liberate its possessions. Even when faced with rebellions in
its "overseas provinces," its only reply was to send in more
and more troops to put down the disturbances and perpetuate
its rule. Not only did the Salazar regime express no prepar-
edness to withdraw, but the policy it followed actually tended
to make its control over the territories greater and commit
all later regimes to their preservation. The native inhabitants
were increasingly assimilated as Portuguese citizens and the
administration was developed to supervise or subdue them.
The system of repression was reinforced to prevent contagion
from independent Africa. At the same time, a steady stream
of peasants and workers from the metropolis brought in new
arms to work the land and, if need be, fight for it.

The situation in Rhodesia and South Africa, as well as
South West Africa under South African administration, was
even more desperate. In these countries the colonizers not

only ruled over the indigenous population, they also lived
amongst them and were solidly entrenched. Since the onset
of decolonization, the settler element had been the backbone
of resistance. This was due less to any out-dated ideology
than a thousand and one practical reasons. The settler had
his farm or business, his shop or mine in Africa. Often, indeed, Africa was his only "home."

Having held sway in Africa for generations and weathered many a storm, the settlers were simply not convinced that
white rule was doomed. For the moment they were still consolidating their hold over the countries. The military forces
and arsenals kept growing. Control of the indigenous population became a fine art and the repressive system crushed any
opposition to the regime. The policy of apartheid was an essential part of this system, for physical separation not only
put the African "in his place," it also made control and defence easier. The "krall" was strengthened and, it was hoped,
made impregnable.

Moreover, cooperation between the three was intensified.
Rather than wait for independent Africa to attack, South Africa
took the initiative. It stepped up its aid to Rhodesia and Portugal and the front became more cohesive than ever. Even
parts of independent Africa were drawn into the system as buf-
fers. Outside the continent, these powers were not forsaken
by their business partners and allies. Thus, aside from the
war effort, life went on as usual for the rulers and the end
was not in sight. As for the Africans, with increasingly
strong repression and defensive operations expanding, independence seemed more remote than ever.

Notes

1. Le Monde, 7 July 1963.

2. Ibid.

A. Portuguese Territories

The first of the European powers to explore and colonize Africa was Portugal, which had small trading stations along the western coast as early as the 1500's. Gradually it carved out one of the largest empires consisting of two major territories, Angola and Mozambique, as well as Portuguese Guinea, the Cape Verde Islands, São Tomé and Príncipe. Portugal was extremely proud of this empire twenty times its size and with a population of thirteen million, but for centuries it had reaped little aside from slave trading and countless small wars. Finally, in the mid-twentieth century, the territories began to flourish and its colonial policy seemed to be paying off. The islands had always done well and now considerable wealth had also been discovered in Angola and Mozambique. The land was farmed and mineral resources extracted, cities grew and industry developed. Several insurrections clouded the picture, but the mass of the population was still kept well in hand. This was certainly not the time to withdraw. Indeed, mentally bound to the notion that Portugal and its territories were one and that the population could be assimilated, it was hard even to conceive of relinquishing them.

The Move Away from Independence.

Portugal had little doubt that hard times lay ahead. During the years when Africans to the north were obtaining freedom, and Portugal was planning for many more years of colonial rule, Lisbon finally got around to taking positive steps to prevent contagion from the liberation movements that were coming ever closer to its territories. There was a series of reforms, belated attempts at removing abuses, and tardy bids to convince the indigenous population that it was a partner in the Lusitanian community. The primary goal of these moves was not preparation for independence, as reforms elsewhere on the continent were designed for largely, but rather to tie the territories to Portugal. That decolonization was not even envisaged for the future is evident in the rebaptization of the colonies as "overseas provinces" in 1951 and their closer integration with the mother country.

211

To put a new face on Portuguese colonialism, the old policy of assimilation was refurbished and accelerated. Although centuries of rule had resulted in major assimilation on the islands, there were only about 40,000 <u>assimilados</u> on the mainland. Salazar's Colonial Act of 1930 did little to change that although it had modernized the administration. So, in 1961, the <u>estatuto do indigenato</u> was simply abolished. From then on, theoretically at least, the natives had the same status as the Europeans. They were given equal rights under common law before the courts. Various social reforms were introduced. And there was some effort to improve education through a scheme for three years' elementary schooling.

Highest priority went to economic development. Most of these often grandiose plans were introduced to improve the position of the local Portuguese and to attract Portuguese and foreign capital. There were two six-year plans, the second of which provided $250 million for Angola and $130 million for Mozambique, largely for infrastructural and colonization projects. But an unprecedented effort came in the midst of the liberation wars, a Transitional Development Plan for 1965-67, entailing an investment of $500 million. Portugal would provide one-third of this from public funds, the rest coming from foreign investors, in which South Africa had an increasing share. Major projects included the Cassanga iron ore mines in Angola, exploitation of the huge oil reserves in Cabinda, and the scheme for building a dam on the Zambezi in Mozambique. This huge dam, located at Cabora Bassa, would be far larger than the Aswan and able to supply electricity to most of southern Africa, irrigate almost four million acres of land and promote industry and mining. Another aspect of these plans was the progressive integration of the "overseas provinces" into the economy of the metropolis. In addition, various measures were taken to reduce trade barriers within the escudo zone.

Despite this, there was no striking change in the lot of the African population. It benefitted relatively little from the economic surge except as poorly paid labor. Most of the cash farming and industry was run by the settlers or with foreign capital and much of the wealth produced was skimmed off for Portugal. Many Africans still fled to avoid heavy labor or the harsh conditions in the mines and plantations. Politically, the Africans had been given no real possibility to express their opinions or share in decisions that affected them. Elections were open only to those with a certain level of Portuguese education and even they could only vote for the one official party, the União Nacional of Prime Minister Salazar. Moreover, all important decisions were taken in Lisbon where the voice of the overseas territories was weak and, in particular, that of the vast majority of their inhabitants. For example, Mozambique sent only seven deputies to the National Assembly, of which one was black. And local administration was in the hands of Governor-Generals appointed by the government or councils elected largely by the settler population. Thus any fundamental opposition had to take extra-legal forms.

To impede this, Portugal did not neglect to accompany its reforms with a reinforcement of the apparatus of control. The courts and police force were able to supervise the territories by means of pass-cards, native labor statutes and residence restrictions. PIDE, the secret police, had an excellent intelligence system and a tight network of informers. Border inspection was designed to avoid infiltration by agitators and censorship kept the population from learning of events elsewhere. Dissenters were discouraged by imprisonment, corporal punishment and torture. Any acts of violence were crushed relentlessly.

Another major element in this move away from independence was the growing influx of Portuguese immigrants. In Angola, the white population had increased from 44,000 in 1940 to almost 200,000 in 1960; in Mozambique it went from 27,000 to 80,000 in the same period. The flow was continuing with more than 10,000 immigrants a year to these two territories.[1] Since they left behind poverty and unemployment, the new colonizers staked their future in Africa. The immigrants, as well as former soldiers, went to colonatos as peasants or to the cities and towns as merchants and workers. They also formed a huge reservoir for the white militia in defence of Portuguese rule. Some of the settlers were even more eager to avoid any withdrawal than the government and might act to influence it.

The Wars of Liberation.

Neither the reforms nor the repression were enough to make the population forsake every wish for independence. As Portuguese control became firmer, hope was often turned into despair and the efforts for independence took a particularly violent form. With no other means available there was an increasing resort to terrorist action. Soon there was rioting in Luanda and in March 1961 an uprising was unleashed in north-

ern Angola. Then the war began in earnest. Another front
was opened in Guinea in 1962 and raids occurred in Mozambique two years later. But the islands remained calm.

Until 1963, the nationalists had been rather successful
in Angola, and by the end of the year they controlled about 6
per cent of the territory. In the following years as many as
50,000 troops were sent in by the government and by 1965 the
freedom fighters were forced back in the northern region although they held on so far as they were able. In the meantime, a new front was opened in the east. During this period
the Angolan liberation armies were being turned into an increasingly effective fighting force, although they were badly
outnumbered and were less well armed than the Portuguese.
Still, they kept up an endless series of raids and ambushes
and made colonial rule a difficult matter.

The struggle in Portuguese Guinea was more of a success. Freedom fighters coming in largely from Guinea harassed the colonial troops and by the end of 1962 had cleared
an area estimated at fifteen percent of the territory. Even
10,000 Portuguese troops could not halt them and the rebels
expanded northwards and soon claimed one-third of the country. In view of this situation, the military budget was increased and Guinea was placed under a military governor. By
1965 the number of Portuguese troops had risen to 20,000 and
the rebels were slowed down. But the fighting continued and
by 1967 the liberation movement claimed to have freed over
half the territory.

Minor guerrilla incidents were reported in Mozambique
early in 1964, but there was little active resistance to the
20,000 Portuguese troops there. There was still little insurgent activity by 1965 when the Portuguese had increased their
troops to 35,000. However, the number of freedom fighters
was also growing and they were better equipped and trained.
There was some subsequent improvement in their military vantage and they gained footholds in the northern districts along
the Tanzanian and Zambian frontiers. But it was hard for
them to break out of those areas and stage attacks further
south.

In 1969, the liberation movements pursued their efforts
and at certain points made headway. Only in Guinea were the
gains really consolidated. Much of the hinterland was freed
and the Portuguese were surrounded in the cities and fortresses, often cut off from one another and scarcely able to coun-

terattack. In Angola and Mozambique the progress was harder to evaluate. The rebels often advanced on one front only to be forced back on another. Portuguese strategy emphasized the reconquering of more valuable parts of the territories, as Cabinda and northern Angola, while containing the freedom fighters in the poorer and exposed parts of eastern Angola and northern Mozambique. It remained to be seen whether the rebellions would be consolidated in those regions and bases established to launch attacks elsewhere or whether the guerrillas would be stopped and eventually pushed back. By then Portugal had between 125,000 and 150,000 troops and was receiving aid from South Africa. Thus, even if it eventually lost Guinea, the most productive parts of the empire could probably be held on the same basis for a long time.

From the start, Portugal had accepted the challenge. As each one of the insurrections broke out, Lisbon hurriedly sent in troops and gradually increased them to maintain order overseas. As long as Dr. Salazar was at the helm there was no doubt that Portugal would show the will. In August 1963, soon after Africa's defiant summit conference, he declared that the metropolis would defend the overseas provinces "to the limits of our human element and of our resources."[2] And his government gave unstintingly of both. The military effort was steadily intensified: compulsory military service was extended, the army and navy were modernized, and the military and civil defence forces in the territories were reinforced. And there was no sign of flagging when Marcelo Caetano became Prime Minister.

So far, Portugal's resources seemed adequate to support the strain of defending an empire of 800,000 square miles. Although it yearly allocated more money to its defence and security budget, reaching a peak of almost $300 million in 1969, the actual military share of the budget had fallen to average about 40 per cent. In exchange, its investors, the overseas settlers and the government itself had been drawing ever greater profits from farming, industry, mining; soon the oil wells in Cabinda are expected to turn over huge profits. Given the economic contribution the overseas provinces made, it was likely that the effort to maintain them as an integral political part of Portugal would continue in the future.

Disunited Fronts.

One of the primary reasons for Portugal's staying power was rooted less in its strength than in the weakness of its
enemies. Portugal was only a small and relatively poor European country with a long tradition of colonial rule. If it were
able to persevere, it was only because, especially under the
monolithic regime of Salazar, it could follow a harshly consistent (if costly) policy, balancing reform and repression and
adjusting military strategy to meet needs. But it was in no
position to face a popular uprising. Fortunately for Portugal
there was no massive and concerted resistance. In fact, its
opponents were badly divided. First of all, the masses of the
population had not been drawn into the struggle for liberation.
This was due partly to repression and ignorance, partly to
rule by tribal chiefs and ethnic differences. There was little
real contact between the nationalists and the general population, or understanding of the former's aims. Warfare had
often been unleashed without the preparation of the populace.
Terrorist raids meant damage and inconvenience followed by
an influx of colonial forces and punishment. As long as the
rebels were forced to attack and withdraw rapidly there was
little chance of their winning the masses to their cause or consolidating their gains. And, to the extent that they were men
from other tribes or classes and not known locally, they were
only received as outsiders. Thus, the biggest obstacles the
opponents to the regime faced were the disunity and even divisions among their own numbers.

The leading nationalist movement in Angola was the
União das Populações da Angola (UPA) of Holden Roberto. It
had its headquarters in Kinshasa (formerly Léopoldville) where
it would draw on the large numbers of refugees. Most of its
members came from nearby northern Angola and, on 15 March
1961, it launched a peasant revolt in that area. Gradually it
expanded a somewhat tenuous control over some of the territory bordering the Congo. This advance gained it considerable
prestige and after its initial successes the major rival, MPLA,
split and part joined the UPA in a Frente Nacional de Libertação da Angola (FNLA) in 1962. The next year it did not
hesitate to proclaim itself the Govêrno Revolucionário da Angola em Exilo (GRAE). And, with the help of the Adoula government, it was able to recruit and equip an army of some
7,000 soldiers.

The rival Movimento Popular para Libertação da Angola
(MPLA) had gotten off to a bad start when its insurrection in

Luanda, in February 1961, aborted. The growing strength of
GRAE, opposition from the Cyrille Adoula regime in the Congo
(Léopoldville) and quarrels among MPLA members, drawn
from urban intellectual and leftist groups, led to a slow disintegration. However, when Alphonse Massamba-Débat came
to power in Brazzaville, it was given a new chance. The
rump MPLA, led by Mario de Andrade and Antonio Agostinho
Neto, established its headquarters on the other side of the
river and formed its own army. It received considerable help
from countries like Algeria, which trained the freedom fighters
and provided equipment. But its main problem was to reach
the battle front since Congo (Brazzaville) had no frontier with
Angola proper. A first expedient was to invade Cabinda, a
small enclave nearby, but no real progress could be made
there. The second possibility was to transit through the other
Congo.

In the meantime GRAE had reached its peak and was
declining. Victories in the field became rarer as the Portuguese concentrated their strength in the strategic north. Then
the Tshombe government was much less helpful and most of
the aid was cut off during the Congolese civil war. This was
a period of unrest at the enforced inaction and there was some
dissatisfaction with Roberto's leadership. But things improved
under General Mobutu. However, GRAE was increasingly concerned by encroachment from MPLA. The latter more "revolutionary" body sought to replace it as the leading movement
and GRAE came under attack for its passiveness and alleged
desire to negotiate with Portugal. The two movements accused one another of arresting their officers and members,
and even assassinating some. The rivalry became fiercest
when MPLA tried to move into the areas that had previously
been held by GRAE. Roberto's army still controlled parts of
the north and could seal off the border. Apparently things
came to such a pass that the freedom fighters fired on one another and some of MPLA's squads were stopped or liquidated.

This friction left room for other movements as well.
There were a number of smaller groups in Kinshasa (Léopoldville) that sought some peaceful arrangement with Portugal and
a movement for Cabinda. But the major development was a
group of younger students and nationalists who were tired of
the quarrelling and futility of the established movements. They
formed the União Nacional para a Independência Total de Angola based in Zambia. UNITA rapidly became known with its
Christmas day raid on Teixeira de Sousa in 1966. It operated
in eastern Angola, often well within enemy lines. Since that

part of the country was less valuable and less well protected, its original successes were impressive.

In Portuguese Guinea there were two major liberation movements. The most important was the Partido Africano da Independência da Guiné e Cabo Verde, based in Conakry. PAIGC launched a guerrilla struggle in 1962 and its army, eventually some 5,000, made fair progress. Its rival, in Dakar, was the Frente de Libertação de la Independência Nacional da Guiné (FLING), which did not open a front and soon left the field. PAIGC's leader, Amilcar Cabral, planned a more thorough campaign than any of his counterparts and the first stage was to rouse and enlighten the people. This work occurred before, during and after operations were spread to any region. While the liberation army advanced the political wing of the movement tried to consolidate the rear. As of 1964, Cabral's forces took over de facto control of certain free zones. Schools and hospitals were set up and the people prepared for independence. The Portuguese were gradually isolated in the capital and various garrisons inland. They were on the defensive and merely tried to hold these bastions. Meanwhile, in the Cape Verde Islands there had not yet been any trouble. Although PAIGC stressed the indivisibility of the territory and had Cape Verdians in its ranks, it was uncertain when the struggle could be spread to the islands.

Originally the Frente de Libertação de Moçambique (FRELIMO) formed by Eduardo Mondlane, had been the only major movement for Mozambique. It set up headquarters in Dar es Salaam and gradually incorporated other exile groups. In September 1964, it launched a general armed insurrection. The call for an uprising was not heeded by the mass of the population and the war was carried on by trained freedom fighters. What worried Portugal most was the considerable support from Tanzania and certain communist countries. Some progress was made but the impact was eventually dulled. Although the army of 8,000 claimed to have won a fifth of the territory by the end of 1967, it was unable to penetrate into the richer southern region. Frustration over the military situation and friction among its diverse elements had led to the creation of the União Democratico Nacional de Moçambique by FRELIMO dissidents in 1963. But UDENAMO was not a serious rival until it joined with smaller groups to form the Comité Revolucionário de Moçambique (COREMO) in 1965. This movement was set up with the support of Zambia, where it was able to launch attacks and open a new front. At the same time, FRELIMO was weakened by internal rivalry and

then, in February 1969, the untimely loss of its most popular
leader, Mondlane.

There was no doubt that the various movements were
all doing some damage and gradually weakening Portugal. By
attacking at different points and working out of different states
the colonial troops were constantly being harassed and hem-
med in. These efforts could have been vastly more effective
if a common front or at least coordinated operations were organized in each territory. Unfortunately, the liberation movements refused to join forces. The only broader association
was the Conferência das Organizações Nacionalistas das Colo-
nias Portuguesas, grouping the "revolutionary" parties like
PAIGC, MPLA and FRELIMO. CONCP did provide some limited political and military cooperation among them, but it was
also a wedge between them and the more moderate movements.
Thus Portugal was allowed to play upon the antagonism by
having agents infiltrate and sabotage the liberation movements
or discrediting them with public opinion. It did not hesitate
to exploit these divisions in the field by shifting troops to halt
an offensive or wiping out a weaker enemy. And, as long as
the opponents outside were divided, there was less danger of
the rest of the population inside uniting against colonial rule.

The OAU and Liberation.

Although the wars of liberation had been going on for
years, the only decisive success was in the smallest territory
of Guinea Bissao. The most obvious reason for the slow
progress of these struggles was that Portugal could still field
more and better armed troops than the liberation armies. The
independent states were aware of this and they had committed
themselves to provide material and financial aid. Some of it
was channelled through the Freedom Fund and the rest directly
by the states. But, in view of the tremendous needs, this
seemed insufficient. At the Cairo Assembly in 1964, the leaders of GRAE and PAIGC complained of lack of support and
Holden Roberto insisted that the "aid received from independent
African countries has not permitted us to face the war as necessary."[3] He then announced that he had no choice but to
seek aid where he could find it, including the communist countries. Other liberation leaders were equally eager to use any
source available.

Assistance to the guerrillas did grow, though a smaller
portion of this aid was channelled through the OAU than had

originally been hoped. Important direct links were established
between the liberation movements and their suppliers and backers in and outside of Africa. At any rate, it soon became
clear that the stocks of modern weapons and equipment were
growing and that considerable aid was reaching the movements
in the Portuguese colonies. More and more freedom fighters
were recruited from among those who fled the colonies and
these men were relatively well trained. Still, there was no
end to the need for more and better material to meet the increasing strength of the Portuguese army. And the need only
grew as more nationalists answered the call and the liberation
forces ceased being rag-tag outfits and formed tough fighting
units.

        The less evident weakness of the liberation fronts were
the divisions which continued to plague them. The primary
task of the OAU Liberation Committee was to resolve any differences and work the liberation movements into common
fronts for each territory and even to develop an overall plan
for the Portuguese colonies. One of its first acts was to establish a good will commission to reconcile the movements in
Angola and Guinea and many similar bodies followed. This
was a formidable task. The movements were often separated
by clashing personalities. Each movement had its historical
leaders who held key posts and often provided important contacts with the supporters. None of them were eager to bow
out or accept lesser positions and the only solution for younger or more dynamic individuals seemed to be a new movement. But there were broader interests and other motives behind each leader. The movements were often recruited from
different regions and social or tribal distinctions arose. One
movement had its roots in the peasantry and another in the
city. If one were also more conservative and the other "revolutionary," it was a small step to ideological divisions which
were sharpened by the allies they found in Africa and elsewhere.

        With these very real differences it was not easy to
bring about cooperation and common fronts. Mergers were
certainly nearly impossible. Thus the Liberation Committee,
from the very beginning, tended to seek other means of operation. Instead of pressing for greater coordination among
the movements in Angola, the good will commission simply
decided to grant exclusive recognition to GRAE. The Congo
(Léopoldville) had already recognized Roberto's government and
the commission was convinced by an impressive display of its
army that this was the best fighting force. MPLA was still in

the doldrums and even its traditional backers in the OAU Committee were willing to present a unanimous recommendation that GRAE be given exclusive recognition. The idea of establishing a provisional government was very attractive to the delegates at the Council of Ministers meeting in Dakar in August 1963. To some it appeared as a visible sign of coming victory. Without considering the disadvanges if the successes ceased or another movement became more effective later on, they agreed to endorse the government-in-exile.

All the member states were urged to recognize GRAE as well and this was eventually done by many. However, rather than disappearing, MPLA was given a new chance only one month later when a revolutionary government came to power in Brazzaville. MPLA was aided and progressively strengthened by various radical countries while GRAE was inhibited by the Tshombe regime and the civil war. By November 1964, the Liberation Committee began reversing its stand and decided to divest GRAE of exclusive recognition. This was not accepted by the Council in Nairobi in March 1965. At that time the Council repeated an earlier resolution urging the reconciliation of MPLA and GRAE and it was clear that the OAU did not intend to condemn the rival. Over the years, actually, MPLA was increasingly backed by the Liberation Committee to the detriment of GRAE. Finally, in July 1968, the Committee meeting in Algiers decided to withdraw its aid from "unrepresentative" or "ineffective" movements and GRAE was included in this category. It was criticized as being less representative than MPLA and asked to become a more "authentic" movement. GRAE was also no longer regarded as a "government." But this decision had no effect on Kinshasa (Léopoldville) which continued its backing of GRAE and refused to open its frontier to MPLA. The decision was also not confirmed by the Heads of State two months later. And the question of OAU support therefore remained open.

The situation in Guinea had never been as painful. The good will commission had also decided not to press for a reconciliation between PAIGC and FLING and it recommended exclusive recognition for PAIGC. Although the point was carried in the Liberation Committee, Senegal managed to block it at the Dakar Council and to obtain recognition of FLING as well. Both movements thus had the support of the Committee and shared the assistance, with much the greater share going to PAIGC. The Nairobi Council decided to look into the matter again and appointed a small military commission of enquiry to visit the front. Although it found that PAIGC was the only

movement actively fighting and recommended that it receive
exclusive recognition, FLING was saved again by Senegal.
But this rivalry had little effect on the campaign in the field
and PAIGC was able to advance smoothly.

The situation in Mozambique was at first the most
satisfactory. Originally the only independent neighboring state
was Tanzania and its government backed FRELIMO solidly,
while discouraging any opposition groups. It had no trouble
having the Liberation Committee grant exclusive backing and
aid. However, when Zambia became independent, joined the
Committee and helped establish COREMO, things changed somewhat. Fortunately, Tanzania and Zambia were on good terms
and the relations between the freedom movements could be developed in relative harmony.

The situation in the three territories also had serious
consequences for the Liberation Committee's general strategy.
The first war was launched in Angola and it made fair headway during the early years. Angola was also the prize colony
and victory there would seriously undermine Portugal's will.
However, the difficulty of the struggle and Lisbon's urge to
resist were underestimated, especially in Angola, where the
largest contingent of troops was sent. Division on the front
also weakened the drive and the Committee's priority to GRAE
turned out to be unwise. More successful struggles were being waged in the poorer colonies like Guinea and Mozambique
where, in addition, there was much less division in the ranks
of the freedom fighters.

The UN and Portugal.

Despite considerable efforts, the liberation movements
were not able to turn the tide. Other forms of pressure were
necessary and the Addis Ababa summit conference had introduced economic and diplomatic sanctions. It decided that the
members should sever their diplomatic and consular relations
and apply an "effective boycott" against Portugal. However,
these measures were not always implemented forthwith. The
year after, trade with Portugal was still three percent of independent Africa's total trade. Similarly, not all the states
had broken off their relations. Thus the Council of Ministers
in Cairo found it necessary "to impress on all African States
that it is indispensable to implement in all its aspects the decision ... to boycott Portugal."

Although not commendable, the position of certain African states was understandable. For countries like the Congo, Malawi and Zambia, an abrupt or complete severance of relations would be expensive and even perilous. Landlocked and largely surrounded by enemy territory, they depended on Portuguese ports for access to the sea. Katanga's wealth had to transit through Angola; that of Malawi and Zambia, through Mozambique. Their economies would be hurt far more by sanctions than Portugal. Therefore, at the Cairo Assembly, President Hastings Kamuzu Banda of Malawi reminded the other Heads of State of his difficulties and publicly refused to break off relations with Portugal.[4] Moreover, it was necessary to remember that even if the remaining trade could be eliminated, this would not have been a crippling blow. No boycott would be a success unless the rest of the world, and especially the main trading nations, were brought into line. For this reason the OAU increasingly worked through the United Nations.

Although the United Nations had been dealing with the situation in the colonies for some time already, it had made little progress.[5] Portugal staunchly claimed that the "overseas provinces" were part of its national territory and rejected any intervention in internal matters. It could not be made to register them as non-self governing territories nor to provide information. Not until the UN's Declaration on Granting Independence and, more particularly, the start of guerrilla warfare in Angola in March 1961, was there any serious action to change the situation. By April, the General Assembly called upon Lisbon to introduce measures and reforms to prepare Angola for independence and established a sub-committee to study the "ways and means" of obtaining compliance with the Declaration. But the situation only worsened and, in December, the General Assembly had to admit Portugal's unwillingness to cooperate and request its members "to deny Portugal any support and assistance which it may use for the suppression" of indigenous elements.[6]

As Portugal brutally put down the rebellion in Angola, there was increasing preoccupation with the condition of the people. In January 1962, the United Nations General Assembly reaffirmed the inalienable right to self-determination of the Angolan people and called upon Portuguese authorities to desist from repressive measures. The Security Council, however, tried to avoid being drawn into the matter. It eventually debated the situation but refused to take a strong stand against Portugal or envisage independence. Still holding the initiative,

the General Assembly urged immediate independence for Angola twice in December 1962. It asked Portugal to hold free
elections and negotiate with the representative political parties.
The General Assembly also requested the Security Council to
take appropriate measures, including sanctions, to secure
Portugal's compliance with the resolutions.[7] But Lisbon only
intensified the military repression.

The creation of the Organization of African Unity led to
a new burst of activity. Only one month after Addis Ababa,
the Committee on Decolonization prodded the Security Council
to consider the possibility of introducing sanctions. In July
1963, at the request of thirty-two African states, the Security
Council met and laid down basic UN policy. It denied that the
"overseas provinces" were part of the metropolis and called
upon Portugal to recognize immediately their right to self-
determination and independence, to cease repressive measures
and withdraw its military forces, to grant a political amnesty,
and to negotiate with nationalist groups "with a view to the
transfer of power." Moreover, although not yet a "threat,"
the situation in the territories was regarded as "seriously disturbing peace and security in Africa" and all states were requested not to offer any assistance, including arms and military equipment, enabling Portugal to continue its repression.[8]

Quite unexpectedly, Portugal seemed to change its
stance and at least expressed interest in a clarification of the
resolutions. There were brief and confidential discussions
with the African states at the United Nations but it did not
take long to discover the misunderstanding. Portugal conceived of self-government as participation of the peoples in the
given structures and not as determination of the structures
themselves. Whereas it might have been willing to introduce
some limited reforms in its "provinces," it would not accept
any desire to modify the structures or seek independence.
The calm during the negotiations was prolonged by the troubles
in the Congo.

Finally, when the campaign was resumed in June 1965,
the African states tried to make up for lost time. Since the
Council resolution (as obviously also the Assembly resolutions)
were not compulsory, they were scarcely heeded by Portugal
or its allies and trading partners. Therefore the Committee
on Decolonization called upon the Security Council "to consider
putting into effect against Portugal the appropriate measures
laid down in the Charter, for the purpose of carrying out its
resolutions."[9] Although the Afro-Asian group demanded a boy-

cott of all Portuguese imports and exports, the Security Council would not go any further. In November, it again requested all states not to offer any assistance or permit the sale and supply of arms and military equipment to Portugal. But this was not made mandatory.[10]

Somewhat as a reaction to this failure, the General Assembly adopted its most far-reaching resolution on the Portuguese territories in December 1965. It appealed to all states to render the necessary moral and material support to the peoples so as to restore their inalienable rights. Portugal was condemned for bringing in large numbers of immigrants and sending workers to South Africa. The measures urged against Portugal included the severance of diplomatic relations and boycott of all trade, the closing of ports and airports, the refusal of military aid and other aid enabling Portugal to continue its repression of the African populations. Lastly, the United Nations High Commission for Refugees (UNHCR) and the relief agencies were asked to increase their assistance to the refugees.[11]

Although this was an impressive resolution, it was purely voluntary. It merely summed up all the demands put forward thus far in the United Nations. It was also a good reflection of the OAU stand. Indeed, the resolution even asked that moral and material support be provided in cooperation with the Organization of African Unity. Since the General Assembly had now gotten into step with the OAU, the Assembly of Heads of State in November 1966 found it unnecessary to present an original resolution of its own. It simply noted that Portugal

> ... continues to defy the resolutions of the United Nations Security Council and General Assembly calling for the recognition of the right of the peoples of the territories under its domination to self-determination and independence and continues to wage colonial wars.

Then it called on all states to implement the Security Council and General Assembly resolutions.

NATO under Attack.

The campaign for sanctions was far from over. Unless they were fully complied with or made mandatory they could

hardly change the position of Portugal. Therefore Africa repeatedly urged broader and stricter measures and it did not
take long to locate the center of resistance. From then on
Africa directed its energy towards overcoming the reluctance
of certain Western states. The offenders were under attack
for several reasons. First, as members of NATO they provided Portugal with arms and equipment. Secondly, as major
trading nations, they made any boycott illusory. And, thirdly,
as permanent members of the Security Council, they prevented
the adoption of compulsory sanctions.

The key states had already been criticized by the first
meeting of the OAU Council of Ministers in August 1963, only
a month after the major debate in the United Nations. The
Dakar resolution "deplores the position taken by the delegations of the United States, the United Kingdom and France during the debates in the Security Council on the questions of
Portuguese colonialism."

However, it was not until two years later that the battle was carried to the UN itself. In its resolution of 10 June
1965, the Committee on Decolonization for the first time singled out and requested the

> ... military allies of Portugal within the framework
> of NATO ... [to] refrain from supplying arms and
> munition and all other forms of assistance so long
> as the Portuguese Government fails to renounce its
> policy of colonial domination. [12]

In December the General Assembly also made special reference
to NATO in its resolution.

Still, as long as East-West relations did not improve
sufficiently to weaken the NATO ties and Western reliance
thereon, there was little chance of preventing the transfer of
arms to Portugal. And, as their ally, Portugal was not without its own means of pressure on the Western states. Portugal and its territories were an integral part of the Western
(and Asian) trading world and a very important supplier or
client. Its partners were loath to cut these ties and the misgivings were strongest in private circles which appreciated the
good profits and investment opportunities in the territories.
They would not heed any mere appeals not to do business with
Portugal and they tried to reinforce their governments' distaste for boycotts.

Success on this front was therefore far from brilliant. There was some restriction of arm sales while Portugal sought other suppliers. It was hard to determine the ultimate use of equipment received through NATO and Lisbon began purchasing certain articles from France and Germany. Economic sanctions were even less successful. Trade and investments kept on rising, Angola and Mozambique supplied or obtained goods from the United States, Great Britain, Germany and even India, and investments came from Europe, America and increasingly South Africa.

When it came to trade, Africa was particularly weak and had no real means of pressure either on governments or private companies. Therefore it worked largely on the diplomatic level trying to convince or brow-beat Western and other states into ceasing certain beneficial relations with Portugal. The battle was still mainly verbal and, despite the summit ultimatum, Africa had not worked out any policy for making the nations of the world choose between it and its enemies. Most offensives were undertaken in the United Nations, where the permanent members and others who blocked measures desired by the OAU came under fire from the African delegates. Steps were also taken to mobilize the Decolonization Committee and the General Assembly to propose African solutions and press them on the Security Council. In 1966, the General Assembly tried to get the Security Council to make the implementation of the Assembly's 1965 resolution "obligatory." Once again, it failed.

Signs of Hope.

For the first time in decades there came in 1968 a political development in Portugal possibly having some effect on this "stalemate." Portugal's colonial policy had been inspired and wielded firmly since 1930 by António de Oliveira Salazar. The will to hold and integrate the "overseas provinces" had come from him. Going against the currents of the modern day, he committed Portugal to the gigantic task of maintaining order and ensuring "normal" conditions in the territories. This was done at great cost to his own country and in spite of much of the world's disapproval and discouragement. A significant question had always been whether, with his passing, Portugal would continue the effort. But the question did not become topical until 26 September 1968, when Dr. Salazar was replaced.

The reply was not long in coming. The new Prime Minister, Marcello Caetano, announced the day after his accession that he would continue his predecessor's policy. He pledged "to neglect nothing, one single moment, to defend the overseas provinces." As in the past:

> ... the armed forces watch over the vast Portuguese territory and in certain parts of this territory they are fighting and struggling against an insidious enemy, legitimately defending the life, security and work of those who stand in the shade of our flag. Law and order is the essential condition so that the honest people can live normally; law and order shall be maintained inexorably.[13]

Without denying the principle enunciated above, Caetano admitted that all life required adaptation. The nature of this adaptation was left open. Judging by his first acts any changes were likely to be minimal. Four of the leading ministers involved in Portugal's colonial policy were maintained in their posts, those for foreign affairs, overseas provinces, finance and armed forces. Later on he stressed that the disappearance of one man would not change everything. The maintenance of Portugal's presence in Africa "is not due, as many people believe, to the personal intransigency of Dr. Salazar, but to the fact that no other attitude is possible." Portugal, the Prime Minister insisted, "is responsible for the security of its populations and cannot abandon its sons, whatever their race and color may be, to the vicissitudes of violence, hatred and international political intrigues." For him, the nationalists in Angola, Mozambique and Guinea were only terrorists who would have collapsed long ago if they did not receive moral and material aid from the neighboring states and help from Soviet, Chinese and Cuban instructors. Portugal's presence in Africa was essential to the defence of Western Europe and the Americas most particularly at a time when the USSR was seeking military bases in the Middle East and North Africa.[14]

Nevertheless, there was something new in the air. This was sensed and interpreted by each in his fashion and in the OAU it seemed a precursor of victory in the field. The policies of Portuguese colonialism and the will to resist every onslaught had been closely attached to the name of Salazar. There was a tendency to presume that soon the military efforts would slacken and that the troops would not be able to hold back the wars of liberation. For the first time in years,

there was satisfaction with the military situation at the Algiers Council in September 1968. The greatest progress had
been made in Guinea but there were also hopeful signs in
Mozambique and eastern Angola. This moved the Council to
"congratulate the African nationalists on their continued progress in the legitimate struggle for the liberation of their
countries." There was even some thought of the post-war
period when the states would be independent and it appealed
to the members to grant additional material assistance to the
liberation movements "to enable them to restore the economy
and organize the lives of the populations in the liberated
areas."

This success may have pushed Portugal to acts of desperation. For the wars were becoming particularly bitter and
the OAU Council of Ministers condemned

> ... the odious crimes of genocide committed by
> Portugal, in flagrant violation of the United Nations
> Charter, through the use of napalm, poison gases
> and other weapons against African peoples fighting
> for their freedom and independence.

Portugal now hesitated less before sending its troops into independent states in pursuit of the freedom fighters or even
bombing camps and villages or exercising other reprisals.
There had been several complaints before the Security Council
from Senegal and Guinea. The Congo (Kinshasa) and Zambia
had also suffered damages. And a sharp warning had been
issued to the Congo (Brazzaville). Thus the OAU further condemned Portugal for acts of aggression against states adjacent
to the territories under its domination.

The United Nations also expected a change. Over recent years it had not been very active and the resolution of
1966 echoed that of 1965, while the resolution of 1967 was a
slight variation on that of 1966. This time, however, the General Assembly proceeded to pass an unusually moderate resolution in the hope that the new government would adopt a different colonial policy. The only innovations of the resolution
of 29 November 1968 were, following the lead of the OAU, to
appeal to all states to prevent the recruitment and training of
mercenaries for use in the colonial wars and to urge the Portuguese government to apply the Geneva convention on prisoners of war in the armed conflicts in the territories. For the
rest, there was the usual demand that the territories be granted independence "without delay," an indication to the Security

Council that the situation was serious and aggravated the explosive situation in southern Africa and the appeal to all
states, especially those of NATO, to refrain from giving Portugal any assistance enabling it to pursue the colonial wars.

Nevertheless, there were valid reasons to wonder
whether any real change was imminent. The progress of the
freedom fighters was encouraging but not decisive and even
the fall of Portuguese rule in Guinea, the least valuable of the
territories, would not lead Portugal to relax its efforts in Angola and Mozambique. The initial impact might even be setbacks on these fronts if the 25,000 troops in Guinea were
transferred there. The United Nations seemed to expect a
change of heart in the new government and a chance to negotiate an improvement in the colonies. But Portugal had not
taken any initiative along these lines and its allies could make
no promises. Indeed, the General Assembly resolution came
after the statements of Prime Minister Caetano announcing that
Portugal would persevere. Hope was not entirely unfounded in
either case, but it remained to be seen whether it would be
fulfilled.

Notes

1. James Duffy, "The Portuguese Territories," in Colin
    Legum's Africa--A Handbook, p. 292.

2. The Times (London), 13 Aug. 1963.

3. The New York Times, 21 July 1964.

4. The Times (London), 21 July 1964.

5. See Patricia Wohlgemuth, The Portuguese Territories and
    the United Nations.

6. General Assembly Res. 1699 (XVI), 19 Dec. 1961.

7. Ibid. 1807 (XVII), 14 Dec. 1962 and Ibid. 1819 (XVII), 18
    Dec. 1962.

8. Security Council Res. S/5380, 31 July 1963.

9. United Nations Doc. A/AC.109/124, 10 June 1965.

10. Security Council Res. 218 (1965), 23 Nov. 1965.

11. General Assembly Res. 2107 (XX), 21 Dec. 1965.

12. United Nations Doc. A/AC.109/124, 10 June 1965.

13. Le Monde, 29 Sept. 1968.

14. Ibid., 29 Nov. 1968.

Colonial and Southern Africa

B. Rhodesia

Rhodesia was a country about one-and-a-half times the size of Great Britain, largely in the highlands, and separated from the sea by Mozambique. Its population consisted of some 200,000 white settlers and over four million Africans. Nevertheless, the whites, who had gained control over the Africans by conquest, divided the whole very much in their favor. Even after the reforms they owned almost half the land, including the best farming areas and ran the mines and the rest of the economy. The country had proven to be rich and the settlers were loath to cede their share to the rest of the population or divide it with them on any but their own terms.

A Country Divided Against Itself.

For centuries the region, formerly the site of the Zimbabwe empire, had belonged to the Mashona people. But driven by tensions further south, caused by an expansion of the white communities, the more warlike Matabele invaded and eventually dominated it. Not long after, the white settlers and "pioneers" erupted into the area in search of more land and wealth and the country was acquired by Cecil Rhodes, by ruse and force, in 1890. The Crown confirmed this by granting his British South Africa Company a Royal charter under which it administered the territory for three decades. There was staunch resistance from the dispossessed Africans, mainly the Matabele, who launched repeated attacks and were joined by the Mashona in the latter phases of the war. However, by 1897, native power had been broken and the settlers ruled over the country in peace. Government was established to meet their needs while the Africans were supervised through the local, salaried headmen.

However, due to abuses, the Crown took over the control although leaving the settlers considerable autonomy. From 1923 on Southern Rhodesia had an unusual status as a "self-governing colony." Under this system Britain retained certain reserved powers, mostly to avoid racially discriminatory laws, and theoretically also the power to suspend the constitution.

Aside from that, the country went very much its own way under the direction of governments elected by the white minority.
Moreover, the settlers tried to extend their influence northwards through the creation of the Central African Federation
in 1953.

Nevertheless, as the rest of Africa became independent,
there were also signs of change in Southern Rhodesia. Under
the chairmanship of Commonwealth Secretary Duncan Sandys,
a constitutional conference was held in February 1961 to update the system of government. The reserved powers were
relinquished but a Declaration of Rights was entrenched in the
constitution and a Council of State was set up to review proposed legislation. An Assembly of 50 upper-roll and 15 lower-
roll seats was introduced to provide representation for the Africans. However, the high income and property qualifications
meant that, in practice, the whites (200,000 population) chose
all the A-roll seats and the blacks (4 million), the B-roll
seats. Any improvement in their position through the electoral
machinery would be long in coming. This timid reform was
widely approved by the Europeans but vehemently rejected by
the nationalists.

Still, the path seemed open for a gradual evolution towards a democratic state, i.e. one in which the black majority would rule. There was talk of partnership and a new deal.
The first real overtures were made before the crucial elections of December 1962. Sir Edgar Whitehead, leader of the
United Federal Party, went out on a limb and proposed the
elimination of racial discrimination, repeal of the Land Apportionment Act and a gradual integration of the races. He envisaged a slow transfer of power to the African electorate
and admitted the inevitability of majority rule in 15 years.
Winston Field's newly formed Rhodesian Front rejected this
platform and, indeed, any participation of the Africans in government. The nationalists demanded immediate majority rule
and eventually boycotted the elections. The reply of the white
minority was to turn towards the more conservative party.
The settler community had become increasingly worried by the
wave of independence that was advancing towards Rhodesia.
And they gave the Rhodesian Front a 2 to 1 majority.

As the other members of the Central African Federation, Northern Rhodesia and Nyasaland, moved towards independence in 1963, there was increasing concern about the future of Southern Rhodesia and demands for its independence as
well. The aim was to become independent with a white minor-

ity government in order to forestall any attempt by London to
impose African control. The struggle split the cabinet and
Field was eventually forced to resign. He was replaced by
Ian Smith, a man who claimed that black majority rule would
not come during his lifetime and committed himself to achieve
independence even unilaterally. In order to determine his
support, a referendum was held in November 1964 on whether
the (white) electorate favored independence under the 1961 constitution. The response was an overwhelming "yes."

All the while the nationalist movement had been growing. After its two precursors had been banned by the government, a third party, the Zimbabwe African Peoples Union was
formed in 1961. It was similar to other movements throughout Africa, with much the same goals and following. It also
attracted some of the more liberal whites, including former
Prime Minister Garfield Todd. But, in August 1963, there
was a falling out between ZAPU leader, Joshua Nkomo, and
some of his earlier supporters. Although the flaming oratory
of Nkomo held the crowds, many of the older leaders and intellectuals left and formed the Zimbabwe African National Union, with the Reverend Ndabaningi Sithole at its head. Despite serious disagreement on leadership and tactics, both nationalist parties insisted that their aim was equality and "one
man, one vote." To cut this threat short the Rhodesian government had many of the nationalists, including Nkomo and
Sithole, arrested and placed under detention.

Still, the Smith regime was not without allies in the
African camp. Working through the tribal chiefs and headmen,
it managed to maintain relative calm among the masses of
tribalized Africans and to isolate them from the contamination
of "Uhuru." In October 1964, Smith was able to call an "in-
daba" in which they even expressed approval of his course.
In addition, Rhodesia was still divided among the Mashona (70
per cent of native population), the Matabele (20 per cent) and
non-local Africans (10 per cent) who worked on the farms and
mines. Finally, along with ZAPU and ZANU, there was also
a legal opposition elected to the Assembly by the Africans who
could and would vote. Although the United Peoples Party was
repudiated by the nationalists, it did not become an apologist
of the regime.

Let Britain Do It!

In view of this disturbing situation, the independent
states of the continent tried to counter Smith's drive for an
"independence" that was the complete opposite of the one they
desired.   Since Southern Rhodesia was still theoretically a colony, they turned to the mother country.   At the summit conference which founded the OAU in May 1963, the United Kingdom was urged "not to transfer the powers and attributes of
sovereignty to foreign minority governments imposed on African peoples by the use of force and under cover of racial legislation."   Later, a resolution asking the United Kingdom not
to transfer sovereignty or military forces to the Rhodesian
Government was initiated by the Decolonization Committee and
brought before the UN Security Council.   Although it was
vetoed by the United Kingdom as interfering with its domestic
jurisdiction, a similar one was adopted by the General Assembly in November 1963.

However, by rejecting the competence of international
bodies, Great Britain accepted the sole responsibility for what
happened in Southern Rhodesia.   It placed itself in the line of
fire between the settlers and their enemies.   Henceforward the
resolutions of the OAU and the demands of the world community were directed at the "colonial power."

As the crisis deepened, the Council of Ministers in Lagos, in February 1964, noting the "critical and explosive situation" in Rhodesia, demanded that the British government "prevent effectively the threat of unilateral independence or subtle
assumption of power by the minority settler regime."   To
guarantee the country's future, it was also asked to convene
a "fully representative Constitutional Conference of all parties
in Southern Rhodesia to decide on the granting of immediate
independence to Southern Rhodesia on the basis of 'one man,
one vote'."   If this were not done, the OAU asked its members to "reconsider their diplomatic and other relations with
Britain."

Here, Britain's bluff was called.   For its control over
Rhodesia was more theoretical than real and it shrank from
using force, the only means of imposing any policy on the
white minority.   However, when the Labour Party came to
power, it took a stronger and clearer stand and one of its first
acts was to warn Smith that a declaration of independence
would be met by full economic sanctions.

For some time the front was rather quiet. The opponents of the Rhodesian regime, the OAU included, merely reiterated previous demands but took no concrete steps. Then, in April 1965, things took a turn for the worse. Smith decided to press the issue. To test his backing, he dissolved the Legislative Assembly and called new elections in order to receive a mandate for unilateral independence. In May, he obtained a clean sweep of the upper-roll seats. The white minority was solidly behind him and was willing to risk seizing independence. Again the elections were largely boycotted by the Africans.

There was a burst of activity in the international organizations. The Decolonization Committee had called on Britain to take urgent and immediate measures to cancel the elections. It was asked to prevent the transfer of military force to Rhodesia and all states were requested to refrain from supplying arms, economic or financial aid to Rhodesia.[1] Public opinion was exacerbated soon after, when a Rhodesian White Paper implied that the United Kingdom would not fully implement sanctions or, even if it did, the economy would not be drastically affected. By June the move had reached the Security Council, which urged all states not to accept unilateral independence and called on Britain to take action to prevent it. At the Extraordinary Council in Lagos, in June 1965, the OAU joined in and called on the British government "to meet its responsibilities" and replace the 1961 constitution with a new one founded on universal suffrage.

The tension reached its peak in October 1965, when Smith indicated he would not wait much longer. On 4 October he went to London to negotiate independence. There the British government insisted he meet certain conditions, namely an improvement in the political situation of the Africans, the end of racial discrimination and gradual progression towards a majority government. On 25 October, in a last minute effort, Prime Minister Wilson flew to Salisbury. But no agreement could be reached.

However, by even negotiating with Smith, Britain laid itself open to charges of ignoring if not betraying African interests. The mood at the OAU Assembly in Accra was clearly one of distrust. The same day that Wilson left for Salisbury, the African Heads of State adopted a statement directed at "the administering power having sole responsibility for the present situation." It deplored Britain's refusal "to meet with firmness and resolution the threat of a Unilateral Declaration

of Independence" and to state categorically that it would only
grant independence on the basis of a majority government.
Once again, Great Britain was urged to suspend the 1961 constitution and to "take all necessary steps including the use of
armed force to resume the administration of the territory."
It was also asked to release the political prisoners and hold a
constitutional conference to obtain universal adult suffrage,
free elections and then independence.

To the very end the fiction of British control over the
situation was maintained and the Assembly resolved that, if
the United Kingdom did not take these measures, it should "reconsider all political, economic, diplomatic and financial relations between African countries and the United Kingdom Government in the event of this government's granting or tolerating
Southern Rhodesian independence under a minority government."
This was a clear enough warning what might happen if Wilson
accepted a compromise rejected by the Africans.

An Alternative Policy.

A second line of policy had already been envisaged for
the OAU at the 1963 summit conference. This was to support
the movements of national liberation and, if power was usurp-
ed by the white minority, the African states were to give

> ... effective moral and practical support to any
> legitimate measures which the African nationalist
> leaders may devise for the purpose of recovering
> such power and restoring it to the African major-
> ity.

Unfortunately, at first the OAU Liberation Committee had assumed that Southern Rhodesia was among the territories that
would be given independence by the colonial power and it received low priority. Eventually the Committee realized its
mistake and hastily tried to strengthen the liberation movements.

However, aside from the slow start, the nationalists
faced a particularly difficult situation. Repression in the country was already strong. The two principal movements had
been banned and the leaders and many of their followers were
in detention camps. The Smith regime used and reinforced
the Unlawful Organizations Act and the Law and Order (Maintenance) Act to inhibit political or other action against the re-

gime. And the Preservation of Constitutional Government Act
made the death sentence mandatory for a wide range of of-
fences. The centers of opposition had no choice but to move
abroad. Then the parties had to convert from basically political to primarily military bodies. Finally they could start
training forces and open a front.

But any guerrilla struggle would be terribly hazardous.
Rhodesia had a professional army of 3,400 men and paramilitary (police) formations with 6,400 men on active service and
28,500 reservists. They were well equipped and trained and,
in case of direct military action, much of the white population
could be mobilized to meet the enemy. The air force of 900
men had a fair number of modern aircraft, including jet fighters, bombers, transport planes and helicopters.[2] Special
units of the police had been prepared to put down riots and
disturbances in the country and considerable forces were sent
to the frontier to bar the way to any freedom fighters trying
to enter from independent Africa. The Rhodesians knew the
terrain and the local population and would put up deadly resistance to any attacks from inside or outside.

The Africans were the overwhelming majority of the
population. It seemed that the tiny settler community could
not resist them for long. The Africans were badly divided,
however; many were still tribalized and obeyed their chiefs
more readily than a nationalist party. And the main handicap
was still the split in the nationalist ranks. There was growing
rivalry between ZAPU and ZANU and the differences in tendency, one more radical than the other, made it harder for them
to agree on joint action. They had somewhat different tribal
and class compositions as well. The most noticeable clash
was between the leaders of these two parties. Joshua Nkomo
and the Reverend Sithole not only refused to cooperate, they
even refused to meet with one another, and quarrels divided
their followers along the line. This division made it difficult
for them to form a common front. It also discredited them
abroad and left the settler regime considerable room for maneuvre at home. The OAU, also uncertain which movement to
support, hesitated.

The Organization of African Unity had repeatedly promised to back the nationalists. At the Cairo Assembly, in July
1964, it even pledged to recognize and support a government-
in-exile. It called on the nationalist movements to "intensify
their struggle for immediate independence." But, first it had
to end the rivalry. The Liberation Committee sent a small

committee to try to heal the rift in August 1964, in vain. The
Lagos Council in June 1965 still expressed deep concern at the
gulf between ZAPU and ZANU and "their refusal, despite all
attempts by the OAU, to form a common front against the
present Salisbury regime." It asked several nearby countries
to help the two movements form such a front and a ministerial
committee made a last minute bid to bring ZAPU and ZANU
together. At the end of July it explored the possibilities of
joint action with the leaders in exile. However, although
ZANU was prepared to discuss cooperation, ZAPU "refused to
meet the other party."[3]

Ian Smith had already intimated that independence was
near and Africa feverishly prepared to meet it. This was the
main concern of the Accra Assembly in October 1965. Aside
from the usual appeals to Great Britain, the Heads of State
seemed to be keenly aware that Africa would have to act as
well. They warned that they would "use all possible means
including force to oppose a unilateral declaration of independence." First priority went to a liberation front in Rhodesia
and they pledged to give "immediate assistance to the people
of Zimbabwe with a view to establishing a majority government in the country." To coordinate all efforts they established a Committee of Five to study and take all necessary
measures to effectively implement the resolution.

Before and after the Assembly there was a flurry of
diplomatic activity as Africa appeared to prepare for all even-
tualities. The Secretary-General of the OAU went from capital to capital. Before Accra he announced that, in case of
UDI, the member states would meet immediately to agree on
positive measures and would recognize and aid a nationalist
government. After the Assembly, he was highly optimistic.
The resolution, he claimed, "answers perfectly the situation"
in Rhodesia. "The people of Africa will be proud of the leaders when they learn of the decisions which have been taken."
But there seemed to be something more. For the OAU "had
not merely adopted a resolution, it had taken concrete action."[4]
What that action was he refused to divulge, but Africa seemed
ready.

UDI - Britain Pays the Bill.

On 11 November 1965, the bubble burst as Ian Smith
solemnly proclaimed a Unilateral Declaration of Independence
for Rhodesia. At the same time a new constitution replaced

that of 1961. It was rather similar but relieved the Legislative Assembly and government of any constraint from the
Crown, including the prerogatives of the Governor and the
right of appeal to the Privy Council, and permitted amendment by a two-thirds vote. This news was accepted quietly by
most of the population, although there were some disturbances
and strikes. They were put down and things rapidly returned
to "normal." The state of emergency was declared and repeatedly extended. Censorship was introduced and communications and movement in and out of the country were strictly
regulated. The Smith regime had things well under control.

In Britain, immediately after UDI, Prime Minister Wilson denounced the "purported declaration of independence ...
as an illegal act" and reiterated that Parliament was the "only
legal authority" that could grant independence. He called it
"an act of rebellion" and stated that his government would have
"no dealings with the rebel regime."[5] A series of economic
sanctions were imposed: embargo on the export of arms and
capital, special exchange restrictions, denial of access to the
London capital market, suspension of Commonwealth trade
preferences, ban on purchases of tobacco and sugar. The
British High Commissioner was withdrawn from Salisbury and
the Rhodesian High Commissioner in London was asked to
leave. Then, on orders from the Queen, the Governor of
Southern Rhodesia, Sir Humphrey Gibbs announced that Smith
and the other ministers ceased to hold office and would be
treated as private citizens. But the United Kingdom refused
to use force to crush the rebels. Wilson only stated that Britain would respond to a request from the Governor for forces,
police or other assistance to help restore law and order.

The Smith regime did not hesitate. UDI had been well
planned and executed. It was backed by most of the white
minority. In short order the realities of power, which had
never really been in the hands of Britain, were put at the
service of the Rhodesian government. Although the country
would be hurt by sanctions, the settlers were willing to accept
the discomfort. And, since the United Kingdom would not use
force, they had little to fear. In reply to British action, the
Governor was divested of his executive powers and replaced by
a man picked by Smith who became the "Officer Administering
the Government." Britain called this an "act of treason," but
could do nothing to keep the regime from freeing itself of all
constraint. The rebellion had succeeded.

The reaction in the United Nations was also prompt.
The General Assembly interrupted its debate and condemned
the declaration. It called on the United Kingdom to take "all
necessary steps" to end the rebellion.[6] The next day, the
Security Council, meeting at the request of Great Britain,
adopted a resolution by 10-0 condemning the Rhodesian declaration of independence and calling on all states not to recognize or aid the illegal regime.[7] London had finally sought
United Nations action since, according to the British Foreign
Secretary, "an attempt to establish in Africa an illegal regime
based on minority rule is a matter of world concern" and because the active support of other states was necessary if the
measures introduced by Britain were to be fully effective.
Nevertheless, he reiterated that "Southern Rhodesia is a British possession and the responsibility lies on Britain."[8] Then,
on 20 November, the Security Council called on the United
Kingdom to put an immediate end to the regime. It also urged
the member states to refrain from supplying arms and equipment and "to do their utmost" to cease all economic relations
and place an embargo on oil and petroleum products. The
Council also asked the OAU to assist in implementing this resolution.[9]

Although UDI was proclaimed only ten days after the
serious warning of the Accra Assembly, it seemed to have tak-
en the OAU by surprise. Africa did not act immediately as
had been threatened. Rather, a week later, the Committee of
Five (or Defence Committee) met in Dar es Salaam to discuss
possible action. It in turn called for an extraordinary session
of the Council of Ministers, which did not meet in Addis Ababa
until 3-5 December 1965. By that time feeling ran very high.
Rhodesia had indeed come under the effective control of a minority regime and it was necessary to accept the challenge.
Talk was not enough and something drastic had to be done.

The OAU conference, a month after UDI, looked very
much like a council of war. The African Foreign and Defence
Ministers had come to work out a plan of attack against the
Smith regime. Although the debates were cloaked in secrecy,
there was no shortage of warlike statements and rumors to indicate the strategy desired by the radical members. Kojo
Botsio, Foreign Affairs Minister of Ghana, chairman of the
meeting, stated that "all that we must do now is to co-ordinate
our action and crush this treacherous act, once and for all ...
Our brothers are looking for us to help ... Their fate is our
fate." Rashidi Mfaume Kawawa of Tanzania added that his
country would fight side by side with Zimbabwe. And the Sec-

retary-General of the OAU reminded the delegates that "our Council is mandated to use force if need be to end the Smith regime."[10]

The radical states seemed to be urging an immediate display of might against Rhodesia under the auspices of the OAU. There were indications that their goal was an African task force with troops from a number of independent states. This force would be both offensive and defensive, since any state serving as a base would need protection against reprisals. There was much less conjecture as to what the moderate states proposed in the place of active intervention. If anything, they would have preferred a well-planned offensive rather than a prompt attack decided hurriedly and impetuously. But the best summing up of the actual state of affairs came from Alhaji Nuhu Bamali, the Nigerian Foreign Minister, who stated that the delegates "had agreed in principle to declare war on Rhodesia ... although we realize we have not yet got the troops to fight."[11] Probably, the moderates also preferred using less violent and dangerous methods altogether, such as sanctions and the traditional moral and material support of local freedom fighters.

Even when the conference was over it was impossible to know what decisions or compromises had been reached. The terse communique announced that the Council had "decided unanimously on concrete measures which will enable an end to be put to the racist regime of the minority European settlers." But there was no clarification of what these measures were. At any rate, a broader plan of action seemed to be in the making. The prerequisite for any action was to strengthen the liberation front and the highest priority was given to the movements in Zimbabwe. It was also necessary to consolidate their operational bases and the Committee of Five was to see what could be done to meet any "emergency" in states neighboring Rhodesia and "in danger of being attacked." It was also to have the members make "military or other contributions." The Committee's future activity was both ominous and vague. For it was to "invite military advisors from Member States in order to study and plan the use of force to assist the people of Zimbabwe." It looked as if this body would determine the military requirements, obtain troops from the various states and plan the coming attack.

In point of fact, it was not until later--when no attack had materialized--that it was evident that the compromise had been against the use of force by independent Africa and in

favor of the more traditional methods. The feasibility of
launching such an attack was analyzed by William Gutteridge
in a study for the Institute of Strategic Studies in London. According to him there was only a reservoir of some 150,000
troops in the independent states south of the Sahara from which
units could be drawn. But the armies were so small and vital that there would have been a danger for domestic security
if many troops left. Even then, a composite expeditionary
force of small contingents would be hard to organize, due to
differences in language and training, varied sources of weapons
and ammunition, and a lack of base installations or airborne
troops. Thus, he deduced, "the apparent conclusion of the
O.A.U. leaders, on the advice of their military experts, that
direct intervention in Rhodesia was not feasible had undoubtedly created a sense of frustration."[12]

The words used in the resolution and communique had
simply masked Africa's inability to come to the aid of brothers struggling for independence. The debates leading to this
admission of impotency had already exasperated many of the
delegates. The other main point, the possibility of using pressure on Great Britain to take a more active stand, was where
the conference recovered its unity and struck. Africa was unable to use force. The United Kingdom was a power that
plainly possessed the military might to crush the Smith regime and did not. Thus certain delegates launched a campaign
to recall the colonial power to its duties. There was already
considerable disgruntlement over London's role in the whole
affair. The radical states had originally sought action against
the settlers, but when this proved impossible it did not seem
unreasonable to get at the settlers through Britain. The
Francophone states had no particular warmth for Britain. And
none of the former British colonies, even the moderates, were
willing to stand up for it. Seizing the threat that had been
brandished several times, apparently without considering the
overall policies of their countries, the Foreign Ministers went
the fatal step further and issued an ultimatum: "If the United
Kingdom does not crush the rebellion and restore law and order, and thereby prepare the way for majority rule in Southern Rhodesia by December 15, 1965, the Member States of the
O.A.U. shall sever diplomatic relations on that date with the
United Kingdom."

This resolution came as a shock. Patience had run
out and there was going to be a collision. For London had already announced that it would not use force. As the ten days
passed, all eyes were on Africa. Some of the Heads of State

hastily rejected the measure and invoked various reasons for not acting. Even Zambian President Kenneth David Kaunda warned that breaking relations would cause difficulties and Emperor Haile Selassie wished to delay action until the Assembly could meet. When the time came, more or less promptly, some of the independent states did sever their relations. However, although the resolution had been adopted almost unanimously, there were only nine in the end: Algeria, Congo (Brazzaville), Ghana, Guinea, Mali, Mauritania, Sudan, Tanzania and the UAR. Obviously, most of the Heads of State felt that the Ministers had been mistaken and they were disavowed. But the OAU was no less embarrassed and its threats deprived of credibility.

The Long Road.

The Organization of African Unity had rarely been in a worse position than when the Council of Ministers met again in February 1966. Relatively few states had broken off relations with Great Britain and no armed struggle to speak of existed. All that remained were the sanctions. And they could not determine the outcome. The Ministers met in an atmosphere of recrimination and disunity.

The radical states, which called for an active struggle against Rhodesia, had let their demands be deflected and accepted a resolution they did not really desire. What they wanted was an open commitment to the use of force or, at least, stronger backing for the liberation movements, especially ZAPU. Algeria circulated a proposal to "intensify the organization ... of the nationalists in Rhodesia with a view to launching armed action within the country and to recognize the ZAPU as the only liberation movement in Rhodesia."[13] However, after feeling the pulse of the meeting, they realized that their demands would be rejected again. There was even a move to reverse the earlier resolution and absolve the members of any obligation to sever relations with Britain. Rather than oppose the other members in a direct clash, the states which had broken off relations preferred withdrawing or participating inactively to accepting decisions they disapproved of in advance.

Nevertheless, the rump Council had a quorum and was able to adopt a modest if inconclusive resolution. Although it admitted that "economic sanctions have not been sufficiently applied to overthrow the illegal minority regime in Rhodesia,"

no alternative course could be suggested. If force was to be
used, then once again this devolved upon the colonial power
and the Council called on the British government to "apply
such effective measures, including the use of force, that would
bring about the immediate downfall of the Ian Smith regime."
No mention was made of the ill-fated resolution on severing
relations. And the compromise on ZAPU and ZANU was "not
to recognize any party and instead to give aid only to such
groups of Zimbabwe fighters who are actively engaged within
Rhodesia in the fight to liberate their country from the colonialist and racist yoke."

     This resolution marked the low point in the Organiza-
tion's campaign. Still, slowly but surely, the various prongs
of the attack had their effect. The boycott did not paralyze
Rhodesia or make it revise its position, as promised by Wilson. Many exports and imports escaped the sanctions without
much difficulty. But they did make life unpleasant and expensive for the settlers. Above all, the bad sales of tobacco hurt
the farmers. With time, as well, small groups of Zimbabwe
freedom fighters began to infiltrate into Rhodesia from Zambia. Although they were rapidly dispersed or captured, this
threat was materializing.

     When the OAU Assembly met in Addis Ababa on 5 No-
vember 1966, almost a year after UDI, there was little to
show for its efforts. However, the frustration was giving way
to a more positive attitude and the crisis had cleared many
ideas. The Heads of State had overcome the initial discouragement and were spurred into closer cooperation so that Africa could finally agree on a joint plan. Almost as a preface,
the resolution "strongly condemns Britain for her refusal to
crush the Southern Rhodesian rebel regime and repeats its demands ... to bring about the immediate downfall of that regime by any means including force." But the emphasis was
no longer there. It was necessary to forget the past and establish a new and stronger policy and one that shared the burden between all concerned: Africa, the colonial power and the
world community.

     The OAU still placed some faith in a policy of sanc-
tions, although it was "convinced that the programme of sanctions ... as conceived and directed by the British government
will not and cannot bring down the illegal regime at Salisbury."
It wanted an expanded boycott and, above all, sanctions that
would be compulsory. Therefore it urged support for a "programme of mandatory and comprehensive sanctions against

Southern Rhodesia under Chapter VII of the Charter of the
[United Nations]."

The freedom fighters had accepted their duty and en-
counters with the Rhodesian forces and limited successes were
reported. In order to boost the efforts the member countries
were asked to contribute to a special Liberation Fund "to enable all Zimbabwe Nationalists to intensify the fighting against
the rebels." And tribute was paid to the "sons of Zimbabwe
who have died in battle with the racist settler regime's usurp-
er forces."

Something had to be done for Zambia as well. Squeezed between the Portuguese territories and highly vulnerable to
retaliation from Rhodesia, it suffered more than any other independent state. Traditionally, 30 per cent of its trade was
with Rhodesia and almost all its trade was routed through Rhodesia and Mozambique. Electricity from the Kariba dam was
essential for mining copper, its major export. So far there
had been some international aid, as petroleum was flown in.
Britain also provided important aid, both financial (loans) and
military (defence of the Kariba dam). China offered to build
a railway through Tanzania to get around enemy territory.
But much more had to be done and Africa had a direct responsibility to this country for its courageous stand. A Committee
of Solidarity with Zambia had been set up in February 1966 to
seek measures of technical and economic assistance. The
member states were now asked to contribute to enable it "to
withstand the effects of UDI" and also "to help all Zimbabwe
freedom fighters more effectively."

One year after UDI, instead of reaching new heights,
the OAU had gone through a tremendous decompression since
the illusions of the first days. It had now settled down for a
long, hard pull, placing considerable emphasis on sanctions
and requiring cooperation with the United Nations and even
Britain.

Britain Seeks a Compromise.

From the beginning, either because it really expected
quick results or because any other policy seemed disastrous,
Great Britain had put its full weight behind a program of sanctions. So great were the expectations that Prime Minister
Wilson, at the Lagos Commonwealth meeting in January 1966,
told his often distrustful, if not openly hostile colleagues that

economic and financial sanctions "might well bring the rebellion to an end within a matter of weeks rather than months."[14] But with time the outlook for success became dimmer.

All the while Britain had been keeping watch over the application of sanctions and, in April, it convened the Security Council to block the possibility of Rhodesia's being supplied with oil through Mozambique ports. It even became the UN's secular arm on 9 April, when the Security Council called on the United Kingdom to prevent "by the use of force if necessary the arrival at Beira of vessels reasonably believed to be carrying oil" to Rhodesia, and empowered it to "arrest and detain" one of the tankers.[15] For the first time in its history, the Council had authorized a member to implement such a decision under Chapter VII of the Charter.

Nevertheless, when the sanctions did not produce the desired results, the African delegates again turned to the United Nations to increase the pressure. Those that were being applied had been undermined by South Africa and Portugal and they were condemned. In order to make sanctions work, Great Britain was asked by the General Assembly to prevent any supplies, including oil and petroleum, from reaching Southern Rhodesia. Going much further, the resolution of 17 November 1966 also asked it to put an end to the regime by all necessary measures, "including in particular the use of force."[16]

The Labour government could hardly mobilize Britain for a greater effort and especially not to use force against the settlers. Aside from the fact that they were "kith and kin," the outcome of such action was more than doubtful. Any but massive intervention might fail under active resistance from the settlers and, if it succeeded, it could well leave Rhodesia without a disciplined force and a victim of anarchy. Thus any British government was open to the possibility of a compromise that, it hoped, would end the conflict to the satisfaction of both settlers and African nationalists.

During the negotiations before UDI, on 21 September 1965, the British government had laid down five principles which "would need to be satisfied before being able to contemplate the grant of independence to Rhodesia." They were:

1. The principle and intention of unimpeded progress to majority rule, already enshrined in the 1961 Constitution, would have to be maintained

and guaranteed.

2. There would also have to be guarantees against retrogressive amendment of the constitution.

3. There would have to be immediate improvement in the political status of the African population.

4. There would have to be progress towards ending racial discrimination.

5. The British Government would need to be satisfied that any basis proposed for independence was acceptable to the people of Rhodesia as a whole.[17]

On 25 January 1966, Prime Minister Wilson added a further principle: "It would be necessary to ensure that, regardless of race, there is no oppression of majority by minority or of minority by majority."[18] Perhaps on the basis of these six principles a settlement protecting the interests of all could be sought.

Despite the fact that Britain had threatened not to negotiate with the illegal regime, informal talks began in London and Salisbury in May. They were merely "exploratory" to determine whether a basis for negotiations existed. However, it soon became obvious that a compromise was being sought and London admitted that it would permit an interim period of direct rule and a transition to majority rule. The talks were interrupted and resumed several times and it appeared that both sides were making concessions. But an agreement was still out of reach. Britain's "last proposals" were submitted and, on 4 November, rejected. Nevertheless, in a final effort to find an "honourable settlement," Harold Wilson met Ian Smith aboard the HMS Tiger off Gibraltar on 2-3 December 1966.

The compromise Wilson offered for a "return to legality" consisted of an interim period--of no more than four months--during which time the legislature would be dissolved and the Governor would appoint a broad-based government with which the United Kingdom could negotiate an independence constitution. During the interim, the Governor would take charge of the armed forces and police and normal political life would be restored. Then a constitution would be drafted guaranteeing the rights of all sectors of the population and providing a

gradual transition from minority to majority rule. Like the
1961 constitution, there would still be a two-roll franchise for
the Legislative Assembly. There would be 33 upper-roll seats,
17 seats reserved for Europeans and 17 lower-roll seats.
There would also be a Senate with 12 European and 14 African
members (8 elected and 6 chosen by the Chiefs' Council). In
order to avoid any backsliding, amendments to the entrenched
clauses of the constitution could only be adopted by a three-
fourths majority of both houses. Moreover, the Judicial Committee of the Privy Council could rule on the constitutionality
of any amendment that might discriminate between the races.
Finally, if the population as a whole approved the constitutional proposals, independence would be granted as soon as possible.

The proposals were not really biased for the European
or African population as such. Rather, they implied two
phases. During the first, the whites, whose educational and
property qualifications gave them most of the A-roll seats,
would still maintain their rule over the country and Smith
could even head the broad-based and successive governments.
All the Africans had won, at the start, was two more seats in
the Legislative Assembly. But this was exactly enough to have
a "blocking quarter" to prevent any backward step. With time,
however, the Africans would raise their incomes and level of
instruction and they would eventually have the majority, and
finally the three-quarters of the Assembly. At this point the
whites would be left with the essential "blocking quarter" but
nothing more.

Thus the compromise entailed a division of power over
time with a gradual phasing out of white rule. The key point
here, of course, was the transitional period. Would it be five,
fifteen or fifty years? How long would it take for the Africans to obtain more income or education and thus political
power? With British and other assistance the process could
be accelerated and take less than a decade. This was far
from immediate democracy, as advocated by the nationalist
movements, but it was much faster than it would be granted
freely by the settlers or might be seized by the freedom fighters. It seemed so rapid, in fact, that the Rhodesian Front
was frightened and demanded more control over the pace of
African advancement. Salisbury also wanted some role for the
chiefs in the lower house and not only the more honorary Senate. Smith and his supporters preferred dealing with the traditional leaders they knew and largely controlled. They also
disliked a direct "testing of opinion" that might disown them.

Quite simply, they were uncertain how they would fare under black majority rule and wished to put off that day as long as possible. And Smith said "no" to the proposals.

The Zimbabwe nationalists were no less suspicious of a sell-out by Britain. Still, even if the compromise did not meet their hopes, the interests of the African population were also covered to some extent. At least a start would be made towards majority rule and the state of exception would end. In the following years a more pacific struggle could be engaged for education and development so that, aided by the force of numbers, the majority could eventually rule. There would be a parallel effort between the nationalist leaders and the chiefs to determine the true representatives of the people. The main demand on the Africans, as it was, was patience and some trust in the colonial power. Although neither ZAPU nor ZANU were willing, the relative calm in Rhodesia indicated that not all the population was in as great a hurry.

The independent states distrusted the repeated negotiations with the rebel government no less than the nationalists. Just after Wilson's "last proposals" to Smith, the Africans again mobilized the General Assembly. On 22 October, it condemned any arrangement that did not recognize the right to self-determination and independence and reaffirmed that any transfer of power to the people had to be on the basis of the principle of "one man, one vote."[19] Somewhat later, the OAU Assembly in Addis Ababa criticized Britain's "hypocritical attitude" and condemned the talks "as a conspiracy aimed at recognizing the independence seized illegally by the rebel settlers." It rejected in advance any regime arising from such talks unless based on majority rule.

Unfortunately, what both the white and black Rhodesians, what the outside world and especially Africa forgot too easily was that the principal advantage to any settlement was that the transfer of power from minority to majority could take place without a clash and the long awaited blood bath. This was one reason why Britain had never ceased looking for a compromise. However, it had always insisted that any settlement must be acceptable to all concerned and this was obviously not the case. The positions on both sides were rigid and any offer was likely to be rejected by either or both. Finally, when the proposals were turned down by the minority regime, Wilson felt that the time had come to go further.

Immediately after Smith's refusal, on 8 December 1966, British Foreign Secretary Brown came before the Security Council and asked it to invoke Chapter VII of the Charter and impose sanctions on certain key products. For the first time in the history of the United Nations, the Security Council determined that a situation constituted a threat to international peace and security and voted the application of selective mandatory sanctions under Articles 39 and 41. All states "shall prevent" the import and export of asbestos, iron ore, chrome, pig-iron, sugar, tobacco, copper, meat, hides, skins and leathers, arms, material for the manufacture of military equipment and (only after the African delegates had won the point) oil and oil products. The states were also asked to prevent the transport of these goods to and from Southern Rhodesia and not to give any economic aid to the minority regime.[20]

Although this was a big step in their direction, Britain's reluctant conversion to mandatory sanctions was not enough to please the Africans. They had had to fight hard to include the most important product and the one point where Rhodesia was really vulnerable--oil and petroleum. Those in the forefront of the struggle, moreover, would accept nothing but the use of force. According to Zambian Foreign Minister Simon Kapwepwe, the only solution was Britain's "military presence and intervention." The Wilson government, he said, rejected the solution because it preferred acting in "collusion" with the racist minority of Ian Smith. He did not hesitate to call Wilson's policy "hypocritical and racist."[21] At the same time, the OAU Secretary-General decried the selective sanctions proposed by London as a maneuvre allowing the Salisbury regime to be consolidated. Further, Diallo Telli stressed that any sanctions had to be backed by military measures. Without a blockade of the coasts of Mozambique and South Africa, they would be a parody.[22]

Shortly after the sanctions were introduced, the Africans seemed to gain their point. On 20 December, Prime Minister Wilson told the House of Commons that he was withdrawing all previous proposals for a constitutional settlement and that there would be "no independence for Rhodesia before majority rule." Britain's terms were now NIBMAR as well.

Repetition at a Higher Level.

Although much had been obtained, the struggle was far
from over. First of all, it was not certain that broad sanctions would bring the Smith regime to its knees, and the sanctions adopted by the Security Council were not very complete.
Any number of products could still get through the loopholes.
Moreover, there was no way of telling how strictly even the
selective sanctions were applied. Estimates varied widely,
from British sources which claimed trade would rapidly be cut
by half to Rhodesian spokesmen who admitted that trade was
down, but not dangerously. The United Nations statistics had
to be taken with a grain of salt as well, for they were voluntary and only covered countries that were proud of their records.

The main point was that no one knew how much of this
trade was being diverted through South Africa or Portugal.
From the start, Pretoria had taken a strictly "neutral" stand.
The day after UDI, Hendrik Frensch Verwoerd told the Nationalist Party that

> ... in accordance with our policy of non-interven-
> tion, we did not try to tell either Great Britain or
> Rhodesia what we thought it should do. Our stand-
> point was that here was a domestic struggle be-
> tween Great Britain and Rhodesia ... But, while
> we will not interfere, we will not allow ourselves
> to be used. We will continue to deal with one an-
> other in economic and other matters as before ...
> We cannot participate in any form of boycott ...
> We intend to preserve friendship with whatever gov-
> ernment the Rhodesian people see fit to choose.[23]

Ever since, South Africa had helped Rhodesia obtain imports
even of oil while its exports of certain goods rose as rapidly
as Rhodesian exports fell. Mozambique was another channel
and the port of Beira was kept open and busy.

In the meanwhile, guerrilla warfare had been launched
and was being intensified. Throughout the spring and summer
of 1967 there were reports of clashes and engagements with
the Rhodesian police. Both ZAPU and ZANU claimed victories
and one group of freedom fighters got as close as a hundred
miles from Salisbury. The main force was sent by ZAPU,
which had several thousand men in training and had already
fielded a few hundred. As of 1968 it also formed joint units

with the South African ANC. Most of its equipment and aid came from Moscow and the East bloc and it was backed by the radical states. It had the primary support of the Liberation Committee. Since Zambia, the main base, had also endorsed its rival, ZANU could do little for the moment. Still, as long as it received aid from Peking and was backed by some of the moderates, it was not out of the running. Of course this rivalry was a handicap to action, but the liberation movements also complained that they were not being helped sufficiently by independent Africa in this crucial battlefield.

The Smith regime had prepared for independence and accepted the dare. It rapidly clamped down on any possible source of disturbance and repression was made stiffer. The death penalty was imposed for the possession of arms of war. To block the freedom fighters, more and more paramilitary police were sent to the border and they tried to intercept them as they crossed the Zambezi. Rhodesia was aided by the arrival of South African anti-terrorism squads and police units. This cooperation was highly effective in the important first phase of resistance. So far there seemed to be no trouble with the tribalized Africans. To immobilize further the nationalist leaders, in 1968, the Rev. Sithole was convicted of incitement to murder Ian Smith and two ministers and jailed for six years, while Joshua Nkomo was simply given five more years' detention.

Despite the outbreak of guerrilla warfare, Britain still hoped to find a peaceful way out of the crisis. Lord Alport had been sent to Salisbury in June 1967 to test the political climate and see whether a situation existed "in which meaningful attempts can be made to reach an acceptable settlement."24 Prime Minister Wilson also authorized the Governor to clarify certain aspects of the Tiger proposals. Commonwealth Secretary George Thomson went to Rhodesia officially and Sir Alec Douglas-Home arrived on a private visit. (Even South Africa's Prime Minister Balthazar Johannes Vorster, who urged a realistic and honorable solution, was thought of as an honest broker). Wilson's minimum demand for any settlement by then was a return to the 1961 constitution. This did not appeal to the Rhodesian Front nor the African nationalists, who demanded full and immediate democracy. But the contacts were kept up.

Thus, when the OAU Council in Kinshasa reviewed the situation in September 1967, it could appreciate some progress, although the basic note was one of dissatisfaction with the slow

rate. The resolution deplored the "total failure" of selective
sanctions and urged that they be made general. It also demanded that they be enforced under Chapter VII of the Charter. There was serious concern with "the recrudescence of
violence and bloodshed in the colony caused by the forces of
repression of the rebel regime." The member states were
requested to raise their contributions to the Special Fund so
that the Zimbabwe nationalists might increase and intensify
their struggle. But the member states also appealed to the
liberation movements "to find a basis for unity, co-ordination
and co-operation, or for the constitution of a common front,
in their struggle to liberate their country." Mention was
made of the "increase in economic and military assistance
openly extended to the rebel regime by South Africa and Portugal." And, finally, the OAU again condemned "any talks between the United Kingdom government and the rebel regime of
Ian Smith without the participation of representatives of the
majority."

This was taken up by the General Assembly early in
November. It also condemned the United Kingdom for not
bringing down the Rhodesian regime and London was asked to
take all necessary measures, "including the use of force."
What was more, the Assembly felt that effective sanctions
would have to be "backed by force" and it urged all states,
"as a matter of urgency, to render all moral and material assistance to the national liberation movements of Zimbabwe."[25]
Although the resolution was carried by a huge majority, this
uncharacteristically hard line was disapproved by most of the
Western countries, which abstained. Nevertheless, Britain
realized that more was needed to alter Rhodesia's stance.
The selective sanctions had only covered about 15 per cent of
Rhodesia's imports and 60 per cent of its exports. Thus, on
29 May 1968, the Security Council unanimously called on the
United Nations members to prevent the import and export of
all goods from Rhodesia aside from medical and humanitarian
supplies. The resolution also covered investments, remit-
tances and emigration. But the Council refused to invoke the
use of force or censure South Africa and Portugal for not complying with sanctions. In addition, it affirmed that the United
Kingdom still had the "primary responsibility" for Rhodesia
while insisting it ensure that "no settlement is reached without
taking into account the views of the people of Southern Rhodesia and in particular the political parties favoring majority
rule."[26]

Meanwhile the situation took a grisly turn for the worse.
Rhodesia had been under attack for some time by the freedom
fighters and there had already been acts of sabotage and violence earlier from within the country. In November 1967, a
number of terrorists had been put on trial for murder and
were eventually condemned to death. With this the whole conflict came to a head. The United Nations and OAU demanded
that the trials be called off and warned against executing the
prisoners. Appeals for clemency were made throughout the
world. At the last minute, the Queen of England reprieved
those condemned. But the breakaway government dared not
show a moment's weakness. Early in March 1968, five of the
men were hung. This time the wail of grief and the anger
that followed appeared to sweep away whatever restraint had
bound the Rhodesian regime and its opponents.

Approaching the Point of No Return.

By then the Rhodesian Front seemed to be controlled
by extremists intent on breaking all links with Britain and introducing a system based on apartheid. They had kept Smith
from accepting the Tiger proposals and were pressing for a
more intransigent position. Moreover, in April 1967, a special congress of the party had adopted a platform including
maintenance of the Land Apportionment Act and, without openly demanding separation of the races, it "opposes compulsory
integration and believes that the peaceful coexistence of peoples can only be achieved when communities have the right and
opportunity to preserve their own identities, traditions and
customs." Increasingly thereafter steps were taken for segregation in sports, schools and public places.

For some time the fate of the country seemed to hang
from the future constitution. In February 1967, Prime Minister Smith had appointed a small multiracial commission to find
a framework for Rhodesia's plural society. In April 1968, the
Whaley Commission reported back. It proposed a two cham-
ber system. The Parliament would have 40 guaranteed white
seats, 20 African seats and 20 elected from a common roll.
The Senate would have 12 white members, 12 Africans and 7
of any race. Initially the whites would carry almost all the
common roll seats and have a strong majority. And the Commission approved of continued white rule due to greater competence and experience. However, as the Africans earned
more money and received a better education, there could theoretically be a parity of the races in both houses. Far from

rejecting such a conclusion, the Commission recommended that there should eventually be parity, without specifying when. This was too much for some of the Rhodesian Front leaders and rank-and-file. They angrily demanded a new draft.

Several months later, after being worked through the party machinery, a new draft was ready. These proposals provided a two stage system. During the first stage, lasting five years, there would be a multiracial Parliament and Senate. Half of the members of the lower house would be Europeans, one-fourth Africans (largely chosen by the chiefs) and one-fourth elected from a common roll. The upper house, divided roughly between Europeans and Africans, could only delay certain bills. Although it was still possible theoretically to reach parity, many of the African representatives would be salaried chiefs. However, in the second stage, the powers would be distributed between the central government and three new "provinces." The Provincial Councils, chosen separately by the Europeans (Asians and Coloured), the Matabele and the Mashona, would only be responsible for certain local affairs. The National Parliament, which dealt with foreign affairs, security, justice, finance, and other matters of the nation as a whole, would include all the races. This stage also set the scene for separate development.

This draft constitution was approved by the Rhodesian Front in September 1968 by a very narrow majority and only because Prime Minister Smith threw his weight behind it. The extremists, who would have preferred racially separated chambers, were unhappy with stage one altogether and wanted a much tougher stage two. The conflict within the party finally ended with the resignation of the extremists in the cabinet. With this Smith and the "moderates" seemed to be in control. For the first time the Prime Minister looked less like a party spokesman than a national leader and stage one, whatever its merits, gave him five years to seek a settlement before taking the dangerous path to apartheid. Moreover, although Rhodesia denied the Privy Council any right to repeal its judicial decisions, there were no more executions of Africans. At the same time a broad section of the population felt some settlement with Britain was the only way out and a Centre Party was formed to this purpose.

Thus it again seemed possible to effect a settlement. Harold Wilson, who had been waiting for a change in circumstances to resume the search for a solution, felt that the time had come to confer with Ian Smith again. From 9-12 October

1968, the two met on board the HMS Fearless near Gibraltar.
The working document was the Tiger proposals. However, the
change was not sufficient and neither side made the concessions expected of it. The differences were as wide as before.
Britain still demanded the right of appeal for the Privy Council while Smith insisted that no external body should have the
final say on the laws of the land or the entrenched clauses of
the constitution. Wilson wanted the African representatives to
be elected directly and popularly and to include Africans in
the transitional government, while Smith demanded some role
for the chiefs and refused to accept a broad-based government
as a step in the return to legality.

Once again the hopes for a negotiated settlement had
been an illusion. But they were more thoroughly dissipated
by Rhodesian action in 1969. On 12 February, Prime Minister Smith announced that there would soon be a referendum on
a new constitutional plan. The party had introduced certain
key changes in the earlier plan to satisfy its more radical
members. The Senate remained as before. This time, however, the Assembly would consist of 66 members elected on
separate racial lists. Fifty would be elected by the white,
Asian and coloured voters and 16 by the Africans, of which 8
would be elected directly and the other 8 chosen by the chiefs
and headmen. Representation was tied to tax contribution and,
as the Africans paid more taxes or improved their educational
qualifications, the number of African seats could increase to
50. Given their low income, it would be long before the African population reached parity. The second major change was
that within five years Parliament would divide the country into
one European and two African provinces with their own councils and powers. Thus an immediate step would be taken towards separate representation and the move towards separate
development was advanced.

According to Ian Smith, the new proposal "entrenches
government in the hands of civilized Rhodesians for all times."
It was interpreted quite differently by Prime Minister Wilson,
who rejected the racial nature of the plan and told Commons
on 18 February that it was "a complete and flat denial" of at
least five of Britain's six principles. London repeatedly
warned Rhodesia that no settlement could be reached on the
basis of such a constitution. Within the country, those who
wished to avoid a break with Britain also urged a negative vote
in the referendum. The Centre Party, representing many of
the business interests, was worried about the effect of further
sanctions and called for continued representation of both racial

communities in Parliament and the institution of a blocking
mechanism either could use to prevent infringements on their
rights.   Most of the churches also asked their members to
vote "no."   And the African opposition in Parliament strongly
rejected any step towards dividing Rhodesia into two camps.
But the Rhodesian Front had no trouble carrying the referendum of 20 June 1968.   Of the predominantly white electorate,
82 per cent were in favor of proclaiming the Republic and 73
per cent supported the draft constitution.

The settlers had clearly expressed their will and authorized the government to steer a new course, accepting the
risks of isolation and opposition from outside.   Neither Smith
nor Wilson placed any more faith in negotiations and Britain
ceased its last diplomatic links with Salisbury.   ZAPU and
ZANU prepared to renew the struggle.   And the OAU conferences in August 1969 devoted most of their time to defining a
policy on Rhodesia.   Yet the task was not easy.   The lengthy
debates in the Council and Assembly showed that the compromise between those who wished stronger action by the independent states or at least massive aid to the guerrillas and
those unwilling to commit themselves further was still tenuous.
Once again the only solution was, as the Emperor pointed out,
to leave the struggle for liberation to the liberation movements.
Unfortunately, they were still divided and, again, it was decided not to choose among them and aid both movements.   Finally, despite the very thorough condemnation of London's
handling of the crisis and although Diallo Telli insisted that
economic sanctions had been a "complete failure," it was necessary to turn towards the United Kingdom and the United Nations to reinforce their action.   On 2 March 1970, the Republic was declared.

Notes

1.   United Nations Doc. A/AC.109/112, 22 April 1965.

2.   Afrique 1967, Jeune Afrique, p. 454.

3.   Africa Report, Oct. 1965.

4.   The Times (London), 23 & 24 Oct. 1965.

5.   BIS Doc. T.80, 11 Nov. 1965.

6.   General Assembly Res. 2024(XX), 11 Nov. 1965.

7. Security Council Res. 216(1965), 12 Nov. 1965.

8. United Nations Doc. S/PV.1257, 12 Nov. 1965, p. 12.

9. Security Council Res. 217(1965), 20 Nov. 1965.

10. The Times (London), 3-6 Dec. 1965.

11. Africa Report, Jan. 1966.

12. The Times (London), 21 April 1966.

13. N. McKeon, The African States and the O.A.U.

14. BIS Doc. T.1, 13 Jan. 1966.

15. Security Council Res. 221(1966), 9 April 1966.

16. General Assembly Res. 2151(XXI), 17 Nov. 1966.

17. Southern Rhodesia - Documents Relating to the Negotia-
    tions between the United Kingdom and Southern Rhode-
    sian Governments, Cmnd 2870, London, 1965, p. 67-8.

18. BIS Doc. T.2, 25 Jan. 1966.

19. General Assembly Res. 2138(XXI), 22 Oct. 1966.

20. Security Council Res. 232(1966), 16 Dec. 1966.

21. The New York Times, 10 Dec. 1966.

22. Le Monde, 10 Dec. 1966.

23. Africa Report, Dec. 1965.

24. BIS Policy Statement, 78.67, 13 June 1967.

25. General Assembly Res. 2262(XXII), 3 Nov. 1967.

26. Security Council Res. 253(1968), 29 May 1968.

C. South West Africa

The huge territory of South West Africa, as big as Great Britain and France together, was originally colonized by Germany in the late nineteenth century. Since the First World War, however, it was administered by South Africa as a mandate. The territory was very thinly settled and only had a population of somewhat over half a million, of which about 15 per cent were whites. Although largely desert, South West Africa had considerable economic potential and was far from poor. But its main significance has recently been that it was becoming a major front in the struggle against South Africa. For, if it could be brought under United Nations administration or made free, its political value as a precedent and its strategic military location would greatly strengthen Africa's hand in the war on its arch enemy.

Mandate or Not?

There had been trouble with South Africa over the mandate from the beginning. Although the Class C mandate placed few restrictions on the mandatory and even provided, according to Article 2, that it "shall have full powers of administration and legislation over the territory ... as an integral portion of the Union of South Africa, and may apply the laws of the Union ... to the territory," South Africa only grudgingly accepted any international accountability. There were several skirmishes with the League Mandates Commission as the mandatory tried to incorporate the territory further but the real problem arose after the League of Nations was dissolved. South Africa then insisted that its obligations under the mandate agreement had also lapsed and it was free to annex the territory.

Thus, from the outset, Pretoria held the initiative in the successor organization and the United Nations had to concentrate on a staying action to keep the territory separate. It tried to maintain some sort of international status for South West Africa. When South Africa adamantly refused to accede to the new trusteeship system, a semblance of the old mandate system was re-created in accomodation. But, this was not so

simple. For South Africa still claimed that the disappearance
of the League had relieved it of its obligations and, at any
rate, it rejected supervision by the General Assembly where
decisions were taken by majority vote and not unanimously as
in the League.

To settle these points, which were of a sufficiently legal nature to warrant reference to the International Court of
Justice, the General Assembly requested several advisory opinions. In 1950, the ICJ replied that South Africa still had international obligations including the submission of reports to
the UN and that it could not modify the territorial status of
South West Africa without United Nations approval. It conceded that South Africa was not obliged to place the territory
under trusteeship. In 1955, the Court added that the two-
thirds voting procedure in the General Assembly was permissible.

However, since these opinions were not binding, South
Africa continued to ignore the demands of the United Nations.
By 1957, the General Assembly realized that some further action was necessary and requested the Secretary-General to explore means of implementing the 1950 opinion. The Committee on South West Africa, which had been established to perform the functions of a mandate commission, was asked to
recommend legal measures to ensure South African fulfillment
of its obligations and a Good Offices Commission was established to enquire into the possibilities of a new agreement on
the international status of the territory.

Then, in June 1960, the African states themselves decided to take a direct initiative. The committee on South West
Africa had reviewed the legal action open to member states of
the United Nations and pointed out that any dispute over the interpretation or application of the mandate could be submitted
to the International Court of Justice (ICJ). Following the predominantly legal tack of the world organization, the second
Conference of Independent African States in Addis Ababa concluded that South Africa's international obligations should be
submitted for adjudication. Ethiopia and Liberia, the only African members of the old League of Nations, expressed their
intention of doing so and a steering committee of four countries including the plaintiffs was set up to determine procedures and tactics. (The case itself was handled by an American lawyer.) The important task of ensuring joint financing
of the rather costly proceedings was later carried over by the
OAU.

On 4 November 1960, Ethiopia and Liberia filed an application for contentious proceedings before the Court. They claimed firstly that South Africa still had international obligations under the mandate and that the United Nations could legitimately exercise the League's supervisory functions. More to the point, they contended that South Africa had violated the mandate, in particular by introducing apartheid in the territory. Africa thus tied up with the basic trend of the period which was to stress the "legal" aspects of a highly political problem and submit them to the World Court.

An Alternative Policy.

Almost at the same time that legal recourse was sought, a new trend was developing. Spurred on by the influx of African states, it was a more typical anti-colonial action. In December 1960, the General Assembly invited the Committee on South West Africa to visit the territory and make proposals leading to independence. Although it was refused entry, it submitted a report that set the tone for the following period. The Committee stated that there had been no change in South Africa's policies and recommended the termination of its administration, the institution of a United Nations presence and eventual independence.

At the end of 1961, the General Assembly proclaimed the right of South West Africa to independence and set up a special committee to work for the elimination of South Africa's political and military control and to prepare the territory for independence. The committee, not surprisingly, was unable to accomplish its mission and reported back that force would be necessary. It added that the population desired UN administration and suggested that a deadline be fixed for independence. Soon after, the functions of this committee were transferred to the Committee on Decolonization and it was obvious that the plan for South West Africa would be the same as for all other dependent territories: rapid independence.

When the Organization of African Unity was created, in May 1963, it sought to draw together the various strands of intentions vis-à-vis South West Africa and give direction to the struggle. Despite any contradiction, the summit conference endorsed both the old and the newer policies: it insisted that South West Africa was under international mandate and let the Court deal with it, while demanding independence. The resolution:

Reaffirms, further, that the territory of South-West
Africa is an African territory under international
mandate and that any attempt by the Republic of
South Africa to annex it would be regarded as an
act of aggression;

Reaffirms also its determination to render all ne-
cessary support to the second phase of the South-
West Africa case before the International Court of
Justice;

Reaffirms still further, the inalienable right of the
people of South-West Africa to self-determination
and independence.

Nevertheless, there was a relative lull while the Court
debated the case. A preliminary objection of South Africa was
rejected in December 1962 and nothing seemed to prevent the
ICJ from giving a ruling. During this time, there was little
activity in the OAU. It condemned South Africa at all meetings, but there were no specific resolutions on South West Africa other than to appeal for financing of the case. The Committee on Decolonization was rather quiet. Although the General Assembly warned that any move to annex all or part of
the territory constituted an act of aggression, it did not take
the offensive. Even Pretoria carefully restrained its policy.
The report of the Odendaal Commission, submitted early in
1964 and proposing territorial partition on the basis of ethnic
groups and closer integration with South Africa, was only accepted in principle and implementation put off to avoid preju-
dicing the Court proceedings.

Time dragged on and no ruling was made. Then, in
mid-1965, the Committee on Decolonization announced that
South Africa was implementing the Odendaal recommendations
and taking preliminary measures of partition. It portrayed
South Africa as a threat to the neighboring African countries
and asked all states to refuse it assistance. Going beyond the
customary reaffirmation of the right of self-determination, it
appealed to all states to give the African people "the necessary
moral and material support to enable them to accede to national independence." It also urged the General Assembly and
Security Council to introduce "positive measures" to assure
respect of the rights of the African populations of southern Africa and to take "appropriate steps to safeguard the sovereignty of the people of South-West Africa and the integrity of the
Territory." It was significant that the Committee suggested

that the necessary measures should be taken in cooperation with the Organization of African Unity.[1]

By December 1965, the General Assembly fell into line. It called upon South Africa to immediately remove its bases and other military installations in the territory and condemned the policy of large scale settlement of immigrants. All states were asked to give the indigenous population the necessary moral and material support in the struggle for independence. And, finally, the Security Council was requested to watch over the situation.

However, the most significant steps were not being taken in diplomatic circles. Without waiting for the World Court to rule nor for the United Nations to propose measures, the peoples of South West Africa began preparing for the future. Of the many groups, two stood out as potential leaders. The Hereros, one of the most dynamic tribes, had long been at the forefront of resistance and had even risen against the German authorities during a bloody war from 1904-1907. The representatives of some 50,000 people (10 per cent of the population) had not ceased sending petitions to the League of Nations and the United Nations. More recently, the largest tribal grouping, the Ovambos, with some 250,000 members (45 per cent of the population), had become increasingly active. They were crucially placed in the north of the country, nearest to independent Africa, although Portugal's Angola lay along South West Africa's northern border.

Closely paralleling this, several nationalist movements were formed as of 1959. First was the South West African National Union (SWANU), originally supported by intellectual and urban groups, the Hereros and the southern tribes. Soon after, the South West African People's Organization (SWAPO) started among the Ovambo peoples. And there were a number of smaller bodies. Although the task was not easy, the Liberation Committee's efforts at coordinating action among them appeared to be obtaining results with the establishment of the South West African National Liberation Front in October 1963. But cooperation in SWANLIF was discontinued and the Committee again had to help each of the major movements separately. Subsequently, as SWANU tended to decline and SWAPO began training a liberation army, it moved towards exclusive recognition of the more effective body.

A Pause for Legal Proceedings.

By then the activity of the World Court had been by-
passed somewhat by events. Nevertheless, each side held
back in the expectation that its theses would be vindicated.
Ethiopia and Liberia charged that South Africa had violated the
mandate agreement--the continued validity of which they expected the ICJ to uphold--through a series of measures and
omissions. It had failed to comply with the provisions on
supervision by refusing to transmit reports and petitions to
the United Nations. It had ignored, moreover, the demilitarization of the territory by establishing military and naval bases
It attempted to modify the terms of the mandate by various ar
rangements integrating South West Africa. And it had impeded the progress of the population towards self-determination,
the right to which was implicit in the League and in current
international standards. But the main contention was that by
following a policy of apartheid South Africa had violated Article 2 (2) of the mandate, providing that it "shall promote to
the utmost the material and moral well-being and social progress of the inhabitants of the territory." Here the effort wa
not so much to prove the intrinsic evil of apartheid, already a
foregone conclusion, but to demonstrate that apartheid per se
was a violation of the mandate and that there existed a genera
rule of international law, or at least an international norm,
according to which all racial discrimination was illegal.

South Africa again replied that the mandate and any international accountability had lapsed with the dissolution of the
League and that it was under no obligation to submit to the
supervision of the United Nations. It argued that it alone was
legally vested with the right to determine the best way of promoting the moral and material well-being of the inhabitants of
the territory and that its measures had been in keeping with
the League mandate. Gradually, going beyond the points of
law, the hearings were turned into a study of apartheid. The
South African barristers tried to provide some insight into the
policy and show that apartheid was not a means of oppression
of the indigenous population merely for the profit of the whites
To the contrary, they insisted that integration, from the so-
ciological and other points of view, would actually have disastrous effects on the well-being and progress of the inhabitants

However, despite the discussions and the lively interes
of world public opinion, the International Court of Justice dismissed the claims on 18 July 1966. By eight to seven, it hel
that the applicants had no legal right or interest in the subjec

atter of their claims. An "antecedent" question made it "un-
cessary" for the ICJ to give a ruling. This was the better
rt of valor. The judges had probably realized after six
ars of litigation that the case was far more political than
ridical and that a ruling on the substance might have shaken
e Court's very foundations. The storm this retreat pro-
ked (including dissident opinions) was certainly less violent
an the reception of any decision as to the moral value or
gal effect of apartheid.

Although there was no ruling, Prime Minister Ver-
oerd immediately claimed that this was a "major victory for
uth Africa." The Africans, for their part, spoke of failure
d betrayal. Without reflecting whether the merits of their
se were such that they would have carried all points, or
w bad would be their position if the Court ruled against them,
ey felt cheated. One expression of this was the statement of
e Ethiopian Foreign Ministry:

> In rejecting the complaints filed by Ethiopia and
> Liberia on behalf of all O.A.U. member states,
> the World Court has failed to safeguard the rights
> of freedom and independence of Africans in South
> West Africa. The verdict will no doubt be in-
> scribed as the most flagrant judgment the Court has
> ever passed on human rights, in particular on the
> rights of the African people.

The reaction was even sharper and more menacing in
e liberation movements. Very belligerent declarations were
sued in Dar es Salaam by both SWANU and SWAPO.
WANU stated:

> We reject absolutely the Court's findings. The
> United Nations was created primarily to provide
> the peaceful solution to international problems. We
> will keenly watch its reaction now. We have re-
> peatedly warned that South West Africa could be
> turned into another Congo.

VAPO was even stronger:

> We believe that there was no need in the first place
> to take this case to the Court. This judgment has
> filled us with disdain and confirmed our belief that
> no fair play could be expected from world organs
> where imperialists play a dominant role. We have

no alternative but to rise in arms and bring about
our liberation.[2]

Whatever Verwoerd's victory may have been, it was
short-lived. For, turning away from the Court, the Africans
and their supporters immediately called for strong political
measures. In the General Assembly debate in September,
they presented an energetic resolution to deprive South Africa
of its mandate. Since Pretoria had failed to meet its obligations, the draft stated, the United Nations would have to terminate the mandate and "assume direct responsibility for the
administration of the Mandated Territory." An Administering
Authority would administer the territory until independence an
the Security Council would be requested "to take the necessar
effective measures to enable the Administering Authority to
discharge its functions.[3] This approach, however, was too
extreme to obtain broad backing in the General Assembly. A
compromise was found by adding certain Latin American
amendments which changed its impact, if not the actual goals

The resolution of 27 October 1966 was a complete
break with the past. After years of effort to prove the continued validity of the mandate, the General Assembly affirmed
its right to take action including the "right to revert to itself
the administration of the Mandated Territory." South Africa
had failed to fulfill its obligations and ensure the moral and
material well-being of the indigenous population. Therefore,
the General Assembly decided, the mandate was "terminated,
South Africa had no other right to administer the territory an
"henceforth South West Africa comes under the direct responsibility of the United Nations." The compromises were that
rather than immediately administering it through a UN Author
ity, there would only be an Ad Hoc Committee for South West
Africa to recommend practical measures for later administration. And the Security Council was not asked to introduce en
forcement action but only to pay attention to the situation.
The onus for implementation was placed on the South African
government which was expected to withdraw and refrain from
any action contrary to the resolution. Despite misgivings in
certain quarters, the resolution was carried by 114 votes to
2.[4]

Although it was scarcely noticed in the general excitement and indignation, the compromise was a rather awkward
one. More than anything it gave satisfaction to the African
states and their only concession was some delay. The concessions of the Western powers were much greater and they

had been put on a path leading towards a direct confrontation with South Africa. Only, this was not a path they would follow readily and even the Communist bloc was not certain how to bring about enforcement. There had also been some discomfort among the legally minded that the resolution was not valid, since the original mandate contained no clause for termination and this was not one of the powers of the General Assembly. This point had disturbed the Soviet Union and France sufficiently to insist that such action was not to constitute a precedent. Thus the main advantage to the compromise was that it put off to a calmer moment the conflicts that were bound to arise over implementation, between the General Assembly and the Security Council and between the United Nations and South Africa.

How to Implement the Resolution.

The major reason for concern, however, was that the resolution might well remain a dead letter. South Africa was firmly entrenched in the territory and its new Prime Minister, Balthazar J. Vorster, lost no time in replying. He pointed out that the decision was illegal and that the General Assembly had no right to take it. His government would therefore do nothing" about the matter and he promised that "We will continue to administer South West Africa as we have always done and we will carry out what has been planned taking into account the demands of the times." He also added that the United Nations would find it impossible to implement the resolution.[5]

South Africa still had the initiative; withdrawal of the mandate had only caused the country to take several steps backward. It no longer hesitated to draw South West Africa further into its own administration and Pretoria gradually assumed the essential functions in the territory. They ranged from taxation to trade and education to labor, without neglecting such key matters as internal affairs and justice. It was very inauspicious that the South African government was also proceeding with its plans to divide the territory into one white block and a dozen smaller areas for different tribal and ethnic groups. On 21 March 1967, the Minister of Bantu Administration, Michael Botha, announced that the Ovambo peoples would be granted self-rule. A semi-autonomous Ovamboland would cover about an eighth of the country, mainly along the northern border with Angola, although the tribe represented almost half of the total population. This plan was rejected by the United

Nations as contrary to its resolutions, but there was nothing
it could do. Soon the Ovambos had their own legislative assembly, executive council and chief councillor with certain
limited powers.

At the same time, South Africa prepared for the coming armed struggle. Although repressive legislation was introduced and the security forces were strengthened, there was
still some resistance and cases of sabotage or attacks. In
June 1967, the Terrorism Act was extended to South West Africa. Then a number of terrorists who had been arrested
earlier were brought to Pretoria to be tried. The trial began
in August and eventually 33 were sentenced, 19 to life imprisonment. However, since the United Nations denied South
Africa any legal authority in the territory, the trials were repudiated by the Decolonization Committee, the Council for
South West Africa, the General Assembly and finally the Security Council. They all condemned the illegal arrests, insisted that the trials cease and the prisoners be repatriated.
The Security Council unanimously condemned South Africa for
the "flagrant violation" of human rights and warned that if it
did not comply with the resolution "the Security Council will
meet immediately to determine upon effective steps or measures in conformity with the relevant provisions of the Charter
of the United Nations."[6] But no measures were taken for the
moment.

The United Nations was thus faced with how to react to
South Africa's defiance of its resolutions and how to alleviate
the rapidly deteriorating situation. Despite the common will
to terminate the mandate there were considerable differences
of opinion about how to implement that policy. The African
members took the initiative at the meetings of the Committee
on South West Africa early in 1967. They demanded that a
special United Nations Council be established to administer the
territory until it could be given independence--no later than
June 1968. South Africa's continued occupation was labelled
an act of aggression and, if it did not withdraw, the Security
Council should take enforcement action under Chapter VII of
the Charter. The Latin American delegates again took a middle ground. There would be temporary United Nations administration but they did not request enforcement action. The
Western proposals merely called for a special representative
to gather information and make contacts. The USSR, for its
part, strongly backed the African demand for independence an
enforcement action. However, it rejected any temporary administration, preferring immediate independence under the

supervision of the OAU.

When no common text could be derived from these four stands, the whole matter was brought before the General Assembly again. For the second time, a compromise was worked out between the Afro-Asian Group and the Latin Americans. The result was a text that eliminated all reference to enforcement action and the condemnation of South Africa as an aggressor. The resolution of 19 May 1967 provided that a Council for South West Africa should take contact with Pretoria to lay down procedures for a transfer of the territory, with June 1968 as a target date.[7] This resolution was adopted by 85 to 2, with 30 abstentions. Among those that abstained were the major powers: United States, Soviet Union, Great Britain and France; from Africa, Botswana and Malawi abstained and Lesotho was absent. The second step towards freeing South West Africa was not taken with the same enthusiasm as the first.

One month later, after lengthy consultations, the General Assembly elected the eleven members of the Council. This body was created to "administer South West Africa until independence." To do so, it was to arrange the transfer of the territory with South Africa, take over the administration, ensure the withdrawal of South African police and military forces and personnel and replace them with personnel under the Council's authority, preferably indigenous people.[8] It was responsible to the General Assembly and had to report back regularly. The Secretary-General also appointed an Acting Commissioner to handle the executive and administrative tasks of the Council.

The Council for South West Africa was not entrusted with an enviable mission and it had trouble getting started. It had been instructed "to enter immediately into contact with the authorities of South Africa in order to lay down procedures for the transfer of the administration of the Territory with the least possible upheaval." This it attempted to do by means of a letter to South Africa. But it only elicited a flat refusal by the Foreign Minister to comply with the "illegal" request. The General Assembly resolution in December urged the Council to pursue its mission by all possible means and it then decided to tackle the second objective, "to proceed to South West Africa with a view to ... taking over administration of the Territory." On 5 April 1968, it finally left for Lusaka, where it tried to find entry into South West Africa. The Council hoped to charter an airplane to fly to Windhoek but was unable

to when South Africa refused landing rights. It later moved
to Dar es Salaam where it met representatives of the nationalist movements.

It had now been amply proven that the South African
government did not intend to cooperate with the United Nations
as it had promised. The Council did not renounce all hope of
entering the territory and taking over the administration, although it admitted that the conditions were not suitable and felt
that only force would compel South Africa to withdraw from
the territory. In order to give it a more modest but practical
contribution to the effort, the General Assembly adopted new
terms of reference in June 1968. It endorsed the Council's
decision to issue travel documents and gave priority to the
tasks of establishing an emergency program of assistance and
training programs for South West Africa. However, the General Assembly did not change the basic goal and it again demanded that South Africa immediately and unconditionally withdraw its military and police forces and administration. But
little could be accomplished without the support of the Security
Council and the resolution urged it to take effective measures
"to ensure the immediate removal of the South African presence."[9]

Two years after it had revoked South Africa's mandate
the United Nations had not found any way out of the predicament. What was worse, the organization was not even united
in its efforts to solve the problem. The original resolution
had been initiated by the African states and the anti-colonial
bloc and, just after the ICJ decision, almost all the members
had been drawn along with them. But this gesture was rarely
followed by action. In June 1968, the scheduled date for inde
pendence, the Assembly symbolically renamed the territory
Namibia, although it would be long before it existed as a sovereign state. The delegates again put forward new and bolder
plans for the future. Many of them urged that the Security
Council introduce economic measures or enforcement action
against South Africa. Others wished that these sanctions be
expanded to include any states which encouraged South Africa
by diplomatic, political, military or economic cooperation.
And some even suggested that once a liberation war had been
launched, a government of Namibia could be established and
recognized and that it could be aided by the United Nations in
its war against South Africa. All these plans were based on
some use of force. But they all overlooked the constant refusal of the Security Council to provide for such force. The

permanent members had repeatedly abstained on General Assembly resolutions and it would take much more to overcome their reluctance. Not even the most audacious resolutions of the General Assembly could change that.

Sharing the Responsibility.

The Organization of African Unity, as well, had been carried away by the General Assembly resolution of 27 October 1966. Meeting in Addis Ababa only one week later, the Council of Ministers tended to look on this as a victory and it made plans for a follow-up. Using much blunter language and brushing over any nuances, it proclaimed that the resolution had "unequivocally terminated the mandate" and signified that "the Government of South Africa has no right whatsoever to exercise authority in any form in South West Africa." The Council's analysis of the situation existing after the UN resolution was that "the continued domination of South West Africa by South Africa constitutes an illegal military occupation of an African sister country." Posed as it was in military terms, the solution to this problem was for the member states "to spare no effort in helping the peoples of South West Africa to rid themselves of foreign occupation" and the Liberation Committee was to "give priority to the termination of the occupation of South West Africa."

The OAU had thus made a call for action. The question was whether it would be heard. Unfortunately, it was unlikely that the Organization could mobilize an adequate fighting force to alter the situation. There was no question of the independent states entering the breach in a hopeless war against the greatest military power on the continent. Internally, it would be increasingly difficult to shake the administration which was massively supported and gradually run from Pretoria. Even guerrilla warfare would be severely hampered by the largely desert terrain and the sparseness of population. Any efforts would be further weakened by divisions. The ethnic groups were scattered over the vast territory and under close control. South African policy had done nothing to dampen the hostility between the tribes and also kept them largely under the traditional chiefs.

As on the other fronts, the struggle was left essentially to the South West Africans themselves. There were several nationalist movements and SWAPO had begun preparing freedom fighters. There was some original uncertainty among its lead-

ers as to the advisability of using force but the first units infiltrated the territory and carried out minor attacks as of August 1966, shortly after the ICJ decision.   Although a number
of them had been captured and were held in prison, many
more joined the nationalists in independent Africa, especially
Tanzania and the UAR, where they underwent training.   They
had the backing of the Liberation Committee and the Organization and a certain priority.   But they were fighting against
greater odds than any of their counterparts and they made little impact for the time being.

      In view of the difficulty expected on this front, the OAU
had no desire to go it alone and referred the matter back to
the world organization.   It was urged that the necessary steps
be taken to give effect to the General Assembly resolution.
The OAU pledged its cooperation to the United Nations in dis-
charging its responsibility towards South West Africa and asked the members to inform the UN Secretary-General of the
"material support" they could provide.   The Kinshasa resolution reinforced this line by placing the struggle on a world
level.   South Africa was defying world opinion by refusing to
comply with UN resolutions and cooperate with the Council.
Therefore, it requested the Security Council "to give all necessary assistance for ensuring the establishment of the United
Nations Council in South West Africa and in carrying out its
mandate satisfactorily."

      The Algiers resolution in September 1968 did not make
any further reference to the liberation wars either although it
did again pledge "total and unconditional support to the people
of Namibia in their struggle."   However, the OAU directed its
efforts even more pointedly through the world body.   Namibia
was defined as "a territory under the responsibility of the
United Nations" and the primary agents were the General Assembly, the Council, the Security Council and, only subsidari-
ly, the OAU.   The main role went to the Security Council and
this body was again called upon to give effective assistance to
the Council for Namibia.   But it was also urged to go much
further, this in accordance with the General Assembly's June
1968 resolution, and "invoke the necessary provisions of Chapter VII of its Charter against the South African regime for its
persistent refusal to hand over the administration of Namibia
to the U.N."   Thus the OAU had come to the same conclusion:
no action was possible without the support of the Security
Council.

Notes

1. United Nations Doc. A/AC.109/126, 30 June 1965.

2. Africa Report, Oct. 1966.

3. United Nations Doc. A/AC.483, 26 Sept. 1966.

4. General Assembly Res. 2145(XXI), 27 Oct. 1966.

5. Africa Report, Dec. 1966.

6. Security Council Res. 246(1968), 14 March 1968.

7. General Assembly Res. 2248 (S-V), 19 May 1967.

8. General Assembly Res. 2248 (S-V), 19 May 1967.

9. General Assembly Res. 2372(XXII), 12 June 1968.

D. South Africa

The real bastion of colonial and settler Africa, however, lay well behind the front lines in the Portuguese territories and Rhodesia. South Africa, independent since 1910
and a Republic since 1961, was one of the largest countries in
Africa, both in size and population. It had untold mineral
wealth and a flourishing agriculture and industry. It was also
the strongest country in the region militarily. Unfortunately,
all these assets were only being used to halt the advance of
independence and equality.

For the prosperity and power were restricted largely
to the white community. Of some eighteen million inhabitants,
only 18 per cent were whites, the rest being African, 69 per
cent; Coloured (mixed blood), 10 per cent; and Asian, 3 per
cent. Nevertheless, the lion's share of the land and economy
belonged to the whites. They also ran the government and
were reorganizing the whole society to maintain their rule.
Over the years a policy of apartheid had been developed and
was being implemented to separate the races and preserve the
status quo. Because of this policy, South Africa had become
the arch enemy of the rest of the continent and a principal
target of the OAU.

The Whites Draw Laager.

South Africa was divided in more ways than one. There
had always been hostility between the white settler population
that gradually pushed back its frontiers towards the north and
the Bantu tribes that streamed into the region from the north.
There was also a barrier between them and the Coloured as
well as the Asians who came as labor. But until relatively
late in its history the initial and deeper division was not the
predominant one. Rather, the struggle for power was between
the Boers (the early settler groups) and the British (both the
Crown and settlers), with the rest of the population on the
sidelines.

The first Europeans landed at the Cape of Good Hope
in 1652. During the following century and a half of Dutch rule
settlers flowed in and many of them struck root and became
pioneers of a growing community. They developed their own
language and customs. In their dealings with the indigenous
population, they tended towards a superiority of white to black
mixed with a certain paternalism. This attitude was carried
into all their fields of interest in South Africa. Later on,
when the Crown took control of the Cape, attracted by its importance for shipping and communications, British settlers
came and gradually pushed back the Boers. Then, in the
1830's, the older stock of settlers opened up the interior during the Great Trek it undertook to free itself of British domination and preserve its way of life. The Boers founded new
republics in the Orange Free State and Transvaal and settlements in Natal, often encountering and containing the African
tribes. They had hoped to escape the encroachment of the
British for ever, but the friction increased and came to a head
in the bitter Anglo-Boer War of 1899-1902.

Although they were defeated by the overwhelming force
of the British army, the Boers did not stop the struggle and
when peace was concluded the rivalry merely assumed other
forms. Considerable progress was made in the economic and
cultural life of the Union and many of them went into politics.
With a new dynamism and their larger population, the Afrikaners had an edge over the British in elections. (About 60 per
cent of the whites today speak Afrikaans and 40 per cent, English.) By 1948, they reached their goal. The Nationalist
Party of Dr. Daniel F. Malan defeated the Union Party of
Field-Marshal Jan Christiaan Smuts. Since then the Boer party has held the initiative in South African politics.

Over the centuries of white expansion there had also
been friction and periodic warfare with the blacks. Successive
waves of migration of the Bantu tribes had led them into the
region and the two forces often met head on. The Boers were
at the forefront of the struggle and a long series of "kaffir"
wars were necessary to assure them peace and tranquility in
the territory they had carved out for themselves after the trek.
Despite bad feelings among the whites, when the tribes rose
against them they forgot their differences and "drew laager"
(an encampment within a circle of wagons). Even the Boer
War was not to upset this alliance. Finally, after more than
a century of disturbances and uprisings, black resistance was
broken and the tribes were pacified and settled in reserves on
the less valuable patches of land. By the beginning of the cen-

tury it seemed that the struggle was over and the whites had
things under control. But the Bantu population did not stop
growing and its very size was a clear threat to white domination. The fear was given much sharper form in the 1950's,
when the Africans to the north began demanding independence
and colony after colony became free under national leaders.

During the same period that much of Africa was re-
covering its freedom, the settler population in South Africa
read the signs of the time to mean that they must act rapidly
to avoid a similar fate. This required tremendous efforts and
a drastic change in the tendencies active until then. For, in
the increasingly mixed society, the minority would have trouble containing the majority and could not resist demands for
increased rights. If it gave in, it would soon be swamped and
the Afrikaner way of life would disappear. The Bantus would
be far more manageable in their own areas and even democracy or independence would be less of a threat.

When the Boers came to power, they immediately recognized the challenge. While launching the successful electoral campaign in 1948, the Nationalist Party stressed that "the
choice before us is one of two divergent courses: either that
of integration, which would in the long run amount to national
suicide on the part of the Whites; or that of apartheid ..."[1]
A policy of "total territorial apartheid" was gradually worked
out by Hendrik Verwoerd, as Minister of Native Affairs. In
1958 he assumed leadership of the party and, as Prime Minister, presided over putting apartheid into practice.

The policy, officially known as "separate development,"
did not in theory imply a political subjection of the Africans.
Each one of the eight major ethnic groups was to be given its
"homeland" where it would be able to develop its own society.
The Bantustans reserved for the Africans would eventually
form the nuclei of separate black communities. There would
also be special areas reserved for the Coloureds and Asians
and each would have its own structures.

Eventually these communities would become self-governing nations and form a Commonwealth with the white nation.
But even then the government of South Africa would conserve
many of the key powers and represent the whole of the country. Moreover, 87 per cent of the land area belonged to the
whites.

Although not all the whites accepted this policy, the opposition United Party of Sir de Villiers Graaff, was certainly
not a counter-pole. This party, largely backed by the English-
speaking and many business sectors, rejected apartheid but endorsed segregation. It too was in favor of white supremacy.
Nevertheless, as the crisis in relations between white and
black grew sharper, it steadily lost ground to the governmental party. Whereas in 1961 the United Party had the support
of just under half the electorate, five years later it was sub-
merged by the Nationalist Party, which won a three-to-one
victory at the polls in 1966. Thus, the white minority was
now solidly behind the policy of apartheid, if not always for
the same reasons.

It was not so much the theoretical differences between
apartheid, segregation, or any other system of white supremacy that mattered, but rather the practical considerations for
staying on top in a country with a vast non-white population.
Although not all the whites were racist or clung to an antiquated system, they all had some vested interest. More often
than not the white South Africans were born there and their
forefathers had come generations earlier. The Afrikaners especially felt as if they were part of the country and neither
they nor the others relished change. Change would be most
painful due to the tremendous drive of this minority which had
given it the land, the wealth and the power. Any move from
minority to majority rule meant the loss of political predominance and much other position and comfort in white life that
had been won over the years.

Everyone realized that apartheid would be hard to implement. For years the trends had been running counter to it.
Only about 40 per cent of the Africans actually lived in the Native Reserves; of the rest, 30 per cent were in white urban
areas and 30 per cent in white rural areas. More and more
Africans were drawn into the white areas and mining and industry depended heavily on them as a labor force. Even the
farms had African hands and help. If they were completely
withdrawn the economy would collapse. How then could the
country be divided physically? Some suggested merely a political separation with homelands the Bantus would leave in
normal times to work in the white areas but where they could
be returned if necessary. Even this was a tremendous task.

The Internal Opposition.

Opposition to apartheid came from various quarters.
Some of the Europeans fought for a democratic society and
formed white or mixed groups to improve relations among the
races. A Liberal Party was created in 1953 by men like
writer Alan Stewart Paton, who worked for the repeal of apartheid laws, and for universal suffrage and an entrenched bill of
rights. The Progressive Party, supported by Harry Oppen-
heimer, desired a qualified franchise based on income or property as a start towards a non-racial society. Despite some
initial success, it ended up with only one member in Parliament. Some of the trade unions also tried to promote freedom of association for the Africans. Since they were placed
under the Bantu Labour Board and could not engage in collective bargaining or strikes, this activity was difficult. Nevertheless, the Congress of Trade Unions included black unions
as well. There were also groups formed in moral opposition
to white supremacy. Here the role of the clergy and certain
churches was important. There was also the "black sash"
womens' organization and numerous individuals from all walks
of life who tried to restore harmony. Unfortunately, these
groups only represented a small portion of the white population and made no headway against government resistance.

The only real opposition could come from outside the
system, among the four-fifths of the population without political, economic or social power. The mainstay of resistance
should naturally have been the Africans. However, they were
not a single people but a group of peoples or tribes and even
during their wars against the Boers they had lacked cohesion
and often been as hostile to one another as to the whites. After defeat and submission, there was little fight left in the
tribes as such. To the extent Bantustanization could return
the Africans to their tribal reserves and place them under the
control of the traditional leaders, what unity there was would
be destroyed and they would be unable to withstand the central
government. The tribalized Africans, at any rate, were a
poor material for opposition. The Asians and Coloureds were
not much better. They had relatively little cohesion and were
in an equivocal position of being slightly better off than the
Africans and thus almost a part of the system. Still, the Indians and Pakistanis had formed an Indian National Congress
to represent them. The Coloureds, although less organized,
had the Coloured People's Congress.

The spark of resistance had to be kindled among the detribalized Africans--the educated, the workers and miners. These groups had been uprooted from traditional society and were more open to ideas of independence and unity. And it was among them that the oldest nationalist movement was founded in 1912. The African National Congress (ANC) had from the start worked against tribalism and prepared the future of the "African" people. Nevertheless, it cooperated with white liberals and upheld the ideal of an inter-racial society. It even formed a Congress Alliance with the Indian National Congress, the Coloured People's Congress and the Congress of Trade Unions. The ANC did not seek to deny the whites or others the rights of full citizenship in the democratic state it wished to establish. Its policy tended to be reformist and conciliatory, although it was driven towards increasingly radical stands by government policy. Because of its approach, it was originally attacked by the Communist Party as a "bourgeois reformist movement." However, after the Communist Party was banned in 1951, many leftists joined the ANC. Still, they were only a minority and the principal leaders, such as Chief Albert John Luthuli, Nelson Mandela and Oliver Tambo were opposed to communism.

The ANC's stand was also rejected by some of the Africans. It was not sufficiently militant for them and, after playing a dissident role within the party, a group of its members broke away in 1959 to form the Pan-Africanist Congress. The PAC was created "to overthrow white domination." But it went further and rejected cooperation with other racial groups. According to its leader, Robert Maugatiso Sobukwe,

> We want to make the African people conscious of
> the fact that they have to win their own liberation,
> rely on themselves to carry on a relentless and de-
> termined struggle instead of relying on court cases
> and negotiations on their behalf by "sympathetic"
> whites ... In short, we intend to go it alone.[2]

The PAC was in a hurry. At its first annual congress, it planned a "status campaign" for courteous treatment of Africans in shops and decided to launch "decisive and final positive action" against the pass laws under the slogan of "no bail, no defence, no fine." This was to be the first step towards the goal of "freedom and independence" for the Africans by 1963. The result of this agitation came quickly. The demonstrations ended with the shooting at Sharpeville, on 21 March 1960, when 74 Africans were killed and 184 wounded. Subse-

quent events led to the declaration of a state of emergency.
After the riots both the ANC and PAC were outlawed and many
of their leaders arrested, and restricted or imprisoned including Chief Luthuli and Sobukwe. Other members went into exile and later formed a loose United Front between the ANC,
PAC and the Indian National Congress.

The Sharpeville riots were a major turning point in the
recent history of South Africa. Serious violence had finally
broken out between the white and black communities. Blood
had been shed and revenge was feared. The whites drew together and the repression was made stronger. The system
was largely based on the Suppression of Communism Act of
1950. Despite the misnomer, the legislation was accurately
aimed against those who were a threat to the status quo. For
the definition Pretoria gave of "Communism" was any doctrine

> ... which aims at bringing about any political, in-
> dustrial, social or economic change within the Re-
> public by the promotion of disturbance or disorder
> ... [or] which aims at the encouragement of feel-
> ings of hostility between the European and the non-
> European races of the Union ...

Under it people could be imprisoned for opposition to apartheid.
Interpretation of the Act by the Minister of Justice was final.
There was also a series of laws against sabotage and terrorism to deal with the more active opponents. And the "90-day
law" even permitted temporary detention, without charges, of
witnesses in security cases.

United Nations Campaign Against Apartheid.[3]

The racial situation within South Africa was a delicate
and explosive problem not only for the people living there. It
was also of concern to the rest of the world community and it
was increasingly internationalized as the Afro-Asian bloc in
the United Nations grew. By 1952, the General Assembly
moved on the broader issue of racial conflict in South Africa
resulting from the policy of apartheid. Until 1960 there was
a steady flow of condemnations and wishes from the UN. Following the lead of the Commission on the Racial Situation in
South Africa, the delegates increasingly stressed that this policy was contrary to the Charter and the Universal Declaration
of Human Rights. The moral onus was placed on South Africa
as a violator of the Charter and its protection under Article 2

(7) (disallowing external interference in a sovereign domestic jurisdiction) faded.

After Sharpeville, however, the situation had become dangerous for continued peace in the region. Although Pretoria insisted this was a domestic matter, for the first time its racial policies were brought before the Security Council at the request of 29 Afro-Asian members. They had hoped to obtain action but, in April 1960, the Council only made a statement "deploring" the killings. Still, it admitted that the situation "if continued might endanger international peace and security" and called on South Africa to abandon its policies of apartheid and racial discrimination. This appeal went unheeded.

Then the anti-colonial bloc, angered at defiance of these resolutions, decided to go further. In April 1961, the General Assembly requested the member states to consider separate and collective measures to impose the resolutions and, in November, it urged the states to take steps within the Charter to bring about change. Finally, in November 1962, the General Assembly for the first time requested specific action: severance of diplomatic relations and a total economic boycott. It also established a Special Committee on the Policies of Apartheid to review the situation and report to the General Assembly and Security Council. This Committee became the watchdog on South Africa and a source of initiatives for action.[4]

When the Organization of African Unity was created, in May 1963, it tried to give a new impulse to the campaign against South Africa. In a resolution on apartheid and racial discrimination, it stressed the need of intensifying and coordinating efforts to put an end to the "criminal" policy of apartheid. To do so, it would try to coordinate "concerted measure of sanctions" and, as a start, it decided to break off diplomatic and consular relations with South Africa and asked for an effective boycott by the African states.

This example, however, would have little effect unless followed by the major trading partners and the allies of South Africa. Thus it was essential to obtain action in the United Nations. For the first time the OAU tried to mobilize the world organization. It made a considerable impact. Within the year the Security Council was convened twice in special session. The first collective effort was aimed at introducing sanctions against South Africa. The session had a limited but impressive success on 7 August 1963. Although rejecting a total boycott, the Council called on the states not to sell arms, ammunition or military vehicles to South Africa. It also asked South Africa to release all opponents of apartheid imprisoned or restricted for their political views.[5]

The shock came a few months later. Pretoria ignored the resolution and brought several African nationalists, including Nelson Mandela and Walter Max Sisulu, to trial on charges of attempting to overthrow the government by violence. In a heated debate in the UN Political Committee, Oliver Tambo told the delegates that the judicial process in South Africa was "genocide masquerading under the guise of a civilized dispensation of justice."[6] Following this, 55 delegations sponsored a resolution to the General Assembly asking South Africa to "abandon the arbitrary trial now in progress" and release all political prisoners held for opposition to apartheid.[7] When the resolution was adopted on 11 October 1963, France, the United Kingdom and the United States objected to this interference in the internal affairs of a member state and abstained on that point. But the Rivonia trials continued.

The full-dress debate in the General Assembly had another interesting aspect. The Africans condemned the evils of apartheid and argued that it was a threat to the peace and that the Security Council should take compulsory measures. The Western powers, especially Great Britain and the United States, countered that there was no immediate threat and that external coercion would only lead the white minority to unite more strongly behind the government. Moreover, expulsion from the United Nations would end direct communication with South Africa and make the search for a solution more difficult. The result of the confrontation between the anti-colonial bloc and the major Western powers was a draw. However, this time there was a third position as well.

The Scandinavians took a stance somewhere between the two extremes and sought to clear the air and restate United Nations policy in a more objective and realistic fashion. The first requirement, before seeking the means, was obviously to determine the ends of any policy. Although the Africans and the General Assembly had repeatedly condemned apartheid, they had never formally stated what the alternative was. Thus the Danish delegate insisted that "rather than simply call for coercive measures the time had come for the Assembly to state openly the ideals by which it is guided and to declare what it wants to see established in South Africa in the place of Apartheid." Without infringing on the rights of the majority the United Nations should also convince the minority that "the end of apartheid and white domination does not mean the end of their existence." Apartheid had to be replaced by a truly democratic and multi-racial society and, during a transitional period, the world organization could help by maintaining law and order and protecting the life and civil rights of all.[8] For the first time it was proposed that a complete review and definition of policy be made.

When the Security Council met it was strongly influenced by this debate in the General Assembly. Once again the demands of direct action by the Africans and the reply that there was still no threat to peace by the major Western powers cancelled out. Nevertheless, the voluntary sanctions were broadened to include equipment for the manufacture of arms. But the most novel aspect of the resolution of 4 December was that the situation should be examined carefully and a genuine solution sought. At the request of Norway, a Group of Experts was set up

> ... to examine methods of resolving the present situation in South Africa through full, peaceful and orderly application of human rights and fundamental freedoms to all inhabitants of the territory as a whole, regardless of race, color or creed, and to consider what part the United Nations might play in the achievement of that end.[9]

Finally, in April 1964, the long-awaited report of the Group of Experts was submitted. The Group itself saw little hope for a compromise since, despite the fact that international condemnation of apartheid was increasing, the South African government was intensifying its policies by new legislation. These forces were on a collision course and inevitable violence "must involve the whole of Africa and indeed the world beyond." To avoid this clash, the Group felt that it was "only on the road of free and democratic consultation and co-operation and conciliation that a way can be found towards a peaceful and constructive settlement." It urged that, as a start, "all efforts be directed towards the establishment of a National Convention, fully representative of the whole population of South Africa, to set a new course for the future." Then the United Nations could offer its good offices to help organize and supervise elections and maintain law and order during a transitional period.

If South Africa balked, however, sanctions might be
needed to bring it to reason. The Group therefore added that
economic sanctions could be effective if universally applied
against South Africa and, to this end, it recommended a "practical and technical study of the 'logistics' of sanctions." If,
by a date stipulated by the Security Council, the South African
government had not replied to the invitation to discuss the formation of a National Convention, "the Security Council should
then take the decision to apply economic sanctions."[10]

There was a definite sting to the report of the Group
of Experts. And it was this "either/or" aspect of the proposals that made the debates in June so desultory and unreal.
The experts had obviously not looked into all possibilities nor
had they given a precise definition of aims and a progressive
plan for attaining them. The United Kingdom considered that
the National Convention was not a first step but rather an op-
timal solution. Its main drawback was that it was bound to
be rejected by South Africa. This implied a resort to the ultimatum at the end of the report, which the British delegate
considered a "somewhat extreme position."[11] Since, for most
of the other delegations, it was a foregone conclusion that
nothing could be done to wean South Africa from the policy of
apartheid, the search for a compromise was forgotten and the
debates focused on the advisability of applying sanctions.

However, when pressed for sanctions, the Western powers again dwelt on the difficulties of determining their impact.
It was uncertain whether the sanctions would be applied universally and, if not, it would be very hard to blockade South Africa's long coastline. In addition, with such an advanced economy, it might take a long time for the sanctions to be felt.
Without committing themselves to the principle of sanctions,
the Western powers did accept the creation of a Committee of
Experts to study the "feasibility, effectiveness and implications" of any measures open to the Security Council.[12]

The Rising Tide of Resolutions.

Although it was flying in the face of world-wide opposition, South Africa's position had not been shaken. It was, indeed, increasingly ostracized in international circles. By
1961 it had left the Commonwealth and it was later expelled
from various international bodies, such as UNESCO, FAO and
ILO. It was also the target of many private conferences on
apartheid. But it hung on in the United Nations even after the

crisis over South West Africa. South Africa was not upset by
the official and political criticism as long as it could get along
economically and militarily. Despite all resolutions and campaigns for a boycott, its trade had not been hurt. Many of its
products, such as gold and uranium, were essential to its
partners and it offered excellent and reliable investment opportunities. To the contrary, most of the Western states, Japan
and some of the socialist countries increased their South African trade. At the July 1964 OAU Assembly in Cairo Kenya
added China to the list.

The main responsibility for keeping South Africa's economy flourishing rested with its major trading partners, the
United Kingdom, the United States and the European countries.
But there was little chance they would cease their trade.
Their businessmen already had an important stake in the country. Of the total foreign investment in 1967 of Ł1,720 million,
almost two-thirds came from Britain and another third from
the United States and Europe. Trade with these countries was
also considerable with almost 30 per cent to Britain, 25 per
cent to Europe and 10 per cent to North America. Because of
the gold bullion market in general and its own negative balance
of payments, the United Kingdom would be doubly hit by losing
its third most important partner.

Militarily, despite the Security Council's 1963 resolution, South Africa continued finding suppliers. Even though
the United States and the Labour Government refused to provide arms, there were others to take their place. The government still obtained aircraft, missiles, naval vessels and
submarines. In addition, although South Africa was not an integral part of the Western defence system, it was too valuable
an ally to lose. It was strategically placed on the important
sea route around the Cape, particularly crucial since the closing of the Suez Canal. And it was a far more reliable stronghold than the recently independent states, most of which spoke
of neutralism while Pretoria preached anti-communism. Of
special interest was the huge naval base at Simonstown.

The OAU had a tremendous task. It intended, among
other things, to set the pace for sanctions. However, at the
Cairo Assembly it was embarrassed to learn that much African trade had not ceased and was instead rising. The leaders
reiterated the demand for sanctions by the African states and
added to them the supply of minerals and raw materials. Potentially more important was the decision to create machinery
to coordinate the sanctions and ensure their implementation,

harmonize cooperation with friendly states and gather informa-
tion on the governments and companies that ignored sanctions.
This task was entrusted to a Bureau of Sanctions within the
Secretariat.

There was little more that Africa could do for the moment. When there was no improvement in the situation by
October 1965, the Council of Ministers decided it was again
necessary to seek international action. It called on the African Group to bring the matter before the United Nations once
more. In particular, the Security Council had to be convinced
that there was a threat to peace in southern Africa and had to
"institute effective economic sanctions against South Africa and
to assist the victims of apartheid and repression." To bring
this about, the members were to help elect to the Security
Council states that supported "effective action."

But the main requirement was still to bring South Africa's allies and trading partners into line. Without them
neither sanctions nor enforcement action would be possible.
France, in particular, was asked to abide by the Security Coun
cil resolutions and stop supplying military equipment. A special appeal was made to the major partners: United Kingdom,
United States, Japan, Federal Republic of Germany, Italy and
France. They were urged "to discontinue their growing economic collaboration with the South African Government, since
such collaboration encourages it to defy world opinion and to
accelerate the implementation of the policy of apartheid."

Yet another tone was heard for the first time. The
Council "invites the South African liberation movements to concert their policies and actions and intensify the struggle for
full equality and appeals to all States to lend moral and material assistance to the liberation movements in their struggle."
Oddly enough, however, the new tone and mention of the final
objective, "full equality," disappeared from the subsequent
resolution, which only laconically "greets all those who are
struggling against apartheid, particularly in South Africa."

This demand for stronger action was followed, although
more slowly, by the United Nations. The Committee of Experts reported back to the Security Council at the beginning of
1965. Although conceding the difficulty of implementation and
noting that the "degree of effectiveness of such measures would
directly depend on the universality of their application and on
the manner and the duration of their enforcement," it emphasized the importance of severing relations and communications,

ceasing trade and placing an embargo on arms, munitions and petroleum.[13] In June, the UN Special Committee on Apartheid went somewhat further and urged South Africa's trading partners, especially the permanent members of the Security Council, to cease immediately all relations which encouraged South Africa to persist in its racial policies.[14] Then, in December 1965, the General Assembly appealed to South Africa's trading partners to cease economic collaboration and drew the Security Council's attention to the fact that the situation constituted a threat to international peace and security, that action under Chapter VII of the Charter was essential to solve the problem and that universally applied economic sanctions was the only means of achieving a peaceful solution.[15]

But the Security Council did not come around to this point of view and could not unless there was a sharp revision in the policies of several permanent members. Neither economic sanctions nor enforcement action were possible without their approval. Great Britain, South Africa's major partner, was not in a very good position to institute either of these measures. Before the Committee of Experts, London had noted that in the first year of sanctions already its balance of payments would show a loss of £300 million and the cumulative damage to its economy would be much greater. Although the United States would be hurt less, it also had considerable economic interests. Moreover, if the sanctions could only be enforced by a blockade, these two countries would be the major contributors to a force that would cost between £70 and 130 million a year.[16] If neither sanctions nor blockade succeeded and military action had to be contemplated, once again it was from them that the greatest effort would have to come.

In addition, they were uncertain whether any action in the United Nations would lead Pretoria to adopt a more conciliatory policy or whether the whites would only be driven to rally behind an extreme position.[17] It was also uncertain whether any measures would avoid or precipitate the long threatened race war. For none of these measures could alter the internal situation of the country but would only weaken it as a whole. Rather than make the white minority reflective, such measures might only aggravate the crisis. Therefore, neither of the major Western powers were eager to push too far.

South Africa Holds Its Own ...

Despite all the pressure brought against it, South Africa continued following the course traced out for it by the Nationalist Party in 1948. The passing of Dr. Verwoerd did not lead to any change and it was even feared that the policy would be hardened when the former Minister of Justice, Balthazar J. Vorster, took his place in September 1966. Before being sworn in as Prime Minister, he announced his intention to push ahead with apartheid. An ominous and forbidding justice minister, known for his role in punishing the opponents of apartheid, he turned out as Prime Minister to be a stern but flexible and dynamic defender of the policy. At the same time, under the stress from within and attacks from outside, the United Party increasingly aligned itself with government policy on major issues like Rhodesia and South West Africa. Occasionally, it even criticized government "appeasement" of black nationalists. Thus the white minority was more united than ever in resisting the pressure against it.

In recent years, the policy of apartheid has been implemented, often brutally, by uprooting tens of thousands of Africans (and others) from the areas they lived in and resettling them in distant Bantustans. The government even accelerated the Bantustanization. Gradually the homelands were taking shape and the first one was created for the Xhosas in the Transkei at the end of 1963. Another was being prepared in the Ciskei. The Transkei had a territorial assembly of 64 traditional chiefs and 45 elected members. But its powers and those of the government were limited to local administration and its laws had to be approved by the President of South Africa. The Coloureds, who were previously represented by whites in the Parliament, would have their own "representative council." The Council, ready in 1971, would have 40 elected and 20 appointed members with limited administrative and legislative powers, mainly for education and social assistance. With this South Africa would have an all-white Parliament. To avoid any "interference" by members of one racial group in the politics of any other, a law of May 1968 forbade mixed political parties and mixed trade unions. This law was accepted by the Progressive Party and the Congress of Trade Unions for their own survival, while the Liberal Party was "temporarily dissolved." Whites were also barred from intervening in Bantu and Coloured bodies. In every aspect of social life, from sports to private receptions, the state was enforcing the separation of races.

Although territorial separation was sought whenever possible, for financial reasons it was difficult to piece together
the scattered areas inhabited by people of the same tribe and
to buy the connecting strips. It was also difficult to remove
the African population from the centers of economy and industry without harming the country's growth. Apparently the government was not able to swim against the current. For the
African population was being detribalized and drawn into the
white areas even faster than official policies to retribalize
them could be implemented. According to the Tomlinson Report, there were 264 separate homelands in 1954.[18] By 1963
only 35 had been consolidated. According to an ILO report,
even if the Bantustans were able to support nine million Africans in another twenty-five years, there would still be about
three-quarters of the larger population that would have to earn
a living in white areas. It concluded that "the present development of South Africa is not leading to the gradual creation
of separate communities, but to an ever-growing de facto integration of the African in the White economy."[19]

Nevertheless, even if it was not possible to separate
the white and black areas entirely, the government still tried
to obtain a political separation. This meant that the Africans
would be migrants in the white areas where they could come
to work but not to live. To this end the various Bantu and
labor laws were reinforced and supervision of the Africans increased. But this was a more serious failure even than apartheid. For although life in the Bantustans was human if hard,
the transient nature of life in a semi-apartheid world was
tragic. Away from their homes and families most of the time,
and unable to strike roots where they worked, the worst consequences arose for the African communities: exploitation for
labor, broken homes, unstable and disrupted lives, crime and
immorality. This introduction to South Africa's way of life
only generated antagonism and hatred in the blacks who outnumbered the other inhabitants of the country two-to-one.

Economically, however, the situation was still brilliant.
Production and income were rising rapidly. Agricultural out-
put was increasing and the country covered most of its own
needs as well as exporting huge quantities of foodstuffs and
fish. Mining was still flourishing and South Africa produced
diamonds, uranium, coal, iron and 74 per cent of the non-
Communist world's gold. Industry was turning out an expanding range of manufactured articles. The only serious weakness was in power supply because of an absence of petroleum,
although electricity was abundant. There was considerable

prosperity and income as a whole grew by over 6 per cent annually. The income was poorly distributed: whites had a
standard of living similar to the inhabitants of the wealthier
countries in Europe, whereas the blacks were only earning a
fraction of that. Even so, black wages were enough to draw
literally hundreds of thousands from the Portuguese territories
and independent states to seek work in South Africa.

Militarily, Pretoria was girding itself for any action by
its enemies within the country or along the border with independent Africa. The army and police force were quickly expanded and in 1967 compulsory military service was introduced.
At that time, the regular army consisted of a permanent force
of 20,000 men, with a citizen force of 50,000, and a further
50,000 in "commando" units. Its 4,000 man air force was
well equipped with fighters, bombers, reconnaissance planes
and helicopters. Even the navy, some 3,500 men, was expanding and had two destroyers, several mine sweepers and
smaller vessels, and soon three submarines. South Africa's
police force consisted of 15,000 Europeans and 12,000 Africans.
In addition, the country was producing some of its own weapons and ammunition and had a factory for small commercial
jets.[20] Impressive as the present establishment was, it was
still growing and a ten year plan aimed at increasing the army
to 100,000. There was also a change in strategy from conventional warfare to protection against a revolutionary war,
i.e. guerrilla and terrorist. During the same period, the defence budget had swollen tremendously. Between 1960-61 and
1965-66, it had gone up fivefold, attaining $322 million.

However, there was one race which the whites were
losing. They could not keep up with the tremendous growth of
the rest of the population. From 1960 to 1965, the black population increased by over 10 per cent; the Coloureds, by 17
per cent and the Asians by 10 per cent, whereas the white
population went up by only 6 per cent. The white minority,
already less than one fifth of the population, was becoming a
decreasing part of the whole. It tried to balance the situation
by immigration. From 1961 to 1966, net immigration of Europeans was 136,000 or about 25,000 a year. To maintain the
proportion of whites in the population, it would have been necessary to have twice this figure annually.[21] If the respective
birth rates did not change, by the turn of the century there
might be 6,750,000 whites and 35,000,000 non-whites in "white"
South Africa.

Thus, the main threat did not reside in the economy or defence but in the political dissatisfaction of the masses. In order to maintain its control over the whole land, the government had to intensify its repression of internal opposition not only to the laws but also to the system. The trials of African nationalists and their white supporters continued. Along with this, there was an increasing number of people imprisoned without trial, held under house arrest or banned. Apartheid's opponents were harshly treated in prison, often put in solitary confinement, and the sentences were crushing. By 1966, about 8,000 persons were reportedly imprisoned for opposition to apartheid. And about 1,200 non-white prisoners, including leaders of the nationalist parties, were held at the Robben Island prison. Since 1963, 420 people had been banned.[22]

... and Counter-Attacks.

But South Africa was not only building up its defences and waiting for Africa to attack. It followed an active policy of aid to its allies in the war against liberation. The guerrilla warfare that had been launched in the Portuguese territories and Rhodesia were also a threat to South Africa. Some of the freedom fighters were trying to infiltrate South West Africa and South Africa and they had to be stopped before they reached the Limpopo River. Militarily, the situation would be much less tenable if any of these territories fell and independent Africa obtained access to a common frontier. Sanctions were also disconcerting, applied against Rhodesia and threatened against Portugal and South Africa; boycotts had to be "proven" ineffective.

Relations between South Africa and Portugal were strengthened as the struggle intensified. To beat the sanctions applied by OAU members, South African Airways was able to fly its planes via Luanda to Lisbon and on. The two might also build a major airport on the Cape Verde Islands. Economic cooperation was broadened and, during a visit to Lisbon in October 1964, Foreign Minister Muller signed an important agreement on trade and communications with Angola and Mozambique. What was most significant potentially was the discovery of oil in Cabinda and the electricity supply from the Zambezi dam. With increased economic integration, even if largely cut off from the rest of the world, the region would be relatively self-sufficient and their economies far less fragile.

There was also some suspicion that a mutual defence pact had been concluded but, even without written documents, the tacit military cooperation could only increase. Soon South African police and instructors arrived in Angola to aid their Portuguese colleagues. There was apparently also a large contingent at the dam site in Cabora Bassa. The contacts were maintained and, in April 1967, the South African Defence Minister visited Portugal to discuss the security of Angola and Mozambique. The visit was returned by Foreign Minister Nogueira in July 1967. The major problems were the security of the Portuguese territories and the need to block infiltration of freedom fighters in South West Africa. Cooperation on these two crucial fronts were to be stepped up.

However, the real front line was in Rhodesia and South African aid to the settler regime was unstinting. There were frequent talks between Smith and Vorster or their assistants to coordinate plans. Despite the embargo, Pretoria intended to maintain normal relations with Salisbury and declared that it would not participate in sanctions or be forced into them, "even if this meant taking risks."[23] But it went much further and soon initiated fast train services to keep Rhodesia supplied. Above all, Salisbury was enabled to obtain more than the minimum amount of oil required. It also got around the sanctions by selling Rhodesian goods. Although hampered by the British blockade, Portugal kept the port of Beira open and helped circumvent the boycott.

More dramatic has been the decision to provide military aid. For some time freedom fighters had been coming in from Zambia. Among them were members of South African movements. They had to be stopped and destroyed at all costs and South Africa did not hesitate. In August 1967 its police joined their Rhodesian counterparts in a major engagement with the "rebels." Within a year there were 300 men fighting with the Rhodesians and eventually armored cars and helicopters were moved in. Portugal, for its part, was not adverse to exerting pressure on the flanks of Zambia or creating an occasional diversion elsewhere in independent Africa by sending its troops across the border.

However, without even using its force, South Africa was able to intimidate its enemies. Its military strength was such that there was no serious thought of sending an "African" army against it. Even an "international" army would be hard put. The figures advanced by Amelia Leiss in Apartheid and United Nations Collective Measures (see Bibliography) showed the ex-

tent of the task. To blockade South Africa's coasts would require 50-60 warships and other support vessels and 300 fighter
and reconnaissance aircraft. The cost for six months would
be $166 million. A successful military intervention would re-
quire 700 aircraft and 90,000 men, at a cost of $95 million
a month, until complete control could be secured in four
months. There would be between 19,000 and 38,000 casualties. And 30,000-45,000 troops would be needed for an extended period of military occupation until a civilian government
could take over. These figures dated from 1965 and would
have to be raised. It was therefore not surprising that neither
Africa nor the world community was eager to come to grips
with Pretoria.

Pretoria's New Look.

But recent policy was even more dynamic and outward
looking. As the strongest and wealthiest country in that part
of the continent, South Africa could exert almost irresistible
pressure on its weak neighbors. Some of them could be tempted to better the lot of their people by cooperating while others
might be chastened. The new tactic of divide and rule consisted of winning friends or at least clients within this zone of
influence. If hostility was met, an iron fist would be used.
Whether or not Pretoria attained all of its aims, it was able
to sow discord in the region and cripple the campaign against
itself.

By the time the neighboring countries became independent, South Africa had considerably hardened its domestic policies and tried to speed along apartheid so that the white minority could remain master in its own house. It was feared
that the relations with independent Africa would be similar and
that any South African government would crudely force them
into compliance. Relations already existed with the High Commission Territories of Basutoland, Bechuanaland and Swaziland.
They were poor and landlocked, dependent, largely on South
Africa, for access to the sea, markets for their produce and
work for thousands of their nationals. This had led to close
economic ties and a customs union. To avoid absorption they
had counted on the protection of Great Britain since the end of
the nineteenth century. When this was withdrawn, accession
to independence was likely to be a mixed blessing unless they
could come to satisfactory terms with their uncomfortable
neighbor.

However, the approach turned out to be entirely different. The South African government offered to help them. It
went to great pains to show that differences of political philosophy need not keep the countries in the southern part of Africa
from cooperating. Proposals were made for financial and technical assistance and closer economic relations. The answer
came on 2 September 1966, a month before Basutoland's independence. For the first time an African statesman, Chief
Leabua Jonathan, was received by a Prime Minister of South
Africa. Back home he told a mass rally that the visit to Pretoria was "an eye-opener and benefit for future relations. I
am convinced that South Africa ... is prepared to live with
you in peace without interfering in your way of life."[24] The
next visit was more significant, for Chief Jonathan was Prime
Minister of the newly-named independent state, Lesotho. In
January 1967 he came to ask economic and technical aid of
Prime Minister Vorster. To the surprise of many, he was
received as the head of a foreign government and his requests
were granted.

Although President Seretse Khama did not go this far,
he could not afford to make his country a center of the struggle against South Africa. Botswana still depended on the good
will of the colonial and settler powers surrounding it. Above
all, he did not want to risk the retaliation that could be expected if his country became a base for the freedom fighters.
In October 1966 the same year Khama's nation, formerly
Bechuanaland, became independent, a number of armed infil-
trators from Rhodesian and South African movements were arrested. At the end of the month the government announced
that it "will not permit Botswana to be used as a base, overtly
or covertly, for violent operations against neighboring states,
however unacceptable to Botswana the policies of those states
may be." In the future such acts would be more severely
dealt with.[25]

The greatest success of the new policy, however, was
a country further north without any common frontier with South
Africa. Malawi was exceptionally poor and overpopulated and
hoped to improve its economic situation through cooperation
with Mozambique and South Africa. On 16 October 1966, Hastings Banda had declared, "I will not be a hypocrite. I cannot
support any boycott of Portuguese Mozambique, South Africa
or Rhodesia because there would be an economic break down
and political chaos here."[26] This may well have been true,
especially since the country was landlocked and dependent on
the port of Beira for access to the sea. However, President

...nda's next step was more compromising. For he sent several of his ministers on missions to South Africa and Portugal ... March 1967. A trade agreement was signed with Pretoria ...d several technical ones with Lisbon. But the political element was uppermost. Foreign Minister Hilgard Muller felt ...at this visit was "of historic importance, and one that should ...rve, we hope, as an example to others that peaceful coexistence is possible in southern Africa among the various nations ...d groups whose internal policies may not necessarily be the ...me."[27] But the bomb came on 10 September 1967, when ...resident Banda confirmed that Malawi would "enter into direct, ...en and formal diplomatic relations with the Republic of South ...rica as from January 1968 if not before that date."[28] This ...s a terrible blow to the Kinshasa OAU Assembly that opened ...e day after and included action against South Africa, Rhodes... and Portugal on its agenda.

In the relationships that were being established between ...rtain independent states and Africa's traditional arch enemy, ...e leaders who felt the attraction of this powerful country ...ost strongly did not regard themselves as the dupes of South ...rican policy. They insisted that a new approach was necessary to turn Pretoria away from its previous practices and to ...ing about a softening of its ideology of white supremacy. ...ter a visit of Sir Seretse Khama to President Banda in Mal...i, from 5-9 July 1967, they adopted a communique which ...plained that in seeking to bring about a change in the think...g of the peoples and countries of southern Africa, the best ...pe lay in contacts and discussions between independent Afri...n states and minority-governed countries. It was necessary ... change the views of the whites, not to shun them. The ...ole problem of apartheid, discrimination or segregation was ...r. For the whites did not know how they would live under ...ck rule.[29]

It was hard to tell if anything was rubbing off. South ...rica had given itself a new look on certain occasions and ...r certain purposes. It had received Chief Jonathan and the ...lawi negotiators with all due honors and had entertained ...m without apartheid restrictions. It even decided to send a ...lti-racial team to the 1968 Olympics. Most striking was ...e debate between the enlightened (verligte) and narrow-minded ...erkrampte) factions of the Nationalist Party. Prime Minis...r Vorster announced that he would continue his new policy ...ward the neighboring countries and attacked the ultra-con...rvatives and "super-Afrikaners" in Parliament. "It is just ...od sense to establish good relations with every country we

can," he insisted.   But he did not cease imposing apartheid on
the non-white population within South Africa and South West
Africa.   And the government continued preparing the Bantustans.   This would eventually create a system in which there
was only one large and powerful state in the south and a hodge
podge of smaller self-governing regions and independent African states, all of which would rely on Pretoria's good will and
would form a barrier or at least a buffer between it and the
adamant rest of the continent.   The final result of this policy
remained to be seen.

Although South Africa could treat its neighbors with kid
gloves, it could also recall them to order if they were not
amenable to such treatment.   Zambia, somewhat more prosperous than the others, was also landlocked and dependent
largely on Mozambique for access to the sea.   It shared various common services and had considerable trade with Rhodesia.
Still, it tried to apply the sanctions.   It was revamping the
whole economy and trade, seeking new means of transport,
and rapidly decreasing its relations with the colonial and settler powers.   It was even becoming one of the major bases for
the liberation movements.   President Kaunda opened his country to the freedom fighters and many of them set off on the
dangerous trip to South and South West Africa from there.
However, due to its precarious encircled position, there was a
limit to what Zambia could do.   And the government tried not
to make the aid too blatant for fear of serious retaliation from
either Salisbury or Pretoria.

This was not an easy task and after the bloody engagements in Rhodesia towards the end of 1967 and the news of
South Africans in the ranks, Zambia seemed to have bitten off
more than it could chew.   In mid-October, Prime Minister
Vorster warned Zambia that Pretoria would strike back if attacked.   If President Kaunda's Zambia ever tried to use violence against South Africa, "we will hit you so hard you will
never forget it."   But neither side really wished to come to
such a pass.   Zambian ministers quickly announced that they
were not training the freedom fighters who went to Rhodesia
and South Africa, although they were not stopping them either.
The day after, the OAU Secretariat issued a statement assuring Mr. Vorster and his regime "that the Member States of
the OAU will certainly not sit idly by while South Africa 'hits'
President Kaunda and his valiant peoples of Zambia.   The resistance would be world-wide."[30]   However, the exchange of
threats ended there, for no one wanted action yet.

3lack Africa on the Defensive.

South Africa was by far the strongest and most solidly
ntrenched of the colonial and settler powers. Its white mi-
ority government could act with impunity within the country
nd it was out of reach of independent Africa. The recent
ears were still a period of consolidation, as preparations
'ere made to withstand any pressure that might arise. Dur-
ng the same period, although Africa had won friends and sup-
ort in its campaign against apartheid and South Africa, it did
ot really make any tangible progress. Thus it was natural
or impatience and dissatisfaction to set in.

The worst tension was within the apartheid country,
/here the Africans and others were increasingly subordinated
) the white society. The brutal methods used to reorganize
he country and to forestall change only heightened the artifi-
ial nature of apartheid and led the Africans, as well, to seek
nore effective and forceful ways of destroying the system.
/hereas the African National Congress had at first preferred
eaceful resistance to the stronger methods of the Pan-African-
st Congress, this division was swept away by the bloodshed
t Sharpeville. Since then, Nelson Mandela brought the ANC
round to an endorsement of the armed struggle as one of the
actics of opposition. In the following years violence was re-
orted to by both groups.

A landmark in the transition to violence was the Rivonia
rials in 1964. For some time the political parties had gone
nderground and had established ties with secret terrorist or-
anizations: the ANC with Umkonto we Sizwe (Spear of the Na-
.on) and the PAC with Poqo. In April, Nelson Mandela, Wal-
er Sisulu and others from the ANC were indicted as the lead-
rs of Umkonto we Sizwe and charged with sabotage as part of
 general plot against the government. A sign of the times
as that Mandela admitted planning sabotage because of "op-
ression" by the whites and Sisulu regarded violence as inevit-
ble. He admitted that he had reverted to a policy of violence
nd sabotage as the "situation was becoming desperate."[31] In
ue course the eight nationalists were convicted of planning
violent revolution" and given life terms and the attorney who
d their defence, Abram Fischer, was soon arrested under
ie 90-day detention law. The government could still crush its
pponents, but in so doing it was only creating more oppres-
ion and desperation.

The clearest lesson for the nationalists was that little could be accomplished within the country and that new forces had to be formed abroad. An increasing number of nationalists left the country. In Algeria and Egypt, in Tanzania and Zambia, or in China, there were several thousand freedom fighters undergoing training or waiting to go into action. The liberation struggle was developing along the lines of the others in Africa. Unfortunately, although a United Front had been formed, there were still two movements. While in exile, under the direction of Oliver Tambo, the larger ANC had managed to maintain its cohesion and was well led and remarkably well disciplined. It formed an alliance with ZAPU and groups of freedom fighters infiltrated Rhodesia. It received primary support from the OAU Liberation Committee. The long wait had not been supported as well by PAC, which split on ideological lines. Although a crisis in leadership was resolved by the Liberation Committee in September 1967, and it agreed in principle to form a united front with ANC, PAC split into two factions the year after. By July 1968, the Liberation Committee had to complain of "great confusion" in the movement and suspend its aid.

But there was little hope for guerrilla warfare or even terrorism. The lay of the land, especially in the north, was unfavorable and the police and army had a close watch on the situation. All that could be done for the moment was to weaken South Africa by isolating it from its trading partners and allies. Although world public opinion had been made sensitive to the racial policies of Pretoria, this was still a long way from convincing the states and businessmen to cease their beneficial relations. Repeated attempts had been made in the United Nations but the results were meager. None of the major partners restricted trade and some had increased it. Despite American and British compliance with the military embargo, South Africa's armed forces were growing. Thus, even if lip service was paid the struggle against apartheid, there were very few acts to speak of.

There was more than enough reason for frustration in Africa. Five years after its creation, the Organization of African Unity was passing through a particularly sobering phase. The progress it had made was largely on paper; little had become reality. Its own resolutions were increasingly pointed but were not always applied. Worse, South Africa was even making inroads on what had been accomplished. The Council of Ministers in Kinshasa, in September 1967, was seriously disturbed by the situation. Even though nothing was admitted openly, a feeling of despair transpired from the resolution.

The Africans had always realized that no boycott would be successful nor even adopted by the Security Council without the backing of certain states. And, despite their disapproval of apartheid, these states were not willing to help Africa effectively. Once again they came under fire: first, the principal trading partners, especially those which still sold military equipment or machinery for producing arms and munition; and then, the three permanent members of the Security Council which "have not complied with the recommendations and appeals of the United Nations General Assembly."

But the greatest problems were closer at home. First of all, apartheid had not been circumscribed in South Africa. The Assembly had to deplore "the extension of apartheid and the very great assistance which the South African Government is giving to the illegal regime of Ian Smith in order to consolidate a further bastion of apartheid."

What was more, Africa had lowered its guard and South African trade was again expanding. It was necessary to remind the independent states to "exercise a more vigilant conrol of their boycott of South African products." Even worse difficulties were created by the member states which established or maintained good neighborly relations with South Africa, in disrespect of OAU resolutions and the most sacred principle of the Charter. This was seen as an open defial and the Assembly denounced the South African "maneuvres to entice the independent African States with economic and financial offers in order to weaken their resolution in the struggle against apartheid."

However, no matter how disturbing the situation, the cause was far from lost. By backing the other colonial and settler regimes, South Africa had slowed down the movement towards independence, but it had also created additional difficulties for itself. Also, although the members of the Security Council denied that apartheid was a threat to peace and refused to adopt mandatory sanctions against South Africa, they were increasingly being forced into a corner on other issues. It was impossible for them to implement the sanctions against Rhodesia or recuperate the mandate in South West Africa--to which they had committed themselves--without reacting against Pretoria. And the struggle on these fronts was making more headway. Thus, the Western powers and the United Nations, despite themselves, might eventually be implicated in a struggle against South Africa.

Furthermore, even if Africa was on the defensive for the moment, things were bound to change. It was only a que tion of time. South Africa was powerful. But its strength could not keep pace with the rest of Africa or the support it could mobilize elsewhere. In particular, no matter how stro Pretoria was, it could not prop up its allies indefinitely. Sooner or later the Portuguese territories or Rhodesia would fall. Then the situation would be quite different. When Sout Africa was surrounded by independent states, when its neighbors were made fortresses to train and defend the freedom fighters, when the sanctions had been spread and were being implemented, the white minority regime would be infinitely more vulnerable. Africa needed only determination and patience to put an end to the regime--as well as an awareness that ill-conceived action could spoil everything.

Notes

1. "Race Relations Policy of the National Party," issued by its Head Office, 1948.

2. Contact, Capetown, 30 May 1959.

3. See Amelia Leiss (ed.), Apartheid and United Nations Co lective Measures.

4. General Assembly Res. 1761(XVII), 6 Nov. 1962.

5. United Nations Doc. S/5386, 7 Aug. 1963.

6. Ibid. A/SPC/80, 8 Oct. 1963, p. 5.

7. General Assembly Res. 1881(XVIII), 11 Oct. 1963.

8. United Nations Doc. A/SPC/82, 9 Oct. 1963.

9. Security Council Res. 182(1963), 4 Dec. 1963.

10. "A New Course in South Africa," United Nations Publication, Sales No. 64.I.13.

11. United Nations Doc. S/PV.1131, 15 June 1964.

12. Ibid. S/5773, 18 June 1964.

13. United Nations Doc. S/6210, 2 March 1965.

14. Ibid. A/5932, 17 June 1965.

15. General Assembly Res. 2054 A and B(XX), 15 Dec. 1965.

16. United Nations Doc. S/6210, 2 March 1965.

17. See George Mudge, Domestic Policies and U.N. Activities.

18. See F.R. Tomlinson, et. al., Report on the Socio-Economic Development of the Bantu Areas, Pretoria, 1956.

19. "Second Special Report of the Director-General on the Application of the Declaration concerning the Policy of 'Apartheid' of the Republic of South Africa," Geneva, International Labour Office, 1966.

20. "Afrique 1968," Jeune Afrique, p. 380; Le Monde, 22 April 1967.

21. "Afrique 1968," p. 377.

22. Issues Before the General Assembly, International Conciliation, 1966 and 1967.

23. United Nations Doc. A/AC.109/L.393, 7 April 1967, p. 65.

24. Africa Report, Nov. 1966.

25. Ibid., Dec. 1966.

26. The Times (London), 17 Oct. 1966.

27. Africa Report, May 1967.

28. Ibid., Nov. 1967.

29. The Times (London), 10 July 1967.

30. Ethiopian Herald, 18, 19, & 20 Oct. 1967.

31. The New York Times, 21 & 22 April 1964.

E. Conclusion

Liberation of the entire continent was Africa's highest goal and it was quite normal that decolonization should be made the primary activity of the Organization of African Uni Towards this end its greatest sacrifices would have to be ma and it was largely on the basis of its performance in emanci pating the continent that the OAU would be judged. Decoloni zation was anything but an academic exercise for the Organi zation. Ever since 1963, it devoted much of its time and energy to this struggle. The supreme bodies repeatedly laid down basic policies and numerous other bodies supervised their implementation. A large share of the financial re- sources was also channelled towards the effort.

Thanks partly to the OAU, the action undertaken agai the colonial and settler powers had a definite impact. The guerrilla units in the field became increasingly effective figh ing forces. New fronts were opened and others expanded. some of the territories the liberation movements gained com mand of extensive areas, in others they at least made life u pleasant for the enemy. Economically, as well, trade was curtailed between most independent states and the settler an colonial powers. The boycott was increasingly supported by the international community and the United Nations had taken the unprecedented step of introducing compulsory sanctions against Rhodesia.

Nevertheless, there were as yet no striking results. No territory had escaped the grip of rear-guard colonialism. Neither the warfare nor the economic squeeze made them re lax their control or seek a way out. To the contrary, even while the struggle was being intensified, the settler and co- lonial powers seemed to be reinforcing their own efforts con mensurate with or beyond those of Africa. A stalemate was reached on many fronts and occasionally the forces of libera tion had been contained. Although they were being hurt, Af- rica's enemies would be able to hold out for some time.

In Search of a Common Policy.

From the start the independent states had judged the situation in southern Africa too optimistically. They were often misled by their own experiences, where a relatively short and limited campaign had persuaded powerful countries like Britain and France to withdraw. They had not expected such determined resistance from a second-rate nation like Portugal or the some 200,000 settlers in Rhodesia. In addition, they were surprised by the speed with which their enemies deployed troops, cut off frontiers and tightened the internal regimes. Their own wishful thinking or propaganda may also have led them to overestimate the militancy and representativity of most of the liberation movements. There was a painful delay before many of them could field even small armies and the response was bitterly disappointing.

Whether they liked it or not, the independent states and the OAU were engaged in a war of attrition that gained ground, but slowly. It required increasingly strong efforts of them and created unexpected strains. If colonialism were to be extirpated from the continent they would have to pool their resources and lay down a policy all would follow. Unfortunately, the brief resolution of the Addis Ababa summit conference was not a strategy but a list of tactics. It included all means-- running from propaganda, diplomatic and economic sanctions, political action, and moral and material support of the liberation movements on down to a generally accepted use of force-- without providing priorities. However, in the long, hard pull, it would be necessary to strengthen the means, use the right methods at the right time and work them into a common plan.

The radicals had always placed the goal of decolonization before all others and they tried to drag the Organization towards use of the most forceful and "effective" means. They took the strongest stands and made the most audacious proposals and offers. At the summit conference, Ben Bella had stated that 10,000 Algerian volunteers were waiting to aid their brothers in Angola. Then, at the first Council of Ministers, he urged that African contingents be sent to the Portuguese territories to "liberate" the populations. To finance the effort, Sékou Touré suggested in Addis Ababa that one per cent of the African national budgets be devoted to the struggle. Finally, in order to undermine the colonial and settler powers, they openly supported the guerrilla warfare of the liberation movements and provided instructors, equipment and funds. However, when the liberation wars did not produce the expected results, there were renewed appeals for more direct intervention.

The moderates, for their part, had a definite preference for the less violent methods. They did not repudiate the use of force, but they left it primarily to the dependent peoples. They rejected any idea of direct African intervention in the territories and backed only the indigenous wars of liberation. Still, even this aid was attenuated. Moderates made relatively small contributions and endorsed mainly the calmer movements. They preferred using other means of pressure first. They wished to try the effect of sanctions fully before resorting to stronger and riskier tactics. They also placed more reliance on the aid Africa could get from outside the continent by world-wide application of sanctions or political pressure. For this reason they tried to work through the United Nations and were willing to leave the responsibility for Rhodesia with Great Britain and for South West Africa with the General Assembly.

For some time the OAU's members followed or preached the methods they thought most effective or appropriate almost haphazardly. There was little control of the extent to which the pledges were put into practice. Thus the level of dedication was much lower than would appear from the public speeches or OAU resolutions. Although Algeria made greater efforts than any other non-border state, it did not send its troops to fight in Angola. And few of the OAU's members made serious inroads in their national budgets to aid the freedom fighters. Although some initial good will was shown, the moderate states eventually left the burden to others and even sanctions were not implemented universally. Reliance on the United Nations and Great Britain was often only the easy way out.

But this dispersed action was no longer possible after the crisis in Rhodesia. As it became increasingly clear that the settler regime would take the risk of declaring independence, Africa was faced with a challenge it could not ignore. Rhodesia was a denial of the policy of peaceful decolonization that had been followed previously and a step backwards in the struggle to free southern Africa. But it was also a case where seemingly a determined push by the population and the independent states could have toppled the settler government and initiated the final phase of decolonization. Awareness had come too late, however, and although there were threats and warnings during the Accra Assembly Africa did not act upon UDI.

The OAU could hardly afford a repetition of this and an extraordinary Council of Ministers was called in December 1965 to work out a common approach. This was actually the first time that there was a serious debate on Africa's policy of decolonization or that the proponents of the different methods had to defend them. This was also a confrontation between two views of decolonization and between the members that held them. The radical states took the initiative. They insisted on throwing more weight behind the "militant" liberation movements, making vastly greater contributions financially and militarily and, since UDI was a challenge to all Africa, even intervening directly. There was talk of mobilizing contingents for an African army.

The moderates were worried about the implications of any direct action. Quite simply, they regarded it as unrealistic. By calculating the cost in men and money of raising an army and airforce capable of defeating Rhodesia alone, it was easy to demonstrate that this would be an intolerable strain. What was more, the demands for direct action were somewhat demagogic. The states proposing this intervention had proven their willingness to make a contribution, but they had not really shown the degree of dedication a war required. The final point was that Africa had been making slow but steady progress through guerrilla warfare. Since the operations were carried out on enemy territory, there was little damage to any independent state. However, if war were declared, the colonial and settler powers would not hesitate to invade the camps of those attacking them. For the first time there would be a real threat to the border countries.

The first round had gone against the radicals and it was clear that the liberation movements would have to carry the brunt of the struggle. Rather than follow this up and force the Organization to increase its aid to the freedom fighters, the members went off on a tangent. The moderates had argued that the "colonial power" was still responsible for the situation. Great Britain was a power that could use force and had failed to prevent unilateral independence. But the radicals knew that neither Britain nor the United Nations could be counted upon to fight Africa's battles. Nevertheless, the Council ordered the severance of OAU's members' relations with London if the rebellion were not crushed forthwith. This decision was doubly bad. When only nine states complied the African community stood divided before the world. And the quarrel distracted Africa from its primary task which was to find a realistic and generally acceptable policy.

It was not until the Assembly of Heads of State in November 1966, a year after UDI, that the debate was continued less passionately. This time the radicals rapidly dropped every notion of direct intervention and accepted that the strongest methods be the use of guerrilla warfare by the liberation movements themselves. They then concentrated on the more valid task of increasing the aid to these movements. Here the limits of moderate dedication became clear. Still, the principle of stepping up action through the freedom fighters and the need of member states to make contributions, and pay their arrears into the Freedom Fund were accepted. Despite the near breach with Britain, the other side of the attack remained reliance on the colonial power and the United Nations to introduce and expand sanctions against the rebel colony.

Africa had finally defined its policy. It only included the tested methods and would not involve Africa in a dangerous adventure. This compromise was less impressive than many earlier statements. Yet it was regarded as a sign of maturity and "realism." Emperor Haile Selassie stressed that this time the resolutions contained nothing that could not be implemented. From the radical camp, President Boumedienne added that the Organization should not be forced to do more than it was capable of.[1] Moreover, and this was essential, the plan was approved and endorsed by all the members. Of course, there were still differences. But at least Africa now had a common framework for action.

Rift Among the Border Countries.

Despite the difficulties, compromises could usually be worked out between the radical and moderate states. But even these compromises were threatened by the admission of a new group of members unable to muster an "absolute dedication" to the emancipation of the continent. These states were dangerously close to the dependent territories and their freedom of action was limited. Even when they desired the independence of these peoples or the rule of the majority in Rhodesia and South Africa, they were not ready to risk their own position by backing the African struggle for liberation.

Although these states did not repudiate the basic principles and aims of the OAU, they were not willing to apply its resolutions and policies. They agreed with the ends--but not the means. From the outset the Heads of State of Malawi, Lesotho, Botswana and Swaziland announced that they would not be able to implement sanctions against Rhodesia. For Hastings Banda, sanctions merely meant "cutting our own economic throats." Chief Jonathan stated that he would not support moves by member states to interfere in the domestic affairs of other countries and would oppose sanctions as this would be "suicidal" for Lesotho. The four also made it clear that they would not let their territories be used as staging grounds for liberation movements or provide a haven on the trip to South Africa. Protecting freedom fighters was only inviting retaliation. Botswana expressed strong concern about the problem of transiting guerrillas at the Kinshasa Assembly. In its view this created a serious danger for the government and it felt that it was incumbent on the OAU to see that the sovereignty and territorial integrity of Botswana were not violated.[2]

What was more disconcerting was that these states were slowly developing their own, very different approach to the situation. They felt that the OAU had to find an even more "realistic" policy. President Banda insisted that "one had to be realistic, for South Africa is here to stay and is the most powerful country in Africa, industrially, economically, financially, and the most militarily powerful."[3] Thus they maintained what relations they had and stressed that the use of force was not a solution to the problems in southern Africa. However, these states also seemed to be making further moves towards South Africa. Economic and political relations were improving and Malawi accepted links it did not previously have. At the same time they were working out an alternative policy. Better understanding was the key and a change in the stand of the settler powers could be sought through contacts and discussions, by learning to live and get along with one another. It was this view of decolonization that shocked the OAU.

This attitude was all the more painful since, in the same region, there were other countries making considerable efforts. True, few of them were as close to South Africa or as dependent on the colonial and settler powers. Yet the fact that they had decided to make sacrifices for decolonization drew a line between them and these more compliant African states. And it was there, along the front, that the split was most ominous and the chances of reaching a new compromise most unlikely. Among the radical states and the more active border countries these members were repeatedly attacked as collaborators. When Pretoria announced that there was going to be an extradition treaty with Lesotho, Radio Brazzaville added the name of Chief Leabua Jonathan of Lesotho to President Banda's of Malawi as the "second traitor who is selling

his own brothers to the white racialists of South Africa."[4]
Hastings Banda replied to his critics in equally biting terms.
He called them "physical and moral cowards as well as hypo-
crites" and charged that "while they are criticizing me for
trading openly with South Africa they themselves are trading
with South Africa secretly."[5]

    This quarrel went even further. Since often these in-
dependent states were more conservative and traditionalist than
most, there was also a split between them and other OAU
members on politics and African ideology. This would not
have been so dangerous if the two most offensive collaborating
regimes were not also rather precarious politically. Chief
Leabua Jonathan suppressed the opposition to stay in power.
Hastings Banda had a falling-out with his progressive ministers in September 1964, only two months after independence.
He accused them of organizing a conspiracy and, as late as
October 1967, one of the rebel ministers entered the country
at the head of an armed band. This opposition was not only
tolerated by other independent states, it was even fostered on
occasion. The ousted Malawi ministers found refuge in Tanzania and Zambia and, in January 1967, they decided to establish a government-in-exile. Thus the two governments, Malawi
and Lesotho, had the additional worries of political threats
from the independent part of the continent.

    Whatever the merits of the case, this sort of hostility
was certainly not serving the cause of Africa. And the primary duty of the Organization of African Unity was to heal the
rift. As it was, the OAU had gotten off to a bad start. The
Liberation Committee, before Basutoland (= Lesotho), Bechuanaland (= Botswana), and Swaziland became independent, supported what it considered the most representative political parties. In each case it was a party in opposition to the conservative ones that won the pre-independence elections. In Accra,
the Council of Ministers endorsed this policy and expressed
concern that "Parties which have openly declared that they
would closely co-operate with the Pretoria regime have assumed control of the governmental machineries in these territories." Not surprisingly, the new states became members of
the OAU under these parties anyway.

    It was not easy to find a place for them within the OAU.
More flexibility than had been shown in the past was required.
From the start the OAU had acted as if all African states were
in the same relative position. Yet it was obviously impossible
for the weak enclaves to impose sanctions on economically

strong racist countries completely or nearly surrounding and landlocking them. Even countries like Congo (Kinshasa) and Zambia felt the need to maintain some relations and trade. Unless the Organization recognized these problems and tried to solve them it could not really fulfill its purposes.

It was doubtlessly difficult to alter policies that had been worked out over years and seemed to be the best ones to produce results. But every policy could allow for special circumstances. For example, it had to be admitted that certain states were in a more precarious position and could not make the same contribution. There was no sense in demanding absolute dedication when little could be done and each attempt only permitted Pretoria and Lisbon to increase their pressure. It was better to formally permit exceptions for these states rather than making them proclaim such exceptions unilaterally. They could be authorized to trade if their economy depended on it. They would not be forced to harbor freedom fighters or launch attacks if their survival was endangered by this. However, by the same token, they should accept some rough supervision so that their trade did not rise or provide channels for getting around sanctions. They could at least be expected not to turn over refugees and freedom fighters within their boundaries.

Then, even while asking the border countries to make a contribution to decolonization, it was necessary to find ways of helping them overcome their own difficulties. If losses due to sanctions were a crushing burden, there should be compensation. If the states were threatened by reprisals, their defence had to be assured. Only in the case of Zambia had the African community as a whole accepted any responsibility. But the Committee of Solidarity was still doing little to relieve it. And this policy would have to be broadened to include other states. The need was finally recognized in September 1968, when the Council requested the Secretary-General to investigate "the nature and form of assistance those African countries genuinely interested in ending whatever economic relations and links with South Africa can be given in order to help them speed up their severing of such links at the earliest possible time."

This way a more valid distinction might be drawn between those that were doing their best and those that were really collaborating with the enemy. President Nyerere of Tanzania had already suggested that such cases "must be judged by Africa in the light of the objective circumstances, and

Africa as a whole must try to distinguish between those states
which embrace their captors and those which seek merely to
survive."[6] This may have been what was intended by the Algiers resolution asking the Secretary-General to ascertain the
"nature and extent of relations" between member states and
the Pretoria regime. However, even for the first category,
it was wiser to start with persuasion. For, by casting them
out, the OAU would only be playing into South Africa's hands
and helping it to "divide and rule."

Malaise on the Liberation Front.

        The basic philosophy of the struggle for liberation was
that it was a joint combat undertaken in common by the dependent peoples and the independent states. The freedom fighters were to be the spearhead of this struggle and launch wars
in each of the territories. The independent states would back
them morally and materially. They were to train and equip
the liberation armies and the neighboring countries would provide bases for launching attacks. Despite any promises or
hopes, however, it was increasingly clear that the independent
states would remain on the sidelines and not intervene. The
increasingly "realistic" policy of the OAU was placing the
heaviest burden on the liberation movements.

        These movements had been interested primarily in the
assistance they could obtain from the independent states.
Speeches and pledges at the summit conference had awakened
hopes of massive aid. A Special Fund was established to finance them. The Liberation Committee called for an aid budget of over four million dollars a year. And the Cairo Assembly made contributions obligatory. Unfortunately, however,
the effort was never fully supported. Many of the moderate
states, in particular, had a poor record. By 1969 the Committee had to complain that only thirteen of the forty-one members were contributing to the Fund.[7] Although the target sums
were rarely reached, the Fund was even so about as large as
the OAU's regular budget. But no matter how high the total
ran, it was never sufficient to meet all the needs of the liberation movements nor did it compare encouragingly with the
vast sums Portugal and South Africa devoted to defence.

        It was not long before the leaders of the nationalist
movements began to complain of the lack of effort on the part
of independent Africa. The support they received was inadequate and they let it be known that they would seek help from

other sources. GRAE's Holden Roberto announced that he
would accept aid from the "devil" if need be. Soon there were
missions to Peking and Moscow as well as various African
capitals. Quieter contacts were also made and over the years
multiple links were established between specific movements
and backers. As the radicals, in particular, lost confidence
in the OAU, they increased direct aid to certain movements,
bypassing the Fund.

Not having received the aid they demanded, the nationalist movements were rather annoyed by the orders coming
from the Liberation Committee. The Committee, which was
trying to give a new impulse to the struggle by working out an
overall strategy, admonished the movements to coordinate and
increase their efforts. It looked into the causes of division
and rivalry and made suggestions--tied to sanctions--to overcome them. This did not please the movements which were,
after all, bearing the brunt of the effort. The fact that the
orders often came from low-level diplomats rankled the leaders of the nationalist movements who bore some actual responsibility for the dependent peoples. They also objected to the
bureaucracy, the inefficiency and the general attitude. On several occasions they suggested that the Liberation Committee be
made a joint venture where they would participate in decisions.
At the Accra Assembly, several movements even requested
that the Committee be disbanded and direct relations established with the Heads of State.

The independent states saw things from a different angle. They were not entirely satisfied that the liberation movements were making the requisite effort. There were too many
groups and subgroups for all to be active and some of the freedom fighters did not seem to spend much time in the field of
battle. There was also an embarrassing congestion of leaders
and staffs in Dar es Salaam and other capitals. The Council
at Accra requested the Liberation Committee "to make a judi-
cious distribution of the freedom fighters in various sectors on
any front and in the border countries ... to avoid a massive
concentration of freedom fighters at the headquarters of the
Committee, which may harm the host countries and the cause
of liberating the continent in every respect."

There was also considerable suspicion that the funds
granted the various movements were not always going to the
best purposes. Some of the leaders seemed to be living too
well and others were spending more time making propaganda
than directing operations. The independent states insisted on

careful supervision of whatever funds they provided and, in November 1966, the Council laid down regulations for the distribution and control of funds. First, the assistance granted any movement should be relevant to the nature of its struggle and had to be devoted solely to the liberation of territories under colonial rule. Of the funds, only 10 per cent would be given the movements in cash for the maintenance of offices or propaganda. The rest would meet the cost of matériel and training and the expenses of running two training centres, one in East Africa and the other in West Africa. Then, before receiving a further allocation, the movements had to submit statements of account with supporting documents to show the use of previous grants.

However, the basic need was still coordination so that the struggle could be made more effective with even the limited means at hand. The original plan was to form common fronts in each territory. This task consumed much of the time and energy of the Liberation Committee. Numerous conciliators and committees were sent to smooth over differences and permit cooperation. Some of these efforts had to be supported or even initiated at the level of the Council of Ministers. It was certainly not easy to overcome the personal, tribal and ideological conflicts. Nevertheless, the Committee gave in too rapidly. Even the first good will mission, after a brief visit to the camps in neighboring countries, abandoned its task of reconciliating the movements in Angola and Guinea. Rather, it decided to grant exclusive or principal recognition to one.

Turning aside from the original goal, the Committee began distributing funds on the basis of "effectiveness." Without denying the need for common fronts, it increasingly tried to integrate all rivals in one movement rather than seek cooperation among equals. This appeared in the new rules, approved by the Council and Assembly in November 1966. They gave precedence to the movements engaged in an armed struggle and, among them, to the movements that established common action fronts or whose struggle had been serious and/or most effective in the previous year. More broadly, priority would be given the liberation movements whose country's independence was more feasible and would in turn be most influential and instrumental in effecting the total liquidation of colonialism in Africa.

The theory behind this was that the other movements, once denied recognition or funds from the OAU would be forced to compose their differences and join the "effective" movement or disappear. The most persuasive arguments could come from the neighboring countries without whose assistance the liberation movements would be deprived of access and operation bases. But the results were very disappointing. Despite all efforts to launch the struggle in Rhodesia, the pressure exerted on both ZAPU and ZANU to make them merge in the crucial moment before UDI was insufficient. The repeated efforts in Angola were also to no avail. After the Committee recognized GRAE exclusively, MPLA was nonetheless able to weather the storm. When the Committee later decided that GRAE was no longer effective, it continued operating as in the past.

It was not hard to explain this failure. First of all, the stakes were too high. Success in a liberation war meant power in the future state. For the backers in and outside of Africa, especially the border states, it meant a friendly neighbor or ally. Thus, once a movement had been formed, there was little chance it would drop out entirely. Secondly, the Committee had wrongly assumed that its decisions would force the unfavored movements to merge or disappear. These groups in fact could still draw on the political and financial assistance of other supporters. For they tended to have their own backers both in and outside of Africa. As long as the liberation movements received more aid directly than through the Freedom Fund, they could afford to brave the demands coming from the Committee.

The Liberation Committee had been mistaken. No matter how difficult it was to reconcile the nationalist movements, it was harder to choose between them or try to suppress one. If any solutions were to be found it had to be based on cooperation. This might start with joint operations and common fronts and possibly end with a merger. It would also provide an essential basis for the cooperation that would be needed in the independent state later on. For these reasons, and also because it could not choose between the movements, the Council of Ministers returned to the policy of common fronts in September 1967, when it decided to bypass the Liberation Committee and set up its own committee to help form a common front in Angola.

Crisis in the Liberation Committee.

Originally the Liberation Committee had been conceived of as a channel for cooperation between the nationalist movements and the independent states. However, when relations were less smooth than had been expected, most of this stress fell on the Liberation Committee and it became a sort of institutional shock-absorber.

The Liberation Committee had been established directly by the Summit Conference. It had originally been endowed with great prestige because of its highly sensitive and crucial task. It was made small and compact so as to act rapidly and efficiently. It had its own staff and headquarters, its own mission and ethos. True, the Committee received instructions from the Council and Assembly. Still, within the broad limits of these vague resolutions and especially during the long intervals between sessions, it made some of the most politically loaded and financially important decisions in the Organization. These decisions could be reversed but they appeared valid and were acted upon by the Committee until modified by a governing body.

The Committee was accomplishing tasks of the greatest importance for the whole Organization and thus the autonomy it claimed soon came under attack. First the Secretary-General claimed and obtained "supervisory power" over the Secretariat of the Committee. More significant was that communications were felt to be faulty with the governing bodies, the Council of Ministers in particular. Many members disliked the aura of secrecy about the Committee's operations and they demanded more detailed reports on its proceedings and financial management. Others felt that administrative costs were too high. This led to a major debate in the Council and eventually an ad hoc committee to examine its functioning.

By November 1966, this general interest and specific investigation resulted in a reform of the Committee. Its budget was made part of the budget of the General Secretariat. It was not allowed to withdraw monies from the Freedom Fund, exclusively reserved for the needs of the liberation movements. The staff of the Committee's Secretariat was made subject to OAU regulations for recruitment, discipline and promotions. The Committee had to submit its accounts to the internal auditing of the General Secretariat and the Accounts Committee of the OAU, the report of the latter being appended to the Committee's report to the Council. The Committee would submit a semi-annual report on allocations, distribution and use of funds to all members of the OAU. And, to satisfy the states that were not on the Committee, any member could send observers to all meetings.

To make the Liberation Committee more influential, it was decided that the members should be represented by senior officials. However, since they were almost always political appointees, often the Ambassador to Tanzania (the Committee's headquarters being in Dar es Salaam), there was still the problem of lack of expertise. Most of the questions had an important military side and the Committee did not have a very good record with its overall or territory-wise strategy. It also needed reliable information about the effectiveness of movements and the situation on each front. In September 1967, the Council decided to establish a Committee of 17 Military Experts to aid it. Although the terms of reference and the relationship with the Liberation Committee were not specified, the experts would probably travel from front to front to investigate the operations and offer advice, and then report back to Committee headquarters. In February 1969 they were asked to review the general strategy of the armed struggle and study the distribution and storage of equipment and improved transit facilities.

But the root of the difficulties was political. As long as the Liberation Committee tried to establish common fronts without discriminating among the movements, there was no trouble. As soon as it attempted to exercise choice, it ran inevitably into friction. Every decision to reduce funds or cease recognition set off complaints from the movement and its backers. What was more serious, however, was a growing bias of the Liberation Committee towards one group of movements. A clear trend developed after the expansion of the Committee in 1965. Most strikingly, there was a gradual revision in the status of GRAE, culminating in the withdrawal of recognition in July 1968. And, although the Council of Ministers was unable to choose between the Zimbabwe movements, the Committee did not hesitate to back ZAPU. Eventually the Liberation Committee came around to supporting all the more "revolutionary" movements: PAIGC, MPLA, FRELIMO, ZAPU, ANC, and SWAPO.

This led to almost permanent controversy over the Committee's decisions. It followed a consistently radical course while the Council of Ministers obeyed the moderates. A collision could not be avoided and, at the Algiers Council in

September 1968, it occurred. This time the moderates demanded an investigation of the Committee's activities and a more drastic reform of its structure. Since all the members paid the budget and had a right to attend as observers, they insisted there was no excuse for excessive secrecy. The Committee should keep all members fully informed of its activities. There were also objections to the composition of the Committee and it was suggested that membership be rotated so that it would not always include the same states. Finally, there were a number of specific complaints about the way funds were distributed, the choice of beneficiaries and a few charges that weapons got into the hands of subversive elements. The campaign was resumed the year after in Addis Ababa and this time yet another committee of experts was set up to consider a possible reform.

The real bone of contention was whether the Committee should become what the November 1966 resolution had claimed it was intended to be: "an executive and managerial body and not a policy-making body." There had always been a tendency for the Committee to increase its influence. It wished to give a general orientation to the struggle and often took crucial decisions in organizing the strategy of liberation. As long as its views coincided with those of the Council this was even encouraged. However, by adopting a radical approach it had alienated the moderate majority in the Organization and the Council began nibbling at its powers and restricting its autonomy. The final result seemed likely to be either a vast increase in membership to permit all states to have a voice or a very strict subordination to the Council of Ministers. Whatever the change, the problem would not be solved but only transferred to another forum. For the Council had repeatedly shown its inability to unify the liberation movements or choose between them. It had never given the Committee detailed and applicable instructions. And any controversy might eventually paralyze both the Committee and Council.

A structural reform would solve nothing. For the problem was not institutional, it was political. A crisis of confidence undermined the joint machinery of liberation in Africa. The liberation movements had not received the aid they needed and they had not made the efforts expected of them. Not only had the moderate states failed to aid the freedom fighters adequately, they had, for reasons of realism or timidity, made their far from drastic doctrine of decolonization the official OAU policy. With this the radicals had switched their backing directly to the more "revolutionary" movements and almost fortuitously had also obtained a majority in the Liberation Committee. In the hands of moderates, rather than being attacked for its radical stands, the Committee might simply have faded out and the OAU would have ceased playing any major role in decolonization.

This meant that it was not necessary to change the institution. It was necessary to use it fully and fairly. If the system created in 1963 had failed thus far, it was because it had never been given a chance. Each partner waited for the other to take the first step. By acting in unison the system could work. The moderates would have to provide funds at a higher level, and without shirking. If they wanted, the radicals could certainly give more, but only through the Fund and without trying to gain special advantages. The African states should also convince all outside states to do the same. With these funds the liberation movements could be solidly financed. With a really concerted political will, the member states would have little difficulty in imposing common fronts on the freedom fighters. Then a serious impulse could be given the struggle.

External Weights in the Balance.

Africa had reached an impasse. The wars of national liberation had been contained or were progressing slowly. Neither economic nor political pressure from the independent states were likely to have any real effect on its enemies. And the struggle might remain bogged down for some time to come. Therefore it was only natural for the African states to seek increased assistance from outside the continent. From the very beginning it was recognized that allies would be needed and the demands on the rest of the world community grew. The question was whether this aid could turn the balance.

The most willing allies were the members of the anti-colonial bloc and especially the Communist states. These countries readily joined in the broad political front against the colonial and settler powers. They could be persuaded to break off relations with Portugal and South Africa and, in most cases, to cease trading with them. What was more important, they could often be counted upon to supply arms and funds for the liberation wars. Unfortunately, this assistance was not as valuable or complete as had been hoped. Many of the states that demonstrated their solidarity could easily afford to do so because they had little to lose. Their relations had never been

very close with Africa's enemies and trade was marginal.
Thus the impact was also very limited. Since these states
had many other problems and demands on their finance even
aid to the liberation movements, although considerable, was
not what it might have been.

The role of the Western states was quite different.
Even if they did not come to Africa's assistance, they could
be as decisive by ceasing to aid and abet the colonial and settler powers. Portugal and South Africa depended on the West
for their military equipment. Their trade was mainly with
Europe and America; any reduction or even stabilization of
trade by major Western nations could be more telling than
total boycotts by other states. Since relations were good if
not warm, Washington or London were still in a position to
proffer advice or express words of caution. Indeed, there
was a tendency for the Western states to play this role: the
American decision to end military sales to South Africa and
Britain's introduction of sanctions against Rhodesia were significant.

But the dedication of the West to this struggle was less
than wholehearted. For, unlike the anti-colonial bloc, these
countries had a good deal to lose. It was hard to reject very
useful allies in the world context. The nationals of the Western powers were carrying on profitable trade and the economy
would have to absorb the cost of a boycott. Moreover, if it
became necessary to go further and introduce a blockade or
enforcement action against their erstwhile friends, it was agai
the citizens of the blockading country who would bear the burden. Finally, they were very uncertain what their recompens
would be. Such action, rather than bringing Pretoria to reason, might lead to a stiffening of its position and a bitter racial war. The West was far from certain that its interest la
in joining Africa's campaign.

In its attempt to rally support from outside the continent, the most convenient channel was the United Nations. Th
African states were particularly well placed in that they already had one-third of the voting strength (over two-thirds
when combined with their friends in the anti-colonial bloc).
Considerable headway was made in the majority bodies like th
Decolonization Committee and the General Assembly. But the
could only appeal for voluntary action. It was much harder t
force the barrier of the Security Council. Some of the perma
nent members were more than hesitant about the wisdom and
feasibility of the measures and unwilling to make sacrifices t

implement them.   Most of Africa's successes were only on
paper.

Nevertheless, there was considerable progress with the
campaign for diplomatic and economic sanctions.   Many countries were willing to cease their diplomatic relations with Portugal and South Africa.   Within the United Nations family, the
two were being ostracized, even disappearing from several
specialized agencies.   There was a constant flow of resolutions condemning them almost unanimously and proposing measures against them.   An embargo was spread from arms and
equipment to cover other items connected with the war effort.
This embargo was even occasionally honored.   Finally economic sanctions were also introduced.   At first they were voluntary and the results none too good.   The break-through came
in December 1966, when, for the first time in its history, the
Security Council adopted mandatory sanctions.   Going from a
selective basis, they were eventually made general.   But the
real problem was to enforce their application.

This was a very slow process.   The Africans were impatient to make greater headway.   They were also irate at the
non-fulfillment of UN resolutions and anxious to have the Security Council make them work.   Thus they constantly turned
their efforts towards enforcement action.   The repression of
the liberation movements, they insisted, was a clear threat to
peace.   But the Western powers did not feel that it was imminent yet.   They were not ready to shoulder the burden of
enforcement action and lead the organization into a dangerous
adventure.   There was no reason to expect a major change in
their position for some time.   And, until they agreed, the
United Nations could not act.

Even the backing of the Soviet Union in such matters
was not exactly what was desired.   Moscow was highly suspicious of any kind of international operation and wary of
United Nations intervention in general.   Its refusal (and that
of France) to pay for the Congo operation was sapping the system on which most action had been based in the past and making it harder to mobilize what would certainly be a much larger and more expensive operation in southern Africa.   Moreover, its support could be embarrassing on occasion.   Rather
than trust the United Nations with the administration of South
West Africa, it proposed that the administering authority be
the OAU.   This, however, was what Africa wanted least.   Giv-
en the material weakness of the Organization, it was more of
a burden than an honor.   The aim was not to go it alone or

run the show but to get help from the United Nations.

Nevertheless, Africa had already maneuvered the world body into a corner on two very delicate issues. Soon the United Nations would have to enforce its demands or back down and lose face seriously. Sanctions had been introduced against Rhodesia and they were being violated by South Africa and Portugal. To make the sanctions a reality, pressure would have to be brought to bear against the two truant states or their coasts would have to be blockaded. Force would have to be used to withdraw South Africa's mandate and control over South West Africa, as well. Pretoria had already announced its decision to stay and considerable pressure would be needed to dislodge it. If the Security Council still refused to act, as was probable, there would be a tremendous discrepancy between words and action in the United Nations.

This gap could readily be explained, since the words usually came from the anti-colonial majorities in the General Assembly and action was a matter for the great powers in the Security Council. The responsibility for this gap and for any clash between principles and realities had to be shared between those who asked too much of the world body and those who refused to give more for its ideals. If the inherent weaknesses of the UN were put under greater stress by new demands and criticism, the world body would be steadily undermined by its own members. This was certainly not in the interest of a continent that relied so heavily on outside support to attain its goals. And it would be unwise for Africa to push the United Nations too far. What was needed was not only the knowledge of what could be gained through the world system but also greater tolerance for its limits.

What Alternative for the Future?

There had been considerable strain on the Organization and on relations between African states because of frustration and anger due to the slow and painful progress of the struggle for decolonization. Things were not likely to change dramatically in coming years. There would again be differences and friction between the radicals, moderates and the new group of states with an unexpected approach towards the continent's enemies. Nevertheless, it was essential for the OAU to find a policy that could be both more effective and generally acceptable.

This time there were three alternatives that could be worked into a joint policy. A stronger, more resolute campaign could be initiated by the independent states, as proposed by the radicals. The same old policy could be followed and gradually strengthened until Africa reached its aims, as suggested by the moderates. Or, it was possible to seek some sort of compromise or more or less comfortable modus vivendi, like the conservatives.

At any rate, the present situation was untenable. Africa was engaged in a strange and limited war that made no headway--a kind of "phony war." Bloody guerrilla operations were being launched within the colonial and settler territories and were repressed by the authorities there. The struggle was murderous and there was tremendous damage and bloodshed. But, aside from an occasional press release, the war was largely unseen and unknown. The struggle was backed by the neighboring African states, where the freedom fighters were trained and armed, whence they launched their attacks and to which they retreated. Periodically, though not too often, a border village was bombed in retaliation. It was uncertain how long this odd status quo would last. Still, for the time being, neither side dared spread the hostilities. The colonial and settler powers had a tremendous potential for retaliation, but they did not want to set off an escalation. The Africans were simply not ready for enlarging their revolutionary activities.

Nevertheless, there was no doubt that much more could be done. Africa had not really thrown itself into the battle. Armed contingents could be sent or an army raised for an all-out attack. These points had been mooted. But a crusade was not probable. What was more likely was that Africa would continue as in the past and gradually intensify its efforts. The guerrillas would push back the enemy mile by mile or at least wear it out. They would be better armed and trained and would receive more backing from Africa. The sanctions would be expanded and greater efforts made to have them implemented. In particular, they might become mandatory. And, eventually, the world community would be less inclined to let South Africa or Portugal persist in their policies.

However, even by following the old course and slowly stepping up the effort, a threshold would be reached sooner or later where the hard and soft lines converged. For the region would become a powder keg and some incident or reprisal might spark a more generalized war. Either the colonial and

settler powers would become nervous and act too sharply or
Africa would feel stronger and move too boldly. One way or
another, some act would start the escalation. The war would
be long and nasty. In its wake it would leave an unprecedented loss of life, destruction of much of the infrastructure and
wealth of the countries involved, and lasting enmity between
races and possibly, continents.

However, there was still the third alternative--one that
had been long forgotten. Because of the stubborness of the
rear-guard colonialists and the bitterness of feelings, the Africans had turned to the weapons that seemed most powerful
and effective. This meant the more violent methods, running
from propaganda to sanctions to warfare. Negotiations had
been discarded as a method, although most of the states (including finally Algeria) had obtained independence in that way.
Compromise was anathema. The mere idea of a settlement
between Rhodesia and Great Britain was loudly and conspicuously rejected, even before the terms were announced and without
waiting to determine whether the basic rights of the population
were safeguarded.

Now this alternative was proposed again. The suggestion came from the states that cooperated with South Africa.
Although any acceptance of a dishonorable or unworthy solution
had to be avoided, compromise as such could be reconsidered.
In many ways it was a valid method. The only worthwhile
question was as to the conditions. If the terms were favorable
to the attainment of Africa's goals, they should not be rejected
out of hand because of principles or suspicions. Obviously the
distance was great between Africa's demands and what the colonial or settler powers were willing to concede. But this
might not always be so. In particular, on certain points which
after all were only secondary, compromises could be reached
without sacrificing anything essential.

For years Africa had been demanding "immediate" independence. The very idea of a transition was denounced. And
yet, a transition could permit a smoother passage from minority to majority rule and, especially, not take any longer than
the hard struggle for decolonization.

In addition, no matter how sacred the self-determination
of the majority was, the colonialists and settlers did have interests to protect. By negotiating a withdrawal or a transformation of the society rather than making vague and blunt demands, those interests could be safeguarded without seriously

inconveniencing the new states-to-be. Portuguese and other investments might be guaranteed in exchange for technical and financial aid. Some guarantee was particularly important for the settlers, since their roots were in the country. As a start, it was necessary to do more than just demand democracy or an end to apartheid and to clearly define the final aims. There would be majority rule under the Africans and probably a multi-racial society. But, would there be entrenched rights for the minorities? Would they have some sort of guarantee of their property? If this were so, support for the African cause might increase abroad and resistance to decolonization might subside in the territories, advancing the day of independence.

Depending on the circumstances, compromise could be as effective a policy in attaining the final aims as any of the more forceful methods. Its main advantage, as opposed to violence, was that it could avert the disaster of serious bloodshed and destruction. It should not be forgotten that even in the case of Algeria, Africa had used both the carrot and the stick. The stick was the guerrilla warfare and sanctions. Harsh language and vain threats did nothing to attain the goal. But there was also the carrot offered by the states which had maintained their contacts with the enemy. The conclusion was a negotiated withdrawal, more rapid and beneficial to all concerned than an uncertain military victory. There was no reason the policy of the carrot and the stick should be forgotten in other conflicts.

Thus the task of the Organization of African Unity was a critical one. It had to think through the whole policy at decisive moments and choose the methods that were best suited to the situation. This meant a choice solely of realistic measures in a combination that was sufficiently flexible to profit from the circumstances. The policy would have to have the widest possible support in the Organization and everything should be done to avoid an open split. Then, once the policy had been chosen, the duty of the African states was to close their ranks and follow it.

Notes

1. <u>Le Monde</u>, 10 Nov. 1966.

2. <u>Africa Report</u>, Nov. 1967.

3. _Ibid._, May 1967.

4. _The Times_ (London), 14 April 1967.

5. _Africa Report_, May 1967.

6. _Ibid._, June 1967.

7. _Ibid._, May 1969.

Chapter IV

Internal Order

The conference of Addis Ababa in May 1963 was a brilliant victory for African unity. The Heads of State met in an atmosphere of reconciliation and optimism for the future. Perhaps it was for this reason that they avoided any discordant note and finally drew up a program that was primarily directed outwards against common enemies: decolonization, non-alignment, liquidation of the sequels of colonialism. Cooperation in these endeavors, it was hoped, would smooth over any differences. The good will of the African leaders could be counted upon to avoid unnecessary clashes.

Relatively little attention was paid to the role the Organization would have to play within the circle of its members. No specific provision was made for positively strengthening their solidarity. There was merely a series of rules to avoid disturbing whatever relations existed. This was a grave omission for, more even than the external aims, good or at least acceptable relations among the member states was the real prerequisite to success. Internal unity was indispensable if the members were to pull together to attain all other goals.

The OAU was not specifically entrusted with maintaining peace and security in the continent and only brief mention was made of peaceful settlement. Even here there was scarcely any reference to the Organization's activities in preventing or settling disputes in Africa. Nevertheless, the events leading up to the summit conference showed that the danger did exist. The continent would not long be free of serious problems. Two territorial disputes clouded the horizon and Morocco and Somalia had already brought forward their claims. The decomposition of the Congo had not yet ceased and, although there was a relative calm, the situation could take a turn for the worse. And the African leaders met with the Togo coup and assassination of Sylvanus Olympio fresh in their minds.

African Disunity.

Faith in Africa's future was undoubtedly justified. The
member states had much in common. They had the same colonial background and were under-developed; they had common
aspirations to liberate the continent and get on with nation
building. This unity was real. But it was only the surface.
Beneath it there were older and deeper realities: an inextricable maze of tribes and races, languages and religions, social
structures and economic ties. Each one of the underlying
units existed and exerted its attraction on the people. Only,
they were both links and barriers. During the period of European colonialism they had been neglected but not eliminated in
the entities established for the purposes of administration.
The result was that, when the states became independent, their
boundaries confined a geographical space whose inner cohesion
was occasionally less binding than that of some of its component parts. Frequently these parts also stretched from one
country to another. In other words, the deeper links were
sometimes at variance with the more recent and superficial
ones, and the product of friction between the different realities of Africa could be discord.

Along with these differences there were also the more
recent ones. As political parties and trade unions were established, as governments were formed and oppositions absorbed or liquidated, political notions were injected in the
whole. Then came the ideological concepts which were rather
hazy but very persuasive excuses for action. With these new
strivings added to the tribal and other rivalries that already
existed, Africa had an explosive mixture that could easily ig-
nite.

Considering that the boundaries between tribes, races
and even nations and kingdoms were usually disregarded when
Africa was cut up into colonies, it was not surprising that
there were many actual or potential border disputes on the
continent. In vain, Africa tried to make just one of the many
factors, the colonial frontiers, the sole criteria to impede a
wave of territorial claims. It could not attain unanimous
agreement. It was still possible for an adjustment to be
sought on the basis of ethnic or historic boundaries, although
other criteria could be put forward as well. However, since
the underlying mosaic was so pervasive and tightly interwoven,
the demands for additions of territory had no logical end. If
all the original or deeper boundaries were restored, no Afri-

can state would be left in its present shape and some would crumble into a multitude of nations or smaller units, making Africa a truly "balkanized" continent.

In the cities and among the educated or detribalized sectors of the population the calls for action were usually political and various interest groups organized to obtain their aims through political parties, trade unions, clubs, etc. In their efforts to modernize the economy or society of the country, the new élites and other nascent classes often turned against the more traditional elements; friction arose between generations as the government tried to pull along and educate or indoctrinate the masses. If a strong opposition to a ruling party emerged or the élites split along ideological lines over the best way to accelerate economic growth or transform the state and society, the situation could rapidly deteriorate, each competing tendency gathering behind it parts of the tribalized masses with but little understanding of the cause they supported.

The deepest rifts arose where the earlier and more coherent units took renewed awareness of their existence. The broader ethnic and religious families, or a combination of both, could reassert themselves in a young state. If strong enough, using modern political tactics, one of them could consolidate its position and win control of the government. If in a minority, it might organize a rival political party or a less formal opposition. However, if it found no redress within the system, a rather audacious grouping might be prepared to throw off the domination by seeking to create a new and independent state. Since this meant a great loss in power and perhaps a further break-up of the old state as other minorities revolted, the central government would probably be forced to combat the separatists and a civil war would ensue.

The worst complications were bound to arise when these tensions were fed from outside. One of the groups could receive backing from friends in a neighboring country or even further off. This might be inspired by sympathy, like-mindedness, blood or annexationist designs. But any efforts to rally this group against the government only made the situation more explosive. If the supporting state decided to intervene openly or secretly, the chances of settling the problem peacefully and quickly diminished. This was particularly true when ideology got involved in the underlying dispute. Then the relations between African states would be sorely strained and a civil war or border clash could escalate into an international war.

Code of Good Conduct.

Africa could only progress and develop if peace were
maintained within the continent. Unfortunately, the causes for
friction and conflict were widespread. No state was really
immune to territorial or political disputes and scarcely any
had a homogeneous racial and religious composition. Therefore it was in their best interest to make the OAU a place
where such difficulties might be discussed and overcome.
Member states could turn to the Organization to obtain a settlement or at least a hearing from the rest of Africa.

Although general rules to govern the relations among
members were a part of any organization, those adopted in
Addis Ababa were more symptomatic. Of the seven principles
enumerated under Article III, the observance of which was
made the primary duty of the member states, five had to do
with aspects of internal order.

Two of these were standard components of international
charters. The OAU was based on the "sovereign equality of
all Member States." To calm the fears especially of the smaller states, every member had an equal voice in the decisions
of the Organization. No other member or group of members
could impose their will or even leadership upon it. The Charter also confirmed the "respect for the sovereignty and territorial integrity of each State and for its inalienable right to
independent existence." It was to have full control over its
domestic and foreign affairs. Its powers extended throughout
the territory. No other state could restrict or replace them
in any way or place.

But the founders of the Organization thought it necessary to go even further in specifying the obligations of the
members toward one another. This was the reverse side of
the foregoing rights or the "thou shalt nots" of the Charter.
These principles were somewhat unusual for international cov-
enants, although they merited universal obedience, and showed
peculiar sharpness. They were a legacy of the troubled historical period preceding the creation of the OAU, when no such
code existed and basic rules of cooperation and coexistence
were flouted.

First was the principle of "non-interference in the internal affairs of States." Each state had the right to determine its own political, economic and social system. It freely
defined its national and international policies. No matter how

deeply concerned by the outcome of domestic crises or the way it might affect them, the other members had to keep out. Any intervention would only aggravate the situation and create serious complications. But the harshest admonition of the Charter was the "unreserved condemnation, in all its forms, of political assassination as well as of subversive activities on the part of neighboring States or any other State." Since each state was alone responsible for its policies, there was no excuse for such undercover action either. Member states had no right to encourage the enemies of any other regime and especially no right to attempt to change its policies by the liquidation of their authors.

Nevertheless, in Africa as elsewhere, disputes were bound to arise and had to be settled. Thus the Charter included the principle of "peaceful settlement of disputes by negotiation, mediation, conciliation or arbitration." Moreover, under Article XIX, the member states "pledge to settle all disputes among themselves by peaceful means." In this way the conflicts could be resolved or at least relegated to processes permitting continued order and tranquility in the continent.

Means of Action.

When it came to the ways and means of maintaining order in Africa, the Charter was strangely silent. A preliminary question even arose as to the Organization's competence. Given the fundamental principle of sovereignty, could the OAU deal with all disputes on the continent, even those seriously affecting peace and security, if this entailed or seemed to entail interference in the affairs of a sovereign state?

During its career, the OAU would often be faced with delicate and controversial issues. It would repeatedly stumble against its own principle of non-interference. And it would have to reply to such questions at various points. Even with disputes or situations manifestly endangering the relations between its members or threatening peace in Africa, the Organization would be uncertain whether it could act without at least the tacit approval of the states directly involved. In addition, its recommendations might or might not be accepted. In a particularly bitter dispute, if the OAU decided on a solution or a course of action, the difficulty of imposing it on the parties involved was obvious.

The Charter provided no clear guidelines. In theory, since even the resolutions of the Assembly of Heads of State were not binding, there was no reason to believe that it could give the necessary orders to its members. More significantly, it would be extremely difficult in practice to make any state implement measures it rejected. But it could discuss any of these matters, express an opinion and counsel appropriate means of restoring harmony.

With guaranteed sovereignty a major obstacle to any envisaged action, it was obvious that the OAU would have to be very careful to find solutions that were broadly acceptable. It would have to develop a very flexible policy to take advantage of every opening. This meant following a soft line most of the time and giving preference to the exercise of good offices and conciliation to arbitration or more energetic "operations." In so doing, the Organization could use any of its legal or political institutions or create temporary bodies for specific purposes.

The Commission of Mediation, Conciliation and Arbitration was designed as the principal organ for dealing with legal disputes. Unfortunately, its Protocol was not adopted until July 1964 and its members were not appointed until October 1965. Thus there was at first no statutory body to handle legal disputes. What was more disconcerting, however, was that even after it came into existence there was a marked reluctance among the African states to submit their disputes to legal settlement. All important matters were or seemed so politically loaded that the states preferred seeking a solution by more flexible political means.

In handling a political conflict, the OAU had three alternatives. They could give it over for settlement at the highest level by the Assembly. But its time was limited and the Heads of State had little opportunity to look into the details of a problem or follow it up. Their authority was greater but they hesitated to associate their names with measures that might ultimately be contested or ignored. The Council of Ministers, the second alternative, was more flexible and could readily deal with conflicts that arose. Its decisions, however, could hardly be imposed upon member states. Thirdly, there could also be set up ad hoc commissions or committees as needed. They would investigate or help the parties towards a solution. But they were responsible to the Assembly or Council where the final decisions had to be taken.

Although the Charter did refer to peaceful settlement of
disputes, it did not consider the possibility that a conflict
might be explosive enough to burst into violence. Despite this
lapsus, the Organization would have to restore peace as well.
Here, too, the approach could be worked out pragmatically.
Only, in this more delicate matter, the barrier of sovereignty
was certain to be even firmer. Obviously, the same bodies
could seek and probably find valid solutions. Even a peace
keeping operation could be planned. But the means of imposing them--already notoriously limited--might be so restricted
as to make any proposal a dead letter. Everything depended
on the good will of the parties. And, if hostilities had already begun, there might be pitifully little of that.

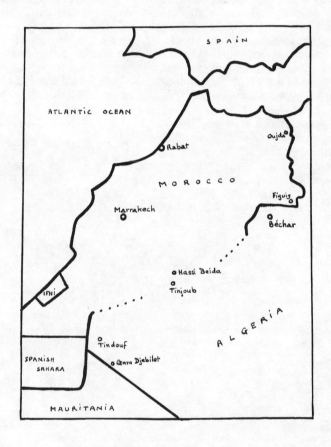

Non-Border Between Morocco and Algeria

A.   Algero-Moroccan Boundary Dispute

Although the conference of Addis Ababa had helped clear the air, there were still many potential disputes in the continent. A recurrent one was the complex of territorial conflicts between Morocco and its neighbors. The former empire had left a rather uncomfortable heritage for the new independent state, which could not always accommodate itself to its restricted borders and still dreamt of a Greater Morocco. For years the monarchy's attempt at recuperating parts of its traditional realm had strained relations in the region. The first act was the campaign against Mauritania. Although no longer a predominant issue, it was the "Mauritanian problem" that caused King Hassan not to attend the Summit. Even when Morocco signed the Charter of African Unity, on 20 September 1963, it did so with the specific reservation that this should not be interpreted as a recognition of existing borders or a renunciation of its rights.[1]

At the same time, a similar problem was building up with Algeria. Despite racial and religious links, common traditions and aspirations for a Maghreb community, one problem had always been pending. No mutually acceptable frontier had been defined between the two countries and, although it was theoretically possible to settle the dispute, a complete deadlock had been reached. Morocco was intent on the restitution of some of the territory. But Algeria refused to cede any of the land it had won from France and even turned a deaf ear to demands for negotiations. This dispute created tremendous friction and drove the brother states apart.

Uncertain Frontiers.

In North Africa and the Saharan basin, most of which was staked out under French colonial rule, there were a number of sources of territorial difficulties. The earlier divisions were rarely respected when the region was cut up into colonies and, since the boundaries only separated parts of the same colonial empire, there was less care in laying down the lines that separated one from another. Some of the boundaries

were only defined on paper, others were altered over the
years and a few did not even exist. This territorial policy
often left a thorny legacy for the successor states. A case
in point was Morocco and Algeria.

Before the French moved into North Africa, a vast
area including part of Algeria and running far south into Mauritania had been nominally subject to Moroccan governors.
Once conquered, this Empire was shorn of its outlying provinces and made a Protectorate while the less nationally conscious and structured Algeria was detached and made constitu-
tionally part of France. However, since the Sahara desert
was regarded as uninhabitable, the French never got around to
demarcating the frontier beyond the northeastern Moroccan
town of Figuig. Even the rough administrative lines (Varnier,
Trinquet) that separated the two were vague and had been
shifted on occasion in favor of Algeria to increase direct control over the region. The longest portion of the boundary was
unclear and contested. [2]

Since much of this territory was traditionally Moroccan,
the Sherifian government began stressing its titles to the land
as soon as it became independent in 1956. Negotiations with
France made no headway and Morocco then approached the Algerians. To avoid embarrassing the GPRA in the midst of
the struggle for independence, these demands were not made
publicly. Rather, they were laid down in a secret agreement
concluded between the King of Morocco, Hassan II, and the
head of the Algerian provisional government, Ferhat Abbas.
This agreement of 6 July 1961 reaffirmed Morocco's support
of the Algerian people in its struggle and went on to recognize
"that the territorial problem created by the boundary between
the two countries, arbitrarily imposed by France, shall be
solved by negotiation between the Government of the Kingdom
of Morocco and the Government of independent Algeria." A
joint Algerian-Moroccan commission was to help seek a solution. [3]

However, when Algeria became independent in July 1962,
Ferhat Abbas and the old guard were rapidly eliminated from
positions of control and a younger "revolutionary" government
under Ben Bella seized power. This regime was not willing
to negotiate or even to admit that a boundary dispute existed.
It would not cede territory won by Algerian arms during seven
years of war. But Morocco refused to let the matter lie. No
sooner was Algeria independent than both sides sent troops into the disputed area and minor skirmishes and incidents oc-

curred. Then, in August 1963, there were more serious
clashes. The nationals of the opposing parties were expelled
from the region. Moroccan troops began concentrating along
the border and Algeria reinforced its posts. Then there was
a deceptive calm.

From Battlefield to Conference Hall.

At the beginning of October, Rabat demanded a "rectification" of the frontier by direct negotiations. There were
talks between the two Foreign Ministers in Oujda, but despite
promises of a normalization, no steps were taken to avert a
crisis. With no peaceful solution in sight, tension rose and
the two armies prepared for the worst. On 1 October, Morocco had occupied the frontier posts of Hassi-Beida and Tinjoub, which it claimed were on its side of the boundary. A
week later, a larger Algerian force dislodged the Moroccans
and took over the posts. Thus, it was hardly surprising when,
on 14 October 1963, major hostilities broke out along the poorly defined frontier. Algeria immediately announced that its
territory had been invaded by a large force with tanks and
planes while Morocco claimed that a battalion of its troops had
"counter-attacked" and "retaken" the frontier posts.[4] The
fighting intensified and the two countries prepared for a pitched
battle. Morocco moved in additional troops and Algeria declared a general mobilization.

The combat went on in the Sahara for a fortnight. It
spread along the frontier as Morocco prepared to attack Tindouf and Algerian troop movements were reported near Figuig.
Despite momentary victories by either side, the Moroccans had
a definite edge over Algeria. They still held Hassi-Beida and
Tinjoub when the front was stabilized, although they could not
take Tindouf. However, by then, the troops had fought themselves to a standstill and little more could be expected of war
as a means of settling the dispute. Although there were sporadic outbursts, new territory could only be taken at the cost
of heavy losses. And no final decision could be obtained by
force anyway. The two parties were tempted to give in to the
many appeals to halt the bloodshed.

Once it was obvious that no more could be gained by
fighting, it was necessary for both to find an appropriate opportunity to put an end to the hostilities without admitting a defeat of their arms. Various sources had proposed their good
offices. There was also the OAU. But the vast majority of its

member states favored the preservation of the territorial status quo (i.e. colonial boundaries) and were decidedly unfriendly toward tampering with frontiers. Algeria had realized this for as soon as hostilities began on 14 October, it seized the OAU Secretariat with the matter. On 19 October, Algeria formally called for an emergency meeting of the Council of Ministers. This did not suit Morocco.

The Emperor of Ethiopia, on a visit to the Maghreb, had immediately offered his services as mediator. On 17 October he went to Marrakech to meet with Hassan II; then he flew to Algeria. As it became increasingly evident that the desert war had been a mistake, he was able to persuade the two Heads of State to seek a way out of the crisis.

Such an opportunity was offered by the invitation to Bamako of President Modibo Keita of Mali to the heads of the two warring parties. On 29 October, they arrived in Bamako with their diplomatic staffs and the delicate and tortuous negotiations began between Hassan II and Ben Bella who at first had refused to meet. The two mediators, President Keita and Haile Selassie, were especially well suited to the task. One was a conservative; the other a radical. Whereas Ethiopia had rejected Somalia's claims, Mali negotiated border settlements with its neighbors. By the next day, apparently bowing to reasons of African peace and unity, the two enemies endorsed the compromise that would restore calm to the region.

The Bamako Agreement of 30 October announced a cease-fire as of zero hour on 2 November. At the same time, the propaganda campaign and interference in the internal affairs of one another would also stop. This was to be followed by a withdrawal of the troops from the frontier and a gradual return to the status quo ante. A demilitarized zone, the limits of which were yet to be determined, would be created by a commission of officers from Algeria, Morocco, Ethiopia and Mali. Malian and Ethiopian officers would supervise the observance of demilitarization of this "no man's land" pending a final settlement.[5] Although there was a new burst of hostilities around Figuig only hours after the cease-fire was to start, the worst was over and the next day the fighting stopped and there was quiet along the frontier.

The primary concern of the Bamako meeting, however, was what happened after that. For the previous situation had proved to be untenable. It was essential for the border dispute to be solved so that a similar crisis would not occur.

The Emperor and Modibo Keita were eager to have the OAU intervene, possibly as a precedent for an African handling of other border disputes, and made a great effort to that end. The real hurdle, of course, was to convince Morocco that the matter should be brought before an African body. The agreement at Bamako provided that the OAU was to call an early meeting of the Council of Ministers to set up a commission of arbitration. Thus both sides had some reason for satisfaction: Algeria, since the troops were supposed to withdraw from the contested zone, Morocco, because the dispute was recognized as such and a peaceful settlement would be sought. Up to the eve of the Council session the latter state remained suspicious however, expecting an "anti-Moroccan bias."[6]

The extraordinary session, held from 15-18 November 1963, was so critical for the future of Africa that it drew all 32 members of the Organization. The Emperor warned them upon their arrival that "Africa's ability to deal with her own problems, free of outside interference or influence is in the balance. Failure would deal a crippling blow ..."[7] Certainly the task of the Foreign Ministers in Addis Ababa was far from easy. The crisis was not yet over. Algeria and Morocco were still on a war footing, their troops along the boundary, and fighting could break out again. The two states were licking their wounds and bitterly suspicious; the one, of any attempt to despoil a fruit of independence, the other, of frustration in the attempt to obtain justice. Most of the delegates were somewhat nervous about the situation and excessively careful not to appear to impose anything on the parties. What they wanted was a return to peace and a chance for Algeria and Morocco to settle the conflict calmly later on. The OAU could not step between the opponents or order them about although it could appeal to their better judgement.

At the conference it was clear that the parties were not in a mood to make any concessions on the substance of the matter. Each Foreign Minister, Abdelaziz Bouteflika of Algeria and Ahmed Réda Guédira of Morocco, laid the blame for the aggression on the opposite party. Morocco wished to recover the territory that had been detached from it during French rule. Algeria refused to cede any of the land it had inherited from France, stressing the danger of such a step for Africa. According to Bouteflika, "to wish to impose unilaterally the least revision of the Algerian-Moroccan border is without a doubt to create a precedent or an unfortunate jurisprudence for the future of many African states."[8] Here the deadlock was complete.

What was decisive, however, was that the two parties were obliged to admit that the resort to war had not settled anything. Actually the recent clash had greatly worsened their relations. The time had come to seek a solution by peaceful means. Thus the Council resolution laid down what it hoped would be the basic rule for all such disputes,

> ... the unwavering determination of the African States always to seek a peaceful and fraternal solution of all differences that may arise among them by negotiations and within the framework of the principles and the institutions prescribed by the Charter of the Organization of African Unity.

Since the two parties had previously been unable to come to any agreement and Algeria still refused direct negotiations with Morocco, it was necessary to set up the commission called for by the Bamako declaration as a go-between. This was to be an "ad hoc" commission since the statutory Commission of Mediation, Conciliation and Arbitration had not yet been established. Its membership was carefully weighed and a rather moderate and neutral body of states was finally chosen: Ethiopia, Ivory Coast, Mali, Nigeria, Senegal, Sudan and Tanganyika.

The Gordian Knot.

With this, the border dispute was no longer a matter for soldiers or diplomats. However, for the jurists as well, it would be terribly hard to find a solution. A first difficulty was that the Commission was not a body of arbitration, as proposed in Bamako. For neither Algeria nor Morocco would have accepted a binding decision on the territorial dispute. At most, the representatives of the seven states could act as a group of mediation or good offices, asking the parties to adopt a given solution or just encouraging them to help find a solution themselves. But no settlement could be imposed on two sovereign states.

Certainly, the Commission's terms of reference did not make its job any easier. Under the Bamako Agreement, its mandate had been defined as:

> a) ascertaining the responsibility for the outbreak of hostilities;

      b)   studying the substantive problem (border prob-
lem) and submitting concrete proposals to the
two parties for the definitive settlement of the
dispute.

It was, of course, excessively difficult for any commission to fix the responsibility for the outbreak of hostilities.
The warfare took place in a sparsely settled desert region with
no neutral observers present. With almost simultaneous action by both armies and contradictory charges of aggression,
it would be hard to prove who invaded or fired first. Without
any clearly delimited frontier, it was impossible to know even
whose territory was invaded.

In trying to settle the border dispute, the Commission
could not make much progress either. The titles and claims
of both parties were mutually exclusive. The Moroccans demanded that the Frnech administrative measures be disregarded and that the territory taken from it by France be returned.
Morocco no longer had such extensive claims as during the
Mauritanian conflict, limiting itself to a specific but variable
area running from Figuig to the scene of the hostilities and,
particularly, the region of Tindouf and the iron mines of Gara-
Djebilet. Here it hoped a satisfactory frontier could be negotiated with Algeria. Algeria, for its part, insisted that the
whole area had been part of its territory at independence and
demanded respect of the "colonial" frontiers. With the lawyers of the Commission, Algeria argued its effective possession and Morocco invoked historicity.

But, although the dispute had been brought before the
OAU Commission, Algeria still denied that any border problem
existed as such. It assumed that the general rule was to respect the intangibility of the boundaries inherited from colonialism, and that this had even been consecrated for Africa with
the signing of the Charter of Addis Ababa. The Charter, however, only included the respect for territorial integrity, and
Morocco countered that it would respect the integrity of Algeria once a frontier had been negotiated between them. Moreover, it insisted that the recognition of a territorial problem
and willingness to negotiate had been layed down in the Hassan
II--Ferhat Abbas Agreement and still bound Algeria.

In these circumstances, even if the Commission had
been able to find one boundary line it considered equitable
through the maze of conflicting claims and shifting frontiers,
it would not have been able to impose it. Morocco demanded

at least a token restitution of territory and the Ben Bella regime in Algeria felt that it was a betrayal of the revolution to
cede an inch. Thus the Commission was not able to impose
its will on the states nor would any proposition it made be
accepted voluntarily.

Rather than cutting the Gordian knot, after a dozen
meetings in member states, and in Algeria and Morocco (although not along the frontier),[9] the Commission turned its
back on it. It very carefully avoided placing any blame for
the outbreak of hostilities. It also did not propose a specific
boundary line. Rather, it tried to bring the two parties together so that they might seek a mutually satisfactory solution
under the Commission's auspices.

It suggested a joint committee including Algeria and
Morocco and some members of the ad hoc Commission to continue the search for a solution. The presence of a third party avoided direct negotiations and might have encouraged a
more objective and vigorous procedure. But Algeria would
have nothing to do with such a committee and the idea was
dropped.[10]

Saber Rattling Along the Border.

Although the ad hoc Commission on the Algero-Moroccan Border Dispute was no closer to a solution than before,
its very existence contributed to a decrease in the tension between Algeria and Morocco. The fact that the Council of Ministers and the Commission were dealing with the conflict made
it possible for both countries to withdraw gracefully and kept
them from endangering a settlement by new hostilities. Each
time the Commission met or appeared before the Council it
reconfirmed the good will of the contending parties and was re-
endowed with their confidence. The very process of seeking
a solution was praised as a victory for African unity.

Nevertheless, even the disengagement in the field was
slow. The Bamako Agreement had ordered a cease-fire and
demilitarization of the frontier region. Within a few days the
hostilities were effectively stopped. But the cease-fire committee was unable to get the two armies to evacuate the positions they had won. The Moroccan troops refused to move out
of Hassi-Beida and Tinjoub and Algerian forces still command-
ed the heights near Figuig. A first attempt at restoring diplomatic relations failed when Algeria tied this to a withdrawal

from the border posts. Finally, on 20 February 1964, an agreement was reached. Algeria would withdraw its troops from Figuig and Morocco would return to the positions it held before 1 October 1963. The highlands near Figuig were to be demilitarized and a no man's land established along the border. Unfortunately, the cease-fire committee was not asked to supervise the implementation of this agreement and, at the request of both parties, it was dissolved in April.

Gradually, there was a return to normal and even some warmth in the relations between the two Maghreb states. In mid-April there was an exchange of prisoners. By the end of May a joint Algerian-Moroccan committee met to restore the situation along the border. The restrictions on movement of persons and goods were ended, the nationals who had been expelled were permitted to resume their activities. By 18 June, diplomatic relations were re-established. Then there was even some talk of a common exploitation of the mineral wealth of the contested area, whose ore had easier access to the sea via Morocco. Economic cooperation was suggested as a solution to the problem and it was hoped that in a broader Maghreb unit the dispute would lose all significance. In May 1965, Hassan II and Ben Bella met near the frontier in Saïdia, where they praised the improvement in relations and decided to meet again.

But the boundary itself was still a festering wound and the many ups and downs in the relations between the two countries were reflected in the dispute as well. Shortly after the Saïdia meeting, Ben Bella was overthrown and the new regime of Houari Boumedienne took a less conciliatory stand. Then, in May 1966, there were reports of Algerian troop movements, immediately denied by the government, and on 22 May important iron mines in the area claimed by Morocco were nationalized. The following day, Rabat accused Algeria of occupying part of the demilitarized zone in violation of the cease-fire. Tension ran high and the events might have taken a turn for the worse. Fortunately, rather than taking the matter in its own hands, the Moroccan government sent envoys to the Emperor of Ethiopia and the President of Mali as guarantors of the settlement and demanded an urgent meeting of the ad hoc Commission.[11] There was no objection to such a meeting from Algiers and the Commission eventually assembled. Although it did not solve the problem this time either, its mere existence had permitted a disengagement on both sides and a new crisis was avoided.

However, the outlook for a settlement was dimmer than ever. President Boumedienne not only repudiated the Hassan II--Ferhat Abbas Agreement, but retracted any concessions that Ben Bella might have made as well. In June 1966, after charges by the National Liberation Front that the United States was building "bases of aggression" in Morocco and Tunisia and threatening Algeria's security, [12] he rejected the Moroccan and Tunisian border claims and insisted that Algeria's frontiers were not negotiable. [13] Then, in February 1967, he added that Algeria would not cede an inch of its territory and would defend its borders with Soviet arms, if need be. [14]

Although the Commission had been able to pacify the disputants on a number of occasions, it had merely postponed any confrontation. Unless a definitive settlement was reached, war could break out again at any time. Unfortunately, any new fighting would now be far worse than the first outbursts, for the end of hostilities in 1963 had marked the beginning of an arms race between the two countries. Algeria's defeat had spurred it on and Colonel Boumedienne spared no effort to strengthen the army. Soon the military establishment was double that of Morocco. A measure of his success was that, by 2 March 1967, Hassan II was sufficiently worried about the situation to ask that U Thant send a commission to North Africa to stop the arms race. [15] More than ever, the OAU had to settle the long-standing quarrel if it were to avoid later friction and possibly bloodshed in the region.

Notes

See Chapter V, A, for the Algero-Moroccan dispute vis-à-vis the great power blocs.

1. Text of reservation in "Maghreb" (Paris), March-April 1964, Vol. 1, No. 2, p. 12.

2. See Anthony S. Reyner, Morocco's International Boundaries: A Factual Background.

3. Le Monde, 23 Oct. 1963.

4. Ibid., 15 Oct. 1963.

5. Ibid., 1 Nov. 1963.

6. The Maghreb Digest, Vol. 2, No. 1, p. 28.

7. The Times (London), 16 Nov. 1963.

8. De Bamako à Addis-Abéba, Algerian Ministry of National
    Orientation, March 1964.

9. See Saadia Touval: The Organization of African Unity and
    African Borders.

10. Le Monde, 31 July 1966 and 4 March 1967.

11. Ibid., 24 & 29 May 1966.

12. The New York Times, 19 June 1966.

13. The Times (London), 21 June 1966.

14. Ibid., 1 March 1967.

15. Le Monde, 4 March 1967.

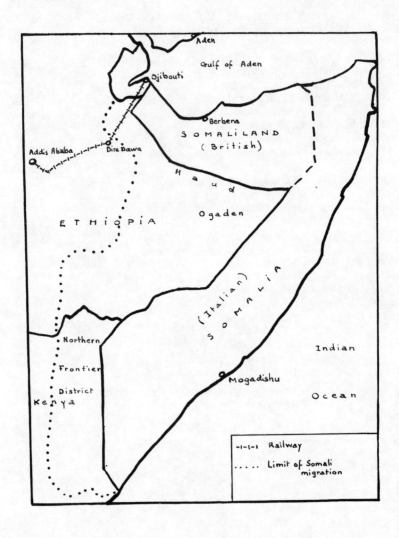

The Somali People

B. Somali-Ethiopia/Kenya Border Dispute

In Africa, the coming of independence often did not solve old problems, it merely gave them new forms. For centuries the group of Somali tribes, settled in the lowlands along the Gulf of Aden and the Indian Ocean, had lived a nomadic life, occasionally waging war against neighboring tribes and expanding their territorial base. After a relatively brief colonial period, in which the European powers also meddled in these quarrels, the Horn entered a new era of independence. However, the Somali people--who had never before been hampered by frontiers--suddenly found themselves divided among four entities: the Republic of Somalia, the French territory, Ethiopia and Kenya.

In the last two cases, the Somalis were included in countries dominated by peoples alien to them, adversaries of earlier days. Rather than remain in these states, they sought to break away and join their brothers in the Somali Republic. Not unsurprisingly, their appeals for self-determination did not move Ethiopia or Kenya. Both could ill afford the loss of these territories. The backing of the demands by the Somali Republic only poured oil on the flames and there was a permanent state of tension among the three neighbors. For years there were clashes with Somali bands and considerable damage and loss of life. But the dispute was potentially more explosive.

Permeable Frontiers.

For centuries peace in the Horn of Africa had been disturbed by periodic fighting among opposing tribes. This rivalry was only aggravated by religious fanaticism when those in the lowlands and along the coast raised the banner of Islam. Only with great tenacity could the people in the highlands hold them back and create the beginnings of the modern state of Ethiopia. However, at the end of the nineteenth century, they were all faced by a greater enemy--European colonialism.

347

Moving into the lowlands along the Red Sea and the Indian Ocean, the European powers brought the "scramble for Africa" to the Horn. Eritrea was taken by Italy and, in the regions inhabited by the group of Somali tribes, British, French and Italian Somaliland were staked out. Although they incidentally helped promote a modern Somali nationalism, the interests of the colonizers were not in the Somali people so much as in their own position, and the boundaries they left showed this. Depending on their relations with Ethiopia and the Somalis they gave or took territory.

More than once Britain ceded or reincorporated in Somaliland huge regions known as Ogaden and Haud. The last treaty, concluded in 1954, left this territory with Ethiopia. Since it was traditional grazing land for the Somalis, their rights were recognized. The Somalis, however, never accepted the agreement. The situation along the frontier with Italian Somaliland was even less clear, for the Italians had never bothered delimiting the frontier, assuming any boundary line was only temporary. In 1934, they made an incident in Walwal a pretext to invade all of Ethiopia. Under Italian domination, another portion of Ogaden was merged with Somaliland and the Somalis were encouraged to move in. After the war, despite repeated attempts bilaterally and in the United Nations, it was impossible to define the frontier between Somalia and Ethiopia.

After the world war, Ethiopia regained its independence while Britain and then Italy retained their positions in Somalia. In the hope of preserving their influence in the region, they voiced support of a greater Somaliland. Although rapidly discarded by the colonial powers, this call was soon taken up by the Somalis themselves. A new Republic of Somalia was created in July 1960 when Italian Somalia and British Somaliland became independent and merged. Both the ruling Somali Youth League and the minority parties supported the ambitious goals of uniting the whole Somali nation in one state. And successive governments followed more or less aggressive policies to do so. In this matter, the undemarcated frontiers were only a marginal factor. For Somalia repeatedly demanded self-determination (and the resulting integration) of all the land inhabited by the Somalis and including French Somaliland, the Ogaden in Ethiopia and the Northern Frontier District in Kenya. This was a vast region, comprising about one-fifth of Ethiopia and one-quarter of Kenya and which would double the size of the Somali Republic.

No sooner was Somalia independent than the relations
with its neighbors became strained.   As agitation for a reunification of the Somalis began, the tension mounted along the
Ethiopian-Somali border.   There were about one million Somalis in Ogaden and most of them were nomads who crossed
the frontier with their cattle, going from one pasturage to another.   Since they had never recognized the boundary line and
resented the Ethiopian presence, they occasionally launched
raids.   The fight was carried on by "shiftas," single or small
groups of Somalis who mingled with the nomads and then attacked their enemies.   To the Somalis they were nationalists;
to the Ethiopians, bandits.   And their acts were met with retaliation and then restriction on the movements and life of all
the nomads.   Occasionally larger units or the army intervened
and there was a more serious flare-up.

The forerunner of friction between Somalia and Kenya
was a prelude to Kenyan independence.   The last wave of Somali expansion had reached the north-eastern part of present
day Kenya and this land was inhabited by some 200,000 Somali
nomads.   In October 1962, the Somalis informed a Crown Commission that they wished to secede from Kenya and join Somalia, but the British refused to take this decision against Kenyan
opposition.   When independence came in December 1963, a
"national liberation front" was created and the Somalis began
a series of raids and attacks that disrupted life in the Northern Frontier District.   Scarcely two weeks later, a state of
emergency had to be declared.

From the beginning the conflict had disturbed the tranquility of Africa.   It was brought up at every major African
gathering and caused the only unpleasantness at the summit
conference of May 1963.   In Addis Ababa, President Aden Abdulla Osman Daar of Somalia pleaded the case of the Somali
nation and urged a reunification of the Somali territories.   He
asked for self-determination for one-and-a-half million Somalis
living under foreign rule.   If an equitable solution were not
found, he warned, "it will constitute a constant source of
trouble in the region, and may affect adversely the friendly relations between the Somali Republic and her neighbors."   He
denied that his government had any "ambitions or claims for
territorial aggrandizement" and only demanded self-determination for the regions inhabited by the Somalis.   However, since
this had steadily been refused before, a peaceful solution
seemed out of the question.   Thus, one way or another, the
Somali government might be forced to fulfill its promise--or
threat--that, "the people of the Republic cannot be expected to

remain indifferent to the appeal of its brethren."[1]

During this time, the raids against Ethiopia and Kenya never ceased. In October 1963, an unusually sharp series of attacks was launched, joined soon by a propaganda campaign by press and radio. Ethiopia then charged that Somalia was sending regular army units into Ethiopian territory to foment disturbances and, by 23 November, the Ethiopian government accused Somalia of a "deliberate policy of expansion."[2] Two days later, when addressing the Parliament, the Emperor warned that "our patience is not limitless."[3] Nevertheless, there was a brief lull. Then the crisis flared up again after incursions by Somali "bandits." Finally, on 7 February 1964, serious fighting broke out between Ethiopia and Somalia. This time it was not mere raids or retaliation but full-scale military hostilities between the armies of both countries.

First Things First.

The battle had been begun not long before an extraordinary session of the OAU was to be held in Dar es Salaam.[4] In view of the urgent need to stop the bloodshed, the Council of Ministers decided to place the dispute between Ethiopia and Somalia, as well as the one between Kenya and Somalia, on its agenda. There was no hope that the long-standing conflicts could be settled. But at least the protagonists had to be separated and a relatively unstable peace restored.

When the Ministers met, on 12 February, the battle still raged along the frontier and showed no sign of abating. The two countries had finally come to grips with one another and neither would retreat. As was expected, Ethiopia and Somalia accused each other of invasion or armed aggression. The Council could not and did not attribute the blame for this. It recognized, in the midst of the fighting, that the most important thing was to bring pressure to bear on both countries to cease the hostilities. After a week of murderous clashes and heavy casualties along the barren desert frontier, both sides realized that little could be gained. Yet it was uncertain whether they were actually ready to stop.

Somewhat grudgingly the parties let reason get the better of the hatred that had been welling up over the years, and they agreed to heed an appeal for peace in the name of African unity. The Council of Ministers was able to adopt a resolution it hoped would stop the tension and the "clashes" along

the boundary. It called upon both states to "order an immediate cease-fire and to refrain from all hostile actions." In
order to calm the tempers, it also asked that measures be
taken to end "all campaigns of provocative or insulting nature,
by all media of communications."

Along the Kenyan border, as well, the situation had
long been tense and raids occurred often. Although Kenya was
not directly involved in the hostilities, it could not let the occasion pass without seeking a solution to the "frequent border
incidents." Since the Council was "greatly concerned that the
continuation of such incidents will inevitably lead to hostilities," it asked the two states "to refrain from further provocative actions and propaganda."

Still, something had to be done to assure that the cease-
fire was actually implemented. Somalia, outclassed by its
rival in men and equipment, was afraid of retaliation against
shifta raids and asked that a demilitarized zone be created and
supervised by neutral observers. Ethiopia, however, did not
want its hands tied in action against the shiftas, who could
readily filter through the net of observers anyway. The length
of the frontier and the size and cost of the supervisory machinery needed to keep the two enemies apart was, moreover,
enough to deter the Council of Ministers. All that could be
done was to ask the diplomatic missions of the African states
in Ethiopia and Somalia "to do their best to assist in the implementation of the cease-fire." Eventually a five-nation committee of ambassadors was formed to keep an eye on the situation.

The restoration of peace still depended on the good will
of the combatants. The Council resolution was adopted on 15
February 1964. That same day Ethiopia and Somalia ordered
a cease-fire, although the actual truce had to be arranged
through the intermediary of Prime Minister Ibrahim Abboud of
Sudan. Very soon, however, fighting broke out again and
Ethiopia and Somalia charged one another with breaking the
truce and launching border attacks. As the hostilities resumed, President Osman of Somalia called for a peace-keeping
force along the frontiers.[5]

The Council of Ministers met again for a regular session in Lagos. As of 24 February the whole matter was discussed anew. The cease-fire was obviously a failure and
something had to be done to impose the OAU's decision. Somalia repeated its request for a demilitarized zone and ob-

servers. To which Ethiopia retorted that neither would be necessary if Somalia renounced its territorial claims and respected international borders. After reviewing the situation,
in particular the difficulty of making the parties cease hostilities or separating them physically, the Council again failed to
give any force to its resolution. It merely congratulated the
Ethiopian and Somali governments for having immediately ordered a cease-fire (which they did not observe) and requested
them to refrain from any action which might compromise its
effective implementation. The praise and advice was a bit
misplaced. For during the month of March there were reports of more fighting, although not on the previous scale.

Another try at ending hostilities was made outside of
the Organization, although in compliance with the request of
the Council of Ministers. As of mid-March, Ethiopian and
Somali representatives met for talks in Khartoum. Despite
continued hostilities along the border, the talks went on and
eventually reached a satisfactory conclusion on 30 March.
Both countries agreed to a new cease-fire and decided that
their troops would be withdrawn 6-9 miles from the border,
under the supervision of a joint commission.[6] They would also end hostile propaganda and would resume direct talks on
the boundary dispute. Despite fresh fighting, the cease-fire
was ordered on 2 April and soon came into effect. Somewhat
later the mixed Somali-Ethiopian cease-fire commission confirmed the withdrawal of the troops.

Although the Ethiopians and Somalis had finally fought
themselves out in large engagements and despite a prevailing
relative calm, the trouble was not over. Small raids and
clashes in both Ethiopia and Kenya did not stop and hardly a
week passed without some occurrence. After relatively serious incidents along the border, in March 1965, Somalia asked
the OAU Secretary-General to appoint a commission to investigate the situation. None was established. Rather, a few
days later, Ethiopia and Somalia agreed to reactivate the joint
commission to help implement the Khartoum agreement. After
another lull, the shiftas resumed their activities and the piece-
meal war continued.

A Further Complication.

In the meanwhile, quite suddenly, a new source of tension arose. To all appearances, Somaliland had been slumber-
ing under the benevolent colonial rule of France. It awoke

dramatically on 25 August 1966, during General de Gaulle's
visit to Djibouti. There were mass demonstrations in the
streets and thousands of people chanted their demand for "total
independence." On 15 September, after serious rioting and
some loss of life, de Gaulle took his stand and announced that
"France knows how to live without the Somali Coast." His
government would "pose no obstacles" if the territory wanted
independence, but it should not count on France's aid if it
severed the links.[7]

At this point French Somaliland became the real bone
of contention between Somalia and Ethiopia. The colony had
long been the fifth point on the Somali star and Mogadishu
made no secret of its claims. But Djibouti was also an essential port and the terminus of the Franco-Ethiopian railway that
connected Addis Ababa with the sea via Dire Dawa. Moreover,
despite its name, the countryside was largely inhabited by
Danakili or Afars, related to the nearby population in Ethiopia.
Ethiopia could not afford to have Djibouti joined to Somalia
and, on 16 September the Emperor stated that "Djibouti indis-
putably is ours and its people know they belong to Ethiopia.
They realize on which side their interests and freedom lies."[8]

As long as the French remained in control there was
peace, but if the colony chose independence, it would probably
be rent in two by the rival tribes and fought over bitterly by
their backers. It had never been so clear that the gaining of
independence could also be a bane to Africa and the OAU was
faced with this dilemma when it met in Addis Ababa in the
autumn of 1966. Somalia and some of the radical states
pressed for independence whatever the consequences might be
and demanded that the OAU supervise the referendum. The
more prudent states were worried about the aftermath of independence and the likely confrontation if France withdrew. The
Francophone states, in particular, wished to avoid any criticism of General de Gaulle or France.

The first position was taken by the Liberation Committee, a hard line calling on the population to seize its "effective
independence" by the referendum and which went on to condemn French intimidation.[9] The ensuing debates in the Council of Ministers were excited but ended differently. The Somali proposal, urging the population to choose independence,
demanding OAU (or UN) supervision of the referendum and
criticizing France, was rejected and the Organization adopted
its most cautious stand ever on decolonization. The Council
resolution of 6 November, approved by the Assembly, merely

asked that the referendum be free and impartial and called upon the population "to unite in confronting its destiny."

However, far from uniting, the Afars and Somalis formed rival political parties and campaigned against one another more than against France. There was a period of serious agitation and the tribes tended to look towards their backers. Ethiopia's lead was that they accept some sort of association with France. Somalia urged independence. But it realized the possible consequences and, early in January, the Somali National Assembly expressed concern at "Ethiopia's threat to annex French Somaliland if that territory chooses independence." Any act of aggression against an independent Somaliland, it warned, would be considered an act of aggression against the sovereignty of the Somali Republic.

The referendum was held on 19 March 1967. Voting followed ethnic lines very closely and the Afars obtained a 60 per cent majority on a platform of continued but looser relations with France. The following day, however, Somalia protested the results to the Secretary-General of the OAU. The vote, it claimed, had been rigged by unjustly expelling thousands of Somalis who lived in the territory. And the Somali Ambassador in Addis Ababa said that the OAU was "evading its responsibility out of fear" and had done nothing to help the "freedom fighters in Djibouti."[10]

Although the crisis subsided it was not over. For the Afars tried to capitalize on their majority and loyalty to France by improving their relative strength in the colony with an eye to the future. At the same time, the "Liberation Front of the Somali Coast," with its headquarters in Mogadishu, decided to resort to armed struggle.[11] The only immediate change was of the colony's name, clearly reflecting the split in what was now the Territory of the Afar and Issa.

Towards a Settlement.

Obviously, the cessation of hostilities after one particularly bad clash was not enough. Lasting peace could not be restored between the countries in the region unless some solution were found to their territorial problems. This required more than a rectification of the frontiers, it entailed a complete redrawing of the map on ethnic lines. This was beyond the means of the OAU in the best of circumstances and it could do little as long as the positions of its three members were diametrically opposed.

While on his way to the conference in Dar es Salaam,
on 12 February 1964, the Somali Foreign Minister Abdullahi
Issa, claimed that "the inhabitants of the area are Somalis
who wish to secede to Somalia, and the only equitable long-
term solution would be a plebiscite to determine their wishes."[12]
In Lagos, he again repeated his country's stand and pleaded
self-determination for the Somalis in Ethiopia and Kenya.
Neither of Somalia's neighbors could deny that the inhabitants
of the areas in question were ethnically Somalis nor that many
of them would have preferred uniting with the Republic. They
knew a plebiscite was dangerous and that, on the basis of its
results, they would then be called upon to cede some territory.
Both Ethiopia and Kenya feared such an amputation for there
was no telling where it would end. The principle of self-
determination did not apply to the independent states of Africa
and, moreover, it was highly dangerous, they warned. What
would happen if every ethnic group tried to redraw the map
in its own interest?

It was not hard to raise the spectre of disintegration
this implied. Ethiopia and Kenya had to discourage such strivings not only in the Somali regions but also in Eritrea and in
Masai lands in Kenya. The Kenyan OAU delegate urged that
the principle of recognizing a state's borders existing at the
time of the gaining of independence be inserted in the Charter.

The Council of Ministers did not try to force the disagreement into the open or lay down any general rules on the
respect of frontiers. Rather, it left the matter to the disputants to patch up as best they could, and suggested "direct negotiations" between each pair of countries. No attempt was
made at finding a permanent solution and no OAU commission
was established to look into the merits of the case. The members were somewhat disappointed at the lack of concrete results
in the Algero-Moroccan border dispute and realized that the
conflict with Somalia was much more complicated and inextricable. The basis of Somalia's claims was even too explosive to handle.

However, as the incursions and clashes continued, each
country tried to put an end to them in its own way. Since
Ethiopia could not guard the whole frontier and prevent all infiltration of shiftas, it could only stiffen the reprisals taken
against them. Kenya launched a more ambitious program in
its North-Eastern Province. The Somali nomads were settled

in modern villages called "manyattas," where they were shown
the advantages of life in Kenya or at least more readily
watched over. By attaching the nomads to the land and preventing the constant movement to and from Somalia, it was
hoped to cut down on shifta activities. To the extent this did
not work, the two countries had to trust to their arms and
just before the hostilities, in November 1963, Ethiopia and
Kenya had concluded a mutual defence agreement and begun
discussions on joint action. Similar discussions and actions
took place over the years.

The Council of Ministers had called for direct talks,
but little more than formalities could be agreed upon by Somalia and its opponents. The underlying problem was as unsolvable as ever. And the accumulated suspicions could not
be dissipated enough to hold worthwhile discussions. Never-
the less, ever since the Dar es Salaam meeting, the Organi-
cation had viewed the situation in the Horn of Africa with concern and this item was kept on the agenda of its various political bodies. It was discussed between the parties or among
all members, but little more than appeals resulted. The other
countries in the region, however, were particularly worried by
the friction and played a more active part in trying to reach
an arrangement. Ethiopian and Somali representatives met
several times in Khartoum and there was even a summit between Presidents Kenyatta, Osman and Nyerere in Arusha, in
December 1965. But no progress was made towards a solution.

Still, the attempts did not cease. They were considerably facilitated when a new man took the head of the Somali
government in mid-1967. Mohammed Ibrahim Egal, who had
to enter the ruling Somali Youth League to become Prime Minister, had not been intimately connected with the claims and
aggressive policy of the earlier governments. He, of course,
could not renounce the principle of uniting the Somalis, but he
could seek to attain this aim in other ways or, to the extent
earlier policies had failed, he could restore some semblance
of peace in the region. Somalia was a terribly poor country
and its military effort was a serious burden on its budget
while preventing a more productive effort at overcoming its
poverty and development. And constant warfare had been to
no one's benefit.

Moreover, Somalia had a much smaller population and
was less heavily armed than either Ethiopia or Kenya, and was
certainly no match for both of them. It could not have im-

posed its claims militarily and could only keep up a harassing
action so they would not be forgotten. Even this was possible
only through backing from the Arab world and the East. However, with the Arab-Israeli war in June 1967, much of this
support evaporated or was proven unreliable. Indeed, this
shock led to a general pacification in the region. At this time
the Eritrean rebels also ceased their activities and returned
to Ethiopia and the friction along the Sudanese border stopped.

Shortly thereafter, there was a definite turn for the
better in Somalia's relations with its neighbors. The Kinshasa
Assembly was the site of a major reconciliation. At the insti-
gation of President Kaunda of Zambia, Kenya and Somalia
signed an agreement on 13 September in which they undertook
to put an end to the fighting and resume diplomatic relations.
The next day this joint declaration was consecrated in a resolution of the Assembly. It reaffirmed the governments' respect of one another's sovereignty and territorial integrity and
the undertaking to settle their differences peacefully in keeping
with the Charter. The Kenyan and Somali governments pledged
to ensure peace and security on both sides of the border "by
preventing destruction of human life and property" and to refrain from hostile propaganda against one another. They also
agreed to meet again with President Kaunda to improve and
consolidate this cooperation. The new turn was reconfirmed
on 28 October, when a "memorandum of understanding" was
signed by President Kenyatta and Prime Minister Egal at the
meeting in Arusha. Along with the above points, it was agreed
to restore diplomatic relations in the near future and to establish a joint commission to examine various issues. Then, on
1 February 1968, diplomatic relations were resumed.

Similarly, after private talks between Haile Selassie
and Mohammed Egal, a joint ministerial commission met in
Addis Ababa. On 23 September, Ethiopian and Somali representatives agreed to "eliminate all sources of tension." They
reaffirmed the Khartoum agreement of March 1964 and decided
to improve relations by the free movement of their diplomats
and equitable treatment of their nationals when travelling. A
joint military commission was to study complaints and quarterly meetings of administrative authorities were to be held
along the frontier in order to increase cooperation.

This time there was a definite improvement in the situation. Nevertheless, was this really the end of the quarrel?
It was hard to believe so, for the earlier leaders had immediately reacted against the "Arusha understanding" with Kenya,

and Egal was expelled from the SYL, although he was later
reinstated and did not lose his position in the government. The
attacks of the opposition were even stronger in view of this
betrayal of the Somali cause. Thus, even on the surface, the
ruling circles were divided on a modus vivendi with Ethiopia
and Kenya. The government would certainly have been unseat-
ed if the agreements had gone beyond the establishment of
relatively normal relations and limited cooperation to include
an explicit renunciation of the Somali claims.

Moreover, an improvement in state-to-state relations
did not get at the roots of the conflict. At the tribal level,
as long as the Somalis were nomads and the ties with blood
brothers stronger than allegiance to the states in which they
lived, even the Somali government could not repress the desire for unification or block action by shiftas. The circumstances that had taught some of the leaders the wisdom of cooperation had not necessarily stilled the deeper urge. This
was borne out in fact since the raids decreased but never
stopped entirely. Probably the backers of stronger means of
settling the Somali problem had only put off their campaign to
a more propitious moment. And the Horn was still far from
a satisfactory and permanent solution. Unless such a solution
were found, the thaw might well be nothing more than a truce.

Notes

1. CIAS/GEN/INF/25, p. 7.

2. The Times (London), 24 Nov. 1963.

3. Ibid., 26 Nov. 1963.

4. For debates in Dar es Salaam and Lagos, see Saadia
      Touval, The Organization of African Unity and African
      Borders.

5. The Times (London), 23 Feb. 1964.

6. The New York Times, 30 March 1964.

7. Africa Report, Nov. 1966.

8. Le Monde, 1 Nov. 1966.

9. Ibid., 1 Nov. 1966.

10. *Africa Report*, April 1967.

11. *Le Monde*, 27 April 1967.

12. *The Times* (London) 13 Feb. 1964.

Revolution in the Congo

C. The Congo Crisis

During its first years, the Organization of African
Unity had met and apparently solved a number of serious problems and its members were increasingly willing to deal with
African issues. Even if that had not been the case, the OAU
could hardly have ignored the events occurring in the heart of
the continent. One of the largest independent states, the former Belgian Congo, dominated central Africa through its size
and location. Some of its provinces were fabulously wealthy
and it was the leading power in the region. But the Congo
(Léopoldville) was certainly in no position to play a positive
role until the internal dissension had been overcome. Until
then, it would only be a tinder box and continual source of
disturbance.

Due to its size and potential, events in the Congo shook
its neighbors. The most direct overflow came from military
operations which made the inhabitants along the borders seek
safety in nearby states. There was also a widespread belief
that as the Congo went, so went all Africa. When allied with
certain ideological trends, conflict in the Congo left no country unaffected. Many found it hard not to take sides. Ultimately, in September 1964, the OAU was called upon to handle
an affair that had been the undoing of African unity before and
might be so again.

New Rebellion in the Congo.

The turmoil following independence had never really
ceased. It seemed that by bringing together the major political tendencies in a government of national unity in August 1961,
a big step had been taken. Only, Cyrille Adoula found cooperation with Antoine Gizenga difficult and he gradually turned
toward the more conservative leaders like Colonel Joseph-
Désiré Mobutu, the head of the army, and Justin Bomboko, his
Foreign Minister. At the same time the two fell out over how
to deal with Katanga and, in January 1962, Gizenga fled to
Stanleyville where he was found and arrested. Then, in January 1963, the Katanga secession was finally crushed by United

Nations troops and the central government again ruled over
the length and breadth of the country.

Nevertheless, all the while there was growing dissatisfaction at the grass roots. None of the promises of independence had been fulfilled. When the Belgians withdrew the administration collapsed and most economic activity ceased. The
peasants suffered most and, especially where cash crops had
replaced subsistence farming, there was hunger and want.
The schools had closed and groups of "jeunesse" agitated the
countryside while the workers were unemployed and demonstrated in the cities. The only ones who seemed to have done
well were those in power. And the politicians out of office,
both to the right and left, seized upon this less articulate protest as weapons against the government. But there was no
real focus for opposition. The Lumumbists were scattered,
Gizenga was in prison and no other leader had arisen.

Still, this disaffection was constantly eroding the center's control over the vast country. The years of strife and
warfare had isolated Léopoldville from many of the provinces.
In fact, the roads and much of the essential infrastructure had
been destroyed and regular contacts were impossible. The administration that might have held the country together had been
disrupted and the army was disorganized and weak. When
combined with the frustration and anger, the central government was clearly in a delicate position. Yet, the plans were
going ahead to draft a new constitution and hold elections.
This might have been a new start. But the old rivalries were
still too bitter and, when the quarrelling deputies seemed likely to frustrate this program, President Kasavubu closed Parliament and gave the government full powers. By October
1963, amidst rumors of a plot, a state of emergency was proclaimed and many of the opposition leaders were arrested.
Others escaped and, just across the river in Brazzaville,
Christophe Gbenye founded a Comité National de Libération.
The CNL's aim was to overthrow the Adoula regime.

In the early months of 1964, the situation deteriorated
still further. The greatest unrest was in the countryside and
fighting broke out in Kwilu. The Armée Nationale Congolaise
(ANC) was attacked by local guerrilla bands led by Pierre
Mulele, who sparked or associated himself with the peasant uprising. Although the ANC was initially able to contain this revolt, new centres were formed in North Katanga and then Orientale and Kivu, the old Lumumbist strongholds. This broader movement, run by Gaston Soumialot, was increasingly suc-

cessful and in June the rebellion approached Stanleyville. At this point it was evident that Adoula could no longer cope with the situation and his resignation was accepted.

From exile, in Spain, Moise Tshombe claimed that he was the only man who could restore order in the country. There was in fact no other candidate and, on 5 July 1964, he was made Prime Minister. President Kasavubu gave him the task of forming a transitional government to prepare the Congo for national elections in nine months and to halt the rising wave of rebellion. Tshombe had returned to seek national reconciliation and, shortly after his arrival, he toured the country and tried to broaden the basis of the central government. In Léopoldville and even Stanleyville he was welcomed as a hero. In a bid to obtain cooperation from the Lumumbists he released Antoine Gizenga and other political prisoners and tried to contact the rebel leaders. All in vain. While he toured Léopoldville with Gizenga and Kalondji, in the eastern Congo, Soumialot denounced his government as illegal. What was worse, the rebellion kept on spreading. The unbroken series of defeats culminated in the fall of Stanleyville on 4 August. As the ineffectual ANC was pushed back, Tshombe was forced to turn from reconciliation to repression in order to save his regime.

The last United Nations troops had been withdrawn from the Congo on 30 June and the central government could only count on the 35,000 man army under now Major General Joseph Mobutu. But this was an army that had been in action ever since independence. It was poorly officered, weak and unnerved. Moreover, it was hopelessly over-extended since the rebels already held one-sixth of the Congo. The ANC could not possibly hold back the rebels over such a wide front, and it repeatedly broke and ran as the menacing hoards approached. In order to strengthen his army, Tshombe called on the Americans for military aid. Also, as in his Katanga days, he began recruiting several hundred mercenaries as a backbone to the Congolese army and he reactivated the Katangan gendarmes. As this aid arrived the ANC became a more effective fighting force and for the first time stopped rebel advances.

The Congo and its Neighbors.

At first the impact of the Congolese crisis on the African scene was relatively limited. But even then there were

dangers of intervention. The flight of refugees abroad was
normal and it could not be avoided that rebels mingled with
them or were given political asylum. However, as passions
rose, it was hard to distinguish between toleration of refugees
and encouragement to rebels and the Congo (Léopoldville) was
increasingly at odds with its neighbors, especially the Congo
(Brazzaville) and Burundi.

Relations were worst between the two Congos. This
was already an old feud. Abbé Fulbert Youlou, when he was
President in Brazzaville, had strongly backed Tshombe and
Kasavubu in earlier phases of the Congo affair. In August
1963, after three days of demonstrations and strikes, he was
forced to resign and was replaced by a violently radical regime. After the "trois glorieuses," Youlou had been imprisoned but many of his followers sought refuge in Léopoldville.
Then, in October 1963, after Parliament was closed and much
of the opposition arrested in Léopoldville, the revolutionary
wing came to Brazzaville and Christophe Gbenye set up the National Liberation Committee (CNL).

When Moise Tshombe returned to the Congo, enmity
flared up between the two capitals. The Brazzaville regime
was accused of harboring unfriendly elements and even helping
the rebels arm and train in camps on its territory. Tshombe,
in return, was accused of supporting Youlou's backers and the
enemies of the regime. Mutual recrimination increased and
was spread by the radio and press. In mid-August, once
again President Alphonse Massamba-Débat charged that the
Tshombe government was smuggling arms into his country as
part of a plot against the regime and was seeking a clash between the two countries. At the same time, Prime Minister
Tshombe warned Brazzaville to stop its subversion in the Congo. Very soon all links were broken between both sides of
the Congo River.

To the northeast, near the province of Kivu where some
of the worst fighting was going on, the tiny Kingdom of Burundi was shaken by the civil war in the Congo. A steady stream
of refugees sought asylum in the country. Among them there
were doubtlessly also rebels, who escaped across the border
only to return and fight again. One of them was Gaston Soumialot, who directed the operations in the eastern Congo from
his headquarters in Usumbura. There was considerable rebel
activity along the frontier and some of the leaders appeared
frequently in Burundi.

Prime Minister Tshombe had already on 16 July 1964
told all foreigners--including Africans--to keep out of the Congo's internal affairs. Only a week later he was forced to take
more drastic measures. The crisis was set off by an attack
on Bolobo, a village on the Congo River to the north of Léopoldville. A force of two hundred men had set out from
Brazzaville to invade the Congo but, after taking the village,
it was repulsed by the ANC. From the documents seized on
Colonel Pakassa, the head of the "CNL Army," Tshombe obtained "incontrovertible proof" of African support of the rebellion.[1] After this he warned Brazzaville and Burundi that he
would expel their nationals or even inflict military reprisals
if they did not cease aiding the rebels.

The OAU Steps In.

Not long after Moise Tshombe returned to the Congo
the first Assembly of Heads of State and Government was held
in Cairo. President Kasavubu had been invited by the Egyptian government, but there was a minor tempest when the delegates learned that he would be accompanied by Tshombe. Certain African leaders bitterly regretted his appointment as
Prime Minister and protested against his appearing at the Assembly. Although it would be quite normal for Tshombe to
attend as Head of Government, there was considerable relief
when he responded to the criticism by boycotting the conference.

That was in July. By the month of September there
was a clamor for the OAU to deal with the situation in the
Congo. The very countries that objected most to his presence
in Cairo began stressing that the civil war was not only a Congolese but also an African affair and that Prime Minister
Tshombe should appear before the OAU. As the rebel position
worsened the demands of the radical countries became more
stringent and various leaders called for an extraordinary session to end the bloodshed and find a "political" solution. At
the same time, they insisted that the mercenaries and Americans be sent home.

Prime Minister Tshombe was not really opposed to a
meeting of the OAU. However, his intention was certainly not
to offer the Congo as an experiment in peace-keeping. He had
his own interests. Tshombe hoped to use the Organization to
get the moral and material backing of the African community.
He wanted to strengthen his hand in the bid for national recon-

ciliation by an endorsement of his own plan. Or, at least, he
wished to prevent any further aid to the rebels by certain
members of the OAU. Since he was somewhat embarrassed
by the disapproval of mercenaries, he might have been willing
to do without them if they could be replaced by troops from
African nations. He had already approached Ethiopia, Liberia,
Malagasy, Nigeria and Senegal to ask such assistance.[2] The
notion of an African "police force" had also been raised. At
any rate, if nothing could be done through the OAU, at least
Tshombe would have an excuse for not changing his methods.

The radicals urged a political solution for very different reasons. The situation of the rebels was growing worse
and the rebel camp needed a respite. If the mercenaries and
American aid were withdrawn the pressure would let up and,
if national reconciliation came about, the Lumumbists could be
integrated in the new government. Eventually they might even
gain a solid foothold within it. A political solution now seemed to open up more possibilities than a military one.

The moderates were less eager to have the OAU intervene actively in the Congo. They supported the central government and they were also adherents of the rule of sovereignty. Nevertheless, they had been asked for assistance and
would have preferred that any aid to the Congo be granted within the framework of the Organization. For the moment, however, they thought it would be best just to send a commission
of inquiry to the Congo to study the situation.

The quarrel between the Congo (Léopoldville) and its
neighbors had also been raised. It had come to a peak when
Prime Minister Tshombe ordered the expulsion of all nationals
of Brazzaville and Burundi late in August. Brazzaville urged
the OAU to intercede in this matter. It and Burundi also
asked to be cleared of the charges made against them and demanded that Léopoldville cease its unfriendly stand and threats
of retaliation.

Despite the contradictory motivation, Africa was agreed
on one point--the OAU should play some role in solving the
Congolese crisis. New requests for a meeting kept on arriving but there were still some qualms about respect for Congolese sovereignty until President Kasavubu himself cabled that
a solution to the Congolese problem should be sought in the
Organization of African Unity. But he made it clear that the
Organization should carefully avoid any intervention in the country's internal affairs.

With surprising rapidity the general wish had become a decision. Soon the Council of Ministers was convened in Addis Ababa, where it met in extraordinary session from 5-10 September 1964. The atmosphere was one of urgency and crisis, overlaid with euphoria--for Africa was finally asserting its political maturity. The United Nations and the great powers had been unable to find a solution and now Africa was itself dealing with the Congolese affair. The portent of their decisions was stressed to the Foreign Ministers by the Emperor of Ethiopia: "It is not only the future of the Congo which hangs in the balance but in a very real sense that of the entire African continent."[3]

The Peace Plan.

No sooner had they met, however, than it became obvious how wide was the gulf between the opposing sides. Nevertheless, by hard bargaining it was possible to work out a tenuous compromise. The points of difference were either overlooked or put aside temporarily and the points of agreement were highlighted. In this way common ground could be found on items like national reconciliation, the mercenaries and relations between the Congo and its neighbors. On this, the Council of Ministers built its peace plan.

Prime Minister Tshombe had always called for national reconciliation and in Addis Ababa he renewed his pledge to restore harmony in the Congo. The only question was: how? He did not insist that the rebels be defeated or crushed, but they were to return to the fold. To bring about reconciliation, the rebels had to lay down their arms and make peace with the government, not vice versa. The radicals wished to start with a cease-fire. Then a provisional government could unite the various factions and prepare the future of the Congo. This was not a task for the present government. Putting the Tshombe/Kasavubu regime on the same footing as the rebels, they suggested clearing the table and beginning anew with a government in which Tshombe, if a member at all, would not be the leader.

No agreement could be reached on what was to follow the cease-fire, but no one argued that the war should continue. The Congolese problem was felt to be "essentially political" and some peaceful means had to be found to restore harmony. Until the fighting ceased, it would be hard to attain any reconciliation. Thus, buttressed on the "solemn undertaking" of the

Prime Minister of the Congo "to guarantee the security of
combatants who lay down their arms," a plan was adopted.
The Council:

> Requests especially all those now fighting to cease
> hostilities so as to seek, with the help of the Or-
> ganization of African Unity, a solution that would
> make possible national reconciliation and the resto-
> ration of order in the Congo;
>
> Appeals to all the political leaders of the Demo-
> cratic Republic of the Congo to seek, by all appro-
> priate means, to restore and consolidate national
> reconciliation.

The Council's plan was very sketchy and provided no
details on arrangements for a cease-fire nor any suggestions
as to how the rebels should come to terms with the government or share in restoring unity. There was no word about
the OAU's role either. As for implementation, the plan was
largely based on requests and appeals and, to work, it required considerable good will on both sides. It also placed a
somewhat greater strain on the rebels. Both sides were to
cease fighting but, once they lay down their arms, the rebels
could count on a guarantee of security only from a man they
hated and distrusted.

When it came to the mercenaries, the shoe was on the
other foot. Prime Minister Tshombe was willing to make concessions. He would stop recruiting mercenaries or even dismiss those already in the Congo, but he insisted that this must
not mean the collapse of law and order. Thus they had to be
replaced by an African force.[4] He wanted to have a number
of African contingents, chosen by the Congo and under its control, although provided under the auspices of the OAU. These
troops would not be used to fight the rebels, he stressed; they
would merely help maintain law and order in the pacified territory. (This would, of course, release the ANC to fight elsewhere.)

The radicals objected that the removal of the mercenaries was a basically patriotic move, for all mercenaries were
the enemies of Africa and a threat to the continent. This sentiment was generally endorsed by the Council, especially since
they were "principally recruited from the racist countries of
South Africa and Southern Rhodesia." Although fighting for an
African government, it could only be feared that in fact the

mercenaries were also fighting against all Africa. In particular, their presence had

> ... unfortunate effects on the neighboring independ-
> ent states as well as on the struggle for national
> liberation in Angola, Southern Rhodesia, Mozam-
> bique and other territories in the region which are
> still under colonial domination, and constitutes a
> serious threat to peace in the African continent.

Given the general disapprobation in the OAU of the role
these foreigners were playing, an appeal was made to the Congolese government "to stop immediately the recruitment of
mercenaries and to expel as soon as possible all mercenaries
of whatever origin who are already in the Congo so as to facilitate an African solution." There was no real counterpart
to this and the radical states successfully blocked Tshombe's
bid to obtain military or other assistance for the Congo.
(Such a resolution failed by one vote.) Nevertheless, he had
considerable leeway, for the mercenaries only had to leave "as
soon as possible."

The Council of Ministers also dealt with the relations
between the Congo (Léopoldville) and its neighbors, the Congo
(Brazzaville) and Burundi. It not unsurprisingly heard a series of charges and counter-charges. Léopoldville complained
of the aid its neighbors granted the rebels, consisting not only
of asylum but also training and arming them. This charge
was denied by Brazzaville and Burundi, which claimed they
were only providing humanitarian help to the refugees from the
Congo. When fighting ceased, especially if the mercenaries
left, the stream of refugees would dry up and relations with
Léopoldville would improve. The Tshombe government simply
had to change its methods and bring about national reconciliation for things to return to normal. To the contrary, they insisted that the Congo cease its threats and demonstrations
against its smaller neighbors.

Since the charges could not be sorted out then and there
the Council decided to act upon the invitations of the three governments to send a "fact-finding and goodwill mission" to their
countries.

The Congo Commission at Work.

When the Ministers finished their debates in Addis Ababa, they left with feelings of elation. They had apparently
just solved another dangerous African problem and elaborated
a peace plan for the Congo. But it took more than a resolution to restore peace. The actual work was left for a special
commission on the Congo.

The Council had decided

> ... to set up and to send immediately to the Demo-
> cratic Republic of the Congo, the Republic of Congo
> (Brazzaville) and the Kingdom of Burundi an _ad hoc_
> commission consisting of Cameroon, Ethiopia,
> Ghana, Guinea, Nigeria, Somalia, Tunisia, U.A.R.,
> Upper Volta and placed under the effective Chair-
> manship of H. E. Jomo Kenyatta, Prime Minister
> of Kenya, which will have the following mandate:
>
> a) to help and encourage the efforts of the Gov-
>   ernment of the Democratic Republic of the
>   Congo in the restoration of national reconcili-
>   ation ...
>
> b) to seek by all possible means to bring about
>   normal relations between the Democratic Re-
>   public of the Congo and its neighbors, espe-
>   cially the Kingdom of Burundi and the Re-
>   public of the Congo (Brazzaville).

Nevertheless, despite its formidable task, the Congo
Commission was not given any material means to attain its
ends. It did not have any machinery for supervising a cease-
fire or to bring together the opposing sides to attain a reconciliation or to normalize relations. All it could count on was
the good will of the parties, the prestige of its members and
its authority as the representative of the African community.

Its greatest weakness, however, was that the Commission's terms of reference were much narrower than the resolution itself. Cease-fire and reconciliation, two items on
which somewhat greater demands were made of the rebels,
were encouraged. But the mandate did not include the appeal
to stop recruiting mercenaries and expel those already in the
Congo, where concessions were asked of Prime Minister
Tshombe. Moreover, the Commission was not requested to

bring about any reconciliation itself but rather to "help and encourage" the efforts of the central government.

Thus, as compared with the resolution, the mandate of the Commission was remarkably lopsided. Eventually the members would have to choose between the letter and the spirit of the resolution, between aid to the Congolese regime and conciliation of that regime with its enemies. The decision, come what may, could not be just to work for the Congolese government. The membership was so arranged as to include those backing both sides in the struggle, that is, to be a "neutral" body. Since three of his most rabid opponents were present: Ghana, Guinea and UAR, it was obvious to Tshombe that the Commission would not be his servant. Moreover, such a degrading and un-African posture was impossible for a high level body, consisting usually of Foreign Ministers and chaired by one of the oldest and most venerable Heads of State.

In view of the urgency of ending the strife in the Congo, the Commission met immediately after the Council session in Addis Ababa. On 11 September 1964, it had already decided to call for a cease-fire. The actual appeal was broadcast by Jomo Kenyatta on 15 September. It was heralded as a major step towards reconciliation in the Congo. But it had not been prepared or organized in any way. There was no specific deadline or time limit nor were any arrangements made to supervise or even observe the cessation of hostilities and security of those who lay down their arms. Everything depended on both sides' good will, which was not forthcoming.

When the Congo Commission met in Nairobi for its first regular session, on 18 September 1964, the members were no longer as optimistic about improving the situation. Nevertheless, they hoped to convince Prime Minister Tshombe to end hostilities and accept a reconciliation. The Commission even seemed intent on starting the national reconciliation on the spot for, when he arrived in Nairobi, Tshombe was unpleasantly surprised to learn that rebel spokesmen were also present and expected to appear before the Commission. As the representative of the legal government, he refused to recognize or even be seated at the same table with the rebels. To the Commission's despair, he could not be made to change his mind and he left Nairobi without seeing the rebels. All the Prime Minister had actually done was to merely present his case again and reiterate the pledges made in Addis Ababa.

No agreement could be reached between the Congo and its neighbors either. Tshombe maintained his charges that the Congo (Brazzaville) and Burundi were harboring and supplying the rebels and that training camps were located in the other Congo. These accusations were rejected, once again, and the two countries complained about the propaganda campaigns directed against them, as well as support of opposition to the regime in Brazzaville.

Although there was a deadlock all around, the Commission could have played a role by visiting the various parties concerned. The first step might have been to visit Burundi and Brazzaville to insure that the rebels were not premitted to abuse their status of refugees and, in particular, that they were not being armed and trained. Then, in Léopoldville, Tshombe could have been asked to neutralize the Youlou backers. In exchange for a cessation of outside interference and an end to backing of the rebels, the central government might have been willing to relinquish the mercenaries and American aid. Eventually, left on their own, both sides in the civil war would have been tempted to end the hostilities and seek a peaceful solution. Nevertheless, despite its very specific mandate, the Congo Commission did not suggest a compromise or even leave to study the situation in the three countries.

The Stanleyville Crisis.

Having failed to attain its goals in Nairobi, the Commission seemed to despair of influencing the course of events in and about the Congo. Its paralysis was due to the foregone conclusion that no political solution could be attained, or even prepared, as long as the war continued. Appearances seemed to prove it right. For all the time it appealed for peace and reconciliation, the fighting went on. The success of the mercenary-led Congolese army eventually put the government in a position of strength. As long as it was winning the war, it had nothing to fear of the Commission and little to gain from its action. Although on increasingly bad terms with the Commission and its Chairman, Tshombe was not worried.

On 5 September, the rebels had proclaimed a "People's Republic of the Congo" in Stanleyville, dedicated to overthrowing the Tshombe government. At its head were Christophe Gbenye as Prime Minister, Gaston Soumialot as Defence Minister and "General" Nicolas Olenga of the Armée Populaire de Libération. When the ad hoc Commission was created, the

rebels flocked to Nairobi to meet with and influence it. A
cessation of hostilities would have consolidated the position of
the new Stanleyville regime and the withdrawal of the mercenaries was vital to their cause. They would certainly also be
part of any new government of national reconciliation. This
willingness to cooperate in seeking a "political" solution had
predisposed some of the Commission and many Africans in
their favor, and Tshombe's enemies were soon referred to as
nationalists.

However, as the tide turned and the war really went
against them, the rebels acted in desperation. As the rebellion was rolled back towards Stanleyville, the leaders decided
to concentrate their forces in the capital and make a stand.
As they retreated, the rebels brought with them most of the
white and Asian population of the region, who were made hostages and then pawns in the struggle. In mid-November, with
its army in rout, the Stanleyville authorities warned of dread-
ful consequences if the ANC did not stop before the city.

Due Mainly to his great prestige, Chairman Kenyatta of
the ineffective OAU peace-keeping Commission was asked to
provide his good offices to save the hostages. Still, in the
midst of the war he did not feel much could be done and he
insisted that he would not help evacuate the civilians unless
the fighting ended on both sides.[5] Finally, however, he gave
in and there was a brief calm as Jomo Kenyatta presided over
the delicate bargaining that began in his country home at Ga-
tundu on 23 November. Talks were held between William Attwood, the American Ambassador to Kenya, and Thomas Kanza, the Foreign Minister of the Stanleyville regime, and attended by the Secretary-General of the OAU.

There was a slim chance that a compromise could be
found to avoid the worst. Nevertheless, it immediately appeared that the positions were far removed from one another.
The rebels had not come just to arrange the release of the
hostages. They sought an end to American and Belgian aid to
the Congo and probably wanted them to bring pressure on the
Tshombe government to cease fire or even negotiate a compromise settlement. As a minimum condition, the Congolese
army (even then massing around the city) had to halt outside
of Stanleyville. Kanza refused to dissociate the evacuation of
the hostages from the general situation, but Attwood had been
authorized only to discuss the safety of the foreign civilians
held in Stanleyville. Jomo Kenyatta tried to save the negotiations. He wanted to prevent any loss of life among the hos-

tages, both for their own sake and to avoid discrediting Africa. But he, too, hoped to have a lever--any lever--to stop the bloodshed in the Congo for the good of all. He urged all sides to cease hostilities so that the negotiations might succeed.[6] He asked the negotiators to try harder, to seek longer for a compromise.

Nevertheless, at dawn on 24 November 1964, the storm broke and Belgian paratroopers landed in the center of Stanleyville. There was little resistence and they were able to liberate most of the hostages, although they came too late for others. Soon after, the ANC entered the city and eventually took it. President Kenyatta was appalled by the turn of events. "A situation which for days past has been tense and threatening ... has finally erupted into tragedy." He had made every effort to reach a solution and there had even been some hope of repatriating the hostages when, without consulting or advising him, the "Belgians and Americans started what they called a 'rescue operation' which led to such bitter consequences."[7]

African indignation at the Stanleyville operation gave new life to the Commission. When it met again in Nairobi, on 27 November, the criticism of Tshombe, as well as of the United States and Belgium, was harsh. In addition, many members lauded the rebels who had been seriously handicapped by the attack and some wished to force the Congo government to form a coalition with them. With no trouble a resolution could be adopted which strongly condemned "foreign military intervention." What was more interesting was that the Commission had been stirred to draw up a comprehensive plan for reconciliation in the Congo. This included a cease-fire, withdrawal of the mercenaries, the end to foreign intervention and a general amnesty. Then, under OAU supervision, there would be a round table conference of all Congolese leaders and free elections.[8] It was hoped that a meeting of Heads of State, proposed by the Congo Commission for the 18th of December, could endorse this plan and make it a reality.

Friction Between the Commission and the Congo.

The President and Prime Minister of the Congo had always stressed that they would not tolerate any interference in the internal affairs of the state. In Addis Ababa, Tshombe had abstained on the Council resolution since it did not give him what he wanted. Still, he promised to cooperate with the ad hoc Commission as long as it respected the Congo's "sov-

ereignty" and adhered to a strict interpretation of its mandate.
However, when the Commission was unable to arrange a reconciliation or normalize the relations between the Congo and
its neighbors at its first meeting, it increasingly turned to
other matters in an attempt to improve the situation. By de-
viating from its mandate, it could not help coming into conflict with the Congolese government.

After the appeal for a cease-fire was ignored, the Commission members began criticizing the Congolese government's
lack of implementation. The Prime Minister was repeatedly
called upon to expel the mercenaries. But this was not part
of the Commission's terms of reference and the resolution did
not even lay down a deadline. What was worse, to ascertain
the possibility of a cease-fire the rebels had been heard in
Nairobi after Tshombe's departure and certain members supported their views on how to attain the reconciliation. At the
same time, the Commission obstinately refused to visit the
Congo to be shown the government's side of the picture.

All this displeased the central government, but the last
straw was when the Commission, straying far from its mandate, decided to send a delegation to Washington to ask the
United States to withdraw its aid to the Congo. On 23 September 1964, in a message to the Secretary-General of the
OAU, President Kasavubu solemnly protested against this "manifest interference in the internal affairs of the Congo." He
accused the Commission of having

> ... called the Congo's independence into question
> by seeking to prevent the execution of agreements
> which the Congo, as a sovereign country and in ac-
> cordance with international law, has made with
> friendly countries.[9]

Later, when the Congo Commission condemned the foreign military intervention in Stanleyville, this was also a clear
if unspoken criticism of the government which allowed the powers to intervene. Prime Minister Tshombe left no doubt that
he had authorized the operation and attacked those who condemned it as intervention. He also rejected the Commission's
resolution and peace plan as adverse to his government. But
he did not rule out all cooperation. "For our part, we always desire frank co-operation with the O.A.U., but only on
the condition that it is in line with the spirit of its Charter--
the respect of the independence and sovereignty of the Member
States."[10]

Nevertheless, as relations with several members of the OAU worsened, Prime Minister Tshombe was increasingly critical of the role of the Commission and the OAU in the Congo. By the time of the Council of Ministers meeting in Nairobi, he made it clear that he categorically rejected the report and recommendations of the Congo Commission. He was particularly sensitive about any suggestion he confer with the rebels. It was already too late for round tables and discussions, he insisted. If the rebels were so sure of their support, let them run in the general elections. That was a better way to prove their popularity than by continuing the civil war. However, given the trouble with some of its members, the Congo would not accept OAU observers at the elections.

African Involvement.

Originally the problem of African intervention in the Congo had been largely restricted to the Congo (Brazzaville) and Burundi. The other moral backers of the rebellion did not play a very active role. Still, there was a temptation for further states to take sides in this internecine struggle whose outcome might determine the future of central and all Africa. To avoid serious complications, the Council resolution of 10 September 1964 had also requested all member states "to refrain from any action that might aggravate the situation."

Despite this resolution, the ideological backers of the rebellion were not willing to look on idly while it was crushed by mercenaries and American aid. As the Tshombe regime gained strength and contained its enemy, support of the rebels grew and the circle of supporters widened. Although at first limited and covert, the bonds of restraint were broken by the fall of Stanleyville. For this was not only a defeat at the hands of the Congolese army but a consequence of the paratroop landing in the city. If the collapse of the "nationalist" forces was to be forestalled and the situation in the Congo stabilized, the rebels had to be aided rapidly and massively. Reacting to the foreign intervention in African affairs, or using it as an excuse for their own, the radical and even some relatively moderate countries greatly stepped up their assistance.

Brazzaville continued playing an active role. There were frequent reports of Chinese instructors at training camps in Gamboma and Impando and increased supplies of money and equipment to the CNL. But it was more important to have a base near the fighting front, and Burundi was a particularly valuable source of aid. All went well until, suddenly, Prime Minister Pierre Ngendandunwe was assassinated on 15 January 1965 and China was implicated in the affair. Some two weeks after, Usumbura[11] broke its diplomatic relations with Peking and the embassy personnel left the country. Then there was calm along one frontier.

However, especially after Stanleyville, new opponents to the Tshombe regime arose in other quarters. The whole radical bloc provided some sort of backing. One way or another they were all involved: Ghana, Guinea and Mali, Algeria and UAR. Ben Bella had immediately pledged "arms and volunteers" to aid the rebels.[12] The main chain of assistance was completed early in December, shortly after General Abboud had been replaced by a more radical regime. The rebels now fled to the Sudan, which became their chief haven. Soumialot was also reported being in Khartoum, when planeloads of weapons began to arrive from Egypt and Algeria. The arms were flown to the south and distributed to the rebel bands.[13] Along with the equipment, there were apparently also Arab instructors and experts in guerrilla warfare. This steady supply was only curtailed when Khartoum discovered that many of the weapons also fell into the hands of its own rebels.

Tshombe immediately charged that Algeria, Sudan and the UAR were aiding the rebels. In a protest letter[14] to the President of the Security Council, he claimed to have "irrefutable evidence" that the rebels were using military material from Algeria and the UAR and also alleged that officers from these countries and Sudan were leading the Congolese rebels along the north-eastern border. To him, this was a "veritable declaration of war."[15] Far from denying this, President Ben Bella proudly announced that he had kept his promise of aiding the insurgents and that Algeria was thus fulfilling its duty to the Congo and to Africa.[16]

As the rebels were forced back towards the Ugandan border, the trouble spread to East Africa. Kenya, Tanzania and Uganda had been relatively quiet during the early crisis, especially since President Kenyatta was the Chairman of the Congo Commission. However, as the rebellion was beaten back by Tshombe's army, they increasingly moved towards the rebels and morally approved of their position. It was also rumored that ships full of Communist arms were docking in Zanzibar. In Nairobi there was a campaign to recruit "volun-

teers" for the rebel forces, former Mau Mau members and ex-
servicemen, to counter-balance the mercenaries. With the
war at its border and its territory bombed, the Prime Minister of Uganda lashed out against Tshombe and the Americans.
Then, on 13 January 1965, Obote of Uganda, Kenyatta, and
Nyerere of Tanzania met Christophe Gbenye at Mbale, Uganda.
There, the three Heads of State made no secret of their sympathy for the rebel cause and even promised support. [17] Finally, after the Sudan stopped its shipments, the aid was chan-
neled through Uganda.

The moderates, for their part, reacted sharply to radical intervention. Although they did not provide material aid
for Tshombe's Congo, they strongly condemned any assistance
to the rebels and increased their moral support of the "legitimate" government. Tshombe also turned towards the Francophone moderates and they eventually took a clear and energetic
stand on the Congo. At the founding session of the Organisation Commune Africaine et Malgache (OCAM) in Nouakchott,
Mauritania, the former UAM states returned to politics as a
group. The final communique of the meeting of Heads of
State, on 12 February, was very much to the point. It criticized the "policy of partiality" of the Organization and considered that the malaise the OAU was suffering was essentially
due to "the lack of respect given to its Charter." This meant
particularly the respect for the sovereignty of states and non-
interference in their internal affairs. Certainly, peace had to
be restored in the Congo, but this could only be done "through
aid to the legal government."

The OAU Bows Out.

In view of the seriousness of the situation after Stanleyville and its inability to impose any solution on the parties,
the Congo Commission had recommended that an extraordinary
Assembly be held on 18 December to lay down a stronger line
and put all its authority behind a complete and ambitious plan
for restoring peace to the region. Although the Emperor of
Ethiopia also called for a meeting, the Heads of State ignored
the appeal and the crisis was ultimately dealt with by the Foreign Ministers attending the UN General Assembly debates on
the Stanleyville operation.

Meeting in New York as the Council of Ministers, they
adopted a resolution on 21 December expressing gratitude and
appreciation to the ad hoc Commission and its Chairman. It

also reaffirmed the original resolution of 10 September 1964
and requested the Commission to continue its mandate. Tacitly admitting that the strict terms of reference did not permit
it to take effective action, at that late date the Commission
was asked "to ensure that all the measures recommended by
the Council for the settlement of the Congolese problem are
carried out." But it went no further. No attempt was made
at removing the weakness and ambiguity of the original resolution itself or laying down a real peace plan along the lines
suggested by the Commission.

Nevertheless, despite its renewed and broader mandate,
the Congo Commission was remarkably inactive after the Stanleyville crisis. It even seemed to have lost contact with the
events. The war between the central government and the rebels was intensified and any concern for reconciliation was increasingly discarded. More and more the African states were
intervening actively in the internal affairs of the Congo and
actually facilitating the bloodshed. Soon all Africa was taking
sides and there was a gradual split into rival camps. But the
Commission took no action and did not even voice criticism.

Its last few meetings were marginal to the crisis.
When it was established in September, the Commission was
supposed to leave immediately for the Congo and its neighbors
to study the situation on the spot. Finally, on 29-30 January
1965, the Commission decided to do so. A first and then a
second sub-committee was sent to make arrangements and to
obtain guarantees of the members' safety. However, due to
the failure of both committees to accomplish that task, the
Commission on the Congo never left Nairobi. All that remained for it to do, as the next meeting of the Council of Ministers approached, was to draw up an official report and recommendations.

Before the Council opened, on 26 February 1965, there
were rumors that the OCAM states or others would boycott the
meeting. The rift between the supporters of the legal government and the nationalists already seemed too great to be
bridged. Nevertheless, both sides came and met in the most
bitter confrontation the OAU had known. The debate was long
and sterile. Prime Minister Tshombe was accused of going
back on his pledge of reconciliation and trying to crush his
enemies. He, in turn, complained that certain members did
not observe the principles of the Charter and blamed the bloodshed and destruction on increased radical aid to the rebels,
making it possible for them to fight rather than seek peace.

The Commission also came in for criticism for its one-sided stance and for never going to the Congo.

The hopes for a compromise rapidly faded. The Commission's report had recommended negotiations between the central government and the rebel leaders. Tshombe, who had come to represent the Congo personally, rejected this proposal and indeed the whole report. He also blocked an attempt at having rebel spokesmen heard by the Council. During the debates, two resolutions were proposed and rejected: one by Cameroun, to grant the rebels a general amnesty in return for surrender, replace the mercenaries with an African force and send OAU observers to the elections; the other by Ethiopia, for the central government to send away the mercenaries, accept a cease-fire and grant an amnesty to the rebels.[18] It was futile to argue any further. The OAU was obviously no longer able to find a solution and the best the Council could do was to avoid an open split in the Organization. For this reason, no decision was taken for the moment and the issue was deferred to the Assembly of Heads of State some half year later. Thus it adopted its briefest (and most disappointing) resolution:

> The Council of Ministers ...
>
> Having discussed the Congo problem thoroughly;
>
> Decides to submit the whole Congo question to the Assembly of Heads of State and Government;
>
> Appeals to all Member States and other powers to refrain from any action that might aggravate the situation.

The OAU played no further role in the Congo and the final decision was a military one. Stanleyville had been a decisive setback for the rebels. Their forces had been concentrated there and were scattered by the paratroopers and the Congolese national army which arrived soon after. This was the beginning of the end and it was clear that the "simbas" and the tribal masses enrolled in the rebellion were no match for the "affreux," the soldiers of fortune Tshombe had recruited to lead his army to victory. The push-back began even as the OAU first dealt with the problem and laid down its plan for reconciliation and, by the time it admitted inability to shape events, the rebel forces were in full rout. They were driven back from Stanleyville to the border with Uganda. As

early as December, Prime Minister Tshombe felt that the revolt had been dismantled and, in June, he claimed that the
rebellion had been crushed for good.

But, it took more than a resolution to end the intervention. The radicals only stepped up their aid to the rebels, no
longer concerned with the criticism of the moderates who, in
the meanwhile, accepted Tshombe's Congo in their midst.
The flow of supplies only ceased when, under the hammering
of the ANC and the mercenaries, the rebel front collapsed.
At the same time the leaders fell out with one another and retired to various radical capitals. There was no longer even
a united rebel government to support morally.

Moise Tshombe was the winner all around. His efforts
and his methods had won the war in the Congo. And during
the first national elections since independence, in March and
April 1965, his Conakat Party had obtained a position of
strength in the National Assembly. He seemed well on the
way to attaining national reconciliation on his own terms. But
the actual denouement was unexpected. On 13 October President Kasavubu dismissed Tshombe. The day after, the Council of Ministers removed the Congolese question from the
agenda. This was its condition for attending the Accra Assembly. However, wearied by the inextricable crises, the
other leaders willingly agreed that the Congo had ceased to be
an African problem.

Epilogue--Revolt of the Mercenaries.

On 25 November 1965, the quarrel between Kasavubu
and Tshombe for leadership of the Congo was abruptly settled
by General Mobutu. Once again he assumed power after a
bloodless coup d'état. For over a year there was relative
calm in the country as the "President General" consolidated
his position and brought about a posthumous reconciliation with
Lumumba, if not with his successors. For most of the revolutionary team stayed abroad and rejected the new military regime. Adopting a hard line Mobutu manifested his independence of the Congo's former backers, especially Belgium, without going to the opposite extreme in seeking allies.[19]

Nevertheless, the ousted politicians were not without a
following. Moise Tshombe, in particular, had rather unusual
supporters in the mercenaries he had recruited for the Congolese army. Some of them, old hands in the Congo, had a
creed of their own and a view of Africa which permitted cooperation and a certain loyalty to him. Possibly sensing this
danger, the central government had already dismissed many
of the mercenaries and planned to disband one of the two remaining units shortly after Tshombe was kidnapped to Algeria.
This plan set off a mutiny of the mercenaries and Katangan
gendarmes, in Kisingani and Bukavu in the north-east, on 5
July 1967. The mutiny soon took a political turn and a rebel
"government of public safety" was set up under Colonel Leon-
ard Monga, a close associate of Tshombe.

This intervention in Congolese affairs was strongly protested and the ANC was sent to capture or destroy the mutineers. However, by early August they had gained control of
Bukavu and dug in. The Congolese army encircled the heavily
entrenched and well armed units but could not dislodge them.
For weeks the 130 mercenaries and 1,000 gendarmes under
the former Belgian planter, Major Jean Schramme, held the
ANC at bay. Despite repeated efforts, President Mobutu was
not able to break their resistance. Still, he was equally unwilling to let them withdraw to nearby Rwanda and escape him.
Thus the siege continued even as the opening day of the OAU
Assembly approached.

Although conditions in the country were very unsettled--
the rebels threatened to march on Kinshasa--the OAU conferences opened on time. Following a campaign against Mobutu
and the Congo in some of the foreign press, this was a welcome triumph of prestige as well as providing a key to the
solution. For the Heads of State also felt that the problem of
mercenaries had to be cleared up for the good of the continent.
A resolution was adopted on 14 September dealing with the
problem both in general and in particular. Part of it offered
the Congo either a face-saving disengagement or aid from the
African states.

It was unanimously agreed that "the existence of mercenaries constitutes a serious threat to the security of Member States." Moreover, the fact that the mercenaries were
white and (although they served African governments) were engaged in combat against Africans, generated racial conflict and
hatred. Thus the Assembly emphasized "the danger that the
presence of mercenaries would inevitably arouse strong and

destructive feelings and put in jeopardy the lives of foreigners
in the continent." The United Nations was asked to take action to eradicate the practice and the states of the world were
called upon to make the recruitment or training of mercenaries a "punishable crime" and to deter their citizens from enlisting as mercenaries.

In the part of the resolution that dealt with the mercenaries in Bukavu, they were given a simple choice. Either
they left the Congo immediately, "if necessary with the help
of the competent international bodies," or the Congo would put
an end to their "criminal acts." If the nercenaries refused
this "generous offer," the OAU member states were urged "to
lend their wholehearted support and every assistance in their
power" to the Congolese government. An ad hoc Committee
of ten states, mainly those bordering the Congo, and presided
over by the Sudanese President, Ismail El Azhari, was to see
to the application of this resolution.

In the case of the mercenaries holding Bukavu, at first
things seemed to be improving. After painstaking efforts a
plan of evacuation had been worked out between the International Committee of the Red Cross and the OAU. The mercenaries would be escorted to an airfield in Rwanda and then flown
to Malta and the Katangan gendarmes and their families could
resettle in nearby African countries. However, before the
plan could be implemented, hostilities broke out again in Bukavu. This time the Congolese launched a powerful attack and
the mercenaries had to fight for their lives. In the midst of
the battle, on 3 November, two more columns of mercenaries
under Bob Denard invaded the Congo from Angola and headed
towards Katanga bearing the effective threat that there would
be new uprisings in the region and a broader front against the
government. This time the Congolese army managed to drive
back the invaders in Katanga, while the mercenaries in Bukavu
retreated to Rwanda on 5 November, where they were disarmed and interned.

There was still the problem of what to do with them.
It had been assumed that they would be evacuated as quickly
as possible. But, on 8 November, Kinshasa refused to allow
the mercenaries to leave Rwanda, fearing that they would return to the Congo or be deployed elsewhere in Africa. Soon
after, it accused Rwanda of complicity with the mercenaries
and asked the members of the OAU not to permit planes evacuating them to overfly their territory until a solution could be
found. President Mobutu then convened the Committee on Mer-

cenaries and his Foreign Minister, Justin Bomboko, declared
that the time for a peaceful solution was past and that the
earlier resolution had become null and void. The new decisions were announced by the Secretary-General of the Organization. Diallo Telli pointed out that the mercenaries would
have to give written commitment that they would not serve in
Africa again. Furthermore, he served notice that they would
not be released until an indemnity had been paid to the Congolese government for the damages they caused. "Justice and
morality require that reparation be made." If the home countries did not compensate, "we will have no choice but to keep
them."[20]

There was no longer much hope of evacuating the mercenaries. Fortunately, something could be done for the Katangan gendarmes and those who accepted Mobutu's guarantee
were able to return to the Congo. No solution had been found
for the others since none of the African countries offered asylum. The Red Cross was increasingly worried about the condition of the internees and uncertain what to do after the about-
face of the OAU. As long as the Organization maintained its
refusal to permit the transit of planes, the mercenaries could
not be flown out, and there was little chance their home countries would pay the ransom demanded by the Congo. The only
"encouraging" sign was that Rwanda, suffering economically
and worried about its security, informed the OAU that it would
have to reach a decision on evacuation very soon.

On 16 December, the Committee on Mercenaries met
again in Kampala, Uganda, during a Conference of East and
Central African Heads of State. This time it went even further afield from the Kinshasa resolution. It asked that the
mercenaries be handed over to the Congo to be put on trial.
Then President Mobutu began demanding that they be extradited
and sent back to the Congo.[21] But President Gregoire Kayibanda of Rwanda had not accepted this deviation from the original plan and insisted that they be evacuated immediately.
From then on the relations between Kinshasa and Kigali (Rwanda) worsened dramatically. The President of the Democratic
Republic of Congo threatened to break off all relations with its
tiny neighbor and, on 11 January, the diplomatic relations
were severed. But Rwanda held out and finally Mobutu merely
accepted written assurances from the mercenaries' home countries that they would not be allowed to return to Africa. On
25 April 1968, the mercenaries were flown out by the Red
Cross.

As for the general problem, a Commission of Inquiry had been set up by the ad hoc Committee at its November session to find out who was behind the activities of the mercenaries in the Congo and elsewhere. It immediately proceeded to the detention camp at Shangugu, Rwanda, where it intended to question the mercenaries. But it did not get very far in its investigation. The United Nations, also, at the request of the African states, debated the problem of mercenaries. Most of the members, including those whose nationals were involved, condemned the practice and expressed the wish that this abuse be done away with. Some of the states concerned, especially Belgium, promised to take stricter measures to prevent their citizens from enlisting as mercenaries. But there was not even a Security Council resolution to show for the effort. However, there was one essential aspect of the question that had been overlooked. There was no doubt that the colonialists and neo-colonialists profitted from and encouraged mercenary activities, but in most cases the mercenaries were actually recruited and paid by the African governments or their oppositions. Even if this was not a very flattering side of the problem, it was certainly one where the OAU had an important role to play.

Notes

1. The New York Times, 2 & 16 Aug. 1964.

2. Ibid., 18 Aug. 1964.

3. The Times (London), 6 Sept. 1964.

4. The New York Times, 7 Sept. 1964.

5. Ibid., 20 Nov. 1964.

6. Ibid., 22 Nov. 1964.

7. The Times (London), 26 Nov. 1964.

8. The New York Times, 28 & 29 Nov. 1964.

9. Ibid., 24 Sept. 1964.

10. The Times (London), 1 Dec. 1964.

11. In some references, the capital city of Burundi is given

          as Bujumbura.

12.   The New York Times, 26 Nov. 1964.

13.   Ibid., 5 & 6 Dec. 1964.

14.   Ibid., 8 Dec. 1964.

15.   Ibid., 28 Dec. 1964.

16.   The Times (London), 8 Jan. 1965.

17.   The New York Times, 15 & 16 Jan. 1965.

18.   Africa Report, April 1965.

19.   In July 1966, President Mobutu ordered the Africaniza-
      tion of the names of many Congolese cities: Léo-
      poldville to Kinshasa, Elisabethville to Lubumbashi, and
      Stanleyville to Kisangani.

20.   Africa Report, Jan. 1968.

21.   Le Monde, 30 Dec. 1967.

D. Subversion

Subversive activities were unfortunately not unknown in the OAU's member states. Serious quarrels or differences occasionally separated the African countries and not all leaders resisted the temptation of influencing events in a rival state. Although there were complaints and accusations of subversion, they were followed by the expected counter-accusations and denials and it was very hard to pin down or eliminate subversion. Only in one case did the Organization of African Unity actually come to grips with the problem.

Nkrumah Sets His Own Trap.

The reason Ghana had to defend itself before the OAU was not so much its relatively active and open campaign of subversion which worried many nearby leaders, but rather a tactical error of Dr. Nkrumah. In his unceasing efforts to make Accra the center of the continent and to impose his concepts on Africa, the Osagyefo had his capital selected as the venue of the second session of the Assembly of Heads of State and Government. Nkrumah's attachment to the success of the conference, where he hoped his ideas would meet with greater acceptance, was his undoing.

For years Ghana has been criticizing the policies in other independent states and especially in the former Community members. In the neighboring countries it had long been engineering disturbances and engaged in activities such as led to the assassination of President Olympio of Togo in 1963. But these threats had not ceased and they only strengthened the cohesion and vigilence of the Francophone moderates. When their leaders met in Nouakchott to create the Organisation Commune Africaine et Malgache, the Ivory Coast presented "irrefutable" proof of Ghanaian intervention in its affairs. This time they decided to press the matter and OCAM planned a counter-attack against Nkrumah.

In the communique of 12 February 1965, the leaders of the new grouping "energetically condemn the action of certain

387

states, notably Ghana, which harbor agents of subversion and organize training camps on their national territory." They therefore decided officially to apprise the OAU of the problem and appealed to the African spirit of the Heads of State of the continent "in order that a climate of cooperation among equals can be substituted as soon as possible for the present climate of mistrust and false leadership through intervention in the internal affairs of the other states."[1]

As the date of the Accra Assembly approached, the moderate states in the region became increasingly vociferous about the threat coming from Ghana. The last straw was the attempted assassination of President Hamani Diori of Niger, on 13 April. The offensive began in earnest on 7 May, when Dr. Nkrumah was taken to task sharply by President Houphouët-Boigny of the Ivory Coast. "We cannot accept that those who speak of the unity of Africa, of continental government and assembly continue to disturb the peace and national unity of other countries." Without beating around the bush, he warned: "We are patient, but our patience has its limits. That is why we have said 'no' to the false prophet, to the fake Messiah Nkrumah, this sick man."[2]

By then the governments of the moderate states were expressing strong concern about the risks of attending an OAU conference in a country that supported their sworn enemies. At a smaller meeting of OCAM Heads of State in Abidjan, Ivory Coast, on 26 May, several of them announced they would boycott the Accra Assembly. The next day, Houphouët-Boigny declared that China was behind most of the subversion in Africa, including the attempt on the life of Hamani Diori, and that Ghana was harboring terrorists and guerrillas trained in Nanking.[3] Then, on 28 May, there was an echo in nearby Anglophone Africa, as President Tubman of Liberia suggested a meeting of Heads of State to deal with the complaints of subversive activities in Ghana against other nations' leaders.

The outlook for the OAU's Assembly was increasingly bleak and it was feared that it could not be held or that the absence of many member states would seriously endanger the Organization's prestige and activities. In order to rescue the conference, Ghana's long-time rival, the Federal Republic of Nigeria, urged a prior meeting to reach a compromise between Ghana and its detractors. Politically akin to the Francophone moderates, but able to communicate with Ghana, Nigeria provided a common ground. At the request of Nigeria's President Nnamdi Azikiwe, and Prime Minister, Sir Abubakar

Balewa, an extraordinary session of the Council of Ministers
was convened to find this compromise. Doubtlessly one could
be found--but only at the expense of Nkrumah.

The Case Against Nkrumah.

At the Lagos Council, from 10-13 June 1965, Ghana
was put in the dock. The policy of its leader was criticized
and condemned by the Foreign Ministers of various African
countries, particularly those that knew it best: Ivory Coast,
Niger and Upper Volta. Togo, long the main victim of Ghanaian activities, was in too weak and exposed a position to join
in the criticism of its uncomfortably big neighbor.

In general, Dr. Nkrumah's Ghana was accused of being
a hotbed of subversion directed against any African leader who
did not follow a policy agreeable to him. Ghana provided the
financing of various oppositional parties and "freedom" movements from the independent states. It harbored rebels and
terrorists and had them trained in special camps by Chinese
and Cuban instructors, where they were taught the art of subversion and guerrilla warfare. Ultimately, these so-called
"refugees" were equipped and sent back to their countries to
wreak havoc and try to overthrow their governments.

The Ivory Coast, bordering Ghana on the west, implicated its neighbor in the continued dissidence of the Sanwi
tribe, a minute kingdom along the common frontier. Sanwi
rebels were received by Ghana which permitted them to continue their political activities and even encouraged a "Government in exile." When a plot to kill Houphouët-Boigny was uncovered in September 1963, it was traced to certain foreign
powers. And similar activities continued.

After Upper Volta snubbed Ghana's overtures for close
relations in 1961, the two countries had drawn apart and the
Voltaic government was increasingly suspicious of Ghana's support to opponents of the regime. Inability to maintain good
neighborly relations was symbolized by the border dispute that
arose in the spring of 1963, when Ghana built a school and
road in an area Upper Volta insisted was on its side of the
border. Despite the appointment of commissioners no solution
could be found until the matter was brought before the Cairo
Assembly in July 1964. As a token of good will, the Ghanaian
representative was authorized by his government to give the
disputed territory to Upper Volta. However, when the commis-

sioners met to demarcate the frontier, no agreement could be reached and the dispute arose anew. But this was only symptomatic of what Upper Volta considered the expansionist designs of its neighbor and the relations were so embittered that President Maurice Yaméogo was reputed to have said that Nkrumah had already appointed a president to succeed him after his assassination. [4]

The situation in Niger was more explosive even. Ever since 1959, when the Sawaba Party was outlawed, its leaders had obtained asylum in Ghana. It repeatedly made threats from Accra until, at the end of September 1964, a letter had been circulated in Niger by Djibo Bakari, former Premier and leader of the "opposition in exile," who urged "passing from verbal violence to armed insurrection and direct violence ..."[5] This time an uprising was attempted and there were a number of terrorist actions. But it was put down by the army and later several "terrorists coming from abroad" were executed. On 27 October, Niger complained of interference from two "coastal brother-states to the south," and threatened to contact the OAU if it continued. [6] In April 1965, the climax came with a hand grenade attack on the life of Hamani Diori.

In his opening speech, Sir Abubakar Balewa had emphasized that the OAU could not tolerate any non-observance of its Charter or permit that some states must live in fear of subversion by other states. Nevertheless, the Foreign Ministers had not come together as a tribunal but to find a way "to save our Organization from its present difficulties without leaving any scars."[7] It was impossible and had never been the intention of the OAU to criticize or condemn the policies of a member, and this was not done to Ghana. However, a compromise could be found to save the Assembly by giving the moderate states satisfaction on the issue of "refugees" and guaranteeing the safety of their leaders.

Finally, without admitting blame, Ghana agreed to "send away from its territory before the next Conference all those persons whose presence is considered undesirable ... and to forbid the formation of political groups whose aims are to oppose any member-state of the O.A.U." In order to verify the application of this resolution, the Council decided to send Joseph Murumbi, its Chairman and Foreign Minister of Kenya, and Administrative Secretary-General Diallo Telli to visit Ghana. They were also to check whether adequate measures had been taken to guarantee the security of the Heads of State.

The Accra Conference.

Despite all these efforts, the Assembly at Accra was
not the gala affair President Nkrumah longed for. What the
moderate states had wanted was to have the rebels sent home,
but Ghana only agreed in Lagos to send them to third countries. However, since no country offered to give them asylum, he decided to let the refugees stay in Ghana and merely
remove them temporarily from Accra for the duration of the
"summit." As things stood, the moderate leaders were dis-
satisfied and they did not feel that sufficient guarantees had
been made for their safety either. In a last minute effort to
talk them into coming, Nkrumah flew to Bamako, Mali, to
meet some of the Francophone leaders. But, in the end,
eight of the OCAM countries stayed away: Chad, Dahomey,
Gabon, Ivory Coast, Malagasy, Niger, Togo and Upper Volta.
The sumptuous and costly state house of Dr. Nkrumah only received 28 of the 36 members of the OAU, of which only 13
sent Heads of State.

Nevertheless, the problem of subversion was placed on
the agenda of the Assembly, from 21-25 October 1965. The
phenomenon was unfortunately not limited to Ghana and its
neighbors and there were similar sources of tension in other
radical states as well. But even they had reason to fear retaliation by an enemy backing their own opposition. Thus the
African states, both perpetrators and victims, could form a
somewhat equivocal front against the threat. This was expressed in a formal "Declaration on the Problem of Subversion" which, since it made no distinction between the members, was accepted by all. However, although it spelled out
the meaning of the Charter principle in great detail and made
the duties of the member states more specific, it did nothing
to increase their obligations or provide sanctions against a
violator.

In conformity with the principle, the Heads of State
solemnly undertook "not to tolerate ... any subversion origi-
nating in our countries against another Member State of the
Organization of African Unity." They were also "not to create
dissension within or among Member States by fomenting or ag-
gravating racial, religious, linguistic, ethnic or other differences." And they were "to refrain from conducting any press
or radio campaign against" members of the OAU.

The African states were also not to be used as a jump-
ing off base for foreign interests and subversion. The Heads

of State agreed

> not to tolerate the use of our territories for any
> subversive activity directed from outside Africa
> against any Member States ... [and] to oppose col-
> lectively and firmly by every means at our dis-
> posal every form of subversion conceived, organ-
> ized, or financed by foreign powers against Africa,
> O.A.U. or its Member States individually.

It was also necessary to guarantee that political refugees did not endanger their home countries, and the Heads of
State undertook to "observe strictly the principles of international law with regard to all political refugees who are nationals of any Member States." The resolution on refugees added
that the member states had "pledged themselves to prevent
refugees living on their territories from carrying out by any
means whatsoever any acts harmful to the interests of other
state members" of the OAU.

In order to avoid or liquidate any problems that arose,
the Heads of State undertook "to resort to bilateral or multilateral consultation to settle all differences ..." and to apply
the procedures laid down in the Charter and the Protocol of
Mediation, Conciliation and Arbitration.

But it was obvious that such a solemn, and unenforceable, declaration could do no more than the Charter had done
to end the problem of subversion. All that had been obtained
by the moderate leaders in their offensive against Nkrumah
was a more explicit statement of principles. This became
evident with a bloody coup d'état in Nigeria in January 1966
when one of the peace-makers of Lagos was slaughtered and
the other took up exile in London. With unseemly haste Accra
recognized the rebels and, according to reports, was in close
contact with the situation.

The denouement came soon after, most surprisingly,
and through no effort of the OAU or OCAM states. For the
next in the series of military coups occurred in Ghana, on 24
February 1966. While away in Peking on a peace mission for
Vietnam, apparently confident that no such thing could happen,
the Osagyefo was overthrown. When the country and the pris-
ons were opened, it became clear that the charges of the
OCAM states were all too well founded and that the "Redeem-
er" stopped at nothing to redeem other states as well. There
was any number of "refugees" and several training camps,

with the basic equipment and personnel, as well as all necessary facilities for the liberation movements of independent Africa.[8]

Notes

1. Victor T. Le Vine, "The Nouakchott Conference," _Africa Report_, March 1965, p. 7-10.

2. _The Times_ (London), 8 May 1965.

3. _Ibid._, 28 May 1965.

4. _The Guardian_, 23 April 1964.

5. _The Times_ (London), 24 Sept. 1964.

6. _Ibid._, 28 Oct. 1964.

7. _Africa Report_, Oct. 1965.

8. See _Nkrumah's Subversion in Africa_; Accra, Ghana State Pub. Corp., Oct. 1966, 91p.

Tribal Nigeria with Original Biafran Boundary

E. The Nigerian Civil War

Nigeria is one of the largest and is by far the most populous country in Africa. It has substantial natural resources and many trained and capable people. This has permitted a slow but gradual development of the economy. In addition, to the casual observer, Nigeria has appeared as a relatively conservative and stabilizing element in African politics. It is a prominent member of the moderate group but has also worked for increased cooperation through the Organization of African Unity. The country has avoided adventures in external and African affairs and has in the past been counted upon to help in crises.

Nevertheless, this solidity was somewhat misleading. Nigerian unity was artificial, imposed more or less willingly on very different ethnic and cultural groups, maintained by British colonial rule and sustained by a mutual desire for independence. To make Nigeria work, a loose federation was established leaving the three major tribes in separate regions, each with considerable autonomy. The center operated on the basis of loose coalitions between the regions. For all this democracy was a must. More important would have been a desire to live and work together and a growing sense of belonging to one nation. With independence, however, even stronger disintegrating forces set in and the history of Nigeria was one of precarious balance, instability and collapse.

Three-Cornered Struggle.

Nigeria had a rather short history as a unit. The British occupation only began near Lagos in the 1860's and it was not until 1900 that the various southern areas were included in a Protectorate of Southern Nigeria. In the same year a Protectorate was declared over Northern Nigeria. But it was not until 1914 that Lord Lugard became Governor General of a united Colony and Protectorate of Nigeria. Despite the theoretical unity, the country was still administered under a system of indirect rule. Each area, and the tribal groupings within each area, continued to develop separately and went their

395

own way. Nevertheless, for simplicity of administration, and
reasons of economic exploitation, the Crown constantly pressed
for greater unity. In the 1940's a regional pattern was introduced and in the 1950's the Northern, Eastern and Western
Regions were given their own legislatures and governments.
Not until 1954 did Nigeria actually emerge as a federation.
During this same decade several steps were taken towards self-
government as well and for the first time the representatives
of the various peoples--not only the colonial officials--met and
got to know one another.

The country had been put together over a long period
of conquest and it was easy to see how little the various parts
had in common. The North consisted basically of a series of
Hausa kingdoms, given some centralization under the Fulani
rulers and united only by Islam. The Yorubas in the West,
on the site of seriously weakened medieval states, had been
partially conquered and were being Islamized from the north
while the British nibbled away in the south. Only the Ibos, a
loosely organized and individualistic people, were able to maintain their freedom somewhat longer. Aside from these three
major groups, there were over two hundred other tribes that
were pieced together in the largest and most variegated colonial structure of Africa.

As independence approached, Britain pressed for commitment to a new federation that would keep its most promising possession intact. This was not a simple matter and it
took many years of hard bargaining to give birth to an independent Federation of Nigeria on 1 October 1960. The greatest reluctance was in the North. The area was controlled by
the traditional Hausa-Fulani aristocracy and in many respects
it had remained feudal and reactionary. Indirect rule had permitted the emirs who already held sway to consolidate their
religious and secular powers and they would not enter a state
that kept them from running their fiefs. The masses in the
North were not much more interested in a common nation with
more dynamic peoples of other races and religions to the south.

In the Federation, the North kept its geographic sphere
of influence, including a large Yoruba minority and other
Christianized tribes, and formed a block with about half the
population and three-quarters of the territory. From this
position of strength it accepted federalism and the forming of
a nation. When independence came, the North was run from
Kaduna by feudal rulers like the Sardauna of Sokoto, who became Regional Premier. Since the Northerners outnumbered

the Southerners, they also had a built-in majority in the federal parliament. One of their leaders, although not a member of the traditional elite, was made Federal Prime Minister --Alhaji Sir Abubakar Tafawa Balewa.

The first sparks for independence came from the East, where Nnamdi Azikiwe had given an impulse to the National Council of Nigerian Citizens and urged a strong and united country. This party was moderately nationalist and progressive. Its strength was among the Ibos. Although it repeatedly tried to become a truly national party, it was not able to rally much support in other regions. Still, despite its relatively liberal backing and tribal audience, it was impossible to govern without northern support and the NCNC formed the early coalitions with the Northern People's Congress (NPC). Azikiwe was made President of the Federation.

The West, the traditional homeland of the Yorubas, was the loser in post-independence days. It was in permanent opposition against the North-East coalition and felt the domination from both sides. At first the Action Group of Chief Obafemi Awolowo successfully governed the region, but he tried to escape this isolation by proning a more radical brand of African socialism and Pan-Africanism to gain a broader base. This bid failed and, in 1962, a plot to overthrow the government was uncovered, a state of emergency proclaimed in the West, and its leaders, including Chief Awolowo and Anthony Enahoro, were imprisoned for treason. After the collapse of the Action Group a distinctly less liberal faction under Chief Samuel Akintola came to power.

National and regional politics were monopolized by the three major tribal units. There were other variations on the theme as well. There was a Middle-Belt in the North, the Tivs and smaller tribes below the Niger River that had not been Islamized. There were also non-Yorubas in the West and about forty per cent of the East were not Ibos. These tribes were worried about the continued domination of the majority tribes. As independence approached several asked the Crown to create new regions but, when this might have delayed independence by two years, the idea was dropped. Still, an alternative to the three-cornered system was one on narrower ethnic lines, giving the minorities--actually about half the population--their own regions. For some minority tribes this was a realistic possibility; others were too small: there were potentially more than 200 such separate groups. A first step was taken however in 1963, when a Mid-West Region was cut

out of the Western Region to provide an area for the Edos and
other non-Yorubas.

Over the years the regions had coexisted, despite disturbances, a coup plot and inter-regional quarrels, but they
had not grown closer together. Each region had its own tribal
composition, its own ruling party, its own government and university, largely separate economies and divergent interests.
If anything, the political system had blocked progress. Regional issues were repeatedly given precedence over national
causes, and the federal government was left to sort out the
differences. Nepotism and corruption were rife. Although the
politicians and middle class had become rather prosperous, the
subsistence farmers and workers were not better off than before independence. And there seemed no way out of the political quagmire by following a timid and irresolute tack.

What tipped the bucket was the census of 1962, rejected
and revised in 1963. The North was given a larger majority
of the population than before. It had thirty million out of a
population of fifty-five million. More than ever this one region could dominate the others. A coalition with the East was
not even necessary. Ties were established with the splinter
party of Akintola in the West. For the first time, the more
natural partners, the progressive forces of the East and West
also formed an alliance on political lines. However, as the
elections of December 1964 approached, after the first nation-
wide strike and bitter electoral campaigning, the country was
drifting towards a violent confrontation. Because of lawless-
ness and irregularities the United Progressive Grand Alliance,
mainly the NCNC and Action Group, decided to boycott the
elections and none were held in the East. The Nigerian National Alliance, primarily the NPC and Akintola's Nigerian National Democratic Party (NNDP), won the occasionally contested elections in the remaining regions. It gained 198 seats as
opposed to only 50 for the Grand Alliance. When President
Azikiwe hesitated to appoint a Prime Minister, the country
seemed close to disintegration. In a final attempt to return
from the brink, rather than impose a coalition based on electoral mathematics, Sir Abubakar formed a "broad-based national government."

Blood Breeds Blood.

The Federation was given a new lease on life. The
leaders of the first decade had agreed to a government that

might hold it together. With enough good will the differences could be resolved and something done to overcome the continued separateness of the tribes and regions. At least, for some time, the administration could be run and current business dispatched. Still, there was little chance that this more conservative government would provide a vigorous policy to solve the old problems and give the country a new impulse. Although most of the groups had retreated from the brink, they were far from happy with the compromise. There was continued friction and disturbances. A last crisis broke out in the Western Region in October 1965. Amidst rising violence, Akintola's NNDP won a huge majority in the hopelessly rigged elections.

Then, on 15 January 1966, the precarious balance was upset. A coup was unleashed by a group of junior officers intent on sweeping away the old regime and introducing a progressive era. Rather than arresting the political leaders in power, the rebellious officers acted blindly and tragically. The Federal Prime Minister, Sir Abubakar Tafawa Balewa, and two Regional Premiers, Ahmadu Bello of the North and Chief Samuel Akintola of the West, as well as many northern officers were assassinated in the most horrible circumstances. It was uncertain what sort of regime would be installed after the coup and, above all, whether the plotters would be able to control the army and the country at large or whether anarchy would ensue. A crisis was forestalled when, a few days later, the highest ranking officer, Major-General Johnson Aguiyi-Ironsi assumed power and set up a provisional military government.

General Ironsi then tried to pacify the country. He had not been involved in the coup, but he hesitated to punish its perpetrators (who had brought him to power). Many of the mutineers were Ibos and most of the leaders and officers killed were Hausas and Fulanis and so long as he did not punish the culprits he was regarded with suspicion in the North. Instead of settling this matter, Ironsi first tried to divert the attention of Nigerians toward more fundamental problems. The old federation had not worked and he hoped to introduce a more unitary system that might replace the precarious and unsatisfactory game of regional politics and coalitions. To overcome division and tribalism he wished to use the army to impose centralization. On 24 May 1966, he suddenly abolished the system of regions. Nigeria was made a unitary state. To counteract particularism, military governors chosen from the different tribes would rotate among the provinces. There

would also be a unified civil service. Later, he promised, a
civilian regime would be elected; until then the National Military Government assumed all powers.

The coup and the General's plan seemed to herald a
better era for many. It was strongly supported by the Ibos.
There was also considerable interest among the Yorubas. The
peoples of the South hated the discredited system and the
changes met some of their demands and aspirations. A coalition of Southerners might have formed to back the plan. However, the reaction in the North was very different. This
looked like a contrived plot. The fact was that General Ironsi
and his advisors were also Ibos, the officers had not been
punished for the coup, and they had killed not only the Federal
Prime Minister but also the Sardauna of Sokoto, the supreme
secular and religious leader. Moreover, the idea of centraliz-
ing the country looked like another scheme for Ibo domination.
Two days after the decree was issued there was rioting in the
northern cities. The first pogroms occurred and many Ibos
were killed or injured. Placards appeared inscribed "We Want
Secession."

Then, on 29 July 1966, while General Ironsi was
touring the country in a bid for unity, there was a mutiny of
northern soldiers. The General and high ranking Ibo officers
were killed. This time the Northerners set up the new government. The man they chose was Lieutenant Colonel Yakubu
Gowon, a Northerner but a Christian from a minority tribe.
On 1 August, he took supreme command of the National Military Government. He saw clearly that unity could not be imposed on the country as long as no foundation existed. Unfortunately for Nigeria, after the stormy political life of the early
years and two coups, he had to conclude that, "putting all considerations to the test--political, economic, as well as social--
the base of unity is not there, or is badly rocked."[1] Thus
his first step was to retract Aguiyi-Ironsi's measures and return Nigeria to the earlier federal system. Later there would
be a constituent assembly, a referendum and elections for a
new civilian government.

This time the coup was felt as a blow against the Ibos.
On the same day Gowon came to power, the Eastern Military
Governor Lieutenant Colonel Odumegwu Ojukwu charged that
"the brutal and planned annihilation of officers of eastern Nigerian origin has cast serious doubt as to whether the people
of Nigeria can ever sincerely live together as members of the
same nation."[2] But the worst was yet to come. The coup

'as almost a signal for the Northerners to act.   Their re-
_ge was terrible.   Rioting broke out and there were massa-
cres of Ibos.   Over a million fled and as many as thirty thousand never reached their tribal homelands.

An Ibo Homeland.

        The Ibos were an educated, modernizing and dynamic
people.   Well before independence an exodus had begun from
the crowded Eastern Region.   Many settled in the Federal and
regional capitals, they were numerous in the civil service and
education.   Ibos ran the railways and the oil refinery in Port
Harcourt, while clerks and artisans could be found throughout
the country.   There was little assimilation and the occasionally overbearing Ibos maintained their apartness wherever they
settled.   This exclusiveness and cooperation through mutual improvement associations only increased their identity.   The return from the diaspora began after the second coup and the
massacres.   The arrival of over a million refugees spread
word of the atrocities.   The Ibos began to withdraw into themselves.   More than ever they were cut off from the broader
Nigerian community.   They also felt persecuted.   The military
government and army had not prevented the pogroms.   How
could they be relied on in the future?

        Above all, those who had suffered and returned home
were wary of accepting the Northern-based government and the
inferior role that might well be theirs under it.   More strongly than others they urged a withdrawal from the Federation.
The Eastern Region was developing rapidly.   Trade and industry progressed and tremendous oil reserves had been discovered.   With these resources, ports and their natural energy,
the Ibos thought they would do better in their own state than
in Nigeria.   This was the only hope for the refugees.   Certainly, at worst, an Iboland would not be less viable than many
other African states.   The problem was that the Eastern Region now consisted not only of eight million Ibos but also five
million non-Ibos, who lived further south in the oil producing
regions, and may have feared Ibo domination in an independent
state.   However, they also had something to gain from the
prosperity of a new state.   And the Ibos immediately tried to
woo them for this plan.

        With each day the Federation crumbled further.   The
federal government could not accept secession.   Without strong
backing from the regions, however, it could not hold the coun-

try together. General Gowon cast about for any formula, less
than a unitary state and short of breakup, to save the country.
Soon after taking power, he convened an ad hoc committee to
elaborate constitutional proposals for the future of the Federation. The conference met in Lagos on 12 September and began its work. At first, it was not very successful. Only the
Mid-West came with a brief for federation.[3] This was the
best way of protecting its minority interests and, when the
idea of dividing the country into smaller, ethnically defined
states was mooted, it had a definite appeal for other minorities, especially the Tivs. But there was surprisingly little
faith in the future of a united Nigeria among the Yorubas and
Hausas.

The Northerners were the first to have a change of
heart. For some time after the first coup, and even after the
second one there had been rumblings of secession. Now the
government was set up by Northern military men and they
hoped to gain under it. Moreover, when the East talked of
independence, the North suddenly realized how dependent it was
on the oil revenue, eastern skills and access to the sea. It
would not accept such an amputation and angrily turned on the
disloyalty of the Ibos. The North was also urged to accept
the new state plan by the Tivs in the army.

The key to the situation was in the West. The Yorubas
had had the worst deal under the old Federation, where they
were squeezed between the North and East. Withdrawal of the
Ibos would have given them work in the administration and
commerce, but the new country would be much poorer. Still,
the Yorubas did not like northern domination either. If the
Ibos left, the Yorubas, a strong tribal group with a large population and area, more advanced and wealthier than their
neighbors, might also seek independence. Even prominent
leaders like Chief Awolowo, who had been released from prison by Gowon, made rather ambiguous statements on the Yorubas' place in the Federation. Others spoke quite openly of a
breach. With an independent South, either as one or two
states (centered around the Ibos and the Yorubas), the North
would be isolated in the more barren interior, cut off from
the sea and possibly bordered by enemy territory. No price
was too great to consolidate a new alliance.

The Ibos would only accept a confederal system with
substantial regional powers and the right to secede. At this
point, for all practical purposes, the East was already autonomous. The Eastern army depended on Colonel Ojukwu and the

Ibos were rapidly reorganizing the administration, business
and other aspects of life.   Preparations for independence went
ahead and the region drifted away from the Federation.   Gowon
tried desperately to find a compromise.   Although Gowon's ad
hoc committee had reduced some of the gaps among the peoples and regions, it had not convinced the Ibos.   There was
another try in early January 1967, at a meeting between the
four military governors and General Gowon at Aburi, Ghana.
It seemed as if a solution had been found, permitting the East
control over its security, some compensation for the loss of
life and property and broad local powers--not including the
right to secede.   Even then, there were differences on the interpretation of the agreement and the trend towards dissolution
was not reversed.   A real shock came when Colonel Ojukwu
ceased paying revenue to the federal government, complaining
that the Ibos had not received the promised compensation.
The federal government retaliated with economic sanctions.

Time was running out and a last attempt was made at
compromise.   A national conciliation committee of leading
personalities from the other regions sent Chief Awolowo to
mediate.   His "peace mission" spoke to Gowon and went to
Enugu to sound out Ojukwu on a new summit meeting of military governors.   On 18 May, he made his proposals: the government would revoke its economic sanctions, Northern troops
would be withdrawn from the East and West, and a new effort
would be made at finding a compromise for all regions.   General Gowon accepted the recommendations and demanded reciprocity from Ojukwu.   The reply was negative.   All the
while there had been mass demonstrations for secession in the
major Ibo cities.   Although Colonel Ojukwu had not been a
prominent advocate of independence, he was also drawn along.
Soon the point of no return was reached.

Realizing what was coming, the Federal Military Government (FMG) reacted strongly.   On 27 May, Gowon promul-
gated a decree decentralizing the country and creating twelve
states out of the former regions.   For the East this meant a
division into one Ibo and two minority-run states.   Another decree abrogated the concessions made at Aburi.   In addition,
Gowon assumed full powers, declared a state of emergency,
banned all political statements and meetings in the country,
tightened control on the press and resumed economic sanctions
against the East.

At this time a 300 member Consultative Committee,
with delegates from all parts of the region, was meeting in

Enugu. This sudden aggravation was poorly received and only pushed the representatives to the brink. They mandated Colonel Ojukwu to declare a free and sovereign state "at an early practicable date." On 30 May 1967, he fulfilled the mandate. He formally declared that the Eastern Region's political ties with Nigeria were "totally dissolved," although it would accept to join in common services or economic unions with other sovereign units of Nigeria or other African states. Henceforth it existed as the independent Republic of Biafra.

The Civil War.

This was the critical moment for Nigeria. So far the FMG could only count on support from the North and certain minorities, but the secession might set off a chain reaction and split the country into its component parts. The greatest danger was in the West. Many of the leaders had not hidden their distaste for the Federation and a partnership with the North would be uneasy. Still, it offered very definite compensations. Forgetting the earlier thoughts of secession, the West, like the North, became a defender of one Nigeria and turned against the East. Already the Yorubas were moving in to fill the vacuum, taking up positions in the administration, business and universities, and even in the army. A decisive step came when Chief Awolowo rallied to the FMG. In June, he decided to accept the top civilian post in the Federal Executive Council as Vice-Chairman and Commissioner for Finance. He was joined by Anthony Enahoro as Commissioner for Information. Eventually the civilian side of the government was composed mainly of men from minority tribes and Christians.

The North had its power in the army. Most of the rank-and-file and many of the officers were Northerners. They felt that the secession could be crushed militarily. Certainly what remained of the Federation had a much larger population and territory, a stronger army and greater financial means. But General Gowon moved slowly. Although he had called the declaration of independence an "act of rebellion which will be crushed," he only decreed a general mobilization and declared a blockade of the eastern ports. He apparently realized that even if war could crush the secession, it could not reintegrate the Ibos in national life. Moreover, any bloodshed was bound to bring permanent bitterness. Therefore he tried economic sanctions first. The "hawks" constantly urged stronger action. Economic pressure would not deter the separatists and Biafra was arming. However, it was not until 6 July 1967, over a month later, that the federal forces launched an attack. This was meant to be a quick "clinical police action."

Despite the military's promises, the troops made no headway. The Nigerian army had never been created for conventional warfare and certainly not on the scale suddenly required. It was only 9,000 strong, with six battalions of infantry, no tanks and few armored cars. It had a tiny navy that could not impose a blockade. And it had no bombers or fighters in its nascent air force. One-third of the officers had been Ibos, and neither they nor the Northerners killed in the coups could be replaced rapidly. The Ibos already had the nucleus of their own army and had been acquiring material. They also had an elderly B-26 bomber. The leadership and organization were good. But it was inferior in size and equipment to the Nigerian army. Still, even if a war between armies would have gone to Nigeria, how could it possibly overcome a population of thirteen million? As the enemy troops withdrew they destroyed the roads and bridges. In no time the Nigerian troops were bogged down.

Suddenly, Lagos suffered a defeat in the Mid-West Region. Ibo-led dissidents in the federal army, under a Yoruba collaborator, Brigadier Victor Banjo, captured Benin on 9 August. Biafra seemed to be expanding westward. Nevertheless, this victory was a poisoned gift. First of all, Banjo decided to create his own state. Then, shortly after the victory of his "Liberation Army," he announced that the Mid-West would be independent of both Biafra and Nigeria. The next objective was to free the West and Lagos of "northern feudalistic control." His long term aim was Nigerian unity under persons interested in the welfare of all, regardless of tribe.[4] Thus the Mid-West had not really been won for Biafra.

Worse, the West had been lost. The Mid-West was a buffer between the Ibos and the rest of Nigeria. The eruption of Ibo soldiers into this region, the advance towards Lagos and the unsolicited offer to liberate the West seriously hurt the Biafran cause. Formerly many of the Yorubas, even those that disapproved of secession, either favored greater autonomy for themselves or were at least not eager for a long and bloody war to hold the East in the Federation. Now an area within their sphere of influence had been attacked and the old rivalry flared up. Chief Awolowo no longer had any trouble persuading the mass of the population to back the war effort.

From its brief and unexpected position of strength, Biafra proposed a compromise. On 30 August, it offered to enter an "Association of States" with one or more Nigerian states. There would be an executive board to supervise joint services like inter-territorial roads, shipping and aviation, customs, diplomatic relations and so on. This solution was immediately turned down by Lagos. It would not tolerate any form of independence, confederation or association. The flexibility was gone and the FMG would accept peaceful negotiations and reconciliation only on the following terms: Biafra had to agree to remain an integral part of Nigeria and renounce its secession, accept the new structure of twelve states and find a leader to replace Ojukwu.

Given the situation, the federal government could hardly expect a positive reply. Biafra had made its independence unnegotiable. And the structure of twelve states which would be imposed if they lost the war was not the sort of compromise the Ibos would accept under any conditions. For it was designed primarily to break their hold on the East. The North was divided into six large states, the West and the Mid-West remained roughly as they were, Lagos was made a state, and the East was divided into three small states. The point was that the three states were so drawn as to leave the Ibos a majority only in the Eastern-Central State while having to contend with other tribes in the two flanking states. Moreover, the Ibo state was cut off from the sea and the oil fields and was in a hopeless economic and defensive position.

A further result of the fatal mistake in Benin was to make the Nigerians feel that Biafra was fighting a war of conquest. The northerners demanded a more vigorous campaign and they were heeded by General Gowon. He changed the strategy from a "police action" to pacify the dissident region to "total war" to crush an Ojukwu-led effort to take over all Nigeria. Even then, Lagos could not have won the war without a tremendous boost from outside. The army was too small and poorly equipped to make real headway against a serious defence. But it was being swollen by rapid recruitment and relatively good pay. The material was modernized and expanded. There was a steady flow of British weapons for the ground forces and then it began receiving Soviet aircraft.

Reluctant Africanization.

Although the civil war in Nigeria, like every phenomenon of dissension and disunity on the continent, was regarded
with concern by the African community as a whole, there was
some uncertainty how to evaluate it.   This was particularly
noticeable in the early months of the war.   If this had been a
political or ideological quarrel, there would probably have
been support for any regime that claimed to be progressive or
revolutionary as in the past.   The first crises and the original coup had been inspired politically and, indeed, Nkrumah
was aware of what was happening and welcomed the fall of the
"retrograde regime."   Biafra also expected the sympathy of
progressive circles, including possibly Guinea and Algeria.
Its leaders stressed the struggle against the feudal and reactionary forces in the North.   Still, even if the Hausa-Fulani
rule was backward and the Ibos considerably more advanced,
so were the Yorubas who supported the government.   Actually,
the war began to look more and more like a tribal feud.

The main inhibiting factor was that, rather than convert the whole country to its view, the Ibos had seceded.   Secession, more than revolution, frightened the African states.
They all had their own dangers of tribalism and separatism.
And they came out unanimously against this threat.   This was
true of both the moderates, traditionally in favor of the status
quo, and the radicals.   But there were definite nuances.   Although all the states disapproved, most of them merely followed events from afar.   Only the UAR and Sudan acted.   They
sold the FMG a number of their aircraft, including bombers,
and Egyptians came to pilot the Soviet fighters and bombers
used by Nigeria.

Elsewhere, there was a growing desire for reconciliation.   On 24 June, President Kenneth David Kaunda of Zambia
had appealed to the African leaders to bring about a peaceful
solution to this "sad problem."   On 8 July, just after the war
began, at a Lusaka, Zambia meeting of Haile Selassie, Kaunda, Kenya's Jomo Kenyatta, Julius Nyerere of Tanzania, and
Milton Obote of Uganda, a joint plea was made to the leaders
on both sides to halt the fighting and reopen discussions.   In
August, a group of prominent Ghanaians appealed to Gowon
and Ojukwu to end the hostilities and seek "an honorable negotiated settlement."[5]   Pressure for mediation rose after the
Mid-West was captured and, at the same time, much of the
incipient support for the Biafran position was stilled.   When
Soviet military supplies began to arrive and the war became

more destructive, public opinion in many countries turned again.

With the escalation of the Nigerian crisis it had become, more than ever, an African affair. Thus there was also mounting pressure for action by the Organization of African Unity. Sharp comments were made in the press. Still the OAU did nothing. There was no extraordinary session. Even when Sékou Touré called for a meeting on problems arising from the Middle East and use of mercenaries, he forgot to include the civil war in Nigeria. The Secretary-General showed little interest in the crisis. Despite months of battle and bloodshed, the Organization persistently ignored the situation. Nevertheless, it had been created to help maintain peace on the continent and it was being discredited by this refusal to act.

The next regular meeting of Heads of State was approaching and it was far from certain that it would deal with the issue. This had not been specifically requested by any body of members. Lagos had already launched a campaign to keep the item off the agenda. It insisted that the secession was an internal affair and could be settled by the federal government alone. Up to the eve of the meeting Nigeria refused to have the matter discussed. It successfully kept it out of the Council of Ministers and it seemed the same might happen in the Assembly. But the leaders who had urged reconciliation pressed for a debate. They realized that Africa had to assume its responsibilities and that the OAU could not afford to remain silent any longer. Finally Nigeria was prevailed upon to have the matter discussed.

During the Kinshasa Assembly from 10-14 September 1967, a debate was held on the civil war. However, the Heads of State did not go very far in their deliberations and were not eager to impose their will on a fellow member. The resolution was prudently couched to avoid any suspicion of intervention in Nigerian affairs. Significantly, it began by reaffirming respect for the sovereignty of member states. Then the Assembly recognized that the situation was an internal affair and, as such, the solution was "primarily the responsibility of the Nigerians themselves." It even expressed its "trust and confidence" in Lagos and offered to explore "the possibility of placing the services of the Assembly at the disposal of the Federal Government of Nigeria."

There was no discussion of Biafra's right to self-determination. Although this right was ardently supported for the colonial territories, it was just as staunchly denied in the already independent states. Nor were the delegates interested in the rights and wrongs, whether the Northerners had pushed the Ibos to secession, or whether the Ibos had unwisely withdrawn. This was of no consequence when it came to national unity. No matter how uncomfortable or unstable the coexistence of various ethnic or religious groups in one country, Africa could not approve secession, fearing it possible in any of the states. Thus, when it came to the question of principle, the Heads of State quickly produced a resolution including a "condemnation of secession in any Member States."

Nevertheless, and particularly because the conflict was so dangerous and even contagious, the African leaders should have sought some means of settling it rapidly. The sooner an attempt was made at reconciling the parties or at least making them reflect whether both would not be destroyed by the war, the more chance there was of saving Nigeria. But the Assembly did not venture to lay down an "African solution" or request a cease-fire. It suggested no compromise and did not even wish for clarification. It merely decided to send a Consultative Committee to the Head of the Federal Government of Nigeria "to assure him of the Assembly's desire for the territorial integrity, unity and peace of Nigeria." This task was entrusted in six Heads of State, all of them from moderate countries of Black Africa, under the chairmanship of the Emperor of Ethiopia. They were: Haile Selassie I, Hamani Diori of Niger, Ahmadou Ahidjo of Cameroon, William V. S. Tubman of Liberia, Joseph-Désiré Mobutu of Congo (Kinshasa), and Joseph Arthur Ankrah of Ghana.

The Mission to Lagos.

This Consultative Committee on Nigeria was by far the highest ranking body ever to represent the interests of the African community. Therefore it was hard to imagine that it would do nothing more than confer with General Gowon and assure him of the Assembly's support. When the resolution was made known, in fact, the expectations in both camps were strikingly different. For some time Enugu had been appealing to the OAU to intervene and it claimed that the mission was coming to mediate. Any African interest in the hitherto neglected conflict was to the good and the appearance of the Committee seemed a tacit recognition that this was not a pure-

ly internal matter. Lagos was on the defensive, it had little
to gain from any gratuitous advice and something to lose if
the mission started talking of peace or reconciliation--ques-
tions brushed over in the Kinshasa Assembly. Thus Chief
Awolowo, head of the Nigerian delegation to the Assembly,
stressed that the mission was only coming to show its solidarity with the federal government.

Judging by the terms of reference, he was right. Still,
the mission's role could easily be expanded if the members
so decided. Even with no power over the FMG, it could be
embarrassing. However, the actual effect was more than anything a question of timing. The consultative mission was originally scheduled to meet shortly after the Kinshasa Assembly
on 27 September. At that juncture, with the war raging nearby and no victory in sight for either side, the six Heads of
State could hardly have limited themselves to their restrictive
and almost degrading functions. A compromise settlement
might have seemed particularly reasonable. Or, at any rate,
the Committee would have strong arguments if it urged a rapid
conclusion of hostilities. In fact, this would have been the
best time to impose a cease-fire or seek a peaceful settlement if any were to be found. Yet, the arrival was postponed,
and then postponed again, partly because of Lagos and partly
because of the hesitation of the Committee members.

All the while, the fighting continued. Equipment was
streaming into Nigeria. When they were powerfully armed,
the federal troops launched their offensive. Biafra had reached its maximum extension and then it began to ebb. After
marching dangerously close to Lagos, it was forced back in
the Mid-West. Shortly after an independent Republic of Benin
had been declared, the forces unexpectedly withdrew and the
federal government resumed control. By the end of September
Lagos had the initiative. The Biafran soldiers were slowly
driven back to the old Eastern Region. Then the federal army
fought its way into this region and attacked it from the south
as well. The offensives by land and sea were successful. On
4 October Enugu fell.

The OAU mission finally met in Lagos on 23 November
1967. Only four of the Heads of State were able to come:
Haile Selassie, Ahidjo, Ankrah and Diori. In a perceptibly
stronger position now, the Federal Military Government was
not inclined to leave the Committee much leeway. The Emperor stressed that its main goal was to preserve the territorial integrity and unity of Nigeria and he urged a peaceful

settlement. This might have meant a policy other than mere
prosecution of the war on the central government's terms.
But General Gowon told the Committee clearly that "your mission is not here to mediate." He held out no hope for a cessation of military operations. Warning that failure to end the
secession in Nigeria would encourage separatism elsewhere in
Africa, General Gowon emphasized that "the most valuable
contribution the mission can make in the present circumstances
is to call on the rebel leaders to abandon secession."[6]

Eventually, after nine hours discussion, he had his way.
The closing communique included no initiative by the mission.
It merely reaffirmed that all secessionist attempts in Africa
were dangerous and that any solution to the crisis must preserve the unity and territorial integrity of Nigeria. Although
the Committee was interested in the government's terms for a
cease-fire, no effort was made to stop the fighting. And the
FMG's peace plan was supported. It was no wonder that Lagos "was in complete agreement with the conclusions reached
at the meeting."

The only point that could be obtained was for the mission to enter into contact with the secessionists. General
Ankrah was mandated to transmit the Kinshasa resolution and
the mission's conclusions to Colonel Ojukwu. However, given
the decisions, there was little hope his efforts would bear
fruit. The message was not an offer of negotiations so much
as conditions it could take or leave. This had been understood by Biafra, distinctly less happy about the outcome. It
had originally asked to cooperate with the Consultative Committee. Now nothing could be expected and the OAU was attacked as an "instrument of the reactionaries." Radio Biafra
announced that the mission was doomed to fail because it had
consulted only one side in the dispute and had "condoned genocide and ... proved itself a rubber stamp by merely endorsing Gowon's warning that their own countries would disintegrate
if they did not rally to his support."[7]

Africa's Worst War.

Although victory was already in sight it was still out of
reach. The Ibos fought desperately and progress was slow.
It would have taken a tremendous additional effort to subdue
Biafra. To shorten the war, General Gowon left open the possibility of negotiations. On 24 December, in a Christmas message to the nation, he reiterated that the conditions for peace

were a renunciation of secession and acceptance of the twelve
states scheme. Aside from that he reassured the Ibos that
they would have full citizenship rights and he guaranteed them
"a future of absolute equality with all other ethnic groups."
However, rather than negotiate with Ojukwu, he called for
peaceful discussions with Ibo leaders "willing to work for national reconciliation, peace and reconstruction" in good faith. [8]

Colonel Ojukwu countered that it was up to the side
that had begun the war to take the first step to end it. He
was not disavowed by anyone on the Biafran side. Actually,
the Ibos had a relatively close-knit and democratic society.
As the war intensified and they were pushed into the heartland,
there was a new resurgence. Whether the non-Ibo minorities
really supported Biafra or not, the common struggle was weld-
ing the Ibos (and some others) into one people. In the hour
of truth they were joined by their most eminent leader of earlier days. Former Nigerian President, Nnamdi Azikiwe endorsed the secession on 16 November. Although he had never
approved of the use of violence to solve political problems,
the civil war had reached a stage where certain "realities of
history" had to be conceded. Since they were not wanted any-
where in Nigeria, the "logical conclusion is to recognize the
natural and inalienable rights of Biafrans to self-determination
and autonomous existence as a free, sovereign and independent
nation."[9]

For some time General Gowon had been holding back
the commanders. He wished to act as the leader of all Nigeria. Realizing that war was driving the Ibos further away, he
tried to avoid wrecking the base of any later union. However,
during this time Biafra was being consolidated as an entity.
So he finally gave in to the military leaders who promised a
rapid victory. The deadline was even fixed at 31 March 1968.
Again the fighting flared up and federal troops moved in to
crush the rebel state. The FMG's matériel had been growing
and by that time its army had a great superiority in arms.
But the fighting was still difficult and although Biafra grew
smaller, it did not collapse. Then there was another stalemate.

To break this resistance the federal army intensified
the war. This was the most generalized and brutal phase.
The military staff had overestimated its capability to defeat
the enemy army. In exasperation, and because it now had the
means to do so, it threw everything into the effort. Jet fighters and bombers and heavy artillery pounded enemy territory.

Modern weaponry was crudely used to bludgeon Biafra into surrender. Towns and villages were bombed; schools, hospitals and markets were blown up. There was also news of atrocities when the Nigerian and Biafran troops met. Lagos was severely criticized for the excesses and, in May, the government decided to curtail the bombing of civilian areas. Then, after almost a year of war, hunger made its appearance. There was even talk of genocide.

Doubtlessly the hatred on both sides resulted in cruelty. Soldiers with little training, untried discipline and good reasons to dislike one another, were engaged in combat. But there were no grounds to believe that the federal government was purposely destroying the Ibo people. The root cause was the war itself. The East had never produced enough food for its people and the blockade prevented imports. Despite the attempts at organizing Biafra, it had limited resources and these were used up. There was no harvest that year. As the food ran short, the civilian population was menaced with starvation. If the war did not end soon, there was a serious danger that it would indeed succumb. Thus, even if there were no deliberate acts of genocide, the outcome might still be an accidental or unintentional destruction of a race.

A Break in the Ranks.

An important consequence of the interminable civil war were the second thoughts in Africa. During its brief war of conquest, Biafra had lost potential political friends. But now there seemed to be less danger of a further break-up of Nigeria than the collapse of one of its peoples. And the longer the bloodshed went on, the more obvious it became that the Ibos could no longer live in harmony with the other peoples of Nigeria. By fighting a year and bleeding themselves, the Biafrans had begun to convince Africa of their will for independence. This led to increasing disapproval of prolongation of the war in influential circles in Black Africa; even to some approval of the Biafran cause. Once assured that this was a genuine effort for self-determination, and not a Katanga-like plot to make off with the oil revenue of Nigeria, radicals like Tanzania and Zambia permitted discreet approval in the press. The moderates, especially those along the coast, more openly deplored the destruction and death.

But the war was disregarded officially by Africa until finally Tanzania, on 13 April 1968, became the first country

to recognize Biafra as "an independent sovereign entity." Only
thus, a government spokesman explained, could Tanzania remain true to its conviction that the purpose of society was
service to man. The Ibos had been rejected by their Nigeria
as had the Jews by Germany. After ten months' fighting they
had proven to the world that they were ready to struggle for
themselves. Tanzania therefore felt "obliged to recognize this
setback for African Unity."[10] The reasons given by President
Nyerere for this unprecedented step were basically humanitarian. He believed that the purpose of the state was to serve
the people and that if the people or a part thereof rejected the
state it had lost its justification. Although Tanzania regretted
that the unity of Nigeria had been destroyed over the previous
two years, he was convinced that unity could not be assured
by force or conquest. A refusal to recognize the existence of
Biafra would have meant tacit support of the war against the
people of the Eastern Region in the name of unity.[11]

This step was immediately condemned by the FMG and
regarded as a "declaration of war amounting to complete severance of relations."[12] But no reprisals were envisaged.
The recognition did not set off a chain reaction and many of
the other leaders disapproved of the action. President Hamani
Diori promptly and categorically declared that Niger would not
recognize the Biafran separatists. His country had a long
common frontier with Nigeria and there were close links between the Hausas on both sides of that frontier. Upper Volta
and Chad also reaffirmed their support of Lagos. Modibo
Keita of Mali warned that the secession was a very serious
precedent for the political unity of every country. President
Léopold Sédar Senghor of Senegal, ruling out recognition, la-
mented the conflict and urged a rapid conclusion. Even Somalia, despite its own demands for self-determination, was on the
side of the federal government. The more active Nigerian
backers, such as Sudan, worried about the impact on its own
separatists, and Egypt as well continued aiding the federal
cause.

As one moved south, however, the educated and often
Christianized élites of Black Africa expressed some solidarity
with Biafra. Lagos was worried about Azikiwe's visit to Kenya and Zambia, whose leaders spoke of the need for mediation.
Togo and Sierra Leone also called for a compromise later.
Favorable comments were heard in Ghana and Gambia. And in
most of the region there was criticism of the bloodshed. In
this region of Africa, only Cameroon, after its long civil war,
situated next to Biafra, seriously disapproved of the secession.

Now that Tanzania had drawn attention to the war going on within the continent, it tried to press the point. Dar es Salaam warned Lagos that if the hostilities did not cease it would have to bring the matter before the OAU or United Nations.

Then things happened. In Gabon, President Albert Bongo declared that it was impossible to look on passively at the genocide of ten million people. It was utopian to believe that Nigeria could subsist in its present form. On 8 May 1968, Libreville recognized Biafra as an independent state. Félix Houphouët-Boigny also denounced the "indifference" of the world at the slaughter in Biafra, where there had already been more deaths in ten months than in three years in Vietnam. It was necessary to see the problem as a human one and, above all, to restore peace. On 14 May, the Ivory Coast recognized Biafra. Then came Zambia on 20 May. Foreign Minister Reuben Kamanga explained that his country was "horrified at the massacre of innocent civilians." "The heritage of bitterness stemming from this horrifying war will make it impossible to create any basis of political unity of Biafra and Nigeria."[13]

The reasons given for recognition in Tanzania, Gabon, Ivory Coast and Zambia were very much the same. No matter how precious unity was, it could not be imposed by force or entail the destruction of a people. Humanitarian considerations prevailed. This was particularly true of the beliefs of Kenneth Kaunda. As for Julius Nyerere, no one had worked harder for unity, and no one was more honest when unity failed. Clearly war and slaughter were not tools for the restoration of unity. Gabon and the Ivory Coast, somewhat to the contrary, had always been opposed to outsized and unworkable federations. For Houphouët-Boigny the collapse of Nigeria was almost a belated justification of the peaceful dissolution of French West Africa.

The skeptics sought in these diplomatic recognitions ulterior motives. However, earlier relations had never been strained and were usually very good. Nothing could be gained by weakening Nigeria and even relatively little from a fully restored Biafra. Moreover, if there had been any material grounds, they only existed as long as Biafra was strong. By the time of recognition, the war had clearly gone against it and there was nothing to entice allies. The influence of outside powers, like China or France, was not the answer, for the other radicals or Francophone states did not follow the

same lead. That the motives were relatively straightforward
may even have been conceded tacitly by Lagos since, aside
from breaking formal relations, there were no reprisals or
serious complications.

Peace Feelers.

During all the strife, cooler heads had remembered
that warfare was a very dangerous and unsatisfactory way of
solving the differences between the former partners of the Federation. Neither Ojukwu nor Gowon had ever ruled out a negotiated settlement. And the pressure on them to hold a par-
ley was mounting. By February, Colonel Ojukwu had informed
two papal envoys that he wanted a cease-fire and a chance to
obtain an honorable peace leaving Biafra guarantees of its internal and external security, although he added that the best
guarantee was still the Republic. At the beginning of April,
Nnamdi Azikiwe launched a peace offensive and announced that
Biafra was prepared to negotiate. This was confirmed by
Colonel Ojukwu who called for an immediate cease-fire and
negotiations without pre-conditions.

Meanwhile, Biafra was growing weaker. Recognition
and moral support had not changed the situation on the front.
Some of the worst fighting had taken place around Onitsha in
March. But on the other hand, federal commanders had not
been able to keep their promise of victory. For some time
Nigeria had also received pressing appeals from Britain to
seek a peaceful settlement. By mid-April, Lagos replied to
Azikiwe's offer and expressed interest in talks. However, at
the end of the month it added the condition that Biafra must
accept that Nigeria was one sovereign country consisting of
twelve states.

Unfortunately, since the beginning of the war the scope
for agreement had narrowed. Too many lives had been sacrificed for Biafra to repudiate secession. Still, it offered to
join in various sorts of links, economic, technical or diplomatic. They could be combined in a loose association. Lagos
was less flexible. The Ibos had to accept integration in a federation of twelve states. The government clung to this formula, which had gone into effect on 1 April, since it was the
main point of commitment for the coalition and especially the
minorities and could not be questioned without dividing its supporters and provoking a constitutional scuffle. But it was not
yet able to disclose the contents of the new arrangement since

there had been no decision on the respective powers of the
states and the federation, sharing of revenue or security and
these essential details would have to be worked out between
the Eastern-Central State and the eleven others after the
war.

Nevertheless, there were alternatives to a relatively
unitary federation and complete independence. These included
a decentralized federation, a confederation or a union. Whatever the name, the relations would have to provide both an
acceptable central power and a sensible role for the various
peoples. It could not start by splitting the most coherent one
among four states. Could a compromise be found? Nothing
was less certain. Still, when seated around a conference table and subjected to pressure by friends and allies or the OAU
the warring parties might have been willing to make enough
concessions to save Nigeria.

That the time was ripe for some sort of discussions
was not perceived by the OAU. Fortunately, the Commonwealth was more active in trying to bring the opponents together. Its Secretary-General Arnold Smith had carefully maintained his neutrality in the conflict. In London and Lagos he
met representatives of the federal government and it also
proved possible to contact the Biafrans. Without arousing
much notice he arranged a preliminary meeting in London.
Secret talks were initiated during the second week in May 1968.
The only item discussed was where to hold the official negotiations and what could be a possible agenda. After Biafra
turned down London and OAU headquarters and Nigeria objected to Dakar and Arusha, they came to an agreement on Kampala, the capital of Uganda. The agenda would consist basically of the conditions for ending hostilities and arrangements for
a permanent settlement.

However, both sides seemed to be playing for time. Nigeria wanted to improve its position militarily and Biafra
hoped for further diplomatic backing. All the while, hostilities continued. The federal troops were moving in on Port
Harcourt where Biafra had its last major airport and control
of the oil fields. Colonel Ojukwu increasingly pressed for a
cease-fire as a prerequisite to serious negotiations. But the
operations continued. On 19 May, the battle raged and Port
Harcourt fell. Two days later the talks began in Kampala.

In his opening speech, President Obote made a strong
plea for a cessation of hostilities. "Whether the war is just

or unjust is no longer the question. The price of failure will
be too much for you, the people you represent and all of Africa." Both delegations seemed to agree. Chief Justice Sir
Louis Mbanefo, the head of the Biafran delegation, felt that
the dispute between Biafra and Nigeria "is a human problem
which must be resolved around the conference table." Anthony
Enahoro, the Commissioner for Information, told the meeting
that the Nigerian government was willing to hold up military
operations once the peace talks had agreed on the terms.
"We are fully prepared to seek peace and unity and fully empowered to seek peace."

        Nevertheless, as of this first encounter the basic differ-
ences came out. Biafra was not ready to sacrifice its sovereignty. "Only sovereignty can guarantee security to the Biafrans." Still, Sir Louis was willing to examine "any other formula which guarantees by constitutional arrangements our
rights." He insisted that a military decision would not solve
the basic issues and urged a three point program of immediate
cessation of hostilities, removal of the economic blockade and
withdrawal of all troops to pre-war positions. Chief Enahoro
would not consider a cease-fire until other conditions had been
satisfied. His view was that

            ... once the rebel army has laid down its arms,
            federally trained police will move into the Eastern
            Region to maintain peace and allay fears and a
            federal constitutional conference of all twelve Ni-
            gerian states, including the three which made up
            the breakaway Eastern Region, would meet to work
            out a new constitution.[14]

        The talks were off to a bad start. In following days
the Nigerian delegation outlined its terms. The first one was
the complete abandonment of secession. Twelve hours after
such a declaration, there would be a truce. Then a "mixed
force" of observers, Nigerians and Biafrans would disarm the
rebels and form a neutral zone along the cease-fire lines.
This plan was flatly rejected by Biafra. The head of the delegation described the proposals as "surrender" and declared
that "we have not come to Kampala to do that." Chief Enahoro concurred with this interpretation. As he told the news-
men, "our position involves that they give in." He added:
"There can be no pretense that there is any solution outside
the concept of one Nigeria. The problem is how to ease it
for the other side."[15] The deadlock was complete and within
a week the conference collapsed.

The OAU Reawakens.

The Kampala talks were a dismal failure. The two
sides had come no closer together. The only positive result
was to show that negotiations were indeed possible and to remind the OAU of its responsibilities. For the Organization
had forgotten that its primary duty was to maintain a presence
and follow the situation closely so as to offer its services at
the right time. Countless lives could be saved and Africa
would show that it was able to handle its own disputes. Now
it was clear that there had been some willingness to seek a
way out of the impasse. The active concern of the Commonwealth sould have been that of the OAU.

The original Consultative Committee was not reconvened for another two months. It held its second session in Niamey, from 15-19 July 1968, at the invitation of President
Hamani Diori of Niger. Only General Mobutu of the Congo
could not come. First, it heard General Gowon's summary of
the developments in Nigeria. Although the federal government
expected a military victory soon, it still preferred a negotiated settlement. The General therefore urged that the Committee have the four recognizers get the secessionist leaders to
attend peace talks. "If the rebel leaders persist in their con-
temptuous attitude to the conference table, the federal government will have no choice but to take over the remaining rebel-
held areas." But Nigeria would not interrupt the fighting to
hold talks. General Gowon insisted that a unilateral cease-
fire would only permit the enemy to reorganize and re-arm.
After the Biafrans surrendered, however, Nigeria might accept an international observer force. This force could come
only at the federal government's invitation and its role would
not be to separate the combatants. It would only be there "to
witness the reassertion of federal authority in rebel-held
areas" and the good behavior of federal troops. Finally, he
outlined the steps taken by the government to relieve the civilian suffering.[16]

The mission of Heads of State then turned to its two
point agenda: relief supplies for the needy and a permanent
settlement of the crisis. Primary attention was paid to relief.
Here they originally took a highly independent tack. The first
drafts apparently included an active plan for channelling relief
to the areas occupied by the secessionists. There would be a
limited truce to establish a demilitarized zone through which
the supplies could be transported. The zone would be determined with the agreement of the parties and would be main-

tained and supervised by an international police force acceptable to both. The FMG was asked to guarantee an air, land
and sea corridor on its own territory leading to the demilitarized zone. Representatives of the relief organizations and
observers chosen by both sides would be stationed in the corridors to examine the shipments and avoid all suspicion.[17]

The final plan was nowhere near as specific. After
consultation with the Nigerian delegation and repeated amendments, the Committee adopted a resolution on 18 July to limit
the "suffering of civilians on both sides." Noting a federal
offer to establish a corridor on its territory, the Committee
merely requested the FMG to set up this "mercy" corridor
without delay and to guarantee the safety and freedom of movement of the agents of the international relief organizations and
of the observers who were to inspect supplies at the collecting
points. A similar appeal was made to the secessionists. But
there were no concrete measures: the demilitarized zone was
not determined, there were no provisions for supervision and
inspection, and no observers were appointed.

Even less progress was made towards a settlement.
Once again the federal government had expressed its interest.
But its conditions had not changed a whit. Even though it conceded that Colonel Ojukwu should be heard by the Committee,
General Gowon was not prepared to meet him. This time the
invitation was widely publicized and Ojukwu immediately announced that he would appear before the Heads of State. Before he arrived, however, the mission adopted a resolution
laying down its aims. The parties were urgently requested to
resume peace talks, under the auspices of the OAU, in order
"to achieve a final solution of the crisis prevailing in their
country, with the objective of preserving Nigeria's territorial
integrity and to guarantee the security of all its inhabitants."

On 19 July, Colonel Ojukwu made a statement to the
Committee. He still supported the original demands of a
cease-fire, withdrawal of troops and an end to the blockade.
But he was ready to negotiate. This was the only point
grasped by the Committee. Both sides had grudgingly admitted
their willingness to resume negotiations and a communique announced that preliminary talks would be initiated forthwith under President Diori. The atmosphere was soon highly optimistic. The Heads of State did not hesitate to proclaim a "success to the O.A.U. and an achievement for Africa." For the
sake of the happiness and honor of Africa, both sides would be
asked to "make sacrifices likely to lead to peace ... We are

convinced that a solution of reconciliation, a solution of unity can ensure the rebirth of this great ensemble which we need so much."

The preliminary talks began in Niamey, Niger, on 20 July on the basis of a three point agenda: arrangements for a permanent settlement, terms for cessation of hostilities and concrete proposals for the transportation of relief supplies to the civilian victims of the war. The actual stress, in this first, low level round of the discussions was on channelling relief to the civilian population. Agreement seemed to be in reach. A demilitarized corridor, controlled by observers from the Committee's members, would run from Enugu to a village under Biafran control. Biafra objected that the observers should include some from the states that recognized it and urged that an airlift be established to bring in supplies more rapidly.[18] It would doubtlessly have been better to strike while the iron was hot and finalize the agreement--or admit none existed, but it had been decided to hold the substantive negotiations in Addis Ababa and, with no concrete decision to boast of, the meeting closed on 26 July.

The second round began in Addis Ababa on 5 August. This phase was held under the chairmanship of Haile Selassie. Colonel Ojukwu came to represent Biafra. Unfortunately, Nigeria did not send General Gowon nor the fairly diplomatic Chief Awolowo, but the inflexible Chief Enahoro. This meant that there would be no dialogue between the only two men who could have reached a settlement. From the outset, it was clear that the discussions would not be easy. The positions were still far removed. Given the circumstances, it would have been wisest to meet behind closed doors, permitting complete frankness. Instead, the initial statements were made in public where a play could be made for world opinion and any demands or conditions would be hard to retract.

In his opening speech, the Emperor insisted: "You cannot afford not to succeed in this task. You must succeed, there is no other alternative." He also cautioned the parties that they should refrain from polemics during the peace talks. The war was now going well enough for Nigeria to comply. Anthony Enahoro briefly recalled Nigeria's desire to restore peace and promised that his government was ready to seek a peaceful solution. It was easy to demonstrate the harmony between Nigeria's policies and the OAU resolutions. He had no trouble calling for a settlement on the basis of the Niamey plan, namely territorial integrity and security.

Colonel Ojukwu could not assume an equally conciliatory
pose. In a lengthy and occasionally impassioned speech, he
went through everything that had passed. We are ashamed of
being associated in an unnecessary and futile war that is discrediting Africa, he began. Then he traced the situation in
Nigeria before independence, the early days, the suspicion as
the major and minor tribes jockeyed for the best positions,
the two coups and the massacres, the bloodshed of the civil
war. He denounced the federal government and he condemned
those that aided it. Finally, after describing the suffering of
the thousands even then dying of hunger, he concluded:

> Our survival cannot be separated from the sover-
> eign independence of our State. No one who has
> studied the past contribution of our people to the
> cause of African freedom and unity can doubt our
> awareness of the need for the whole of Africa to
> unite. Nevertheless, we have learnt by bitter ex-
> perience that unity must come in stages through co-
> operation and mutual understanding ... In fulfil-
> ment of that purpose we offer to discuss with Ni-
> geria the closest form of association which does
> not detract from our right to ensure security at
> home and abroad.[19]

Once again, a war of words had been launched. The
apparent agreement of Niamey vanished. Chief Enahoro called
the speech provocative and Colonel Ojukwu, unable to meet his
counterpart, left Addis Ababa. The talks continued. The Nigerian delegation presented its terms for settlement. This
plan covered only the Eastern-Central State, the one reserved
for the Ibos, as the Rivers and South-Eastern States had already been reintegrated. After the renunciation of secession
and disarming of the rebel forces, that State would enjoy the
same status as the others. An Ibo Federal Commissioner and
Military Governor would be appointed and would participate in
the Federal Executive Council and Supreme Military Council.
The State administration would be in the hands of the people
and the security would be entrusted mainly to Ibos. The federal army would only intervene in case of a threat to law and
order and there was the possibility of an external observer
force. The Ibos would be absorbed again into the civil service, police and armed forces, and there would be a general if
incomplete amnesty.[20]

But the Biafrans were not interested in the terms for
readmission to the Federation. They wished to maintain their

sovereignty. In order to determine the margin for fruitful
negotiations, the Emperor asked the delegation to outline its
"minimum requirements" for security. According to Dr. Eni
Njoku, they were: Biafran control of its own army and police,
the right to an international personality and membership in international organizations, and the power to conclude international economic agreements and manage its own resources, industries and economic development. These demands covered
the whole of Biafra. The only concessions were for maximum
economic cooperation and common services with Nigeria.[21]

Rather than see whether a start could be made at building a bridge between them, within the week both parties decided that no solution was possible. Since the conference in
Niamey, each had become more intransigent. The federal
army continued its successes in the field and the commanders
wanted another few weeks to end the war. During the interval
as well, France had suggested that the conflict be settled on
the basis of self-determination of the "Biafran people." This
was not much, but it instilled new hope in the secessionist
leaders.

If the two sides were to be brought to an agreement,
it was necessary for Africa to make a stronger effort. Haile
Selassie, who represented the Committee and the OAU during
these talks, felt the hope for peace slip out of his hands. A
new start had to be made. The Emperor attempted to con-
vene the full Committee on 15 August so that the six Heads of
State might try to obtain concessions on behalf of the whole
African community. He also invited the attendance of General
Gowon and Colonel Ojukwu, the two indispensable participants.
Nigeria was asked to cease hostilities during the meeting.
But none was held. Soon the time had run out. On 17 Au-
gust, the federal army received orders for the final offensive.

As of the second week, the Emperor turned to the only
item on which some agreement might be attained--the initiation
of relief operations. This had become increasingly urgent.
The number of people dying each day had reached frightening
heights and world public opinion was indignant. Haile Selassie
gave this matter top priority and he held numerous meetings
with the delegations, now at a lower level, to urge them on.
Twice he made compromise proposals and twice they were examined and amended by the parties. The path was long and
tortuous.

The objective was to provide relief as broadly and rapidly as possible, and the Emperor proposed the establishment
of land, sea and air corridors. The corridors would be demilitarized and placed under the supervision of the Red Cross
and the OAU. Guarantees were included to avoid abuses.
But the stumbling block lay elsewhere. Rather than accept a
"package deal" that gave both sides some satisfaction, each
party turned down the corridor its opponent preferred. The
Nigerian government objected to the airlift since it felt that
arms and mercenaries might be flown in as well. Biafra
feared that food sent through Nigerian territory would be poisoned. Each claimed that the other would gain some military
advantage and they rejected one another's proposals. Finally,
after five weeks of meetings, the conference adjourned on 9
September without having found any solution.

The "Ostrich" Assembly.

The failure of the Addis Ababa talks coincided with Nigeria's final offensive. To the end, General Gowon had maintained that he preferred a negotiated peace. The military
leaders were eager to resume operations and felt that the rebellion could be crushed in two weeks. By the beginning of
September, before the conference had concluded, they
launched violent attacks on all fronts. After a major battle
Aba was taken. Only Owerri and Umuahia remained. Biafra
seemed to be in its death pangs. The territory had been reduced to a fifth its original size. In this "redoubt" there
were still six million people. Yet no real steps had been tak-
en to establish land or air corridors for relief. The humanitarian organizations were desperately trying to get food and
medicine to them. Repeatedly, their flights were banned and
transport planes fired at. More than ever there was talk of
genocide.

To disprove this, the Nigerian government asked six
observers to come to the country and follow the advance of the
federal troops. They were invited from Canada, Poland, Swe-
den, Great Britain, the United Nations and the OAU. Their
verdict was "no genocide." They admitted that all war was
grisly but insisted that the federal troops had behaved well.
Still, a handful of men could not observe the whole front.
Moreover, this was beside the point. For the deaths were
not provoked by combat so much as by bombing and starvation.
Attacks on civilian targets were well-known publicly. The
whole world bore witness to the refusal of leaders on both

sides to compromise on a plan to rescue the civilian population. The whole world saw how the "peace talks" of Addis
Ababa, loudly heralded by the OAU, had been futile.

It was in this atmosphere that the Assembly opened in
Algiers on 13 September 1968. It started very inauspiciously
for Biafra. In the part of his address on imperialist threats,
President Houari Boumedienne of Algeria included an attack
against the "machinations directed at Nigeria aiming to disintegrate that great African state, the unity and cohesion of
which we were and are so proud." He blamed the crisis on
a foreign conspiracy. Without putting his finger on the culprits, he linked the Katanga secession with the situation in
Nigeria and claimed that the same states and organizations
that supported Katanga were now aiding the Biafran secessionists. Despite his regret at the suffering, he also implied the
"political and religious organizations that today are raising
their voices to lament, or to threaten and criticize, moved by
fallacious humanitarian considerations they did not express toward other human tragedies that shook whole countries for
years." All this, he indicated, prevented the restoration of
unity, the only means of putting an end to the crisis in Nigeria.[22]

This speech led to a first clash. President Kaunda refused to accept a vice-chairmancy because he had been "lump-
ed with the imperialists." In open session he declared: "I
feel the whole issue has been prejudged." Later the four
states that had recognized Biafra explained their reasons for
taking this step. They spoke out for a resolute and courageous people. Still, even then, they were on the defensive and
somewhat apologetic, since they were not hostile to Nigeria
as such. Nor did they favor secession. What they objected
to were the means used to preserve unity and they felt im-
pelled to condemn the bloodshed. Far from restoring unity the
warfare and hatred it engendered was making later unity impossible. But none of them pressed the matter and a breach
was carefully avoided.

Nigeria also avoided any quarrel. When arriving in Algiers, Chief Awolowo announced that his delegation would not
make an official protest against the four recognizers. In the
Assembly he described the underlying reasons for the civil
war, which were tribal more than anything. Although regretting the war, he insisted that the rebellion had to be crushed.
According to him, the best way to end the suffering was for
Biafra to surrender so that the federal government could rein-

tegrate and save the population. His government was even
then preparing measures for the future.

Among the other delegations, some were enthusiastic
supporters of the Nigerian cause. Others were often less concerned with the situation in Nigeria than the impact a successful bid for secession would have at home. They did not want
a dangerous precedent. Most members were also unhappy
about the war. They wanted peace to be restored. However,
since the defeat of Biafra seemed near, many of the delegations hesitated to intervene in any way. There were few
qualms about Biafra's fate and even a tendency to feel that
right was somehow allied to might. The only wish was that
the conclusion would come as rapidly as possible.

The debate lasted only a few hours. Once again, it
was held in very general terms that contributed little to clari-
fying the problem. Moreover, the concern with fundamental
principles kept the conference from doing something about
lesser matters that could have been tackled, and perhaps
solved. There was no serious thought of ending the hostilities, bringing together the leaders on both sides and holding
negotiations under stricter OAU control. There was no discussion of how to lessen the suffering by opening relief corridors. This was reflected in the rather inexplicit draft resolution of the Consultative Committee. It was limited to generalities and appeals. The Ivory Coast demanded a more specific resolution as much as one attuned to Biafran needs. It
urged both parties to take steps towards an immediate cease-
fire and a definitive settlement and called upon all concerned
to co-operate in delivering relief supplies.[23]

These demands were turned down or left vague in the
final resolution. Still, it very sketchily covered the various
aspects of the problem. First, it appealed to the secessionist
leaders to "co-operate with the Federal authorities in order to
restore peace and unity in Nigeria." In this connection it proposed a cessation of hostilities, asked the FMG to declare a
general amnesty and "co-operate with the O.A.U. in ensuring
the physical security of all Nigerians alike, until mutual confidence is restored." It asked all parties to cooperate in the
speedy delivery of relief supplies to the needy. But it left
out the indispensable details that could have given the resolution real significance. There was no deadline, no plan of implementation and no supervisory machinery for the cease-fire.
It was not clear what role the OAU would play in ensuring
security. And, despite weeks of discussion, no plan was rec-

ommended for providing relief.

Once again, the Organization had avoided the shock and possible disintegration of a direct confrontation. Speakers on both sides carefully refrained from poisoning the atmosphere and the rather colorless resolution was adopted overwhelmingly (against four negative votes and two abstentions). But it papered over the cracks more than actually furthering a solution. For Nigeria, everything had gone smoothly and, in the final session of the summit, Chief Awolowo noted the conference's success in "staving off the threat of division." He thanked the states that voted with Nigeria for supporting the principle of territorial integrity and avoiding maneuvres that would split Africa. Henceforth every African state must be considered an "organic entity," all secession condemned, and the OAU respect existing governments. The analysis of Rashidi Mfaume Kawawa, Tanzania's Vice-President, was quite different. Algiers was "one clear example in history where eminent leaders decided to evade the real issue by playing the ostrich game" and merely siding with the federal authorities.[24]

Towards Peace in Nigeria.

About this time the Nigerian government was convinced that the secessionist regime would soon collapse. Its army penetrated ever further into the redoubt. But this still ignored the nature of the war. For some 80,000 federal troops not only had to defeat a somewhat smaller army, they had to pacify a region some hundred miles square and a population of five million. This "redoubt" was less a fortress that could be captured than a maze in which an army easily got lost. The federal troops only occupied the main roads and villages. All around them, just a few hundred yards away, the dense forest was held by the Biafrans. Nevertheless, the federal army could deprive the enemy of its capital by taking Umuahia and it could interrupt the shipment of weapons by destroying the Uli airstrip. Actually, it had been progressing smoothly with this objective until mid-October, when Biafra suddenly began receiving more supplies. Again it had enough ammunition to slow down the advance.

The war continued unabated. All the while Nigeria was being ruined. The death toll rose and the effort cost hundreds of millions of pounds. The country was troubled. Sacrifices were not always accepted and there had been tax riots in the

West. Sometimes there was political unrest. The military
regime disrupted the normal administration and development.
In the East, things were much worse. The region had been
a battlefield and was completely devastated. There may have
been a million dead and other millions crushed by the war.
It would take years for the country to recover. This should
have been sufficient reason to think of ending the hostilities,
but neither side would give in.

Fortunately, by then the humanitarian organizations had
managed to curb the wave of starvation. Planeloads of pro-
tein foods were flown in and distributed. However, when the
last airstrip fell, not only the rebel arms supplies but also
relief would cease and a particularly acute crisis would ensue.
Meanwhile, as their troops advanced, the federal government
reintegrated parts of Biafra. Some two million Ibos had come
under federal control. The relief agencies were able to feed
them and the government tried to persuade them that they
would not have an inferior status in the Federation. It also
wished to convince the Ibos in the redoubt that they had been
misled by propaganda and that there was no danger if they
surrendered. But many were still engaged in what they saw
as a war for survival and the indiscriminate bombing did not
make them believe otherwise. Even after major fighting
ceased, it would be hard to overcome their hostility.

Still, from time to time, there was a flickering hope
of peace. Colonel Ojukwu, whose troops were slowly being
pushed back by a considerably better armed force, repeatedly
demanded a cease-fire as a preliminary to serious negotiations. These appeals were echoed by others as Christmas
1968 approached. Various statesmen called for a truce as a
step towards peace. The Emperor of Ethiopia urged that hostilities be suspended for a week, and his appeal was seconded
by Prime Minister Wilson and the Pope. General Gowon, who
did not want Biafra to use this breathing spell to prepare its
defence, finally agreed to a 48 hours truce. In the end, there
were only 12 hours without combat. The pleas for a cessation of hostilities increasingly fell on deaf ears as the federal
government decided it would have to "fight for peace" in the
face of foreign intervention.

Although there were other initiatives, the circle of possible mediators was thinning. Nigeria now insisted that it
would accept only a settlement based on the Algiers resolution.
But this was both vague and geared to the needs of the federal
government. Moreover, the OAU's past behavior indicated

that in the event of negotiations it was not likely to take an
independent stand or seek concessions. Prime Minister Wilson also desired a peaceful solution, but he would not put any
pressure on Lagos to attain it. Colonel Ojukwu did not heed
the advice to reduce his terms either. Although much of his
backing came from France, he ignored President de Gaulle's
hint that Biafran self-determination be sought within a union
or confederation. When he called upon President Nixon to
mediate, he forgot that Washington was most concerned with
the suffering of the civilian population and had no desire to intervene.

For some time, any proposals were more an article of
propaganda than a sign of willingness to seek a compromise.
Nevertheless, during the months of stalemate, both sides may
have been prepared to save the country from collapse. This
was uncertain. Still, there was one body created specifically
to test this willingness. The Consultative Committee had its
mandate extended and expanded in Algiers. Yet it remained
inactive for months. Any African interest in a settlement was
limited to brief initiatives or a few words of counsel. The
four recognizing nations continued their support of Biafra and
their appeals for negotiations were suspect. An OCAM plan,
worked out in January 1969, did not get very far since that
body was equally divided. President Senghor, a more neutral
figure, also sought a solution. He recognized that "in this
fratricidal war, the Nigerians are not the only guilty ones";
all the Africans were guilty, "passively." First he requested
an immediate cease-fire followed by negotiations. As for the
aims, "once the principle has been admitted of Nigeria's in-
tegrity--I do not say unity--the question of whether it shall be
federal or confederal is not worth the life of a single person."[25]

Finally, from 17-20 April 1969, the Consultative Committee met in Monrovia. The chances for its having success
in exerting its influence had never been so slim. By then the
federal government seemed assured of victory and showed little interest in a peaceful settlement. Shortly before the meeting it had launched a major offensive against Umuahia. It was
announced that General Gowon could not attend and Colonel
Ojukwu, forced to defend his capital, was unable to come.
Tacitly admitting the situation, the Committee merely drew up
a declaration calling on both parties to accept, "in the supreme interest of Africa, a united Nigeria which ensures all
forms of security and guarantee of equality of rights and privileges to all its citizens." Once endorsed by both parties, it

proposed a cessation of the fighting and the opening without
delay of peace negotiations with the good offices of the OAU.
This text was readily approved by the Nigerian delegation.
But Biafra had not sent its representatives to surrender to
Nigerian unity. And the declaration came to naught.

Unexpectedly, Biafra did not collapse. To the contrary,
its troops had filtered through the Nigerian lines and surrounded a number of key positions. Soon after they attacked Owerri and Onitsha and some units crossed the Niger while others
continued south coming ever closer to the oil fields and Port
Harcourt. The federal side no longer had the initiative and it
again used its overwhelming supremacy in the air to fight
back. The targets were much the same, the only visible sym-
bols of Biafra, such as markets, schools and hospitals, while
the soldiers were hidden by the forests. The air force also
attacked Red Cross planes provoking a serious crisis and the
suspension of relief flights. The weapon of starvation was
brandished. Despite the desperate attempts of Count von Ros-
en's tiny force of single motor planes, it was impossible to
pin down the growing number of MIGs and other aircraft. But
the Nigerian air force could not stop the soldiers on the
ground either and the war continued implacably.

There was now a greater need than ever for a compromise solution. The Pope's visit to Uganda in August 1969 offered an excellent opportunity to resume discussions. Colonel
Ojukwu immediately urged a cease-fire and talks while sending a delegation to Kampala. Although refusing any cease-fire,
the federal government did not reject the possibility of an en-
counter. Pope Paul's insistence on the need to halt the bloodshed and his willingness to do everything he could to provide
a meeting ground impressed the Nigerian delegation. Yet, in
the end, there was no meeting.

The efforts of Dr. Azikiwe to find a compromise were
even less successful. Earlier in the year he had proposed a
peace plan, under United Nations supervision, including an
arms embargo, a general armistice and an end to the blockade, followed by a plebiscite in Eastern Nigeria so the people
could decide on unity or independence. This plan was sharply
rejected by Lagos. Then, late in August, he put forward a
considerably different plan in Monrovia, Lagos and London, accepting the Federation but providing considerable autonomy for
the states, each with its own police force and the right to conclude agreements among themselves within the federal structure. He also called on his Ibo brothers to stop fighting and

live in peace with the other Nigerians. This plan was not far
removed from the Aburi agreement, only it came too late,
when the hatred and deaths could not be forgotten in Biafra,
and the former leader of the East was rejected by the new
regime.

Certainly the federal government welcomed Azikiwe's
return. But it did not endorse his plan or show any willingness to make peace either. If anything its position had become stiffer. Men like Anthony Enahoro and some of the
younger military were increasingly influential and General
Gowon was under fire for his moderation. They were willing
to use any and all means to put a rapid end to the conflict.
Yet, although they could reject any initiatives for peace they
could not defeat the Biafran army. If peace were to be attained it had to be imposed from outside.

This could have been the mission of the OAU. Its
Committee had not met since Monrovia but the summit in Addis Ababa might have been the ideal place to act. This time,
the delegates recognizing Biafra, especially the Ivory Coast
and Tanzania, insisted that the conflict be given top priority.
During the Committee's session and the Assembly it was debated at length. General Gowon again reaffirmed his acceptance of a peaceful solution within the framework of a united
Nigeria and the Biafran delegation, through its contacts behind
the scenes, urged that negotiations begin immediately without
prior conditions. Yet, few of the members pressed for direct
negotiations, and most insisted that the earlier resolutions
must form a basis for any talks. They came out strongly for
a guarantee of the principle of unity. The prospects of secession worried them almost as much as Lagos and they did
not want an independent Biafra. Thus the conclusion was de-
ceiving.

The resolution of 10 September 1969 did call for a
cease-fire, while reiterating its stand on secession and seem-
ing to make this a condition. The resolution

> ... appeals solemnly and urgently to the two par-
> ties involved in the civil war to agree to preserve,
> in the overriding interest of Africa, the unity of
> Nigeria and accept immediately a suspension of
> hostilities and the opening without delay of negotia-
> tions intended to preserve the unity of Nigeria and
> restore reconciliation and peace that will ensure
> for the population every form of security and every

guarantee of equal rights, prerogatives and obligations.

But the real weakness was that the Assembly failed to back
up its appeals with machinery for a cease-fire and negotiations. Once again, by default, the decision was left to the
force of arms.

But this seemed to be a long and costly process. Despite terrible suffering, Biafra was still holding on. In Nigeria, riots and incidents as well as the calmer views of General
Gowon showed that not everyone supported the war at all costs.
Yet the generals and the hawks on both sides could not be
stopped by local unrest and humanitarian concern nor the half-
hearted attempts of various African leaders to seek a compromise. The only serious effort at bringing both sides together
was made by Emperor Haile Selassie of Ethiopia, with seemingly little support from the rest of the OAU. It collapsed on
18 December when the Biafran mission left Addis Ababa after
waiting for the Nigerians, while the leaders on both sides demanded the preconditions that had always been rejected, a
cease-fire or prior acceptance of Nigerian unity.

By then the Nigerian army had launched another offensive. This time it was effective. The army had grown in
size and had more material for its land and especially air
forces. The Biafrans, after thirty months of war, were greatly weakened and morale was low. With its troops pressing in
from all sides, Nigeria made a lunge for Owerri, the last
large village, and the Uli airstrip. Backed by artillery and
bombers it took Owerri on 10 January 1970 and Uli was pounded into rubble. The same day there was a council of war
among the Biafran leaders. This time Ojukwu, admitting that
conventional warfare was no longer possible yet hoping for a
guerrilla effort, was in the minority and he decided to leave
the country and place all powers in the hands of the Chief of
Staff, General Philip Effiong. Two days later, as the Biafran
army collapsed and the population fled, he called for peace.
This was accepted by General Gowon, who announced that the
time had come for national reconciliation and reiterated his
offer of an amnesty. On 15 January, a mission arrived in
Lagos to sign the act of surrender, a purely military function
and not the result of negotiations as Chief Enahoro pointed out.
Biafra ceased to be.

But only the war was over. If the Nigerians acted too
crudely there was still the possibility of guerrilla action or

sabotage and General Ojukwu, who had escaped abroad, would
see to it that nothing passed unnoticed. It was also necessary
to rehabilitate the refugees, build up the economy and return
to a civilian regime. Yet even this was not enough, for the
war had solved none of the earlier problems of Nigeria. It
was still a huge conglomerate of tribes. The relations between the Ibos and Yorubas was now one of distrust and towards the northerners maybe of hatred. Could the Yorubas
and Hausas, never more than a loose coalition during the war,
work out a policy other than just keeping the Ibos down?
Could a role be found for those Ibos and others who, under
the pressure of war, had begun to form a nation? Would a
new balance be reached with the many minority tribes, some
now come to power in the twelve or more states of the new
Nigeria? And, were the leaders capable of finding policies
for peacetime which would give the country the positive and
constructive approach it had never had before? There was no
doubt, it would be far harder to win the peace than it had
been to win the war.

For Diallo Telli, as for Nigeria's most unconditional
supporters, "Africa has obtained one of its greatest victories."[26] But how much greater this would have been if it had
been obtained earlier, and more peacefully. The OAU's poli-
cy--that of Africa--had been one of excessive timidity and
missed opportunities. Throughout the crisis there had been
moments of deadlock when a concerted effort could have
brought the opposing sides closer together. Then, as Biafra
weakened, it could have stepped in to impose negotiations
which would have shortened the war. But in the end its resolution only served to permit General Effiong to surrender
briefly to African Unity. With the death of Biafra and two
million Africans, it was hard to see how one could speak of
"victory."

Notes

1. <u>Africa Report</u>, Oct. 1966.

2. <u>Ibid.</u>

3. "Understanding the Nigerian Crisis, A Public Statement by
   the Government of the Mid-West State," <u>The Economist</u>,
   20 July 1968.

4. <u>Africa Report</u>. Oct. 1968.

5. Ibid., Oct. 1967.

6. "Report on the O.A.U. Consultative Mission to Nigeria,"
    Nigerian National Press, 1968.

7. Africa Report, Jan. 1968.

8. Ibid.

9. Ibid.

10. The Herald Tribune, International Edition, 15 April 1968.

11. The Observer, 28 April 1968.

12. Herald Tribune, 15 April 1968.

13. Ibid., 21 May 1968.

14. Ibid., 24 May 1968.

15. Ibid., 25 May 1968.

16. Ibid., 17 July 1968.

17. Le Monde, 19 July 1968.

18. Ibid., 26 July 1968.

19. "Address of Colonel Ojukwu on 5 August 1968," Biafran
    Ministry of Information.

20. "Federal Peace Efforts," Federal Ministry of Information,
    1968.

21. Le Monde, 14 Aug. 1968.

22. "Revue de l'O.U.A.," Dec. 1968, p. 6.

23. West Africa, 21 Sept. 1968, p. 1117.

24. Ibid., p. 1117 and 1089.

25. Le Monde, 2 Jan. 1969.

26. Journal d'Egypte, 22 Jan. 1970.

F. Conclusion

In its few years of existence, the Organization of African Unity was repeatedly called upon to help preserve the peace and tranquility of the African continent. It handled several boundary disputes and dealt with one of the worst crises in the Congo and an even more explosive one in Nigeria. On occasion, it had to call its own members to order and attempt to restore good relations among African states. It would doubtlessly continue playing this role in the future.

Although its successes were not numerous or dramatic, the OAU's contribution could not be measured only by what it had done. Equally important was what it avoided. The Organization's very existence prevented some conflicts from arising and kept others from spreading. Even when it could not bring about an improvement, by keeping inevitable disputes from worsening it had already proven its value.

But the OAU was in a rather poor position for these activities. It had not received the authority or powers to act effectively to maintain internal order. It could not make its members desist from hostilities or settle their differences peacefully. Even less could it influence the government and opposing factions in an internal dispute. Much depended on the parties. The Organization could only create an atmosphere in which to end a dispute or propose and work for valid solutions. But its means of pressure were few.

Updating the Charter.

Already, by the time the first Assembly met in Cairo from 17-21 July 1964, two serious border conflicts had broken out--each of which led to violence. Several principles of the Charter had been disregarded and war had opposed African states though fortunately, action by African leaders and the OAU had calmed the hostilities. Still, the Heads of State felt the need to fill in the gaps in the principles affirmed in the Charter.

Obviously, the principle of "territorial integrity" was not sufficient when there was some question as to just where the border ran between two jealous neighbors. An attempt at clearing the situation was made by adopting a resolution on border disputes among African states. Since there was already a rule followed by most of the members, the Assembly went a step beyond the Charter and solemnly declared that "all Member States pledge themselves to respect the frontiers existing on their achievement of national independence." Although this important corollary was adopted by acclamation, its value was uncertain. There were cases where no frontier or several had been drawn and others where the interpretation or demarcation was contested. More particularly, it had been impossible to consecrate the respect of colonial frontiers in the Charter to begin with and this was still rejected by the two states most directly concerned: Morocco and Somalia.

Although the Charter of African Unity laid down the principle of peaceful settlement of disputes, the original summit conference had not inserted an article prohibiting the use of force. This oversight may have been due to excessive optimism. After war had broken out twice in the course of a year, a stronger stand was felt necessary. Repudiating the recent past, the Assembly proclaimed that "all Member States herewith renounce war and the use of armed force, except in self defence, as instruments of national policy in dealing with other African States or as means of reaching national goals with respect to other African States." It even provided that "measures" could be taken against any member found by the Assembly or Council to have violated its commitments under the Charter or this resolution.

These two resolutions and the principles they embodied were important additions to the credo of the Organization. However, in practice, they had the same inherent weakness. Whereas the Charter was at least binding, if unenforceable, the resolutions were not even binding. Even though the "non-aggression resolution" envisaged concerted measures against a state violating it, there was little chance that this would happen in the future and any state threatened with action by the OAU would most strongly reject it as an infringement of its sovereignty. These resolutions were condemned to be largely academic. The principle of the inviolability of frontiers inherited from colonialism could have been invoked in the Algero-Moroccan and Somali disputes. The use of force and subversion could have been condemned in other cases. But this was never done. No state was ever openly criticized or threatened

even with ostracism for violating any of the Organization's
principles.

The Process of Settlement.

Although it could not use a heavy hand, the OAU did
make a contribution to maintaining order in the continent. Owing to its very existence it became easier to avoid disputes
and clear up those that arose. The periodic meetings encouraged Africa's leaders to discuss their problems and often to
solve them. Informal, behind-the-scenes contacts permitted
them to iron out differences. Potential disputes were occasionally nipped in the bud. Others, such as the exchange of
Guinean and Ghanaian nationals (although not those from the
Ivory Coast), could be settled by the parties concerned or
through the good offices of other states. Certain border affairs were also calmed.

As an official forum, the OAU provided even greater
services. The members could bring their problems and disputes before the supreme bodies and African opinion would be
focused on them. Even if no action was taken, the fact that
the continent and the world were aware of a conflict made the
parties more eager to solve it. If the parties could agree
that the matter was an "African problem," the OAU would seek
an "African solution." Here the full weight of African diplomacy and public opinion came into play. On behalf of the
broader community, the Organization could go further and seek
more effective means than the parties themselves. And, if a
compromise were not too much against their interests, the
parties more willingly accepted an African solution for the
sake of African unity than one they had haggled over or imposed on one another and which might involve a loss of face.

The context in which disputes could be handled most
readily turned out to be the Council of Ministers. The Foreign Ministers were accustomed to such activities and could
easily be called into extraordinary session. Soon the Council
became Africa's chief trouble shooter. The Assembly was
used less often. Although it had greater prestige and authority, it was unwieldy and hard to mobilize. Usually it preferred mere confirmation of an agreement reached by the
Council. However, certain crises seemed too delicate or had
important repercussions and could only be dealt with by the
Heads of State.

In most cases no settlement could be reached at first, especially after hostilities, and the Assembly or Council had to establish subordinate bodies. An ad hoc committee, or a group of the Commission of Mediation if the states agreed, could then study the situation, undertake investigations, help the parties find a solution or propose one. It could meet more often and would be fairly flexible. To give it greater authority, the members were chosen among senior officials, eminent jurists, Foreign Ministers or even Heads of State and men like Kenyatta and the Emperor of Ethiopia acted as African "elders." The bodies were meant to be neutral and were broad enough to include all various tendencies. Ultimately, the resolutions of the subordinate bodies and even the Council of Ministers could only be imposed--if at all--by a strong stand of the Heads of State.

The Balance Sheet.

The first challenge to the OAU was the dispute between Algeria and Morocco. Through the good offices of the Emperor of Ethiopia and the President of Mali, it was possible to obtain a cease-fire which was later sanctioned by the OAU. The Council then set up a special Commission to deal with the border dispute. Unfortunately, no progress was made towards a final solution, i.e. an agreed boundary line, and the parties could not even be brought together to seek an agreement under the Commission's auspices. However, the fighting had ceased and despite friction and an arms race did not resume. With the renewal of the Arab common front, the conflict was temporarily forgotten.

After extensive warfare along the Somali-Ethiopia border, it was possible to achieve a disengagement, although this required several injunctions by the Council and the good offices of a member state. This was followed by sporadic clashes between shiftas and the authorities in Ethiopia and Kenya. Nevertheless, it left time for the parties to reconsider their positions and seek a solution. With the general pacification in the region after the Arab-Israeli war, Somalia came closer to its neighbors and the situation improved rapidly. It could only be hoped that the solution proved lasting.

One of the most dangerous crises dealt with by the OAU was the civil war in the Congo. Although primarily internal, it seriously affected the peace and security of the whole continent. The question of competence was waived when President

Kasavubu invited the OAU to deal with this "African problem." However, the issue of sovereignty was a considerable obstacle to its activities thereafter. The Council's compromise on the internal dispute was highly ambiguous and by not following a carefully balanced approach, the Congo Commission eventually came under criticism for its role. Neither its appeals for a cease-fire nor its attempts at reconciliation succeeded. The relations between the Congo and its neighbors, as well as serious African intervention in its internal affairs, aggravated the situation. And the final solution was reached when one side was victorious in the field. With peace restored by force, both the internal dispute and its external ramifications ceased.

The situation during the Nigerian civil war was roughly similar, but Africa's attitude was completely different. After ignoring it for some time, the OAU finally decided to deal with the matter at the Kinshasa Assembly. Even then, the services it offered were very modest. It empowered its Consultative Committee merely to assure the federal government of its assistance. Very slowly it realized that steps such as a cessation of hostilities and relief were essential, but it never considered the substantive dispute or proposed a compromise solution. Rather, the Organization seemed to await the final, military conclusion.

No mention was made in the OAU of another civil war, the long and deadly one in the Sudan.

As for foreign intervention and subversion, the OAU was occasionally able to bring pressure to bear on its members. International disapproval or condemnation of such acts did have some effect. But criticism was not enough to stop a regime intent on spreading its ideas and influence. If the underlying differences were not smoothed out, the interference was bound to resume.

Success or Failure?

As is clear from its record, the Organization was always most successful in the first phase of action intended to maintain internal order, namely putting an end to active hostilities or intervention. The crisis could sometimes be kept from spreading, the fighting ceased and the parties brought to the conference table. However, when it came to the second phase, finding a solution to the problem and settling the dispute definitively, there was little success. No borders were drawn, reconciliation was urged but not imposed or accepted, subversion or intervention often resumed after initial temporary success in stopping it. The OAU's task was not finished as long as peace and harmony were threatened and a conflict could start again.

What was far more serious was that the OAU had steadily decreased its efforts. Whereas it appointed a commission to seek a settlement between Algeria and Morocco, there was no body to study and inform the Organization of the situation in the Horn. The OAU drew up an ambitious if impracticable peace plan for the Congo: a cease-fire, a reconciliation, a reminder to the warring parties of their pledges; the creation of a true African presence. During the civil war in Nigeria, however, the OAU went to the other extreme and its presence had little significance.

Possibilities of Action.

One thing had to be admitted: all the OAU's activities were characterized by its weakness. The Organization had few material means or sources of pressure upon its members. It did not have the military or financial force to run a real peace-keeping operation. Nor could it impose decisions. Only when contending nations realized that they could not get what they wanted did they call upon the OAU to restore peace or seek with them a solution. And the only solution a nation would accept was one it already desired--or a second best. Very much depended on good will.

It was important to recognize this because each attempt at imposing a solution had failed. The most visible failure came when the Congo Commission forgot its limits and tried to impose a solution on Prime Minister Tshombe. Neither a cease-fire nor reconciliation could be forced on opposing sides. Politics was the art of knowing and doing what was possible. The OAU enjoyed its successes when rival parties were simply encouraged to define and then accept their own terms. By helping them find a solution, and then consecrating it on the altar of African unity, the OAU had a definite role to play.

But the Organization could increase its chances of success. First of all, it had to deal with every dispute. No matter how fruitless or dangerous it appeared, it was better to attempt settlement than to let a dispute deteriorate. Moreover,

the sooner it acted the better, for the most realistic solution might best be found before hatred and passion accumulated and clouded the acceptable terms. A constant African
presence was essential. The Organization and, in particular,
a special body established to deal with a specific conflict,
would have to follow the situation closely to avoid aggravation
or to take advantage of any unexpected opportunities of
improvement.

It was necessary always to pay close attention to timing. The best moment to offer services was when there was
a draw. When the parties were of equal strength and neither
could overcome the other, both would be most willing to compromise. Even after one party had seized the initiative, there
were periods of deadlock and stalemate when a settlement
might seem reasonable. The last opportunity was just before
the defeat of one side, and a political conclusion might prove
more satisfactory than a military victory.

Then the Organization would have to deal with substantive issues. It was essential to see the problem as it really
was, if necessary by sending committees of enquiry or hearing both sides, and not as the members felt it was. Each
conflict had its own peculiarities and nothing was gained by
treating it as a precedent. Fear of territorial adjustments or
tribalism was not a sufficient reason to ignore legitimate
claims and aspirations. On this basis the OAU could seek
feasible solutions. The next, and most difficult step was to
obtain acceptance from the parties. This could be done first
by emphasizing the advantages of a settlement, any settlement,
over the continuation of a conflict. Warfare harmed both
sides and internal strife only led to lasting bitterness. But
a temporary disengagement was not enough. As long as the
underlying causes had not been resolved, the conflict could
flare up again. Finally, it had to convince both sides of the
advantages of the proposed compromise, and the compromise
had to be designed to provide both sides with some advantage.

If the parties were still unwilling to accept a settlement, the other member states should seriously consider
whether pressure was not appropriate. The OAU had few resources and an attempt at imposing a solution by force was
bound to fail. Still, the Organization could certainly exert
greater pressure than it had in the past. Moral pressure
would be felt. The parties could be censured for their in-
transigence. Diplomatic pressure was also possible, and a
threat from the member states to sever relations and cease

support would not leave the belligerents indifferent. Even economic sanctions were possible in some cases. This procedure was realistic, but it required considerably more imagination and courage.

For it to work, it was also essential to develop a feeling for compromise. In the OAU, the members and any bodies dealing with a conflict had to be neutral. This did not mean a mixture of states on both sides nor a group of unconcerned states, but a body consisting of members that earnestly desired a solution. Then, the parties had to be open to compromise. They could not expect to obtain all their demands, some of which were unreasonable in any circumstances. Unfortunately, the experiences in seeking internal order in the Organization all too often showed that some of its members took sides or even intervened and that the parties were very inflexible. Only if this changed was there real hope for maintaining internal order.

Chapter V

African Non-Alignment

After having shaken off the yoke of colonial domination, nothing was more natural than for the newly independent states to define their own policies in all domestic and international affairs. Some of them continued very close and cordial relations with the former colonial power, whereas others broke completely and turned elsewhere for friends and allies. But none of the states wished to find itself again in a position where it could not determine its basic options alone. By insisting to be the masters of their own destinies, all the African states considered themselves to be non-aligned.

Whether or not this was true of each individual state, it was basically valid for them all when they acted as a unit. Since some leaned one way and some another, the tendencies cancelled out and Africa as a whole could find a policy that, if not always equidistant from the blocs, at least followed none closely. In order to determine its own course, Africa needed a forum where each state would be able or would be encouraged to cast aside its external connections for the sake of the continent. This was one of the services the Organization of African Unity hoped to render. There the member states could seek a policy that was non-aligned quite simply because it was African.

Early Non-Alignment.

Originally, non-alignment--as conceived of by its founders and philosophers--was a stance somewhere between that of the major blocs. In practice, it was rarely in the middle, but at least there was considerable leeway for choice. To avoid serious conflict, the uncommitted states tried to find a peaceful solution or compromise for each issue. This was not neutrality or passiveness and an active policy was to be proposed on each matter. Nevertheless, any action was always on the terms of the two super-powers. Driven by repulsion rather than attraction to American and Soviet policies, the non-aligned group could still do nothing more than propose solutions to the problems raised by others and then await the ultimate approval or rejection of their solutions.

On this background, the Charter of African Unity laid down its final principle: "affirmation of a policy of non-alignment with regard to all blocs," but gave no indication of what this meant in practice. Some of the blanks were filled in by a resolution on non-alignment adopted by the Council of Ministers in February 1964. On the one hand, it recalled the importance of coexistence between different systems of government and ideologies and the need to maintain international peace and security. On the other, it stressed more specific concerns such as the unity and solidarity of the member states and the freedom, stability and prosperity of Africa. To attain these various aims it was recommended that the African states cease their commitments as soon as possible and follow a coordinated, non-aligned foreign policy. Such a policy would be prepared by direct consultations.

But the only attempt at active measures stemmed from the summit conference's resolution on general disarmament. On a world level, it appealed to the great powers and, in particular, the Soviet Union and the United States, to reduce their conventional weapons, end the arms race and sign an agreement for general and complete disarmament under strict and effective international control. It also objected to the accumulation of nuclear weapons and testing thereof and urged greater efforts for the peaceful use of atomic energy. At home, it demanded "the end of military occupation of the African continent and the elimination of military bases and nuclear tests." It also affirmed the principle of making Africa a nuclear free zone. A year later, at the Cairo Assembly, the Heads of State adopted a "Declaration for the Denuclearization of Africa," in which they solemnly expressed their will "not to manufacture or acquire control of nuclear weapons."

However, this brand of non-alignment was soon forgotten. No treaty on denuclearization was ever signed or even negotiated. After France stopped its nuclear tests in the Sahara and the states which wished to rid themselves of military bases did so--while those which did not, maintained them--the urgency of such issues dwindled. There were no other campaigns and few consultations.

In addition, as long as there was no direct threat to
the continent, the OAU had little say about the external policies of its members. It had to trust that they would be
sufficiently anxious to avoid entangling alliances and dangerous
commitments. Each state was allowed to choose its friends
and allies abroad and to look after its own non-alignment.
Since the options varied widely, the OAU could scarcely lay
down a hard and fast line as to what sort of mix was necessary to remain non-aligned and any criticism of a member's
policy would only have led to friction. The Organization was
not there to police its members but to serve them.

Africa for the Africans.

However, there was another aspect of the division of
the world into two huge rival blocs which was more threatening. It was possible for one or both of the blocs to take too
close an interest in what was going on in the continent. Rather than play an active role in world affairs, Africa found it
more important to keep outside powers from intervening in its
own affairs. For cold war involvement would only embitter
the differences and inhibit cooperation while undermining the
continent's independence.

The desire to free Africa of all foreign interference
was the mainspring of much of the Organization's activity.
Often it was felt instinctively and there was no need to work
out a conscious policy to prevent every attempt of meddling in
the continent. Nevertheless, it was necessary to think ahead
in order to avoid the cold war before Africans became en-
meshed in conflict and, above all, it was vital to the OAU to
know where the dangers might arise. For the responsibility
had to be placed not only on the outside powers that interfered
but also the African states that allowed or asked them to do
so.

This was the virtue of a resolution adopted by the Cairo Assembly on "good-neighborliness." Despite its somewhat
misleading title, this document laid down the ground rules of
a new, more specifically African non-alignment. First of all,
the member states were warned to avoid all commitments that
tended "to inject into Africa foreign rivalries or bloc politics."
This, of course, did not mean that they could not enter into
agreements for their defence, freedom or development with
outside powers. However, they had to see to it that such undertakings did not "threaten the peace, tranquility and develop-

ment of Africa as a whole ... or interfere with the rights, freedom and integrity of other African States." The members also had to discourage the cold war actively. In their relations with non-African countries and especially the major powers, they

> ... shall at each and every opportunity restate the determination of Africa not to become involved in foreign disputes or conflicts, nor to become the battlefields in any fight for world power, and not to allow any African region, State or problem to become part of any struggle for world power.

This was a rather tame declaration and not a fiery Monroe Doctrine, and correctly so. After the tremendous wave of decolonization had liberated most of the continent, there was little chance that external powers would force their way brutally into Africa as had been done earlier. The new methods were more subtle and disguised. Although quite eager to expand their influence, the greater and lesser powers were reluctant to act without first receiving an invitation. Thus, the main duty of the member states was to exercise restraint and resist the temptation to disregard non-alignment. Once an outside power had entered the continent, however, more active measures would be necessary.

Unfortunately, it was often difficult to avoid involvement. One standing invitation was the continued need of assistance in all the independent countries. When it came to development, the whole African community (including those most bitterly attacking neo-colonialism) realized that essential aid could only be obtained from the more advanced and prosperous part of the world. Financial and technical assistance was repeatedly requested and granted. This even spread into delicate areas like defence and military support. Although the African states asked that aid be given without "strings," it was hard to keep from drawing closer to one's benefactor.

This danger also arose in connection with decolonization, for the continent was not strong enough to emancipate the remaining territories itself and the liberation movements needed substantial funds and equipment. What they could not obtain in Africa they had to seek elsewhere. Since more backing came from one side than the other, there was a growing indebtedness towards one of the blocs. But decolonization was a sufficiently sacred goal not to require repayment in full and the leaders of the nascent states were wary of accepting new chains while fighting to throw off the old ones.

There was perhaps a service the OAU could perform to help its members maintain their non-alignment. Various schemes had been proposed for channelling aid to the developing countries. It had been suggested that it be made multilateral to avoid ties or that a central body, like the United Nations, act as a barrier between the donor and beneficiary. Here the OAU might also have a role to play. The Organization was already doing something of that sort in the field of decolonization, where the Liberation Committee managed a Fund that was to finance and arm the freedom fighters while neutralizing the money and supplies it received. And, at critical moments, the OAU could help out a member which preferred obtaining specific and limited assistance from within the continent.

African Solutions to African Problems.

The most serious invitation to outside meddling arose when conflicts broke out on the continent. Fortunately, these disputes usually had a concrete basis and with sufficient good will and some give-and-take a solution could be sought. It would be possible in each case to judge the opposing viewpoints calmly and try to find a compromise. If none could be found, the dispute might rest in abeyance or lead to friction. It might even end in warfare. But, as long as the parties knew what they wanted and what they could reasonably hope to obtain, there was a very good chance of finding a solution or at least avoiding unnecessary damage and bloodshed.

However, if some global ideology got mixed up in a dispute, the whole matter might be blown up into something it definitely was not. Such a distortion was particularly distressing in Africa. Basic views did not differ drastically from country to country. All the states had escaped from colonialism, belonged to the anti-colonial group and fought more or less zealously for liberation of the continent. All sought to develop the economy and modernize the society. None adhered to capitalism or Communism outright or denied the virtues of democracy, and most proclaimed some sort of African socialism and had one-party states. The similarities were great enough for them to support the broad African ideology of the Charter of African Unity. And there should have been no reason for extraneous or irreconcilable ideological quarrels.

Nevertheless, ideology could not be entirely avoided.
There were differences on policy and outlook. Many of the
African leaders increased the differences by trying to give an
impetus to their countries through a national ideology. This
was further complicated by rigidity in the body politic due to
the one-party system. Governments willing to maintain relations with both East and West externally were rarely willing
to permit different opinions at home. By not tolerating opposition and being painfully sensitive to criticism, every minor
difference was made serious. When at odds with another
state or faction, there was a tendency for each side to justify
its stand in political terms. But these ideologies were still
undergoing gestation or were closely tied to circumstances.
Moreover, even when they were widely promoted by the leaders, they were not really understood or adhered to by the
masses, especially the still tribalized sectors. Thus it was
unwise to invoke them needlessly.

Still, the fact remained that the dangers were greatest
wherever a conflict between African states or within one
state was combined with ideology. In such cases, the country
and continent tended to fall into rival groups. They would
slide towards cold war confrontation when one side, often the
weaker, appealed to a friendly power already aiding it to make
an increased effort in the moment of crisis. Desperate, the
African state might have to accept stronger conditions than it
would ordinarily desire. Or, if the great power was afraid
of a reversal in the local or general balance of power, it
might force its aid on the protégé. At any rate, if support
were forthcoming, this would give the African adversary persuasive reasons to solicit and possibly to obtain backing from
the opposing bloc. With this would begin escalation.

The Congo Trauma.

The greatest danger of interference was thus connected
with conflicts inside Africa. The task of the Organization of
African Unity was not only to find a solution or compromise
to a dispute but also to avoid contagion and disruption from
the outside world. Left to themselves, the Africans might
well reach an agreement. Aggravated by the cold war, things
would be far more difficult.

The need to develop this aspect of non-alignment became evident at an early date. This was driven home by the
tragedy in the Congo. It had scarcely been free a few days

when the Belgians returned to their former colony. In order
to have the troops withdrawn and to avoid further complications, the African states called upon the United Nations. However, behind the Belgian screen, a secessionist regime had
already been established and was being consolidated in Katanga. When Prime Minister Lumumba differed on how to end
the secession, wishing to crush it rapidly by force, and accepted a Soviet offer of aid, he took a dangerous step. The
situation deteriorated further when Kasavubu broke with Lumumba and appealed to the United States to help support the
government. Soon the Gizenga regime was operating in Stanleyville, and the central government, in Léopoldville, each
with its friends and allies. Even the United Nations, by following one policy instead of another or by doing nothing appeared as a tool of outside interests.

Ideology rapidly crept into the conflict and the super-
powers mistook political and tribal quarrels for part of the
world-wide struggle between the two blocs. This atmosphere
was pervasive and the Congo was turned into a major battlefield of the cold war. Gradually, the control over events
slipped out of Congolese and African hands.

The experience in the Congo was conclusive. If the
cold war got mixed up in an African conflict, it would rapidly
distort and swell the actual problem. Bitter and extraneous
ideological issues would make it harder to find a practicable,
and African, solution. By forgetting their original aims, the
leaders and people might end up fighting for goals they could
not attain and causes they did not desire.

Even worse, by introducing the great powers in an African conflict, the means of destruction were increased tremendously. The relatively poor African countries with small
armies and limited equipment could not fight as long or cause
as much damage to each other as they could with the powerful
weaponry of outside backers. With a steady stream of arms
and matériel, the cannon fodder being available locally, the
struggle would be drawn out and deadly.

Finally, if a solution were found to such a conflict, it
would not have been worked out by the African parties concerned nor would it reflect a genuine victory in the field. It would
largely be imposed by the powers, more interested in their
own relations than the merits of the situation or the good of
Africa. Having ignored the realities, the solution was likely
to be unstable and always in danger of being contested or re-

opened.

After the Congolese crisis, there was a dramatic reaction to all foreign intervention and non-alignment was given a very special meaning. It was clearly directed outwards and aimed at shielding the continent so that the Africans could settle their own problems. In the future they would reject and condemn any attempt by foreign powers or the United Nations to intervene in African affairs. In times of crises the continent might even seek to isolate itself. But it remained to be seen whether Africa would succeed where others failed.

A. Escalation in the Maghreb

During the seven long years Algeria had fought for its
liberation, it was backed morally and materially by Morocco.
It was not until after this struggle that major differences came
to light between the war-hardened FLN and the traditionalist
monarchy. The regime of Morocco's Hassan II, a relatively
conservative government, had already assumed a rather cautious stance in national and international affairs. In Algeria,
Ben Bella, to the contrary, quickly installed a strong dictatorship, launched a policy of socialization and nationalization, and
took a hard line on all questions of domestic and external policy. This led to a growing ideological gulf in the Maghreb.

It also led to a reversal of alliances. Originally Morocco had obtained support for its claims on Mauritania from
the East. Its army had been equipped and trained by these
countries. However, the flirt with Moscow was brief, for as
soon as it became independent Algeria seemed a more natural
and valuable ally. Morocco turned back to the West, especially the United States. At the same time, given the territorial
dispute, Algeria determined to strengthen and modernize its
own army. This was rapidly made a priority by the national
liberation army which played an important role in national life.
When Algeria asked the Soviet Union for aid, the reply was
affirmative.

Denaturation of a Boundary Dispute.

Serious fighting broke out in the Sahara on 14 October
1963. In an amazingly short time, it gripped more than just
the professional or "popular" armies. The next day, after
initial setbacks, a general mobilization was decreed in Algeria
to meet the "invasion." President Ben Bella donned his uniform and called upon the people to join the war effort. Men
flocked to the recruiting centers and thousands of veterans
were re-enlisted. All the while Morocco moved more troops
and equipment to the front.

451

Appeals to patriotism only fed the animosity between the two peoples. As the positions became stabilized in the field, the conflict was carried to the air waves in a campaign of propaganda that rapidly degenerated into vituperation and personal insult. Morocco was attacked as a backward and greedy monarchy trying to rob an idealistic and socialistic soldier-people of the fruits of its struggle for independence. Algeria was portrayed as a parvenu and ingrate, lightly forgetting Morocco's precious aid during the war. Both the King of Morocco and President of Algeria were described in the most unflattering terms.

The situation was particularly critical since, at the same time, the Algerian Government was faced with a "counter-revolution" in the Kabylia region in the mountains not far from Algiers. When hostilities broke out with Morocco, President Ben Bella criticized Morocco's border policies at the same time as he did the internal revolt and pointedly linked the two, even speaking of "collusion" between his enemies.[1] Morocco may well have counted on this struggle to create a diversion and to weaken Algerian resistance during the confrontation in the Sahara. But the contrary happened. Internal differences were patched up in order to meet the national enemy and Algeria turned more resolutely and angrily against Morocco.

The border dispute rapidly escalated to engulf the two peoples. The split roughly along ideological lines and a similar weakness in both countries for soliciting aid from the great powers already contained the seeds of the cold war. From the start the former colonial power, France, refused to take sides, trying to remain on good terms with both states. However, with an ideological conflict in the making, the greatest dangers were elsewhere. Shortly after the outbreak of hostilities, Ben Bella announced that "foreigners" were piloting the Moroccan planes and the rumor spread swiftly that American planes were flying the Moroccan troops to the combat zones. Hundreds marched on the USIS cultural center to protest.[2]

Although Washington denied the reports, Algeria had a pretext for much less hypothetical aid from the Soviet Union. Throughout the hostilities, its army continued to receive Soviet equipment. Most of it was shipped from Cuba and the UAR and had supposedly been ordered before the warfare. Still, there was no doubt that Algeria was being armed rapidly and massively nor was there doubt as to where this aid was

coming from. The cost of the war may have been borne more
easily with a Soviet loan of $100 million, followed by a Chi-
nese offer of $50 million in long term credits.[3] What was
worse, since Algeria was not familiar with the material, it
had to be accompanied by technicians and instructors and perhaps other personnel.

Although Western diplomats warned of an East-West
arms race as each shipment of Soviet supplies arrived in Algeria, and Morocco reportedly sought Western arms to keep
stride,[4] there was relative restraint. In particular, the
United States did not give in and send new arms to Morocco.
Washington warned all concerned not to provoke an East-West
confrontation in North Africa, but it apparently did not think
the time had come to go any further.[5] The Kennedy administration did not want to push Algeria into the Soviet camp nor
to endanger future relations. Moreover, for the time being,
Morocco was still better equipped militarily. Only a decisive
change in the relative strength of the combatants might have
forced the hand of the United States.

Despite their moral or material backing, the two super-
powers stayed largely on the side lines. The Soviet Union
also avoided a direct confrontation with an African state by
channelling most of its aid through Cuba and the UAR. Its
smaller partners, however, were much more active. Egypt
left no doubt about its backing of Algeria and introduced its
own presence in the region. Less than a week after the fighting began, Morocco announced that it had captured five Egyptian officers with the Algerians in a Soviet-type helicopter.[6]
As the hostilities continued, the Algerian forces were apparently joined by Cuban volunteers and troops from the UAR.

Relations became increasingly stormy. On 21 October,
Morocco accused the UAR of "aiding the Algerian aggressor"
in the conflict.[7] It gradually became convinced that Egyptian
troops were participating in the attacks.[8] On 31 October
Rabat severed its diplomatic ties with Havana for sending arms
and troops. Although it did not go so far with the Arab states,
the Moroccan ambassadors were recalled from Cairo and Damascus because of the "extreme hostility" shown Morocco, and
a break was hinted at if their attitude continued. No action
was taken against the Soviet Union, whose participation was
much less flagrant.

For the moment it seemed that more energetic measures would not be necessary since a cease-fire had already

been agreed to and the conflict would soon be brought before a
special meeting of the OAU. Nevertheless, this was not the
end. Despite the calm in the Sahara, Egyptian destroyers
paid visits to the port of Algiers as a sign of solidarity and,
more ominously, a military mission under General Ali Amer
was sent to Colomb-Béchar (near the site of hostilities). The
most disconcerting element to the Moroccans was that by the
slow introduction of troops there were soon 300 to 500 Egyptian soldiers on Algerian territory.[9] By the 15th of November, when he appeared before the Council of Ministers, the
Moroccan Foreign Minister did not have to mention names
when he struck out against foreign intervention in the conflict
and attacked a "third country, a member of the Organization,"
for giving aid to Algeria in the midst of the warfare and for
violating the Charter of the OAU.[10]

The First "African" Affair.

Despite earlier signs of friction between Morocco and
Algeria, it came as a tremendous shock to Africa when, less
than six months after general idealism at Addis Ababa, hostilities broke out. There had been some hope that the parties
would agree to a cease-fire until the negotiations in Marrakech
collapsed on 17 October 1963. By then the dispute had apparently escaped its masters. By permitting the territorial conflict to get out of hand, and by turning to big power allies to
obtain a victory in the field, Algeria and Morocco were leaving the door wide open to more serious complications. Advancing from moral backers to material supporters, the great
powers could have pushed their intervention much further.

If this danger was not clearly perceived by the Algerian and Moroccan leaders, too deeply involved in the conflict,
it was recognized rapidly by other African nations. Appeals
soon came from the Maghreb and Arab world. Even before
the outbreak of the worst fighting and often thereafter, President Bourguiba of Tunisia called for an end to hostilities and
offered his services. By 20 October, a meeting of the Arab
League Council in Cairo called upon the two states to cease
the combat and decided to send a commission of mediation to
Algeria and Morocco. Not long after, President Nasser himself proposed a summit of the four Maghreb states and the
UAR to restore peace.

Although some of these appeals to fraternity may have
moved the Algerian or Moroccan Heads of State, none of the

potential peace-makers was acceptable to both. Tunisia already had political differences and a boundary dispute of its own with Algeria. And the Arab League and Nasser had disqualified themselves as mediators in advance. At the same time as they made their offers, the League adopted a stand largely following the Algerian line and President Nasser had even denounced the "aggression" against Algeria and supported its military efforts.[11]

Another candidate was the United Nations. The world body debated the situation and, on 18 October, U Thant offered his good offices. The Moroccan government indicated for some time a desire to submit the dispute to the United Nations. However, it was clear to all that there was an appreciable danger of great power involvement in that forum. Whether they liked it or not, it was hard to ban cold war polemics and politics from any body they were members of. Fortunately, neither the United States nor the Soviet Union were particularly eager to be drawn into the conflict. Probably Washington and Paris prevailed on the King to turn elsewhere. And the OAU was given a chance. (See Chapter IV, A.)

Notes

1. The New York Times, 16 Oct. 1963.

2. Ibid., 16 Oct. 1963.

3. Ibid., 6, 10 Oct. 1963.

4. Ibid., 31 Oct. 1963.

5. Ibid., 1 Nov. 1963.

6. Le Monde, 22 Oct. 1963.

7. Ibid., 23 Oct. 1963.

8. The New York Times, 28 Oct. 1963.

9. Le Monde, 13 Nov. 1963.

10. The Times (London), 16 Nov. 1963.

11. Le Monde, 22-24 Oct. 1963.

B. Arms Race in the Horn

From the beginning the prospects for peace between the
Republic of Somalia and its neighbors had been very dim. As
of independence, its leaders in Mogadishu backed the right of all
the Somali peoples to unite in a greater Somali nation-state.
However, since this would entail a considerable loss of territory for Ethiopia and Kenya and they refused any change, there
was bound to be a serious dispute. None of the parties really
had much faith in a peaceful solution and each tried to
strengthen itself for the confrontation. Each state wished to
be thoroughly prepared diplomatically and militarily when the
time came. However, by building up their forces and seeking
allies, they only spread the danger. For aid was to be found
not only in Africa but more so in the real seats of power outside the continent.

The Search for Allies.

The fact that the territorial dispute sprung from a deeper urge for self-determination made it all the more explosive.
The situation was not eased by the inclusion of the contestants
in broader units as well. The Somalis were fervently Muslim.
Ethiopia and Kenya, to the contrary, were dominated by ethnic
groups that were often Christian. There were also differences
between the ways of life and incipient ideologies on both sides.
These differences were further accentuated or distorted under
the pressure of the dispute and this eventually led the antago-
nists to gravitate towards different camps in Africa and in the
world.

Faced with a common threat from Somalia, Ethiopia
and Kenya were quite naturally allies. They had to defend
their cause diplomatically and, more and more frequently, to
ward off the attacks of shiftas and prevent violations of their
territorial integrity. Their regimes were relatively stable and
the leaders came from the older generation of the traditional
ruling circles. They usually followed a moderate policy in international affairs and internally. Both politically and especial
ly territorially, they represented the status quo, as neither

456

country could afford the amputation of the Somali territories and a possible disintegration. On the point of territorial integrity they were supported by the community of African states, equally worried about the impact of such a precedent.

Valuable as African backing was morally and diplomatically, it was of little help in a military confrontation and both Ethiopia and Kenya were eager to be able to throw back any attack. By the time Somalia became independent, in 1960, Ethiopia had already received considerable military assistance from the United States and had a large and well-equipped army. It even had a budding air force. Kenya was still a British colony, its army trained and armed by Great Britain, and for some time after independence, it was officered by expatriates. It continued to enjoy the benefit of logistic aid against the shiftas. Nevertheless, both Ethiopia and Kenya prided themselves on being non-aligned and to some extent they did receive other forms of aid from the Communist bloc. The Emperor, in particular, played an active role in winning support for his country and he conferred not only with Kennedy and de Gaulle, but also Nasser and Chou En-lai to explain his position.

Somalia also fit into a broader regional context. Although not of Arab stock, the Somalis had been converted to Islam and were proudly part of the Muslim world. Since the Arab circle was a non-exclusive and expansive one, there was room for a gradual integration by Somalia. Of course, the main concern of Mogadishu was to obtain help against the two states that blocked its reunification. This could be had from some of the leading Arab capitals, like Cairo and Damascus, and with its allies it formed a crescent around Ethiopia from the Sudan, along the Red Sea and into Somalia. In exchange for this aid, Somalia embraced Arab causes, entered the radical wing of the African states and directed its non-alignment eastwards.

Objectively, tribal and nomadic Somalia was no more promising soil for transplanting Communism to Africa than its neighbors. It had many dynamic and volatile leaders who promoted various socio-economic schemes or reforms. Still, its radicalism was clearly rooted in a national and not a class struggle. There actually was some hesitation in the Communist bloc. But neither side had much choice. Somalia was unable to obtain from the West the military aid it wanted in order to enforce its claims. Of the former colonial powers, Italy could not provide the quantity desired and Great Britain

backed Kenya.   London was increasingly criticized in Somalia
for this and, by March 1963, Mogadishu decided to sever its
diplomatic relations.   The United States was too well established in Ethiopia to offer arms that might eventually be turned against its ally.   Thus, in its bid to receive aid, Somalia
quickly realized that the only place to get what it wanted was
among the enemies of Ethiopia's and Kenya's allies.   The
Communist powers were not seriously committed in the region
and, as late comers, they were looking for a foothold.   Not
just the Soviet Union was interested and Somalia rapidly became a major beneficiary of Chinese aid and advice.

        Somalia's military build-up began at independence.   It
immediately received generous support from Egypt, which
pledged to equip 5,000 soldiers and provide £5 million worth
of light arms.[1]   Much more was forthcoming from China.   A
major turn in the road came early in August 1963 when, after
a stop-over in Cairo, Prime Minister Abdi Rashid Shermarke
left on a good will visit to China.   While there, he signed a
military aid pact and was promised equipment and instructors.
But there was one last opportunity to maintain the balancing
act between East and West.   Shortly after the pact with China,
the United States was for the first time moved to propose
military aid to Somalia.   This possibility seriously worried
the Emperor who flew to Washington to have the offer retracted.   However, although the United States again confirmed its
support of Ethiopia in the border dispute, the offer was maintained.

        Ultimately, it was the Somali government that took the
decision.   In November, it turned down the military aid of the
United States and other Western nations as too late and inadequate and accepted a larger package from the Soviet Union.
The thirty million dollars worth of military equipment, enough
to arm an "internal security" force of 20,000, was a significant boost in its strength.[2]   Soviet aid was needed, according
to Prime Minister Shermarke, because of Ethiopian "provocation" and to cover the costs of looking after the Somali refugees.[3]   Although Somalia repeatedly protested that its policy
of non-alignment was still intact and objected to wide-spread
misinterpretation of its acceptance of this aid, it had taken a
decisive step.   Its neighbors, however, did not find this entirely negative, since the Soviet presence would counterbalance
the growing Chinese influence.   They hoped that Moscow would
dampen Somalia's eagerness to follow any adventurous policies
encouraged by China.

But the influx of military aid was a danger in itself. The Horn of Africa had now become a powder keg. For years raids had been occurring in the contested areas, but they had only been sporadic and annoying forrays by small groups of nomads or irregulars. Then, the shiftas became more active and their attacks assumed larger proportions. Shortly after it obtained the Soviet military aid, this campaign was openly backed by Mogadishu and regular troops were reported in the region. Ethiopia was deeply concerned about the situation and, at the end of the year, hurriedly ratified its mutual defence pact with Kenya. It was not surprising that the opposing sides ultimately made contact and large-scale fighting broke out on 7 February 1964.

Return From the Brink.

For Somalia and Ethiopia (as well as Kenya, a very interested on-looker), this was a struggle that might seal the fate of three nations. Fortunately, however, neither the United States nor the Soviet Union had any real stakes in the victory of either side and neither wished to upset the balance in the region irremediably or unleash a wave of territorial claims they would be called upon to support or combat. Although they wanted to aid their friends, they were not ready to make enemies in Africa. And they held back from intervening in a fruitless war in which they had little to gain. China may have thought otherwise, but even it did not really prod them on.

That the great powers did not desire war was made clear from the start. Only days after the fighting broke out, Premier Khrushchev appealed to both sides to reach a peaceful settlement and the United States called for an end to the fighting. After the failure of the first cease-fire, there was a dangerous moment when President Osman hinted at American "connivance" and the British were implicated in a clash along the Somali-Kenyan border. Then Ethiopia and Somalia accused one another of using non-African troops.[4] However, all these charges were denied and Ethiopia announced that it had not invoked its defence pact with Kenya nor obtained aid from the United States or Israel. At the beginning of March, Soviet Deputy Foreign Minister Yakov Alexandrovich Malik arrived on a surprise visit to Ethiopia, after having been to Somalia earlier. And even Chou En-lai, who was in Mogadishu shortly before the hostilities broke out, had been to Addis Ababa first in an effort to strengthen China's ties with Ethiopia. Thus, it

could reasonably be assumed that the great powers were urging restraint on the belligerents.

More even than they, the rest of the African community wanted a return to peace and feared the effect of prolonged
hostilities and that the great powers might not always remain
aloof.   There was also some concern that the matter would
be brought before the United Nations and that it would become
entangled in the cold war there.   The Organization of African
Unity seemed far safer.

Almost as soon as the hostilities broke out, the Emperor of Ethiopia informed the other African Heads of State of
the dangerous situation.   At the same time, Somalia lodged a
complaint in the United Nations against Ethiopia's "armed aggression" and called for an immediate meeting of the Security
Council.   On 9 February, Haile Selassie asked the OAU to
consider the Somali "aggression" and urged an extraordinary
session of the Council of Ministers.   The next day, Somalia
got into step and also asked the OAU to deal with the conflict
without, however, withdrawing its complaint from the United
Nations.   Even while travelling to the OAU meeting in Dar es
Salaam, where the matter would doubtlessly be handled, Somali Foreign Minister Abdullahi Issa indicated that the dispute
was not yet an African one exclusively.   He warned that "Somalia will take her case to the United Nations if she fails to
obtain satisfaction from the O.A.U."[5]

Somalia was obviously worried about how its border
conflict with Ethiopia and Kenya would be received by the Foreign Ministers of Africa.   Realizing that most of the independent states opposed redrawing the frontiers inherited from colonialism and that none would openly support such drastic
changes as those advocated in Mogadishu, it still preferred
avoiding the OAU and using a forum where it was certain of
at least some support.   Even as the Council of Ministers met,
on 12 February, Somalia appealed to the Secretary-General of
the United Nations to send a commission to the area to determine the responsibility for the hostilities and supervise the
cease-fire the OAU was bound to recommend.[6]

But the United Nations had shown no wish to encroach
on the OAU.   U Thant went along with the African delegations'
preference for an African solution and, even while appealing
to the Somali and Ethiopian governments to resort to peaceful
settlement, he referred to the OAU.[7]   The major effort in
Dar es Salaam was therefore to convince Somalia that the dis-

pute should be dealt with in an African context. The Council eventually had to call upon both parties not to bring the issue before any other international organization. And it was successful. Somalia gave in and its complaint with the United Nations was left pending. To mark a point for the future, the resolution of 15 February expressed the conviction "that the Unity of Africa requires the solution to all disputes between Member States be sought first within the Organization of African Unity."

Notes

1. Philippe Decraene, Panafricanisme, p. 87.

2. The New York Times, 14 Nov. 1963.

3. Ibid., 1 Dec. 1963.

4. Ibid., 19 & 20 Feb. 1964.

5. The Times (London), 13 Feb. 1964.

6. Ibid., 13 Feb. 1964.

7. The New York Times, 10 Feb. 1964.

C. Tanganyika Mutinies

Most of the new African states were unusually fragile. Much of their cohesion and strength resided in two institutions: a single-party government and the army. Small and unimpressive in absolute terms, the army was the best organized and disciplined force, disposing of relatively modern and powerful equipment. It was often the backbone of the state internally and could impose order and tranquility. It was also the only means of protection against outside interference. When obedient to the government, it enabled the country to overcome many of its difficulties and develop. When opposed, it was occasionally able to replace the government. If, however, the army became disorganized or purposeless even momentarily, the whole country could be dragged with it into anarchy.

The Trouble Spreads.

Early on 20 January 1964, the troops of the Tanganyikan Rifles stationed just outside of Dar es Salaam rose against their officers (British for the most part) and arrested them. Then they left their barracks and entered the capital, where they surrounded the state house and by dawn controlled all the strategic points in the city. From this position of strength, they presented their demands for the removal of all expatriate officers and an Africanization of the army as well as an increase in pay. When the ministers with whom they parleyed promised favorable treatment of the demands, most of the soldiers agreed to return to their barracks. The next day, the units in the provinces repeated this operation, on a smaller scale, and also returned to their barracks. Within days there were sitdown strikes in the armies of neighboring Kenya and Uganda.

Unfortunately, the difficulties were not over with the acquiesence of the ministers. The momentary disruption of law and order had rapidly been seized upon by others as an opportunity for looting and rioting. The trouble-makers were joined by some members of the army and even the police and serious insecurity reigned in the capital. Along with considerable material damage, this sudden outburst left a number of dead and injured. Despite various efforts, it was impossible for the local authorities fully to restore order.

Since there had also been disturbances in the Kenyan and Ugandan armies and most of Tanganyika's police force élite was in Zanzibar, President Nyerere had little choice but to call on the former colonial power to put an end to the chaos and disarm the soldiers. Early on 25 January, British troops were moved in by helicopter and rounded up and disarmed the mutineers and rioters. But this was not the end of the matter; the army could no longer be trusted or the mutineers reinstated, and it was necessary to build up and train a new force. This would take time and Tanganyika could scarcely keep the British troops that long if it did not want to run certain risks.

Even while the disturbances were going on, the mutiny had started to take on a political coloration. Not only the soldiers were aggrieved by the fact that independence had not dramatically changed their lot in life. Worse trouble was stirred up by dissident civilian elements that began conspiring with the leaders of the mutiny. Soon there were rumors of a Communist plot or even a "popular revolt." With the return of Great Britain so strikingly to its former colony--some 600 troops and the aircraft carrier Centaur anchored in the bay-- the government had put an end to the mutiny. But it increasingly lay itself open to the charge of inviting in neo-colonialism.

Serious international complications also cropped up immediately after the British arrival. The situation could not have been more delicate. On 12 January, only two weeks earlier, a violent uprising and massacre had been unleashed by the Negro population in Zanzibar. The Sultan was deposed and a pro-Communist government came to power on the island. Some of its leaders had reportedly been trained in China and Cuba and the new regime was immediately supported by the Soviet Union. Making no secret of its ideological tendency, it proclaimed a "People's Republic." Nevertheless, the new Zanzibar leaders were seriously worried by the presence of British troops and ships at no great distance from the coast. On 26 January, the Soviet Union had already warned against any "forceable acts against the new Republic of Zanzibar by those who do not wish to abandon their former colonial privileges." Such acts, it added, would be "full of dangerous consequences."[1]

The day after the Soviet warning, the Tanganyikan government admitted that it was "very much disturbed to see there had been attempts to introduce cold war politics into the disturbing events in Tanganyika."[2] With the threat of great power involvement increasing, President Nyerere turned to the only ally that could help him maintain his country's political balance, the African community as a whole.

A Helping Hand.

When the Tanganyikan government called on the other African governments to attend an extraordinary meeting of the OAU in Dar es Salaam, it stressed that the East African mutinies were not only a danger for the three countries but for all of Africa and African unity. Similar events could happen elsewhere and it was essential for the Organization to know how to react and to help the countries concerned avoid more serious consequences. Although an ordinary session of the OAU was scheduled to be held only two weeks later, everyone was aware of the urgency and the Foreign and Defence Ministers were able to meet from 12-15 February 1964.

His fellow Heads of State in Kenya and Uganda, in much the same situation, had not shown the same desire as President Nyerere to introduce an African presence. This was because of the stricter policy of non-alignment he had been following for some time and a number of special circumstances in Tanganyika. It could not be forgotten that Dar es Salaam, as the headquarters of the Liberation Committee and of various freedom movements in southern Africa, was the focal point of the struggle against the colonial and settler powers. Even if the British presence did not prevent these activities, it could have an inhibiting effect on a cause that concerned all Africa. More important, owing to the situation in Zanzibar, the escalation of threats between the great powers had already begun and one of them was on Tanganyikan soil. If the British troops were not removed, the threats might have taken a more concrete form and the region would become an object of cold war controversy.

Appearing before the Council of Ministers, President Nyerere admitted the humiliation of his country at the mutinies and added that the "enemies of African liberation will continue to mock at Africa while any African State relies on outside troops to safeguard its citizens." By calling in Great Britain to put down disturbances his own government could not handle, Tanganyika had been saved from one threat only to fall into another. "The presence of troops from a country deeply involved in the world's Cold War conflicts," he stressed, "has serious implications in the context of African nationalism, and our common policies of non-alignment."[3]

In its moment of need, Tanganyika had to turn to an ally that was able to act rapidly and send a force to quell the mutinies. Time was of the essence and it was doubtful that any African state or the OAU could have come to its assistance. The Organization was still rudimentary and could not mobilize a force under its auspices without interminable delay for meetings and approval by various states. The precedent of the United Nations in the Congo did not encourage Tanganyika to call on the Security Council.

However, now that law and order had been restored, it was much easier merely to obtain African troops to replace the British ones. Ghana seized the opportunity to propose an African high command and a force of intervention to rescue nations like Tanganyika. But the government was intent on recuperating its full freedom of action and did not want any OAU peace-keeping force. Since the Congo crisis, indeed, no African state was willing to receive an even partially autonomous force on its territory. What Tanganyika wanted was a loan of units from other African armies until such time as it could rely on its own army again. The task of the OAU was one of intermediary and it was not deemed necessary to set up any body to supervise or even advise during the operation. Nevertheless, the moral role of the Organization in making the arrangements and the aura of unity with which they were surrounded were very important.

Eventually, it was decided that the British should be replaced by three battalions of African troops and an air wing. The Tanganyikan government would at all times be in charge of the operation. It would choose the states from which to ask this aid; the troops would stay only six months (until a new national army was trained) unless requested to stay longer; and all the African troops would be under its direction and control. Any details of the operation and costs would be worked out between the Tanganyikan government and the states concerned. Already, by 23 March, the first Nigerian units began to arrive and the British started withdrawing. Ethiopian units came somewhat later. Soon there was no trace of Tanganyika's painful tumble into unwanted and dangerous alignments.

Notes

1. The Times (London), 27 Jan. 1964.

2. Ibid., 28 Jan. 1964.

3. Ibid., 13 Feb. 1964.

D. Cold War in the Congo

The real test case for African non-alignment was the Congo. It had already been the scene of a great power confrontation, directly and through the United Nations, and it was still looked upon as a key to the continent. The government of national unity had ended the open rivalry and there was a brief lull, but foreign interests were never distant. And sufficient ideological material had been injected in the quarrel to make any conflict in the Congo part of the cold war. It would take considerable self-restraint by the Congolese and strenuous efforts by the Organization of African Unity to avoid intervention.

The short history of the Congo Republic was not promising. Since independence, the competing factions, rather than seek compromise or cooperation, had resorted to the help of outside powers to strengthen their position and overcome their enemies. This was true of all: Katanga, the Lumumbists and the central government. Even the conclusion of the first phase of the crisis was not a serious attempt at cooperation. Only because neither the central government nor the Lumumbists felt strong enough to run the country was a compromise accepted. When the rivalry resumed--eventually bursting into a chaotic civil war--there was every reason to fear that the opponents would again look beyond Africa for backing. The ideological tinge given the conflict domestically could only make the entrance of the great powers more rapid.

Cold War in the Congo?

When Moise Tshombe returned to the Congo, in order to reconcile and unite, the rebellion was spreading. It was carried from Kwilu into Orientale and Kivu provinces, the former Lumumbist strongholds, and eventually reached Stanleyville. The Armée Nationale Congolaise (ANC) was then in no position to stop the rebel wave and thus Tshombe's primary concern was to strengthen it. To do so, he turned towards his earlier friends and the traditional backers of the central government.

467

Most of Léopoldville's support came from the United States and, to a lesser extent, Belgium. Only a few weeks after Tshombe came to power, President Johnson decided to send Under-Secretary William Averell Harriman to Belgium to confer on the Congo and weighed the requests for more military aid. By 11 August, Washington announced that it planned to increase its military and economic aid and would provide air and ground transport equipment to the Congo for "transport functions" only. Neither power was to send troops. However, the United States soon went further and sent a number of light bombers, to "assure Congolese internal security." By mid-September there were already 34 US military aircraft in the Congo as well as a contingent of servicemen to guard them and assorted instructors and advisors.[1] At the same time, Tshombe began recruiting white mercenaries from among the Belgians and South Africans to spearhead his army and reorganized the gendarmes.

The return of the former Katangan leader provoked an immediate reaction from the Soviet Union. The day after Tshombe's arrival, Moscow warned that he was a threat to the territory's peace and soon began speaking of a "puppet regime." Shortly thereafter, it also complained that the United States was meddling in Congolese politics. When aid began to arrive, moreover, the Soviet Union denounced American and Belgian "armed intervention" in the Congolese civil war and criticized the American "machinations" for adding to world tension. Moscow hinted that it might also aid the rebels.[2] However, its support of the rebels had not awaited this public denunciation; the Soviet Union had taken its old place as backer and supplier of the left-wing opposition and the rebellion it led.

But a relative new-comer was far more active. China had already become pleased with the "excellent revolutionary situation" in the Congo under Cyrille Adoula and felt the insurrection was developing along the lines of the war in Vietnam.[3] This time it made a serious bid to influence the course of events in the continent and seemed to be acting on a dictum of Mao Tse-tung: if we take the Congo, we shall hold the whole of Africa. For some time China had been backing all branches of the Congolese rebellion. Pierre Mulele, who started the guerrilla campaign in Kwilu, was trained in China and had just recently returned from Peking. Taking advantage of the enmity between Léopoldville and certain neighbors, especially Brazzaville, China moved into a number of countries surrounding the Congo. Through its embassy in Brazzaville,

China gave aid to Gbenye's National Liberation Committee and had a hand in running the training camps. Relations with Brazzaville progressed so well that by 23 November 1964 it was able to conclude a Treaty of Friendship and Co-operation. There was also a suspiciously large staff (including experts in guerrilla warfare) at the Embassy at Usumbura, where the leader of the rebellion in the eastern Congo, Gaston Soumialot, had his headquarters. Near the scene of the worst fighting they were able to advise and supply the rebels. By 1 August, Tshombe declared that he had "incontrovertible proof" of support and financing of the CNL by China, and referred to the weapons and documents seized after the attack on Bolobo.[4]

It was clear enough that the Congo was being turned into a battlefield of the cold war. This trend could not be stopped by Prime Minister Tshombe's appeals or threats to foreign powers to keep out of the internal affairs of the country. Escalation was inherent in each new arms shipment to either side. The United States, increasingly suspicious of the Soviet Union and especially China, gradually stepped up its aid to Tshombe. The greater the reverses that the rebels suffered, the more China and the Soviet Union threw matériel into the fray.

Escalation was not inevitable: the Soviet Union had been rather discreet about its aid and the United States let itself be drawn into the conflict largely because of fear of Chinese involvement. Left to themselves the Americans and Soviets might have limited or avoided the escalation. Yet, as long as the rebels could obtain Chinese arms and therewith defeat the central government's army, the United States saw no choice but to back Tshombe. Briefly there seemed to be a last chance of disengagement. Léopoldville asked a number of African states for troops and it appeared that one or another might accept. Washington hailed this appeal for African troops and might have been willing to cover the costs of the operation.[5] Tshombe was encouraged to turn towards Africa and there was even some talk of an OAU "police force." With such a force, he promised, the Congo would be able to dismiss the mercenaries.[6] But Moscow (and the radicals) opposed the plan and this African presence never materialized.

The Congo Commission and Foreign Intervention.

When the Council of Ministers met in Addis Ababa, it had hoped to insert the conflict in an African context and to

relieve the external pressure. But it was not able to find an
alternative policy to permit Prime Minister Tshombe to forgo
foreign assistance in his attempt to restore order. The Council did not provide any massive plan of peace-keeping either,
whereby the Organization of African Unity would move in and
separate the parties while isolating the Congo from the outside
world. The resolution of 10 September 1964 merely included
a strong appeal "to all powers at present intervening in the internal affairs of the Democratic Republic of the Congo to
cease their interference." No action was envisaged to implement this appeal aside from the suggestion that the diplomatic
missions of the member states "impress" the need on the intervening powers.

This point was not included in the terms of reference
of the OAU Commission established to deal with the domestic
and African aspects of the crisis. Nevertheless, the Congo
Commission did not see how its other tasks could be accomplished as long as foreign powers continued to intervene and
fed the civil war. With outside backing, the struggle was
made more bitter and the resistance of the opponents strengthened. Already, after its first meeting in Nairobi, the Commission felt the need to act. On 22 September, President
Kenyatta explained that

> ... it is the feeling of the Commission that with-
> out the withdrawal of all foreign military interven-
> tion in the Congo, the Commission cannot find the
> right atmosphere for a solution. We find that while
> the Congo is still supplied with the material of de-
> struction the peace we intend to make in the Congo
> cannot be achieved.[7]

Although all intervention had to be withdrawn, the Commission unfortunately did not plan a comprehensive drive
against all the intervening powers. For the moment it was
only intended to send a delegation to President Johnson of the
United States to ask him to stop American military support of
the Tshombe regime. But the Commission did not indicate
that other visits would follow or even point out which other
states had to be discouraged from intervention.

This one-sided approach was sharply criticized by the
Congolese government and the mission to Washington was rejected as interference in the Congo's internal affairs by President Kasavubu on 23 September. The same day, Washington
informed the OAU that it "could not agree to discuss our aid

to the Congo without the participation of the Congolese Government at whose request our aid is given."[8] The Americans
were particularly annoyed that they, who were openly helping
the legal authorities put down a rebellion, had been singled
out and that no mention was made of those secretly aiding the
rebels, especially China.

The climate in Washington when the mission arrived on
24 September was distinctly chilly. Still, the delegates were
received by the Secretary for African Affairs, G. Mennen
Williams, and managed to negotiate with Secretary of State
Rusk. There were even some tentative results to show for
the effort. As a token of cooperation with the OAU, it was
suggested that the American planes should be disarmed and
grounded during the time the Commission was trying to bring
about a reconciliation. The State Department insisted that
there were no reasons of prestige or gain underlying its action in the Congo. However, if the Commission desired a
withdrawal of American assistance, it was essential to find
some means of filling the gap left by the withdrawal.

For this offer to be effective, it was indispensable for
the OAU or its Commission to provide some compensation for
American concessions. Since the Council of Ministers had so
recently failed to create an African force or to impose a
cease-fire and settlement in the Congo, there was little chance
the Organization could fill the gap. But another follow-up was
possible. After visiting the United States, it was only natural
to urge that equal concessions be made by the other side in
the cold war. Washington might have been willing to cut back
its aid to Tshombe if Moscow and Peking did the same with
the rebels. To ascertain this, and show its impartiality, the
next urgent step should have been for the Congo Commission
to send a delegation to the Soviet Union and China. This it
never did. The possibility of agreement with the United States
was missed.

The Stanleyville Operation.

All the while the Tshombe regime had been pursuing
the war. With the mercenaries, aircraft and steady supplies
of military equipment, it was possible to make the Congolese
National Army a tougher fighting force and to throw back the
rebels. Slowly but surely the ANC closed in on the rebel
capital. At the same time the rebels stiffened their position
and prepared for a pitched battle. As they retreated, they

brought with them the foreign population of the region and
eventually concentrated some 1,500 whites and Asians in and
about Stanleyville. There were teachers, doctors, missionaries and nuns, businessmen, and traders. However, as the
war turned against them--owing largely to Western aid--the
differences became blurred and many of the rebels wished to
wreak vengeance on the white population in their hands or use
them as a bargaining point. At the beginning of September,
General Olenga announced that he was holding all the white
men, women and children in Stanleyville as hostages against
air raids by the Congo government.[9]

        Certain actions of the rebels seemed irrational and
did not bode well for the safety of the hostages. Tension
rose when a medical missionary, Dr. Paul Carlson, was
accused of being an "American major" and tried for spying.
Then the rebel radio blamed the United States and Belgium for
the air raids and put all the whites under house arrest. Finally, the rebel leaders demanded that these states cease their
"participation" in the fighting as a condition for freeing the
hostages. The crisis broke in mid-November, when they decided to execute Carlson as a spy, although agreeing in principle to negotiate with the American Consul. Secretary Rusk
warned the rebels that they would be responsible for Carlson's
life, but he also tried to avoid the worst and urged the OAU
to save him and the other foreigners in a message to Kenyatta.

        In the meanwhile, the ANC was preparing to attack.
Soon government troops led by the mercenaries would open the
drive and the prospects for the hostages were not good. However, when Gbenye offered to hold talks with the United States
in Kenya and the various representatives arrived in Nairobi,
there was a glimmer of hope. But the rebels wanted more
than just the evacuation of the civilians, they demanded a
cease-fire. This demand was also made by President Kenyatta. The Americans and Belgians refused to negotiate the
safety of the hostages under pressure and they would not, or
could not, halt the Congolese army on the threshold of the decisive battle. Almost as they started, the discussions reached an impasse.

        In Stanleyville, the situation had become terribly con-
fused and unpredictable. The rebel radio began broadcasting
threats of a horrible fate for the hostages if the ANC came
into sight. Passions were aroused in Europe and America and
the governments were called upon to save their nationals.

Meanwhile, the United States and Belgium, in agreement with the Congolese government, had been mobilizing for a "rescue mission." Two battalions of Belgian paratroopers and American transport planes gathered on the British island of Ascension (St. Helena). Then, on 24 November, the paratroopers were dropped at dawn, just in time to save most of the hostages although some had already been killed. Soon the ANC invested the city and began follow-up operations.

This last minute rescue was greeted with a sigh of relief in the West. But it unleashed a vast wave of indignation and hatred in Africa. Messages of protest and anger flooded the ad hoc Commission when it met for the second time in Nairobi, three days later. The operation had been a rude awakening for the delegates. Years after independence, it was still possible for foreign powers to openly intervene and determine the course of events in the continent. They had been severely shocked by the arrival of American planes carrying Belgian paratroopers to the heart of Africa. The purpose of the mission was largely forgotten.

After expressing bitter criticism in its debates, the OAU Commission "strongly condemns and protests against foreign military intervention in the Congo" by the United States, Belgium and Britain. Clearly on the defensive, the three countries tried to stress the purely "humanitarian" aspect and denied this was an act of intervention since it had been authorized by the Congo. This was confirmed by Prime Minister Tshombe, who explained that "the humanitarian Belgian action was authorized by my Government, and was received with great satisfaction by the majority of the population." He then attacked the Soviet Union and the Africans who condemned the operation. Insisting that the intervention came from other quarters, he added that China was still giving the rebels machine-guns and ammunition.[10]

The debates in the United Nations throughout December were no less impassioned. There was nearly complete agreement among the African delegates that any interference in the continent's affairs was dangerous and reprehensible. Even some of the more moderate outdid themselves in proving their African patriotism by condemning the United States, Belgium and Great Britain. Tshombe was also severely taken to task for permitting the operation and profitting from the rebel defeat. Some of the delegates complained that a strong enough effort had not been made to settle the matter peacefully before intervening. Others went so far as to speak of planned ag-

gression and hint at an insidious imperialist plot for crushing
the rebels and recolonizing the Congo. Relatively few supported the Congo's right to authorize the mission or showed understanding for the attenuating circumstance of the need to
save the hostages. Particularly disconcerting were the definitely racist overtones of the most abusive statements and accusations. Each side tended to count its dead and salve its
injured pride while remaining indifferent to the losses of the
other.

        In their own defense, the US and Belgium stressed the
fact that for a long time intervention had been rife in the Congo and that others were as or more guilty than they. They
had given their support to the legal government and they had
requested an authorization before landing in Stanleyville.
Others were aiding the rebels and showed little concern for
the consequences. The culprits were not only outsiders like
China and the Soviet Union, but also African countries like
Brazzaville, Burundi, Algeria, Ghana, Sudan, and the UAR.
In the light of their own behavior, the most scathing critics
of the Stanleyville operation could hardly make a convincing
plea for non-intervention and this task fell to the moderates.

        Despite the animated debate, little could be done. The
state directly concerned, the Congo, had authorized the action
and gained from it. Moreover, by 29 November, the hostages
had already been flown out, the paratroopers were evacuated
and the operation was liquidated. When the Africans held
their own meeting as the Council of Ministers of the OAU,
from 16-21 December, all that could be done was to adopt a
resolution condemning the "recent foreign military intervention
in the Democratic Republic of the Congo, which is disturbing
the peace and security of the African continent." All powers
involved in the Congo were also urged "to cease such inter-
ferences in order to enable the Organization of African Unity
to work for the achievement of national reconciliation." But
no action was proposed.

        The African Ministers then called upon the Security
Council of the United Nations "to condemn the recent foreign
military interventions which had compromised the efforts being made by the O.A.U. to secure national reconciliation in
the Congo." Despite the fury of the preceding debates, there
was only a muffled echo in the Security Council resolution of
30 December, which merely deplored the "recent events" in
the Congo and requested all states "to refrain or desist from
intervening in the domestic affairs of the Congo."

The OAU Takes Over.

Terribly little could be done about the Stanleyville affair, especially since it was now a thing of the past. Then,
for some reason, Africa's wrath was deflected to the United
Nations. There was little to reproach in the second phase of
the Congolese crisis. After having left the peace-keeping
force in the Congo an extra year at the request of the Adoula
government, the last troops were withdrawn and the UN maintained only its technical assistance. When Tshombe came to
power and appealed for military aid, the Secretary-General
had opposed large-scale military aid to the Congo and spoke
of the "undesirable consequences" it could have. Again, just
before the Stanleyville operation, he warned about "undesirable
consequences."[11] There had never been any question of the
United Nations' intervening. In reply to Tshombe's early request that it help curb infiltration by communist agents in the
Congo, U Thant had admitted that the situation was "very bad,"
but he did not see any new role for the world organization.[12]

Nevertheless, in their urge to be sole masters of the
continent, the Africans also turned against the United Nations.
Taking advantage of the possibility offered by the Charter,
they demanded that the Congolese affair be transferred to the
OAU. Meeting in UN Headquarters in New York, the Council
of Ministers made two other pleas to the Security Council on
21 December: "to recommend an African solution to the Congo problem" and "to recommend to all Powers concerned that
they co-operate with the O.A.U. in order to facilitate the solution of the Congolese problem."

Although neither its top officials nor the great powers
showed any desire to have the United Nations become entangled in major operations in the Congo again, this was a
disavowal of the world body. In a week the matter was
clinched and the OAU was recognized as the appropriate tool
for dealing with the Congo. The Security Council resolution
of 30 December repeatedly referred to the OAU resolution on
the Congo and reaffirmed certain of its articles. It "encourages the Organization of African Unity to pursue its efforts ..."
and "requests all states to assist the Organization of African
Unity in the attainment of these objectives." More generally,
the Security Council was "convinced that the Organization of
African Unity should be able ... to help find a peaceful solution to all the problems and disputes affecting peace and security in the continent of Africa."

The OAU had now taken over from the United Nations and renewed its appeal against foreign intervention. But it did not keep the initiative. No further action or even proposals were forthcoming from the Congo Commission. Yet, it was clear that a major wave of intervention had begun. After Stanleyville, the Soviet Union had charged that the airdrop was "gross active intervention" and China spoke of a "brutal crime." However, rather than deter them, this was a sign that they had to act quickly to avoid a collapse of the rebels. China promised to take "all possible measures" and increased its supplies. This time not discreetly, the Russians provided the arms that were being channelled through the Sudan and, according to Communist bloc sources, the Soviet Union helped pay the airlift by Algeria and the UAR.[13]

The United States was now much less active. Earlier already the Americans felt that the war had turned in favor of the central government and the Stanleyville clash was decisive. They had also realized the danger of backing even a legitimate government in such a bitter quarrel and became extremely cautious. The message was put across pointedly after the rescue operation when, following Kenyatta's condemnation of this intervention, groups of angry demonstrators stoned the American, Belgian and British Embassies in Nairobi. In face of the criticism heaped on them and Tshombe in the general hate campaign that followed, Washington was embarrassed about giving open support. It only tried to explain the humanitarian nature of the mission and protested that the rebels were even then obtaining weapons from the USSR and China, as well as certain African states.

Although this growing intervention was notorious, it was not picked up or criticized by the Congo Commission in the months before the Council of Ministers. And, after this, the Nairobi meeting in February 1965 was too divided to do more than make a weak appeal to the "other powers" not to aggravate the situation.

Notes

1. The New York Times, 13 & 18 Aug. and 24 Sept. 1964.

2. Ibid., 13 & 26 Aug. 1964.

3. Ibid., 25 June 1964.

4. _Ibid._, 2 Aug. 1964.

5. _Ibid._, 19 Aug. 1964.

6. _Ibid._, 7 Sept. 1964.

7. _Ibid._, 23 Sept. 1964.

8. _Ibid._, 24 Sept. 1964.

9. _Ibid._, 4 Sept. 1964.

10. _The Times_ (London), 1 Dec. 1964.

11. _Ibid._, 21 Aug. and 22 Nov. 1964.

12. _The New York Times_, 22 Aug. 1964.

13. _Ibid._, 26 & 27 Nov. and 7 Dec. 1964.

E. War in Biafra

Secession and the consequent civil war in Nigeria seem
ed to contain the seeds of a much broader crisis. As the state
threatened to dissolve there was fear that the quarrel would
not be limited to the Nigerians but that the rivals would seek
and find allies more than willing to benefit from the circumstances. Indeed, Biafra was pointedly (although misleadingly)
compared with Katanga by its opponents and General Gowon
expressed concern that his country would become another Congo.

Although basically a split on tribal lines, the civil war
had other dimensions. The North was largely Muslim; the
East, Christian or animist. The North was still feudal and
backward; the East had long prided itself on a progressive out
look. The Ibos were possibly the most modernizing and dynamic people in Nigeria. But the Federal Executive Council,
with Commissioners from many minority or Christian tribes,
and especially the Yoruba participation in the war effort blurred the lines. Still, even if neither side was willing to commit itself ideologically, Biafra looked towards the more enlightened countries for aid and Lagos instinctively turned to
the usual supporters of the status quo.

On Their Best Behavior.

Great Britain had long been proud of its most brilliant
possession in Africa and then of the federation and great democratic experiment its colonial administrators had created.
The relations with independent Nigeria were also very close
and warm. When the crisis broke out there was genuine dis-
appointment. However, Britain had interests and ties in all
parts of the country and tried to keep out of the internal conflict. It chose a policy of neutrality in order to preserve
the most possibilities of future action. Although it did not
wish to take sides, London preferred the older and more con-
genial leaders in Lagos to the new men in Enugu. From the
start the Foreign Office warned the Ibos that it could not approve of secession by Biafra.

478

By the same token, it would seem that the rest of the Federation had some claim to aid from its ally. Nevertheless, at first Britain was reluctant to provide any support. This attitude was hard to maintain as the war went against the federal government and Lagos repeatedly appealed for arms to stop Biafra's advance and as protection against its tiny air force, the old B-26 bomber that menaced the capital. But it was not until fully a month after hostilities began that London accepted to send a "small quantity" of "defensive" arms, mainly anti-aircraft guns.[1] However, once this new policy of active neutrality was initiated there was a tendency to send ever greater amounts of material. Although it wished to restrict its participation, Britain remained a major supplier of the army it had created.

The United States and other Western powers also tried to maintain their neutrality, and it was much easier for them to avoid being drawn into the war. Washington regretted the tragedy in a friendly state and one of the stabilizing elements in Africa. But Nigeria was not really in its sphere of influence and it wished to avoid unnecessary involvement. It did not provide military aid. And, although it did not conspicuously condemn Biafra, it offered no encouragement. When Enugu tried to force its hand by sending a mission to Washington, the delegation was sent away and the State Department stressed that it did not recognize Biafra's existence. There were occasional rumors of sympathy or aid to the Biafran cause later. So, as the war entered its eighth month, the United States set things straight by confirming that it recognized Lagos as the only legal government in Nigeria and had "in no way encouraged, supported or otherwise been involved" in the secessionist movement.[2]

Rather unexpectedly, when the Federal Military Government did obtain massive aid and air coverage, it came from the Communist bloc. On 23 August, Lagos announced that Nigeria had acquired Soviet aircraft and military equipment as well as technical assistance "on a strictly commercial and cash basis." The Soviet Union delivered sixteen MIG-17 and seven Czech Delfin fighters, joined by three Ilyuchin-28 bombers procured by way of the UAR. It was reported that 165 military personnel and technicians accompanied the shipment. Radio Biafra immediately charged that Lagos had joined a "diabolic collusion" with Moscow to "communize Nigeria and Africa" and that Gowon had "traded massive Soviet military aid to Nigeria for a contract assigning Nigerian oil concessions to the USSR." But this aid caused concern in other quarters as

well.   Washington issued a statement in which it expressed
regret that the Soviet Union was sending extensive shipments
of jets to Nigeria.   Moscow had thus injected an "element of
great power competition in the internal affairs of a friendly
state."3

Some years earlier, in a similar context, the Soviet
Union could have been expected to appear on the side of a progressive regime and, from the start, Biafra had carefully underlined its "progressivism."   At any rate, it was improbable
that Moscow would have helped rescue what was still an Anglo-
American fief.   But its ideological foreign policies had not
paid off in Africa and this time it took a more realistic and
calculating approach.   It may have been true that any Nigerian
government would remain under the domination of the conservative pro-British North.   However, since the former regimes
had kept out all Soviet influence, it clearly had nothing to lose
and something to gain by becoming the supplier of a hard-
pressed government.   This would be an entry in the larger
and more important part of the country even if Biafra remained independent.   And, by waiting until August, it was possible
to test the wind: Lagos was open to Soviet overtures for
closer links, its army was able to win the war, and it was
actively or passively backed by the whole African community.
This new stand even gave the USSR a certificate of good conduct as the champion of existing regimes.   It also fit in particularly well with the new policy of aid to the Arab and Muslim states.

At any rate, with overwhelming superiority in the air,
the federal forces rapidly turned the tide of the battle and the
Biafran army was rolled back.   More even than Great Britain
or the United States, the Soviet Union took its stand as the
guarantor of the central government and the status quo.   In a
personal message on 16 October, Prime Minister Kosygin assured General Gowon of "Soviet support in preserving Nigeria's
unity and in developing economic and cultural contacts."   He
added that he opposed all interference in the internal affairs of
states in Africa.   Two weeks later, a £20 million credit was
announced.4   From then on there was a constant barrage of
propaganda against Biafran secession and the alleged backing
of imperialist and neo-colonialist forces seeking to divide Africa.

Although the war dragged on for months, Biafra was
not able to convince any of its more or less natural allies to
help it.   The pleas against Hausa-Fulani imperialism did not

convince the Communist East or the liberal West. It had little success in bargaining away its natural wealth with greedy
powers or private interests. Even if some such opportunism
could have been expected while Biafra was winning the war,
there was considerably less enthusiasm for backing a loser.
However, after it had been thrown back to its own territory
and was on the defensive, it started receiving more aid. This
came from an equally unlikely source. Biafra purchased material from arms merchants and weapons and ammunition were
flown in regularly to Port Harcourt. The essential link was
Portugal, which permitted or promoted an operation that used
bases in its African possessions. Lisbon had no sympathy or
illusions about Biafra, but the longer the war lasted the more
it embarrassed independent Africa and diverted attention from
the colonies.

There was also some danger of another serious case of
mercenaries. An old Congo hand like Colonel Mike Hoare had
visited Biafra, where he found the position hopeless and even
warned his erstwhile colleagues to keep out so the fight would
be short. But he was not heeded and former Katanga and Foreign Legion types came. A commando brigade was set up under Rolf Steiner. This time mercenaries appeared from a
new source as well. Nigeria had a growing air force and no
pilots. These were provided by the UAR and Egyptians flew
the jet fighters and bombers that pounded Biafra.

Despite early fears, Nigeria was saved from the cold
war. To the contrary, there was a new sort of competition
between the great powers. In a way, it was the scene of what
Radio Biafra called the "British-Soviet conspiracy." For the
first time both major blocs were on the same side in an African crisis. With the Communists backing the wrong camp
ideologically, there was less hostility than tacit acceptance or
rivalry for Nigeria's favor. The West could hardly reproach
the Soviets for helping the central government crush a secession. And it may well have preferred sharing this dubious
honor. Moreover, since Africa also backed Lagos, there was
no complaint of interference.

Humanitarian Intervention.

The Nigerian civil war was one of the most destructive
in recent history. At first it was a forgotten war. Then finally public opinion realized its extent. The Biafrans had been
driven back to the Ibo heartland and, rather than surrender to

the federal troops, most of the civilians followed the army and were crammed into an increasingly small area. They were harrowed not only by artillery fire but also heavy bombing. Six million refugees and displaced persons lived in that narrowing circle. Food had run short and they faced starvation, especially among the aged, women and children. Soon there were thousands dying each day. Within a year, there were probably 100,000 casualties. The second year it neared a million. And there was considerable anxiety that the war might conclude with the disappearance of a whole people.

The dimensions of this disaster were first seen by the humanitarian and charitable organizations. Before the governments ever came to admit the existence of such a crisis, these voluntary agencies set up a call for help. As soon as the fighting broke out, the International Committee of the Red Cross (ICRC) dispatched representatives to both sides to safeguard the rules of war. It worked for the protection of prisoners of war and observation of the Geneva Convention on civilians. But the prisoners were not always given quarter and violations were numerous. Then the bombing of Biafra began. The targets were chosen rather indiscriminately and included hospitals, schools, churches and markets. Thousands of civilians died. Thus the Red Cross had to intervene time and again. All too often its protests fell on deaf ears. By then it was busy with the greater problems of malnutrition and disease.

Resistance was low and the civilian population succumbed to starvation. At this point many other humanitarian organizations launched their operations. Protestant churches in Scandinavia and Germany and the Catholic agency Caritas ran an unprecedented campaign to send food and medicine, and eventually coordinated their relief operations through Joint Church Aid. Oxfam in Britain and other independent bodies appealed for donations. UNICEF sent aid. Considerable help came from the American government which supplied foodstuffs and cash. It was joined by many other governments, especially in Scandinavia, France and Britain. But more funds, public and private, were constantly needed in an operation that ultimately ran into several hundred million dollars.

Soon relief supplies were arriving in Lagos, Fernando Póo and São Tomé. Although it was relatively easy to distribute them to the "liberated" areas, it was hard to reach the remnant where more and more people were living precariously Often foodstuffs accumulated in depots while a few hundred

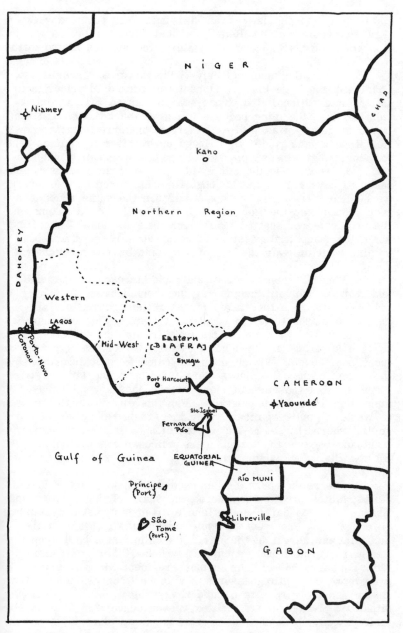

Nigeria, Biafra, and Their Neighbors

miles away the population was starving. The tremendously
difficult problem of the Red Cross and the other bodies was to
find some means of channelling aid to the victims of the war.

During the month of July 1968, the pressure built up.
Originally the Nigerian government had agreed in principle to
let the International Red Cross send planes to Biafra, but it
went back on the offer because it feared mercenaries and arms
would be flown in as well. Rather, it preferred sending relief along a land route from Enugu or by river to Biafran held
territory where the supplies would be taken and distributed by
the Red Cross. On the other side, the Biafran leaders refused to have relief pass through Nigerian territory. They
were afraid the federal troops would use the same route to attack, could stop the flow of supplies at will and, it seems,
the people feared that the food would be poisoned. Mutual
suspicion made it impossible to reach an agreement and bargaining went on over the use of air, land or river corridors.

Finally, when no agreement could be reached, the ICRC
and Joint Church Aid decided to run the blockade. The
boldest action was thus taken by the relief agencies. They
chartered planes to fly in supplies at night. They were prepared to ignore government demands if this was the only way
to save hundreds of thousands of lives. Unfortunately, even
then, not enough food and medicine came for all. During
these operations, the planes were fired upon and landing strips
bombed. But the humanitarian organizations accepted these
risks to succor the population. For this, they won the praise
of Western public opinion. They also reaped the anger of Nigeria, where they were under suspicion by the federal government and became the targets of a vicious press campaign
against Biafra's "partners in crime."

The relief operations enjoyed the support of the United
States, which provided an increasing share of the supplies and
finance, offered cargo planes and exerted diplomatic pressure
on occasion. President Johnson had already singled out the
humanitarian aspect of the war. He called upon both sides to
let international relief reach the civilians. For some time
after January 1969 it seemed that President Nixon would take
even more energetic measures. Various Congressmen visited
Biafra and their reports painted a very bleak picture of the
situation. Nixon himself had expressed concern over the "terrible tragedy." "Genocide is what is taking place right now--
and starvation is the grim reaper."[5] Nevertheless, despite
appeals from the public and suggestions of Colonel Ojukwu,

Washington did not seek to influence either side politically or offer mediation and restricted itself to humanitarian aid.

By the end of the year the humanitarian agencies seemed to have stemmed the tide of starvation and were providing essential relief for several million people. But new problems arose with the independence of Equatorial Guinea in 1968, the closest base and the one used by the ICRC. Under pressure from Lagos, and then because of internal disturbances, the flights were suspended repeatedly and much of the aid ceased. Thus a further base was opened in Dahomey on 1 February 1969 and soon afterwards, President Francisco Macias[6] of Equatorial Guinea authorized a renewal of flights from Santa Isabel. At the same time, a more serious crisis was building up, for Lagos had obtained aircraft for night missions and the relief planes might be destroyed. So far the Nigerian government had tacitly accepted these flights but it never approved and they were undertaken at the risk of the relief agencies.

The situation took a sharp turn for the worse in May 1969. At the beginning of the month a relief plane crashed near Uli and several weeks later the head of ICRC operations, Ambassador August Lindt, was arrested at the airport in Lagos. He was later released. Then, on 5 June, a clearly marked Red Cross plane was deliberately shot down by a MIG and the following day the Nigerian government announced that it would not permit night flights. The International Red Cross accepted this decision and its supplies to Biafra ceased while it sought a new basis for its operations. Attacked as a spy and agent of the Western powers by the local press, it was also harassed by the government. August Lindt was declared "persona non grata" while the Nigerian Red Cross prepared to take over the control of all operations in the country. Temporarily the Joint Church Aid also decided to suspend its flights.

Since the relief operations began it had been possible to avoid the worst. Without being able to feed the population adequately at least the number of deaths could be reduced and basic care provided. When the flights ceased the few reserves very rapidly disappeared and kwashiorkor and other forms of malnutrition ravaged the population. There was no more medicine in the hospitals. And the physical destruction of Biafra resumed. The efforts and money from the outside world had only provided a brief respite for hundreds of thousands of refugees. As the death rate rose alarmingly there were renewed efforts from the West and several African countries to reach

a new modus vivendi. Appeals were made in Washington,
Paris, the Vatican and the United Nations. Eventually Mi-
chael Steward restored the contacts between the Red Cross and
Lagos. General Gowon's offer to permit day flights was hailed
as an unparalleled act of clemency and the head of the Foreign
Office challenged Biafra to reciprocate.

Yet the situation was not that simple. Biafra had undoubtedly benefitted from night flights which covered the arrival of arms. But day flights implied a distinct advantage
for Nigeria. There was reason to fear that Lagos could use
relief flights as cover for an attack on Uli. Moreover, the
offer of day flights included the condition that each plane pass
by an airfield in Nigeria so that its cargo could be inspected.
Aside from a loss of time, this meant that Lagos would control the flow of supplies to its enemy. In its repeated attempts at working out a more balanced plan, the ICRC met
with little understanding and in mid-September it had to accept
the Nigerian offer, immediately rejected by Biafra.

Nevertheless, a solution could have been found. Some
of the complaints implied a misuse of the relief facilities.
The Biafrans might introduce arms or the Nigerians tamper
with supplies. This could have been prevented by inspection
at the take-off and landing points or accompanying shipments
by land or river. To dissipate any suspicion representatives
of both parties could participate. There was also the question
of military advantage. Each side put forward plans that hampered the opponent's operations and feared it would not demili-
tarize any corridors. This could have been dealt with by a
neutral committee defining the corridors and observers to control them. All this could have been organized by the Red
Cross and, to lend any plan greater authority, the OAU could
have set up a permanent committee and inspection and observation teams including representatives of states recognizing and
rejecting Biafra. However, rather than accept such arrangements, each side sought to impose its plan and the OAU, despite several attempts, never tried hard enough to make them
cooperate.

France and Biafra.

It was only rather late in the war that any extra-African power expressed support of Biafra. For over a year
France had looked on in silence. The government carefully
kept out of the conflict although this stance was not always

taken by individuals. There were mercenaries in Biafra and rumors that French companies sought commercial advantages and particularly oil concessions. But Nigeria was still of very secondary interest. French investments there were only 10 per cent of the total and only 30 per cent of this was in the East. True, there were many potential gains if Biafra remained independent. Yet the first gestures of solidarity came at a time when no gains were to be had. Biafra was only a fifth its original size and there seemed to be no hope it would survive. There was also some doubt whether the Ibos would survive either.

It was then that France acted. On 31 July 1968, a first allusion was made to the self-determination of the "Biafran people." Later on de Gaulle insisted that a military victory could not settle the problem. Only a political solution would provide a satisfactory conclusion. And this had to take into account the personality of the Biafran people. For some time public opinion had warmed to the cause and now the government seemed to gravitate towards recognition. This led to friction with Nigeria and riots, especially in the North, where France was denounced for encouraging Ojukwu. Although the support was still only moral, there was a rabid press campaign against interference in Nigerian internal affairs. It reached a peak on 9 September, when President de Gaulle expressed his views on the problem. After questioning the validity of federal systems that grouped different and even opposed peoples, he turned to the situation in the Federation of Nigeria.

> Indeed, why should the Ibos, who are mainly Christians, who live in the south in a certain way and who have their own language, why should they be subject to another ethnic fraction of the Federation? For that is what is happening. As soon as the colonizer withdraws his authority in an artificial federation, one ethnic element imposes its authority on the others.

> Even before there was the present drama of Biafra, one could wonder how Nigeria could live, in view of all the crises the Federation was going through. And now that there is this heinous, shocking drama, now that Biafra has proclaimed its independence and that the Federation, in order to bring it to heel, is using warfare, blockade, extermination and starvation, how can one conceive that the peo-

ples of the Federation, including the Ibos, will
resume their life in common?

In this affair, France has helped Biafra to the extent of her capabilities. She has not taken the action which for her would be decisive: recognition
of the Biafran Republic. For, she feels that the
gestation of Africa is, above all, the affair of the
Africans. Already some states in East and West
Africa have recognized Biafra. Others seem to be
pointing in this direction. That is to say that, for
France, the decision which has not been taken is
not excluded in the future. Besides, one can imagine that the Federation, realizing the impossibility
of remaining with its present organization, may
transform itself into some union or confederation
in which would be established both Biafra's right
to self-determination and the bonds that would remain between it and the whole of Nigeria.[7]

This statement was severely criticized in Lagos, and
France was increasingly seen as behind all efforts to aid Biafra. It was accused of pure mischief-making and trying to
blackmail the rest of the Francophone states into recognizing
the break-away regime. But it was hard to conclude that
Gabon and the Ivory Coast, which had recognized Biafra several months earlier, acted at France's behest. For their leaders were no less doubtful about the viability of outsized federations. Nor did they feel that the price of unity should be the
destruction of a people. Perhaps it was they who used their
influence to have de Gaulle protest and draw the world's attention to the situation.

President de Gaulle's words had a considerable impact.
Colonel Ojukwu expressed his gratitude for the courageous
stand and France was praised as Biafra's closest friend. It
was hoped that other states would follow the lead and for some
time a number hesitated. It was this slender hope that gave a
new vigor to the campaign and stiffened the position of the
Biafran leaders. Still, in the end, the secessionist regime
was no less isolated.

Of course, moral disapproval of the war could not
change its course. Self-determination had become a question
of fire-power and the army was running short of ammunition.
For some time it had fought with the stocks bought before and
just after secession, arms captured from the enemy or made

in crude shops.   But the war was unexpectedly long and the
landing strips fell to the federal troops until only Uli was left.
As of mid-October 1968, however, things began to change.
The Biafran soldiers were increasingly well armed and took
the initiative again.   They did not have as much material as
he federal troops, but they managed to consolidate the front.
This was traced back to supplies of French weapons, apparently flown in from Libreville and Abidjan with French cooperation if not direct aid. [8]

Biafra received a second wind.   However, by then, the
rebel nation had been reduced to only part of the former Ibo
heartland.   No matter what happened, it was improbable that
it would expand and certainly not into the minority tribe areas
where the federal government was well entrenched.   What
then was the purpose?   France would never get hold of the
oil concessions.   There was not much chance of a mishappen
and landlocked Biafra eventually being born.   All that remained was that it would become a slightly stronger party in the
war.   But it would have been tragic if the resurgence led only
to that.   The other alternative was Biafra as a party to negotiations.   If the Ibos were not crushed militarily, they would
not be forced to surrender and accept whatever settlement was
imposed on them.   They could negotiate a compromise that to
some extent satisfied them and one they would be more likely
to honor.

Towards an African Solution?

In order to avoid intervention in African affairs, it was
necessary for any conflicts to be settled by the Africans themselves.   Unfortunately, this sort of action was not forthcoming.
The Organization of African Unity did not touch upon the problem until its Kinshasa meeting in September 1967, two months
after the war had begun.   Rather than go immediately, the
consultative Committee did not arrive in Lagos until six weeks
later, and the first serious attempt at mediation in Niamey
came after a year of bloodshed.   This meant that others had
to think of compromise or urge an end to the war.   Initiatives
were actually taken by Great Britain and the Commonwealth,
the Vatican and the United Nations.   And the meaning or very
existence of an "African solution" had to be reassessed.

Actually, it was the bleeding of Biafra that aroused
awareness of its cause.   More and more it became known--
especially in the Western world--that a people was fighting for

independence and being crushed by overwhelming force. To
avoid sharing this responsibility several European countries
placed an embargo on arms to both sides. There was also
interest in mediation to end the war. The bases for such a
solution were not very clear and no state espoused an independent Biafra. Still, its position might be strengthened by
such action.

The first real initiative for peace came from the Vatican. Three quarters of the people living in the Eastern Region were Christian and, of them, half were Catholics. But,
for all men the Pope appealed for a cease-fire as Christmas
approached. Then, on 22 December 1967, two papal envoys
arrived in Lagos to try to arrange a truce. They were also
received by Colonel Ojukwu and, on 9 February, he announced
that Biafra was prepared to accept a cease-fire and negotiate
an honorable peace. Frequently thereafter Pope Paul VI offered his services as mediator and, during his visit to Uganda
in August 1969, success seemed within reach. Having expressed his distress at the conflict consuming Nigeria, he did
everything in his power to bring the two sides together. Delegations were present from both Nigeria and Biafra and yet,
they did not meet. Nor was this the end of Vatican efforts as
the hierarchy sought ways of ending or alleviating the suffering.

A more successful attempt was made by the Commonwealth, which could claim particular interest in a settlement
since Nigeria was a member. The loose organization tried to
handle conflicts in an informal way that aroused little attention
and anxiety. This time it was the Secretary-General, Arnold
Smith, who managed to serve as a go-between. For some
time he was active contacting the authorities on both sides in
order to hold a meeting. It was not until May 1968 that it
came about. The discussions in London and the conference in
Kampala, held at his initiative and partly under his chairmanship, merely led to mutual accusations between the two enemies and a refusal to compromise. Some sort of pressure
was needed to bring the sides closer together.

One source of pressure was Britain, as it appeared to
be having second thoughts. Her Majesty's Government had
continued supplying arms and ammunition regularly to Nigeria.
This was its duty as a friend and ally. Still, it was surprisingly apologetic. It insisted that it sent only 15 per cent of
the total (while opponents claimed 50 per cent). In public,
the Commonwealth Secretary George Thomson defended the

policy by stressing that Britain only sent equipment in "carefully controlled quantities," provided none of the aircraft responsible for the worst damage, and explaining that most of the victims did not die of the war but of famine. As a positive argument, London maintained that it could restrain Lagos and calm the war or help negotiate peace. Then the Government offered Ł250,000 for relief and sent an official mission under Lord Hunt to see how the refugees could be aided. Meanwhile, it faced an increasingly irate public. Some sectors were disgusted at the deaths sacrificed to "unity." Demonstrations had been initiated by Biafran students, and they were soon joined by others. The Labour Party was under attack from its own left-wingers and repeatedly side-stepped any major debate.

Some of the campaign in Britain was pro-Biafran or humanitarian and the government had solid political reasons for backing Nigeria, reasons that were shared by the Conservatives. And it was willing to participate in any rescue operation, while blaming every failure on Ojukwu. But Labour had claimed to have some leverage with Lagos, and it was repeatedly challenged to prove this and shorten the war. Unfortunately, it was not in a very good position to mediate. Britain had had the closest relations with people on both sides. Originally it would have been able to work for a settlement. However, since it had become a busy supplier of the Nigerian army, it was seriously distrusted if not hated in Biafra. Eventually efforts were made. In June 1968, Lord Shepard was the first government official to meet with a Biafran representative. Later, the Commonwealth Secretary left for Lagos with a personal message from Prime Minister Wilson. Still little changed. There was a faint hope of an international force as a means of reassuring the Ibos after the war. Apparently London also obtained, although quite briefly, a let-up in the bombing of civilian areas.

Nevertheless, even this attitude unsettled Lagos enough to launch a diplomatic counter-offensive. It played down the dimensions of the tragedy in Biafra and levelled its own charges of atrocities. Chief Enahoro came to London to defend his position. At the same time, he warned Britain of "grave consequences" if it stopped supplying arms to the federal government. For then "Nigeria would be compelled to turn elsewhere and this might involve British interests."[9] Moreover, it was already late for an effective British threat or even a useful lever. The Soviet Union was rapidly becoming the major supplier. With no internal difficulties, Moscow was able to give freely and throughout it kept supplying equipment, including jet fighters and bombers. It confidently posed as Nigeria's surest ally. Even if Britain slowed down, the USSR could have made up the difference. In exchange, Lagos had come around to signing economic and trade agreements, confided some of its development projects and even moved closer to the Soviet Union diplomatically.

There was little chance the Labour government would alter its position basically in the last phase of the war. Still, Prime Minister Wilson continued proding for a solution. Emissaries were sent to Lagos and Addis Ababa; General Gowon and the Emperor of Ethiopia were consulted on the possibility of negotiations. Finally, at the end of March 1969, Wilson went to Lagos himself. The initiative was rather awkward, since he did not plan to mediate or influence the Nigerian government, but merely to study the situation. He also mentioned that he might meet Colonel Ojukwu, a move that was poorly received by both parties and eventually came to naught. Wilson hoped to obtain more facilities for relief operations and securities for the Ibos after the war. His major goal seemed to be further peace talks, bringing together both leaders. But he did not propose any terms since he insisted that this was a matter for Africa and the OAU. On his way back, he stopped over in Addis Ababa and spoke to the Emperor briefly. Doubtlessly he offered his services to promote the Consultative Committee's work.[10]

He also spoke of an embargo of military supplies. This was the most important idea that had been voiced by a foreign statesman since the beginning of the crisis. The civil war in Nigeria, like every war in Africa, had been able to continue only because of the steady supply of weapons. Neither side had its own arms industry and the fighting was fed by aid, first to Lagos and then to Biafra. Once a stalemate had been reached, as happened at the beginning of 1969, further shipments only increased the intensity of the combat. It would take another big step in the escalation on one side to turn the tide again. However, if all shipments ceased, the two sides would have to stop fighting and seek a political settlement. It remained to spread the embargo to the other powers or introduce a blockade if need be; but practical aspects were the least difficult to solve. After the two years of warfare, there seemed to be some willingness among the supporting powers to slow down the war. It was less certain how the warring parties felt. Earlier, Azikiwe had included an embargo in his plan, and the Biafrans could thus avoid military defeat. A peaceful conclusion also had advantages for Nigeria as a whole. This was definitely something for the OAU to look into. But the Monrovia session of the Committee did not follow it up.

The only other quarter from which an initiative for peace could come was the United Nations. Yet the world organization remained silent longest. Despite the bloody warfare, no delegation brought the matter before the Security Council or the General Assembly. It was recognized that it would not be easy to restore peace and the members were worried about the consequences of another peace-keeping operation. Perhaps fearing also the alienation of OAU members, the UN had passed over the matter as an internal affair and an African affair as well.

So long as the Organization did nothing to end the worsening crisis, the pretext by the UN of deferring to the other's competence was only partially valid. As the war dragged on, the pressure grew. The Scandinavian states, Canada and Israel spoke of bringing the matter before the Security Council. Ultimately, what had been admitted in private occurred and the consensus in the world body was so solidly against action that it was never even submitted. Thereafter the discontent tended to focus on the Secretary-General, who was increasingly criticized for passiveness. But the fault lay much more with the member states, whose responsibility it was to demand action. The Secretary-General could, of course, have made appeals to the world's conscience. Instead, he preferred trying to convince those people in the best position to do something, the African Heads of State and Government.

At the Algiers Assembly, the most stirring call for action was made by U Thant. In words that troubled his audience, he described the situation:

> If I am unable to conceal my concern about developments stemming from the persistence of colonial and racial policies in Africa, even less can I refrain from expressing my distress and dismay at the mounting toll of destruction, starvation and loss of life resulting from the tragic fratricidal strife in Nigeria over the past year. As has been verified from impartial sources, a very large number of people, combatants and non-combatants alike, are either dying or undergoing acute suffering; many,

particularly children, are dying from, or are on
the verge of starvation. In the name of humanity,
it is essential that everything be done to help relieve the impact of this tragic conflict.

He then outlined the Organization's first steps and confirmed that "the O.A.U. should be the most appropriate instrument for the promotion of peace in Nigeria." He paid
tribute to the efforts of the OAU and its Consultative Committee. But he also stressed that the only way to end the plight
of the people was through a cessation of hostilities and the
negotiation of a permanent settlement. He concluded: "It is
my earnest hope that, pursuant to the practical steps and procedures thus far agreed upon, fruitful negotiations will take
place leading to a just solution which would guarantee the security of all the people of Nigeria."[11]

Once again, the matter was referred to the Organization of African Unity. No other state or international organization was prepared to replace it, although some offered their
cooperation. It was still up to the OAU to respond to these
calls. In the absence of any such effort, however, General
Ojukwu turned to the United Nations and then the neutral
states of Europe to mediate. But they were not eager to intervene either and early in December Bern agreed to take action, probably jointly with the other neutrals, only if both
sides consented.

At the same time, due to public disgust at the continuing bloodshed, Prime Minister Wilson was facing renewed
criticism of his policy. He defended the policy as the only
possible one and warned that other sources would replace British arms sales. He also sent Maurice Foley, Secretary for
African Affairs, on a fact-finding mission to Lagos, but not
Biafra, while Lord Carrington, Opposition leader in the House
of Lords, visited Biafra and Lagos. Yet no initiative for mediation materialized. A showdown was reached when many
members of both parties signed a motion calling on the government to revise its policy. Despite increasing dissatisfaction,
Wilson weathered the storm and, on 10 December, won approval for his policy in the House of Commons by 170 to 86.
The Soviet Union faced no such problem as it increased its
supplies to Nigeria.

The various sources of arms to Biafra, never clearly
identified but suspected to be France and the colonial powers
of southern Africa, also continued if at a slower pace. Biafra

even built up a little airforce to attack the enemy.   But open
support, except among Western public opinion, was waning.
The International Red Cross did not resume the forbidden
flights and there was some fear that the various church agencies would cease their flights, until Joint Church Aid firmly announced it would continue as long as the need existed.
On 4 January 1970, U Thant called on the "magnanimity" of
General Ojukwu to comply with the OAU resolution and seek
peace while adding, with a reference to Katanga, that the
United Nations could not accept the principle of a secession in
one of its member states.

Then Biafra collapsed.   Radio Moscow spoke of a "victory of the progressive forces of the African continent over
imperialism."   In the West feelings were mixed.   Above all,
among those who condemned as well as those who backed Biafra, there was a sigh of relief that finally the war had ended
and the bloodshed would cease.   The uppermost concern now
in London, Paris, Washington and the Vatican was to find
some means of protecting the innocent and rehabilitating the
refugees.   Pope Paul spoke somewhat hastily of a danger of
genocide but an even greater threat was that now that Uli had
fallen and the relief organizations' supplies stopped, there
would be increased suffering and starvation among the masses.
The Red Cross and Caritas wished to step up their aid, the
United Nations was called upon to act, and President Nixon offered massive aid while Maurice Foley went to Lagos to seek
some arrangement.

Then, on 13 January, General Gowon told the relief organizations to keep their "blood-stained money" and that Nigeria would handle the crisis alone.   The only authorized
bodies were the Nigerian Red Cross and the National Rehabilitation Commission.   Nigeria would accept no aid from
France, Portugal, Rhodesia or South Africa, because of their
hostile attitude, nor would it permit relief operations by those
who had worked illegally in Biafra, including the Joint Church
Aid, Caritas, and the French and Scandinavian Red Crosses.
For some time, it was hoped that the more neutral role of the
International Committee of the Red Cross would enable it to
coordinate operations but the authorization never came.   Time
was of the essence, yet it was clear that relief work would be
slower and more costly.   Food and medicine had to be flown
into Lagos, taken by truck to the former redoubt and distributed.   Thus, while the federal government resumed control over
the area and kept its sovereignty inviolate, the refugees strug-
gled to stay alive until help came.

Notes

1. Le Monde, 11 Aug. 1967.

2. The Herald Tribune, International Edition, 7 Feb. 1968.

3. Africa Report, Oct. 1967.

4. Ibid., Jan. 1968.

5. Ibid., 21 Sept. 1968, p. 1118.

6. Full name given in some references as Francisco Macias
    Ngnema.

7. Press Conference of 9 Sept. 1969, French Embassy, New
    York.

8. Le Monde, 17 Nov. 1968.

9. The Herald Tribune, International Edition, 13 June 1968.

10. House of Commons Debates, 2 April 1969, Hansard, p.
    486-500.

11. United Nations Press Release SG/SM/998, 13 Sept. 1968.

F. Conclusion

Originally, non-alignment had been a broad principle of the newly independent states and the line to follow in each case was more often than not uncertain and contested. The Charter provided no indication as to the Organization's role and, indeed, it would have been hard to tell in advance what it could do under varying circumstances. Nevertheless, the OAU gradually developed its own brand of non-alignment. Although nowhere near as ambitious as the original aspirations, it was a definite contribution to the well-being of the continent.

The OAU did not become a body to inspect and approve the policies of its members in foreign affairs. Rather, it tried to protect Africa from outside interference at critical moments. Resistance and discipline were low in the midst of crises and serious conflicts. At such times, individuals or states were tempted to accept assistance or curry favor outside the continent. If they wished to avoid or free themselves of commitments, they could turn to the Organization for help (and perhaps receive comparable assistance as well as aid in disentanglement). If there was a clear threat of involvement in a crisis or conflict, the African community could in concert try to convince those concerned to renounce the foreign assistance. Also, the OAU could attempt to persuade outside powers not to mix in African affairs.

Africa's Experiences.

The danger of interference in the continent's affairs was not as pervasive or permanent as had been feared, although it did become a serious problem in every conflict the Organization had to deal with. In times when the general status quo on the continent seemed likely to change, interested states sought to maintain their position or improve it by backing one of the sides. This was almost inevitable in "ideological" quarrels or where the stakes were high. Africa's potential wealth and might were tempting the outside powers to try to influence the outcome; the present military weakness of the independent states made it easier to do so.

Nevertheless, despite its very limited means, Africa was surprisingly successful at keeping its conflicts out of the cold war. In several cases, disputes were calmed before any intervention took place; in others the great powers remained on the side lines and supplied only arms or finance. Only in one case was there direct intervention. This record was most impressive when compared with the rest of the third world, where the great powers were wont to wage the cold war. Africa was in a far better position than the Middle East, Latin America or Asia. It had no Palestine, no Cuba and no Vietnam. These examples showed Africans the importance of maintaining the vigilance and discipline of the continent.

In the two boundary disputes, the involved parties tended to forget strictly territorial claims and injected an element of ideology. Still, they had been persuaded to end the hostilities rather than calling on their allies which, incidentally, were not very eager to intervene. Moreover, the conflicts were eventually brought before the African rather than the world organization. Although no settlement was found, the great powers were satisfied that things were in African hands.

The Tanganyikan mutinies provided a simple exercise in non-alignment. By sending African troops to replace the British ones, it was possible to save President Nyerere from slipping into an aligned, and contested, position despite himself. By limiting the British stay in its former colony, a Soviet reaction was made pointless.

OAU action in the Congo was less successful, particularly because Africa and the Organization were themselves too committed. No solution could be found to the civil war or to the bad relations between the Congo and its neighbors. The conflict had become too bitter and the parties refused to compromise. As the war dragged on, the positions only stiffened all around until finally there was no willingness to compromise in Africa. Both sides in the civil war repeatedly asked and received moral and material aid from the leaders of the rival super-power blocs. Since Africa in general was also polarized, some states backing the "legitimate" government and some, the "nationalists," it was in no position to give a lesson to outside powers or discourage their interference.

Nevertheless, the OAU's attempt at introducing a non-alignment and non-intervention policy in the Congolese crisis was far from a failure. First of all, there was broad agreement on the attitude toward foreign intervention. The only ef-

fective decisions taken by the Congo Commission were to send
a mission to Washington and to condemn the Stanleyville operation. Surprisingly, despite its original rejection, the United
States did finally receive the mission and even expressed willingness to reduce its assistance if Africa provided some counterpart. Then, by forming a united front after Stanleyville,
the OAU found it possible to have the "rescue" operation liquidated in short order. The most conclusive victory was
against the United Nations, when the world body decided to
leave the Congolese affair entirely in the hands of the OAU
and Africa.

This policy would have been more successful if the
OAU had not ignored the basic rule of non-alignment--impar-
tiality. By condemning Tshombe more loudly than the rebels,
the OAU Commission lost the confidence of the Congolese government. By sending a mission only to Washington, without
criticizing those supporting the rebels, the Commission lost
the trust of one of the great powers. Nevertheless, both
Tshombe and the United States might have been ready to halt
or even reverse the escalation if they felt that the other side
would also make concessions. In demanding unilateral meas-
ures--of those backing the recognized government--the Commission and the OAU missed the opportunity to obtain a genuine disengagement and relieve the stress and bloodshed in the
region.

In the Nigerian civil war, despite superficial similarities to the Congolese, the situation was very different. Although the internal struggle was even more bitter, it was far
less ideological. Neither side proclaimed its adherence to an
alien ideology or had a clear claim on the great powers.
Both were more reluctant to trade future advantage for military equipment. The African states maintained a united, if
somewhat inactive front. And, when assistance came, the
bulk of it went to the central government, which was supported by world ideological opponents, Great Britain and the Soviet Union. Biafra received much less aid and was never
openly backed. With the same policy followed by the great
powers and the African states, non-alignment seemed a success.

The OAU Gains Recognition.

Over the years non-alignment in this sense became a
part of OAU policy. Its value was even conceded explicitly or

tacitly by much of the world community. The clearest success was with the United Nations. Under Articles 52 and 53
of its Charter, regional bodies such as the OAU were given a
role in the settlement of disputes and a lesser one for the
maintenance of peace. But it was not certain that it would
actually play this role. Only with time was the Organization
accepted as the most neutral or least dangerous body in which
to handle conflicts. Its main advantage over the United Nations was that the cold war could be avoided. Moreover, the
Africans preferred settling disputes in their own way rather
than receiving decisions from a body in which the great powers had the strongest voice.

When the King of Morocco and the President of Algeria
could be persuaded to submit their dispute for settlement by
the OAU, this was an important precedent. The Council resolution on the matter later expressed "the imperative need of
settling all differences between African States by peaceful
means and within a strictly African framework." However, it
took more than that to bring the highly explosive border dispute between Ethiopia and Somalia into an African context.
Somalia had serious misgivings about entrusting the issue to
an organization that was overwhelmingly against any change in
the territorial status quo, and sought instead the backing of a
great power. Nevertheless, sufficient pressure could be
brought to bear on Somalia to have the matter dealt with by
the OAU.

The test case was the Congo. Despite the risks, the
member states unhesitatingly decided to bring the crisis into
an African framework. At the Council of Ministers in September 1964, the members were "deeply conscious of the responsibilities and of the competence of the Organization of African Unity to find a peaceful solution to all the problems and
differences which affect peace and security in the African continent." The United Nations quietly acquiesced. The great
powers, however, continued aiding the opposing sides. Finally,
after the Stanleyville operation, the member states insisted
that the problem be given an "African solution." On 30 December 1964, the Security Council went even further and accepted the broad principle that "the Organization of African
Unity should be able, in the context of Article 52 of the Charter, to find a peaceful solution to all the problems and disputes affecting peace and security in the continent of Africa."
Its only duty toward the world body was to provide information
on its action.

Thus, within less than two years, the OAU was solidly established as the primary arbiter of conflicts and crises on the continent. This view prevailed during the Nigerian civil war as well and was declared most emphatically by Prime Minister Wilson, who told his opposition that "this is a conflict between Nigerians and, if outside help is needed, the Organization of African Unity is the appropriate agency for mediation."[1] (But there was reason to believe that this reflected less a desire to let the Africans solve their own problems than a lack of alternatives and a fear of being caught in the conflict.)

The inherent right of Africa to settle its conflicts did not lead the great powers to refrain from all intervention. Actually, the quantity of arms supplied to Nigeria was far larger than that received by both sides in the Congo. And the struggle to gain the good will of Lagos was as active, if less visible, than the endeavors to impose a government in Léopoldville. The combined front of East and West against Biafra was hardly less damaging than the earlier phase of the cold war. Although this was rarely remarked by the African states, also supporting Lagos morally and somewhat relieved that aid might permit it to end the war, the new situation was not a real improvement. The danger of uncontrollable escalation or ideological bitterness lessened. But the certainty of broad support did not lead one side to compromise or the other to accept defeat. And rivalry between the supporting powers led to a gradual increase in the means of destruction. The decisive difference was that rather than balancing the forces, this combined effort gave a tremendous advantage to one side. More than ever, it was not the parties nor the broader African community so much as the intervening powers that determined the outcome.

Africa's Policy.

Each time a conflict arose on the continent there was some danger of outside interference. There was always some political difference between the sides which could be blown up into an ideological dispute of a broader nature. This distortion might be wrought by the parties themselves in a bid to obtain assistance or by outsiders in the hope of increasing their influence in Africa. This meant that the Organization had to act on two fronts, internally and externally, to avoid the cold war.

To play its role the Organization had to be unbiased. Unless both sides to any dispute felt they would receive a fair hearing and just consideration of their arguments in the African body they would not entrust it with a matter that concerned them so intensely. Then it was necessary to condemn all involvement, from either side in the cold war, and to show Africa's will to free itself of this interference. In particular, the OAU and its members had to avoid taking sides, for this would only give the opponents another reason to seek allies abroad. Certainly the OAU could not expect successfully to ward off intervention while it or some of its members intervened. Their first duty was therefore also self-discipline. If Africa itself split into rival groups and backed the parties this would only introduce a small cold war in the continent that could usher in the big one.

It was necessary in addition to convince the great powers that there was less to gain than to lose by mixing in African affairs. Although the OAU could make its strength felt against its own members, this was insignificant when brought to bear against the leaders of the world blocs. No policy of restraint could be imposed upon them. Nevertheless, they could be given food for thought. Intervention had been very expensive in the past. By supporting one faction or state, each power had made enemies of the other: too many embassies had been closed and relations severed to make this attractive. And the outcome of African crises was so unpredictable that often both blocs were losers. By forming a united front Africa could reinforce the message and show the great powers that even if intervention in the continent's affairs got them the friendship of the side they supported, it could entail the opposition of the rest of the community.

The OAU had a considerable ally in the lassitude and indifference of the great powers. If no appeal was made by an African state or the situation in the country did not strongly attract interference, the rest of the world was often willing to let Africa solve its own problems. There was no reason to believe that the foreign powers were constantly seeking pretexts to intervene. What they wanted more than actually changing the balance in their favor was to avoid any serious loss. They were usually willing to refrain from playing an active role in a crisis if their opponents did the same. Even if already involved in a conflict, the great powers might be persuaded to withdraw on a reciprocal basis. Each side could move out roughly at the same time and to the same extent without giving an advantage to the other side. They would be particularly willing to do so if the affair were then dealt with by Africa as a whole rather than being left to fester.

Recently it had become necessary to develop a policy toward the newer phenomenon of a combined front of East and West. This was likely to be increasingly frequent if the cold war relaxed and the major powers accepted concerted action outside their immediate spheres of influence. Here it was even harder for Africa to react since, in most cases, the member states supported the same side and the great powers appeared as the secular arm of an impotent OAU. This kind of intervention would be rejected only if Africa realized that its primary aim was still to avoid an aggravation of the crisis and to reach an African settlement. For this interference also led to rigidity and refusal to compromise, greater destructiveness and, for the losing side, the conviction of being defeated unfairly. The great powers could determine the winner but they could not remove the underlying causes and, when they were occupied elsewhere or the cold war resumed, the conflict might be reopened. In the interest of Africa, it was necessary to pursue a more genuine, if more difficult non-alignment.

"An African Personality."

Promising and valuable as it was, this restricted variety of non-alignment was still largely defensive or negative. If Africa really wished to create a personality on the world scene it had to return a bit to the original idea of non-alignment and seek a positive contribution. Very rarely since its creation had the OAU dealt with an issue that was not purely African. Disarmament had only been considered as it affected the continent and when the situation was relatively satisfactory the issue was dropped. Even with other questions of a broader nature, there was always some connection with Africa.

A case in point was racial discrimination. This matter was usually seen in the context of the struggle against South Africa and other settler or colonial powers. Nevertheless, the African states also tried to erase the sequels of discrimination in their own countries or expressed "deep concern" about the situation in the United States. A special resolution on racial discrimination was adopted at the Cairo Assembly. It regretted the "continuing manifestations of racial bigotry and racial oppression against Negro citizens of the United States of America." Then it went on to urge the American government to

intensify its efforts "to ensure the total elimination of all
forms of discrimination based on race, colour, or ethnic origin." This was the first specific reference to the plight of
brothers on the other side of the Atlantic. It was also the
last for the time being and there was no follow-up nor even
any further resolution on the subject.

The Palestinian situation conserved an ambiguous relationship to the Organization of African Unity. Although several of its members were thoroughly committed on the issue,
the other states managed to keep it largely marginal. They
resisted being drawn into the campaign of the Arab countries
and often maintained excellent relations with Israel. Meeting
after meeting, from Cairo to Kinshasa to Algiers, the Arab
leaders launched attacks against Israel as an imperialist and
neo-colonialist stooge, drawing close parallels between their
struggle against Israel and Africa's struggle against South Africa. Finally, after the defeat and loss of territory of one of
its members, the OAU adopted a statement. The most significant aspect of the Kinshasa declaration, however, was not so
much the "sympathy" expressed to the United Arab Republic
as the fact that the OAU left action to the United Nations. Despite renewed efforts this stand was not altered in Algiers.

When it came to issues that were strictly non-African,
although of crucial importance for the peace and security of
the world, the OAU consistently remained on the side lines.
A notable precedent was made at the Accra Assembly when
certain states tried to include items on Kashmir and Vietnam
in the agenda. The prior meeting of the Council of Ministers,
both in the political committee and plenary, refused to recommend any resolution on these two points because they were
Asian issues. This decision was maintained by the Assembly,
which added that the items could best be discussed at the
forthcoming Afro-Asian Conference. This pretext was only
partly valid, especially when the Conference was twice postponed. For, in all issues affecting world peace and security,
Africa could adopt its own position as well rather than just
being the appendage of a broader front.

Nevertheless, for the moment, the member states felt
that they had enough problems as it was: decolonization, internal order and development. It was far more difficult to
find a common denominator or establish a joint African policy
on other matters. Moreover, any pronouncement on such issues might cost Africa sympathy and support for its primary
aims. Thus it was agreed to keep them out of the Organiza-

tion, let each member go its own way and, if need be, have the issues dealt with in other forums.

One day, however, it would be normal for the OAU to become more active and outward-looking. It could define and then defend a policy on disarmament, peace-keeping or action in any number of political crises. This was necessary if ever Africa hoped to play a valid role in international affairs. Indeed, this too was a purpose of the Charter: the Organization of African Unity shall "promote international co-operation, having due regard to the Charter of the United Nations and the Universal Declaration of Human Rights."

1.   House of Commons Debates, 2 April 1969, Hansard, p. 485.

Chapter VI

Development

The struggle for liberation was hardly concluded when the leaders and peoples in the newly independent states turned to the next major challenge: the need for progress and development in all possible fields. Cooperation in economic, social and cultural matters increasingly became a part of the programs adopted by the various African organizations, the Afro-Malagasy states, and the Casablanca and Monrovia groups. By the time of the Summit Conference, it was agreed unanimously that the Organization of African Unity should be a major tool in reaching a higher level of well-being.

The Preamble spoke of the Heads of States' "responsibility to harness the natural and human resources of our continent for the total advancement of our peoples in spheres of human endeavour." It was certainly not one of the lesser tasks of the new organization "to coordinate and intensify their co-operation and efforts to achieve a better life for the peoples of Africa." Still, the scope of its activities was made exceptionally broad and unusually energetic efforts would be necessary to get the member states to "co-ordinate and harmonize their general policies" in these fields: economic (including transport and communications), education and culture, health, sanitation and nutrition, science and technology, and defence and security. To which were added social, labor, legal and refugee.

To pursue its activities in these spheres, the OAU was given a number of specialized commissions, established by the Assembly and responsible to it, and composed of the respective ministers. Other commissions or groups of experts could also be created as needed. The work of the various bodies was to be coordinated and followed up by the Council of Ministers. And, to service this machinery, the Secretariat would have to establish the necessary divisions to provide the general documentation and handle specific tasks.

A Heavy Assignment.

When the Organization of African Unity was founded in
Addis Ababa, the lists of tasks the Heads of State suggested
for each field were certainly long and ambitious.   They could
not all be tackled at once and much of the work had to be left
to the states or other organizations.   The OAU could only play
an auxiliary role.   First it was hampered by its limited powers towards its members.   Then its activities would be seriously restricted by the lack of funds and staff.   The Organization was not wealthy to begin with and the technical projects
could be rather costly in men and money.   Since most of its
staff and funds were already committed to the political side,
it was necessary to impose very strict discipline.

The first step might have been to examine the various
lists and divide the tasks into broad categories.   The simplest
to handle, although not making a serious dent on the situation,
were the preparatory ones.   This meant taking stock of what
existed and what was needed, increasing understanding among
the members and preparing minds for later action.   There
could be surveys of agriculture and industries, studies of research facilities and armed forces, information about national
social and health legislation, teaching of English, French and
Arabic, or an exchange of professors, students and technicians.
Such activities entailed relatively low expenditures, could be
undertaken with or even without the active participation of the
states, and in no way infringed on their rights.

A gradual transformation could be wrought by measures
of coordination and harmonization.   It was possible to establish federations or confederations of trade unions or professional associations, run joint campaigns to eradicate rinderpest or malaria, harmonize development plans or social security legislation, or set up a payment union or free trade area.
The structures of the states or national units would be left
basically as they were and the governments or private associations would take their decisions freely.   But they would exercise a mutual influence on one another and try to make their
structures increasingly similar while working at the same time
for the same goals.

The most decisive action was through integration.
There might be an African military academy or university, an
African trade union or press agency, a currency zone or common market.   Here, new structures would embrace and replace the old ones.   This granting of broad power to the bodies

running the joint operation involved a considerable restriction
on the states' powers and thus resistance from vested interests. It would not be easy to get the states to agree to
create the machinery in the first place.

This was very important since almost every task could
be tackled at any of the three levels. For example, when it
came to inter-African trade, it was possible merely to publish
reports on the various markets and opportunities. Customs
procedures could be simplified or harmonized. Or, a free
trade area could be created by reducing the tariff barriers between members but leaving them otherwise free as concerned
their economic and trade policies and tariffs towards third
states. Finally, a common market could be established by
removing all duties internally to form a single market and
setting up a uniform tariff wall outwards. This would be followed by free movement of currency and labor, harmonization
of social and commercial legislation and a coordination of economic and trade policies as the members were welded into a
unit. In the process the joint machinery would be reinforced
progressively to regulate the functioning of the common market and, to some extent, to relieve the governments of their
former prerogatives.

Before making any choice, the Organization would have
to study the situation. It would have to find out what had already been done or was being undertaken by other bodies and
states. It would have to determine what remained to be done.
And then, above all, it would have to examine itself and decide what could be done best by the OAU. At this point, it
might realize that it was still a small organization faced with
huge tasks. In the lists of tasks it might find it wiser to
start with the modest ones of preparation and coordination. It
might decide to move slowly. This should be especially so in
light of its own history. For the OAU was only created on a
relatively low level of unity--coordination and harmonization of
policies--after having been blocked in greater unity by the un-
surmountable obstacle of sovereignty.

Priorities and Program.

Nevertheless, when the various specialized commissions
assembled to lay down their terms of reference, they did not
stop to consider the difficulties. Rather, they were carried
away by the urgency and importance of these matters for the
continent. And they ended up by adopting all the items pro-

posed by the Addis Ababa summit conference and more. True, this was only a list of prospective tasks and there was much to be done. Unfortunately, some of the Ministers were too enthusiastic while others were overly conscientious, and the result was always that the commissions had trouble selecting priorities among its many tasks. When they did make a choice, it was not based on cost-benefit considerations nor even on feasibility.

In the end, the Economic and Social Commission, with a nine point list, requested studies on all but concentrated on the question of a free trade area or common market. Similarly, other items were given priority by the other commissions. Among them were the uniting of the African trade union movement and a Pan-African news agency. The Secretariat also wanted an emblem for the OAU. There was still the whole range of activities of the Commission for Technical Cooperation in Africa that had to be continued. And considerable efforts would be made over a wide front in defence and for refugees.

There was more of a hodgepodge of objectives than a logical and integrated program. The various items were not of equal importance for the continent. Some were quite easy to accomplish and others terribly hard. Some were short term and others long term. In particular, the establishment of a common market would take years and required more staff and finance than the whole OAU Secretariat had at its disposal. Therefore it was clearly necessary to work out an order of priority for the items chosen by the various commissions and to fit this into the overall program of the Organization.

The only bodies that could establish priorities and a program were the Council of Ministers and the Assembly. One of the Council's duties was to coordinate the work of the technical bodies and to point out any financial or staff limitations. However, since it was usually absorbed in more pressing political activities, it rarely got around to this. Even then, this disparity of interest should have intimated the general low priority for all technical matters. Once again, rather than wait for the situation to clear, the commissions made the OAU a launching pad for hastily prepared and hazardous ventures. Although the projects had varying fates, little success could be expected in the short run and the stature of the OAU was not enhanced by such uncoordinated efforts.

The Political Element.

What the Organization needed most was a basic philosophy towards this work. An effective approach to such matters might have been technocratic: a relative unconcern with
extraneous elements as long as projects made progress. The
commissions were basically technical and, even though the
ministers were not always experts or even technically-minded,
once the projects had been chosen they should have been left
to professionals and specialists able to disregard all other
considerations than the best means to attain the ends. The
governing bodies, however, the Assembly and Council of Ministers that supervised these activities, were highly political.
And they were likely to judge progress from a very different
angle.

Moreover, the OAU as a whole was a predominantly
political organization. This had its positive side. For it was
often stressed that the OAU, unlike the more strictly technical
bodies on the continent, could provide the political will for
success. Once the Heads of State had endorsed a project, the
efforts to undertake and accomplish it should be much greater.
But the choice of projects and the means to achieve them were
not always the best. And politics could get in the way. At
most, it was a mixed blessing.

Among the technical items, some had a significant political aspect or were bound up with political objectives. This
at least assured considerable interest. The OAU worked more
actively at them and the governing and specialized bodies rallied support. The Defence Commission and the Commission
on Refugees benefitted most. Their work was a necessary
foundation for success in matters like decolonization, non-
alignment and internal order. Since they were essential tools
for attaining political goals of the OAU they received very high
priority. The economic projects that provided concrete links
between the member states were also rated highly. For these
links had to support the political structure and pave the way
for unification of the continent. Likewise, in the field of education, the establishment of a news agency, so closely connected both with information and propaganda, was given precedence.

However, by fixing priorities politically, the more
strictly technical fields which were no less important for the
well-being of the continent were neglected. This was true of
transport and communications, but even more so of health.

There were liable to be few if any real attempts at coming to grips with these matters. It was also possible for the political side of the work at hand to overshadow the more technical or humanitarian aspects. To the problem of refugees, there was a tendency to seek political solutions rather than human ones. When domestic options and ideologies were at variance or relations with the outside world got involved, the problems confronting the OAU became much more complicated. Often, on particularly delicate items, there could be so much rivalry and controversy that rather than expediting matters the political element impeded all progress.

A common approach was not made easier by the very differing attitudes among the member states as to the ultimate goals and methods. The stumbling block was the controversy over "neo-colonialism." The OAU had grown out of the two urges: independence and unity. For some, an acceptable degree of both had already been attained with national sovereignty and some loose Pan-African organization. Faced with the tasks of development, to obtain the technical and financial aid they needed, they were willing to welcome back the former colonial power or other states that could help them, referring to the Charter objective of "international co-operation." Others felt that it was necessary to carry the struggle for liberation into further areas, not only economic but social, cultural and other. The struggle had to assume new forms to counter the new phenomena of interference in African life. They also demanded that unity be more exclusive and objected to close relations with non-African powers. They invoked the determination in the preamble "to fight against neo-colonialism in all its forms."

Nevertheless, in any given case, it was not easy to agree on what was neo-colonialism. The trouble was that neo-colonialism, analyzed by its opponents as a much subtler influence than old-fashioned colonialism, was often accepted by the states afflicted with it. For some, massive technical or financial support was "assistance" and for others it was "neo-colonialism." For some, close trade relations was just business, for others it was neo-colonialism. For some, use of a European language was a handy vehicle in a multilingual society, for others it was neo-colonialism. More specifically, the radicals often warned against these manifestations as concealing deeper threats while the moderates felt they were helpful despite any risks.

This extension of decolonization was pervasive. An educational reform or the revision of textbooks entailed weeding out "colonial subjects" and the "colonial bias," which had to be replaced by a course of studies adapted to African needs and pride and books stressing the African personality and solidarity. Even a seemingly innocuous field like communications or transport was not free from it. A proposal for an African post and telecommunications network or for better inter-African plane connections implied a decreasing reliance on communications through London or Paris and plane connections via Geneva or Rome. Even the most "technical" measures could be politically loaded.

In some ways, this was a wise reaction. For Africa had to be careful not to fall into new traps or let itself be subjected again by outside powers. Often it was a useful defensive mechanism. To some extent, this approach was suitable when trying to attain certain goals, especially those of integration, where the policies often implied excluding foreign interests and possibly injuring them. A cartel of primary producers, its own companies and industries or a common market might well improve Africa's position at the expense of others. And they could only be accomplished through a purely African body. With other, less ambitious projects, this approach could be harmful. For the African states needed huge injections of financial and technical assistance from the advanced countries. They could not develop rapidly enough by their own means. Fear of neo-colonialism often meant an unfortunate tendency to reject what came from without even if it were useable and to make it harder for African states to cooperate with those in a position to help them. It led some to destroy the old before the new had been created.

Before the Organization could make real progress on many points, it was necessary to work out this contradiction from Africa's past and one which was also embedded in the Charter. Over the years, the governing bodies were rarely able to make an official pronouncement on neo-colonialism, either to define it or to condemn it. This was because of the great divergency of views within the membership. Although the conflict was often muted, it was always there. It kept the OAU from becoming an active platform against neo-colonialism but it also prevented the OAU from becoming a solid foundation for development. It frequently led the radicals to scorn the minor schemes of the moderates, while the moderates refused to embark on the major ventures of the radicals. In the Secretariat, as well, some of the higher officials had been raised in the hard school and their views contrasted sharply with those of the more technical personnel. Thus, as long as no conclusion was reached, the OAU was liable to dissipate its energy fruitlessly rather than tackling the many tasks that awaited it.

A. Economics

Immediately after obtaining independence the African states launched vast campaigns to promote the development of their countries and peoples. This matter was given top priority internally and, despite all difficulties, it was essential for the new leaders to make concrete and measurable progress. Many of the activities also offered a promising soil for broader cooperation. With cooperation much of the duplication or competition of unregulated efforts could be avoided. It would be easier for the continent to diversify its economies, to industrialize and to enter into effective trade. Beyond this was the ambitious goal of integration. First regional and limited it could expand to a continental arrangement with far-reaching links.

Many of the ideas for cooperation were still vague. Yet there was a growing recognition of the need for Africa as a whole to plan its future. The summit conference decided to include economic activities in the new Organization of African Unity. But the terms of reference suggested hardly made up a coherent program. Rather, it was a somewhat haphazard mixture of all the ideas and pet projects of the African leaders. This ran from the marketing boards of the cautious gradualists to the African monetary zone dear to President Nkrumah, and included the idea of an African economic community that had caught everyone's imagination.

On none of these points were the Heads of State innovators. The projects they suggested were not specifically African nor were they all equally feasible or adapted to African conditions. They joined the general movement for development that had been building up and was often channelled through the United Nations. Already several limited attempts had been made, some successfully, at forming customs unions and monetary zones under the aegis of the former colonial powers. More truly African efforts were the projects of the Afro-Malagasy Union and the Entente. But the major outlet for the ideas and efforts of the continent was the Economic Commission for Africa. There was no need for the OAU to start from scratch. To the contrary, it was essential for it to fit into the broader scheme of things.

The ECA and the OAU.

The beginning of specifically African efforts at developing the continent could hardly come before 1958, the year in which the process of decolonization really got under way. It was in that year that the United Nations Economic and Social Council decided to establish a regional branch in Africa. The Economic Commission for Africa (ECA) was created, with headquarters in Addis Ababa, on 29 April 1958. It was designed to promote economic and social development and cooperation among the countries of the region. However, at first, it was visibly an emanation of the world organization. It was responsible to the UN's ECOSOC and was financed from the regular UN budget. Along with the relatively few independent states, its membership included the colonial powers. Other members of the UN, including the United States and Soviet Union, also attended its meetings as observers. And it was largely staffed with foreign experts.

This anomaly occasionally diverted the African states from their economic tasks and the political struggles of the day tended to flow over into the ECA. Gradually it underwent a parallel decolonization. Portugal and South Africa were evicted. The other colonial powers were made associate members and their importance decreased as more and more African states became independent. In 1962, Robert Kweku Atta Gardiner, a Ghanaian, returned from his UN Special Representative post in the Congo and actively assumed ECA direction as Executive Secretary. And, as the staff grew, it was relentlessly Africanized. The independent states increasingly fashioned the ECA's policies on their own while leaving the last word--and only the last word--to the parent body in New York.

Then the Economic Commission for Africa began to prepare its technical work. First it had to take stock of the actual conditions in Africa. The continent was huge and still amazingly unknown. Thus the ECA sought to increase Africa's knowledge of itself and of its real needs by initiating a number of surveys of agriculture, industry, trade and transport. Then it studied the flow of aid and organized technical assistance. It also contributed to training. Finally, after this spade work had been done, the ECA began to launch concrete projects on commodities, transport or even social problems.

But its major concern was to take the far-flung and largely
separated states and work them into a whole. This implied
a broader and deeper integration of its members.

To rally support for the economic development of the
continent, the OAU, its highest political body, could also play
an important role. But, what would it be? By the time of
the Addis Ababa conference in May 1963, the ECA had already
shown its ability to handle economic tasks. The Heads of
State praised the progress in setting up the Dakar Institute of
Economic Development and Planning and the forthcoming Conference of African Ministers of Finance, that met in Khartoum
and eventually set up the African Development Bank. Nevertheless, the list of items for economic work they gave the
OAU Economic and Social Commission overlapped considerably
with what was even then being done by the ECA. To sort
this out, those gathered at the summit merely decided to set
up a preparatory economic committee to study these matters
with "all the necessary support and assistance" of the ECA.

A number of working documents had been drawn up by
the time the Economic and Social Commission was constituted
in Niamey, Niger, from 9-13 December 1963. There was no
lack of enthusiasm when the ministers arrived to inaugurate
this new, high-level body which they felt could give a real
boost to the economic development of the continent. They
were tired of the slow and painstaking efforts of more technical bodies and hoped that the OAU could provide the decisive
impulse. Without hesitation they adopted the Heads of State's
whole list of desiderata as their terms of reference. They
merely reorganized them somewhat to show their own momentary priorities:

> 1) the coordination of national development plans,
>   beginning with a scientific study of ways of
>   achieving this;
>
> 2) the creation of a free trade zone of member
>   states, beginning with the standardization of cus
>   toms procedures;
>
> 3) the conclusion of payments and compensation
>   agreements among member states;
>
> 4) the creation of inter-African road, air and sea
>   companies;

5) the creation of a Pan-African telecommunications union;

6) the establishment of a common external tariff;

7) a monetary zone with a central bank of issue;

8) a joint stabilization fund to support the prices of primary produce; and

9) an organization of African trade fairs and exhibitions.

The tasks the Economics Ministers set for themselves could hardly have been more ambitious. Still, they did make some effort to list the items not only in the order of importance but also of feasibility, starting with some of the more practicable tasks. Although the list was very uneven, at least it put a free trade zone before a common external tariff, and only planned to start by standardizing customs procedures. And only the first five items were to be given priority attention. Nevertheless, the Commission was in a hurry and it aimed at nothing less than "concrete achievements." When it asked the Secretariat for studies, its requests covered all nine items.

At the same session, the Economic and Social Commission (the Commission) set about defining its relationship with the ECA. Its resolution noted that it was "basically a policy-making and executive body while the role of the Economic Commission for Africa is generally limited to technical and advisory functions." It thus decided to "set up close co-operation on a complementary basis" with the ECA and requested the latter body to "proceed with its studies and investigations." However, at the same time, it called upon its member states to have the ECA "pay particular attention" to the items on the OAU program and priorities. This meant that the ECA could do the homework of the OAU Commission. And, in fact, since the Secretariat did not have the staff for the various studies, most of the work was entrusted to the ECA.

The Economic and Social Commission did not hold its next session until a year later, from 18-22 January 1965, in Cairo. By then it had realized that a more permanent structure and larger staff were necessary to carry on its activities. It also half admitted that the OAU could not do everything itself and so weighed the respective contributions of the national

governments, other organizations and the OAU Commission
and Secretariat. Without determining its exact role, it went
ahead and called upon the Secretary-General to appoint a committee of experts to study the measures needed to set up regional or continental common markets, free trade areas and
customs and payments unions. This time it had decided to
tackle the toughest items. And it was in no mood to wait.
As a first step, the committee was to draw up a list of products that could come under free trade right away.

The need for official relations with the Economic Commission for Africa was felt even more keenly at this second
meeting. The ministers called for "a draft agreement or arrangement that defines in a precise manner the framework of
co-operation between the O.A.U. and the E.C.A." The terms
of this cooperation were still complementarity; that is, a division of authority and labor as proposed by the first session.
This was expressed clearly enough by the Assistant Secretary-
General for Economic Affairs, Gratien Pognon, at the ECA's
seventh session in Nairobi, in February 1965. He reminded
the delegates that the role of the OAU had been defined as
planning and execution and the ECA's role as technical and advisory.

Unfortunately for the OAU, however, it was increasingly hard to hold its Commission meetings and the Economic and
Social Commission was unable to have a third session. The
committee of experts was not established either. And the economic division only had a staff of five. Thus the Economic
Commission for Africa kept the initiative. The fragility of an
relationship of subordination was abundantly clear. Without
any real difficulty the agreement signed with the ECA, on 15
November 1965, was based on complete parity. It provided
for reciprocal consultations and an exchange of observers at
all organized meetings as well as closer cooperation in matters of documentation and statistics.[1]

The Economic and Social Commission met no more and
could not provide directions for the Organization. But there
was still an urgent need for some economic activity. At this
point a basic change occurred in the structures. To fill the
gap the Addis Ababa Assembly, in November 1966, decided to
have a third committee established within the Council of Ministers to deal with economic tasks among others. In its few
days of deliberation, however, Committee C could not do the
indispensable preparatory work and it was the Secretariat that
replaced the old Commission by providing background material

and suggestions.

Only this time, rather than follow the orders of the competent ministers, the Secretariat tended to take the lead and give guidance to the Council. Occasionally what it did was simply to increase its work load and prestige. For example, the resolution on intra-African cooperation, like many others, could be traced back to a report of the Secretariat showing the importance of trade and integration. The only action demanded was that the Secretariat write another report on the conditions for establishing an inter-African market. Whether this reading matter would accelerate the creation of such a market was doubtful, but at least the Secretariat had legitimized its initiative and created a further job for itself. That there was some wishful thinking in the Secretariat as well was shown by a resolution urging regional stocks of food grains to free the continent from dependence on the rest of the world.

However, the Secretariat also launched one of the few projects that might succeed. This was the last and most unassuming of the items on the list of priorities--an African trade fair. The Commission had tried to work its way down the list and never reached it. With time, this was seized upon by the Secretariat as a joint African venture that would be rather easy to accomplish with little cost. A document outlining the advantages of such a fair in promoting inter-African trade and creating links between the participants was presented in Kinshasa in September 1967 and the Council advised the Assembly to have the Secretary-General organize an All-African Trade Fair as soon as possible. Preparations could be made by a small staff and the Secretary-General or an Assistant could provide an OAU presence. The cost would be borne by the host government and that honor could circulate from state to state.

The African Common Market.

Even before the Economic Commission for Africa was founded, the question of integration and a common market had become topical. This was a normal task for any African economic body, but it was pressed upon the ECA by external circumstances. On 25 March 1957, the Treaty of Rome established the European Economic Community. However, at the request of France, this European common market was opened to include the territories with which it or other members had "special relations." This system of association included

eighteen African colonies: Burundi (UN trusteeship-Belgium,
then part of Ruanda-Urundi), Cameroun (French), Central Af-
rican Republic (Fr. Oubangi-Chari), Chad (Fr.), Congo (Braz-
zaville) (Fr.), Congo (Kinshasa) (Belg.), Dahomey (Fr.),
Gabon (Fr.), Ivory Coast (Fr.), Malagasy (Fr. Madagascar),
Mali (Fr. Soudan), Mauritania (Fr.), Niger (Fr.), Rwanda
(UN-Belg., part of Ruanda-Urundi), Senegal (Fr.), Somalia
(UN-Ital.), Togo (UN-Fr.), and Upper Volta (Fr.).

These territories were made associates in a system
based on mutual benefit. According to the Treaty of Rome,
"the purpose of this association shall be to promote the economic and social development of the countries and territories
and to establish close economic relations between them and
the Community as a whole." There would be a reduction of
tariffs in Europe for goods from the associated countries, thus
giving them a privileged position in the market as compared
with their competitors. They would also benefit from a large
Development Fund. In exchange, they were not yet expected
to lower their own tariffs, but rather to grant the other members of the EEC the same preferential treatment as the colonial power.

Association was one of the burning subjects of debate
in the early days of the ECA. It was strongly attacked as
neo-colonialistic from the outset. The associates were warned
that they would remain economically subjected and that development was a pipe dream. Europe would keep them in the
position of primary producers for goods it needed rather than
permitting industrialization and diversification. The Eurafrican
relationship prevented closer and broader links with the rest
of the continent, as a further disadvantage. This came to a
head at the ECA's fifth session in Léopoldville in February
1963. A resolution was submitted by a combination of Anglophone and Arab states which decried "the application of a discriminatory tariff" against developing countries not associated
to the EEC (Britain not being a member, its colonies were not
associates). It also took note of "recent developments ...
tending to perpetuate a sharp distinction between two groups of
independent African countries." But the eighteen held their
own and it was decided only to investigate the situation.

The UAM members in particular would not be deterred
by these attacks nor take advice from states that had not
proven their ability to work together or to create an African
common market. After weighing profit against loss, the eighteen decided to seek another period of association. The new

agreement was freely negotiated by the now independent states, which actually took the initiative, and the new Yaoundé Convention was signed. The system that came into force on 1 June 1964 was better adapted to their needs. Although tariffs would be reduced by Africa, the associated states were allowed to retain or introduce duties for development or fiscal purposes. European duties on their primary products were largely eliminated. And the new Development Fund, some 730 million dollars for five years, would be devoted to diversification and industrialization. The associates ran the system together with the European members, on a parity basis, through joint machinery: Council, Committee, Parliamentary Conference, and Court of Arbitration. The solidarity between the African states was strengthened by their internal customs union and the need to work out common policies and tactics toward their partners. Moreover, an opening to the rest of the continent was provided by enabling them to form customs unions with non-associates. The EEC also took a step toward the other African states by lowering tariffs on certain of their products and by permitting other forms of looser association or bilateral agreements.

The complaints of neo-colonialism died down with time. What the associates got was aid, preferential treatment and even integration. The other states could hardly deny the benefits. Some of them had Commonwealth preferences or close trade relations with East or West and the criticism often sounded like sour grapes. The turnabout came when certain states realized the advantages and tried to obtain them as well. The first to take the step was Nigeria, by far the most populous and dynamic state in the region, when it decided to negotiate with the EEC for its own kind of association at the end of 1963. There was also some interest in East Africa and the Maghreb countries sought an arrangement since all had had close relations with Community members. (In July 1966, Nigeria concluded an agreement for limited association, followed by Kenya, Tanzania and Uganda in July 1968, and Tunisia and Morocco in March 1969.)

From this point on the African states ceased their attacks and became more positively committed to overcoming the difficulties by creating their own economic community. The Economic Commission for Africa had already adopted a major resolution on economic integration at the Léopoldville session. It immediately got to work studying the technical, financial and institutional aspects of the problem. It set up groups of experts and gradually evolved its own philosophy of integration.

Traditionally, common markets were thought to be beneficial
to the extent that the member states had complementary
economies. Unfortunately, in Africa, the economies were
largely competitive and there was, in fact, little trade. But
integration was needed to provide the larger market required
if the continent was ever to industrialize and diversify. Thus
integration was a prerequisite to development.[2]

Given the distances and differences among states, as
well as the problem of sheer size, the ECA wisely decided to
divide the continent into a number of sub-regions for its integration schemes. Then it made the feasibility studies and
worked out alternative plans. After the ECA staff had found
a likely arrangement for the region, it convened meetings and
conferences to have the units created. It even drummed up
political support and obtained acceptance by the governments.
Often, in the last stage, the sovereign states or OAU intervened to preside over the founding of the communities. But
there was no doubt where most of the credit went.

In 1965, the ECA began a key cycle of sub-regional
meetings on economic cooperation. The best spot was in East
Africa, where three members had already founded a "common
market" in 1964. An ECA meeting was held in Lusaka, Zambia, in November 1965, which recommended that the governments create an Economic Community of Eastern Africa. An
interim Council of Ministers of such a Community was established and by May 1966 it signed Terms of Association. The
states then involved, covering much of the region, were ten:
Burundi, Ethiopia, Kenya, Malagasy, Malawi, Mauritius,
Rwanda, Somalia, Tanzania and Zambia. Others were bound
to follow. The plan was for a progressive elimination of all
trade barriers and the establishment of a full customs union.

The work in West Africa was slow to start with and no
meeting was held for the sub-region until October 1966. But,
by May 1967, Articles of Association could be signed in Accra
This was a binding international agreement but it was only a
pre-treaty. It merely stated the intention of creating an Economic Community of West Africa for Dahomey, Gambia, Ghana
Ivory Coast, Liberia, Mali, Mauritania, Niger, Nigeria, Senegal, Sierra Leone, Togo and Upper Volta. The group's interim Council of Ministers, in November 1967, was more ambitious and decided that the ultimate aim should be to develop
cooperation in all fields and a provisional secretariat was set
up to draft a treaty. These states, joined by Guinea, held a
major conference in Monrovia in April 1968. With considera-

ble fanfare a ministerial meeting followed by a summit decided
to establish a regular organization for cooperation in West Africa.

Central Africa, which already had a rather advanced
customs union for most of its members, was not able to move
ahead. The meeting in April 1966 only recommended that the
governments in the region set up a ministerial committee to
study institutional arrangements for economic cooperation.
The problem was to fit the Congo (Kinshasa)--much larger
than its neighbors--into the existing structures. The North
African region was still at the stage of pre-feasibility studies.
Even the Maghreb, with an intricate institutional setup, was
only turning out reports. And relations with Egypt and Sudan
were quite limited.

Despite its greatly reduced activities, the OAU did not
wish to lose track of the movement towards integration. In
particular, a time would come when the various regional groupings had to be melted into a continental one. Then the political will required would be much greater than for the original
faltering steps. In September 1967, after the process was
well under way, the Council of Ministers recalled the importance of economic cooperation. It was convinced "that the future of the O.A.U. and the solidarity of the African peoples
are indissolubly linked with the establishment and development
of every kind of organized trade on a continental scale in Africa." But it stressed that the formation of such units could
only be "a phase in the establishment of an expanded African
market covering the entire continent." Elsewhere the regional
groupings were reminded to keep the OAU informed about their
activities. For the moment, though, it only instructed the
Secretariat to draft a study on the creation of an intra-African
market.

By the September 1968 Council of Ministers, the Organization took a surprisingly sober and modest view of the situation. It noted that although the need for economic cooperation
had been grasped a great deal of effective work still remained
to be done and that, despite resolutions adopted in the past,
the volume of inter-African trade had not increased apprecia-
bly. It also admitted that many of the goods available inside
Africa were, for various reasons, imported from outside. To
improve the situation the member states were asked to help
the Secretariat compile information needed to expand inter-
African trade and to submit reports of their experiences in any
groupings they created. Such regional groupings would have to

be broadened to include new members and extended to cover
a greater range of economic sectors and commodities.   And
promotional efforts, such as businessmen's meetings, publicity
programs and trade fairs could be launched.   The task given
the Secretariat was

> ... to assemble and disseminate any statistical and
> accounting data relevant to the economic integration
> of Member States, to draw up in particular an in-
> ventory of the agricultural and industrial resources
> of those States and to make a study of their respec-
> tive fiscal and customs systems as well as of their
> import and export structures, in order to help
> Member States in their efforts to integrate.

But political will, increased publicity and reductions in
tariffs would not always be enough to hold together the emerging economic units.   The ECA tried to give them a solid basis
for integration by nurturing a complementarity in the economies.   This could be done by harmonizing development plans
and encouraging regional projects that created solid economic
links.   One approach was to make the states trade with one
another by locating different industries in different states.
The most important effort was made for the iron and steel industry in West Africa.   Rather than have many small, redun-
dant plants in various countries, a major one could be established to service the region.   After careful preparation and
repeated meetings, it was decided to create a West African
Iron and Steel Authority.   The counterpart for this was, naturally, other schemes for other industries so that each state
in the region would have something to offer.

Trade and Aid.

Somewhat later, trade became the most active front in
the struggle for development.   The African states lived largely on their sales of primary products and raw materials to
the more developed countries, from which they then imported
finished goods.   However, they were startled and angered by
the conclusions of an analysis that showed that, although the
trade of the developing countries was increasing, it was not
keeping up with expansion elsewhere.   Their share in total
world trade was thus falling and, in addition, most of the
trade was with the advanced states rather than with the rest
of the third world.   What was worse, the prices the developing countries received for their goods was decreasing relative-

ly to what they paid for industrial and other goods from outside. This degradation of the terms of trade threatened their
very existence.

This analysis, prepared largely by the Argentinian
economist Raul Prebisch, was a cause for dismay. The efforts at developing their countries by increasing sales of their
own goods and using the receipts to promote growth did not
seem to be paying off. Still, the developing countries would
not beg for aid. They only claimed what they felt was rightfully theirs and demanded a transformation of the trade structures that put them at a disadvantage. What they wanted was
trade on a more equitable basis. Given their bad starting
position this also included preferences for the first manufactured and industrial products of their infant industries.

Tacitly admitting some of these claims, the members
of the United Nations decided to hold a World Conference on
Trade and Development. It was hoped that some of the problems could be thrashed out and a new deal obtained for the
developing countries. The points under discussion would include the need for increasing the trade of the developing countries, both among themselves and with the developed countries,
in primary commodities as well as manufactured goods; measures for ensuring stable, equitable and remunerative prices
for their exports; and measures for gradually removing tariffs
and other barriers which had an adverse effect on their trade.
Finally, the conference would seek to establish any methods
and machinery found necessary. [3]

The Heads of State were also aware of the problem.
And the list of economic tasks included "the restructuralization
of international trade." They recognized the importance of the
World Trade Conference and welcomed it. This opportunity
had to be seized and the summit resolution

> ... urges all States concerned to conduct negotia-
> tions, in concert, with a view to obtaining from
> the consumer countries real price stabilization and
> guaranteed outlets on the world market so that the
> developing countries may derive considerably great-
> er revenue from international trade.

The first session of the OAU's Economic and Social
Commission in December 1964 also encouraged the member
states to participate actively and suggested a number of pointers for a joint approach. The OAU states were asked to use

the forum to present the developed countries with the following
demands:

1) to abandon the reciprocity clauses in their economic arrangements with African states;

2) to adapt "most favored nation" clauses to the
particular needs of each developing country;

3) to grant preferential treatment to growing African industries;

4) to maximize the use of raw materials as opposed to synthetics;

5) to work toward the abolition of all discriminatory regulations covering imports from developing countries;

6) to replace existing international trade organizations (i.e. GATT) with a single new body equipped to deal with Africa's needs; and

7) to avoid all present practices by the "economic
blocs" of the industrialized states which are
prejudicial to the economies of African countries.[4]

The Trade Conference was held in Geneva from 23
March to 16 June 1964. Its Final Act confirmed the original
analysis and objectives and also outlined a much more detailed
program for attaining them. But the main decision was to establish a permanent organization, United Nations Conference on
Trade and Development (UNCTAD), to pursue these aims.
With its occasional full meetings, a large governing Board,
and technical bodies on commodities, manufactures, shipping
and finance, UNCTAD was a very ample piece of machinery to
analyse and plan and, ultimately, to bargain. UNCTAD I also
indicated that appeals would be made to the good will of the
advanced countries so that increasingly favorable compromises
might be reached. A first significant suggestion was that the
advanced countries try to provide financial resources to the
developing countries at a minimum level as close to one per
cent of gross national income as possible.

Nevertheless, despite the principles and resolutions
adopted, there were few concrete results and disillusionment

gradually set in.   The whole arrangement seemed a bit flimsy.
The traditional principle of reciprocity had been shelved and
the only question was the level of gains for the third world.
The developing countries therefore urged far-reaching commitments while the advanced states tried to limit their losses.
Once the debates centered on a fair share of trade and an
equitable remuneration for goods, terms that were hard to define economically, they moved ever further into the realm of
economic bargaining and politics.   Thus, at the same time the
developing countries demanded more, they were afraid that the
advanced countries would go back on what had already been
promised.   The attitude at the second session of the Economic
and Social Commission in January 1965 was one of vigilance.
To keep a watch on the situation and plan a joint policy, the
Commission set up an ad hoc Committee of Fourteen consisting mainly of the African members of the Board.

The Committee of Fourteen met jointly with the ECA
Working Party on Inter-African Trade which provided the economic expertise and documentation while leaving the OAU to
look after the political coordination and impulse.   There was
a first meeting at the end of March in Addis Ababa and an extraordinary meeting, just before the convening of the governing Board, from 22-29 August 1965 in Geneva.   The latter
meeting may have been responsible for the reportedly well-
coordinated and effective stand of the African delegations and,
if so, it was unfortunate that more joint ECA/OAU meetings
did not follow them up.

But the task of the OAU Committee of Fourteen was
not that simple.   On the whole the interests of the developing
countries coincided and a joint approach could be worked out
towards the advanced countries.   What complicated matters
was that one group of advanced countries had already worked
out temporarily satisfactory relations with a group of developing countries.   Association with the European Economic Community had already given the eighteen associates much of what
was being asked of the other developed countries.   There was,
of course, little chance that the associates would renounce the
preferences they already enjoyed and the aim had to be a global preferential system in which they would receive at least
equivalent advantages.   However, since the associates (and
those who enjoyed Commonwealth preferences) already had
more than could be gotten from UNCTAD for some time, they
tended to let others take the initiative as long as their interests were not harmed.   Since the number of associated and
other states with or seeking special relations with some out-

side economic bloc was high in Africa, the Committee had to
carefully balance its policies rather than just follow a hard
line.

Africa was not working alone in UNCTAD. From the
beginning the nations took sides and three basic groups crys-
tallized: the so-called Group of Seventy-Seven African, Asian
and Latin American countries, the market economies, and the
centrally planned economies. The group of developing countries, which soon had many more than 77 members, already
had a large majority and kept the initiative. Even though it
could adopt any decisions it wished, it was clear that, since
implementation was voluntary, it should not demand more than
could be reasonably expected. It was helped by a certain ri-
valry--more than emulation--between East and West, although
this was of limited value when demands affected both. Still,
it was not long before a gap arose between what the developing countries wanted and what the advanced countries were
willing to give.

Looking back on the early years of UNCTAD, the developing countries were not very happy. The time had been
devoted to rather wordy discussions with those in a position to
help them. But the actual assistance was relatively limited.
Although sometimes higher in absolute terms, the aid from
the advanced countries was further than ever from the one per
cent of national income requested. And no start had even been
made at a reorganization of world trade to improve the sales
of traditional exports or promote the diversification of economies. Still, although this was far from promising, the Seventy-Seven decided that the next major round should be devoted
to negotiating on a number of specific items so as to achieve
"practical and concrete results." And the long preparation for
UNCTAD II began.

This turn was reflected in the OAU. In November 1966
the Addis Ababa Assembly decided "to co-ordinate the positions
of African leaders in order to guarantee the success of the
second World Conference on Trade and Development, both with
respect to solidarity among developing countries and to negotiations among the latter and industrialized countries." Nevertheless, during the following period, its economic work almost
ground to a halt and even the Committee of Fourteen was largely inactive. The view of the Kinshasa Council was in September 1967 already less encouraging. In a brief resolution on
UNCTAD, it noted that the developed countries "are making a
concerted effort to delay the implementation of the recommen-

dations and resolutions of the First World Conference." However, UNCTAD II was coming up and the OAU had to prepare for it as well. The Group of Seventy-Seven had decided to hold a conference of African, Asian and Latin American Ministers of Economic Affairs to lay down a common stand. Thus the Council urged the African states to meet before that conference in Algiers "to adopt a uniform position and co-ordinate African views regarding the agenda." Such a meeting was arranged and, with the counsel of the OAU and ECA, an African Declaration was adopted and merged with those of the other two groups.

The Economics Ministers Conference was opened by President Boumedienne of Algeria on 10 October 1967. In a very stiff speech he expressed his views on the distressing situation in the developing countries and did not hesitate to point his finger at those he held responsible. He charged the United States and Europe with "pillaging" the resources of the third world in the guise of "peaceful coexistence." Increased development aid, he felt, should be considered as "simple restitution of part of the debt incurred by Western countries in the course of their odious exploitation."[5]

His words did not dominate the conference as such. The delegates were economists and this was not their language or field. They left the political aspects of the problem to others and did not seek to pin down any culprit. Nevertheless, in their own way, they reflected the prevailing mood. They too drew a dismal picture of the foregoing period during which the situation in the developing countries had only worsened. The rate of economic growth had fallen off and the disparity with the affluent world was only sharper. This meant that "the lot of more than a billion people of the developing world continues to deteriorate as a result of the trends in international economic relations."

The Charter of Algiers, adopted on 24 October, was a thirty page program of measures to redress the situation. Two weeks' work had gone into preparing this list of demands directed at both capitalist and socialist countries and spelling out in some detail how they should help the developing world. Among other things, the developed countries were asked a) to conclude a number of commodity agreements to stabilize markets and prices, b) introduce no new tariff or non-tariff restrictions and gradually remove existing ones on commodity exports from developing countries, c) negotiate a general system of preferences on a non-reciprocal basis for unrestricted and duty-free access of their manufactures to markets of the developed countries and d) increase the flow of public and private capital.

There was considerable depth to the analysis and justification for many of the items, but this was only one side of the problem. The Algiers Charter cited the failure of the advanced countries to aid the poorer nations. Great stress was placed on the international community's "obligation to rectify these unfavourable trends and to create conditions under which all nations can enjoy economic and social well-being." But it did not really go into the failures or missed opportunities of the developing countries. Although they insisted that the "primary responsibility for their development rests on them," there was no definition of this responsibility nor of their duties during the process. Therefore, as a basis for bargaining, the Charter was valid. But it could only be one pillar of any future joint program of action. What was needed most was not so much a campaign against the advanced countries as an alliance with them against underdevelopment as such.

When the Council of Ministers next dealt with the matter, UNCTAD II had already begun. The resolution was again prepared by Committee C, whose members were more often politicians than economists. This statement therefore contrasted sharply with the Algiers Charter. More than anything, it simply gave vent to wide-spread impatience and pessimism. The resolution of 20 February 1968 noted with regret "that in the proceedings of UNCTAD II the developing countries are encountering opposition in their efforts towards achieving changes in the iniquitous terms of trade which have always prevailed due to the rigid attitude and lack of realistic understanding on the part of developed countries who are resistant to the necessary changes being demanded by the developing countries." It urged on the members of the African Group, in cooperation with other groups, to "spare no effort in the defence of African Trade interests and the implementation of the objectives of the Algiers Charter." Since flexibility might have been a better policy at that point, stressing the more essential items and dropping others so that some agreement could be reached between widely divergent starting positions, this resolution did little to relieve the atmosphere.

UNCTAD II deliberated from 1 February to 29 March 1968 in New Delhi. It did not take long to realize that the positions of the developing countries and both the market and centrally planned economies were as far apart as ever. Frus-

tration only grew as the Group of Seventy-Seven tried to impose the points it had proclaimed in the Charter.   Soon a
deadlock was reached and the rest of the second UNCTAD conference was just an attempt at putting the best face on things.
No commitments for preferences on primary and manufactured
goods had been attained and the time had not even come for
actual negotiations.   The only apparent accomplishment was to
insert in the new list of aims a series of targets that had no
more chance of being attained than the previous ones.   For
example, despite the unmistakeable indication of the advanced
states that they would not be able to increase their aid to development for many years to come, the Final Act raised the
level of aid requested to one per cent of gross national product.   The only point on which the OAU received satisfaction
was somewhat extraneous to the debates.   South Africa was
suspended from UNCTAD "until it shall have terminated its
policy of racial discrimination."

At the Council of Ministers in Algiers, from 4-12 September 1968, there was a long debate on UNCTAD II.   What
was clear was that the conference "did not satisfy all the aspirations of the countries of the Third World in general or of
Africa in particular."   The delegates were especially annoyed
that the conference had never really gotten off the ground and
had been just another display of forensics.   "The negotiations
called for so insistently did not materialize and ... the basic
demands of the developing countries were left unsatisfied."
When they sought the reasons for this they were only able to
cite one, "the lack of political will on the part of the developed countries."   The Council did not enquire into the causes of
this lack of will nor consider how it could be overcome.
There was also no thought of making UNCTAD a more cooperative venture.

Rather, the conclusion drawn by the OAU was that Africa and the third world had to increase their "effectiveness."
A three point plan was suggested.   There should be an institutional reform of UNCTAD.   Then, ministers of the Seventy-
Seven should meet again in Dakar to coordinate the views and
safeguard the common interests of the developing countries.
The African Group would meet first to harmonize the views
of its members, especially as concerned the thorny question of
preferences.   Finally, it was recommended that the twelve African members of the Board constitute an OAU Committee of
Experts empowered "to ensure the implementation of the policies set forth in the Algiers Charter, and to propose to O.A.
U. Member States appropriate methods for successful negotia-

tions within UNCTAD." Here the OAU and ECA Secretariats were requested to extend all possible assistance.

UNCTAD was a rather special combination of trade and aid. But the advanced countries of West and East as well as various international organizations were more directly able to help the developing countries of Africa obtain both the technical and financial assistance they needed. Although there were many divergencies among the members of the OAU, there was full agreement that every effort should be made to increase this aid absolutely and also relatively, since the more recently independent continent of Africa was at first neglected. Bilateral aid was, of course, left to the members. But the OAU was interested in multilateral aid, especially from UN bodies.

Although the OAU had not actively campaigned for increased aid, the member states and the UN African Group had been encouraging this for years. They had also been very successful. Although technical assistance had originally been rather small, it was growing and Africa was soon first among the five continents. By the time the OAU was founded, Africa was receiving fourteen million dollars worth of technical assistance a year from the various UN programs and agencies. But it was much lower on the list for financial aid. By 1963, although Africa had obtained one billion dollars in loans from the World Bank and its affiliates, it was not enough for a broad scale and rapid campaign of development.

At the Council of Ministers in September 1967, it was suggested that Africa could do much better for itself if it presented a common front rather than undertaking isolated or individual actions. The resolution on industrialization, along with urging participation of the member states and the Secretariat in work by UNIDO (UN Industrial Development Organization), recommended

> ... a co-ordinated and collective stand towards the capital exporting countries and the aid-giving international organs such as the International Bank for Reconstruction and Development [IBRD] and its affiliates and the U.N.D.P. (Special Fund) with a view to bettering our bargaining position vis-à-vis these organs, thereby enhancing the flow of more financial resources into the continent and influencing favourably our borrowing terms in the way of longer maturity dates and lower interest rates.

Then, in September 1968, the African Executive Directors and Governors of the International Monetary Fund and the IBRD were encouraged to coordinate their efforts in order to secure better conditions for Africa.

However, there was another source of aid that had still not been tapped. All the African countries were developing or under-developed. Yet there were big differences between them. Some were more advanced technically, even if only one step ahead of others. And they would be in a position to offer assistance to the member states that had to overcome similar problems somewhat later. They could thus provide experts and technicians, particularly well acquainted with African conditions, less expensively than the industrialized countries or international organizations. The states of the continent were also not equally poor. The coastal ones or those with abundant natural resources were often better off than their neighbors. Certainly a small OAU program of technical and financial assistance would be a welcome addition and could greatly strengthen solidarity in Africa.

By September 1968, the Organization was ready to take its first timid steps in this direction. A number of states had, on their own initiative, already introduced bilateral arrangements for technical assistance; a report of the Secretariat suggested that these arrangements be expanded. The Secretariat was also asked to collect information on the availability and need for cadres. It would only act as a clearing house, relaying the information to interested member states. But a further institutionalization was bound to follow. It was much less certain when the OAU would be able to introduce financial assistance as well.

Notes

1. UN Document A/6174.

2. See Arthur Hazlewood, <u>African Integration and Disintegration</u>.

3. General Assembly Res. 1785 (XVII), 8 Dec. 1962.

4. <u>Africa Report</u>, March 1964.

5. <u>Ibid</u>., Jan. 1968.

B. Trade Unionism

From the very beginning, the trade union movement in Africa had been divided. The unions sprung up at different times and were shaped to resemble differing structures in the metropolitan or "fraternal" (usually American and Soviet) unions that helped them grow. The young unions adopted differing ideologies, roughly classifyable as moderate, Christian or radical. Thus there was considerable contrast from state to state and even within each country. This was only aggravated by close relations with the three international centres: the International Confederation of Free Trade Unions (ICFTU), the International Federation of Christian Trade Unions (IFCTU), and the World Federation of Trade Unions (WFTU).

The strivings towards continental unity had been strongly felt in the trade union movement as well. But the situation was even more difficult than with sovereign states since there were often more than one union or tendency in each state and internal rivalry only aggravated continental divisions. Even after the founding of the OAU, there were still two antagonistic Pan-African organizations. The All-African Trade Union Federation (AATUF) included the unions from radical states as well as splinter groups of an even more rabid stamp. The African Trade Union Confederation (ATUC) consisted of moderate and Christian unions of most of Francophone Africa and the moderate Anglophone countries and represented a substantially larger number of workers and unions than its rival.

Although both continental groupings stressed unity and were deliberately open to all unions that accepted their views, there was little desire to merge. Each had a specific clientele and had membership provisions that inhibited adhesion from unions of the opposite tendency. ATUC was less doctrinaire and permitted its members to follow their own policies on most matters. But it was rejected by those unions that disapproved its links with the ICFTU and criticized any attachment to non-African centres. AATUF had taken a very strong stand on disaffiliation, which it proclaimed as a duty of members and non-members alike, and it was this point that became the official stumbling block to unity.

534

One Step Forward, Two Steps Back.

Nevertheless, it was clear that the feud had to cease if the trade union movement wished to play an important and constructive role in nation-building and African unity. The culmination of the governmental efforts for unity was the Addis Ababa summit conference in May 1963. There, the Heads of State forgot their differences and quarrels and formed one single organization. Pressure built up for the trade unions to do the same. And the summit resolution on labor matters prescribed the aim of establishing an African Trade Union.

Soon after, at the 1963 International Labor Organization (ILO) session, the unions showed their basic agreement when they walked out over the question of South Africa. The atmosphere seemed to clear and, finally, representatives of both AATUF and ATUC met in Dakar to discuss the possibility of merging. On 19 October they issued a joint communique recommending the unification of national trade union organizations and the realization of their independence of the internationals. They also agreed to hold a preparatory meeting in Algiers in January 1964 to choose the time and site of a founding congress of a unified African labor movement. But the meeting was postponed and never took place.

The two African organizations then fell back into their old rivalry. In April 1964, the African Regional Organization of the ICFTU met in Addis Ababa. It adopted a resolution on African labor unity, which it strongly supported, and proposed as the basis thereof a confederation of union centres, each having the right to affiliate internationally as a sign of solidarity as well as a projection of the African personality. One could hardly claim that the moderates were holding out their hand, but the reply was unfortunate. For, in June 1964, the AATUF meeting in Bamako passed a resolution stopping further discussion with ATUC on the question of unity. It also adopted an even more revolutionary charter that lay down a "doctrine, orientation and principles" it considered a condition to membership and the violation of which was subject to sanctions.

At that point the OAU appeared on the scene. At the Cairo Assembly, in July 1964, AATUF appealed for exclusive recognition. This was not acceptable to the majority and no suggestion was made of granting the same status to both organizations. Rather, the matter was referred to the Economic and Social Commission for further consideration. When the

Commission met in Cairo, in January 1965, it received a report from the Secretary-General analyzing the differences between AATUF and ATUC and suggesting that joint meetings be
held under the auspices of the OAU. It was hinted that sooner or later the governments would have to intervene to accelerate the reconciliation. Acting on the conclusions of this report, the Commission requested the Secretary-General to help
the two bodies meet under the auspices of the OAU in order to
seek ways of attaining unity. It also intimated that the split
was due solely to affiliation with trade union organizations outside Africa and called upon the unions to be inspired by the
principles of the Charter, especially that of non-alignment,
when seeking unity and independence. The Commission was
soon eclipsed, but the Secretary-General continued making suggestions and he proposed there be a joint meeting in Accra
just before the Assembly.

        Although the OAU intended to narrow the gulf and over-
come differences, its first steps were part of the old rivalry.
AATUF, which represented a minority although vociferous
group of unions, could hardly be the sole spokesman in OAU
councils. Neither the report nor the resolution espousing
AATUF's view on affiliation were acceptable to ATUC which did
not wish to meet in Accra, the headquarters of the rival organization. And even AATUF was suspicious of the Secretariat's meddling in union affairs. The OAU initiatives were short-
lived and the cause of unity in the trade union movement was
temporarily forgotten.

        There were, of course, periodic feelers for unity. The
ordinary Congress of ATUC in Lagos, from 5-8 October 1965,
brought together 30 trade union organizations from 23 countries. They adopted a resolution asking their new officers "to
initiate all measures and make all necessary contact with secretariats of the All-African Trade Union Federation with a view
to achieving pan-African trade union unity" on the basis of the
Dakar communique and taking into account the wish expressed
by the Economic and Social Commission. ATUC even instructed its new bureau "to study desirable statutory changes" that
might facilitate unity. This time it did not stress the question
of affiliation. Rather, ATUC invoked another principle when
reaffirming "its faith in African unity and its conviction that
authentic trade union unity must be founded on the independence
and liberty of each member organization to determine its own
policies ... in accordance with the Charter of the Organization
of African Unity stipulating non-interference in the internal affairs of Member States."

Still, no concrete progress was made. As late as February 1968, the AATUF executive bureau decided to resume its contacts with ATUC and take up the dialogue to attain unity. What it envisaged, however, was a trade union movement that was profoundly African and disaffiliated from the international organizations. The centres adhering to the single African organization of the future would have to be disaffiliated from the internationals.[1] Thus, as long as each rival clung to its own principles, there was little reason to expect any change in the situation.

An OAU-type Compromise.

It would be a terrible over-simplification to claim that nothing prevented a merger and that all that was needed was good will. The differences were fundamental and deep. The underlying ones were ideological. ATUC included the more moderate and traditional unions concerned with the welfare of the individual workers. It was pragmatic and evolutionary. It stressed working conditions and bread and butter issues. It did not want to be regimented into government plans of development although it was willing to participate in planning and decisions and to cooperate in implementation. Its policies presupposed a relatively liberal economy and a certain degree of democracy. And its unions fought for national autonomy and independence from the government. Although it did not stress political initiatives, ATUC did support the general African stand on decolonization, non-alignment and neo-colonialism.

AATUF, on the other hand, represented the newer trend of militant trade unions that put national interests before the welfare of the workers. These unions were often integrated in the state structure or at least toed the government line. They had much more articulate economic and political goals, such as strong socialism, condemnation of Western imperialism and criticism of American policy in Vietnam. The AATUF charter clearly reflected this outlook. Socialism was the economic objective but the path was largely political. The role of the trade union was "first of all political" and its aim was "broadening the consciousness of the masses in adding a revolutionary social content to their conceptions of the national liberation struggle." However, the action of the trade unions varied with the country they were in. In those following a "revolutionary course," they were to look after the economic management, training of competent political, economic and social leaders, and "revolutionary orientation" of the country. But, in those

"under the domination of neo-colonialism and reactionaries,"
they were to work against the government and rally the masses
to "an authentic revolutionary political party." It was on this
basis that "African trade unionism could become an independent
and united ... movement within the framework of a well-de-
fined doctrine authentically African."

It was this militant policy of AATUF, contrary to the
assumption of its charter, that embittered and hardened the divisions. For the ATUC unions were not willing to accept the
dictation of the radicals. They especially resented this pressure since they represented a broader base of workers and
more states. Ever since the days of Sekou Touré's UGTAN,
and after AATUF's Secretary-General John K. Tettageh
had threatened to crush them, the ATUC members suffered
raiding, the creation of splinter unions, attempts at imposing
AATUF ideology and all sorts of strong arm tactics. They had
also witnessed the emasculation of free trade unions in certain
countries. They refused such domineering and would not be
brought into a larger unit on these terms. Since the radical
states were clearly behind the "revolutionary" unions, the mod
erate unions received support from their own governments,
which preferred them to local unions working along the lines
suggested by AATUF.

Despite the outlooks and methods, the differences between the two continental organizations had become somewhat
less sharp with time. Both agreed that unity in the trade
union movement was desirable and that the trade unions had to
play a dynamic role in political, social and economic life. It
had been, thus far, the point of affiliation that blocked unification. The ATUC unions had repeatedly insisted on their right
to determine all policies including affiliation. They benefitted
from ties since ICFTU and IFCTU provided training and even
financial support. However, as the unions became organized
and stronger and were backed by legislation and financed by
the check-off, they were increasingly independent of internation
al aid as well. Still, they saw no reason to cease such relations or isolate themselves. In AATUF the policy had been
pointedly anti-affiliation. The charter permitted neither AATUF
itself nor its members to affiliate internationally. But they
were allowed to maintain fraternal relations "with all the work
ers and all trade union organizations of the world." In practice this had meant close contacts with WFTU, where they obtained training and other sorts of assistance. It also made
the question of formal affiliation somewhat academic.

Certainly there were still differences. But they were no greater than those between the states before Addis Ababa. A solution could have been found in the same way. First, it was necessary to forget old grudges. Then a broad platform could be defined, similar to that of the OAU to include decolonization, non-alignment, and development. It would also have to include certain guarantees for cooperation. But the key to unity could only be the actual foundation of co-existence in the continent: the principle of non-interference. This would permit the equal and sovereign unions to determine their own policies without fear of reprisal or raiding. Then the policies of the joint organization could be worked out democratically, with one vote per union or on some proportional basis according to the number of members. Non-affiliation would have to be a compromise, as in the OAU, whereby the Pan-African organization was not aligned but its members could have what relations they desired. Indeed, as long as the unions did not see eye-to-eye, a system like the OAU was the only workable basis for unity.

Could it be achieved? Considering that they demanded much more than the moderates, the radicals would have to relax their militant policies and bow to majority decisions that might often go against them. What they, and all the workers, would obtain in exchange would be a united, viable and positive movement. This was far better than the divided and quarreling groups that existed. And, where they could convince the moderates to go along with them, the efforts of the trade unions would be much stronger and more successful. Thus they had to take the same dare as the radical states.

The Council of Ministers in Kinshasa, in September 1967, returned to the question and asked the Secretary-General to organize a meeting to reconcile the trade union centres. But it was not until 12 March 1969 that representatives of AATUF and ATUC met in Algiers to draw up a program and methods for achieving unity. This agreement was endorsed by the Conference of Labour Ministers which called upon the trade unions, the member states and the OAU to work for its implementation. The most important element was the national governments and their pressure could be decisive. Still, it remained to be seen whether the trade union movement would finally be united.

1.   Le Monde, 20 Feb. 1968.

C. Technologia

There was also a whole range of activities, including social, transport and communications; education and culture; health, sanitation and nutrition; and scientific, technical and research, which could make a definite contribution to the development of Africa. The ministers concerned were acutely aware of the potential importance of these fields and they tried to draw the Organization into extensive campaigns. With so much to be done, the specialized commissions hoped to give an immediate and powerful impulse to new and older projects. They drew up impressive work programs and planned to reorganize and expand the necessary structures.

But none of the fields seemed that attractive or urgent to the governing bodies and, after a brief round of conferences, the work fell into neglect. The reason was apparently that the OAU did not have the staff or funds to handle it. But, in fact, the highest priorities were simply not there and the more technical activities had to be downgraded. First the programs and then the structures were restricted. Few of the projects were ever launched and even fewer were completed. Even the commissions stopped meeting and, to follow up some of the ongoing work, the Council of Ministers and Secretariat provided interim machinery.

Social, Transport and Communications.

The Economic and Social Commission met twice, first in Niamey in December 1963, and then in Cairo in January 1965. However, from the beginning, the social aspects were largely overshadowed by the economic plans. The Commission was run mainly by the Economics Ministers and projects like integration or trade received the greatest attention. Nevertheless, a number of ideas had been expressed for work on labor and social questions.

First priority went to labor and particular interest was shown in uniting the two trade union associations, ATUC and AATUF. But there was some concern for more general aspects as well. The first session of the Commission called for the establishment of an African labor office that would have broad tasks of harmonizing social legislation, vocational training and other activities. The Inner-African Labour Institute, part of the Commission for Technical Cooperation in Africa known as the CCTA, was thought of as a building block for a later structure.

However, before even starting their work, the members of the Commission were somewhat annoyed to find that they had a potential rival in the Conference of African Labor Ministers. This body, created by the ILO, was more highly specialized in labor matters and also met at ministerial level. Nevertheless, the Ministers of Economics at the second session did not hesitate to inform their colleagues that the OAU Commission was "the proper forum in which the authorities on Labour and Social problems may co-ordinate and harmonize their activities." They therefore recommended "that in the future, all preoccupations of the Conference of African Labour Ministers be an integral part of the agenda of the sessions of the Economic and Social Commission of the Organization of African Unity."

Since the Commission was not able to hold a third meeting, it could not make good its claim. As in the past Africa's labor leaders maintained their contacts through ILO meetings and annual conferences and the Conference of African Labor Ministers. Yet the importance of close relations with the ILO was such that an agreement on cooperation was signed by the OAU and ILO on 26 November 1965. Then, at their sixth session, the Labor Ministers turned towards the OAU. The Kinshasa Council of Ministers, in September 1967, authorized the Secretariat to coordinate the activities of the Conference and to service further meetings by sending out invitations and preparing documents on the agenda. The first session under OAU auspices was held in Algiers from 10-15 March 1969. But the activities were still largely restricted to defining a policy toward the ILO. The Council resolution on labor recommended that the member states choose African nationals to represent their governments, employers and workers in the ILO and that they present a united front there in order to defend African interests. Then the Conference urged more active participation in the ILO and, particularly, more African seats in the committees and governing body.

Second priority went to youth. The OAU hoped to associate young people with the ideals of African unity. The Economic and Social Commission considered the possibilities of

unifying the youth movements and running activities such as
festivals, jamborees and work camps. It wished to draft statutes for a Pan-African Youth Organization and to organize an
African Scouts Union and an annual African Sports Game. Little came of this through the OAU although some headway was
made within the movements themselves.

The fields of transport and communications were originally dealt with by the Economic and Social Commission and
at its first session the ministers lay down a program including
cooperation in land, air and sea transport, the creation of African companies and organizations and especially the establishment of a Pan-African Telecommunications Union. To this
purpose the Egyptian government had convened a meeting of
Communications Ministers and this was brought to the attention
of the Heads of State attending the Cairo Assembly in July 1964.
They decided that the field was sufficiently important to warrant a new Commission on Transport and Communications,
which was established at the Cairo meeting in November 1964.

The first act of the new Commission, however, was to
deny any interest in an African Telecommunications Union
since it considered itself to be "the sole competent Organization for studying, in a spirit of African development as a whole,
the decisions and the programmes of co-operation and progress in those technical fields." But the Commission recognized the importance of the work of international organizations
in these fields. It also realized that technical and even financial assistance would be necessary to carry on its own projects. It therefore requested its members to increase the number of African seats in the Administrative Board of the International Telecommunications Union (ITU) and to participate
more actively in the Universal Postal Union.

The Commission on Transport and Communications presented a very impressive program. The foundation for these
activities would be the Rome and Dakar Plans drawn up by the
ITU. The magnitude of the tasks the Commission tackled
could be judged from some of the items like laying a coaxial
submarine cable, using artificial satellites and installing a system of transmission by micro-waves to link member states.
It also lay down a basic principle of Africanization of links:
"communications between any two African member states should
be established either directly or via another African member
state wherever this is possible, and that all traffic inside Africa be routed through member states." In order to prepare
and then implement these projects, it asked the Secretariat to

stablish three offices on post, telecommunications and trans-
ort.

None of the Commission projects were launched. For-
unately, other organizations were increasingly interested in
ossibilities of cooperation in these fields. The Economic
'ommission for Africa had invited the OAU to participate in
.s own activities and the Organization was asked to help run
 joint meeting on telecommunications in Africa in March 1966.
'here was a follow-up resolution at the Kinshasa Council in
eptember 1967. Obviously unfamiliar with the technical as-
ects of the problem, the delegates limited themselves to crit-
zizing the colonial network which linked the former colonies
) the mother countries rather than one African state to an-
ther and urging cooperation to develop a new network. But
nly very general and vague pointers could be given. After
sking that this work be given "the priority it deserved," the
ouncil recommended better individual and joint utilization of
xisting and future installations, training adapted to African
eeds and standardization. None of these recommendations,
owever, would be useable until presented in sufficient detail,
iving explanations and specifications.

The Economic Commission for Africa had been actively
orking at improved road and maritime transport for the con-
nent. For years it had planned a trans-Saharan highway and
:her links between African countries. It also tried to consoli-
ate the inland rail, highway and waterway networks and to in-
rconnect the railway and road systems, paying special atten-
on to the landlocked countries. Yet when the Kinshasa Coun-
l dealt with these matters, no reference was made to the
ork of the ECA and other bodies. The Council only recalled
at the task of the Commission on Transport and Communica-
ons was to draw up plans and coordinate policies in these
elds. This was already a weak basis for its recommenda-
ons, which were largely pious wishes unless backed up by
udies and financing: highway networks should be extended
d improved, legislation should be coordinated, ways and
eans should be found to develop multinational use of river sys-
ms and lakes and so on. And there were more pious wishes
e year after. The only valid suggestion had been to keep the
AU Secretariat informed of all regional links envisaged so it
uld disseminate the information and increase knowledge and
us use of these links.

In November 1964, an African Air Transport Conference
d met in Addis Ababa, attended by the International Civil

Aviation Organization (ICAO), ECA and the OAU. The purpose
of the meeting was to establish an African Civil Aviation Organ and the member states insisted that the OAU be consulted
on the measures to establish such a body. Unfortunately the
project got bogged down in a jurisdictional quarrel among organizations and the ICAO draft statute was rejected by both the
OAU and the ECA, who circulated an alternative text. The
Council of Ministers later expressed its ire and insisted

> ... that ICAO's role in air transport development
> in Africa should be confined to the technical aspect
> of Civil Aviation, and that the economic aspects and
> priorities should be worked out and handled by the
> O.A.U. and the E.C.A., so that the purely African
> interests are never lost sight of.

It then recommended that the OAU/ECA text be the basis of
discussions. The African bodies won the battle and the three
agreed on a new draft statute. But the OAU came out on top
as the convener of the constituent meeting of the African Civil
Aviation Organ at the beginning of 1969.

Education and Culture.

The Educational and Cultural Commission was able to
meet twice. It met in Léopoldville in January 1964, and again
in Lagos in January 1965. It began its career by formally absorbing the already existing meetings of Ministers of Education
held by UNESCO. However, there was no desire to supplant
the United Nations Educational, Scientific and Cultural Organization in the fields where it was doing such useful work for
Africa and the Commission expressed its appreciation thereof.
At its second session, it tried to work out an agreement. But
given UNESCO's broader field of activity, it was necessary to
establish a framework including the OAU Scientific, Technical
and Research Commission as well. UNESCO even suggested
that the two OAU Commissions be merged "as a means of facilitating co-operation and co-ordination with UNESCO."

Rather than draw up its own plan of education, which
would have required considerable preparation and study, the
Educational and Cultural Commission merely adopted UNESCO's
Addis Ababa Plan. This was a comprehensive schedule for educational development throughout the continent with common
targets for expanding instruction to the whole school age population. A major goal was to increase the number of children

attending primary school by five per cent a year. The Commission wished to play a role in implementing this plan but, in addition, it also established its own program of work. It proposed to handle specific items like teacher training, language problems, schooling of nomadic populations, higher education, financing of education, illiteracy and vocational guidance. Around the corner there was also a fundamental reform of education to adapt it to post-independence needs while promoting African aspirations and unity.

The Commission decided upon a number of concrete projects as a start. In order to overcome some of the language barriers, it desired the creation of two institutes to give crash courses in English and French. A more ambitious project was an Institute of African Studies as the first branch of a future African university. The Secretariat was asked to set up a committee of experts to examine the operation and structure of such an institute. And a number of lesser items were entrusted directly in the Secretariat. It was asked to encourage activities that promoted African unity such as music and drama festivals, journals, inter-African games and so on.

The program of work was obviously a long-term affair. In order to prepare its activities the Commission decided to establish two committees of experts to study proposals. Since the Commission only met once a year, it also tried to introduce a more permanent existence in the Secretariat. It referred to the need to establish "common machinery to give expert educational advice to Member States for the solution of common problems." This advisory service would be able to follow up the work of the Commission and put the results of committee suggestions to practical use. It might even have been the nucleus of a later educational service providing technical assistance among the African states.

In the end, this machinery was never established and the OAU could not even set up the expert committees. UNESCO, however, had not curtailed its activities in favor of Africa and the meetings of Ministers of Education continued. It was even suggested that UNESCO and the OAU hold a joint meeting. The Conference on Education and Scientific and Technical Training in Relation to Development in Africa was held in Nairobi in July 1968. Despite its notable lack of accomplishment and its minute education division, the OAU did not hesitate to press its views. And, once again, it had an impact on the decisions. The delegates of 36 states, including many ministers, established the priorities for a reform of primary educa-

tion, stressed the need to train more African professors for
secondary schools and urged a greater bias towards scientific
and technical training. Although UNESCO Director General,
René Maheu, cautioned that they could not count on a serious
increase in external aid and that the African governments
would have to step up their own efforts, the delegates also
adopted several resolutions calling on UNESCO and other organ
izations to provide additional aid.

Highest priority, however, was not given to general education or culture but to information. It was there that the
OAU eventually made its only concrete effort. First it took
advantage of the existence of three bodies in the field of information. They were the Union of African News Agencies (UANA),
set up at a UNESCO-sponsored conference in April 1963, the
Union of National Radio and Television Organizations of Africa,
founded in 1960, and a militant group, the Pan-African Union
of Journalists. The three had formed a coordinating committee on mass communications media in December 1964. At the
second session of the OAU Educational and Cultural Commission, in January 1965, the coordinating committee was adopted
as its "sub-committee of information."

Then the Commission decided to launch the only project
which was actually supported by the Organization. This was a
Pan-African News Agency (PANA) entrusted with "collecting
and disseminating truthful, objective and impartial news about
Africa in the African and world press, radio and television."
The various African newspaper, radio and television authorities
depended largely on the international press agencies and foreign sources in general for the news they disseminated. It was
widely felt that this news had been prepared by biased Western
or Communist agencies. It seemed impossible to make decisions based on such information and the differing tendencies
only increased the ideological gap between African states. It
was hoped that by working on a continental scale the OAU
could set up an African agency to obtain reliable information
and to spread unbiased or possibly "Africa-biased" information
to the outside world.

Nevertheless, within an African agency there would still
be problems. On what basis would information be compiled
and selected? When Africa had a common stand this would be
relatively easy. However, if it were disunited, there could be
considerable friction. It would have been hard to sort out the
reports, denials, accusations and counter-accusations in the
Congolese crisis then going on. The process of selection

would be very delicate and to some it might appear one-sided.
But, if everything were printed, then much of the information
would be mutually contradictory. Thus there were definite political obstacles to creating such an agency. There were economic ones as well. The cost of a powerful radio station, offices throughout the world, a huge staff, correspondence and
cable fees were forbidding when compared with the cost of using established agencies.

Perhaps for these reasons the members stalled. The
Secretariat, in cooperation with UANA, had accomplished its
work and prepared the background documents and statutes for
an agency that had already been given a name and initials:
PANA. But the founding meeting could not be held. The original demand for a meeting had been made in January 1965 and
an appeal was made at the Accra Assembly. Still, despite the
Secretariat's efforts, it was not able to convene a committee
of experts until December 1965. After investigating the technical and economic aspects of PANA, they proposed that the Organization go ahead and set up the agency. It would draw on
African national press agencies for African news, have corre-
spondents abroad and use both English and French. But nothing was done. Two years later the Union of African News
Agencies met in Addis Ababa. The Executive Committee asked
that PANA be established and insisted that it was still "technically possible." Whether it was financially and politically possible remained to be seen.

In another area, what originally seemed a rather simple
matter also dragged on. The Secretariat wished to have an
emblem as a symbol of the OAU. The Council of Ministers
agreed and, in July 1964, it asked the Secretary-General to
"appeal" to African artists to submit sketches. The emblem
was to "promote consciousness of the purposes and objectives
of the Organization among the peoples of Africa." But very
few sketches were received. The Secretariat therefore decided to run a contest and offer a prize. The Educational and
Cultural Commission approved of the idea and offered a prize
of $5,000 to the winner. The deadline was 30 July 1965 and
the best design would be chosen by a panel of experts. This
time the nine experts sent by member states were able to examine a huge collection but they were unable to agree. The
prize sum was changed and the deadline postponed several
times in the following years. In September 1969, Diallo Telli,
the Secretary-General finally got an OAU emblem.

Although it had not been mentioned in the program, a very good start for a cultural policy was made by the Negro Arts Festival held in Dakar in April 1966. This was the fulfillment of an old dream of Léopold Sédar Senghor and a demonstration of the cultural variety and maturity of the Negro world. Once such a festival was held, fortunately, it was bound to encourage others. The idea was taken up by the Secretariat and suggested to the Council of Ministers in Kinshasa. It was approved and the Secretariat was asked to initiate work on an All-African Cultural Festival of African drama, folksongs and instrumental music. This time the contents would be somewhat different with the inclusion of other non-Negro strains of African culture.

As of September 1967, the Secretariat and an eight-country committee began drawing up the plans. The Council announced that Algeria would be the host and invited all the member states to participate. Since the festival was supposed to be self-financing the only problem seemed to be the initial budget. Officially it was estimated as one-and-a-half million dollars and unofficially as some five million and, after appealing to the various international bodies and member governments, a contribution of more than half-a-million dollars had to be advanced by the Organization. It was considerably less difficult to obtain over four thousand artists from forty-one states and six dependent territories. The display of African cinema, theatre, dance, music, painting, sculpture and handicrafts was a tremendous success and the vast symposium on African culture turned out a "progressive" charter. From 21 July to 1 August 1969, Africa celebrated its cultural wealth, past and present, and gave a thought to the future.

Health, Sanitation and Nutrition.

The specialized commission in this field met only once, in Alexandria in January 1964. It failed to meet again when no quorum could be obtained on two occasions. From the start it was less demanding than the other specialized commissions. The Ministers of Health merely requested a number of papers from the Secretariat concerning a standardization of health legislation, statutes, terminology, training of medical personnel and public health activities. Ultimately they would help coordinate the struggle against endemic and epidemic diseases. But no projects were suggested. And the only machinery they asked for was a Public Health Division in the Secretariat consisting of an office of documentation and information and a pool of experts.

Health was one of the fields in which international co-operation had been most effective and fruitful. This may have been why the delegates were less eager to forge their own instruments of action in the OAU. They merely praised the work of the World Health Organization and showed a desire to cooperate with it while avoiding waste. The resolution urged that the OAU Health Commission and the WHO "should actively co-ordinate their activities and programmes through a formal agreement with a view to achieving maximum efficiency and economic use of available resources--human and material." Cooperation was also sought with the FAO (Food and Agriculture Organization) and UNICEF. But cooperation with the WHO was hampered by the fact that its regional structure cut Africa into three parts with some states included in the Near East and others in Europe. Therefore, the Commission requested the establishment of a common African Office. At the same time, it urged that South Africa be excluded.

It was quite clear from this session how hard it was to combine different specializations in one commission. The delegates present came from the public health sector. There was lively interest in health and sanitation but little in nutrition. Cooperation with the WHO was strongly urged; coordination with the FAO was asked incidentally. Health received priority in this commission as economics and education did elsewhere. Unless sufficiently large delegations could be sent to deal with all aspects of a commission's work, possibly even by forming several sub-committees, the treatment would be very uneven.

For almost three years, there was silence on health and nutrition. Finally, in September 1967, the Council of Ministers adopted resolutions on the subject. But they were obviously not the work of experts on health or agriculture. The resolution on hygiene and health made very general comments on the frequency of communicable diseases and the fact that they did not respect frontiers and recommended a system of continental or regional co-operation to combat diseases, forgetting the campaigns even then being carried out by the WHO. The only concrete suggestion was that the member states encourage the manufacture and use of pharmaceutical products from African countries. Given the limited pharmaceutical industry this would be impractical in most cases and only benefit a few more advanced countries. The resolution on the establishment of regional stocks of food grains also went about the problem the wrong way. Although potentially Africa could grow more than enough food for its population, it did not produce enough at the present time. There was little sense in lamenting that occasionally member states had "to obtain food from outside Africa to cover abnormal conditions." The thing to do was to increase agricultural production sufficiently to cover needs and not to worry about establishing regional stocks of grains that were usually in short supply.

Scientific, Technical and Research.

The most dynamic body turned out to be the Scientific, Technical and Research Commission, rapidly dubbed the STRC. It met officially for the first time in Algiers, in February 1964, and again in Lagos, in January 1965. However, under different titles and in different capacities, much the same people met on other occasions as well. And, despite a decline, some real work was being accomplished. Nevertheless, this was the only commission for which the original summit conference did not suggest terms of reference and the two sessions devoted some time to defining a program. Among the ideas mooted were research on vegetable fibres and aid to the campaign for eradicating rinderpest. The emphasis was practical so as to support the development of industry and technology by research on new and better ways of exploiting natural resources, improvements in agriculture and mining, or production and conservation of fish. The Commission also suggested an inventory of research centers and activities and a list of research workers and technologists in Africa. There were indeed so many possibilities for work by the STRC that it decided to set up an ad hoc committee to draw up its program for the next three years.

Any broad program of research, however, required a solid institutional basis, and the Commission wanted an ample structure. It was the only body that asked for its own headquarters and secretariat, although "supervised" by the OAU Secretariat. The Commission, consisting of ministers, was to remain the supreme organ. But it would be advised by a Scientific Council for Africa, where the member states would be represented by scientists. It would also have an Executive Committee of at least ten members to look after the administration, program and budget. The Commission urged the creation in each country of a national scientific organization to formulate scientific policy and coordinate scientific activities locally while remaining in liaison with the STRC for the promotion of continental activities. And, finally, the Commission hoped to establish an African Academy of Science.

However, it was another matter that actually determined
the future of the STRC. In the place of terms of reference the
summit conference had referred to the CCTA and the transformation it was undergoing. The Commission for Technical Cooperation in Africa South of the Sahara was founded in January
1950 by the colonial powers as a structure to handle the administrative and financial problems of technical and scientific
cooperation. It met once a year to make unanimous recommendations to the governments. The Scientific Council for Africa, consisting of independent experts, was established to advise it. The CCTA was given a Secretariat in 1952, headquarters in London in 1954, and in the ensuing years various
offices, commissions or committees were set up for specialized tasks. They were active in fields such as animal health,
tripano research, phyto-sanitation, soils, mechanization of agriculture, geology, surveying and mapping, housing, community
development, labor and even social sciences. These bodies
held conferences and seminars and undertook studies or projects like the climatological atlas and locust and pest control
campaigns. Some of this was financed by a Research Fund.
Then, as of 1958, the CCTA began promoting technical assistance and training through a Foundation for Mutual Assistance.
This was not a fund but only a channel to inform the governments of worthy projects that required financing. Over the
years the CCTA accomplished a considerable amount of work
itself. But its major contribution was to encourage and help
the governments to cooperate and launch joint projects.

As of 1958, however, a crisis was developing in the
CCTA.[1] The original members were Belgium, France, Great
Britain, Portugal, the Rhodesias and South Africa. However,
when the wave of independence broke the CCTA was joined by
an increasing number of new African states. In 1962 a basic
revision occurred and the independent states were made the
only full members, Belgium, France and Great Britain were
made associate members and Portugal and South Africa were
expelled. The limitation "South of the Sahara" was dropped to
permit an expansion to the whole continent. The Africanization was continued after moving the headquarters to Lagos by
electing an African as Secretary-General. Nevertheless, the
transformation was not rapid nor complete enough and the
CCTA had some trouble adopting a new convention.

At the summit conference the possibility of absorbing it
appeared as an alternative to many. To the extent this institu-

tion could be drawn into the Organization of African Unity it
would have a tremendous head start in these fields. But no
final decision was taken. The resolution merely decided to
"maintain the CCTA and to reconsider its role in order to
bring it eventually within the scope" of the new Organization.
However, the "eventually" of the Heads of State was soon by-
passed by the Council of Ministers. At its first session in
Dakar, in August 1963, it already announced its intention "to
give the CCTA an African character and to integrate it in the
O.A.U." Without waiting the Ministers requested the Provisional Secretary-General to negotiate the transfer of the powers of non-African countries to the OAU and urged that "practical steps be taken for the effective integration of the CCTA
in the O.A.U."

The Secretariat immediately began negotiating the withdrawal of Belgium, France and Great Britain. The main problem was that they had largely financed the work of the CCTA
and Africa might not be able to keep up the budget. A compromise was reached in Lagos, in November 1963, when the
three governments agreed to withdraw from the CCTA but to
"consider sympathetically" requests for technical and financial
aid. This, however, implied a slower transition. The first
session of the Scientific, Technical and Research Commission
was not willing to bargain and demanded a rapid integration of
the CCTA. Without even trying to tie up loose ends the resolution recommended that the integration take place on 1 October 1964 and that it "should not await final decisions on the
transfer of assets and jurisdiction, which will continue to be
discussed between former members of the CCTA and O.A.U."
The final disengagement was more abrupt. The Council of
Ministers in Cairo recommended integration take place on 31
December 1964 at the latest and, since the European powers
decided to end their support of the budget as of December
1963, a special appeal had to be made to the OAU members to
finance it through 1964. On 26 October, the OAU Secretary-
General informed the administrative committee of CCTA that
it could make no binding decision beyond 31 December 1964
and asked it to recommend a program of activities to the forth
coming STRC meeting.

When the STRC met in January 1965, the CCTA had already been integrated in the OAU. Its staff would form the
"nucleus" of the STRC staff, its program was to be continued
primarily by the STRC and its budget financed by the OAU.
It was also decided to keep the CCTA headquarters in Lagos
and to have the bureaus outside the continent "brought back to

Africa." Steps were taken to expand the membership to all
the independent states and to adapt the program to their needs.
It might also be necessary to update the program to include
newer fields of research like desalinization of water and peaceful uses of nuclear energy. At any rate, the absorption of the
CCTA was regarded as a major victory for the OAU and it was
expected to give real momentum to the STRC.

Nevertheless, the Scientific, Technical and Research
Commission did not meet again after Lagos. Only the Scientific Council for Africa (CSA), carried over from the CCTA
and largely replacing the STRC, continued its annual meetings.
The actual fate of the CCTA was a well kept secret. Its headquarters and some of the offices still existed and certain projects were followed up. The EEC Development Fund and
United States AID had agreed to finance a rinderpest control
campaign run by the STRC. But it was impossible to judge the
level of this or any other work. The OAU made no mention
of its activities during the years after integration. Not until
the Kinshasa Council was there any mention of scientific matters at all. Then the CSA submitted two conventions to the
member states for approval. First was a Phyto-Sanitary Convention for Africa, designed to control and eliminate plant diseases. Somewhat later an African Convention on the Conservation of Nature and Natural Resources, prepared at the OAU's
request by the International Union for the Conservation of Nature and others, was ready for approval.

Going beyond the old structure, CSA also suggested new
units. Its second session, in April 1967, proposed that training and research institutions or "centres of excellence" be established for training highly qualified personnel and undertaking
research in scientific disciplines. It saw rather far since it
suggested institutions for: geology, geophysics and mineralogy;
climatology, meteorology and hydrology; human medicine and
pharmacology; food sciences and technology; veterinary medicine; physics and mathematics (including electronics); and
oceanography, marine biology and fisheries. The Kinshasa
Council, notwithstanding the dimensions of the undertaking, approved the proposal in principle. It requested the Secretary-
General to gather the relevant information and provide details
on costs and possible external aid. However, a concrete offer
was also made. The Democratic Republic of the Congo was
willing to turn its "Centre Nucleaire Trico" in Kinshasa into a
regional center for the utilization of radio-isotopes in medicine,
agriculture and biology. The Council approved the offer and
called upon the member states to "encourage in every way the

expansion and functioning not only of this Centre, but also of
the other African Centres which exist for the same purpose."

The idea had originally emanated from the Secretariat
and it made rapid progress. It was amended and put forward
by the CSA and approved by the Council of Ministers in September 1967. Then it was returned to the Secretariat for pre
paratory work. The matter was brought up and endorsed at
the Nairobi Conference on Education. By September 1968, the
Council of Ministers could agree that the establishment of
training and research centres be part of a joint OAU/ECA pro
gram and decide to appoint an OAU committee responsible for
the setting up of "centres of excellence" in Africa. This time
the Secretary-General was requested to take appropriate action
to implement the recommendations of the Nairobi Conference
and to contact the inter-African and international organizations
and UN specialized agencies "which can help in any way in the
early establishment of the required centres."

Still, it was legitimate to have some doubts about the
solidity of work in these fields. Although the conventions and
the offer of the Kinshasa center were encouraging, the possibility of creating a dozen new research centers was very remote. The main problem was still finance. The original
structure inherited from the CCTA was expensive enough. Th
headquarters in Lagos had a staff of a hundred, there were
about thirty offices, commissions and committees, and research was costly. The structure and budget were already as
heavy as that of the OAU itself. Thus it was not at all certain that Africa could or had maintained it at anything like the
previous level. This was particularly doubtful since these
were low priority items when seen in the general context of
the Organization.

Yet the financial problems went even deeper. The Scientific, Technical and Research Commission did not meet agai
after Lagos but it was replaced largely by the Scientific Council for Africa. Unfortunately, however, attendance had been
falling off and the second session in Addis Ababa sounded the
alarm. The CSA recalled that there was no such problem before since the old CCTA met the full costs of members attend
ing its meetings. Therefore it urged the OAU to set up a cen
tral fund to cover at least the travelling expenses of members
In view of the importance of this work, the Council of Ministers accepted the proposal in principle while asking the Secretary-General to study the financial implications. This situation was particularly disconcerting since the STRC had ceased

meeting owing to the absence of delegates. There was all the
more reason to fear that the CSA could also be asphyxiated by
poor attendance. And, if both Council and Commission were
out of operation, the former CCTA offices and the on-going
activities would either have to continue without authoritative
supervision or grind to a halt.

1. See Immanuel Wallerstein, The Early Years of the O.A.U.:
   Search for Organizational Preeminence.

D. Defence

One of the stronger motives when the independent states created the Organization of African Unity in 1963 was "to defend their sovereignty, their territorial integrity and independence." For this they were willing to coordinate and harmonize policies and increase cooperation. It was not that long ago that Belgium had re-entered the Congo and there was a threat of "recolonization" by far bigger powers. Even if this was admittedly an exception and it was unlikely that another state would be openly invaded, the chances that an outside power would be invited in to help a government in bad straits were much greater.

There were yet other reasons for concern with defence and security. For the members had accepted very strong commitments to "eradicate all forms of colonialism" and especially to bring about the "total emancipation of the African territories which are still dependent." It could not be excluded that far-reaching measures would be taken one day in connection with non-alignment, peace-keeping and especially aid to the dependent peoples. This showed that in many respects the OAU had been designed for conflict: protection against outside powers, efforts to avoid entangling alliances and domination, action to prevent discord among the states and the struggle to liberate the continent. What would be its role?

Defining Defence.

Even at the Addis Ababa conference most of the questions were left open. Should Africa's policy be purely defensive or also offensive, internal or external, passive or active, coordinated or unified? No clear stand was taken and there was not even a resolution hinting at the aims in the field of defence. Still, some of the questions were answered although only tentatively during the debates on activities and institutions In each instance the Heads of State as a whole preferred the less demanding of the alternatives. It was interesting that, aside from President Nkrumah, no one proposed a joint defensive structure or suggested mutual defence arrangements such is existed in the Casablanca and Brazzaville systems.

There were, to the contrary, many pressing appeals to come to the aid of the dependent peoples and even declare war against their oppressors. But the independent states were not ready. Although they accepted to succor the freedom fighters and back their efforts, there was to be no active intervention or even a corps of volunteers. Still, even by providing a haven and equipment, certain states were risking retaliation and might be drawn into the struggle. For independent Africa, as well, there was some danger of disputes within or among members. If such conflicts broke out it might be necessary to intervene sufficiently to restore peace. However, given the respect of sovereignty, there was little the Organization could do.

When it came to the means of assuring defence and security, the assembly showed no desire to establish an "African army." Even the idea of a Board of Heads of Staff, possibly the embryo of a military staff for a later army, was not acceptable and the Ethiopian draft was amended. The final decision was in favor of a Commission of Defence Ministers--no different formally from the other specialized commissions. The machinery for the liberation struggle was more complete. Yet it was entrusted to politicians with little knowledge of guerrilla or conventional warfare. And the summit had not conidered the eventuality of peace-keeping operations.

But none of these answers was immutable. This was made clear by the leaders who supported the stronger of the alternatives. Kwame Nkrumah had given special importance to the establishment of joint defensive machinery and he was not satisfied with the compromise. Sékou Touré and Ben Bella called for active intervention on the side of the freedom fighters and they disapproved of the compromise on decolonization. Many of the radicals continued campaigning for stronger measures at early meetings and particularly at the Defence Commission in Accra. President Nkrumah offered to play host to its first session, from 29 October - 2 November 1963, in the hope of influencing the decisions on machinery and activities.

The Ghanaian delegation again proposed a "Union High Command," very much the opposite of what had been decided at the summit. The plan consisted of an army and military staff, not subject to the individual states but rather following the orders of a "union government." Since this government had not been created the orders would have to come from the Assembly of Heads of State. It would have its own headquar-

ters and a staff to prepare any military operations. This pla
was not seriously discussed so shortly after it had been reject
ed in Addis Ababa. The Defence Ministers did not feel competent to take a decision and preferred having the item passed
on to the next Assembly. Nevertheless, they did sense the im
portance of their position and requested a special relationship
with the Heads of State. Rather than being subordinated to th
Council, the Commission wished to serve as a consultative or
gan and send recommendations directly to the Assembly.

The debate was revived by events in Africa. This per
iod was one of the most explosive and the calm was repeatedl
broken by all sorts of conflicts: border disputes, civil strive
mutinies and a new offensive in the colonies. By the Lagos
Council of Ministers in February 1964, Nkrumah and Touré
felt that events had proven their point. Ghana and Guinea agair
pressed for the creation of an African army and high comman
They insisted that only such a force could have "properly intervened" in the rash of border disputes, mutinies and coups.
Other countries wished to step up the assistance to the liberation wars. But the same problems arose over all the proposals. Who would pay for any force (and how much would it
cost)? What country would command or determine its action?
And under what circumstances would it act and at whose request? These questions could not be answered and it was
again decided to refer the matter to the Heads of State.[1]

However, what the proponents of stronger action had n
realized was that events were actually proving them wrong.
In neither of the territorial disputes could the OAU intervene
until the parties had fought themselves out and were willing to
be separated. Algeria and Morocco had accepted a small tean
of officers to inspect the demilitarization of a no man's land,
but even this group was soon disbanded. After lengthy deliberations the Organization decided that it could not intervene
along the Ethiopia-Somalia border since one of the parties rejected this; even if both had agreed, the OAU found that the
size and cost of the operation would be prohibitive. Even in
the mutinies in East Africa, the three states had called on the
former colonial power first and only Tanganyika accepted African troops--merely through the intermediary of the OAU, th
Organization having no real responsibilities in the operation.

Somewhat later, there were even more decisive precedents. In the Congo affair, the community of states saw how
difficult it was to maintain peace. Two sorts of action were
proposed: the central government wished to station contingent

from other states in the pacified areas while its opponents desired a major operation under the OAU to separate the combatants and impose a cease-fire and reconciliation. However, since the members disagreed sharply, the radicals deprived Tshombe of any aid while he and the moderates prevented any conceivable intervention in the Congo's internal affairs. At the same time, the drive of the liberation movements was blunted and they were often contained. Finally, in the Rhodesian crisis, the idea that had so often been voiced of actively intervening to aid the liberation movements was finally presented formally and turned down by the majority. Africa was in no position to wage war on the colonial and settler powers and this fact was accepted.

By the first Assembly in Cairo, in July 1964, all of these issues were on the agenda in one form or another and the debate was reopened. President Nkrumah was there in person to plead the urgency of a "union high command" to overcome many of these difficulties. Ben Bella made an impassioned appeal for aid to the liberation movements. But no extraordinary measures were taken this time either and, on the whole, the Heads of State were inclined to let things drift. Interest in effective machinery even flagged to the point where the Defence Commission could not attain a quorum late in 1964. It had to be reconvened and eventually met in Freetown, Sierra Leone, from 2-4 February 1965.

Organizing Defence.

The proposals made in Freetown showed what sort of contribution could be made in practice. There were suggestions for simple forms of cooperation in military training: exchange of officers and students, teaching of African unity in the curricula, joint maneuvres and the establishment of a joint African military academy. The idea was also put forward of creating an African Defence Organization. Although it went nowhere near as far as Nkrumah's plan, this implied much more than a mere Commission. It was also a relatively acceptable and realistic response to many of the questions.

The African Defence Organization, as described by the OAU press release, would be a body for "maintaining peace and security in Africa." Africa here meant only the independent states. The machinery could be set in motion to aid "one or more Member States who have been victims of extra-African aggression or who suffered serious internal trouble or in the

case of a conflict between two or more Member States." Thus
the system would be basically defensive and internal. It could
protect the states from external aggression or engage in peace-
keeping operations. It would only become involved in the struggle for liberation to the extent one of the border states was
attacked by a colonial or settler power.

The system was entirely voluntary. The African force
would consist of one or more units freely ear-marked by the
member states from their own national forces and placed at
the disposal of the OAU for specific operations. It was stressed that the force would "be used only at the express request"
of the member states. Even the modalities for action, determined by the Council of Ministers, would have to be "consented to by the recipient countries." This meant that from start
to finish the states concerned would be free to accept or refuse the services of such a body. They could request the
force whenever they were in need of it; they could reject it
again when the need ceased or if they disapproved of any aspect of the operation.

But the mechanism was not automatic. Once a request
for help had been received by the Secretariat, it was necessary
to convene the Council of Ministers. The Council would have
to approve the request and then work out the nature of the action. The Council's decision would have to be accepted by a
majority of states including the recipient states and those supplying the troops. Operational plans were to be prepared within the Secretariat's Defence Department and, in particular, by
a Committee of Defence Experts the Secretariat pledged to establish promptly. It was to handle all technical questions such
as the coordination of the different national units. It was also
the only permanent part of the African Defence Organization.

Since these decisions were made with two border disputes, the Tanganyikan experiment, and the Congolese crisis
as a background there was a feedback from the OAU's first attempts at peace-keeping. This was reflected primarily by the
stress on the voluntary nature of the system. No action could
be imposed on a member state and none of the states would
accept global and prior commitments in this matter. It would
be necessary in each individual case to work out some ad hoc
procedure within the broad framework. But this aroused some
doubt as to the conditions under which the Defence Organization would act and an African force be created.

In conflicts between two or more member states, since a force could only be used with the consent of all the parties, it had to be assumed that they already admitted that the military phase was inconclusive and were willing to permit a disengagement. A cease-fire could be established then and it could be supervised by a force sent to patrol the border or a demilitarized zone. Internal troubles could, in some cases, be smoothed over by such a peace-keeping body. But this would assume that a requesting government would have things well under control before the appeal was made, otherwise the operation would appear as interference in internal affairs. In serious or controversial disputes, a majority might not be found in the Council. Such a force could also become necessary in case of aggression against a member state by Portugal, Rhodesia or South Africa, although given Africa's limited military establishments, it was uncertain what sort of action could be taken.

Despite the original hopes and some fanfare from the Secretariat, the system was not put into use. There were a number of conflicts and incidents in which some force could have been established, but none was approved by the governing bodies. Moreover, even the modest and voluntary African Defence Organization failed to obtain a majority in the Council and Assembly. Interest in such projects and willingness to accept commitments dipped even further in the following years. The Defence Commission did not meet again and no Committee of Defence Experts was established. The OAU Secretariat had one expert briefly but no division was built up until later. This, of course, did not mean that the system could not be taken out of mothballs when needed.

It was far less certain how decolonization fit into the picture. As the struggle intensified, the OAU began creating various bodies of a military nature that originally had nothing to do with the Commission or "defence." A committee of military experts was to advise the Liberation Committee on the military side of its activities, both to determine the effectiveness of the wars of liberation and to plan a broader strategy. There was also the Committee of Five on Rhodesia. With time there was greater concern about the security of the nearby states. Thus the Committee of Five was also interested in the defence of Zambia. As the number of freedom fighters trained and working out of bases in the independent states grew, so did the nervousness and retaliation of the colonial and settler powers. There were more and more incidents along the borders. And South Africa had already warned Zambia that it might strike back.

The Algiers Council realized that the member states themselves were increasingly being included in the field of combat. It condemned Portugal "for the acts of aggression committed against the independent States adjacent to the territories under its domination." However, the threat was more pervasive and for the first time the OAU had to think of mutual defence. The Council of Ministers therefore solemnly declared that "any agression on any O.A.U. Member State by the colonialist and racist regimes of Portugal, South Africa and Rhodesia is regarded as an aggression on all the Members of the Organization." This statement was still largely symbolic since it only committed the members morally and Africa had no serious military force to back it up. But a decisive step had been taken.

1.   See Norman J. Padelford, <u>The Organization of African Unity</u>.

E. Refugees

The emergence of a new Africa was not a smooth process. One regrettable by-product was an increasingly serious
problem of refugees. Even before the struggles for liberation
were launched, groups of refugees settled in nearby territories
where they hoped for a better life. When warfare broke out
and repression became stronger, the flight of refugees grew.
Whole families, villages or tribes left their land and sought
safety elsewhere. As decolonization spread, wave upon wave
of refugees arrived in the independent states. Most of them
came from the Portuguese colonies with increasing numbers
leaving Rhodesia, South Africa, and South West Africa.

Peace and quiet did not always reign in the young states
either. A new source of refugees was created when friction
and turmoil disrupted life in the independent countries. Tribal
clashes after the fall of the Tutsi monarchy in Rwanda was a
striking case. But it was little compared to the results of internecine conflict in the Congo since independence. Civil war
in the Sudan and especially in Nigeria added tremendously to
the number of people in distress. Unfortunately, it would take
time for all internal differences to be worked out and no end
was yet in sight. Moreover, the trend to one party systems
and strong leaders offered the opponents of a regime little
choice but to remain silent or go into exile.

The Situation in Africa.

The process of decolonization and the adjustment to independence was accompanied by an irregular but steady growth
in the number of refugees. Even statistically the problem was
alarming. On 9 October 1967, the Secretary-General of the
OAU announced that there were some one and a half million
refugees in Africa.[1] This figure of Diallo Telli was double
that of the United Nations High Commissioner for Refugees,
which only included those fortunate enough to have obtained an
international status. As of 1 January 1967, the UNHCR had
recorded some 735,000 international refugees in Africa.
303,800 of these refugees came from Angola, 61,000 from

Portuguese Guinea, 20,000 from Mozambique, 74,000 from the Congo (Kinshasa), 159,000 from Rwanda and 115,000 from the Sudan.[2] But the scattered political refugees from other states were not counted nor was so large a group as the half million Somalis from Ethiopia and the Northern Frontier District which the Republic of Somalia claimed to have absorbed. Above all, the record did not include the Biafrans.

The most worrying aspect of the problem was that the tide was not receding. The exodus grew from year to year. The number of refugees within the competence of the UNHCR in January 1964 was 400,000. By 1970, only some six years later, it had grown to almost a million. These figures were soon dwarfed by the misery in the ill-fated Republic of Biafra. Most of the Biafrans were not officially refugees since they had not escaped across an international boundary. However, they were uprooted and without a home. The war left millions of displaced persons. Thus, although the number of Congolese and Rwandans levelled off, they were more than made up for by movements from the dependent territories, Sudan and especially within Nigeria. It was also disconcerting that the number of refugees from the dependent territories had been passed by those from the independent states showing that disturbances there could be as bad a source of refugees as colonial repression.

The refugee problem was a heavy burden for Africa, particularly since it was so unevenly shared. The countries nearest the scene of conflict were suddenly flooded by huge numbers of people who needed food, clothing and housing. Since most of them would not be able to return home for years if ever, the country of asylum had to keep on providing for their welfare and often finally absorb them. This had never been an easy task and it was particularly hard on the relatively poor countries of Africa. In some places it could not be coped with and the country fate had chosen to be host was unable to meet the needs. According to the UNHCR by 1967 there were 357,000 refugees in the Congo (Kinshasa), 156,000 in Uganda, 79,000 in Burundi, 61,000 in Senegal, 43,000 in Central African Republic, 33,000 in Tanzania and 5,600 in Zambia.

In view of the situation, it was not long before the Organization of African Unity was called upon to play a role. The original demand grew out of the friction between Rwanda and Burundi. After the Hutus had taken power in Rwanda many of the Tutsis withdrew to the Kingdom of Burundi. Those that left in 1959 had not given up all hope of reconquest, however, and they made several armed incursions in their former homeland. After a particularly serious clash in December 1963, there was a violent reaction from the Hutus, who slaughtered some of the remaining Tutsis while others fled. Burundi protested to the OAU. Although this bloodshed was not dealt with by the Lagos Council of Ministers in February 1964, it did act on a request of countries receiving Rwandan refugees and decided to set up an ad hoc Commission to deal with the matter. The terms of reference of the ten nation Commission were to examine:

> a) the refugee problem in Africa and make recommendations to the Council of Ministers on how it can be solved;

> b) the ways and means of maintaining refugees in their country of asylum.

The Commission's tasks were partly political and partly humanitarian. The political side was further complicated by a certain duality in Africa. There was no inherent difference among people made refugees by a variety of causes. The OAU could not improve on the very neutral definition of the 1951 Convention on Refugees, adopted in another context and for people from other continents. An African refugee was also a person who,

> ... owing to well-founded fear of being persecuted for reason of race, religion, nationality, membership of a particular social group or political opinion, is outside the country of his nationality and is unable or, owing to such fear, is unwilling to avail himself of the protection of that country.

Nevertheless, the Organization had to act very differently depending on whether the refugees came from an independent state or a dependent territory. Those from independent Africa would be treated as other refugees in the past. Once the crisis was over, they could be repatriated and, if not, they would be resettled elsewhere. Meanwhile they had to be neutralized as much as possible and kept from disturbing relations with their former country. If from a dependent territory, since the colonial and settler regimes were enemies, the mass of refugees could be left as a sign of discontent while individuals joined the liberation movements. Then, once the last bastions had fallen, they could return home.

While everyone waited for the underlying problems to be solved, the refugees had to be maintained in their countries of asylum. Despite the hospitality and generosity of the local population and the national governments, refugee needs often exceeded resources and international aid had to be requested. Emergency aid was usually organized by the Office of the High Commissioner for Refugees. In the internal strife over Biafra the agent was the International Red Cross. But this was just the beginning. The refugees could not be kept in camps indefinitely or until they were able to return home. Something had to be done to give them a relatively normal life and permit them to become largely self-sufficient. Since most were of peasant stock, where land was still available they could form their own communities and soon make a living from what they grew. During this transition, and to provide training and schooling that might improve their lives, an operational program normally would be worked out between the humanitarian agencies and the governments.

All of this was terribly expensive. It was usually too great a burden for the governments of the few states which actually received the refugees. A crowded country like Burundi or a small one with large refugee groups like Uganda was hard put to care for them. Even the others could not handle the problem alone. They were often aided by the High Commissioner for Refugees and by 1967 more than 18 million dollars had been allocated for work in sub-Saharan Africa. Africa's share of the aid was constantly rising. But this was less than one-third of the total voluntary aid for refugees. The rest came from humanitarian organizations like the Red Cross and agencies of the Catholic and Protestant churches. Still, there was a need for assistance from the African countries that were not directly affected.

Towards a Policy.

Soon after its creation the Refugee Commission visited a number of camps in Burundi, Tanzania and Uganda to obtain a better understanding of the problem. In a brief round of meetings its members rapidly sketched out a pragmatic solution. Then, in order to have a carefully worded and binding document to govern the action of the African states, the Cairo Council of Ministers requested the Commission to draft a convention on all aspects of the problem of refugees in Africa. The Commission provided a first draft for the Nairobi Council. To improve on it a committee of legal experts was set up by the Council and it produced its first draft for the Accra Assembly in October 1965. A second draft was finished in September 1966.

For some time, the OAU's refugee work was concentrated on this draft convention which was supposed to embody a specifically African approach to the problem. This was not easy, since one category of refugees was similar to those elsewhere in the world and could be covered adequately by the United Nations Convention. As most of the drafts were rough copies thereof it was not really necessary even to adopt an African convention. The other category was quite different. But it was hard to find appropriate wording to cover the case of the refugees from dependent territories and a convention for both could be contradictory, since what was forbidden one was often demanded of the other.

Despite considerable work on an African convention, none was approved. As time passed, the Assembly found it necessary to fill the gap by urging all member states to accede to the Convention on the Status of Refugees of July 1951 and then the Protocol on the Status of Refugees of January 1967. Only somewhat over half the members had actually signed the convention although others acted on it in practice. Some, however, were reluctant to accede, the opposition being occasionally fundamental, and the Council and Assembly had to make their request repeatedly. Although no real support had been mobilized for an African or the United Nations convention, the work of the Commission and expert committee was useful in crystallizing ideas and seeking to define the problem in Af-. rica.

Fortunately, most of the African states followed a very open policy towards the refugees. It was generally accepted that they should be received and not turned back at the border. Every effort was made to care for people from the dependent territories or those fleeing hostilities or other turmoil in the independent states. Even political refugees had little trouble obtaining asylum. These ideas were given expression in the draft convention of September 1966. It included the basic principle that "the grant of asylum is a peaceful and humanitarian act and shall not be regarded as an unfriendly act by any Member State."

For the refugees from independent states, the ideal solution would be voluntary repatriation. Once the causes had been removed or the situation which drove them away became

quieter the refugees could return home. But they would not be
forced to do so. At its first meeting, on 6 June 1964, the
Commission recommended "that refugees expressing the wish
to return to their country of origin shall receive all the necessary assistance to enable them to do so." This idea was tak-
en up by the Heads of State at the Accra Assembly, in October
1965, where they solemnly pledged "to endeavour to promote,
through bilateral and multilateral consultations, the return of
refugees with the consent of both the refugees concerned and
of their countries of origin." The Commission also examined
various details of the process of repatriation including the
proclamation of welcome, principles of return and restoration
of normal rights, supervision of the return, and safety measures.

Although the Commission had hoped to play a key role
in organizing and supervising the repatriation of refugees, it
was usually kept on the sidelines. The actual arrangements
were made on a government-to-government basis. The outcome was very different for the Congolese, Sudanese and
Rwandan refugees. The Congolese returned slowly after the
fighting died down. In the case of refugees from the Sudan,
agreements were reached with Uganda and the Congo to organize the repatriation of refugees who wished to return home.
The agreement with Uganda even included a six-man committee
to interview the refugees and work out a plan of repatriation
and reintegration in the Sudan. Until impartial observers
could be appointed, the members of the OAU Refugee Commission were to send representatives to act as a provisional observer team. But the efforts were in vain and the flow of
refugees from the Sudan continued.

The situation with the Rwandan refugees went from bad
to worse. The Tutsis were still a threat and, in November
1966, the Rwandan national guard turned back bands of war-
riors trying to enter the country while the government accused
Burundi of being a base for these raids. Burundi denied this
and claimed it was only providing asylum to the victims of a
"genocide" perpetrated by the Hutus.[3] Soon after, the Assembly of Heads of State met in Addis Ababa and asked the Congo
to reconcile its two neighbors. Not until March 1967 was General Mobutu able to hold a meeting with Rwanda and Burundi
at Goma, Republic of the Congo (Kinshasa). First it was
agreed that the dissident refugees would be disarmed. Then
the three governments "decided to establish a tripartite standing political commission to recommend suitable measures for
helping the refugees to return to their country of origin."

They also agreed that "no refugee shall be sent back to his country of origin against his will."[4] However, the commission was long inactive and in the end relatively few Tutsis returned home.

Clearly, if the refugees could not be repatriated they should leave the temporary camps and settle in the country of first asylum or elsewhere. This policy was followed widely and by 1968 half a million refugees had been resettled by the High Commissioner's Office and various operational agencies. The OAU made no contribution to this work. Actually, it was less concerned with how the refugees were settled than where. For, if not carefully supervised or resettled, they might become a danger. If the refugees engaged in political activities or, especially, if they abused their status by attacking the country of origin or partaking in subversion they could seriously damage relations among member states. That this threat was not imaginary was shown repeatedly by trouble along the borders of certain states with political or minority problems: Rwanda, Congo, Sudan, Ethiopia and Kenya. It was particularly dangerous during a civil war as in the Congo.

The most serious complications arose when other countries espoused the cause of dissident groups as above and in Nkrumah's Ghana. [See Chapter IV, Part D.] This latter case led to a debate on subversion at the highest level, first in Lagos and then at the Accra Assembly in October 1965. At the same time, the debate on refugees also hinged on this aspect and the resolution reminded the member states that they 'had pledged themselves to prevent refugees living on their territories from carrying out by any means whatsoever any acts harmful to the interests of other states, Members of the Organization of African Unity."

This prohibition of subversion was incorporated in the draft convention on refugees. It stipulated that

> ... member States undertake not to allow refugees residing in their respective territories to commit any hostile act against any Member States of the O.A.U., either through the media of the press, the radio, with arms or any other media which may cause friction between the Member States.

However, since the pledges could be violated, a more pragmatic solution was sought. By removing the refugees from the border zone and resettling them where they could cause no

harm, a lot of the friction would be avoided. The tactic de-
vised by the OAU was simple and effective: "refugees must be
settled, as much as possible, far from the frontiers of their
countries of origin, for obvious security reasons."[5]

The solution was quite different for the refugees from
dependent territories. They obviously could not return to their
country of origin as long as the struggle went on. Rather
than resettle them, they were often left in areas along the
frontier and near the scene of combat. Many of the men were
recruited and trained as freedom fighters and this side came
under the Liberation Committee. Others had to be taught various professions in order to help administer and develop the
new states after independence. The difference in origin and
destiny, however, made the attitude towards refugees in the
OAU fundamentally ambivalent. This was shown by the Accra
resolution on subversion which concluded with the reservation
that, although the member states were urged to avoid political
action by refugees from independent states, they were "to continue to guarantee the safety of political refugees from non-
independent African territories, and to support them in their
struggle to liberate their countries."

Cause and Effect.

Although the general principles concerning refugees had
been defined, the OAU was not able to adopt a convention.
For a while the Commission and expert committee ceased meeting. The Refugee Bureau in the Secretariat even stopped turning out reports. And the Organization marked time until the
International Conference on the Legal, Economic and Social Aspects of African Refugee Problems, held in Addis Ababa from
9-18 October 1967. The initiative for the meeting came from
the High Commissioner for Refugees and the Dag Hammarskjöld Foundation which sought to bring the African governments together with the many inter-governmental organizations
and non-governmental agencies that were active in the field.
It was hoped that a broader and better coordinated program
might be organized to care for the refugees. But the OAU
was also a convener. From the start, the Secretary-General
tried to take the lead. He immediately drew the conference
into the gambit of the OAU's work by claiming that "more than
an encouragement, more than a promise, it is the crowning of
efforts which have been made since the creation of our Organization."

In his speech, Diallo Telli then tied the problem of refugees to the struggle against colonialism. For he defined the cause as one of the

> ... disastrous and inhuman sequels bequeathed our Governments and our peoples by the colonial and racist systems which prevailed throughout the Continent as a whole and which continue to oppress, under the abominable conditions of which everyone is aware, the greater part of Southern Africa.

There was not a word about the people fleeing internal strife in the independent states nor the terrible war in Nigeria. This side had not been overlooked by reference paper No. 1, which traced the problem back to another aspect of decolonization, namely that "with this went the imperial power that kept incipient tribal, racial and religious differences at bay." The reference paper No. 1 also stated that decolonization had provoked rising expectations and near instability in some states. But the OAU analysis was adopted, namely that the solution to the refugee problem

> ... depends increasingly on the abolition by all possible means and particularly through international pressure of racist regimes and policies of repression practised in the Southern part of the continent, the non-independent territories and by minority government. [6]

The campaign was pursued by an important delegation led by the Assistant Secretary-General in charge of political questions, Mohammed Sahnoun. Since the representatives of the twenty-two governments had a greater say in decisions than observers from the many humanitarian agencies, it was relatively easy for the OAU's position to be imposed when a specific policy was articulated. Ambassador Sahnoun was even elected spokesman of the conference. Ultimately, the solution proposed for handling refugees was also along OAU lines. Asylum was basically accepted. The first attempt should naturally be to voluntarily repatriate them and an appeal could be made by the Secretary-General, as well as the government concerned, inviting refugees to return home with assurances of their welfare. The alternative was settlement, especially on the land, as this would permit eventual self-sufficiency and 'help eliminate tensions" that could arise among states. It was also agreed that refugees shall "abstain from any subversive activities against any African Country, except for countries under colonial and racist minority domination."

When it came to the humanitarian aspects of caring for and resettling the refugees, the OAU had little to add. The Secretary-General did not even admit any responsibility for a contribution. Diallo Telli had put the blame on colonialism. The refugee problem was, "first and foremost, the direct responsibility of the colonial and ex-colonial powers of Europe." Since it was a threat to stability, peace and security, the international community in general, and the European powers in particular were "under a political and moral obligation to find adequate solutions to it." Thus the focus was on the response of the international organizations and voluntary agencies. Although their aid was recognized and praised, it was considered insufficient. Ambassador Sahnoun called on the African states to exert greater diplomatic pressure on the traditional contributors outside Africa to increase assistance. He also asked that there be more African members in the Executive Committee that determined the UNHCR's programs of assistance and general policy.[7]

Again the conference endorsed the OAU. It also stressed "the moral and political obligation of the international community to find adequate solutions to this problem in view of the potential threat to peace and stability in Africa and throughout the world." It urged the United Nations to increase the African membership in the Executive Committee and expressed a hope for greater aid to the refugees. It even proposed that the OAU Refugee Bureau be regularly informed of financial assistance granted by voluntary agencies. But these demands were hardly necessary. The United Nations promptly elected another African member to the Committee. And the UNHCR, which had always shown great willingness to expand its program towards the continent, was already devoting more than half its budget to African refugees. Coordination had been very close on an informal basis and it had, among other things sent legal experts to advise on the draft convention. The voluntary and humanitarian agencies were also willing to step up their assistance without being pressured and unprecedented efforts to save the Biafrans were soon being made.

The endorsement of its theses may have been a triumph for the Secretariat. Only it was of dubious value as long as they were based on half the truth. The causes of the refugee problem were the evils of colonialism; failings of the independent states were overlooked. The effect was that Africa had not admitted its collective responsibility towards the refugees of the continent. The conference did recommend that every African government agree to take some refugees and an inter-African committee for refugee migration was suggested. But there was no clear plan for sharing the burden. The Secretariat did not offer to channel or initiate such work either. This meant that the main source of relief would still be the international and humanitarian agencies. Unfortunately, this analysis was also the worst possible basis for cooperation. For the non-African donors required a more honorable and appealing role than expiation for past sins.

The only task the Secretariat claimed for the OAU was the establishment of a Bureau for the Placement and Education of Refugees. This was a sort of clearing house to advise the refugees on possibilities of training and education and later to help recruit the professional cadres among them. However, although the coordination of efforts could be accomplished by the OAU, the actual scholarships, training and jobs would be offered by various governments, organizations and philanthropic agencies. Since the bulk of the aid would not come from the OAU or Africa in general, there was a rather top-heavy structure at first. The Bureau would only have two full-time staff members at the outset, yet it would be advised by both a Consultative Board and a Standing Committee composed of representatives from the OAU, ECA, UNHCR, ILO, and UNESCO. What was to the good was that the Organization had finally undertaken a concrete task to aid refugees directly.

Dereliction of Duty.

Even while the Organization was consolidating its position institutionally, the most serious crisis the continent had witnessed was steadily deteriorating. The Eastern Region of Nigeria was slowly contracting under the attacks of the federal army. The already crowded region eventually shrank to an area about a fifth its pre-civil war size. Living here were some eight million people, mostly Ibos who had refused to seek safety in Nigeria. By remaining with their army and leaders they were exposed to bombing and starvation. Unless food and medicine were supplied the whole population might waste away.

The plight of these people aroused the concern of many humanitarian and charitable agencies. Through the Red Cross, World Council of Churches, Caritas, UNICEF and other bodies, it was possible to raise millions of dollars from individuals and governments. Soon relief was being sent towards Nigeria. But it was not easy to reach the victims. The main difficulty was that the federal government and the secessionist leaders could not agree on arrangements for channelling supplies into Biafra.

What was needed was an African intermediary with sufficient authority to impose on both sides an elementary respect for the rules of war and the rights of the civilian population. The ideal body for this would have been the Organization of African Unity. But the members had no desire to intervene and the Secretary-General did not draw their attention to the need. Yet, the need was so great that the Consultative Committee on Nigeria had to ignore its very restrictive mandate. At the Niamey meeting, with the consent of both sides, it discussed the problem of sending food, medicine and clothing to the affected areas. The resolution of 18 July 1968 appealed to the parties to help establish "mercy" corridors, to facilitate the transport and distribution of supplies and to guarantee the safety and free movement of the agents of the relief organizations and observers. Talks on ways and means began at the end of July. They were continued under the Emperor of Ethiopia throughout the month of August but there were no concrete results.

One of the reasons was that although the Committee had considerable prestige it had little expertise. Moreover, the Heads of State were unable to meet often or at length. At this point, the Refugee Commission or another body should have been convened to seek an arrangement. First it had to define land, sea and air corridors. It would have to determine the routes and conditions of their use. Later it could provide inspection and guarantees to ensure that there were no abuses. The observer teams might include members from states that recognized Biafra. Once a solution had been found, the Consultative Committee could be reconvened to impose it. At any rate, the Organization should not have relaxed its efforts until a system of facilitating relief was found.

The other side of the problem was the provision of aid to the civilian population. The Niamey resolution also "urgently appeals to all Member States of the Organization of African Unity to assist in this massive humanitarian relief effort." Certainly the OAU should have been the first to urge and organize an African campaign for donations. This was a task for the Secretariat. But Diallo Telli showed little interest in the situation and did not initiate any action. Most of the mem

er states individually were hardly more active. This poor
esponse was regretted by the OAU observers in Nigeria.

> The participation ... in humanitarian and other re-
> lief activities in the Nigerian crisis is strongly
> recommended as the absence of such physical and
> material contribution may give ground to detractors
> bent to undermine the role of the Organization. It
> is advisable that all African states, through the co-
> ordination media of the Organization of African
> Unity, offer voluntary relief workers of their na-
> tionals to assist the Nigerian Red Cross and the
> Nigerian Rehabilitation Commission.[8]

Unfortunately, the Organization did not rise to the chal-
enge. Its members and officials remained hesitant or indif-
erent. The only activity of the Refugee Commission during
his period was to continue its somewhat academic labor on the
onvention. Finally, in September 1968, the Draft Convention
n the Status of Refugees in Africa was adopted. It still had
o be signed by the Heads of State and above all ratified by
heir governments before it could come into force. Even more
ffort was necessary for it to have some effect. And it was
ot a very encouraging sign that the convention was adopted in
he midst of a crisis creating untold suffering for refugees.
n Algiers neither the Council nor the Assembly seriously dealt
ith the problem in Nigeria. The Secretariat could have
aised money and supplies. The Organization could have press-
d for a compromise to channel them towards the sick and
tarving. And the member states could have prevailed on both
ides to end the tragedy. But, rather than use already exist-
ng machinery and make a serious attempt at restoring the
ituation, the Assembly merely "appeals further to all con-
erned to cooperate in the speedy delivery of humanitarian re-
ef supplies to the needy."

Notes

United States News Bulletin, Addis Ababa, 10 Oct. 1967.

AFR/REF/CONF. 1967, No. 1, UNHCR, Geneva.

Le Monde, 20 Nov. 1966.

AFR/REF/CONF. 1967, No. 4, UNHCR, Geneva.

5. Diallo Telli Speech, 9 Oct. 1967.

6. Recommendations of the Conference, UNHCR, Geneva.

7. Ethiopian Herald, 12 Oct. 1967.

8. "Final Report of Observers Team in Nigeria," Lagos, Federal Ministry of Information, 1968.

F. Conclusion

Unlike the political activities where the Pan-African movement already had considerable experience, the Organization of African Unity was constantly breaking new ground in its technical activities. Never before had an organization representing the whole continent attempted to cover such a vast sphere of action. It was not surprising, given the size of the task, that the first tries were impulsive and disorderly. It proved impossible to tackle the ambitious projects selected by the Commissions and often by the Secretariat with the staff and funds available.

Almost no concrete results marked this initial period. Only a few projects of the CCTA were brought to fruition and several others of the Council/Secretariat made progress. Nevertheless, even in its present form, the Organization could make use of its considerable prestige and its excellent vantage point to promote technical activities. First it had to explore its possibilities and find a valid role, a relatively modest one for the time being. Then it had to restore or even expand the original machinery so that serious work could be done. Doing both, it had to keep in mind that there were already numerous other international organizations, sub-regional groupings and private associations serving Africa and that only through cooperation could the many problems be solved. On this basis, the OAU could make a comeback.

Expansion and Contraction.

Originally the summit conference and the commissions had reviewed the problems faced by Africa and established a list of priorities with the most important--and most difficult-- at the top. In the general atmosphere of hope and enthusiasm of the first years of the OAU, the specialized commissions immediately began working on the top priority item or, more often, items. They wished to give them a tremendous boost and expected quick results. However, by their very nature, none of these projects could bear fruit at once. More often than not, they also exceeded the possibilities of the commis-

577

sions. The Economic and Social Commission, like the others, eventually asked itself what the commissions and the OAU could and could not do in these matters. When it took stock of its resources, it may have hesitated, but it was already committed to a long-term project like a common market and it forged ahead.

Often the commissions became involved in tasks they could not handle in a few days of irregular meetings. They tried to make up for this by requesting studies from the Secretariat. But the understaffed offices provided for each of the many fields were not able to turn out the documentation either. Not even the preliminary studies were made for many of the projects. The commissions tried to create institutions, draft conventions and work out plans for the future, forgetting that this could only be a starting point. The Organization still had to find staff and new funds. Then the members had to be fully convinced of the need and willing to make the necessary efforts

The specialized commissions hastily concluded that nothing could be done without a larger structure. They asked for permanent councils, expert committees and study groups. They wanted the departments and divisions of the Secretariat to be expanded. What they did not grasp was the relatively low priority of their fields. The OAU was primarily a political body and little was left over for the commissions. Rather, the Organization ultimately decided to reduce the technical machinery. An Institutional Committee had been studying the structure and it presented its recommendations to the Council of Ministers in November 1966. Among those approved was one to merge the seven commissions into three while preserving most of the fields of activity. The Economic and Social Commission would include transport and communications, and an Educational, Scientific, Cultural and Health Commission grouped the more technical, but poorly assorted fields of three earlier bodies. The Defence Commission was maintained but the Commission of Jurists was dropped. It was also recommended that the commissions only meet every second year.

Still, even on this basis, it was hard to reactivate the technical side of OAU operations. For some time the commissions simply did not meet. There was even some doubt as to whether they should be continued at all. Some of the member states felt that the OAU should be not only primarily but exclusively a political body. Others stressed that concrete links in the technical fields were essential as a foundation for the political activities. However, it was already too late to go

ack on the decision of the summit conference and the debate
oncluded in favor of stop-gap machinery. The Addis Ababa
ssembly decided that in the future the Council of Ministers
hould convene three committees, the third being "specially
ommissioned to give detailed consideration to the various as-
ects of African economic, social and cultural co-operation in
rder to recommend all common action capable of speeding up
rogress in these fields."

This was a basic mutation in the structure for, rather
han just coordinate the work of the Commissions, the Council
as replacing them temporarily. But the Council's possibili-
.es were even more limited. Although it only met twice a
ear, it was supposed to give careful consideration to a vast
umber of items. For example, in Kinshasa, after debating
ssues like Rhodesia and Namibia, the Council adopted thirty-
ree resolutions on technical questions. The following session
as less ambitious but its half-a-dozen items were dealt with
somewhat greater detail. It was even more significant that
e delegates changed. Although other ministers and experts
ould attend Council meetings, the representatives usually came
rom the Foreign Office. This led to an unfortunate decrease
competence and an increase in politicization. The interim
olicy of the Organization became less reasoned and objective
nd more aggressive.

At this point the Secretariat stepped in. The Assembly
ad instructed it to undertake surveys on the problems and
rospects of economic and social cooperation. However, it
ften seized the initiative and included very specific proposals.
ince its reports to the Council were the only basis for deci-
ions, its draft resolutions were often adopted in the absence
f anything else. Still, its contribution was of uncertain value.
ometimes it was an exercise in make-work or wishful think-
g. But the main defect was that some of the top-level staff
as apparently more politically-minded than technically quali-
ed. The reports and resolutions often worried less about
oncrete solutions than past or future dangers of neo-colonial-
m.

Some things did get done. The on-going matters like
e operation of the CCTA, relations and joint meetings with
e ECA, UNESCO and other bodies, and the drafting of con-
entions were supervised and directed. The Council/Secretari-
t was even able to launch projects like a Trade Fair and a
ultural Festival. The most encouraging trend was in the eco-
omic field where the Secretariat was set at tasks like collect-

ing and disseminating information. This sort of preparatory
work was essential for later progress in integration, trade
promotion and technical assistance. Another advantage was
that all these tasks could be handled easily by civil servants
and politicians. Moreover, since the items were not too big
for it, the Organization was put on the right track.

But it was obvious that few real accomplishments could
be expected unless the specialized commissions were restored
Since they were an integral part of the Charter the malaise
was particularly noticeable. In Kinshasa, in September 1967,
a resolution was adopted by the Council and later approved by
the Assembly underlining the need to strengthen intra-African
cooperation in the economic, social, cultural, scientific and
technical fields. The importance of this cooperation as a
"sound foundation of solidarity" was recognized. The Secretariat was asked to hold a series of meetings before the next
session of the Council and the governments were requested to
participate regularly. However, although the resolution was
twice adopted by the member states, the commissions were
not reconvened until the end of 1969 and beginning of 1970, an
then only for the purpose of making recommendations.

Leadership or Partnership?

It soon became obvious that the OAU could not accomplish its ambitious tasks alone. It had a staff of only about
two hundred of which less than seventy were professionals.
Even with half of them working in the various technical fields
especially CCTA and economics, many of the divisions such a
social, health or transport, would have no more than one or
two experts to run them. The budget was also devoted large
to administration and political work. At most a third would
be available for the technical activities and much of this woul
be eaten up by meetings and the skeleton staff. But the OAU
could also draw on the far greater resources of various international organizations, sub-regional groupings and private associations. They all had their own specializations, traditions
and pride. The OAU added the specifically African ingredient
and its political dynamism. There was thus a basis for coop
eration.

Despite its inferiority in staff and funds, the OAU was
in some ways superior to the other regional groupings in specialized fields for it covered the whole continent at the highes
level. This claim of supremacy was never made as such by

he Heads of State. No resolution was adopted calling for a
ubordination of other bodies. However, trouble unavoidably
rose from the fact that the Economic Commission for Africa
nd other bodies had much the same terms of reference as the
AU's commissions. Since these commissions decided to di-
ect the actual preparation and implementation of projects
hemselves, there was bound to be either duplication or com-
etition.

At first there was a rather active campaign to estab-
sh the primacy of the OAU. However, the Organization was
learly in no position to impose any sort of order when, with-
1 two years, its commissions had already succumbed. With
me the official claims of preeminence were toned down. The
greements signed with the ECA and ILO, a model for any
hers, were based on complete parity. But this was only a
rmal solution and the struggle went on behind the scenes.
he Secretariat undertook a subtler campaign within other bod-
s in or concerning Africa to impose its philosophy. The
implest expression thereof was Diallo Telli's, namely that the
AU was the organ of "conception" while the others were re-
ponsible for "execution."

This claim was met with disbelief or uneasiness in the
lready established bodies. They all had their own activities
nd clientele and expected quite another sort of relationship.
he test case was the Economic Commission for Africa. Long
fter the agreement of cooperation had been signed, the OAU
as still trying to impose its leadership. At the ECA's eighth
ssion in Lagos, in February 1967, the Secretariat's repre-
entative again pointed out that the work of both bodies over-
pped and hinted that there were difficulties. He insisted that
e function of the OAU was primarily political, and consisted
f planning and implementation, while that of the ECA, which
as more technical, consisted of the preparation of studies and
e gathering of information. The OAU should therefore ex-
mine the ECA's program of work and indicate which matters
felt were within its exclusive province.[1]

There was also some friction with the various sub-
gional groupings (and even non-governmental bodies). The
ember states had increasingly created and supported smaller
ner-African units to accomplish specific tasks and they did
t want strict OAU supervision. An early attempt at placing
em under the Organization had been made at the first Coun-
l of Ministers in Dakar, in August 1963. There, all that had
en done was to recommend that any such groupings follow the

principles of the Charter. The later attempts came from the Secretariat. For some time the Secretary-General complained about division or snubbed OCAM and the Entente. But the regional units were too important a part of governmental plans to be subordinated to the OAU.

This was clearly a struggle between Secretariats.[2] To some extent, it left the states indifferent or annoyed. The OAU's governing bodies had never demanded supremacy. Rather, they repeatedly called for cooperation with all other organizations. When the Secretary-General insisted on deference towards the OAU, it was largely on his own. His action even met with passive resistance from the governments. They did little to impose supervision on the international organizations and sub-regional groupings and preferred letting them continue their work as usual. If there was duplication or competition, it could only come from the OAU entering fields that were already being serviced by other bodies. Thus they witheld the funds necessary to expand the Secretariat or did nothing to overcome the crisis in the commissions. The end result was that very few activities were undertaken by the Organization and duplication was avoided. But this was certainly not the best way of solving the problem.

If it had so desired, the OAU could have obtained a definite predominance. For its bodies included all the independent states and met at the highest level: Heads of State, Foreign Ministers, and other ministers. In the other organizations the delegates were lower-ranking and received instructions from them. If the political leaders had wished stricter dependence they could have imposed it. This was evident for the sub-regional groupings but it also held true of the United Nations family and especially the regional branches of the specialized agencies and the ECA. For the African states had 100 per cent of the votes in the regional and a third of the votes in the parent bodies. By laying down its own policies and having them propagated by the delegates, the OAU could influence the decisions taken within other institutions and determine the effective relationship.

Nevertheless, cooperation was obviously a better policy Indeed, any rivalry would have been foolish since the other organizations had greater experience and expertise. They also had a much larger staff and budget for their restricted fields. When the OAU was established, with the Economic and Social Commission as one of its lesser bodies, the Economic Commission for Africa already had a staff of 250, including 85 pro fessionals. Its budget was many times that of the OAU and it was drawn from the regular UN budget, largely paid for by the rest of the world. The same was true of the specialized agencies. It would have been unwise to let the still rudimentary OAU machinery try to direct the activities of such large and effective ventures.

Furthermore, rivalry was basically unnecessary. These bodies were also working for the good of the continent. In addition, they were quite willing to cooperate with the OAU. A prime example was the Economic Commission for Africa. From the beginning, the OAU "has come to depend upon the ECA Secretariat to do its economic and social work, a relationship which the Commission has encouraged and which is facilitated by the location of both organizations in Addis Ababa."[3] Aside from providing reports and studies, the ECA often seconded personnel to service OAU meetings. It included the OAU in its own conferences on economic cooperation, telecommunications and transport. It provided the economic know-how for the work of the Committee of Fourteen. And other organizations followed suit.

But the Organization still had to provide a framework for cooperation with its partners. Certainly an observer or consultative status could be created for the international and sub-regional organizations and many private associations. There was no reason why the various bodies should not attend most meetings of the commissions and committees and even make suggestions and recommendations. Although the status, whatever it was, would be predominantly for "African" organizations, it did not have to be exclusive. Since most of the aid to refugees came from external agencies, for example, it might be helpful if they were regularly informed of the work of the Refugee Commission.

Coordination and Harmonization.

Within a few years the Organization had come full circle. The most suitable role turned out to be the very one included in the Charter: coordination and harmonization of the policies of the member states and cooperation with other bodies and the outside world. The OAU had always been well placed to coordinate the many activities being undertaken on the continent. Unfortunately, the commissions had mistakenly assumed that this coordination had to be at the level of integration and set about creating their own common markets and

universities. If no previous foundation had existed, this might
have been necessary. However, since considerable progress
had already been made before the OAU, the wisest policy would
have been to study the situation and see where the various efforts could be better coordinated and on-going policies harmonized. Most of the projects could simply have been left to
their initiators. The Organization would only have had to intervene to avoid rivalry or barriers to later continental integration.

The basic role of the Secretariat would then be information. Beneficial relations could be established with the mem
ber states, the ECA, the specialized agencies and the various
sub-regional groupings. This could then be expanded to some
of the professional and private associations. Through these
channels the Secretariat could obtain data and documentation on
all the work that was being accomplished in the continent.
This would be compiled and analyzed, and then sent to the appropriate authorities, the most important being the various institutions of the OAU. The Secretariat could also draw up
plans for specific projects, but only at the request of these
bodies and not on its own initiative.

On the basis of this information, the specialized commissions could study the situation in their own fields. They
could see what work was being done by a multitude of organizations, groupings and governments. Then they could determine where there were weaknesses and gaps or duplication
and waste. They could suggest that certain activities be harmonized or that a new project be launched. The Commissions
should not seek to introduce their own projects or take over
the direction of existing ones. Only in cases of clear failure
or unreasonable delay should they ask that the OAU implement
an activity itself. Their recommendations would be addressed
to the governing bodies.

The Council of Ministers and the Assembly of Heads of
State, on the basis of the information and recommendations,
would be able to accomplish their own tasks of coordination.
First, within the Organization, the Council of Ministers would
have to weigh the relative priorities of the various commissions depending on the work at hand and the budget. It could
prompt greater activity or restrain undue ambition. It could
also promote increasing cooperation between the OAU and the
other organizations active in Africa. Ultimately, the Heads
of State would have to decide to what extent the policies of the
member states should be coordinated. The Assembly could

all on the member states to undertake a given project or
void duplication or competition with another one. It could
rge that any groupings be expanded in membership or extend
nto other fields. It would stress possibilities of harmoniza-
ion and conclude conventions on essential matters. Then it
vould try to work all the on-going activities into a logical
vhole and determine which projects deserved priority.

But the primary responsibility rested with the member
tates. As in the past, they could take the initiative without
vaiting for the OAU. The Negro Arts Festival, sports meets
nd professional conferences had been held this way. Any
tate could offer to host certain projects, such as the Cultural
'estival and the Trade Fair, on behalf of the other members.
'ollectively, they could continue supporting regional groupings
ɔ solve specific problems and to obtain more intimate cooper-
tion. But these groupings should not be made exclusive nor
ecome blocs and pressure groups that competed with others.
'inally, the states had to accept their moral, if not legal ob-
.gations towards the OAU. They had to participate actively
ι its institutions and meetings and, once they had defined a
rogram that was acceptable to the largest number, they had
ɔ provide the necessary funds.

This kind of role might not seem as impressive as the
arlier concept but it would be more realistic and ultimately
ιore effective. It took advantage of what had already been
ɔne and what was being done rather than starting from
cratch. It was a more solid and constructive one than right
fter the Summit. And the down-grading of its activities did
ɔt mean that the OAU would not play a leading role later on,
nce it had acquired the essential experience and had the staff
nd funds it needed. With time, there would be greater pres-
ure for harmonization and coordination in Africa. The real
hallenge would come when the individual projects, as yet
ɔarse, had to be fit into a larger whole. Only the Organiza-
on of African Unity could provide such a continental plan.

Notes

, Annual Report 1965-67, Economic Commission for Africa,
       p. 131-132.

, See: Immanuel Wallerstein, The Early Years of the
      O.A.U.: Search for Organizational Preeminence.

3. Robert W. Gregg, "U.N. Regional Economic Commissions
    and Integration," International Organization, Spring
    1966, p. 227.

Chapter VII

African Unities

A. Regionalism

The Organization of African Unity was established in
May 1963 as the one All-African organization. But it is far
from being the only organization on the continent. Given the
vast geographical extent of Africa there was bound to be any
number of smaller, more compact groupings. And, despite
the many facets of OAU activities, there is still room for
more highly specialized bodies. Some of them already exist
and others will be created later. What was necessary from
the beginning was to have some coordination of these bodies
and their activities to prevent duplication or even rivalry. It
was hoped that this task could be handled from Addis Ababa.

Any real coordination of the continent's activities requires a united political will. Unfortunately, there are serious divergencies. The member states do not always have the
same aims and priorities and normally reach full agreement
only on some of the points brought up in the OAU. In most
cases a joint policy could be defined for limited and specific
purposes. But, at certain times especially during crises, the
underlying political differences tended to separate and regroup
and there were clashes between opposing ideologies. This did
lead to highly dangerous breaches in the common front. The
OAU was created to heal the rift between the Casablanca and
Monrovia blocs and it can not afford to allow a similar split
in the future.

These are not the only differences that had to be reconciled to preserve unity. There are amazingly thick walls
among the states using English, French or Arabic as official
or vehicular languages. There is a vague geographical separation between regions like eastern and western and northern
and central Africa. Going more deeply, there are tribal and
ethnic divisions. There are branches of the Muslim, Chris-

587

tian and animist religions. And there are broader racial and
religious differences between Arab and Black Africa. Within
each one of these groupings the links are very strong, often
more so than ties with those on the outside. This solidarity,
if wisely channelled, could be a boon to African unity. If un-
checked, it could give rise to separatism.

The OAU and Regionalism.

The Charter of African Unity contains no provision making the OAU the highest African body and requiring compatibil-
ity with it nor does it impose any integration of other bodies into the Organization. However, since the Heads of State are
ultimately responsible for all the institutions in Africa, they
may create, dissolve, coordinate or decentralize as they wish.
It is certainly not in their interest to have wasteful duplication
or futile opposition between a regional or specialized body and
the OAU. Therefore, one of the first tasks was to define the
relationship between the fledgling organization and other African bodies.

Since one of the driving motives for creating the Organization of African Unity was to end the political divisions that
split the continent into feuding blocs, it was necessary for the
OAU to be the supreme political authority and possibly the
only one. But many other non-political groups and institutions
came to exist that did not seriously threaten the unity of the
continent and which contributed to its growth and development.
Even if they can be done without at a later stage, their pro-
moters do not wish to destroy them without knowing what they
would be replaced by. Moreover, to lay the foundations for
unity, many leaders put their faith in a gradual approach,
moving from the economic to political sphere or from regional
to continental units.

In an effort to remove the worst abuses of the past,
the first Council of Ministers of the OAU, meeting in Dakar
from 2-11 August 1963, adopted a resolution on regional groupings. There had always been very different tendencies at
work and it was not easy to reconcile them and even more
difficult to unambiguously lay down on paper the exact relationship between the OAU and all other bodies. The solution,
advocated by radical states, like Guinea and Ghana, as well
as Nigeria, was quite simple: the previous organizations
would be disbanded. There was no longer to be any body that
could oppose its policy to that of the OAU. The few group-

ings that subsisted would have to be non-political and strictly regional. A Guinean draft resolution specifically mentioned the abrogation of the Casablanca, Monrovia and UAM Charters and provided that "geographical realities and economic and social conditions common to neighboring states" were to be "the sole justification" of groupings and sub-groupings.[1]

The main target was clearly the Afro-Malagasy Union which stretched from Mauritania to Madagascar. Although its members might have been willing to cease their political activities, they would not be summoned to do so and, above all, they had rather important economic and cultural links to preserve. Some of them spoke of harmonization or even an eventual merger with the OAU, but they would not be pressured into foresaking the UAM altogether. Finally, after a very stormy debate, the fourteen states were able to have their way. The Council decided against simple suppression of the existing organizations and a second criteria was added to satisfy the Afro-Malagasy states.

Ultimately, the only point on which there was general agreement was that the OAU should be the political body for Africa. But, even this was not laid down as a hard and fast rule. The resolution merely omitted "political" in the list of activities it suggested for the permissible groupings. The basic characteristics of such groupings were that they

> ... be in keeping with the Charter of the O.A.U. and meet the following criteria:
>
> (a) Geographical relations and economic, social and cultural factors common to the States;
>
> (b) Co-ordination of economic, social and cultural activities peculiar to the States concerned.

However, the resolution did not determine the actual relationship between the OAU and the regional groupings. First of all, it was simply recommended that they be compatible with the Charter of Addis Ababa. At most, the member states were invited when setting up groupings to conform to the principles or even "to contemplate the integration of already existing bodies into the specialized institutions of the O.A.U." But the Organization was given no supervisory powers. There was no requirement that other bodies consult with it or even inform it of their decisions. And the provision that the treaties of such bodies be deposited at its seat was a mere formality.

Whereas, in Dakar, some of the members were opposed to permitting regional groupings but accepted them as a
practical or temporary necessity, the attitude became more
positive with time. The increasing activities and success of
such non-political groupings and the collapse of the OAU's
specialized commissions made them an essential part of Africa's institutional machinery. At the Council of Ministers in
Kinshasa, in September 1967, a resolution was adopted on regional economic groupings. By then it was recommended that
the member states encourage the formation of such groupings
by all appropriate means. However, the problem was less to
create these bodies than to coordinate them. The final objective was a continental system and, although the early groupings were to become stepping stones, they were not always designed to facilitate later integration. Even if the OAU was
not empowered to impose coordination on them, the members
were asked to promote an exchange of information through the
Secretariat.

The Conversion.

The Dakar resolution called for an evolution or adaptation to the new situation. But the demise of many of the political groupings has often been quite abrupt. The radicals took
the lead and even before the Council meeting President Sékou
Touré announced the formal dissolution of the Ghana-Guinea-
Mali Union on 3 June 1963. Since this Union had never really
existed in practice its passing was hardly noticed. The All-
African Peoples' Organization also faded away and some of its
clientele and activities were assumed by the Afro-Asian People's Solidarity Organization. And, despite its articulate
Charter and institutional paraphernalia, the Casablanca group
simply broke up. The same happened to the rudimentary Inter-African and Malagasy Organization of the Monrovia group
which had been formed while awaiting a new continental body.

The more successful groupings, however, did not disappear that readily. Both the Afro-Malagasy Union and
PAFMECSA had shown their promise and ability to handle
problems and were even expanding. They were taken to task
by Guinea and Ghana. President Nkrumah, now a bitter enemy of regionalism, denounced them as a threat to continental
unity. On 4 June 1963, he warned that "regional associations
and territorial groupings can only be other forms of balkaniza-

tion unless they are conceived within the framework of continental union." His criticism included not only the UAM but PAFMECSA and even East African Federation. President Nyerere, who had never approved of the blocs and steadily worked for broader unity, was willing to end this venture and, on 25 September, PAFMECSA was disbanded by its chairman, Kenneth Kaunda.

The Brazzaville group was another matter. The Union Africaine et Malgache had been a going concern ever since its creation and the regular meetings at Heads of State and other levels had permitted its members to work out a common stand on many questions. Its economic cooperation organization (OAMCE) and the post and telecommunications union (UAMPT) had been particularly active and had many concrete projects and acts of harmonization to their credit. Only the defence union (UAMD) was unable to come to grips with its primary role of planning a joint defensive structure although it did handle lesser points. It was not easy to dissolve such links for the sake of an untried organization and it was clear that the Dakar resolution would not produce a sweeping change in the members' attitude towards the UAM.

For almost a year the leaders of the Afro-Malagasy Union were divided over its future. Most of them eventually agreed with the Dakar resolution and conceded that the Union should cease its political activities. President Senghor led the campaign to give the OAU a chance by dismantling the more exclusive and objectionable links between the members. A smaller group centered about Houphouët-Boigny felt that a purely economic body was not viable. Stronger cement was needed to hold together states so widely separated geographically and with different economic partners and interests. Finally, at a summit conference in Dakar, the decision was taken. Papering over the differences, the communique of 10 March 1964 announced the unanimous decision of the Heads of State to work solely in the economic, technical, cultural and social fields and to create an organization called the Union Africaine et Malgache de Coopération Economique.

The Charter of the UAMCE was signed by the fourteen members at a further meeting in Nouakchott, from 28-30 April 1964. The new organization was to replace the former OAMCE and UAMPT and to continue their activities. The defence union was let lapse. UAMCE's structure was similar to the UAM. Its supreme body was a Conference of Heads of State and Government. A Council of Ministers prepared the

conferences, supervised application of decisions and dealt with
questions referred to it. There were also seven technical
committees which were purely advisory. The general secretariat had its seat in Yaoundé, Cameroon, and although it was
left open to all African states, it already had a definite membership.

The Moderates Return to Politics.

     For more than a year there was excellent cooperation
in the Organization of African Unity. A series of crises including the Algero-Moroccan border dispute, the clashes between Somalia and Ethiopia/Kenya and the mutinies in Tanganyika had been faced and joint policies adopted to deal with
them. There was growing solidarity among the states in their
efforts to solve the problems that threatened the peace of the
continent and in working for the liberation of the dependent
territories. Any differences among members of the former
blocs were secondary and could readily be overcome in the in
terest of unity of action.

     However, in July 1964, the OAU tackled a problem tha
was incomparably more delicate: the civil war in the Congo.
Although strife there had previously contributed to a hardening
of the Casablanca and Monrovia blocs, it was confidently assumed that the OAU would provide a common forum in which
to obtain an African solution. But there were significant differences. The radicals were angered by the return of Moise
Tshombe and his bid to bring about "national reconciliation."
His terms were not acceptable to the rebels nor their sympa-
thizers. The moderates, to the contrary, again came out in
favor of the central government and supported whatever policy
it chose. Thus there were soon two alternative "African" solutions, depending on which side one backed in the civil war.

     Unfortunately, rather than thrashing out a real compro-
mise, the Council of Ministers merely included the often contradictory desires of all in its resolution of 10 September
1964. It did not take long for the peace plan to fall apart.
Almost as soon as the Congo Commission began its work it
was faced with divergent interpretations of its terms of reference. Also, it made an enemy of Tshombe. Léopoldville re
peatedly criticized the interference and one-sidedness of the
Organization and its Commission. The moderate states also
withdrew their support. To the radicals' way of thinking, the
OAU was not doing enough to end the war and integrate the

rebels in a new government so they too began looking elsewhere.

The climax came after the Stanleyville operation of 24
November 1964. The following period witnessed an open split
in the African ranks. The members no longer hesitated to
take sides in the struggle. The radicals reacting bitterly to
the near collapse of the rebel government and attributing this
to the intervention of foreign powers, began stepping up their
aid. The rebels, who had been supported more or less secretly by Brazzaville and Burundi, were now openly backed by
states that did not hide their intervention. Algeria, Egypt and
Sudan were sending in weapons and apparently personnel.
Strong moral and some material support also came from
Ghana, Guinea and Mali. And, in the later stages, Tanzania,
Uganda and Kenya moved towards recognition.

The reaction of the moderate states to this was to ac-
centuate their support of the central government and to re-
claim their freedom of action. Some of the more adamant
wished to create an organization permitting political cooperation as well. Finally, at a summit conference in Nouakchott,
the Dakar decision was reversed. The new Organisation Commune Africaine et Malgache (OCAM) was presented on 12 February 1965 as "a regrouping of African states within the framework of the O.A.U." It was to strengthen cooperation and
solidarity among its member states and to accelerate their development in the political, economic, social, technical and
cultural fields. The important point was the addition of political activity.

OCAM initiated its career with a pronouncement on the
Congo affair. The communique lay the blame for an aggravation of the situation on a "policy of partiality" in the OAU.
The malaise was caused by disregarding certain of its principles, namely sovereignty and non-interference. This was also
the first time that a large group of states expressed support
of the central government. Without formally endorsing
Tshombe's policies, they affirmed the "urgent necessity of
bringing peace back to the Congo-Léopoldville by aid to the
legal government."[2] Not long after, President Tsiranana of
Madagascar attacked the African states that refused to have
any contact with Premier Tshombe and affirmed that "the newly formed OCAM is ready to mediate in the Congo dispute if
both sides agree."[3] Obviously, both sides would not agree.
But OCAM's criticism of the OAU and the action of some of
its members was significant.

By the time of the Nairobi Council, the situation was indeed grave. There were rumors that the OCAM states would not come or that the radicals would officially recognize the rebels. There was fear of a split in the OAU and its ultimate collapse. In fact, the Organization was on the brink of a serious crisis. Since the Foreign Ministers could do nothing for the Congo they tried to forestall the threat to the OAU by passing the problem on to the Heads of State. Fortunately, in the interval before the next Assembly, things changed completely. The rebels were pushed back and finally beaten and Tshombe emerged briefly as the winner. His consecration came in May 1965, when the Congo was received as a member of OCAM. However, on 13 October, Tshombe was dismissed by President Kasavubu. With this the Congo issue was struck from the agenda, the radicals were ready for a reconciliation and the near split became a thing of the past.

But there was another prong to the moderate states' counter-offensive. They had long criticized and feared the policy of President Nkrumah, which included intervention in the affairs of other states. The communique of 12 February presenting OCAM also condemned the subversion from Ghana and announced that the OAU would be seized with the matter. This time the campaign was launched with the support or connivance of the English-speaking moderates as well. President Tubman of Liberia suggested that a meeting look into the complaints of Ghanaian subversion. Then the Nigerians, who had also been a target of Dr. Nkrumah's ire, proposed that such a meeting be held in Lagos. On 26 May, at the request of Houphouöt-Boigny, the OCAM states most directly concerned consulted in Abidjan and agreed to attend the Lagos meeting. There, Ghana was put in the dock. However, when their demands were not complied with, many of the Francophone states stayed away from Accra.

Nevertheless, these political activities were not to the liking of all OCAM members. Brazzaville was still on rather bad terms with Léopoldville but remained in OCAM because of the other links. Moktar Ould Daddah, then Chairman of OCAM, increasingly disapproved of its return to politics. All along he had felt that OCAM was a possible "competitor" to the OAU and might undermine its authority. He objected to the Abidjan meeting and, in July 1965, Mauritania withdrew from the political OCAM while continuing its cooperation in other fields.

Radical Disarray.

With the end of the Congolese civil war, the rift in Africa was healed and the improvised blocs lost most of their cohesion. There was renewed unity. At almost the same time, another crisis was welling up in Southern Rhodesia where a settler government had taken power. In the face of this the Africans forgot old differences. The eventuality of a unilateral declaration of independence was discussed and supposedly prepared for by the Accra Assembly. But, when it came on 11 November 1965, Africa was taken largely unaware. Not until December was an extraordinary meeting called to lay down a common policy. This time the Council of Ministers found another compromise, one that did not really make either side happy. The radicals had urged very strong action against the Smith regime by Africa itself. The moderates preferred having Britain act against the rebel colony while holding African action in reserve (or avoiding it altogether). The compromise was to break off diplomatic relations with Great Britain if it did not crush the rebellion by 15 December 1965.

This was an unfortunate solution. It was not in the interest of either the radicals or the moderates to cease relations and was of doubtful value to the Zimbabwe people. Still, the decision was adopted unanimously by the Foreign Ministers as the only strong measure they could agree upon to avoid an open split in the ranks. When it came to implementation, however, the compromise had its worst consequences. For, in the end, only the radical states severed relations: Algeria, Congo (Brazzaville), Ghana, Guinea, Mali, Mauritania, Sudan, Tanzania and the UAR. They naturally reacted angrily to the fix they were in owing to the moderate states' failure to apply the resolution.

Relations between the members were very strained when the next meeting of the Council was held on 28 February 1966. Tension ran particularly high since, only four days earlier, there had been a coup d'état in Ghana and two delegations arrived in Addis Ababa, one reconfirmed by President Nkrumah from Peking, the other sent by the National Liberation Council. Either because they refused to be seated with the new Ghanaian regime or out of dissatisfaction with action on Rhodesia, many of the radical states walked out of the meeting or stayed without participating. But this did not paralyze the "rump" Council and the moderates still had a quorum and proceeded to adopt resolutions in the absence of the radicals.

It was not until the Addis Ababa Assembly in November 1966 that tempers had cooled sufficiently for the members to seek a genuine compromise. The radicals admitted that direct intervention by Africa was not feasible and the moderates were willing to provide somewhat stronger backing to the liberation movements. This compromise was still rather meek and did not really please the radical states, but they had little choice other than to accept it. Whereas at the start of the crisis the radicals seemed to have the initiative, it was now clear that it was the moderates who determined policies in the OAU.

The radical leaders had also become worried about the "successes of imperialism and neo-colonialism" in Africa and were particularly disturbed by the series of military coups resulting in even more moderate regimes and culminating in the fall of Nkrumah. The coup in Ghana became a rallying point for the radicals. The sharpest reply came from Sékou Touré who made Nkrumah his co-president and threatened Ghana with war. Then Julius Nyerere, the Osagyefo's antithesis in many ways but sharing some of his ideals, made a major speech warning against the consequences of these changes that blunted Africa's drive.

The radical movement was in a very uncomfortable position. Its leaders were deeply concerned about the situation in Rhodesia where they wished to make stronger efforts (although not always so great as they claimed), but they could not have their own way in the OAU. They were uncertain whether the circumstances warranted a separate policy outside of the Organization or merely further efforts at stiffening the official policy. And, at the same time, the political tide seemed to be turning against them. Eventually they recognized the need to meet to agree on a common stand. But the radicals were already less dynamic and less organized than they suspected and the "revolutionary summit" was not held until 4-6 April 1967. The conference in Cairo was attended by Houari Boumedienne, Moktar Ould Daddah, Julius Nyerere and Gamal Abdel Nasser. Although Sékou Touré sent a representative and Massamba-Débat and Modibo Keita ensured the others of their support, the showing was poor.

The meeting dealt primarily with the Rhodesian affair but came to no clear-cut decisions. It did not go back on the earlier demands and reaffirmed that "the use of force is the only effective means to end the racist regime in Rhodesia."[4] But it was uncertain what force was meant: force by Britain (according to the OAU resolution), the United Nations, or Af-

rica itself (as they had previously urged). It would seem to
be one of the former as the only direct call for action came
when President Nasser appealed for an uprising of the Zimbabwe people. To this end, the radical states promised to increase their aid to both ZAPU and ZANU. Thus the leaders
stuck very much to the OAU policy, only deciding to make a
somewhat greater contribution, rather than striking off on
their own.

Unlike the Francophone moderates, the radical group
did not try to set up a regular institution or adopt a charter.
Both Nasser and Nyerere insisted that the meeting should be
held within the framework of the OAU and that a new "bloc"
should not be formed. Moreover, it proposed to examine the
cleavage in the OAU and seek means of strengthening the common body. Nevertheless, there was some speculation that a
front of progressive African states would be created. The alliance could only be political, since the potential members were
unwilling (or unable because of distance) to engage in any other
activities. After Cairo there was a brief flurry of reports.
There was supposed to be a meeting of revolutionary parties
in Algeria. However, the radicals proved incapable of creating an organization or even holding a regular series of conferences. The later meetings, in twos and threes, were less
publicized and the main concern was to restore relations with
Britain in a dignified manner. By mid-1968 this step had been
taken by all concerned.

Although it was eventually possible to find a half-way
house for the radicals and moderates on most questions of decolonization, there was a more painful rift in the southern
part of the continent. Differences among the states bordering
the zone of combat were more difficult to resolve. Friction
and antagonism grew between those at the fore of the struggle,
like Tanzania and Zambia, and those willing to cooperate with
South Africa and its allies. As the refusal to support an active OAU policy verged on collaboration with Africa's enemies,
the chances of healing the rift and finding one policy for all
diminished.

Radicals vs. Moderates.

What is in a label? Quite a bit, judging by the way
some states pre-empted the tag "revolutionary" and left much
less enviable titles for the others. Nevertheless, all the African countries were basically revisionist[5] or revolutionary.

They were all interested in a decisive change in status. Some
were more militant or simply made more noise, but no state
idealized its present situation in all respects or failed to encourage change somewhere. There was an urgent desire
throughout Africa to come of age, to enter the modern world
and to play a worthy role internationally. Still, there were
certain attitudes and policies that characterized different states
and leaders and these tendencies could be traced more readily
by using some terms. The simplest and most neutral were
radical, moderate and conservative. To give them a more
specific meaning they have been used in connection with the
activities of the OAU to show where the member states agreed
and acted in unison and where they became radical or moderate.

It is not easy to classify the African states since, basically, they have so much in common. The Program of Addis
Ababa was and is sincerely desired by all. All the states
want an end to colonialism, all want some elbow room in international affairs, all want to develop economically and social
ly, and none wants intervention in its own internal affairs.
Even more specifically, all support the struggle for liberation,
all seek some degree of non-alignment, all are "socialists"
and hope to mobilize the masses, and all are worried about
the next coup d'état. The internal regime is not the key either, for all praise democracy and tend to create one-party
states in which opposition has steadily been eliminated. Finally, although little progress was made, all pledge themselves
to African unity.

If differences are to be found, it is not in the quality
or degree of "revolution" but in the priorities and approach.
The radicals are at the forefront of the struggle for liberation;
they aid the militant movements and give more arms and instructors. Some have felt that this should be the primary or
the only real task of the Organization and constantly offered
stronger plans to turn the tide. For the radicals, the use of
force is to be encouraged and they have even suggested that
the independent states throw themselves into the battle. The
radicals have been far more active in international politics and
try to play a role on the world scene. They also insist on
the need for a non-aligned policy not only in their own countries but throughout Africa. When crises break out within the
continent, they more readily line up on the side of like-minded
forces, whether governments or dissidents. Although the radi
cals also have been deeply concerned about the economic situa
tion, they are not able to do as much compared to the moder-

ates because of the amount of their time, energy and money
that has already been allocated to decolonization and politics.
Some of the leaders have worked out impressive schemes for
vast continental structures, but they were rarely put into practice.

The moderates are far less concerned with decolonization. (And the conservatives, rather similar in other respects,
have reasons to cooperate with South Africa and Portugal.)
Although the moderates do accept force, it is as an ultima ra-
tio and they insist it be wielded by the oppressed peoples
alone. (The conservatives refuse to be involved in such measures and are sceptical about the results.) The moderates are
amazingly quiet about foreign policy and their relations are
limited to a few, old friends. In inter-African affairs, they
show greater respect for sovereignty and rarely wish to intervene in another country's problem. Nor would they stand for
intervention in their own domestic affairs. The moderates
and conservatives are far more concerned with the tasks at
home. They devote much of their effort to bringing about
change in the economic field. True, their "economism" has
made the moderates blind to certain causes, but it also has
enduced them to work with others for specific goals. Even if
they refuse to commit themselves on far-reaching integration
with uncertain aims, they have not hesitated to enter into
strictly limited groupings that could grow. In the end, they
have gone much further than the prophets of unity.

One could hardly claim that either the radicals or the
moderates always have chosen the best policies. When it
came to decolonization, the radicals offered a nobler and more
self-sacrificing program and one that would have sped independence more than the moderates' hesitation. Some of the
proposals were not realistic and some of the offers were not
honored, but the radicals were on the right track if all other
concerns could be put aside. Unfortunately, they could not.
It has always been necessary, even in the most "revolutionary" countries, to weigh guns against butter or decide what
initiatives can be made abroad at the expense of domestic improvement. Here the moderates have had a more workable
alternative. The radicals are correct when they stress the
dangers of foreign entanglement; the moderates are no less
right when they stress the benefits of cooperation with the outside world. Unity can be achieved faster if the states would
accept some loss of sovereignty. None of the states are really willing to do this and so a more gradual approach, expend-
ing great effort to keep the OAU functioning, is wisest. The

best thing for the radicals and moderates is not to prove who
is right but to learn from one another and to work out joint
policies so that they can advance together towards the common
goals.

It was easy to see in what manner the policies of the
two groups of states vary. The radicals are militant and
make quite a show of what they do. They are dynamic and
expansive, insisting that others follow their lead. They have
pushed ahead and clamored for rapid results although their
choice was often restricted by great doctrinal purity. The
moderates are rather calm. They move slowly, step by step.
They are more pragmatic and willing to join forces with others,
even those of differing views. Not attempting to teach others
lessons, they do not like to be taught either. Given the drive
of the radicals and the reserve of the moderates, it almost
comes as a surprise to learn that the latter represent over
two-thirds of the membership and that they are the ones that
really run the Organization.

Taking individual states and leaders, it is hard to decide in fact which are the most revolutionary. There is no
doubt that some, such as Algeria, the UAR and Tanzania, support the liberation movements very actively, but others also
contribute. Economically, the greatest upheaval has not been
where socialism was purest but where growth and industrialization were most rapid. Thus the Ivory Coast was turning
out a new middle class and a new proletariat faster than any
of its more rabid neighbors. Socially, the secularization of
Muslim countries renovated the old society more than any mobilization within the existing structures, and Habib Bourguiba
has gone furthest on that path. The quietest and most "moderate" of the radicals, Julius Nyerere, has gradually gained
the reputation he deserves as the most consistent and courageous. Often, also, the edges blurred, with expansive moderates like Tsiranana and pragmatic radicals like Keita, while
some leaders have tried to combine development and decolonization, such as Kaunda.

It is no simple matter to list the membership of either
camp since the alignments change frequently and there are always marginal members. Nevertheless, two major African
crises provide an indication. The hard core of the radicals
were those backing the rebels in the Congo and those urging
direct African intervention and the use of force in Rhodesia.
More specifically, they included the states that severed relations with Great Britain. The radicals consisted partly of a

Black African wing: Ghana, Guinea and Mali. The Arab wing was led by the UAR and Algeria and assembled protégés from the broader Islam circle: Mauritania, Somalia and Sudan. A newer group consisted of Tanzania and Zambia, deeply engaged in the struggle for liberation but less keen on traditional items like non-alignment and neo-colonialism. With the disappearance of Nkrumah, however, there was already an unbalance in the radical camp, with a preponderance of Arab-Muslim states.

The hard core of the moderates were the ones that supported Tshombe or who wanted to let Britain determine the pace of the struggle against the Smith regime. The moderates included the older generation of leaders from the former English and French colonies. Among the principals of the latter were Houphouët-Boigny and Senghor, and the real strength was in OCAM. The English-speaking group was less well organized, although it was occasionally represented by Azikiwe or Tubman. And a special place was reserved for Haile Selassie as an elder statesman. There were also countries, Ghana the best known of them, where the army had turned out the political leaders and then tried to put the country's affairs in order with more rigid administration and greater economic concern.

The membership of moderates and radicals is very fluid. Tenure of office in Africa is at best uncertain; a coup d'état can alter the official policy of a country overnight or, rarely, a gradual change could bring a country from one camp to another. The most striking example was the coup in Ghana, where the mainstay of the radical camp was replaced by a military government eager to strengthen relations with its moderate neighbors. Brazzaville moved towards the radicals when Abbé Youlou was ousted. Morocco left the old Casablanca bloc when its partners ceased backing it on Mauritania and when Algeria, much more radical, became its enemy on the border question. But there were any number of other changes in person that could imply a change in regime. On the wall of the conference room of Africa Hall, in Addis Ababa, where the OAU Assembly and Council often meet, there is a huge mural of the Heads of State and Government who attended the historic summit conference in 1963. This was a pointed reminder of the changes that had taken place in the following years. For many of those who attended were now deposed or dead.

Regional Renaissance.

        Shortly after the creation of the OAU the various politi
cal organizations of the continent had been dissolved or converted and it looked like the beginning of the end of regionalism. Since the OAU had top-level specialized commissions in
most technical fields, it could be assumed that these would
rapidly take the lead and obviate the need for any other bodies or at least provide general control and coordination of
those that remained. However, despite these early prediction
the contrary happened. The institutions that existed expanded
and new ones were created. These bodies sprang up in all
parts of the continent and in the most varied specializations
although much of the activity is now economic and little as ye
has been done on a comparable scale in social or cultural
fields. Rather than fade away, African regionalism had been
infused with new life.

        The basic reason for this is the sheer immensity of th
continent. Economic relations of the developing countries
simply do not extend much beyond the neighboring states. So
cial and cultural ties are not extensive. Even political relations do not link all the states. Thus there is more cohesion
on a regional level and most matters can be undertaken with
greater chances of success in smaller groupings. Other units
not strictly regional in the geographical sense, are bound by
close relations that originated during the colonial period or th
struggle for independence. Despite distance there was enough
solidarity for the member states to undertake certain tasks
without waiting for the others.

        One of the main reasons for the growth of regionalism
was the failure of the OAU to provide a true continental frame
work for such activities. When the commissions fell into dis
use it was clear that the states had to act on their own if any
thing was to be done. This, however, led to a disorderly
growth of formations. The resultant groupings have not always been rational economically. Links were determined tradi
tionally or even fortuitously. They were sometimes incomplete or overlapped with one another. Since there was usually
a political undercurrent, organizations have ended up as rival
This was not so much to attack one another as to offer better
conditions and woo economic satelites in order to expand the
sphere of influence of a large or dynamic country. With time
and circumstances, these groupings have become more genuinely regional, sensible and viable.

The African countries had already laid the foundations for regionalism before the creation of the OAU. Several bodies have remained intact and even expanded over the years, such as the Entente and the Equatorial Customs Union. Others have developed along lines very similar to less successful attempts of earlier days, especially in East and Central Africa and in the Maghreb. There have arisen also a number of more restricted groups based on river or lake basins. The first is the Senegal River Basin Commission of Guinea, Mali, Mauritania and Senegal. It was founded in July 1963 with an Interstate Ministerial Committee for the improvement of the river basin, and includes further sub-committees on administration and legal affairs, navigation and transport, and power and agriculture. The Act of Niamey of October 1963 provided for free navigation and economic cooperation among the states bordering the Niger River. Cameroon, Chad, Dahomey, Guinea, Ivory Coast, Mali, Niger, Nigeria and Upper Volta then established a Commission and permanent secretariat to coordinate studies. A simpler Commission has been set up for the Lake Chad basin in May 1964. It includes Cameroon, Chad, Niger and Nigeria. Although the Nile Waters Agreement was signed back in 1959, the potential members of the grouping--Sudan, UAR, Kenya, Tanzania and Uganda--have been slow in creating machinery.

One of the oldest and most effective bodies, the Economic Commission for Africa, is also continental but has long since decided that a regional approach would be best to solve the problems of economic integration and development. For the ECA's planning purposes, independent Africa has been divided into four rough areas, each with a sub-regional headquarters: East Africa (Lusaka), West Africa (Niamey), Central Africa (Kinshasa) and North Africa (Tangier). Later a fifth might embrace Southern Africa. There are, of course, no strict geographical, economic or other demarcation lines, but this division of the continent has simplified the work and provides more manageable building blocks. In each of these regions, the ECA was actively promoting integration and encouraging common markets and other units.

West and Equatorial Africa.

For a long time the only grouping in West Africa that prospered was the Entente. It was strongly supported by its members who initiated new measures for harmonizing economic

policies. The main cement, the solidarity fund, was turned
into a mutual aid and loan guarantee fund to encourage foreign
investment. The Ivory Coast decided to forego its share for
five years and the other partners derived even greater benefit.
Thanks to its flexibility and the decision to deal with governments rather than individuals, a number of political upsets
could be absorbed without shaking the organization. The Council of Understanding was not disrupted by the Dahomey coup in
October 1963, although for some time the new regime flirted
with the idea of a Benin Union with Ghana, Nigeria and Togo.
It also adjusted to the coups d'état that followed and even to a
majority of military regimes. After the pressure from Ghana
let up, the until-then silent partner, Togo, was able to join
officially in June 1966. More recent meetings have discussed
the possibility of cooperation with Ankrah's and Busia's Ghana.

          Under the impulsion of Houphouët-Boigny, the Entente
tried to take a decisive step to integrate the economies and
peoples. In December 1964, the Heads of State of the Ivory
Coast, Niger and Upper Volta (joined later by Dahomey)
reached agreement on a project of "organic fusion." This
meant a common citizenship for the nationals of these states,
free movement, free access to the civil service and to private
property, the right to vote and eligibility. The nationals of
each state would have the same rights and obligations in all
four states. Had it worked, this attempt at "multinationality"
might have been the origin of a federation or broader national
state. But it met with considerable resistance from the civil
servants and workers of the Ivory Coast, who feared a tremendous influx of outsiders. Although the project had to be
withdrawn, Houphouët-Boigny did not repudiate the idea and
announced that he would wait until OCAM and the OAU made
similar gestures.

          Ghana, Guinea and Mali did not emulate their moderate
rivals. In spite of sporadic talk of solidarity, the three continued drifting apart and did not even have close informal relations. What was worse, they rejected all overtures from
other states and blocked attempts at expanding cooperation
throughout the region. Although Modibo Keita was rather conciliatory and tried not to make enemies of his moderate neighbors, his country had embarked on a socialist course and a
degree of autarchy that stifled trade even with Senegal and
Mauritania. Sékou Touré was far more doctrinaire and was
unable to cooperate with leaders of differing views. In August
1964, a West African Free Trade Area had been worked out
between the Heads of State of Liberia, Sierra Leone, Guinea

and the Ivory Coast but it was stillborn. Moreover, for political reasons and real or imagined offenses, Touré began attacking the leaders of the OCAM states and, in particular,
Presidents Senghor and Houphouët. The most disruptive force,
however, was Ghana. President Nkrumah systematically condemned all regional units for balkanizing the continent and was
particularly sharp against the Entente and OCAM. Thus
broader unity was not possible in the region until 24 February
1966.

With the fall of Nkrumah there was a slow but distinct
change. Mali was the first to escape from its isolation. Already in June 1963, the rift with Senegal was officially ended,
but there was little trade. Still, they were anxious to restore
economic relations. The first serious attempt at cutting
across ideological barriers came with the adoption of the new
convention of the West African Customs Union in March 1966.
This unit, originally created in 1959, consisted of Dahomey,
Ivory Coast, Mauritania, Niger, Senegal, Upper Volta and
Mali. Now these states were ready to establish a common
external tariff and permanent institutions including a General
Secretariat, Council of Ministers and Committee of Experts.
Then, in February 1967, Mali decided to return to the franc
zone and once again economic cooperation became possible.

For some time Sékou Touré continued and even stiffened the old course. However, without repudiating the Osagyefo,
he eventually had to recognize the new situation. After having
repeatedly refused to attend meetings of the Senegal River
Commission, Touré suddenly made a bid to take the lead.
The meeting in Labé, Guinea, at the end of March 1968,
created at his insistence an Organisation des Etats Riverains
du Fleuve Sénégal, of which he was the first President. The
OERS had very ambitious machinery consisting of an annual
Conference of Heads of State, a bi-annual Council of Ministers,
a consultative interparliamentary council and a secretariat in
Dakar. The scope was expanded to include the physical development of the basin, planning and economic development of
the region, and educational, cultural and social affairs. Politics would probably not be forgotten either. But Sékou Touré
went even further and proposed political unity among the four
states: Guinea, Mali, Mauritania and Senegal. He followed
this up with a plan to merge Guinea and Mali in one nation
and state. Although stressing Mali's eagerness for such a union, Modibo Keita admitted that this still required "solid preparation."[6]

Now that political considerations no longer overruled economic logic, it was possible to forge ahead. The major breach in the old divisions resulted from the patient efforts of the Economic Commission for Africa to promote integration. Finally, in 1967, the countries in the sub-region signed the Articles of Association for an Economic Community of West Africa. However, with the new wind of unity blowing strongly, even this framework seemed too restrictive to the ministerial meeting and summit convened in Monrovia in April 1968. The delegates drafted and signed the Protocol for a West African Regional Grouping. This time the nine founder members included Guinea, but most of the Entente states had not come. Still, it was assumed that the fourteen states in the region would eventually join. The new Protocol incorporated the Articles of Association and the grouping would be primarily economic. The members wished to strengthen cooperation in industry, agriculture, transport, communications and power, and to expand and liberalize trade. But it was bound to flow over into other spheres of activity. There would be cooperation for the free movement of workers and joint action in education, training, health and research. Politics might follow. The structure consisted of a Conference of Heads of State and Government, a Council of Ministers, an Executive Secretariat and various subsidiary bodies. The contents and operation were to be defined more precisely at a conference in Ouagadougou the year after. Yet this plan also remained in abeyance.

In Equatorial Africa things started off well. The original customs union between the Central African Republic, Chad, Congo (Brazzaville) and Gabon spread to include Cameroon in February 1964. The other Congo could not join then because of the civil war and rivalry with Brazzaville. By December, the five members agreed to go ahead and progressively constitute an Union Douanière et Economique de l'Afrique Centrale. UDEAC intended to eliminate all barriers to trade, have a common customs tariff, coordinate development plans and harmonize investment codes and financial systems (including a joint central bank). Special arrangements were made to help the poorer, landlocked countries by distributing industrial projects equitably and refunding part of the duties and taxes collected at ports. An excellent example of practical cooperation was the common oil refinery at Port-Gentil in Gabon. Supervision would come from a Council of Heads of State, a Management Committee and a General Secretariat. The UDEAC treaty came into force on 1 January 1966.

This Central African Customs and Economic Union was
sually given as an example of sensible economic integration
⌐ Africa.[7] However, quite suddenly, it split up. Rather
⌐an join the groupings, the huge Congo (Kinshasa) formed a
⌐val body with Chad and the Central African Republic. The
vo states had not benefitted as much as expected from
DEAC and they may have received a better offer. General
⌐obutu's visit to Bangui in February 1968 resulted in a Proto-
⌐l of the United States of Central Africa. Then, on 2 April,
⌐e three leaders adopted the Charter of the Union des Etats
⌐ l'Afrique Centrale (UEAC). This was a very ambitious pro-
⌐ct. The Union of Central African States intended to establish
⌐ common market and harmonize industrialization, development,
⌐ansport, telecommunications and even defence. From the
⌐art General Mobutu spoke of a "reality," but for the moment
⌐EAC only consisted of a President and Secretariat. The Un-
n would require considerable machinery to handle its tasks.
⌐oreover, there was traditionally little trade among the three
⌐d even no infrastructure for such relations. The Congo's
⌐ly port was badly placed to service its partners.

It was hoped that the new UEAC would extend eastwards
⌐ Rwanda and Burundi and also draw the other UDEAC mem-
⌐rs into the Congo's sphere of influence. But Congo (Brazza-
⌐lle), Cameroon and Gabon showed no interest in foresaking
⌐e older body and the new creation remained highly artificial.
⌐ genuine compromise might have been found, and had indeed
⌐en sought in the ECA, to integrate the Congo (Kinshasa) into
DEAC or some new body, but as long as politics and prestige
⌐d priority little could be done. To further complicate the
⌐tuation, after considering its interests, the Central African
⌐epublic returned to UDEAC in December 1968 and left the re-
⌐aining members physically separated from one another. The
⌐suing escalation of threats and reprisals made it even hard-
⌐ to find a solution.

⌐st Africa and the Maghreb.

With East African unity, things got worse before they
⌐t better. In June 1963, the Heads of State of Kenya, Tan-
⌐nyika and Uganda had pledged to establish a political federa-
⌐on by the end of the year. But the goal was well out of
⌐ach and they had to settle for a functional approach based on
⌐e common services left by Britain. This was worked into a
⌐st "common market" in 1964. Nevertheless, each of the
⌐ates increasingly looked after its own interests. Kenya,

which had been the center of the colonial structure, seemed
get most out of the arrangement and an effort was made at
improving the position of Uganda and Tanzania. Attempts we
made at inducing investors to go to the other members and
Arusha, in Tanzania, was made the headquarters of any futu:
economic unit. Nevertheless, Kenya continued developing mo
rapidly and to protect themselves the other two put up tariff
barriers and introduced their own currencies. Free movement was restricted and the common services were threatene
To save the links that remained, a special commission was e
tablished to draft a new treaty more evenly sharing benefits.

This treaty of the East African Community was signed
by Kenyatta, Nyerere and Obote in Kampala, Uganda, in Jun
1967. The fifteen year treaty initiated a system with no internal duties and a common external tariff, and decentralized
and relocated the common services. To compensate Tanzani
and Uganda, there were transfer taxes, fiscal incentives to
harmonize industrial development and a development bank to
which all contributed equally while Kenya withdrew less. Th
Community was placed under the direction of an East African
Authority of the Presidents of the member states. They we
aided by several Councils of Ministers on the common marke
communications, economic consultation and planning, and research. There was also a Tribunal and Legislative Assembl
Thus the East African threesome were off to a new start. I
addition, this common market of thirty million people might
serve as a regional pole. Other states could negotiate their
participation or association in the Community and formal ap-
plications have come from Burundi, Ethiopia, Somalia and
Zambia.

Presidents Kenyatta and Nyerere also introduced a se
ies of political conferences in East and Central Africa. The
were meant to promote good neighborly feelings among the
states of the region. The first one was convened in Nairobi
at the end of March 1966. It was followed periodically by
other meetings at the Heads of State or Foreign Ministers
level. Those attending the first were Burundi, Central African Republic, Chad, Congo (Brazzaville), Congo (Kinshasa),
Ethiopia, Kenya, Malawi, Rwanda, Somalia, Sudan, Tanzania
Uganda and Zambia. Among the issues discussed were the
situation in the Portuguese territories, Rhodesia and South A
rica, disputes among the members, the refugee problem and
unity as well as technical cooperation. Although most of the
were also on the OAU agenda, the conference was not intend
as "an attempt to form a regional grouping or to usurp the

functions of the O.A.U."[8] No permanent machinery was established but the conferences wished to adopt concrete measures and two Commissions were set up to see to their implementation. One dealt with security problems caused by the
colonial and settler powers and the other with economic, transport and communications questions.

No region was so emotionally proud of its common heritage as the Maghreb and talks on unity never really ceased.
For the time being, the region consisted of Morocco, Algeria,
Tunisia and Libya, with Mauritania as a potential member. A
meeting in September 1964 decided to establish regular machinery. Soon there was a Maghreb Council of Ministers for
Economic Affairs, a Standing Consultative Committee, a Permanent Secretariat and specialized sub-commissions on industry, commerce, transport, post and telecommunications, tour-
ism and statistics. The four states agreed upon a system of
privileged economic relations and decided to promote the harmonization of customs and industry. In subsequent meetings
agreements were reached on the export of esparto grass, harmonization of the iron and steel industry, a marketing body
for agricultural products (especially citrus fruits and wine) and
air transport. Unfortunately, no common stand could be taken
towards the European Economic Community and not all their
agreements have been put into practice.

In the Maghreb, political and ideological differences
have been strong enough to block even loose economic cooperation. After the Arab-Israeli war, however, there was a striking improvement in relations. In September 1967, King Hassan made a state visit to Algiers where he attended the OAU
Assembly. Then, after a series of consultations among Ministers and technicians, President Boumedienne paid a visit to
Morocco in mid-January. The reconciliation was consecrated
with a treaty of "brotherhood, good neighborhood, and cooperation." The terms of this twenty-year, renewable treaty were
very general. It offered cooperation "in all fields" and specialized bilateral commissions would later suggest initiatives.
Although there was no specific mention of the border conflict,
this problem, still unsettled, was temporarily forgotten. At
least it was agreed that any differences would be submitted to
joint commissions and violence was forbidden as a means of
settling disputes. The treaty was regarded by Boumedienne
as "a new page and the end of the period which was characterized by the 1963 events."[9] A less formal step was taken in
Rabat at the Islamic Summit of September 1969, when King
Hassan and Moktar Ould Daddah quietly agreed that Morocco's

territorial claims would lapse. In May 1970, the Algerian and
Moroccan leaders announced that the boundary dispute was closed.

The Afro-Malagasy States.

Another institution, although not strictly regional, more
than made up for this with greater harmony, even solidarity,
in other respects. The oldest and most successful unit still
is the Organisation Commune Africaine et Malgache (and its
two ancestors). The common denominator here was and is po
litical moderation and the primacy of economics. OCAM is
rooted in the former French colonial world and grew out of
the federations and customs unions and the franc zone. But it
spread and other links were established. Considerable progress was made through UAM and its successor, UAMCE, before these states set up OCAM. Despite its modest aims this
group has gone further than any other and much further than
the OAU in the various non-political fields.

Although the Organisation was active from the very
month of founding, in February 1965, it was still necessary to
adopt a Charter and establish the organization formally. This
process dragged on for over a year. The next major meeting
was in Tananarive from 12-18 January 1966. It was originally intended that the Heads of State should sign the Charter but
agreement could not be reached and the Foreign Ministers
only initialled it, while Brazzaville did not even do that. It
was not until the 27th of June 1966 that the summit could be
held on the island of Madagascar and the Charter signed. The
members were: Cameroon, Central African Republic, Chad,
Congo (Brazzaville), Congo (Kinshasa), Dahomey, Gabon,
Ivory Coast, Malagasy, Niger, Rwanda, Senegal, Togo and Up
per Volta.

OCAM's purpose was "to strengthen co-operation and
solidarity between the African and Malagasy States in order to
accelerate their economic, social, technical and cultural development." But it went somewhat further since it would coordinate activities in these fields and also facilitate "inter-
state consultations on foreign policy." The organization was
open to any independent sovereign African state that requested
admission and accepted the provisions. It had three main institutions. The Conference of Heads of State and Government,
the supreme body, could discuss all matters and adopt majority decisions in the technical fields. For political recommendations, however, decisions had to be unanimous. The Counci

of Ministers, consisting usually of Foreign Ministers, was responsible to the Conference and would implement cooperation among the members according to the directives of the Conference. The Administrative General Secretariat, with headquarters in Yaoundé, was to ensure the administrative functioning of the organization under the authority of the Chairman of the Conference. The Secretariat also assumed the activities of the UAMPT and Air Afrique.

The machinery of OCAM was thus very similar to that of the OAU and consecrated it as the standard structure in Africa. Nevertheless, there were several significant differences. OCAM was still a classical body with a strict respect for national "sovereignty and the fundamental options of each member state," and some of its decisions had to be taken unanimously. However, once adopted, they were binding on the members. In the OAU majority decisions were the rule, but even unanimous ones were not obligatory. The role of the Chairman-in-Office of the Conference was also rather novel. This post rotated annually but was more than just honorary, for the Chairman represented OCAM between meetings and could be entrusted with specific tasks and missions. He became a roving ambassador and trouble shooter and also kept an eye on the Secretariat. The role of the Secretary-General, elected for only two years, was downgraded to make way for more dynamic and authoritative action by the Chairman.

The major concern was still economic cooperation and integration and new measures were taken regularly. The Dakar meeting in March 1964 discussed items like a common market, joint insurance fund, multilateral fund of guarantee for private investments, and payments and compensation union. Unlike the OAU, a start was made with the simpler, more practicable ones. The UAM conventions on the movement of persons, diplomatic representation and technical assistance were carried over. Conventions on double taxation and on mutual administrative assistance in customs and exchange were adopted. In June 1966, at Tananarive, an agreement was concluded on sugar, whereby the producers (Brazzaville and Malagasy) would receive privileged treatment in the partner states. Similar agreements were in the offing for meat and cotton. There was further coordination of policies through the African and Malagasy Coffee Organization (OAMCAF). Ideas still being mulled over included a multinational insurance company and a joint shipping line (on the same basis as Air Afrique, one of the few airlines that was expanding and making a good profit).

But no point was more important than relations with the
European Economic Community. President Hamani Diori of
Niger, in his capacity of Chairman, went on several missions
to inform Europe of feelings in Africa and to criticize insuffi-
ciencies or abuses. Basically, OCAM states at the Niamey
meeting, from 22-23 January 1968, approved associate membership in the EEC, after a decade's experience with the system, and expressed the will to conclude a third agreement.
The principal concern was to increase benefits through expanded trade with Europe, commodity guarantees, aid for industrialization and a larger Development Fund. To prepare their
bargaining position, the members decided to set up national
committees and a Coordinating Council. On 29 July 1969 a
new Convention of Association was signed.

The fourteen states also went beyond the economic
sphere. In January 1966, they created a student movement,
the Mouvement des Etudiants de l'Organisation Commune Africaine et Malgache (MEOCAM), to neutralize the troublesome
Fédération des Etudiants d'Afrique Noire en France (FEANF),
which followed a policy most often critical of the moderate
leaders. OCAM also planned to establish regional vocational
training centers for veterinarians and agricultural engineers.
Then, in August 1967, the first steps were taken towards
creating a press agency.

A very long term goal was the ambitious project close
to the heart of Léopold Sédar Senghor. As early as 1955 he
had spoken of the formation of a "commonwealth à la française." The idea of promoting a Francophone community was
broached at the Tananarive conference and was accepted by
the Heads of State. The community would be based on an already existing affinity drawn from a period of common history
traditions and culture. Above all, it was a "spiritual community of countries using French as a national, official, or working language. The use of French is therefore one of the most
important criteria, and the only standard of definition for
francophonie." This community would be open to some thirty
countries with over 200 million inhabitants, much of them from
Africa. Presidents Senghor and Diori tried to win support for
this on various trips. The greatest success was with President Bourguiba of Tunisia. But the idea did not appeal to
radical leaders like Boumedienne and Touré. Although France
viewed the move with "sympathy and interest," de Gaulle
awaited events and did not want it interpreted as neo-colonialism. The organization that might house francophonie was as
yet uncertain. However, at the OCAM meeting in January

968 a step by step approach to its achievement was intro-
uced. It would be prepared by numerous meetings of Franco-
hone ministers and parliamentarians, professors and students.
"hen, in March 1970, an Agency for Cultural and Technical
'ooperation was founded in Niamey.

Political issues of particular concern to the members
'ere also debated privately or publicly. A recurrent problem
'as the coups d'état in the member states, with which OCAM
ried to act with flexibility and caution, desiring to return a
ountry to stable rule and not provoke withdrawal. It also
trove to settle disputes among members. In 1963, UAM had
estored harmony between Brazzaville and Gabon after a ser-
es of riots, and between Dahomey and Niger after the recip-
ocal expulsion of nationals and a minor border dispute. In
'iamey, OCAM tried to reconcile General Mobutu and Presi-
ent Gregoire Kayibanda of Rwanda during their clash over the
lercenaries. In Kinshasa, from 27-29 January 1969, it over-
ame a series of conflicts in central Africa. The feud between
'DEAC and UEAC had embittered relations throughout the re-
ion. Friction and then reprisals upset even the normal eco-
omic currents between the Central African Republic, Chad
nd Kinshasa. With the execution of Pierre Mulele and the
essation of traffic on the river, the two Congos were again
stranged. In addition, OCAM took initiatives in highly deli-
ate "African" issues like the Congolese civil war and Biafra.
'wing to dissatisfaction with the OAU's handling of the first
risis and with its inertia on the second, OCAM began to seek
olutions elsewhere.

Although OCAM was open to all African states, and was
ius potentially continental like the OAU, there was no chance
would cease representing a sectarian, though large, group
f states. Even so, there was the danger of duplication or
ompetition. Its Charter stipulated that OCAM would act in
the spirit of the O.A.U." and the preamble added that the
lember states were faithful to the principles and objectives
f the OAU. If limited to fields in which the OAU was not
articularly active, namely those included in the 1963 resolu-
on and covered by the UAMCE, there would have been no
eal problem. Overlapping was avoided by the fact that the
AU had almost no economic, social or technical work. But,
ince OCAM had been created specifically to pursue political
:tivities as well, the two could come into collision.

Nevertheless, the Charter of African Unity did not rule
it other bodies and the Afro-Malagasy states were free to

establish any machinery they desired. The actual relationship
would have to be worked out with time. The OCAM leaders
denied that there was any threat of overlapping or conflict.
According to President Tsiranana:

> It has never been our intention to obstruct the work
> of the O.A.U., as some have unconvincingly im-
> plied, but on the contrary to consolidate it. At
> present OCAM regards itself, and should be re-
> garded by everyone, as a party in a political as-
> sembly ... The work of any assembly is based on
> the mutual concessions of parties moving in the
> same general direction, and it is in this spirit that
> we enthusiastically provided the O.A.U. with what
> is now one-third of its effective support.

Thus OCAM was a party within the OAU, or, to quote Houphouët-Boigny, "a nucleus and a unifying force."[10] What this
meant more strictly was that OCAM was a well-coordinated
group of states that had already reached a considerable degree
of agreement on the policies they followed within the OAU.
Since it encountered far looser groups there, this made OCAM
a strong organization within the Organization.

North-South Tension.

       Although less noticeable than the political, linguistic or
even geographical lines, the racial and religious divisions were
potentially the most dangerous. For some time they had been
amazingly well suppressed or ignored, but they had never been
erased. The continent consisted broadly of an Arab-Muslim
and a Black African area. The line of demarcation was not
sharp and the religious borders plunged much further south
than the racial ones. Still, there was a rough if poorly defined separation between north and south.

       Originally, the movement of solidarity had been racial
and not everyone in Black Africa wished to expand it. Reluctance was particularly strong on the East coast where the reactionary Arab sultanates were hated. There were occasionally bitter debates on the subject terminating with the complaint
of "Arab first, Arab last." Nevertheless, there were also
compelling reasons for the movement to embrace the whole
continent. Considerable aid for decolonization in southern Africa could be obtained from the north. These states, in turn,
certainly hoped to spread their influence southwards. What-

ver the motives, both sides accepted the dare and on the
whole the partnership was successful.

Within the OAU there was no hard and fast Arab group.
There were only five strictly Arab states and they were divided both between the Maghreb and Egypt and on moderate-
radical lines. Even if united this was too small a minority
to be effective. However, they were often joined by states
like Mauritania, Somalia, Sudan and lately Nigeria. With nine
members the unit was now a significant minority and could exercise pressure on other countries with a large Muslim popu-
ation. But this group only formed on specific issues. Thus
the convening of an Islamic Summit in September 1969 seriously embarrassed the states with a mixed population and most of
those in Black Africa stayed away.

Usually the Arab-Muslim states acted no different from
the other members. The Maghreb states participated actively
in the OAU and sometimes even put their attachment to Africa
first. A decisive success for the young Organization was, indeed, to handle the Algero-Moroccan border dispute in the
place of the Arab League. Egypt, although repeatedly placing
the Arab world before Africa, was anxious to make a good im-
pression. Realizing that too energetic a policy might frighten
its partners, it was very restrained and acted more like an
advisor or older brother than a leader. Several of the countries that straddled the dividing lines also tried to serve as
bridges between the two worlds. This policy was followed
most consistently by Mauritania and by the largely Muslim
countries just south of the Sahara.

On the whole, the situation was calm. But it was in
a state of unstable equilibrium. The Arab-Muslim civilization
had through the centuries repeatedly advanced from the east
and north into the sub-Saharan regions and whereas the Arabs
had conquered only as far as the Maghreb, and the Arab world
strictly speaking ended with the Sahara, that desert was a sea
traversed by caravans and Islam moved across it. Taken up
by warrior tribes in the savanna, it gave them a new impulse
in their age-old attempt to rule the Negroid tribes further
south. Islamization also followed the Nile. The spread of
both the Arab language and culture and the Muslim religion was
not over; it continued in the Sudan and elsewhere. Islam was
the religion most rapidly making converts in Africa.

It is not surprising that tensions should have arisen.
There were sometimes disturbances and even raids or revolts.

The Sudanese civil war was the worst example. It dragged on
with no hope of peace and most of the Sudanese governments
did nothing to end it except install tougher efforts at repression. This was a dirty and savage war and, despite occasional press reports, there is now little knowledge how many villages have been destroyed and how many southerners killed.
In the Horn of Africa there was also trouble in northern Kenya
with the Somalis, and especially in Ethiopia, with the Somalis
in the east and the Muslims in Eritrea. As of 1966 Chad was
raided by armed bands coming from Sudan. Only with French
assistance could this bid for an "Islamic Republic" be blocked.
Even the arabization in Mauritania worried the Negro minority.
In Zanzibar the reverse happened. A revolutionary but primarily nationalist movement overthrew the sultan and there
was a massive slaughter of Arabs. This uprising of the vast
majority against the ruling minority was sudden and lightning
swift and no less quickly forgotten.

Still, despite occasional outbursts, the situation was
relatively quiet during the early years of the OAU. The main
concern was with decolonization of the rest of the continent,
and the dependent territories were concentrated in the south.
Thus the Black Africans were the petitioners and they seriously needed the help that came from the north, often more than
elsewhere on the continent. Moreover, Black Africa did not
return the favor and help the Arabs with their own "decolonization" of Palestine. Since Black Africa was very clearly the
debter it could not make greater demands on its benefactors.
Many things were overlooked in the bargain, one of them being the violence in the Sudan. However, in 1967, the situation
changed dramatically and some of the underlying problems rose
to the surface.

At first there was only minor friction over the policy
toward Israel. The Arabs had never ceased their war against
the Jewish state and they repeatedly called on the rest of Africa to back them. But they did not make this a quid pro quo
for cooperation in the OAU. They even played it down and despite their verbal attacks at various meetings, especially the
Cairo Assembly, they did not make an issue of it. All the
while the Black African states had been establishing good and
friendly relations with Israel. Israel was a relatively safe
and valuable source of aid and its presence spread in Africa.
Ghana began the move in 1957, soon followed by Guinea and
eventually most of the moderate and radical countries south of
the Sahara. And backing from Nkrumah and other leaders was
decisive in warding off the early attacks.

The crisis began with the six day war in June 1967. Most of the African states had disapproved of the provocation that led to the war and some felt that the Arabs got what they deserved when their armies were defeated. There was considerable embarrassment at the extent of the disaster, but the majority of the states tried to keep out of the quarrel. The reaction after the war was bitterly disappointing. The Muslim states spoke out for the Arab cause but, further in Black Africa, Guinea was the only state to expel the Israelis (Touré had even offered to send troops) while Tanzania and the other radicals showed some moral support. The moderates did not even do that. Although Guinea and Somalia demanded an extraordinary session of the OAU, most of the members preferred having the matter handled by the United Nations. Even at the General Assembly debates, the Black Africans often were not at the side of their Arab brothers. Relatively few of them endorsed the extreme Arab position and most voted for a compromise resolution that gave satisfaction to neither party. In particular, although France voted with the Arabs, many of the OCAM states refused to follow Paris.

But the Arabs had been transfigured by the defeat. They turned inwards and became more intensely Arab than before. Obsessed by the struggle with Israel, they wished to draw others into the crusade, but at the same time they became less involved in African causes and less able to contribute to continental affairs. At the first Assembly after the war, the Arab members launched an all-out campaign to bring the OAU into line against Israel. The comments in Kinshasa were very pointed and finally, on the last day, the Arab and Muslim states obtained a statement on the matter. This "declaration" of 14 September 1967 could hardly have been more non-committal given the circumstances. It reaffirmed the principle of territorial integrity and expressed concern at "the grave situation that prevails in the United Arab Republic, an African country, whose territory is partially occupied by a foreign power." The Assembly offered its "sympathy" to the UAR, yet it decided to work towards an evacuation of its territory through the United Nations. This was clearly not enough and the matter was taken up again at the Council of Ministers in Addis Ababa. In February 1968 the Arabs finally got what they wanted: the condemnation of Israel as an aggressor and the call for an immediate and unconditional withdrawal of Israeli forces from the occupied territories.

Still, the Arabs must have sensed that Black Africa was not with them, for instead of adopting resolutions normally,

they resorted to unusual maneuvers to have them voted. Even
though the item was not on the agenda, the Kinshasa declaration had been steam-rolled through the Assembly just before
closing. It was presented and, despite protest, quickly put to
a vote by a Sudanese chairman. [11] The stronger Council reso
lution was adopted by acclamation rather than a regular vote,
a procedure which although endorsed by Diallo Telli was not
permitted by the Rules of Procedure. If the Foreign Minister
of the Ivory Coast was correct that about fifteen states disapproved of the resolution, [12] there was a good chance that it
would never have been adopted or only in greatly modified
form.

The key test, however, was the Assembly in September
1968. A two-thirds majority was necessary and the members
were particularly wary of irregularities. This time the leaders met in Algiers, the heart of Arab resistance, from whence
President Boumedienne urged a continuation of the war. Although more reserved, he drew striking parallels between the
situation in Palestine and on the continent. Then he spoke of
the Zionist threat to Africa.

> Even now we are enduring aggression against the
> U.A.R. where parts of its territories are occupied
> and where it is still repelling the attacks of im-
> perialistic Zionism and replying to its provocations
> This Zionist imperialism has expelled a whole peo-
> ple from its land and is now pursuing its expan-
> sionist policy to the detriment of other peoples in
> the region. [13]

The other Arab leaders also pressed for a strong condemnation of Israel. But their appeals were not heard and the rather neutral resolution did not even mention Israel by name.
Although it referred to aggression, it significantly dropped the
demand for an immediate and unconditional withdrawal of foreign troops. This withdrawal was now subjected to the terms
of the Security Council resolution of 22 November 1967. The
OAU's support of the Arab cause was lukewarm and indirect.

Another dramatic issue had also brought racial and religious differences to the fore: the bitter and devastating
civil war in Nigeria. Internally there was a clear division on
racial lines with the Ibos fighting primarily the Housas and
northern peoples; religion played a secondary role. Although
the broader African situation was not as clear, there seemed to
be similar lines dividing the continent's sympathies. The

states that immediately came to the support of Lagos are
Egypt and Sudan. The four countries that recognized Biafra
are all from Black Africa. In addition, the states that were
sympathetic to the Biafran cause, either along the West coast
or in East Africa, were deep in Black Africa while those that
promptly announced they would not recognize Biafra had large
Muslim populations.

Ten years after the Pan-African alliance between Arab
and Black Africa, the relations are no longer as smooth as
they have been. There is little danger of a breach in the common front, but it is undergoing greater stress. Much depends
on how the attitude toward Israel develops and whether the
members were pressured into going further than they wanted.
Above all, it was essential to attain a reconciliation in the
states along the dividing lines, the most critical tests being a
solution to the problems of Nigeria and the southern Sudan.
Only thus could the hatred cease and the bridges be rebuilt.

Notes

1. Clyde Sanger, Toward Unity in Africa, p. 274.

2. Bulletin de l'Afrique Noire, No. 360, 17 Feb. 1965.

3. Ethiopian Herald, 21 Feb. 1965.

4. The Times (London), 7 April 1967.

5. Vernon McKay, African Diplomacy.

6. Le Monde, 2 April 1968.

7. See: A. G. Anguilé and J. E. David, L'Afrique Sans
    Frontières.

8. The Nationalist, Dar es Salaam, 2 April 1966.

9. Le Monde, 6 Feb. 1969.

10. Journal of Modern African Studies, Oct. 1968, vol. 6,
    no. 3, p. 421-425.

11. Le Monde, 17 Sept. 1967.

12. Ibid., 28 Feb. 1968.

13. <u>O.A.U. Review</u>, Dec. 1968, p. 6.

B. Towards Continental Unity

One of the most striking phenomena on the international scene in recent years has been, without a doubt, the speed and certainty with which the African states united to forge their own instruments of action. Unlike the emerging countries on other continents and even the older nations, the newly formed states of Africa were able to overcome their differences sufficiently to found organization after organization until a satisfactory solution was reached. Many of the joint ventures soon disappeared but, despite their lack of experience, it took only five years from the first Conference of Independent African States to the founding of the Organization of African Unity. With the establishment of what has turned out to be a lasting and even successful body, the Africans were moving towards unity.

The level of unity attained at Addis Ababa was defined by the Charter as merely the coordination and harmonization of national policies in a broad range of fields. The OAU was created as a tool to help bring this about and through its institutions and meetings, the member states tried to lay down Pan-African policies. Although this was not always possible, the members were becoming increasingly familiar with the advantages of a common organization. There was more give-and-take and increased willingness to cooperate. The OAU itself was also growing into the framework provided by the Charter and was becoming accustomed to its functions.

The Charter stipulated that the first purpose of the Organization was to "promote the unity and solidarity of the African States." This it did through its very existence and through its activities. On occasion, however, it was necessary to deal with unity per se and improve the existing machinery to better achieve the ends. Sometimes it was even necessary to decide whether the Organization was adequate or whether a higher level of unity, beyond mere coordination and harmonization, should be sought.

Continental Leadership.

Although not fully recognized, the creation and consolidation of the Organization of African Unity was a major
achievement for the young African states.   The natural tendencies for division had been suppressed, if not eliminated, and
there was a genuine will for cooperation.   There were, of
course, crises and near crises during its existence.   But each
time the African states stopped before the brink and it was
possible to save the Organization.

It was already a considerable accomplishment for the
OAU to ignore the potential sources of division in order to
bring all the states on the continent together into one organization.   Crossing barriers of many sorts, geographical and
linguistic, racial and religious, the OAU made only one demand on its members--that they be African.   This criteria
was not purely geographical and included the moral element of
Pan-African nationalism.   It implied a dedication to liberation
of the rest of the continent and a specific platform.   But the
platform was broad enough and fundamentally desirable enough
for all states to accept it even if differing on means to the
end.   It was also restricted enough not to look into the creden-
tials of members nor make demands that they be radical or
moderate, pro-East or pro-West, but only pro-Africa.

The OAU welded together by far the greatest number of
states theretofore in Africa.   Not only were over forty countries willing to work together towards the same ends, but they
were sufficiently in agreement to make this cooperation valid
and effective.   In so doing they showed an amazing resistance
to the policy that had been the undoing of the continent for centuries: divide and rule.

What makes the OAU strikingly different from other international organizations, however, is the level of membership
of the governing and subordinate bodies.   Its Assembly con-
sists of Heads of States and Government; its Council, of Foreign Ministers or other ministers; and its commissions and
even committees, of ministers or senior officials competent in
the appropriate fields.   This difference in degree creates an
important difference in kind, for when the delegates to these
meetings are the highest representatives of the states they give
the Organization a prestige and authority it would not otherwise have.   The OAU is quite different from an organization
consisting only of representatives who have to report back to
their governments before taking any decisions and whose deci-

sions, even then, are subject to rejection. Delegates to the
OAU are already the key members of the governments and the
link with the member states was direct.

What Africa has, then, is a sort of composite government: some forty ministers in all the specialized fields, some
forty Foreign Ministers in charge of inter-African and international affairs, and some forty Heads of State and Government.

Within the OAU, the Ministers of Transport can prepare necessary plans in the field of transport, and the Ministers of Defence or Economics can do the same in their fields.
These recommendations would then be forwarded to the Council of Ministers where the Foreign Ministers, acting much
like Prime Ministers, would try to balance them and prepare
a feasible program covering all fields. They would also add
their own resolutions on political matters and keep the Heads
of State up to date on what was happening throughout Africa.
Material preparations and various background documents would
be provided by the Secretariat. On this basis, the regular
summit conference would then take the appropriate decisions
for the Organization.

Once the decisions had been taken, the Assembly of
Heads of State, the Council of Ministers and the other bodies
of the Organization would then be entrusted with implementation in their own countries.

But only one side of the composite government is really effective: the machinery for reaching joint decisions. For
there is a considerable gap between decision-making and implementation, which is very weak, the compliance of the member states being voluntary. The OAU goes as far as any non-
supranational body can go--but no further.

Although this is a far cry from the total unity urged by
certain leaders, it is a rather good start. As the ministers
are expected to work out plans in their own fields, and these
are then inserted into an over-all program by the Heads of
State, there should be a keen awareness both of Africa's needs
and its means. And because decisions are made at the highest level by persons endowed with broad powers in each state,
it may be assumed that they would largely be enforced. When
the Heads of State, Foreign Ministers, and the Ministers of
Transport, Defence and Economics return home from the OAU
they should be morally bound to seek to impose on their own

governments the policies they championed at the OAU.

Given the political structure in most of Africa, the only real spokesmen of the countries are the Heads of State and their ministers. Thus all the power in the Organization goes to the governments and none to the people. Their interests may not always have been defended by the leaders, but it is not for the OAU to inquire into this. For, in order to accomplish its aims, the Organization had no choice but to accept whatever situation existed in member states.

Heads of State and the People.

Unlike the Charter of the United Nations and many other historic documents, the Charter of African Unity made no pretension of creating an organization for the people as opposed to the leaders. The Charter boldly began "We, the Heads of African State and Government ..." and its contents were clearly molded to fit their needs. Alongside the general objectives of the OAU, there were a number of principles, such as the ones on assassination and subversion, which showed the concern of the leaders with their personal position and that of their regime. Others, on sovereignty and territorial integrity, showed a desire for maintenance of the status quo. This was certainly legitimate in trying to spare Africa unnecessarily brutal and frequent disruptions. Although by pushing things to their extreme, a strict interpretation of the Charter would, as Borella pointed out, have led to making the OAU a "Holy Alliance" of the governments in place against all forms of opposition in which they were prone to see foreign support and intervention.[1]

But the first principle has never been applied that strictly. There have been innumerable acts of political violence on the continent, including bloody coups d'état and even assassinations, and in most cases they were briefly condemned. However, by virtue of sovereignty, these internal changes have generally been ignored by the other states as long as they were not directly affected. The principle does not cover the Head of State as a person so much as the "leader" of a state. Even if snubbed for some time, a new ruler and regime are always recognized. Actually, the policy of recognition of most African states is extremely flexible and the only major problem arose in connection with President Nkrumah. He was overthrown shortly before the Council of Ministers in February 1966 and there were two delegations present when the meeting opened. The majority of the members opted for the government in effective control and, although several delegates walked out of the meeting in protest, it was not long before General Ankrah was accepted by all.

The principle of territorial integrity, to the contrary, is honored meticulously. National unity is no longer a mere slogan, it is a dogma. After the early recognition that colonial boundaries were highly artificial there was a short-lived dream of sweeping them away to form larger units. But no one was willing to take the first step, although exchanges of territory could often have created more rational and homogeneous states. There were too many divided tribes, peoples and economic or social units. And it may have been for this reason that the governments have reacted so blindly to any danger of territorial loss and possible break-up of the state. They dread a "balkanization" that might conceivably turn Africa into a mass of small and unviable states highly dependent on foreign powers.

The danger occasionally came from outside, when a neighboring state claimed part of the national territory. It could be on historical grounds, as with Morocco, of for ethnic reasons, as in Ethiopia and Kenya. But it has rarely happened that any state would cede even an inch of territory to obtain a settlement. Other dangers have come from within: when one of its component peoples decided to break away from a state. Here there was an even greater threat of disintegration. Anarchy in the Congo permitted more than one tribe to think of making its province a state. The southern Sudanese also preferred secession to assimilation. And the most striking example was the struggle of the Ibos to found the Republic of Biafra.

These phenomena also correspond to another aim that was not avowed at the summit conference. In order to create modern and united states most of the leaders declared war on tribalism. For years they have been trying to break or at least channel the traditional power of the tribes. They fear that the tribe could become a dangerous counterforce to the government's authority. Nevertheless, the tribe is basically a group of people with a feeling of identity among themselves and of distinctness from others. Beyond blood links, they have a common social, cultural, economic and political structure. This structure may not be modern, but it is often more solid than that of any state and provided a basis for nationalism. Among Africa's leaders, however, there is little willingness to recognize the tribes as a group of people with any rights other

than those granted by the governments or that the urge to run
their own affairs may in any way be legitimate.

Although it was quite correct to stress the dangers that
arose for the states and the leaders, it seemed equally correct to admit the rights of the peoples. An early version
of the Charter included the proposition that "the aim of govern
ment is the well-being of the governed." This was quickly
withdrawn and the preamble only referred to the notion that
"freedom, equality, justice and dignity are essential objectives
for the achievement of the legitimate aspirations of the African
peoples." Unfortunately, however, this statement was mainly
for external consumption. These goals were incorporated in
Africa's campaign against apartheid, racial discrimination and
colonialism. But they were and are remarkably absent in the
domestic policies followed by OAU members.

Serious racial problems and even acts of genocide have
taken place in Africa: the civil war in the Sudan, the massacre of the Tutsis in Rwanda, destruction of much of the Arab
population of Zanzibar, the killing of civilians in Biafra; there
were lesser incidents as well. Yet, the OAU has never really come to grips with the problem. It has not investigated
any of these events, made open criticism or drawn the public'
attention to them. There has also been little effort to promote
democracy; the peoples were left to the fate determined by
their governments. Gradually, as these rights were ignored
and violated in independent Africa, scepticism began to spread
outside the continent about even the justified complaints of the
OAU against the colonial and settler powers.

Thus the Organization's failing has not been to oppress
the peoples--something it was incapable of--but rather that it
paid insufficient attention to their needs and made no provision
for their participation. If the Organization of African Unity
is ever to have a powerful or lasting effect, it has to work in
depth. It must not forget the masses and cater only to the
needs of the ruling élites. Rather it has to provide an outlet
for the peoples so that they, too, may participate in its action
At the same time the OAU should educate them to the possibilities of greater and truer unity. For the moment, the OAU
still appears as a ceremonial meeting of African leaders to
debate policy loftily. As long as those at the grass roots neither gain from nor contribute to this policy their interest is
bound to be limited.

Nkrumah and Unity.

There were serious imperfections in the OAU as established. No one saw that more clearly nor criticized it more
severely than Kwame Nkrumah. In the beginning his sugges-
ions had envisaged a supranational body with the power to
ake binding decisions. He urged a strong structure with col-
ective organs and a popular assembly. He also proposed that
he foundations of unity be solidly entrenched on the pillars of
a joint military command and a common economy. To press
his aims, he spoke of unity to the peoples and demanded their
participation. But his appeals were turned down in Addis
Ababa.

Nevertheless, Nkrumah kept on devising plans to
strengthen or completely replace the OAU by what he called a
"Union Government of Africa." As time, and events, passed
his proposals were toned down, although he never changed the
itle of the body he proposed. In Cairo, at the first Assembly in July 1964, Ghana made another proposal for union government. This plan recognized state sovereignty and merely
aimed at coordinating continental policies in defence, diplomacy and economics. Even then, the other leaders hid behind
he principles of the OAU and a decision was avoided. The
plan was sent to the specialized commissions to study the various aspects of African unity and report back to the Council.
The Foreign Ministers were then to examine the conclusions
and submit their own report to the second Assembly. With
he disappearance of the commissions, however, this task was
never accomplished.

As the next Assembly approached, Nkrumah increased
his efforts and pressure to adopt a new organization or at
least a basic reform of the old one. To house the conference
he had a magnificent State House built in Accra as a future
Capitol of Africa. He warned his colleagues that soon the
OAU "must decide to create machinery for an All-African Union Government, or it must decide to exist as a talking
hop."[2] When the conference finally opened, on 24 October
1965, he was ready with a new plan. "I am more convinced
than ever," he announced, "that Africa must unite to constitute one single state under a Union Government. That is the
viewpoint I expressed in Addis Ababa in 1963 and last year in
Cairo. I still insist in this ..."[3]

This time, however, he was much less ambitious (or
more cautious) than in the past and he suggested a rather sim-

ple formula. He did not even call for a major reshaping of
the OAU but rather an additional institution that could fit into
the existing structure. This was an Executive Council, appointed by the Assembly to look after its work in the interval
between meetings. The Council was not permanent itself and
only the President and Vice-President, elected by the Assembly, would meet periodically to review the work of the Executive Council when not in session. Nkrumah called this an
"executive arm" of the Heads of State. It would be able to initiate policies and make recommendations to the Assembly and
governments on questions concerning the purposes and objectives of the OAU. But the wording was left sufficiently vague
to intimate that the Executive Council would have considerable
powers without really defining the extent of those powers or
its actual relationship to the Assembly. President Nkrumah
also announced that he would ask the next Assembly to amend
the Charter so that binding decisions could be taken with a
two-thirds majority. [4]

This project was discussed at length in Accra. Some
of the leaders approved of the principle but wanted further
clarification before taking a final decision. Others were already worried that a door was being opened to supranationality.
Eventually it received 18 votes, or six short of the required
majority. Thus the Assembly put the matter aside and adopted a very terse resolution. It took note of the Ghanaian proposals concerning the establishment of an executive body of
the OAU and the following discussions and "requests Governments of the Member States of the OAU to examine that problem in order to express their opinions at the next session of
the Assembly."

In this way the project was politely deferred. However
before the Addis Ababa Assembly, there was a coup d'état in
Ghana and Kwame Nkrumah was eliminated from the official
African scene. Despite the Assembly's resolution to do so,
his project was not even discussed; certainly if it had it would
have come to a similar conclusion. For, although this was
his least ambitious proposal, Nkrumah's project was vague
enough to seem to counter traditional notions of sovereignty.
The states were less willing than ever to delegate powers to
a restricted group some of them would not belong to. They
were not interested in increasing the competences of any institution. And they definitely did not want binding decisions.

It is difficult to modify the Charter. Nevertheless, the
OAU has been flexible enough to find ad hoc solutions to many

f its problems. Some of the advantages of an executive coun-
il have already been obtained through the Council of Minis-
ers. This body has gradually assumed the task of represent-
ng the Heads of State on all matters, political and otherwise,
etween sessions. With three committees, it is rather well
quipped to coordinate and follow up the work of the Assembly.
 may make recommendations, supervise (but never control)
mplementation and even take political initiatives.

Thus, Nkrumah's last proposal for unity failed as well.
 the final analysis, his position in the movement towards
nity was very uncertain. There was no doubt that he was the
ajor champion--or rather prophet--of unity and that he had
endered a great service by keeping in mind the need for unity
nd proposing plans, some aspects of which might be refur-
ished later on. Only, his plans were increasingly modest.
lthough each of them was presented as the ultimate solution,
 veil of words hid their real contents. "Union government"
ventually had little meaning as its scope was restricted and
nded as a glorified "executive council" without executive pow-
rs. The greatest loss was in totally discarding the popular
lement and offering no role to the masses.

At the same time, Nkrumah also caused a great dis-
ervice to unity which may even have outweighed any hypothe-
cal future benefits. His insistence on far-reaching unity was
ften an obstacle to his acceptance of the level of cooperation
e OAU actually achieved. He never really became a relia-
le backer of the Organization and at first refused to cooper-
te with the Liberation Committee. What was worse was his
outing of the code of good conduct that was the condition sine
ua non of cooperation. More than any leader, he violated
e OAU's principles and Ghana was the only state that was
dicted by the other members. By disregarding the sover-
ignty of others and trying to impose his leadership rather
an accept a partnership, he only enhanced division. His dis-
ppearance permitted cooperation and unity to resume.

he Facts of Unity.

Nkrumah's vision was doubtlessly appealing and may
en have contained an ideal solution. Its basic weakness was
ot the ultimate goals so much as its lack of practicability.
here was simply no foundation for the plans he put forward.
frica was not ripe for greater unity.

For this reason only a body with limited powers like
the OAU could be a success. Its institutions are very flexible
and can be adapted to needs. An African willingness to work
for the good of all has grown and a routine has been established which encourages the states to work together for common ends. If stronger demands had been made or if the
states felt any constraint, suspicions and resistance would
have arisen.

The most dismaying fact, however, is that even existing machinery is not being used fully. The specialized commissions have ceased operations and the Council and Assembly
are not always attended by Foreign Ministers and Heads of
State. The productivity of the meetings in real terms is rather low. If anything, there was a tendency to restrict the Organization. At the Algiers Assembly in September 1968 the
member states agreed to amend the Charter by reducing the
specialized commissions to three. Tunisia even proposed the
Assembly of Heads of State should only meet once every three
years and the Council of Ministers once a year. It also asked
that all the specialized commissions be abolished since the
OAU had neither the funds nor staff to make them effective
and the members already belonged to the United Nations specialized agencies. This would have meant a drastic reduction
in the OAU's activities, both in time and extent, and these
amendments were overwhelmingly rejected. Unfortunately, the
member states have not adopted the sort of decisions that
would have given the OAU a chance to realize even its inherent potential.

The Organization is only a reflection of the situation in
the continent. Throughout Africa, despite the active sowing of
earlier days, the harvest of cooperation is meager. True,
there has been some success, even organic unity. After
United Nations plebiscites it was possible to unite British Togoland with Ghana and parts of British Cameroons with French
Cameroun and Nigeria. Pan-Somalism also wedded two colonial territories at independence. As long as they did not contradict any deeper ties, these units worked well.[5] But this
is largely a thing of the past. Not much progress has been
made since the states became independent and they and their
rulers have vested interests to defend. This validated Nyerere's warning that unity was easier before independence than
after.

Over the years, the mystique of unity has faded. The
same words are mouthed but there are few concrete achieve-

ments to point to. The only recent act of political integration
was the merging of Tanganyika and the off-shore islands of
Zanzibar and Pemba to create a single federal state: the
United Republic of Tanzania, proudly proclaimed on 23 April
1964. It was the work of President Nyerere of Tanganyika
and Rashidi Kawawa of Zanzibar (who became Vice-President
of Tanzania) and resulted from a special political constellation
and the fact that the islands were not self-sustaining unless
they united with the mainland or accepted a non-African role
as the showcase of an alien power. No other major step towards political unity has taken place since the OAU was established. Even Gambia continued its separate existence,
financed by the former mother country, while discussions went
on as to the formation of a future Senegambia. In April 1967,
a start was made with a treaty of association and some scant
machinery for consultation.

There have also been numerous attempts of a more partial nature. Many of the African leaders have staked their
hopes for unity on an economic approach and any number of
schemes were worked out for the integration of neighboring
states through common markets, customs unions and more
limited units. No matter how encouraging many of them
seemed the sudden disruption of UDEAC showed that even the
most promising experiments were fragile. There was only
one noteworthy attempt at carrying the economic process further. This was the daring plan of establishing multinationality
in the Entente. Its failure showed that the time had not come
for this degree of unity.

During the same period, unfortunately, the trend towards the disintegration of African states has been as strong,
or stronger. The civil wars in the Congo were finally
crushed but the situation in the Sudan has only deteriorated.
The most tragic case is the collapse of Nigeria. Composed
of three relatively large ethnic groups with little in common
and a long history of rivalry and enmity, the nation's attempt
at cooperation through democracy failed, and the attempts at
imposing it through military dictatorship were even worse.
Ibos proclaimed the Republic of Biafra and fought for it to the
extent that it appeared that the first nation was being born in
Africa as the result of popular effort and not the decision of
colonizers. However, since comparable divisions existed elsewhere and tribalism was a threat to all, the split has aroused
panic and blind reactions in the other states. The OAU broadly condemned any such manifestation of disunity in Africa rather than seeking to understand it or lay down a concrete policy

to overcome it.

The only hope for genuine unity will be a wide-spread feeling that the old borders are too narrow. Yet governments are plagued by political difficulties expressing fundamental divisions and the leaders have considerable trouble in ruling even the smaller states. In addition, the people are not mature enough for greater unity. In many cases they do not yet regard themselves as citizens of a state but rather as members of a tribal, social or religious group that has lost as much as it gained by inclusion in a national unit. Even if resistance is not the general rule, neither is discipline and patriotism. This meant that the national foundations were not strong enough to support a heavier continental structure.

With the task of nation-building far from over and the very existence of the states still fragile, the African leaders are in no mood to consider relaxing sovereignty. The member states increasingly demand bodies of the whole rather than restricted ones and they hamstring those that had too much power. This happened with the Commission of Mediation and the Liberation Committee. It also kept the Secretariat from becoming a guiding force.

Financial Crisis.

Not only was Nkrumah's plan too ambitious, the Organization of African Unity itself seemed to have aimed too high from one point of view. Its basic institutions and activities were accepted by the members. But there was serious concern about the rapid expansion of its budget. Within two years of its founding, the OAU was already in a crisis.

During the first year, the Ethiopian government at the behest of His Imperial Majesty graciously provided the staff and building for a provisional secretariat. This staff began much of the essential work and laid the foundations of the Organization. It framed the basic documents of the Secretariat and other institutions. It also drafted the reports and organized the first meetings of the various bodies, so that they could adopt rules of procedure and determine their terms of reference. This running-in period required a tremendous amount of work. It was also very costly. Nevertheless, at the first Assembly in Cairo, the Emperor announced that Ethiopia would underwrite these expenses.

The second year was not quite so busy. There was a low transition from a provisional to permanent Secretariat. iallo Telli and his assistants took over control. The staff rew and the Organization began to take shape. However, it as very difficult to get the member states to agree to a budget and provide the funds. It was not until the Council of Ministers in Nairobi, in March 1965, that the first budget ould be adopted. In the meanwhile the money needed to run e Organization had to be advanced by the Emperor (and ultimately repaid). Thus, for nearly two years, a single state overed the expenses of the OAU.

The first ordinary budget was adopted for a period of fteen months, from March 1965 to May 1966. It amounted almost $4,500,000. Then the campaign for contributions egan. A resolution was adopted in Nairobi calling on the members to pay their dues. A more urgent appeal was made Lagos, in June 1965, stressing the serious nature of the nancial crisis. However, by the end of the financial year, ly 87 per cent of the total sum had been paid in.[6] The eed to get these contributions was a major headache for the ecretariat and also entailed additional and unnecessary work d expense. But the OAU could do no more than make appeals. Although the members "agree to pay their respective ntributions regularly,"[7] the Charter offered no possibility of nctions such as withdrawal of the right to vote or eventual xclusion. Any state could refuse to pay its share with immunity.

The Accra Assembly, in October 1965, was overshadved by concern for the future of the OAU. The financial risis was deepening and Diallo Telli sounded the alarm. any members had not paid dues and the Organization was tting into debt. But the response was not a renewed effort. ather, the Council of Ministers and the Secretary-General ught ways of limiting expenses. The matter was so critical at it was brought before the Heads of State to confirm the ouncil's decisions. The Assembly laid down the basic premise that the budget of the OAU was a "heavy burden" on the member states and asked that major reductions be made. In e meantime, the member states would meet their financial ligations under the budget and the Secretary-General would y to effect savings. However, it was recommended that en future budgets were drawn up, "due consideration should given to the limited resources of Member States."

A serious review of the OAU's structure and operations became necessary in view of its uncontrolled growth and the refusal of members to accept further financial demands. Two advisory committees were established for this purpose. The Institutional Committee had to deal with the problems created by the expansion of the main institutions and the proliferation of non-statutory bodies. Since the creation of the OAU there had been a rapid snowballing of commissions and committees and repeated meetings of the various bodies. There had also been an unfortunate tendency to create new ad hoc bodies rather than give tasks to already existing institutions. Partially owing to the advice of the Institutional Committee, it was decided to reduce the number of specialized commissions from seven to three by dropping the Commission of Jurists and merging the others. These commissions were not permitted to establish the multitude of expert committees and permanent secretariats they clamored for and much of their preparatory work was to be done by the permanent Secretariat. Fewer ad hoc bodies would be created in the future and even the Algero-Moroccan Commission limited its activities.

These decisions drastically reduced the size of the Organization and hence its budget. This made the work of the Committee on Budgetary and Financial Matters easier and the subsequent budgets have been kept much lower. The Committee also had to deal with a problem raised by the smallest members, such as Rwanda and Gambia. According to the Charter, contributions were to be made in accordance with the scale of assessments of the United Nations and no member was to be assessed more than 20 per cent of the yearly regular budget. But this UN scale, in which most of the African states were in the lowest category, did not make a sufficient distinction between the poorest. Thus the Council of Ministers in March 1967, decided to work out a different scale for the OAU. The new scale would also be based on national product and income but would have finer shades of difference between the limits of 1/2 of 1 per cent (Gambia) and 10 per cent (UAR).

Thanks to the work of these two committees, by November 1966 it was possible to present a draft budget that was acceptable to the members. This austerity budget of $1,700,000 showed the extent to which the activities of the OAU would be curtailed. Even before then, the Secretariat had cut back the work and it was possible to put aside $2,154,000 or almost 40 per cent of the previous budget. With these savings the budget for 1966-67 could be covered en

irely and the members were not asked for contributions dur-
ng that period.[8]

As of then the Secretariat faced much closer scrutiny
of its accounts and estimates by the Budgetary Committee and
Council of Ministers. The struggle was resumed in February
1967. The draft budget submitted by the Secretariat showed
an increase in expenditure. The Council of Ministers demanded suitable explanations for this increase, and when they could
not be given, it distrustfully requested further information on
the financial state of the Organization. Finally, in view of the
"apprehension shown by most delegates," the Council decided
only to renew the previous budget. If the Secretariat were
able to justify an increase, the supplementary credits could be
voted later. Otherwise, the budget would be kept at the same
ow level for 1967-68 as well. But even at this level not all
the members complied with their obligations promptly or fully.

The next year there was an unexpected upswing. The
Secretariat and the Budgetary Committee realized that the budget was already dangerously low and permitted no expansion
of activities. They fought tooth and nail for a higher budget
and they obtained $2,300,000 for 1968-69. Diallo Telli was
elated. "For the first time we have a normal and regular
budget in accordance with the aspirations of the O.A.U. I
would call it a propulsion budget. It is a real balloon going
up in the air."[9] But it soon came down again. The growing
ack of confidence in the OAU and its staff was reflected in
the debate over the 1969-70 budget. Once again it fell below
the two million mark.

There is no doubt that Africa is a poor continent and
the OAU, expensive. Still, there are reasons to doubt that it
is too heavy a burden on its members. The African states
engage in all sorts of undertakings, many of which have been
more costly and less beneficial than the OAU. For example,
the huge State House in Ghana and the "African village" in
Kinshasa cost more than the regular OAU budget itself for
many, many years. Moreover, in the past just one member
state, Ethiopia, had been able to cover the total expenses of
the Organization during the busy years after Addis Ababa.
The Emperor also made the premises available for the temporary headquarters and offered the site for a new headquarters
building. It did, of course, profit more from the Organization's presence. Yet there seems to be no reason why the
other African states were not able to make their own contributions regularly to the functioning of the OAU during the follow-

ing years.

It may be pointed out that the budget figures only cover
ed the bare essentials. Contributions to the Freedom Fund
and the new headquarters building were kept separate. And
there have been virtually no operational expenses since the
OAU has not really embarked on any projects. The money in
the regular budget only represents the cost of salaries for a
modest-sized staff, various administrative expenses and the
cost of holding conferences. Although originally there were
conferences every few weeks, soon the OAU began convening
only often enough to keep going. The decrease in conference
costs more than made up for the increase in staff costs. The
budget had already fallen as low as it could without crippling
the Organization.

Quibbling about budgetary expenses probably represents
less an inability to pay than hidden disapproval of purposes for
which the money was spent. This was more a way of expressing general dissatisfactions and disappointments with
the OAU. It is standard practice for a member state that disagreed with decisions of an international organization to exert
financial pressure on the body concerned. But the stress on
poverty in Africa seems to show a more general disenchantment. A solution to the financial troubles of the Organization
would have been not to reduce its machinery but to let it undertake tasks for which the member states were willing to pay

Realism and Courage.

The Organization founded in Addis Ababa seems to be
at an appropriate level of unity to correspond to the situation
in Africa. The time has not come for a further step and the
basic barrier is still sovereignty. Nevertheless, Africa has
shown a unity of purpose and action that was rare in the third
world and in the more "advanced" countries as well.

The first years were ones of enthusiasm and, to some
extent, wishful thinking. The OAU seemed to be the ultimate
tool. The member states did not hesitate to set the Organization to all tasks facing the continent. They wished it to be a
weapon to destroy not only colonialism but even neo-colonialism. It was a forum in which to settle internal disputes and
also to present the world with an African policy. And, finally,
it was to promote development in every field of human en-
deavor. Thus the OAU was soon dangerously overextended and

:ould not make a serious contribution in any field.   Moreover,
t rapidly exceeded the funds members would donate.

A reaction to this was to narrow down the activities
ınd make a maximum effort in one.   The radical states urged,
ınd the moderates acquiesced, that the OAU become an organi-
:ation devoted primarily to decolonization.   Technical activi-
ies and even peaceful settlement were neglected.   Meetings of
he governing bodies debated the situation in the various terri-
ories and called for increasingly strong measures against the
:olonial and settler powers.   But it was rarely possible to
urn the resolutions into acts.   At the same time, the cam-
»aign conducted in the United Nations was blocked by the veto
ınd even then many states did not implement the sanctions.
Angered by these failures, some of the OAU's members wished
o strike a powerful blow that would turn the tide, but such a
»low went beyond Africa's means.

Thus the limits to OAU activity became increasingly
:lear.   Still, within the limits, there were many possibilities.
:ven if the OAU can not form an army to aid the liberation
novements, it can channel money and material.   Not able to
;end troops to end a conflict, it can provide observers once a
ruce had been reached.   Even if it should fail to settle differ-
›nces within a state or between states, it can seek reconcilia-
ion.   If it can not construct a common market or university,
t can at least give help and encouragement to states consider-
ıg forms of cooperation.

This lesson was learned in the first few years and
·ealism became the order of the day.   However, this realism
»ften turned into timidity and passiveness, and the OAU has
»een used less than is possible, or even necessary.   Thus
·ealism had to be tempered with courage.

First it is necessary to correct the balance in the pro-
;ram of activities.   Although a broad consensus and consider-
ıble action may be attained on political matters, it is ex-
remely difficult for the OAU to reach agreement or even to
ındertake minor projects in many other fields.   Member
;tates tend to go their own way rather than work through the
:ommon body.   In the few cases where the OAU has assumed
·esponsibilities it has had negligible success in mobilizing its
nembership.   This leaves the OAU a rather lop-sided instru-
nent for generating unity.   United on "common enemy" issues,
he members were less inclined to work for positive and con-
:rete links among themselves.

So far the solidarity in the struggle for liberation has been strong enough to help the Organization weather any storm. The ties may at times seem broken and the OAU ready to founder, but when a new urgent call comes for aid, the states will doubtless reform their ranks. However, by its very nature, decolonization will not be a permanent problem for the Organization. It has to be replaced by new, positive links in the many other, less political fields. There are any number of projects the OAU is capable of achieving and each one of them could have consolidated the links among members.

More imagination is also needed to eliminate its blind spot. The people of Africa are only on-lookers at the work of an organization that had supposedly been created for their greater well-being. Few of the activities affect them directly and they are never consulted during times of decision-making or the formulation of policy. They should be given some way of participating. A consultative or observer status could be designed to associate the already existing "peoples' organizations" in the work of the OAU. Such a status could be given to all sorts of men's, women's, and youth organizations as well as religious, cultural and professional bodies. A particularly valuable one would be the trade unions of Africa. They would have a chance to cooperate with the institutions of the OAU and, at the same time, help to promote the aims of the Organization among the African peoples.

A further step might be to deal with problems that arise with individuals and not only the states and their leaders. Those who need help most are the refugees, but more attention has to be paid to the average citizen as well. Since human rights and democracy are widely praised in the independent states there seems to be no barrier of principle. Thus there should have been no objection to laying greater stress on them, possibly by adopting an African Declaration of Human Rights. This would, of course, have to be coupled with a limited right of petition and supervisory machinery. Then, some time in the future, it might be possible to add an institution truly representative of the people.

A final act of courage would be to tackle the most bitter and inextricable problems and not only the more normal or traditional ones. The OAU can not afford to stand aside and let the citizens of a member state slaughter one another. It can not merely sanction the results and accept the winner as the legitimate authority. No matter what dangers, the OAU has to create a presence and seek solutions to fratricidal wars

ke those in Nigeria or the Sudan. Cowardice would only dis-
redit the OAU and Africa. Success might be far off and
are, but the worst failure is to do nothing.

There are still many challenges that can be met by the
rganization of African Unity as it exists. They do not re-
uire major changes in structure or amendments to the Char-
r. What is needed is greater realism and courage. The un-
xpected result of such an approach might be that, far from
eakening the Organization, the states and peoples would more
learly realize how precious it is.

Notes

. François Borella, Le Régionalisme Africain en Crise,
       AFDI, 1966, p. 769.

. The Sunday Express (London), 24 May 1965.

. Opening Speech at OAU Assembly, 24 Oct. 1965.

. The Times (London), 24 Oct. 1965.

. See: Arthur Hazlewood (ed.), African Integration and Dis-
       integration.

. Marchés et Travaux d'Outre-Mer, Paris, Nov. 1966,
       p. 2963.

. Charter of the OAU, Art. XXIII.

. Marchés et Travaux d'Outre-Mer, loc. cit.

. Africa Report, April 1968.

Annexes

641

CHARTER OF THE ORGANIZATION OF AFRICAN UNITY

We, the Heads of African States and Governments assembled in the City of Addis Ababa, Ethiopia;

CONVINCED that it is the inalienable right of all people to control their own destiny;

CONSCIOUS of the fact that freedom, equality, justice and dignity are essential objectives for the achievement of the legitimate aspirations of the African peoples;

CONSCIOUS of our responsibility to harness the natural and human resources of our continent for the total advancement of our peoples in spheres of human endeavour;

INSPIRED by a common determination to promote understanding among our peoples and co-operation among our States in response to the aspirations of our peoples for brotherhood and solidarity, in a larger unity transcending ethnic and national differences;

CONVINCED that, in order to translate this determination into a dynamic force in the cause of human progress, conditions for peace and security must be established and maintained;

DETERMINED to safeguard and consolidate the hard-won independence as well as the sovereignty and territorial integrity of our States, and to fight against neo-colonialism in all its forms;

DEDICATED to the general progress of Africa;

PERSUADED that the Charter of the United Nations and the Universal Declaration of Human Rights, to the principles of which we reaffirm our adherence, provide a solid foundation for peaceful and positive co-operation among States;

DESIROUS that all African States should henceforth unite so that the welfare and well-being of their peoples can be assured;

RESOLVED to reinforce the links between our states by establishing and srengthening common institutions;

HAVE agreed to the present Charter.

ESTABLISHMENT

Article I

1. The High Contracting Parties do by the present Charter establish an Organization to be known as the ORGANIZATION OF AFRICAN UNITY.

2. The Organization shall include the Continental African States, Madagascar and other Islands surrounding Africa.

PURPOSES

Article II

1. The Organization shall have the following purposes;
   a. to promote the unity and solidarity of the African States;

b. to co-ordinate and intensify their co-operation and efforts to achieve a better life for the peoples of Africa;

c. to defend their sovereignty, their territorial integrity and independence;

d. to eradicate all forms of colonialism from Africa; and

e. to promote international co-operation, having due regard to the Charter of the United Nations and the Universal Declaration of Human Rights.

To these ends, the Member States shall co-ordinate and harmonize their general policies, especially in the following fields;

a. political and diplomatic co-operation;

b. economic co-operation, including transport and communications;

c. educational and cultural co-operation;

d. health, sanitation, and nutritional co-operation;

e. scientific and technical co-ooperation; and

f. co-operation for defence and security.

PRINCIPLES
Article III

The Member States, in pursuit of the purposes stated in Article II, solemnly affirm and declare their adherence to the following principles:

1. the sovereign equality of all Member States;

2. non-interference in the internal affairs of States;

3. respect for the sovereignty and territorial integrity of each State and for its inalienable right to independent existence;

4. peaceful settlement of disputes by negotiation, mediation, conciliation or arbitration;

5. unreserved condemnation, in all its forms, of political assassination as well as of subversive activities on the part of neighbouring States or any other States;

6. absolute dedication to the total emancipation of the African territories which are still dependent;

7. affirmation of a policy of non-alignment with regard to all blocs.

MEMBERSHIP
Article IV

Each independent sovereign African State shall be entitled to become a Member of the Organization.

RIGHTS AND DUTIES OF MEMBER STATES
Article V

All Member States shall enjoy equal rights and have equal duties.

Article VI

The Member States pledge themselves to observe scrupulously the principles enumerated in Article III of the present Charter.

INSTITUTIONS

Article VII

The Organization shall accomplish its purposes through the following princi pal institutions:

1. the Assembly of Heads of State and Government;
2. the Council of Ministers;
3. the General Secretariat;
4. the Commission of Mediation, Conciliation and Arbitration.

THE ASSEMBLY OF HEADS OF STATE AND GOVERNMENT

Article VIII

The Assembly of Heads of State and Government shall be the supreme organ of the Organization. It shall, subject to the provisions of this Charter, discuss matters of common concern to Africa with a view to co-ordinating and harmoniz ing the general policy of the Organization. It may in addition review the structure functions and acts of all the organs and any specialized agencies which may be created in accordance with the present Charter.

Article IX

The Assembly shall be composed of the Heads of State and Government o their duly accredited representatives and it shall meet at least once a year. At the request of any Member State and on approval by a two-thirds majority of the Member States, the Assembly shall meet in extraordinary session.

Article X

1. Each Member States shall have one vote.
2. All resolutions shall be determined by a two-thirds majority of the Mem bers of the Organization.
3. Questions of procedure shall require a simple majority. Whether or not a question is one of procedure shall be determined by a simple majority of all Member States of the Organization.
4. Two-thirds of the total membership of the Organization shall form a quorum at any meeting of the Assembly.

Article XI

The Assembly shall have the power to determine its own rules of procedure

THE COUNCIL OF MINISTERS

Article XII

1. The Council of Ministers shall consist of Foreign Ministers or such other Ministers as are designated by the Governments of Member States.
2. The Council of Ministers shall meet at least twice a year. When requested by any Member State and approved by two-thirds of all Member States, it shall meet in extraordinary session.

Article XIII

.   The Council of Ministers shall be responsible to the Assembly of Heads of tate and Government. It shall be entrusted with the responsibility of preparing onferences of the Assembly.

..   It shall take cognisance of any matter referred to it by the Assembly. It shall e entrusted with the implementation of the decision of the Assembly of Heads of tate and Government. It shall co-ordinate inter-African co-operation in accordan-e with the instructions of the Assembly and in conformity with Article II (2) of he present Charter.

Article XIV

1.   Each Member State shall have one vote.
2.   All resolutions shall be determined by a simple majority of the members of the Council of Ministers.
3.   Two-thirds of the total membership of the Council of Ministers shall form a quorum for any meeting of the Council.

Article XV

The Council shall have the power to determine its own rules of procedure.

GENERAL SECRETARIAT

Article XVI

There shall be an Administrative Secretary-General of the Organization, who hall be appointed by the Assembly of Heads of State and Government. The Ad-ninistrative Secretary-General shall direct the affairs of the Secretariat.

Article XVII

There shall be one or more Assistant Secretaries-General of the Organization, ho shall be appointed by the Assembly of Heads of State and Government.

Article XVIII

The functions and conditions of services of the Secretary-General, of the ssistant Secretaries-General and other employees of the Secretariat shall be overned by the provisions of this Charter and the regulations approved by the ssembly of Heads of State and Government.

1.   In the performance of their duties the Administrative Secretary-General and the staff shall not seek or receive instructions from any government or from any other authority external to the Organization. They shall refrain from any action which might reflect on their position as international officials responsible only to the Organization.

2.   Each member of the Organization undertakes to respect the exclusive character of the responsibilities of the Administrative Secretary-General and the staff and not to seek to influence them in the discharge of their responsibilities.

COMMISSION OF MEDIATION, CONCILIATION AND ARBITRATION

Article XIX

Member States pledge to settle all disputes among themselves by peaceful means and, to this end decide to establish a Commission of Mediation, Conciliation and Arbitration, the composition of which and conditions of service shall be defined by a separate Protocol to be approved by the Assembly of Heads of State and Government. Said Protocol shall be regarded as forming an integral part of the present Charter.

SPECIALIZED COMMISSIONS

Article XX

The Assembly shall establish such Specialized Commissions as it may deem necessary, including the following;
1. Economic and Social Commission;
2. Educational and Cultural Commission;
3. Health, Sanitation and Nutrition Commission;
4. Defence Commission;
5. Scientific, Technical and Research Commission.

Article XXI

Each Specialized Commission referred to in Article XX shall be composed of the Ministers concerned or other Ministers or Plenipotentiaries designated by the Governments of the Member States.

Article XXII

The functions of the Specialized Commissions shall be carried out in accordance with the provisions of the present Charter and of the regulations approved by the Council of Ministers.

THE BUDGET

Article XXIII

The budget of the Organization prepared by the Administrative Secretary-General shall be approved by the Council of Ministers. The budget shall be provided by contributions from Member States in accordance with the scale of assessment of the United Nations; provided, however, that no Member States shall be assessed an amount exceeding twenty percent of the yearly regular budget of the Organization. The Member States agree to pay their respective contributions regularly.

SIGNATURE AND RATIFICATION OF CHARTER

Article XXIV

1. This Charter shall be open for signature to all independent sovereign African States and shall be ratified by the signatory States in accordance with their respective constitutional processes.

2. The original instrument, done, if possible in African languages, in English and French, all texts being equally authentic, shall be deposited with the Government of Ethiopia which shall transmit certified copies thereof to all independent sovereign African States.

3. Instruments of ratification shall be deposited with the Government of Ethiopia, which shall notify all signatories of each such deposit.

ENTRY INTO FORCE
Article XXV

This Charter shall enter into force immediately upon receipt by the Government of Ethiopia of the instruments of ratification from two thirds of the signatory States.

REGISTRATION OF THE CHARTER
Article XXVI

This Charter shall, after due ratification, be registered with the Secretariat of the United Nations through the Government of Ethiopia in conformity with Article 102 of the Charter of the United Nations.

INTERPRETATION OF THE CHARTER
Article XXVII

Any question which may arise concerning the interpretation of this Charter shall be decided by a vote of two-thirds of the Assembly of Heads of State and Government of the Organization.

ADHESION AND ACCESSION
Article XXVIII

1. Any independent sovereign African States may at any time notify the Administrative Secretary-General of its intention to adhere or accede to this Charter.

2. The Administrative Secretary-General shall, on receipt of such notification, communicate a copy of it to all the Member States. Admission shall be decided by a simple majority of the Member States. The decision of each Member State shall be transmitted to the Administrative Secretary General, who shall, upon receipt of the required number of votes, communicate the decision to the State concerned.'

MISCELLANEOUS
Article XXIX

The working languages of the Organization and all its institutions shall be, if possible African languages, English and French.

Article XXX

The Administrative Secretary-General may accept on behalf of the Organization gifts, bequests and other donations made to the Organization, provided that this is approved by the Council of Ministers.

The Conucil of Ministers shall decide on the privileges and immunities to be accorded to the personnel of the Secretariat in the respective territories of the Member States.

CESSATION OF MEMBERSHIP

Article XXXII

Any State which desires to renounce its membership shall forward a written notification to the Administrative Secretary-General. At the end of one year from the date of such notification, if not withdrawn, the Charter shall cease to apply with respect to the renouncing State, which shall thereby cease to belong to the Organization.

AMENDMENT OF THE CHARTER

Article XXXIII

This Charter may be amended for revised if any Member State makes a written request to the Administrative Secretary-General to that effect; provided, however, that the proposed amendment is not submitted to the Assembly for consideration until all the Member States have been duly notified of it and a period of one year has elapsed. Such an amendment shall not be effective unless approved by at least two-thirds of all the Member States.

IN FAITH WHEREOF, We, the Heads of African State and Government have signed this Charter.

Done in the City of Addis Ababa, Ethiopia this 25th day of May, 1963.

ALGERIA

BURUNDI

CAMEROUN

CENTRAL AFRICAN REPUBLIC

CHAD

CONGO (Brazzaville)

CONGO (Leopoldville)

DAHOMEY

ETHIOPIA

GABON

GHANA

GUINEA

IVORY COAST

LIBERIA

LIBYA

MADAGASCAR

MALI

MAURITANIA

MOROCCO

NIGER

NIGERIA

RWANDA

SENEGAL

SIERRA LEONE

SOMALIA

SUDAN

TANGANYIKA

TOGO

TUNISIA

UGANDA

UNITED ARAB REPUBLIC

UPPER VOLTA

The OAU Member States

State	Capital	Colonial Power	Independence
Algeria	Algiers	France	1962
Botswana	Gaberones	Britain	1966
Burundi	Usumbura	Belgium	1962
Cameroon	Yaoundé	France/Britain	1960
Central African Republic	Bangui	France	1960
Chad	Fort Lamy	France	1960
Congo, Republic of the	Brazzaville	France	1960
Congo, Democratic Republic of	Kinshasa	Belgium	1960
Dahomey	Porto Novo	France	1960
Ethiopia	Addis Ababa	--	--
Equatorial Guinea	Santa Isabel	Spain	1968
Gabon	Libreville	France	1960
Gambia	Bathurst	Britain	1965
Ghana	Accra	Britain	1957
Guinea	Conakry	France	1958
Ivory Coast	Abidjan	France	1960
Kenya	Nairobi	Britain	1963
Lesotho	Maseru	Britain	1966
Liberia	Monrovia	--	1847
Libya	Benghazi, Tripoli	Italy	1951
Malagasy Republic	Tananarive	France	1960
Malawi	Zomba	Britain	1964
Mali	Bamako	France	1960
Mauritania	Nouakchott	France	1960
Mauritius	Port Louis	Britain	1968
Morocco	Rabat	France/Spain	1956
Niger	Niamey	France	1960
Nigeria	Lagos	Britain	1960
Rwanda	Kigali	Belgium	1962
Senegal	Dakar	France	1960
Sierra Leone	Freetown	Britain	1961
Somali Republic	Mogadishu	Italy/Britain	1960

The OAU Member States (cont.)

State	Capital	Colonial Power	Independence
Sudan	Khartoum	Anglo-Egyptian	1956
Swaziland	Mbabone	Britain	1968
Tanzania	Dar es Salaam	Britain	1961
Togo	Lome	France	1960
Tunisia	Tunis	France	1956
Uganda	Kampala	Britain	1962
United Arab Republic	Cairo	Britain	1922
Upper Volta	Ouagadougou	France	1960
Zambia	Lusaka	Britain	1964

PROTOCOL OF THE COMMISSION OF MEDIATION
CONCILIATION AND ARBITRATION

PART I

ESTABLISHMENT AND ORGANIZATION

Article I

The Commission of Mediation, Conciliation and Arbitration established by Article XIX of the Charter of the Organization of African Unity shall be governed by the provisions of the present Protocol.

Article II

1.   The Commission shall consist of twenty-one members elected by the Assembly of Heads of State and Government.
2.   No two Members shall be nationals of the same State.
3.   ThfMembers of the Commission shall be persons with recognized professional qualifications.
4.   Each Member State of the Organization of African Unity shall be entitled to nominate two candidates.
5.   The Administrative Secretary-General shall prepare a list of the candidates nominated by Member States and shall submit it to the Assembly of Heads of State and Government.

Article III

1.   Members of the Commission shall be elected for a term of five years and shall be eligible for re-election.
2.   Members of the Commission whose terms of office have expired shall remain in office until the election of a new Commission.
3.   Notwithstanding the expiry of their terms of office, Members shall complete any proceedings in which they are already engaged.

Article IV

Members of the Commission shall not be removed from office except by decision of the Assembly of Heads of State and Government, by a two-thirds majority of the total membership, on the grounds of inability to perform the functions of their office or of proved misconduct.

Article V

1.   Whenever a vacancy occurs in the Commission, it shall be filled in conformity with the provisions of Article II.
2.   A Member of the Commission elected to fill a vacancy shall hold office for the unexpired term of the Member he has replaced.

Article VI

1.   A President and two Vice-Presidents shall be elected by the Assembly of Heads of State and Government from among the Members of the Commission

who shall each hold office for five years. The President and the two Vice-Preisidents shall not be eligible for reelection as such officers.

2.   The President and the two Vice-Presidents shall be full-time members of the Commission, while the remaining eighteen shall be part-time Members.

Article VII

The President and the two Vice-Presidents shall constitute the Bureau of the Commission and shall have the responsibility of consulting with the parties as regards the appropriate mode of settling the dispute in accordance with this Protocol.

Article VIII

The salaries and allowances of the Members of the Bureau and the remuneration of the other Members of the Commission shall be determined in accordance with the provisions of the Charter of the Organization of African Unity.

Article IX

1.   The Commission shall appoint a Registrar and may provide for such other officers as may be deemed necessary.

2.   The terms and conditions of service of the Registrar and other administrative officers of the Commission shall be governed by the Commission's Staff Regulations.

Article X

The Administrative expenses of the Commission shall be borne by the Organization of African Unity. All other expenses incurred in connection with the proceedings before the Commission shall be met in accordance with the Rules of Procedure of the Commission.

Article XI

The Seat of the Commission shall be at Addis Ababa, Ethiopia.

PART II

GENERAL PROVISIONS

Article XII

The Commission shall have jurisidiction over disputes between States only.

Article XIII

1.   A dispute may be referred to the Commission jointly by the parties concerned, by a party to the dispute, by the Council of Ministers or by the Assembly of Heads of State and Government.

2.   Where a dispute has been referred to the Commission as provided in paragraph 1, and one or more of the parties have refused to submit to the jurisdiction of the Commission, the Bureau shall refer the matter to the Council of Ministers for consideration.

Article XIV

The consent of any party to a dispute to submit to the jurisdiction of the Commission may be evidenced by :

(a) a prior written undertaking by such party that there shall be recourse to Mediation, Conciliation or Arbitration;

(b) reference of a dispute by such party to the Commission; or

(c) submission by such party to the jurisdiction in respect of a dispute referred to the Commission by another State, by the Council of Ministers, or by the Assembly of Heads of State and Government.

Article XV

Member States shall refrain from any act or omission that is likely to aggravate a situation which has been referred to the Commission.

Article XVI

Subject to the provisions of this Protocol and any special agreement between the parties, the Commission shall be entitled to adopt such working methods as it deems to be necessary and expedient and shall establish appropriate rules of procedure.

Article XVII

The Members of the Commission, when engaged in the business of the Commission, shall enjoy diplomatic privileges and immunities as provided for in the Convention on Privileges and Immunities of the Organization of African Unity.

Article XVIII

Where, in the course of Mediation, Conciliation or Arbitration, it is deemed necessary to conduct an investigation or inquiry for the purpose of elucidating facts or circumstances relating to a matter in dispute, the parties concerned and all other Member States shall extend to those engaged in any such proceedings the fullest co-operation in the conduct of such investigation or inquiry.

Article XIX

In case of a dispute between Member States, the parties may agree to resort to any one of these modes of settlement : Mediation, Conciliation and Arbitration.

PART III

MEDIATION

Article XX

When a dispute between Member States is referred to the Commission for Mediation, the President shall, with the consent of the parties, appoint one or more members of the Commission to mediate the dispute.

Article XXI

1. The role of the mediator shall be confined to reconciling the views and claims of the parties.

653

2.   The mediator shall make written proposals to the parties as expeditiously as possible.

3.   If the means of reconciliation proposed by the mediator are accepted, they shall become the basis of a protocol of arrangement between the parties.

PART IV

CONCILIATION

Article XXII

1.   A request for the settlement of a dispute by conciliation may be submitted to the Commission by means of a petition addressed to the President by one or more of the parties to the dspute.

2.   If the request is made by only one of the parties, that party shall indicee-that prior written notice has been given to the other party.

3.   The petition shall include a summary explanation of the grounds of the dispute.

Article XXIII

1.   Upon receipt of the petition, the President shall, in agreement with the parties, establish a Board of Conciliators, of whom three shall be appointed by the President from among the Members of the Commission, and one each by the parties.

2.   The Chairman of the Board shall be a person designated by the President from among the three Members of the Commission.

3.   In nominating persons to serve as Members of the Board, the parties to the dispute shall designate persons in such a way that no two Members of it shall be nationals of the same State.

Article XXIV

1.   It shall be the duty of the Board of Conciliators to clarify the issues in dispute and to endeavour to bring about in agreement between the parties upon mutually acceptable terms.

2.   The Board shall consider all questions submitted to it and may undertake any inquiry or hear any person capable of giving relevant information concerning the dispute.

3.   In the absence of agreement between the parties, the Board shall determine its own procedure.

Article XXV

The parties shall be represented by agents, whose duty shall be to act as intermediaries between them and the Board. They may moreover be assisted by counsel and experts and may request that all persons whose evidence appears to the Board to be relevant shall be heard.

Article XXVI

1.   At the close of the proceedings, the Board shall draw up a report stating either:

(a) that the parties have come to an agreement and, if the need arises, the terms of the agreement and any recommendations for settlement made by the Board; or

(b) that it has been impossible to effect a settlement.

2. The Report of the Board of Conciliators shall be communicated to the parties and to the President of the Commission without delay and may be published only with the consent of the parties.

PART V

ARBITRATION

Article XXVII

1. Where it is agreed that arbitration should be resorted to, the Arbitral Tribunal shall be established in the following manner:

(a) each party shall designate one arbitrator from among the Members of the Commission having legal qualifications;

(b) the two arbitrators thus designated shall, by common agreement, designate from among the Members of the Commission a third person who shall act as Chairman of the Tribunal;

(c) where the two arbitrators fail to agree, within one month of their appointment, in the choice of the person to be Chairman of the Tribunal, the Bureau shall designate the Chairman.

2. The President may, with the agreement of the parties, appoint to the Arbitral Tribunal two additional Members who need not be Members of the Commission but who shall have the same powers as the other Members of the Tribunal.

3. The arbitrators shall not be nationals of the parties, or have their domicile in the territories of the parties, or be employed in their service, or have served as mediators or conciliators in the same dispute. They shall all be of different nationalities.

Article XXVIII

Recourse to arbitration shall be regarded as submission in good faith to the award of the Arbitral Tribunal.

Article XXIX

1. The parties shall, in each case, conclude a *compromis* which shall specify:

(a) the undertaking of the parties to go to arbitration, and to accept as legally binding, the decision of the Tribunal;

(b) the subject matter of the controversy; and

(c) the seat of the Tribunal.

2. The *compromis* may specify the law to be applied by the Tribunal and the power, if the parties so agree, to adjudicate *ex aequo et bono*, the time-limit within which the award of the arbitrators shall be given, and the appointment of agenst and counsel to take part in the proceedings before the Tribunal.

Article XXX

In the absence of any provision in the *compromis* regarding the applicable law, the Arbitral Tribunal shall decide the dispute according to treaties concluded between the parties, International Law , the Charter of the Organization of African Unity, the Charter of the United Nations and, if the parties agree, *ex aequo et bono*.

Article XXXI

1. Hearings shall be held in *camera* unless the arbitrators decide otherwise.
2. The record of the proceedings signed by the arbitrators and the Registrar shall alone be authoritative.
3. The arbitral award shall be in writing and shall, in respect of every point decided, state the reasons on which it is based.

PART VI

FINAL PROVISIONS

Article XXXII

The present Protocol shall, after approval by the Assembly of Heads of State and Government, be an integral part of the Charter of the Organization of African Unity.

Article XXXIII

This Protocol may be amended or revised in accordance with the provisions of Article XXXIII of the Charter of the Organization of African Unity.

IN FAITH WHEREOF, We the Heads of African State and Government, have signed this Protocol.

Done at Cairo, (United Arab Republic), on the 21st day of July, 1964.

ALGERIA	MALI
BURUNDI	MAURITANIA
CAMEROUN	MOROCCO
CENTRAL AFRICAN REPUBLIC	NIGER
CHAD	NIGERIA
CONGO (Brazzaville)	RWANDA
DAHOMEY	SENEGAL
ETHIOPIA	SIERRAL LEONE
GABON	SOMALIA
GHANA	SUDAN
GUINEA	TOGO
IVORY COAST	TUNISIA
KENYA	UGANADA
LIBERIA	UNITED ARAB REPUBLIC
LIBYA	UNITED REPUBLIC OF TANGA-
MADAGASCAR	NYIKA AND ZANZIBAR
MALAWI	UPPER VOLTA

THE GENERAL SECRETARIAT

PART I

Rule 1

The General Secretariat, as a central and permanent organ of the Organization of African Unity, shall carry out the functions assigned to it by the Charter of the Organization, those that might be specified in other treaties and agreements among the Member States, and those that are established in these Regulations.

Rule 2

The General Administrative Secretariat shall supervise the implementation of decisions of the Council of Ministers concerning all economic, social, legal and cultural exchanges of Member States:

(i)   keeps in custody the documents and files of the meetings of the Assembly, the Council of Ministers, of the Specialized Commissions and other organs of the Organization of African Unity;

(ii)   within its possibilities, the General Secretariat shall place at the disposal of the Specialized Commissions the technical and administrative services that may be requested. In case a session of a Specialized Commission is held outside the Headquarters of the Organization, at the request of a Member State, the General Secretariat shall conclude agreements or contracts with the Government of the Member State on whose territory the Session of the Specialized Commission is being held, to guarantee adequate compensation of the disbursements incurred by the General Secretariat;

(iii)   receives communications of ratification of instruments of agreements entered into between Member States.

(iv)   prepares an Annual Report of the activities of the Organization;

(v)   prepares for submission to the Council, a report of the activities carried out by the Specialized Commission;

(vi)   prepares the Programme and Budget of the Organization for each Fiscal Year, to be submitted to the Council of Ministers, for its consideration and approval.

Rule 3

The General Secretariat of the Organization of African Unity is the Secretariat of the Assembly, of the Council of Ministers, of the Specialized Commissions and other organs of the Organization of African Unity.

Rule 4

The Organization of African Unity has its Headquarters in the City of Addis Ababa.

Rule 5

The Headquarters for the official use of the Organization, for objectives and purposes strictly compatible with the objectives and purposes set forth in the Charter of the Organization. The Administrative Secretary-General may authorize the celebration of meetings or social functions in the Headquarters of the Organization when such meetings or functions are closely linked, or are compatible with the objectives and purposes of the Organization.

PART II

THE ADMINISTRATIVE SECRETARY-GENERAL AND

THE ASSISTANT ADMINISTRATIVE SECRETARIES-GENERAL

The Administrative Secretary-General

Rule 6

The Administrative Secretary-General directs the activities of the General Secretariat and is its legal representative;

Rule 7

The Administrative Secretary-General is directly responsible to the Council of Ministers for the adequate discharge of all duties assigned to him.

Rule 8

The appointment, term of office and removal of the Administrative Secretary-General are governed by the provisions of Articles XVI and XVIII of the Charter and of the Rules of Procedure of the Assembly.

Rule 9

The participation of the Administrative Secretary-General in the deliberations of the Assembly, of the Council of Ministers, of the Specialized Commissions and other organs of the Organization shall be governed by the provisions of the Charter and by the respective Rules of Procedure of these bodies.

Rule 10

The Administrative Secretary-General shall submit reports requested by the Assembly, the Council of Ministers and the Commissions.

Rule 11

The Administrative Secretary-General shall furthermore:

(i) carry out the provisions of Article XVIII of the Charter, and submit Staff Rules to the Council of Ministers for approval;

(ii) transmit to Member States the Budget and Programme of Work at least one month before the convocation of the sessions of the Assembly, of the Council of Ministers, of the Specialized Commissions and of other organs of the Organization;

(iii)   receive the notification of adherence or accession to the Charter and communicate such notification to Member States, as provided in Article XXVIII of the Charter;

(iv)   receive the notification of Member States which may desire to renounce their membership in the Organization as provided in Article XXXII of the Charter;

(v)   communicate to Member States, and include in the Agenda of the Assembly, as provided in Article XXXIII of the Charter, written requests of Member States for amendments or revisions of the Charter;

(vi)   establish, with the approval of the Council of Ministers, such branches and administrative and technical offices as may be necessary to achieve the objectives and purposes of the Organization;

(vii)   abolish, with the approval of the Council of Ministers, such branches and administrative and technical offices as may be deemed necessary for the adequate functioning of the General Secretariat.

The Assistant Administrative Secretaries-General

Rule 12

The appointment, term of office and removal of the Assistant Administrative Secretaries-General are governed by the provisions of Articles XVI and XVII of the Charter and the Rules of Procedure of the Assembly.

Rule 13

The Administrative Secretary-General shall designate one of the Assistant Administrative Secretaries-General who will represent him in all matters assigned to him.

Rule 14

One of the Assistant Administrative Secretaries-General shall exercise the functions of the Administrative Secretary-General in his absence, or because of any temporary incapacity of the Administrative Secretary-General, and shall assume the office of the Administrative Secretary-General for the unexpired term in case of a definite vacancy. In case of definite vacancy, the Council will designate one of the Assistant Administrative Secretaries-General who will replace the Administrative Secretary-General provisionally.

PART III

ORGANIZATION OF THE GENERAL SECRETARIAT

Rule 15

The General Secretariat has the following departments:
(i)   the Political , Legal and Defence Department;
(ii)   the Economic and Social Department;
(iii)   the Administrative, Conference and Information Department.
The Administrative Secretary-General shall create divisions and sub-divisions, as he may deem necessary, with the approval of the Coucil.

PART IV
FISCAL RULES
Rule 16

The Administrative Secretary-General shall prepare the Programme and Budget of the Organization as provided in Article XXIII of the Charter, and shall submit it to the Council of Ministers for scrutiny and approval during its first ordinary session.

Rule 17

The proposed Programme and Budget shall comprise the programme of activities of the General Secretariat of the Organization. It shall include the expenses of the Assembly, of the Council of Ministers, of the Specialized Commission and of other organs of the Organization.

Rule 18

In formulating the Programme and Budget of the Organization the Administrative Secretary-General shall consult the different Organs of the Organization of African Unity.

The proposed Programme and Budget shall include:
  (i)   a list of contributions made by Member States in accordance with the scale established by the Council of Ministers and by reference to the provisions of Article XXIII of the Charter;
  (ii)   an estimate of various incomes;
  (iii) a description of the situation of the Working Fund.

FINANCIAL RESOURCES
Rule 19

Once the budget is approved by the Council of Ministers, the Administrative Secretary-General shall communicate it to the Member States, with all pertinent documents, at least three months before the first day of the Fiscal Year. The budget shall be accompanied by a list indicating the annual contributions assigned by the Council to each Member State. The annual contribution of each Member State becomes due on the first day of the Fiscal Year.

Rule 20

The Administrative Secretary-General is the Accounting Officer of the Organization and shall be responsible for the proper administration of the Budget.

Rule 21

The Administrative Secretary-General shall submit to Member States a quarterly statement on payments of contributions and outstanding contributions:

Rule 22

There shall be a General Fund, in which the following amounts will be entere.d
  (i)   annual contribution of Member States;

(ii)   miscellaneous income, unless the Council of Ministers determine otherwise;

(iii)   advance from the Working Fund

From such General Fund all expenditures established in the budget shall be et.

Rule 23

The Administrative Secretary-General may establish fiduciary funds, reserve unds and special funds with approval of the Council of Ministers. The objectives nd limitations of these funds shall be defined by the Council of Ministers. These unds shall be administered in separate accounts, as provided in special regulations pproved by the Council of Ministers.

Rule 24

The Administrative Secretary-General, may accept, on behalf of the Organiza- ion, gifts, bequests and other donations made to the Organization, provided that uch donations are consistent with the objectives and purposes of the Organization, nd are approved by the Council of Ministers.

Rule 25

In the case of monetary donations for specific purposes, these funds shall be reated as fiduciary or special funds, as provided in Rule 22. Monetary donations or no specific purposes shall be considered as miscellaneous income.

Rule 26

The Administrative Secretary-General shall designate the African Banks or anking Institutions in which the funds of the Organization shall be deposited. he interests accrued by such funds, including the Working Fund, shall be entered s miscellaneous income.

ACCOUTING

Rule 27

The accounts of the Organization shall be carried in the currency determined y the Council of Ministers.

FINANCIAL SUPERVISION

Rule 28

The Council of Ministers shall be responsible for the supervision of the nances of the Organization.

Rule 29

The Administrative Secretary-General shall submit to the Council of Ministers ny matter relating to the financial situation of the Organization.

PART V

MISCELLANEOUS

Rule 30

The Administrative Secretary-General shall submit to the Council of Ministers for its approval, at the earliest possible moment, the complete Regulations governing the Accounting Method of the Organization, in accordance with established international accounting practices.

AMENDMENTS

Rule 31

These Regulations may be amended by the Council of Ministers by a simple majority subject to the approval of the Assembly.

V

The OAU Conferences

Assembly of Heads of State and Government

Summit Conference of Addis Ababa, 22-25 May 1963.
First Ordinary Session, Cairo, 17-21 July 1964.
Second Ordinary Session, Accra, 21-25 Oct. 1965.
Third Ordinary Session, Addis Ababa, 5-9 Nov. 1966.
Fourth Ordinary Session, Kinshasa, 11-14 Sept. 1967.
Fifth Ordinary Session, Algiers, 13-16 Sept. 1968.
Sixth Ordinary Session, Addis Ababa, 6-9 Sept. 1969.

Council of Ministers

Pre-Summit Conference, Addis Ababa, 15-21 May 1963.
First Ordinary Session, Dakar, 2-11 Aug. 1963.
First Extraordinary Session (Algero-Moroccan Border Dispute),
   Addis Ababa, 15-18 Nov. 1963.
Second Extraordinary Session (Tanganyika Mutinies and Ethio-
   pia-Kenya-Somalia Conflicts), Dar es Salaam, 12-15 Feb.
   1964.
Second Ordinary Session, Lagos, 24-29 Feb. 1964.
Third Ordinary Session, Cairo, 13-17 July 1964.
Third Extraordinary Session (Congo), Addis Ababa, 5-10 Sept.
   1964.
Fourth Extraordinary Session (Congo), New York, 16-21 Dec.
   1964.
Fourth Ordinary Session, Nairobi, 26 Feb.-9 March 1965.
Fifth Extraordinary Session (Subversion), Lagos, 10-13 June
   1965.
Fifth Ordinary Session, Accra, 14-21 Oct. 1965.
Sixth Extraordinary Session (Rhodesia), Addis Ababa, 3-5 Dec.
   1965.
Sixth Ordinary Session, Addis Ababa, 28 Feb.-6 March 1966.
Seventh Ordinary Session, Addis Ababa, 31 Oct.-4 Nov. 1966.
Eighth Ordinary Session, Addis Ababa, 27 Feb.-4 March 1967.
Ninth Ordinary Session, Kinshasa, 4-10 Sept. 1967.
Tenth Ordinary Session, Addis Ababa, 20-24 Feb. 1968.
Eleventh Ordinary Session, Algiers, 4-12 Sept. 1968.

Twelfth Ordinary Session, Addis Ababa, 17-22 Feb. 1969.
Thirteenth Ordinary Session, Addis Ababa, 27 Aug.-6 Sept.
  1969.
Fourteenth Ordinary Session, Addis Ababa, 27 Feb.-6 March
  1970.

Draft Convention on the Status of Refugees in Africa

Preamble

We the Heads of State and Government,

Noting with concern the existence of the growing numbers of refugees in Africa and desirous of finding ways and means of alleviating their misery and suffering as well as providing them with a better life and future,

Recognizing the need for an essentially humanitarian approach towards solving the problems of refugees,

Aware, however, that the refugee problems are a source of friction among several Member States, and desirous of eliminating such discord,

Anxious to make a distinction between a refugee who seeks a peaceful and normal life and a person fleeing his country in order to subvert it from outside,

Determined that the activities of such subversive elements should be discouraged, in accordance with the Declaration on the Problem of Subversion and the Resolution on the Problem of Refugees adopted at Accra in 1965,

Conscious that the Charter of the United Nations and the Universal Declaration of Human Rights have affirmed the principle that human beings shall enjoy fundamental rights and freedoms without discrimination,

Considering that the Member States should co-ordinate and harmonize their general policies and grant refugees minimum legal rights,

Convinced that the efficiency of the measures recommended by the present Convention to solve the problem of refugees in Africa necessitates close and continuous collaboration between the Organization of African Unity and the United Nations High Commission for Refugees.

Have agreed as follows:

Article I

Definition

1.   For the purposes of this Convention the term "refugee, shall mean every person who, owing to well-founded fear of being persecuted for reasons of race, religion, nationality, membership of a particular social group or political opinion i outside the country of his nationality and is unable or, owing to such fear is unwilling to avail himself of the protection of that country, or who, not having a nationality and being outside the country of his former habitual residence as a result of such events, is unable or, owing to such fear is unwilling to return to it.

2.   In the case of a person who has more than one nationality the term "a country of which he is a national" shall mea each of the countries of which he is a national and a person shall not be deemed to be lacking the protection of the countr of which he is a national if, without any valid reason based o well-founded fear, he has not availed himself of the protectio of one of the countries of which he is a national.

3.   This Convention shall cease to apply to any refugee un der this Convention if:

    (a)   he has voluntarily re-availed himself of the protec tion of the country of his nationality; or

    (b)   having lost his nationality he has voluntarily re-acquired it; or

    (c)   he has acquired a new nationality, and enjoys the protection of the country of his new nationality; or

    (d)   he has voluntarily re-established himself in the country which he left or outside which he remaine owing to fear of persecution;

    (e)   he can no longer, because the circumstances in connection with which he was recognized as a refu

gee have ceased to exist, continue to refuse to
avail himself of the protection of the country of his
nationality;

(f) he has committed a serious non-political crime outside his country of refuge after his admission to
that country as a refugee;

(g) he has seriously infringed the purposes and objectives of this Convention.

4.   The provisions of this Convention shall not apply to any
person with respect to whom there are serious reasons for
considering that:

(a) he has committed a crime against peace, a war
crime, or a crime against humanity as defined in
the international instruments drawn up to make provision in respect of such crimes;

(b) he has committed a serious non-political crime
outside the country of refuge prior to his admission
to that country as a refugee;

(c) he has been guilty of acts contrary to the purposes
and principles of the Organization of African Unity;

(d) he has been guilty of acts contrary to the purposes
and principles of the United Nations.

Article II

Asylum

1.   Member States shall use their best endeavours consistent with their laws and constitutions to receive all refugees
and to secure the settlement of those refugees who, for well-
founded reasons, do not want to return to their country of origin or nationality.

2.   The grant of asylum to refugees is a peaceful and humanitarian act and shall not be regarded as an unfriendly act
by any Member State.

3.   No person shall be subjected by a Member State to
measures such as rejection at the frontier, return or expul-

sion, which would compel him to return to or remain in a territory where his life, physical integrity or liberty would be threatened for the reasons set out in Article 1, paragraph 1.

4.   Where a Member State finds difficulty in continuing to grant asylum to refugees, other Member States shall consider, in a spirit of African solidarity and international co-operation, appropriate measures to lighten the burden of the Member State granting asylum.

5.   Where a refugee has not received the right to reside in any country of asylum, he shall have a prior claim to temporary residence in any country of asylum in which he first presented himself as a refugee pending arrangement for his resettlement in accordance with Article II, paragraph 4.

6.   Every refugee has duties to the country in which he finds himself, which require in particular that he conform to its laws and regulations as well as to measures taken for the maintenance of public order. He shall also abstain from any subversive activities against any state whatsoever.

Article III

Prohibition of Subversive Activities

Member States shall undertake to prohibit refugees residing in their respective territories, from attacking any Member State of the Organization of African Unity either through press or radio, with arms or through any other activities which may cause tension between the Member States.

Article IV

Non-Discrimination

Member States shall apply the provisions of this Convention to refugees without discrimination as to race, religion or country of origin.

Article V

Religion

Member States shall accord to refugees within their territories treatment at least as favourable as that accorded to their nationals with respect to freedom to practice their religion and freedom as regards religious education for themselves and for their children.

Article VI

Residence Prior to this Convention

Where for reasons and circumstances set out in Article 1 of this Convention an individual has been residing in the territory of a Member State prior to the date of entry into force of this Convention, subject to the provisions of Article 1 of this Convention, such period of residence shall be considered to have been lawful residence within the territory of a Member State, and such an individual shall be considered a refugee within the terms of this Convention; provided that the rights and benefits accorded to such a refugee by virtue of this Convention shall not have any retroactive effect.

Article VII

Movable and Immovable Property

Member States shall accord to a refugee treatment as favourable as possible and, in any event not less favourable than that accorded to aliens generally in the same circumstances, as regards the acquisition of movable and immovable property and other rights pertaining thereto, and to leases and other contracts relating to movable and immovable property.

Article VIII

Right of Association

As regards non-political and non-profit making associations and trade unions the Member States shall accord to refugees lawfully staying in their territory the most favourable treatment accorded to nationals of a foreign country, in the same circumstances in accordance with the laws of the Member States.

Article IX

Liberal Professions

Each Member State shall accord to refugees, lawfully staying in their territory, who hold academic or professional qualifications recognized by the competent authorities of that State, and who are desirous of practicing a liberal profession, the most favourable treatment as that accorded to nationals of a foreign country.

Article X

Identity Papers

Member States shall issue to refugees in their territories standard identity papers in accordance with the Schedule to this Convention.

Article XI

Travel Documents

1.   Subject to Article 3, Member States shall issue to refugees lawfully staying in their territories travel documents in accordance with the Schedule to this Convention for the purpose of travel outside their territory, unless compelling reasons of national security or public order otherwise require. Member States may issue such a travel document to any other refugee in their territories; they shall in particular give sympathetic consideration to the issue of such travel documents to refugees in their territories who are unable to obtain a travel document from the countries of their lawful residence.

2.   Travel documents issued to refugees under previous international agreements by parties thereto shall be recognized and treated by Member States in the same way as if they had been issued pursuant to this Article.

Article XII

Transfer of Assets

Member States shall, in conformity with their laws and
regulations, permit refugees to transfer assets, which they
have brought into their territory, to another country where
they have been admitted for the purpose of resettlement.

Member States shall give sympathetic consideration to
the application of refugees for permission to transfer assets
which are necessary for their resettlement in another country
which they have been admitted.

Article XIII

Refugees unlawfully in the Country of Refuge

Member States shall not impose penalties, on account
of their illegal entry or presence, on refugees who, coming
directly from a territory where their life or freedom was
threatened in the sense of Article 1, enter or are present in
their territory without authorization, provided they present
themselves at the first available opportunity to the authorities.

Member States shall not apply to the movement of such
refugees restrictions other than those which are necessary and
such restrictions shall not be applied until their status in the
country is regularized or they obtain admission into another
country. Member States shall allow such refugees a reasonable period and all the necessary facilities to obtain admission
to another country.

Article XIV

Repatriation

No refugee shall be repatriated against his will.

In examining the question of repatriation of refugees,
appropriate arrangements shall be made by the Member State
which has granted them asylum for ascertaining the free will
of return of the person concerned, and, in co-operation with
the country of origin, shall make adequate arrangements for
the safe return of the refugees.

671

Article XV

Expulsion

1.   Member States shall not expel a refugee lawfully in their territory save on grounds of national security or publi order.

2.   The expulsion of such a refugee shall be only in purs ance of a decision reached in accordance with due process c law.   Except where compelling reasons of national security otherwise require, the refugee shall be allowed to submit ev dence to clear himself, and to appeal to and be represented for the purpose before competent authority or a person or p sons specially designated by the competent authority.

3.   Member States shall allow such a refugee a reasonab period within which to seek legal admission into another cou try.   Member States reserve the right to apply during that period such internal measures as they may deem necessary.

Article XVI

Co-operation of the National Authorities with the

Organization of African Unity

In order to enable the Administrative Secretary-Gene of the Organization of African Unity to make reports to the competent organs of the Organization of African Unity, Mem ber States undertake to provide the Secretariat in the appro priate form with information and statistical data requested c cerning:

(a) the condition of refugees,
(b) the implementation of this Convention and
(c) laws, regulations and decrees which are, or may hereafter be, in force relating to refugees.

Article XVII

Co-operation with the United Nations High Commission

for Refugees

1.   Member States shall co-operate with the United Nations High Commission for Refugees.

2.   In accordance with Resolution AHG/Res.26, Member States shall, save as herein provided, apply the provisions of the U.N. Convention of 28 July 1951 relating to the status of refugees, irrespective of the dateline and of any geographical limitation as provided in the Protocol on the Status of Refugees of 31 January 1967.

3.   The present Convention shall be the effective regional complement in Africa of the 1951 United Nations Convention on the Status of Refugees.

Article XVIII

Settlement of Disputes

Any dispute between parties to this Convention relating to its interpretation or application, which cannot be settled by other means, shall be referred to the Mediation, Conciliation and Arbitration Commission of the Organization of African Unity, at the request of any one of the parties to the dispute.

Article XIX

Signature and Ratification

1.   This Convention is open for signature to all Member States of the Organization of African Unity and shall be ratified by Member States in accordance with their respective constitutional processes.

2.   The original instrument done if possible in African languages in English and French, all texts being equally authentic, should be deposited with the Administrative Secretary-General of the Organization of African Unity.

3. The instruments of ratification shall be deposited with the Administrative Secretary-General of the Organization of African Unity.

Article XX

Adhesion and Accession

Any independent sovereign African State, member of the Organization of African Unity, may at any time notify the Administrative Secretary-General of its adhesion or accession to this Convention.

Article XXI

Entry into force

This Convention shall come into force as of the day of deposit of the instrument of ratification by two-thirds of the Member States of the Organization of African Unity.

Article XXII

Denunciation

1. Any Member State may denounce this Convention at any time by a notification addressed to the Administrative Secretary-General of the Organization of African Unity.

2. Such denunciation shall take effect for the Member State concerned one year from the date upon which it is received by the Administrative Secretary-General of the Organization of African Unity.

Article XXIII

Amendment

This Convention may be amended or revised if any Member State makes a written request to the Administrative Secretary-General to that effect; provided that the proposed amendment is not submitted to the Assembly of Heads of State and Government for consideration until all Member States have

een duly notified of it and a period of one year has elapsed.
uch an amendment shall not be effective unless approved by
t least two-thirds of all the Member States.

Article XXIV

Notifications by the Administrative Secretary-General

of the Organization of African Unity

The Administrative Secretary-General of the Organiza-
on of African Unity shall inform all Members of the Organi-
ation:

(a) Of signatures and ratifications in accordance with
Article 19.
(b) Of adhesion and accession in accordance with Article 20.
(c) Of entry into force in accordance with Article 21.
(d) Of denunciations in accordance with Article 22.
(e) Of requests for amendment in accordance with Article 23.

IN FAITH WHEREOF, WE the Heads of African State
nd Government have signed this Convention.

Glossary of Acronyms

AAPC	All-African Peoples Conference
AAPO	All-African Peoples Organization
AAPSO	Afro-Asian People's Solidarity Organization
AATUF	All-African Trade Union Federation
ABAKO	Alliance des Ba-Kongo (Léopoldville)
AFRO	African Regional Organization (within ICFTU)
AID	Agency for International Development (USA)
ANC	African National Congress (South Africa)
ANC	Armée Nationale Congolaise
ATUC	African Trade Union Confederation
CCTA	Commission for Technical Cooperation in Africa (south of the Sahara)
CIAS	Conference of Independent African States
CNL	Comité National de Libération (Congo)
CONCP	Conferência das Organizações Nacionalistas das Colonias Portuguesas
COREMO	Comité Revolucionário de Moçambique
CPP	Convention People's Party
CSA	Scientific Council for Africa (CCTA; continued STRC)
EACSO	East African Common Services Organization
EEC	European Economic Community
ECA	Economic Commission for Africa (UN)
ECOSOC	(UN) Economic and Social Council
FAO	(UN) Food and Agriculture Organization
FEANF	Fédération des Etudiants d'Afrique Noire en Fran
FLING	Frente de Libertação de la Independência Nacion da Guiné
FLN	Front de Libération Nationale (Algeria)
FMG	Federal Military Government (Nigeria)
FNLA	Frente Nacional de Libertação da Angola
FRELIMO	Frente de Libertação de Moçambique
GPRA	Gouvernement Provisoire de la République Algérienne
GRAE	Govêrno Revolucionário da Angola em Exilo
IAMO	Inter-African and Malagasy Organization ("Monro via Group")
IBRD	International Bank for Reconstruction and Develo ment

CAO	International Civil Aviation Organization
CFTU	International Confederation of Free Trade Unions
CJ	International Court of Justice
CRC	International Committee of the Red Cross (Swiss nationals only)
FCTU	International Federation of Christian Trade Unions
LO	International Labor Organization (UN)
MF	International Monetary Fund
TU	International Telecommunications Union
EOCAM	Mouvement des Etudiants de l'OCAM
IPLA	Movimento Popular para Libertação da Angola
AACP	National Association for the Advancement of Colored People (USA)
ATO	North Atlantic Treaty Organization
CNC	National Council of Nigerian Citizens
IBMAR	"No Independence [for Rhodesia] Before Majority Rule"
NDP	Nigerian National Democratic Party
PC	Northern People's Congress (Nigeria)
AMCAF	OCAM coffee organization
AMCE	Organisation Africaine et Malgache de Coopération Economique (sub-div. of UAM)
AS	Organisation de l'Armée Secrète (Algeria)
CAM	Organisation Commune Africaine et Malgache
ERS	Organisation des Etats Riverains du Fleuve Sénégal
NUC	United Nations Operation in the Congo
AC	Pan-Africanist Congress (South Africa)
AFMEC(S)A	Pan-African Freedom Movement of East and Central (and Southern) Africa
AIGC	Partido Africano da Independência da Guiné e Cabo Verde
ANA	Pan-African News Agency
SA	Parti Solidaire Africain (Congo-Kwilu)
DA	Rassemblement Démocratique Africain (Party of African Representatives in French Assembly)
TRC	(OAU) Scientific, Technical and Research Commission
WANLIF	South West African National Liberation Front
WANU	South West Africa National Union
WAPO	South West Africa People's Organization
ANU	Tanganyika African National Union
AM	Union Africaine et Malgache
AMCE	(see OAMCE which superseded UAMCE)
AMD	UAM Defence
AMPT	UAM Post-Telegraph
ANA	Union of African News Agencies

677

UDEAC	Union Douanière et Economique de l'Afrique Centrale
UDENAMO	União Democratico Nacional de Moçambique
UDI	Unilateral Declaration of Independence (Rhodesia)
UEAC	Union des Etats de l'Afrique Centrale
UGCC	United Gold Coast Convention
UGTAN	Union Générale des Travailleurs d'Afrique Noire
UNCTAD	UN Conference on Trade and Development
UNESCO	United Nations Educational, Scientific and Cultural Organization
UNHCR	United Nations High Commission for Refugees
UNICEF	United Nations Children's Fund
UNIDO	UN Industrial Development Organization
UNITA	União Nacional para a Independência Total da Angola
UPA	União das Populações da Angola
UPC	Union des Peuples du Cameroun
USIS	United States Information Service
WCC	World Council of Churches
WFTU	World Federation of Trade Unions
WHO	World Health Organization (UN)
ZANU	Zimbabwe African National Union
ZAPU	Zimbabwe African People's Union

Bibliography

Some documentation on the various African organizations can be obtained from their secretariats although, in the political bodies, there is a tendency to impose considerable secrecy about the activities. A first "OAU Review" was issued in May 1964 and a new series was initiated in December 1968. Aside from that, almost everything of interest--including the "secrets"--can be found in one source or another. Good coverage is provided by newspapers such as The Times (London), The New York Times and Le Monde. Valuable information and articles, not all of which are listed below, also appear in Africa Report, Africa Research Bulletin, Afrique-Genève, The Economist, International Conciliation, International Organization, Jeune Afrique, Journal of African History, Journal of Modern African Studies, and Revue Française d'Etudes Politiques Africaines. Full citations for the footnotes in the preceeding text can be found in this bibliography, which is classified as follows:

A. Background
B. The OAU
C. Decolonization
D. Peaceful Settlement
E. Non-Alignment--World Relations
F. United Nations
G. Development
H. Regionalism
I. National Unity

A. BACKGROUND

1. Borella, François. "Les Regroupements d'Etat dans l'Afrique Indépendante," Annuaire Français de Droit International. 1961, p. 787-807.

2. Carter, Gwendolen M. (ed). Politics in Africa: Seven Cases. New York, Harcourt Brace, 1966, 283 p.; in which see:
    Liebenow, J. G. "Which Road to Pan-African Unity? The Sanniquellie Conference"; and
    Rothchild, D. S. "A Hope Deferred: East African Federation."

3. Emerson, Rupert. "Pan-Africanism," International Organization. Spring 1962, vol. 16, no. 2, p. 275-290.

4. Hama, Boubou. "Enquête sur les Fondements et la Genèse de l'Unité Africaine," Présence Africaine. 1966.

5. Hazlewood, Arthur (ed). African Integration and Disintegration. London, Oxford Univ. Press, 1967, 414 p.; in which see:
    Hoskyns, Catherine. "Pan-Africanism and Integration."

6. Hodgkin, Thomas, and Ruth Schachter. "French-Speaking West Africa in Transition," International Conciliation. May 1960, no. 528, p. 375-436.

7. Hooker, James R. Black Revolutionary: George Padmore's Path from Communism to Pan-Africanism. London, Pall Mall Press, 1967.

8. Hoskyns, Catherine. The Congo Since Independence, January 1960-December 1961. New York, Oxford Univ. Press, 1965, 518 p.

9. Kloman, Erasmus, Jr. "African Unification Movements," International Organization. Spring 1962, vol. 16, no. 2, p. 387-404.

0. Legum, Colin. _Pan-Africanism: A Short Political Guide_. London, Pall Mall Press, 1965, 362 p.

1. ----------. (ed). _Africa: A Handbook_. London, Anthony Blond, 1965, 558 p.

2. Loewe, H. "Interafrikanische Zusammenschlüsse bis zur Organization Afrikanischer Einheit 1963," _Zeitschrift für Auslandisches Offentliches Recht und Völkerecht_. Feb. 1964, vol. 24, no. 1, p. 122-155.

3. McKay, Vernon. _Africa in World Politics_. New York, Harper and Row, 1962, 468 p.

4. Nkrumah, Kwame. _Africa Must Unite_. New York, Praeger, 1963, 265 p.

5. Padmore, George. _Pan-Africanism or Communism? The Coming Struggle For Africa_. London, Dennis Dobson, 1956, 279 p.

6. Schachter-Morgenthau, Ruth. _Political Parties in French-Speaking West Africa_. London, Oxford Univ. Press, 1964, 445 p.

7. Segal, Ronald. _African Profiles_. Harmondsworth, England, Penguin Books, 1962, 352 p.

8. Strauch, Hanspeter. _Panafrika: Kontinentale Weltmacht im Werden?_ Zürich, Atlantis, 1964, 416 p.

9. Zartman, I. William. _International Relations in the New Africa_. Englewood Clifts, Prentice-Hall, 1966, 175 p.

B. The O A U

Bonzon, Suzanne. "L'OUA d'Addis-Abéba à Kinshasa," _Revue Française d'Etudes Politiques Africaines_. Oct. 1967, p. 20-39.

Borella, François. "Le Régionalisme Africain et l'Organisation de l'Unité Africaine," _Annuaire Français de Droit International_. 1963, vol. 9, p. 838-859.

Boutros-Ghali, Boutros. "The Addis Ababa Charter," _International Conciliation_. Jan. 1964, no. 546, 62 p.

4. Boutros-Ghali, Boutros. L'Organisation de l'Unité Africaine. Paris, Armand Colin, 1969, 197 p.

5. Cervenka, Zdenek. The Organization of African Unity and its Charter. London, Hurst, 1969, 253 p.

6. Elias, T. O. "The Charter of the Organization of African Unity," American Journal of International Law. April 1965, vol. 59, no. 2, p. 243-267.

7. Gam, P. "L'OUA, L'Organisation de l'Unité Africaine, Revue Juridique et Politique. April-June 1966, vol. 20, no. 2, p. 295-334.

8. Lampué, P. "L'Organisation de l'Unité Africaine," Année Politique et Economique. Dec. 1963, vol. 36, p. 421-433.

9. McKeon, N. "The African States and the OAU," International Affairs. July 1966, vol. 42, no. 3, p. 390-409.

10. Markakis, Dr. John. "The Organization of African Unity A Progress Report," Journal of Modern African Studies. Oct. 1966, vol. 4, no. 2, p. 135-154.

11. Padelford, Norman J. "The Organization of African Unity," International Organization. Summer 1964, vol. 18, no. 3, p. 521-542.

12. Sanger, Clyde. "Toward Unity in Africa," Foreign Affairs. Jan. 1964, vol. 42, no. 2, p. 269-281.

13. Smets, Paul F. "La Charte d'Addis-Abéba ou l'Organisation des Patries," Revue de Sociologie. Brussels, 1964, no. 2, p. 311-350.

14. Wallerstein, Immanuel. Africa: The Politics of Unity. New York, Random House, 1967, 274 p.

15. ----------. "The Early Years of the OAU: The Search for Organizational Preeminence," International Organization. Autumn 1966, vol. 20, no. 4, p. 774-787.

C. DECOLONIZATION

1. Barber, J. Rhodesia: The Road to Rebellion. London, Oxford Univ. Press, 1967, 338 p.

2. Carter, Gwendolen M. (ed). South Africa's Transkei: Politics of Domestic Colonialism. London, Heinemann, 1967, 217 p.

3. Davis, John A., and James K. Baker. (eds). Southern Africa in Transition. New York, Praeger, 1966, 427 p.

4. Duffy, James. Portugal in Africa. Harmondsworth, England, Penguin Books, 1962, 240 p.

5. Dugard, C. J. R. "The Organization of African Unity and Colonialism," International and Comparative Law Quarterly. Jan. 1967, vol. 16, pt. 1, p. 157-190.

6. Feit, Edward. African Opposition in South Africa. Stanford, Calif., Stanford Univ. Press, 1967, 223 p.

7. First, Ruth. South West Africa. Harmondsworth, England, Penguin Books, 1963, 269 p.

8. Green, L. C. "South West Africa and the World Court," International Journal. Winter 1966, vol. 22, no. 1, p. 39-67.

9. Gupta, Anirudha. "The Rhodesian Crisis and the Organization of African Unity," International Studies. July 1967, vol. 9, no. 1, p. 55-64.

10. Legum, Colin, and Margaret Legum. South Africa: Crisis for the West. New York, Praeger, 1964, 333 p.

11. Leiss, Amelia C. (ed). Apartheid and United Nations Collective Measures. New York, Carnegie Endowment for International Peace, 1965, 170 p.

12. Margarido, Alfredo. "L'O.U.A. et les Territoires sous Domination Portugaise," Revue Française d'Etudes Politiques Africaines. Oct. 1967, p. 82-106.

13. Mtshali, B. Vulindlela. Rhodesia: Background to Conflict. London, Leslie Frewin, 1968, 255 p.

14. Mudge, George Alfred. "Domestic Policies and U.N. Activities: The Cases of Rhodesia and the Republic of South Africa," International Organization. Winter 1967, vol. 21, no. 1, p. 1-23.

15. Segal, Ronald (ed). Sanctions against South Africa. Harmondsworth, England, Penguin Books, 1964.

16. Spence, J. E. Republic under Pressure: A Study of South African Foreign Policy. London, Oxford Univ. Press, 1965, 132 p.

17. Wohlgemuth, Patricia. "The Portuguese Territories and the United Nations," International Conciliation. Nov. 1963, no. 545, 68 p.

18. Ziegler, Jean. La Contre-Révolution en Afrique. Paris, Payot, 1963, 244 p.

D. PEACEFUL SETTLEMENT

1. Austin, Dennis. "The Uncertain Frontier: Ghana-Togo," Journal of Modern African Studies. June 1963, vol. 1, no. 2, p. 147-162.

2. Castagno, A. A. "The Somali-Kenyan Controversy: Implications for the Future," Journal of Modern African Studies. July 1964, vol. 2, no. 2, p. 165-188.

3. Drysdale, John. The Somali Dispute. New York, Pall Mall, 1964, 183 p.

4. Elias, T. O. "The Commission of Mediation, Conciliation and Arbitration," British Yearbook of International Law. 1965, p. 336-354.

5. Lewis, I. M. "The Problems of the Northern Frontier District of Kenya," Race, 1963.

6. Mariam, Mesfin Wolde. "Background to the Ethio-Somalian Boundary Dispute," Journal of Modern African Studies. July 1964, vol. 2, no. 2, p. 189-220.

7. Reyner, Anthony S. "Morocco's International Boundaries: A Factual Background," Journal of Modern African Studies, Sept. 1963, vol. 1, no. 3, p. 313-326.

8.   Skurnik, W. A. E. "Ghana and Guinea, 1966--A Case Study in Inter-African Relations," <u>Journal of Modern African Studies</u>. Nov. 1967, vol. 5, no. 3, p. 369-384.

9.   Strauch, Hanspeter. "L'O.U.A. et les Conflits Frontaliers," <u>Revue Française d'Etudes Politiques Africaines</u>. Oct. 1967, p. 59-81.

10. Touval, Saadia. "The Organization of African Unity and African Borders," <u>International Organization</u>. Winter 1967, vol. 21, no. 1, p. 102-127.

11. Wild, Patricia Berko. "The Organization of African Unity and the Algerian-Moroccan Border Conflict," <u>International Organization</u>, Winter 1966, vol. 20, no. 1, p. 18-36.

12. Zartman, I. William. "The Politics of Boundaries in North and West Africa," <u>Journal of Modern African Studies</u>. Aug. 1965, vol. 3, no. 2, p. 155-174.

E.   NON-ALIGNMENT - WORLD RELATIONS

1.   Brzezinski, Zbigniew (ed). <u>Africa and the Communist World</u>. Stanford, Calif., Stanford Univ. Press, 1963, 272 p.

2.   McKay, Vernon. <u>Africa in World Politics</u>. New York, Harper and Row, 1962, 468 p.

3.   ---------- (ed). <u>African Diplomacy: Studies in the Determinants of Foreign Policy</u>. New York, Praeger, 1966, 210 p.

4.   Martin, Laurence W. (ed). <u>Neutralism and Nonalignment: The New States in World Affairs</u>. New York, Praeger, 1962; in which see:
        Good, Robert C. "The Congo Crisis: A Study of Post Colonial Politics," p. 34-63; and
        Lefever, Ernest W. "Nehru, Nasser and Nkrumah on Neutralism," p. 93-120.

5.   Rivkin, Arnold. <u>The African Presence in World Affairs</u>. New York, Glencoe Press, 1963, 304 p.

6. Zartman, I. William. "Africa as a Subordinate State System in International Relations," International Organization. Summer 1967, vol. 21, no. 3, p. 545-564.

7. ----------. International Relations in the New Africa. Englewood Cliffs, N.J., Prentice Hall, 1966, 175 p.

F. UNITED NATIONS

1. Hovet, Thomas, Jr. Africa in the United Nations. Evanston, Ill., Northwestern Univ. Press, 1963, 336 p.

2. Iturriaga, José Antonio de. "L'Organisation de l'Unité Africaine et les Nations Unies," Revue Générale du Droit International Public, 1965, p. 370-394.

3. Karefa-Smart, John. "Africa and the United Nations," International Organization. Summer 1965, vol. 20, no. 3, p. 764-773.

4. Kay, David. "The Politics of Decolonization: The New Nations and the United Nations Political Process," International Organization. Autumn 1967, vol. 21, no. 4, p. 786-811.

5. Spencer, John H. "Africa at the UN: Some Observations," International Organization. Spring 1966, vol. 16, no. 2, p. 375-386.

6. Strauch, Hanspeter. "Les Relations entre l'Organisation de l'Unité Africaine et l'O.N.U.," Revue Française d'Etudes Politiques Africaines. Oct. 1967, p. 40-58.

G. DEVELOPMENT

1. Davies, Ioan. African Trade Unions. Harmondsworth, England, Penguin Books, 1966.

2. Dumont, René. False Start in Africa. New York, Praeger, 1966, 320 p.

3. Friedland, William H., and Carl G. Rosberg (eds). African Socialism. Stanford, Calif., Stanford Univ. Press, 1964, 300 p.

4. Green, R. H., and K. G. V. Krishna. <u>Economic Co-operation in Africa</u>. London, Oxford Univ. Press, 1967, 160 p.

5. Hazlewood, Arthur (ed). <u>African Integration and Disintegration</u>. (q.v.s: A. Background) in which see:
   Hazlewood, Arthur. "Economic Integration in East Africa;"
   ----------. "Problems of Integration Among African States;"
   Robson, Peter. "Economic Integration in Equatorial Africa."

6. Legum, Margaret. "Africa's Divided Workers." In Legum, <u>Pan-Africanism</u>, (q.v.s: A. Background) p. 81-92.

7. Plessz, Nicolas G. <u>Problems and Prospects of Economic Integration in West Africa</u>. Montreal, McGill Univ. Press, 1968, 100 p.

8. Segal, Aaron. <u>East Africa: Strategy for Economic Cooperation</u>. Nairobi, 1965.

9. Thomas, L. V. <u>L'Idéologie Socialiste et les Voies Africaines du Développement</u>. Paris, Livre Africain, 1966, 300 p.

10. Zack, Arnold M. "Trade Unions in Africa." In Legum, <u>Africa: A Handbook</u>, (q.v.s: A. Background) p. 447-457.

H.   REGIONALISM

1. Anguilé, A. G., and J. E. David. <u>L'Afrique sans Frontières</u>. Monaco, Paul Boru, 1965.

2. Borella, François. "Le Régionalisme Africain en 1964," <u>Annuaire Français de Droit International</u>. 1964.

3. ----------. "Le Régionalisme Africain en Crise (1965-66)," <u>Annuaire Français de Droit International</u>. 1966.

4. Cox, Richard. <u>Pan-Africanism in Practice--An East African Study, PAFMECSA, 1958-1964</u>. London, Oxford Univ. Press, 1964, 95 p.

5. Currie, David P. (ed). Federalism and the New Nation of Africa. Chicago, Univ. of Chicago Press, 1964, 440 p.

6. Foltz, William. From French West Africa to the Mali Federation. New Haven, Conn., Yale Univ. Press, 1965, 235 p.

7. Hazlewood, Arthur (ed). African Integration and Disintegration. (q.v.s: A. Background) in which see:
    Robson, Peter. "Problems of Integration between Senegal and Gambia";
    Julienne, Roland. "The Experience of Integration in French-Speaking Africa"; and
    Hazlewood, Arthur. "The Economics of Federation and Dissolution in Central Africa."

8. Michel, Hubert. "La Politique Africaine des Etats de Maghreb," Revue Française d'Etude Politiques Africaines. March 1968, p. 41-62.

9. Nye, Joseph S., Jr. Pan-Africanism and East African Integration. Cambridge, Mass., Harvard Univ. Press 1965, 307 p.

10. Rosberg, C. G., Jr., and A. Segal. "An East African Federation," International Conciliation. May 1963.

11. Sabatier, Robert, and Jacques Baulin. The Arab Role in Africa. Harmondsworth, England, Penguin Books, 1962.

12. Tevoedjre, Albert. Pan-Africanism in Action: An Account of the UAM. Cambridge, Mass., Harvard Univ. Press, 1965, 96 p.

13. Welch, Claude E., Jr. Dream of Unity: Pan-Africanism and Political Unification in West Africa. Ithaca, N.Y., Cornell Univ. Press, 1966, 396 p.

14. Zartman, I. William. "The Sahara--Bridge or Barrier? International Conciliation. 1963, no. 541, p. 42-50.

I. NATIONAL UNITY

1. Anber, Paul. "Modernization and Political Disintegration: Nigeria and the Ibos," Journal of Modern African Studies. Sept. 1967, p. 163-180.

2. Bonfanti, Adriano. "Soudan--Noirs et Blancs, Dixième Parallèle," Revue Française d'Etudes Politiques Africaines. Jan. 1966, p. 24-42.

3. Carter, Gwendolen M. (ed). National Unity and Regionalism in Eight African States. Ithaca, N.Y., Cornell Univ. Press, 1966, 565 p.

4. Coleman, J. S., and C. G. Rosberg. (eds). Political Parties and National Integration in Tropical Africa. Berkeley, Calif., Univ. of California Press, 1964.

5. Hazlewood, Arthur (ed). African Integration and Disintegration. (q.v.s: A. Background) in which see:
   Ardener, Edwin. "The Nature of the Reunification of Cameroon";
   Lewis, I. M. "Integration in the Somali Republic"; and
   O'Connell, James. "Political Integration: The Nigerian Case."

6. LeVine, Victor T. The Cameroons from Mandate to Independence. Berkeley, Calif., Univ. of California Press, 1964.

7. Lewis, I. M. The Modern History of Somaliland. London, Weidenfeld and Nicolson, 1965, 234 p.

8. Schwarz, Frederick A. O., Jr. Nigeria: The Tribes, The Nation, or the Race--the Politics of Independence. Cambridge, Mass., Massachusetts Institute of Technology Press, 1965, 316 p.

9. Shepherd, George W., Jr. "National Integration and the Southern Sudan," Journal of Modern African Studies. Oct. 1966, vol. 4, no. 2, p. 193-212.

Index

691

Attwood, William, 374
Awolowo, Chief Obafemi, 66, 397, 402-405, 410, 421, 425, 427
Azikiwe, Nnamdi, 29, 75, 81, 101, 388; Biafra: 397-398, 412, 414, 416, 430-431, 492

Bakari, Djibo, 390
Balewa, Sir Abubakar Tafawa, 74, 133, 135, 149, 388, 390, 397-399
Balkanization, 51, 82, 96, 110, 329, 590, 625
Bamako agreement, 338-340
Bamali, Nuhu, 243
Banda, Hastings, 223, 296-297, 309-310
Banjo, Brigadier Victor, 405
Basutoland, see Lesotho
Bechuanaland, see Botswana
Belgium, 57-58, 61, 64, 373-374, 385, 468, 472
Bello, Ahmadu, 396, 399-400
Ben Bella, Ahmed, 377; Algero-Moroccan dispute: 336, 338, 343, 451-452; decolonization: 77, 142-143, 153, 305, 559
Biafra, 404-433, 478-496, 499, 501, 564, 573-575, 618-619, 631
Black Power, 13, 26
Boganda, Barthélémy, 111
Bomboko, Justin, 60, 361, 384
Bongo, Albert, 415
Botha, Michael, 269
Botsio, Kojo, 242
Botswana, 295-297, 308-312
Boumedienne, Houari, 308, 425, 529, 609-610, 618
Boundaries, artificial: 87, 89, 116, 140, 328-329; intangibility: 139-141, 341, 355, 436, 625; peaceful arrangement, 76, 389-390, 455. See also Algero-Moroccan dispute, Somalia dispute
Bourguiba, Habib, 67, 145, 454, 600
Bouteflika, Abdelaziz, 339
Brazzaville Group, decolonization: 48-49, 50-52, 55-57, 60-63, 77; unity: 94-97, 102, 104-106, 589
Brown, George, 252
Budget, 187, 632-636
Budgetary Committee, 635-636
Burundi, Congo II: 364-366, 369, 370-372, 377; refugees: 564-566, 568-569
Busia, Kofi, 604

Cabinda, 212, 215, 217
Cabral, Amilcar, 218

694

Guinea, 66-67, 76, 89-91, 117, 371, 377, 604-606
Guinea Bissao, 214-215, 218-219, 564
Gutteridge, William, 244

Habte-Wolde, 140-141
Haile Selassié I, 77, 245, 308, 338-339, 343, 601, 632-633, 635; Algero-Moroccan dispute: 338-339, 343; Biafra: 407, 409-411, 421-424, 428, 432, 492; boundary dispute: 350, 353, 357, 457-458, 460; at summit: 26, 129, 134-135, 137, 141, 147-148
Hammarskjöld, Dag, 59, 62, 64, 184
Harriman, Averell, 468
Hassan II, 125, 335-336, 338, 343-344, 451, 608-610
Headquarters (OAU), 189
Health, Sanitation and Nutrition Commission, 548-549
High Commission for Refugees, see UNHCR
Hoare, Mike, 481
Houphouët-Boigny, Félix, 139, 142, 147, 388, 415; unity: 48, 110, 130, 591, 604, 614
Human rights, 267, 282, 285, 626, 638
Hunt, Lord, 491

Ileo, Joseph, 58-59
Information work (OAU), 546-547, 678
Institutional Committee, 173-174, 578, 634
Inter-African and Malagasy Organization, 78, 106-107
International Civil Aviation Organization, 543-544
International Confederation of Free Trade Unions, 69-70, 534-535, 538
International Court of Justice, 151, 180, 262-268
International Federation of Christian Trade Unions, 534, 538
International Labour Organization, 291, 535, 541, 573, 581
International Monetary Fund, 533
International Telecommunications Union, 542
Ironsi, General, see Aguiyi-Ironsi
Islam, 456-457, 478, 615-616
Islamic Summit, 609, 615
Israel, 34, 51, 107-108, 138, 167, 459, 493, 504, 616-619
Issa, Abdullahi, 355, 460
Italy, 348
Ivory Coast, 110-111, 387-389, 415, 426, 431, 488-489, 600, 604, 618

Japan, 287
Johnson, Lyndon, 468, 470, 484
Joint Church Aid, 482-485, 495
Jonathan, Chief Leabua, 296-297, 309-310

698